PERSONALIZING
PHYSICAL EDUCATION
AND
SPORT PHILOSOPHY

EARLE F. ZEIGLER
Ph.D., LL.D.

Professor and Dean
Faculty of Physical Education
The University of Western Ontario
London, Canada

ISBN 0-87563-102-9

Published By
STIPES PUBLISHING COMPANY
10-12 Chester Street
Champaign, Illinois 61820

DEDICATION

To Peter Spencer-Kraus, a bright, perceptive,
sensitive spirit who came to the University of
Illinois from England in the 1960's to study physical education and sport philosophy in the context
of philosophy's "Age of Analysis." He gave and
found friendship, respect, and love and would
have undoubtedly made a significant contribution
to both the profession and discipline of physical
education and sport. A traffic accident ended his
life when he went back home for a while before
embarking on a doctoral program. Many of us
felt the loss deeply, both personally and professionally . . .

PREFACE

A writer must always ask himself, "Is the writing of this book necessary or even advisable?" In this instance the author thinks that such an effort was advisable; you, the reader, will in time decide whether this collection of material was necessary or advisable. At the time these words are being written, the writer has been "professing" and teaching physical education and sport for well over thirty years. Further, he has been teaching and writing about what might be loosely called "physical education and sport philosophy" for just about a quarter of a century. Let's hope that it hasn't been "one year's experience repeated twenty-five times!"

This volume is actually a collection of some of the articles and chapters that have been published by the writer over the past fifteen years since he became somewhat more consciously involved in physical education and sport philosophy as a sub-disciplinary area of the field. Careful reading and analysis of this material will undoubtedly offer the reader a type of historical experience--viewed, of course, through the eyes of one fallible and persistent physical educator-- coach--philosopher--administrator. Study and discussion of these papers will also serve as an introduction to physical education and sport philosophy as it has evolved. In this prefatory essay the writer will present (1) a reasonable statement of the field's objectives in the twentieth century; (2) a chronological statement describing the types of sport and physical education philosophizing that have been carried out; (3) the types of people who have been writing this material; (4) a brief explanation of the author's background and approaches to the topic at hand; and (5) how the reader can interpret these essays and relate them to himself/herself as the perplexing issues and problems of the day are confronted.

It is a truism to state that the field of physical education and sport has made enormous progress in the twentieth century on this continent. Ford Hess, in his study completed at New York University in 1959, assessed American objectives of physical education in the light of historical events. Between 1900 and 1919 he identified what he labeled as the "health or hygienic objective" as most important. The 1920's were seen as a decade when a "socio-educational objective" became the dominating goal, and this was followed in the 1930's by a trend toward increased emphasis upon what Hess called a "socio-recreational objective" as most important in physical education. Quite obviously, with such an all-out conflict as World War II, "physical fitness" almost inevitably became the main objective of physical education in the period between 1939 and 1945. Immediately after the War ended, despite continuing international tension and other wars, there was a de-emphasis on physical fitness per se, and the trend seemed to be in the direction of what might be called "total fitness" in the years from 1950 to 1960.

If one attempts to state what have been the main objectives of physical education in the past fifteen years, he is immediately confronted by his inability to obtain historical perspective. Most certainly there has been a strong disciplinary emphasis. At the same time both health and recreation have strengthened their movements toward independent--and yet allied--professional fields. One might argue that the main objective has been to decide what it is that physical education does--and then to make a better attempt to carry out our professional responsibilities in an improved manner. However, such a statement is nowhere nearly precise enough because of the many issues and conflicts that are unresolved. But more about this later . . .

In looking at "what has gone before" in regard to physical education and sport philosophy, in the 1800's and early 1900's there seemed to be a combined "common sense and rational thought approach." This was followed by what might be identified as a "normative philosophizing approach" from the late 1920's to the 1950's. In some rare instances this "principles of physical education era" has carried on even to the present time. Then in the mid-1950's a few physical educators seemed to "key in" on what might be called the "philosophy of education systems approach" that employed a "structural analysis technique." Concurrently in the late 1950's and down to the present day, there have been those who have attempted a "theory-building approach" with some success. This developed to a degree along with a burgeoning of interest in so-called structural analysis--an approach or technique that draws implications from metaphysical analysis to a specific philosophy of education with resultant inferences for physical education and sport. The author in the early 1960's added a step to this technique which may have made it more "palatable" to those who require that philosophy be somewhat more "scientific" or objective. In connection with the employment of the structural analysis technique to draw implications for physical, health, and recreation education from the educational philosophy of reconstructionism, he gathered available scientific evidence to lend support to his work.

Two other approaches were begun in the 1960's as well--one involving a phenomenological-existentialistic technique and method that has attracted a considerable following, and the other involving a philosophy of language--language analysis approach that has been experimented with by approximately a half dozen people in the field on this continent to a greater or lesser extent.

The question must be asked (and answered) additionally about the calibre and background of the person who has sought to write physical education and sport philosophy. At first this person had no background in philosophy at all, or at best may have had an introductory couse in philosophy, in theology, or in philosophy of education somewhere in his or her past. Then there was a period when a number of self-made philosophies appeared--people who read extensively, audited courses, etc. (an approach that was followed to a degree by the author after his study in the history and philosophy of education at Yale). As these men and women became thesis advisers, they encouraged their students to take minor programs in amalgams of philosophy and philosophy of education.

In the late 1960's many students began to avoid philosophy of education courses almost completely and turned to semi-sequential series of courses in the department of philosophy itself. This led very soon to the need for undergraduate minors or even major programs in philosophy. Still another stage has begun, and this is characterized by graduate students within the field of physical education obtaining the master's degree in philosophy on the way toward the Ph.D. degree in physical education. Lastly, and even more so since the advent of the Philosophic Society for the Study of Sport, the few fully prepared philosophers who became interested in sport in the early 1960's have grown to a substantive minority within the Society. (The author has also felt it most beneficial to qualify for membership in the American Philosophical Association and the Philosophy of Education Society.)

All of the above-mentioned developments have taken place most mostly since the advent of the first few doctoral studies within the field that had alluded to physical education philosophy (however, interpreted)--those by Arthur Esslinger at Iowa in 1938 and by Margaret Clark at New York University in 1942. The author of this volume appeared on the scene in the mid-1940's as a part-time graduate student in the history and philosophy of education at Yale studying under the eminent John S. Brubacher. At the same time the writer was working full-time in physical education and athletics at the same institution as a teacher and coach. When he moved to Western Ontario in 1949, he began to teach the "principles course" in physical education using the established texts of the time (Williams, Brownell, et al.). As helpful as they were, he soon realized that there "must be a better way." He began to search for implications for physical education, health, recreation, and athletics from his background in educational philosophy (which at that time stressed the "systems approach"). It was just at this point that Professor Richard Morland of Stetson University was working on his "monumental" dissertation in physical education philsosophy at N. Y. U., and some of the early doctoral studies were carried out with Dr. Eleanor Metheny at Southern California.

This author began in 1959 to outline what he thought was to become the first philosophical foundations text in the field. He was subsequently amazed to discover that Craig Davis was carrying out a similar project at Southern California and had "beat him to the punch." (Indeed Dr. Davis' book would have still come out a bit earlier than this author's even if Prentice-Hall hadn't moved the publication date of Zeigler's text back from 1963 to 1964.) This move had been made so as not to conflict with a similar, but much more "principles-oriented," text by Cowell and France that was also scheduled for 1963. What happened after this is more recent history, and perhaps too complex and space-consuming to repeat here.

(This writer has led an almost too complex professional life--in his opinion--since he entered the field in 1941. Everything considered, the variety of experiences may have stood him in good stead, however. He began as a physical educator-coach even before he acquired his specialized professional education in physical education at the undergraduate and graduate levels (at Arnold College and Columbia Teachers College, respectively). He has been a practicing administrator on four different occasions (and is currently so involved on a presumably half-time basis). His disciplinary interests have ranged from philosophy to history to administrative theory and to the international and comparative aspects of physical education and sport. More recently he has embarked on a learning experience in sociology, anthropology, and the other behavioral sciences.)

The articles and papers included in the present volume have been written over a period of thirteen years and cover a wide range of topics in physical education and sport. The author's approach has typically been personalized and related to values. He is "addicted" to the concept of as much freedom as possible for the individual in an evolving democratic social system, society, and culture. He sees himself basically as a physical educator-coach with a deep interest in philosophy (and secondary interests in the other sub-disciplinary areas mentioned above). The term "physical education" is disturbing to him only because it implies a mind-body dichotomy which he feels that psychologists have quite thoroughly disproved.

Since the late 1940's in his philosophical writing, the author has employed sequentially, and at times concurrently, a common sense approach, a normative approach, a structural analysis approach (while favoring pragmatism) and, more recently, has been following a more eclectic philosophical methodology including certain techniques of historical and descriptive methods; of the philosophy of language; of pragmatic structural analysis; and occasional normative philosophizing that "defies careful analysis."

All of the above may lead the prospective, but wary, reader to say, "All right, I understand what has gone before, so to speak, and

I may be willing to admit that there is a need for a book that reflects the writing of one physical education and sport philosopher over a decade or so, but is there a plan that will allow me to follow the progression of articles and ideas in a way that will have meaning?" Hopefully the answer to this question is a strongly affirmative "yes!"

An important point for us all to keep in mind as we listen to anyone philosophizing about physical education and sport, or writing about it, is it's not what you <u>say</u> or <u>write,</u> but in the final analysis it's what you do that counts! On the other hand Morland and others have stressed time and again that the <u>recurrent themes</u> in a person's writings help us discover what he really believes (or what he thinks he really believes). Thus, the articles and papers herein have been grouped under a number of different headings--or <u>recurrent themes</u>-- which admittedly overlap in a variety of ways. These headings (or themes) are as follows; (1) physical education and sport in historical persoective; (2) personalizing physical education and sport philosophy; (3) sport and athletics; (4) professional preparation; (5) the disciplinary emphasis; (6) the meaning of physical education; and (7) the future.

The author has identified ten stances currently held by many in the field which he feels should be eliminated (they "have got to go"). The first he calls "The Shotgun Approach to Professional Preparation," which is characterized by an undergraduate major program designed to prepare a man or woman to be a generalist to the extreme. Secondly, the writer has decried what he calls an "Athletics Über Alles Approach" in which interscholastic and intercollegiate athletics' advocates seek to assume far too large a place in an educational program and in the process athletics becomes "the tail that wags the dog." Thirdly, the author has criticized perennially what he has labeled as "The Women Are All Right In Their Place Approach" exhibited until perhaps most recently by the large majority of male physical educators and coaches.

The fourth problem or prevailing stance is the sharp division that seems to have developed between "God's anointed"--the disciplinary-oriented "intellectual giants" living off the profession but run running it down at every opportunity--and the large majority of professional workers in the field who think these professors are really not doing much that is truly worthwhile anyhow. The fact of the matter is that the professors with esoteric interests are mostly erstwhile physical educators themselves who have "lost sight of home base." Conversely, it is desperately important for the professional workers to be made aware of the urgent need for a sound body-of-knowledge upon which to base their professional task.

The remaining six "stances" will not be discussed in any detail. Their import may be gleaned by the reader from the slogans that have been created for them (as follows): (5) "The Password Is Treadmill Approach"; (6) "The Name That Was Good Enough For My Father Approach"; (7) "The Let Joe And Mary Do It Approach" in regard to who should teach (or do something) about the continuing lack of elementary school physical education programs; (8) "The Mickey And Minnie Mouse Curriculum Approach"; (9) "The I Must Have My Pound Of Flesh Approach" to the idea of a required program in physical education; and (10) "The I'm Not Really Academically Respectable Approach"--so why fight it.

It is always a pleasure to express gratitude, appreciation, and friendship to people from whom you have learned, with whom you have shared experiences, and to whom you have perhaps taught something. Wihtout attempting to categorize individuals on this basis, the author will simply list a number of names--of those in philosophy, philosophy of education, and physical education and sport philosophy only--who belong in one or more of these categories:
J. S. Brubacher, R. B. Morland, H. J. VanderZwaag, P. J. Galasso, J. W. Keating--and then alphabetically--S. Abe, P. Arnold, J. W. Bell, M. Bouet, T. Brameld, C. K. Brightbill, H. S. Broudy, Pat Cavanaugh, M. C. Clark, Sue Cook, J. Daly, E. C. Davis, B. J. Diggs, J. R. Fairs, W. P. Fraleigh, W. K. Frankena, E. Gerber, L. J. Huelster, L. Holbrook, A. H. Johnson, F. Keenan, S. Kleinman, P. Lawson, Hans Lenk, W. J. L'Heureux, C. H. McCloy, F. McMurray, K. Meier, E. Metheny, V. C. Morris, B. Mutimer, J. B. Nash, R. G. Osterhoudt, G. Patrick, K. Pearson, S. Ross, A. Sheedy, D. Shogan, D. Shwayder, D. Siedentop, H. Slusher, P. Smithells, P. Spencer-Kraus, R. Stone, C. Ulrich, Fred Will, Paul Weiss, and Sokichi Yoshizawa. I will be forever grateful to all those who wrote the many articles and books I have read.

Earle F. Zeigler
London, Ontario
January, 1975

TABLE OF CONTENTS

Table of Contents (Continued):

PART III
SPORT AND ATHLETICS

Table of Contents (Continued):

PART IV
PROFESSIONAL PREPARATION

Table of Contents (Continued):

PART V
THE DISCIPLINARY APPROACH

PART VI
THE MEANING OF PHYSICAL EDUCATION

PART VII
THE FUTURE

Table of Contents (Continued):

Appendix
FOR FURTHER READING

Part I
PHYSICAL EDUCATION AND SPORT
IN HISTORICAL PERSPECTIVE

Selection #1

THE IDEA OF PHYSICAL EDUCATION IN MODERN TIMES

To express the "idea of physical education in modern times" is an exciting assignment, but one that seemed much simpler when first considered in a casual way.* In the first place it would be ridiculous to define the term in such a way that it might not apply for the entire world. Obviously, physical education means "many things to many people," and it may well be said that we are presenting a "blurred image to a bewildered public."

With this particular topic--the idea of physical education in modern times--"idea" will be taken to mean "the conception of" or "the nature of." "Physical education" will be accepted as a program which is offered by certain departments in schools and colleges throughout the world, as well as the activity carried on both formally and informally by parents, community leaders, and an individual himself. It can and does often include health education, physical education, recreation, safety education, dance, sport and competitive athletics, and other types of activities. All of this leads one to think that perhaps "physical education" has become a highly unsatisfactory name--everything considered. And lastly, considering this paper's topic, "modern times," which may have begun about 1500 A.D. (McNeill, 1963, xii), will be defined as the twentieth century for the purposes of this presentation.

One last introductory statement should probably be made. With a topic like this it is difficult to determine where history leaves off and philosophy begins. Although the writer has a sincere interest in both aspects of the field, his preference is to place greater emphasis on the philosophical aspects of the topic. This will be done in the first half of this paper, but a historical summary in the form of an allegory will be included at the end. The assumption is that the major points to be emphasized will be made more forcefully that way.

---

* A paper presented initially to the Philosophical and Cultural Foundations Area of the Physical Education Division of the American Association for Health, Physical Education, and Recreation, St. Louis, Missouri, April 1, 1968. This article appeared in several journals (in one instance under a title not approved by the author). It had been sent originally for the consideration of A. W. Willee in Australia, who published it under its original title. "The Idea of Physical Education in Modern Times," in The Australian Journal of Physical Education, 43 (June-July, 1968): 17-24.

Philosophical Analysis

The philosopher approaches his task typically in at least one of three ways: (1) speculatively, (2) normatively, or (3) analytically (Frankena, Philosophy of Education, 1965, p. 10). He may speculate about what we know and believe about the universe and our own sphere of human affairs within this framework. He may approach these questions normatively and evolve a systematic and coherent plan whereby a human may live. Lastly, and it should be stressed that there are a number of different methods and techniques within each of these three approaches, he may seek to analyze other philosophical approaches critically and to make comparisons. In this latter approach he will probably attempt to clarify concepts and to present evidence that seems to bear out one philosophical position or another. Finally, he may go so far with critical analysis that he will decide that language analysis and a type of semantics should be his primary task (Zeigler and VanderZwaag, 1966, p. 78).

Five Meanings of Physical Education

No matter which of the three approaches is employed primarily by a philosopher of physical education and sport, he should at least recognize the ambiguity of the term "physical education," and the fact that it may mean any one of five things:

(1) the activity of physically educating carried on by teachers, schools, and parents (or by oneself),

(2) the process of being physically educated (or learning) which goes on in the pupil or child (or person of any age),

(3) the result, actual or intended, of (1) and (2),

(4) the discipline or field of enquiry that studies or reflects on (1), (2), and (3) and is taught in departments, schools, and colleges of physical education,

(5) the profession whose members practice (1) above, try to observe (2) taking place, attempt to measure and/or evaluate whether (3) has occurred, and base their professional practice on the body-of-knowledge developed by those undertaking scholarly and research effort in the discipline (4). (Adapted from Frankena, Three Historical Philosophies of Education, 1965, p. 6, with some modifications.)

Thus, without even considering "the idea of" physical education in relation to its objectives, the professional physical educator can readily see how important it is that he communicate more effectively with his fellow professionals. Where this problem in language leaves the layman is immediately obvious.

A Plethora of Objectives

That this field, whatever it is called by anyone, has had a
plethora of objectives espoused by its leaders must be considered
one of the "understatements of the year." Because of the field's "defensive posture" occasioned by many attacks against its gradual
"intrusion" into the curriculum, leaders in physical education have
claimed that an adequate physical education can cure everything from
"soiled characters to chilblains." Notable among these leaders who
have defined certain objectives, starting in the early 1920's, have
been Hetherington (1922), Bowen and Mitchell (1923), Wood and
Cassidy (1927), Williams (1927), Hughes (with Williams in 1930),
Nash (1931), Sharman (1937), Wayman (1938), Esslinger (1938),
Staley (1939), McCloy (1940), Clark (1943), Cobb (1943), Lynn (1944),
Brownell and Hagman, Scott, Bucher, and Oberteuffer (all in 1951).
There have been many other statements since that time, but 1951
seems like a good year to stop. One could categorize and then enumerate the various objectives proposed for the field, and the list
would be really impressive. Hess' assessment of the objectives of
American physical education from 1900 to 1957 in the light of certain
historical events assisted this author. The major objectives in the
sequence in which they appeared (according to Hess, 1959) were:
(1) the hygiene or health objective (1900-1919); (2) the socio-educational objectives (1920-1928); the socio-recreational objectives (1930-
1938); the physical fitness and health objectives (1939-1945); and the
trend seemed to be in the direction of "total fitness" and international
understanding from 1946-1957.

The Need for Consensus

It seems quite obvious that the profession should take positive
steps to plan and then work for consensus among the conflicting
philosophies of physical education extant in the Western world. This
is especially true with a field that now seems to be redoubling its
efforts to relate to other countries in all of the world's hemispheres.
It would not seem to be wise to export the present "mass confusion"
on the matter of objectives. Not many people will be fooled for very
long with such an approach. Delineation of one's own personal
philosophy on the part of each physical educator will help, but the
employment of optimum methods for the achievement of greater
agreement with our colleagues at home and abroad must be carried
out for the best possible outcome. Still further, the East and the
West should meet--and just as soon as possible. (Burtt, pp. 272-273).

The Need for Verification of Objectives

Most recently, physical educators have realized the need for
the development of a "body-of-knowledge" through a greatly expanded

program of scholarly and research endeavor in a variety of sub-discipline (Zeigler and McCristal, 1967). Some of our scientists had realized this earlier, especially in the physiological area and certain aspects of psychology. But now relationships are gradually being strengthened with such disciplines and sub-disciplines as anatomy, sociology, history, philosophy, comparative and international education, anthropology, and administrative theory (within the behavioral sciences and educational administration) as well (Zeigler, 1967).

As the "body-of-knowledge" increases, and inventories of scientific findings from the various sub-disciplines to which the field is relating improve in both quantity and quality, it will become increasingly possible to verify whether a planned program of physical education does actually result in the achievement of the many objectives which have been stated. Maybe then the field will be able to achieve consensus on certain "common denominators" in the "education of an amphibian" (Huxley, 1964) or a "naked ape" (Morris, 1967). What seems to be really important in regard to the classification of a "relatively hairless ape," in addition to the obviously still prevailing legacy from ancestors, is that man has now become "almost non-apelike" and that there remains ample opportunity for all sorts of differential development in the eons which lie ahead. (Simpson, 1968) Physical education has a significant role to play in this development, no matter what the field decides to call itself. The following allegory will perhaps explain the "basic nature" of physical education from both a historical and philosophical standpoint.

The Basic Nature of Physical Education (An Allegory)

Blank, sometimes designated as _____, but who really should be called tnemevom (which is quite difficult to pronounce), has had both a glorious and a shameful existence. He is a part of the very nature of the universe, a fact which is incontrovertible. He is involved with both the animate and inanimate aspects of the cosmos. His is a basic part of the fundamental pattern of living of every creature of any type that has ever lived on earth. Early man knew he was important, but he was often not appreciated until he was gone, or almost gone. Civilized man used him extensively in the early societies, as did the Greeks and the Romans and all others. Some used him vigorously, but others used him carefully and methodically. He was used gracefully by some, ecstatically by others, rigorously by many when the need was urgent, and regularly by most who wanted to get the job done. He was called many things in various tongues. But strangely enough, he was never fully understood.

The time came when he was considered less important in life, although people still admired him on innumerable occasions. Some seemed to understand him instinctively, while others had great difficulty in employing him well. He was eventually degraded to such an extent that well-educated people often did not think that he had an important place in their background and preparation for life. Many gave lip service to the need for him, but then would not give him his due. Other appreciated his worth, but felt that he was less important than many aspects of education. But he persisted despite the onset of an advanced technological age. Some called him calisthenics. Others called him physical training. A determined group called him gymnastics. A few called him physical culture, but they turned out to be men of "ill repute." Others felt that he had been neglected in the preparation of man for life; so, they did him a favor and called him physical education.

The Aftermath of a New Name. He prospered to a considerable degree with this name, although it caused him considerable embarrassment because it classified him as a second-class citizen. But he struggled on. Then a strange thing happened. As a result of this modicum of prosperity, he developed offshoots. (Two of these offshoots - his brothers - had, of course, been with him for thousands of years. They were known as dance and athletics.) These were two new offshoots. One soon became known as recreation, and the other was called health and safety education. Our hero helped to develop them quite a bit and, of course, they in their gratitude helped him too (while maintaining the dependency of youth).

Then one day after some great wars and other strong social forces had their influence on society, physical education, who was still a second-class citizen among educators, discovered that his offshoots (recreation and health and safety education) had grown large and important in the world. They were anxious to become first-class citizens, and they made loud noises on occasion to inform all men that they deserved priority in life--and men, at least a goodly portion of them at any rate, recognized that they were right. But times change slowly, and the education of men was not yet greatly affected by this recognition.

During roughly the same period of time, two other phenomena occurred which held great import for physical education. His brothers, athletics and dance, had been performing so well that they had over a period of time grown strong and powerful as well. Athletics (or sport, as it seems to be called on continents other than North America) looked at him and said, "What a dull clod art thou!" What athletics meant was that physical education, or blank, or _____, or tnemevom (which is quite difficult to pronounce) wasn't very exciting, as he usually involved repetitive exercises and endurance activities which promoted muscular strength, flexibility, and cardiovascular efficiency. Sadly enough, dance (his other brother) seemed to feel the same way. He realized that he had a responsibility to teach young people about himself in schools, but it was so much more thrilling to perform for the cognoscenti, and even the multitudes. Thus, he proclaimed that he was an art, and he wanted to join his brother arts in performing centers which were springing up in communities and on college and university campuses.

The Unhappy Plight of Physical Education. Physical education, or blank, or _____ , or tnemevom felt very sad, and he became worried. He looked back at his long heritage, and he recounted to himself the tale that has just been told to you. He felt important-- at least to himself. He figured that he had been misjudged, since his motives were pure. He wondered if he has been stupid, because people often seemed to treat him as such. He knew that all people still needed him (hadn't a great president been shocked by his absence?), but his very name--physical education (both words thereof, in fact)--made many seemingly intelligent people's lips curl. Thinking about the proverbial rose, he wondered if he would "smell as badly" with another name. After all, the U. S. Tire and Rubber Company was now known as UniRoyal, and people didn't look down on it. What should he do?

Time for Reflection. And then he began to think deeply, as deeply as he, a second-class citizen, could think. His identical twin sister, that lowly female creature who was really part of him (but who often made different noises as she went her own way), had been telling him for some time that he couldn't see the forest for the trees. She said, "Physical education; blank; sometimes designated as _____ ; but who should really be called tnemevom (which is quite difficult to pronounce), we have really been fools, and we merit our plight. We have been so stupid that we haven't been able to spell what we really should have been called--tnemevom it is, to be sure, but we have had it completely reversed!

Crestfallen, but with a rising sense of elation, tnemevom came to life all at once. He saw the light as explained to him by his identical twin sister. He took a deep breath, tensed his muscles, and executed a back somersault with a half twist. He assumed new dignity almost immediately, as he realized that he now had a new name (that was quite simple to pronounce), and it was MOVEMENT! From that day forward, he vowed that he would carry out his function more purposefully than ever before. He recognized that he could still relate effectively to his brothers and/or offshoots, as well as to his own identical twin sister (the person known formerly as a woman physical educator). But, more importantly, he realized that there was more to him than push-ups and jogging, as truly important as these parts of him might be. He sensed that he had physiological aspects, anatomical aspects, historical aspects, philosophical aspects, sociological aspects, psychological aspects, and so many other aspects that he couldn't count them on the fingers of his two hands.

The Hard Road Ahead

This was an important realization for MOVEMENT (formerly spelled tnemevom), but he didn't rush off blindly to proclaim his glory to the world. He had learned his lesson. This time he would spell his name correctly, and he would rest his case for recognition on a sound scientific base. He defined himself to the best of his ability and decided that "the interaction of man and his movements" (Paddick, 1967, p. 70) described his function quite well. Thus, a disciplinary body-of-knowledge could conceivably come from the "human movement sciences" (Kenyon, 1968, p. 16), or perhaps the human movement arts and sciences. Having reasoned so deeply, our hero looked around for his twin sister (that lowly female creature who was really part of him, but who was fidgeting rather impatiently at the moment) and said, "It's a hard road that lies ahead, and we may be unfit for the task. But if it is to be traversed, we must do it together. If we deserve to reach the goal we have dreamed of, we may get there some day. However, let's not debate the issue too long, since the sun is already quite high in the sky."

General Bibliography

1. Bowen, W. P. and Mitchell, E. D. The Theory of Organized Play. New York: A. S. Barnes and Company, 1923.

2. Brownell, C. L. and Hagman, E. P. Physical Education: Foundations and Principles. New York: McGraw-Hill Book Company, Inc., 1951.

3. Bucher, Charles A. Foundations of Physical Education. St. Louis: The C. V. Mosby Company, 1952.

4. Burtt, Edwin A. In Search of Philosophic Understanding. New York: The New American Library, Inc., 1965.

5. Clark, Margaret C., "A Philosophical Interpretation of a Program of Physical Education in a State Teachers College." Ph.D. dissertation, New York University, 1943.

6. Cobb, Louise S., "A Study of the Functions of Physical Education in Higher Education." Ph.D. dissertation, Teachers College, Columbia University, 1943.

7. Esslinger, Arthur A., "A Philosophical Study of Principles for Selecting Activities in Physical Education." Ph.D. dissertation, State University of Iowa, 1938.

8. Frankena, William K. _Philosophy of Education_. New York: The Macmillan Company, 1965.

9. _____. _Three Historical Philosophies of Education_. Chicago: Scott, Foresman and Company, 1965.

10. Hess, Ford A., "American Objectives of Physical Education from 1900 to 1957 Assessed in the Light of Certain Historical Events." Ed.D. dissertation, New York University, 1959.

11. Hetherington, Clark. _School Program in Physical Education_. New York: Harcourt, Brace and World, Inc., 1922.

12. Huxley, Aldous. _Tomorrow and Tomorrow and Tomorrow_. New York: The New American Library, Inc., 1964.

13. Kenyon, Gerald S., "On the Conceptualization of Sub-disciplines within an Academic Discipline Dealing with Human Movement." A paper presented at the Annual Meeting of the National College Physical Education Association of Men, Houston, Texas, January, 1968.

14. Lynn, Minnie L., "Major Emphases of Physical Education in the United States." Ph.D. dissertation, University of Pittsburgh, 1944.

15. McCloy, C. H. _Philosophical Bases for Physical Education_. New York: Appleton-Century-Crofts, Inc., 1940.

16. McNeill, William H. _The Rise of the West_. Chicago: The University of Chicago Press, 1963.

17. Morris, Desmond. _The Naked Ape_. New York: McGraw-Hill Book Company, 1967.

18. Nash, Jay B. (ed.). _Mind-Body Relationships_ (Vol. I). New York: A. S. Barnes and Company, Inc., 1931. (This was the first volume in the Interpretations of Physical Education Series; of interest, also, is _Character Education Through Physical Education_, 1934.)

19. Oberteuffer, Delbert. _Physical Education_. New York: Harper and Row, Publishers, 1951. (The Second Edition in 1962 was in collaboration with Celeste Ulrich.)

20. Paddick, Robert., "The Nature and Place of a Field of Knowledge in Physical Education." M.A. thesis, University of Alberta, April, 1967.

21. Scott, Harry A. Competitive Sports in Schools and Colleges.
    New York: Harper and Row, Publishers, Inc., 1951.

22. Sharman, Jackson B. Modern Principles of Physical Educa-
    tion. New York: A. S. Barnes and Company, Inc., 1937.

23. Simpson, George Gaylord, "What Is Man?" (A review of The
    Naked Ape by D. Morris), The New York Times Book Re-
    view, Feb. 11, 1968.

24. Staley, Seward C. Sports Education. New York: A. S. Barnes
    and Company, 1939.

25. Wayman, Agnes R. A Modern Philosophy of Physical Educa-
    tion. Philadelphia: W. B. Saunders Co., 1938.

26. Williams, Jesse F. The Principles of Physical Education.
    Philadelphia: W. B. Saunders Co., 1927. (The first
    edition of this significant work.)

27. _____ and Hughes, W. L. Athletics in Education.
    Philadelphia: W. B. Saunders Co., 1930.

28. Wood, Thomas D. and Cassidy, Rosalind. The New Physical
    Education. New York: The Macmillan Company, 1927.

29. Zeigler, Earle F., "History of Physical Education and Sport,"
    FIEP Bulletin, 3-4, 41-45, 1967.

30. _____ and McCristal, K. J., "A History of the Big Ten Body-
    of-Knowledge Project in Physical Education," Quest, IX,
    79-84, December, 1967.

31. _____ and VanderZwaag, H. J. Physical Education: Re-
    constructionism or Essentialism. Champaign, Illinois:
    Stipes Publishing Company, 1966.

PERSISTENT HISTORICAL PROBLEMS OF PHYSICAL EDUCATION AND SPORT

The presence of serious-minded men and women at this First International Seminar on the History of Physical Education and Sport --professional people assembled from so many different countries in the world--attests to the significance of such a meeting as this Seminar.* Despite the fact that all of us considered it important to be here, it is probably true that there would be as many different interpretations of the field's functions as there are delegates present here at the Wingate Institute in Israel. This should not concern us unduly, however, as there are undoubtedly some common denominators upon which we can agree (even if there is considerable concern by some as to what constitutes an acceptable name for what it is that we are).**

What are some of these common denominators in physical, health, and recreation education (including sport)? One stands out more clearly than any other--the belief of the large majority that regular physical education periods should be required for all school children through sixteen years of age (approximately). A second point of agreement is that a child should develop certain attitudes toward his own health in particular and toward community hygiene in general. Thus, certain basic health knowledge should be taught in the school curriculum. We can find agreement also on the worthy use of leisure.

Still further, professionals within the field would argue to a man that physical vigor is important. Beyond this we cannot go, however, since there would be no general agreement among the men, or between men and women, about what constitutes physical vigor or fitness. There are no world standards for physical fitness, only national norms in some cases which give us present status--nothing more.

---

* A paper presented to the First International Seminar on the History of Physical Education and Sport, Wingate Institute, Israel, April 9-11, 1968. (Published in the Proceedings).

** No apology will be offered for calling the field "physical, health, and recreation education (including sport)" at this moment. From one standpoint it could be explained that such a title reflects the philosophically progressivistic bias of the author. It does intimate that we are concerned with many aspects of the total education of man throughout life. If we grant the seemingly widely accepted unity of the human organism, then it follows that there is no such thing as physical education.

Even the role of competitive sports for boys and girls is an area in which there is some agreement. We feel generally that boys and girls at some stage of their development should have an experience of this type. But we can find no general agreement at all beyond this rather meaningless statement; there is quite a difference between a ten-year old playing marbles competitively and a fifty-four year old man wrestling competitively at the national level.

The matter of remedial exercise for physical defects that can be corrected in this way offers us another opportunity for a bit of agreement, but we can't decide who should attend to this, or when or where. Lastly, we agree that the area of character and/or personality development is important, but substantive evidence as to the effect of physical education and sport on such development is relatively negligible. The time is long overdue when this field should be able to present to the public far greater agreement on what it is that physical educators accomplish for the education of youth! (Zeigler, 1964, pp. 287-88).

The Body of Knowledge Project

The world is on the threshold of an exciting, if also a highly frightening, time. But even though man may be looking both hopefully and fearfully ahead, there is an ever-present need to become increasingly aware of the past. It was to this point that René Maheu addressed himself in the Foreword to the History of Mankind, the first global history of mankind, planned and written from an international standpoint by experts of world-wide reputation, and produced under the auspices of UNESCO:

> At a time when man is preparing to launch out from this planet into space, it is well that History should hold him in contemplation of his trajectory through the ages. Never before, indeed, has he shown so searching a curiosity about his past or such jealous care to preserve its vestiges . . . Be that as it may, never more than now, when man finds himself hurtling at vertiginous speed towards a wondrous future, has there been a great need for the function of memory to ensure for mankind the appropriation of its creative actuality . . . To evoke this retrospective awareness is the first thing that this work which we now have the honour of introducing to the public sets out to do; it is an attempt to sum up the heritage of civilization to which we owe our present élan. (Hawkes and Wooley, 1963, xi).

These statements about man "hurtling towards a wondrous future," "launching out from this planet into space," and yet "contemplating his trajectory through the ages" may well be applied to the situation of the field of physical education and sport at the present time. The effort to define the field as a discipline, so that a body of knowledge may be developed upon which the profession may practice and build its theory, may well assist man quite substantially to realize a "wondrous future" both on this planet and in space. Thus, the kinesiologists, exercise physiologists, psychologists, and sociologists within our field, for example, should be able to help us discover how man moves, and what happens to him when he moves. But it will be largely up to those interested in the historical, philosophical, and comparative aspects of physical education and sport to assist the profession to "contemplate the trajectory" of physical education, sport, human movement, kinesiology, or human motor performance through the ages. Some of you may be unwilling to accept responsibility for the inclusion of history, philosophy, and comparative (or international) education as applied to physical education and sport within your sphere of operation as a professional person. Naturally, this must be your own choice. The point being made, however, is that it is extremely difficult, if not impossible, to consider history, or philosophy, or comparative education without automatically encountering knowledge from one or both of the other two disciplines.

A Need to Specialize. This dilemma should not frighten professional physical educators who by necessity have been perennial "jacks of all trades" from the very beginning. It does not mean that quasi-historians, for example, are going to be forced to master the disciplines of philosophy and comparative education as well. It does mean, however, that a sport and physical education historian will need to maintain a continual awareness about what is taking place in the other two fields--and especially in regard to the points where the disciplines may impinge on one another.

At the same time there is a great need for vastly increased specialization within history, or philosophy, or comparative and international education as applied to this field. If it is maintained that physical education and sport represent an important phase of man's culture, it is absolutely imperative that competent historians record faithfully and analyze carefully what has transpired in this area. As Woody has stated, those who have written about education and history seem to have slighted "physical culture" through bias:

> Despite the fact that lip-service has been paid increasingly to the dictum 'a sound mind in a sound body,' ever since western Europe began to revive the educational concepts of the Graeco-Roman world, there is still a lack of balance between physical and mental culture, both in school programs and among those who write of education. This is

> evident in many quarters, even where a certain universal-
> ity of outlook ought to reign. Turn where one will, it is
> impossible to find physical culture adequately presented in
> books dealing with the general history of education. Writ-
> ten in keeping with a dominant rationalism, these books
> have been concerned chiefly with intellectual movements
> and institutions for mental improvement. (Woody, 1949,
> vii).

If this assessment is even reasonably substantially true, the field of
physical education truly has its work cut out for it.

And lest the occurrence of this First International Seminar
should tend to make those present even the least little bit self-
satisfied about progress in this direction, several perhaps embar-
rassing questions should be asked: (1) What percentage of those present at this Seminar spend even one-quarter (25%) of their working
time each week adding to the body of knowledge about the history of
physical education and sport?; and (2) How many others throughout
the world, not present here, could answer this question affirmative-
ly? Still further, are educational historians now assisting physical
education and sport historians--consciously or unconsciously? Or
for that matter, what help is coming from historians? And beyond
this, can the field continue to rely on those laymen, perhaps sportsmen of one type or another, who have an inclination to write sports
history of varying quality?

The Cause Is Not Yet Lost. That there should be serious concern about the present need for a greater amount of historical
investigation in this area is self-evident, and this concern grows
somewhat greater when it is understood that there doesn't appear to
be anywhere nearly full awareness of the need. There can be encouragement, nevertheless, from the knowledge that "as late as 1880
there were only eleven professors of history in American colleges,"
and as Muller also pointed out that:

> Our age is nevertheless more historically minded than any
> previous age, and has a much longer, wider, clearer view
> of the past. Its contributions to historical knowledge, over
> the last hundred years, are among its most honorable
> achievements. (Muller, 1952, pp. 33-34).

Persistent Historical Problems in Physical Education

More careful description and delineation of some of the persistent historical problems of physical education and sport is perhaps
the most important professional goal of this author. He would like to
be able to say that the idea for this approach came to him in a brilliant

flash of insight while standing on a high mountain top, but, alas, the derivation of the idea occurred in a much more prosaic manner. Although it is true that many of the ideas for the specific problems listed below did originate with him and some of his colleagues and graduate students, and that some adaptations have been made, the credit for this unique approach in educational history and philosophy must go to John S. Brubacher, long-time professor of the history and philosophy of education at Yale, and more recently at The University of Michigan in Higher Education. Thus, it is the adaptation of the approach, the selection of certain of the persistent problems, and the delineation of the implications for this specialized field that may possibly be considered as new contributions.[1]

Such an approach as this does not really represent a radically different approach to history. The typical major processes are involved in applying historical method to investigation in the field: (1) the data are collected from primary and secondary sources; (2) the collected data are criticized; and (3) an integrated narrative is presented which is based on critical inquiry for the entire truth. This approach does differ markedly, however, when the organization of the collected data is considered: it is based completely on the problem areas of the present and an effort to illuminate them for the student of physical education and sport. Thus, a conscious effort is made to keep the reader from thinking that the subject is of antiquarian interest only. The student moves back and forth from early times to the present as different aspects of the subject are considered, say, in the chapters of a book--a "longitudinal" approach as opposed to a strictly chronological one. These persistent problems, then, are ones that recur again and again down through the ages, and they will in all probability continue to occur in the future. A problem used in this sense (from its Greek derivation) would be "something thrown forward" for man to understand or resolve. The following are persistent historical problems of physical, health, and recreation education (including sport) as seen by the author and his associates at the present time:

1. Values (Aims and Objectives) - throughout history there have have been innumerable statements of educational aims, and almost invariably there was a direct relationship with a hierarchy of educational values present in the society under consideration. In general

---

[1] For further information the reader is referred to the following books: J. S. Brubacher, A History of the Problems of Education. New York: McGraw-Hill Book Company, 1966; and E. F. Zeigler, Persistent Problems in the History and Philosophy of Physical Education and Sport. Englewood Cliffs, New Jersey: Prentice-Hall, Inc., 1968.

educational philosophy, values have been either subjective or objective (i.e., do values exist in the world whether man happens to be present to realize them or not?). Physical education and sport has been viewed as curricular, co-curricular, or extracurricular.

2. The Influence of Politics - the kind and amount of education has varied throughout history depending upon whether a particular country was a monarchy, an aristocratic oligarchy, or a type of democracy. Experimentalism (pragmatic naturalism) in education, and this applies to physical, health, and recreation education as well, can flourish only in a type of democratic society. Educational essentialism, and this includes its implications for physical education and sport, may be promoted successfully in all three types of society.

3. The Influence of Nationalism - the influence of nationalism on this field throughout history is obvious. If a strong state is desired, the need for a strong, healthy people is paramount. There have been many examples of this type of influence as far back as the Medes and the Spartans, and as recently as some twentieth century European and Asian powers. In a democratic society, however, it is extremely difficult for a government in power to promote nationalism except by indirect and less effective means. During wartime, for example, the basic educational objectives are threatened when the government of a democracy attempts to dictate that physical education and sport be employed to promote physical fitness and national policy.

4. The Influence of Economics - in past times education has prospered when there was a surplus economy and declined when the economic structure weakened. Furthermore, educational aims have tended to vary depending on how people made their money and created such surplus economies. One of the problems of advancing industrial civilization has been the uneven distribution of wealth bringing educational advantages of a superior quality to some. Education "of the physical" can be promoted under any economic system. In largely agrarian societies, much physical fitness can be gained through manual labor, whereas in industrial societies some means has to be developed whereby all will maintain a minimum level of physical fitness. The more individual freedom is encouraged in a society, the more difficult a government will find it to demand that all citizens be physically fit.

5. The Influence of Religion - the church has had a strong influence on education throughout history, but there is evidence that the power of the church over the individual is continuing to decline in the twentieth century. The Christian religion can be recognized for the promulgation of principles in which man was considered valuable as an individual. A society must decide to what extent it can, or should, inculcate moral and/or religious values in the public schools. In

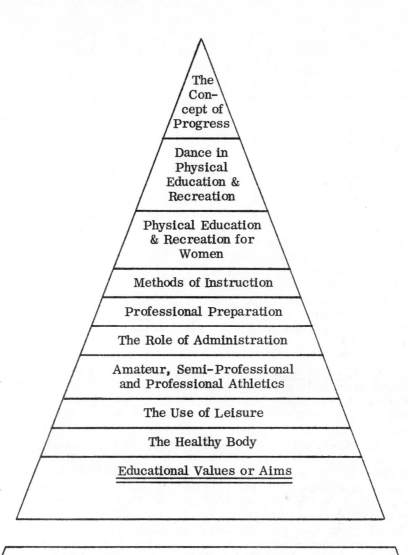

The
Con-
cept of
Progress

Dance in
Physical
Education &
Recreation

Physical Education
& Recreation for
Women

Methods of Instruction

Professional Preparation

The Role of Administration

Amateur, Semi-Professional
and Professional Athletics

The Use of Leisure

The Healthy Body

Educational Values or Aims

HISTORICAL EVOLUTION OF SOCIAL FORCES
(Politics, Nationalism, Economics, Religion)

SELECTED, PERSISTENT, HISTORICAL PROBLEMS
OF PHYSICAL, HEALTH, AND RECREATION EDUCATION
(including SPORT)

keeping with a trend toward separation of church and state, the question remains whether the church has the flexibility to become that unique social institution needed to effect necessary changes in the social environment. Physical, health, and recreation education (including sport) have not been supported significantly by religious organizations in the past. In fact, with the promotion of a mind-body dualism, the opposite has often been the case. Fortunately, this attitude seems to be changing to a degree.

6. The Healthy Body - a study of past civilizations indicates that the states of war or peace, as social influences, have had a direct bearing on the emphases placed on personal and/or community health. Freedom from disqualifying defects, strength, and endurance are important to men who want to win wars. When a particular war has ended, a society may then be able again to focus greater attention toward a more healthful environment at home. It is profoundly disturbing that so many people in the world cannot profit from the outstanding progress that has been made in public health science. There is still disagreement as to a definition of health and as to the place of health instruction in the school curriculum. Which agency, the home, school, or community agency, should play the greatest role in this area?

7. The Use of Leisure - this persistent problem has a relationship to the influence of economics on a society - both education and recreation prospered in times past when there was a surplus economy. In most of the world's twenty-one civilizations the average man has had to work very hard to earn a meagre living. Certain classes, rulers, priests, and nobles, were the first to enjoy anything like extended leisure. Even in the Middle Ages life still held many inequalities for the masses, although recreation did begin to take on a broader significance. Wars, the fact that times change slowly, and the power of the Church prevented the concepts of political democracy and socialism from taking hold. Then, too, the natural sciences had to be advanced enough so that advanced technology could lead men into an industrial revolution, which has lowered man's working hours so markedly. Now we hear about cybernation and automation, and education for leisure would seem to warrant serious consideration. The extent to which such preparation is included in the school's curriculum depends quite largely on prevailing educational philosophy.

8. Amateurism, Semi-Professionalism, and Professionalism in Sport - the motivation behind participation in games and sports through the ages has been so complex that there is really no general agreement on the matter. Man has taken part for fun, for recreation, for self-expression, for health, for exercise, for competition, for money, and probably for other reasons not readily discernible. There was even an early relationship of sport to religious observances. Even in the earlier days the aspect of over-specialization

- 18 -

because of the desire to win (and perhaps the material rewards) has tended to "tarnish the lustre" of the amateur ideal. There are so many different definitions of an amateur extant in the world today that it is impossible to keep up with them. It may well be that we will have to re-evaluate some of our treasured, basic assumptions about the amateur code in sport, which views the matter on the basis of polarities. There is need for a semi-professional category in which the athlete will not be viewed as something "dirty and degraded." There is a need further for a professional sportsman who will be taught to devote his life to a social ideal--to serve his fellow man through his contributions to the many phases of a sport's development. Under the right auspices all types of sport can hold value for the individual. Sport can be a "socially useful servant."

    9. The Role of Administration - social organizations, of one type or another, are inextricably related to man's history as a human and social animal. Superior-subordinate relationships evolved according to the very nature of things, as man produced goods, fought wars, organized his society politically, formed his churches, and developed a great variety of formal and informal associations. A central theme seems to have been that of change--change that was made to strengthen the organization administratively. It was only recently that "administrative thought emerged as a differentiated field of sustained writing, conscious observation, abstract theory, and specialized terminology." (Gross, 1964, p. 91). Education has become a vast public and private enterprise demanding wise management based upon sound administrative theory. The "organizational revolution" has meant that educational administrators have been forced to create a greater amount of bureaucracy. Educational essentialists tend to believe that there are valid theoretical principles of administration that should not be violated. Educational progressivists, conversely, tend to view administration as a developing social science--a science that is gradually providing man with a body-of-knowledge about human relations and the decision-making process. Administrators of physical education and sport organizations need to understand this development thoroughly.

    10. Professional Preparation - the idea of professions (with accompanying preparation for this type of service) has its origins in antiquity in the very early societies. Professional preparation of teachers to any considerable extent is a fairly recent innovation. In early times the most important qualification for the position of teacher was a sound knowledge of the subject. In the Middle Ages there was no such thing as professional education to be a teacher, at least in the sense that certification is needed today to teach in the publicly-supported institutions at certain levels in particular countries. It was in Prussia where the most headway was made in improving teacher education in the late eighteenth and early nineteenth centuries. This system was copied extensively elsewhere. Significant advances

in the theory of pedagogy occurred through the influence of Pestalozzi. In America, for example, the normal school became a well-established part of the educational system. In the twentiety century this organization has progressed to college and/or university status. Professional education eventually achieved status at the university level, but it is required for public school teachers only--not at the college or university level. Generally speaking throughout the world, professional preparation for physical education is included at the normal and/or technical school level. University recognition has been achieved at some institutions in England, Japan, and the United States, for example, but there is much progress to be made.

11. <u>Methods of Instruction</u> - the educational curriculum has been influenced strongly by a variety of political, economic, philosophical, religious, and scientific factors. In curriculum construction, therefore, a primary task is to determine which subjects should be included because of the recurring interest that has been shown among educators and laymen for their inclusion at some educational level. Primitive and pre-literate man undoubtedly learned through imitation and through trial and error. When writing was invented in the early civilizations, memorization played a large part in the educational process. Tradition and custom were highly regarded, and the importance of precept and proper example were significant aspects of both physical and mental culture. In the Near East Jesus was evidently a very fine teacher, but Christian religious leaders who followed him presumably employed less exciting teaching methods with an emphasis on formality and dogmatism. Toward the end of the Middle Ages, educational methodology is said to have improved considerably. With the onset of the Renaissance, there was greater recognition of individual differences, and the whole spirit of this period was much more humanistic. Physical educators need to understand that the concept of a mind-body dualism has prevailed in many quarters down to the present day. A physical educator should determine for himself what influence that content has on method; do they go hand in hand? Shall physical education and sport (or whatever part of it is included in the curriculum) be taught formally, semi-formally, or informally. The persistent problem remains: how can the student be motivated so that learning will occur most easily, and so that it will be remembered?

12. <u>Physical Education and Recreation for Women</u> - throughout history women's physical education has been hampered not only by the concept of the place of physical education in a particular society, but also by the place that women themselves held in most societies--and by the ideas that men and women have had about the limitations of women because of their anatomical structure and their role in the reproductive process of the human race. Aristotle, for example, felt that they were generally speaking weaker, less courageous, and incomplete, and that they had been fitted by nature for subjection to the

male. Plato held a different view; he believed that women should have all types of education similar to the pattern he prescribed for men (including the highest type of liberal education, and even preparation for warfare). Throughout history, with notable exceptions in the cases of Crete, Sparta, later Rome, and certain individual instances, practically all women were considered inferior. In the twentieth century, certainly one of the significant social trends has been woman's "emancipation." Many women are now conceived of as having an intellectual function depending in many cases upon her individual qualifications. More democratic theories of state have fostered equalitarianism. Many people feel that men's physical education and women's programs should more nearly approximate each other. The norm projected by society for women tends to be retrogressive; and it has been modified by what many consider to be unfortunate societal influences. For example, most women are quite concerned about their appearance, but it is often maintained by a artificial devices, and they are rarely physically fit. If our total field has advantages to offer to women, educators should see to it that they receive these opportunities.

13. Dance in Physical Education and Recreation - in all ages people have danced for personal pleasure, for religious purposes, for expression of the gamut of emotions, and for the pleasure of others. An analysis of the dance forms of a civilization can tell a qualified observer much about the total life therein. In primitive societies types of rhythmic expressions were "instinctive satisfiers" of man. Dance was most often serious in nature and only incidentally served physical fitness, health, and recreation. It served a purpose in Roman civilization, but its status was below that given it by the Greeks. During the Middle Ages dance had very low status probably due to its corruption in the later Roman era. The place of dance began to rise again during the Renaissance; different types and forms have waxed and waned over the centuries. The twentieth century has witnessed a truly remarkable development in the dance, as the body is gradually being rediscovered as a means of communication through the dance medium. There is still much room for progress. For example, a significant body of research knowledge is lacking. Still further, an improvement of the interaction between the dance teacher and the professional performer would add further strength to the development. Articulation within the dance curriculum among the various educational levels is needed. On the North American continent modern dance especially seems unacceptable to the majority of male physical education teachers (and hence to the boys and young men in their classes as well). As both an art and as a social function, dance will probably always be with us and will reflect the dominant influences of the age in which it is taking place.

14. The Concept of Progress - any study of history inevitably forces a person to conjecture about man's progress. Certainly there

has been progression, but can this be called "progress?" To ascertain if change may be called progress, it is necessary to measure whether advancement has been made from worse to better (for example). A criterion must be recommended by which progress may be judged. It is true that man has made progress in adaptability and can cope with a variety of environments. It is probably safe to assume that man on the whole is the pinnacle of evolutionary progress on this earth. Throughout the course of history until the Golden Age of Greece, a good education had been based on the transmission of the cultural heritage. During the Roman Empire and the Middle Ages such an educational pattern continued, despite the fact that from time to time certain educational theorists offered proposals of greater or lesser radical quality. Thus, when a society declined, those involved in the educational system had relatively few useful ideas about social rejuvenation. Despite the forces of the Renaissance and accompanying humanism, followed by the gradual introduction of science into the curriculum, the same traditional educational pattern kept the school from becoming an agent of social reconstructionism. In physical education and sport, it is vitally important to search for consensus among the conflicting philosophies of physical, health, and recreation education (including sport). The field has been proceeding "amoeba-like" for far too long considering the body-of-knowledge that is amassing. It is fortunate that there is more agreement in practice than in theory.

Conclusion

And so this discussion has proceeded full circle through brief summaries of some fourteen persistent historical problems back to the common denominators that were presented at the outset of this paper. Having stated these common denominators, it would appear that the time is long overdue when the field should be able to present fairly concrete evidence of far greater agreement to the public in relation to what it is that we do. The goal should be the discovery of what contributions physical education and sport can make to the development of man. Then, based upon its system of values, a particular society will accept or reject this evidence and promote that type of a program which the people will support. Based upon the scientific evidence from the discipline, and the enlightened support of intelligent laymen, the professional's task is to administer the program of physical education and sport so that maximum benefits will accrue to the greatest number of people possible. This task belongs to us alone.

Selected References

Gross, Bertram M. The Managing of Organizations. 2 vols. New York: Crowell-Collier Publishing Company, 1964.

Hawkes, Jacquetta and Wooley, Leonard. History of Mankind. (Vol. I: Prehistory and Beginnings of Civilization). New York: Harper and Row, Publishers, 1963.

Muller, Herbert J. The Uses of the Past. New York: The New American Library of World Literature, Inc., 1954.

Woody, Thomas. Life and Education in Early Societies. New York: The Macmillan Company, 1949.

Zeigler, Earle F. Philosophical Foundations for Physical, Health, and Recreation Education. Englewood Cliffs, New Jersey: Prentice-Hall, Inc., 1964.

Selection #3

VIGOROUS PHYSICAL EDUCATION AND SPORT AS ESSENTIAL INGREDIENTS IN AMERICA'S PATTERN OF PHYSICAL ACTIVITY

The twentieth century in the Western world, despite the inroads of war, has been characterized by a great surplus economy.* Education for "the worthy use of leisure," as an organized structure of our democratic educational system, however, has not kept pace with the developing economy. Many otherwise intelligent people, refusing to recognize the place that wholesome recreation must have in a madcap society, display a perplexing lack of a leisure philosophy. Hard work, industriousness, and unremitting toil are vital in the "race to the moon," but the ability and the desire to relax and take part in recreative activities are equally as important for a daily renewal of vigor and a complete life.

In addition, children and young people in the United States are "enjoying" a way of life which is not conducive to the achievement of a strong, supple body that is healthy enough to withstand many of life's stresses and strains. We are told that a great many of our boys cannot do one pull-up; that only twenty-five percent of our elementary school children receive regular, organized physical education classes; that only fifty percent of our high school youth get such instruction regularly; that draft statistics in World Wars I and II showed high rejection rates; that the average adult female is sixteen pounds overweight, and that the average male is twenty pounds overweight; a and that many people twenty-seven years of age are old "physically," insofar as large muscle-group strength, flexibility, and circulorespiratory efficiency are concerned.

Young People Are Not Rugged Enough

Boys and girls today just aren't rugged enough. Our way of life has changed to such a marked degree that we are actually depriving our children of experiences which heretofore were commonplace. Children on this continent have demonstrated conclusively that their muscular strength and endurance are low. Translated into simplest terms, it would appear that we are mistakenly "coddling" our children. The late Dr. C. H. McCloy of the State University of Iowa, certainly one of the foremost people in the physical education field,

---

* A paper requested for the Youth Development Issue of the Michigan Osteopathic Journal, Vol. XXX, No. 8:19-22, October, 1965.

doubted if "more than one-fifth of our physical education classes in the schools of today include enough exercise of a vigorous nature to contribute materially to any significant organic stimulation."

Kennedy Followed Beliefs With Action

The late President John F. Kennedy, even before his election, gave Sports Illustrated a most important story about his belief in the importance of physical fitness of our youth. Soon after his election, he followed his beliefs with action. The President's Council on Physical Fitness is still guiding itself by these words taken from a "Presidential Message to the Schools on the Physical Fitness of Youth":

> The strength of our democracy is no greater than the collective well-being of our people. The vigor of our country is no stronger than the vitality and will of our countrymen. The level of physical, mental, moral, and spiritual fitness of every American citizen must be our constant concern.

> The need for increased attention to the physical fitness of our youth is clearly established. Although today's young people are fundamentally healthier than the youth of any previous generation, the majority have not developed strong, agile bodies. The softening process of our civilization continues to carry on its persistent erosion.

Americans Are "Running Scared"

"So far, so good," you say. This is true! Admittedly, many of us are "running scared." We see pictures of Russians taking calisthenics instead of coffee breaks, of Russian athletes breaking world records, and of exceptionally well-conditioned Russian women performing flawlessly in track and field, as well as in gymnastics. Couple this with the various other aspects of the Cold War, and it is quite simple to realize that perhaps we should re-double our efforts along the lines of physical fitness.

The Program in Michigan

Observation of the boys' and girls' programs of health, physical education, and recreation in Michigan public schools over a period of seven years led to the conclusion that the program in Michigan is not significantly better than the hypothetical national average. This may be good enough for some whose educational philosophy allows no room in the core curriculum for this subject-matter field. It should not be "good enough," however, for those educators who subscribe to the concept of a "sound mind in a sound body." Even this ideal does not necessarily imply "the worthy use of leisure," which looms so large in so heavily an industrialized state.

Lest the reader think that a "blast is being loosed" at colleagues on the elementary and secondary levels, let me hasten to say that this is only partially so. One of the major difficulties appears to be that old "bugaboo" that goes by the name of "administrative feasability." To be sure, many of the teachers may not realize the potentialities of which they are capable, but we can't argue the fact that administrative leadership tends to be deadening and stifling in many instances. The state consultant, to give one example, is thoroughly competent and knows what the ideal health, physical education, and recreation program should look like, but for a number of reasons he is not in a position to demand that the "ideal" be approximated.

Let us look at the situation briefly before attempting to offer specific suggestions drawn from a number of school visitations. Frankly, our secondary schools do not seem to be able to cope with the demand for all sorts of sports and games. In the high schools one usually finds a good interscholastic athletics program, a fair to poor required physical education class program, an almost non-existent intramural sports program for the average male youngster, and a deficient voluntary physical recreation program. Generally speaking, community recreation program leaders have tried to fill the gap in "intramural games and sports" and have left inter-community competitive leagues to all sorts and kinds of "outside organizations." The resultant heterogeneous outcome looks something like a patchwork quilt with a few disturbing holes in it.

Unfortunately, there appears to be little or no articulation among the three levels of education before college or university. Elementary school children (grades 1-6) are not getting rugged physical education activities in school, nor are they learning sports skills. Some youngsters are getting varying levels of attention outside of school through private organizations and community recreation programs. The junior high school picture (grades 7-9) is better in regard to regular health and physical education classes (but still not good!) and, in some cases, a considerable amount of interscholastic athletics competition is going on. This latter emphasis, along with junior high school marching bands, has been sharply criticized by Dr. James B. Conant recently. I do not sense this as a serious problem in Michigan, however.

Awareness of Growth and Development Pattern Needed

It is simply not possible to discuss physical fitness and sport for children and youth intelligently, unless we are fully aware of the entire pattern of child growth and development. For example, what are the growth and development characteristics of a ten-year old, or a thirteen-year old? Some people think that a normal, healthy youngster should be playing tiddly-winks most of the time, while others go so far as to encourage regional and national tackle football tournaments for elementary school children. Your children and mine are of the utmost importance to you and me, and we want to be certain that we are "doing right by them." If you want to find out what a person really thinks, take a look at what he is encouraging his own children to do, and why.

Adequate Physical Development Important

From the mental hygiene standpoint, a child or an adult who is physically undeveloped tends to feel a sense of inferiority, which may well affect his social responses. From a completely practical standpoint it may be pointed out also that a person without a normal amount of muscle is much more susceptible to fatigue than an individual with adequate musculature. A fatigued organism is simply not ready for the burden and demands of everyday life. Such a person is more subject to colds and minor infections. Much more serious is the fact that the flabby child or adult usually has a heart that is weak and is not ready for emergencies. In this regard I am not thinking necessarily of the strain of a street fight or a fire in the home. It could well be a question of the organism "mobilizing to do battle" against some infection like pneumonia. As McCloy said often, "Adequate strength is good life insurance." Our immediate concern should be that we are not giving youth a program which guarantees either strength or endurance.

We Do Not Know All The Answers

Right now I should be able to say that we know absolutely that a particular program must be followed by all. Although the opinions of the majorities of physicians, authorities in physiological and psychological research, and eminent physical educators point very definitely toward a reasonable amount of exercise and competition at the very least, in a number of ways these opinions are based on conclusions which have not always been proved scientifically and repeatedly. Furthermore, recent summer youth fitness schools conducted at universities like Illinois, Michigan, and Oregon are presenting solid evidence that we have been too over-protective in the types of activities that have been recommended for elementary school youth.

Guarantee Youth The Best Type of Sport Experience

Certainly this is not a black or white issue. It is not a case of being for or against sport for children. It is more a matter of guaranteeing our youth the best possible types of experiences through the medium of games and sports. Although vigorous physical activities are recommended by most authorities, unfortunately sound elementary physical education programs exist in only a relatively small percentage of public schools in the United States. The fact is that leadership, facilities, and class time are generally not available.

Don't Immediately Criticize Those Who Sponsor Sport for Youth

For this reason it seems rather unjust for anyone to automatically criticize people who sponsor leagues and tournaments for youth. The leadership is all-important, as this will probably be the deciding factor as to the worth of the activity to the boy or girl. The school should have a prior claim to children during the school year. Community recreation directors, or anyone else, should never fight "for us of the same bodies" during that time of the year when school is in session. Instead more attention should be devoted to other age groups, where there is most assuredly a great need for the development of active and creative program activities in all areas of recreational interest.

Athletics Offer Ideal Setting for Teaching and Learning

The late Harry M. Scott, in his excellent book of the 1950's entitled Competitive Sports in Schools and Colleges, pointed out that the highly emotionalized situations in athletics afford the ideal setting for teaching and learning to take place, but he stressed further that there is nothing inherent in this type of activity which guarantees that this learning will necessarily result. Programs should be organized so that the real-life drama of athletics will actually become a part of the general education of youth.

He emphasizes further that we should never encourage a boy or girl to become too narrow a specialist early in his/her sports career. No athletic program should exploit the athletic abilities of the youth. From another standpoint he tells us that the degree of organic vigor accruing to the individual is lessened when the purpose behind the participation is social recreation and increased when the element of serious competition is introduced. Stressing the need for sound leadership and sportsmanship education also, Scott believes that since actions are conditioned by understandings and appreciations, it is necessary that all players should be provided with guidance and instruction in personal conduct both as participants in and spectators at athletic contests.

Parents Should Speak Out

If parents are truly concerned about their children's physical fitness, they will make their wants and needs known to the schools They will tell their principals and superintendents that every child deserves a fine program of health, physical education and recreation. This should include an intramural competitive sports experience as well, even if this interferes somewhat with the varsity teams' practice time. After all, who ever heard of -- say -- five or ten percent of the advanced students in English setting absolute priority over the remaining ninety percent. Many children are quite completely deficient in athletics and physical recreational skills. Interscholastic athletics, conducted by sound educators, make a fine contribution-- but only if they "crown" an outstanding program of health, physical education, and recreation for every child.

The Public Needs Convincing

Somehow, the President's Council on Physical Fitness, as well as others concerned at the state and local levels, are going to have to convince parents and school personnel that the physical welfare of all our youth is so important that every child should have a regular physical education class daily. This will be no mean task for a number of reasons. In the first place, we are living in an "era of new conservatism," despite what a number of administrators in power are saying about "new frontiers." Many educators, especially those at the college and university level, think that this means a return to "old frontiers" presumably long since discarded.

Youth Needs Fitness Motivation

If we want youth to be fit, the answer appears to be quite straightforward: we must motivate them by somehow interesting young people in the whole idea of sport and physical recreation as a basic part of the North American culture (Canadian and U. S.). Patterning our schools after those in Russia is assuredly not the answer! We can't return to unnatural activities from another era in our history that didn't really work then either. In our health, physical education, and recreation programs we must evaluate progress according to the individual's own growth and development pattern. Routinized calisthenics and distance running need to be seen as a means to an end. We should offer remedial instruction to the youngster who needs it. There is a real need here. Over and above this, we should instruct youngsters in a variety of individual, dual, and team sports skills. If he or she acquires proficiency through excellent instruction along the way, the "battle will be mainly won." As young people and adults we take part in those activities in which we excel to at least some degree. Give a man or woman a physical recreational sports skill, and this person will continue to take part in that activity throughout life. Such a man or woman will make the opportunities for healthful play somehow. In so doing he or she will build and maintain a foundation for so-called physical fitness throughout one's entire life.

An Ideal Program

Now for some of the specifics which relate primarily to the junior high and high school levels, although there are some implications here for the elementary grades as well. I believe that every school system should develop a curriculum guide or syllabus with some of the following suggested headings:

1. Aims and Objectives - rarely, if ever, do I find a written statement of long range aims and immediately realizable objectives for the health, physical education, and recreation program.

2. Medical Examination - there is usually no policy about such an examination for all students and subsequent assignment to physical education activities on this basis. We usually don't even ask for a statement from the family physician.

3. Physical Education Classification - such classification of students to get some sort of homogeneous grouping in the various classes is practically non-existent. In many instances one finds boys and/or girls from all grade levels taking part in the same activity at the same time.

4. Individual or Adapted Program - there are many young people in our classes with remediable defects, but there is not time and there are no facilities to do anything about this problem.

5. Health Education - there seems to be no general understanding of the recognized three-pronged approach to this program feature (i.e., health services, health instruction, and healthful school living). I have yet to find a really active health committee within a high school with representation from those who should be involved (i.e., the janitor, the principal, etc.).

6. Required Physical Education Class Program - here we face a situation where conditioning is not adequate; sports instruction is not varied enough nor in sufficient detail; and elective opportunities are not sufficiently available to upperclass students.

7. Intramural Athletics - administrators should consider the appointment of an interested teacher on a part-time basis to administer the "athletics for all" program under the department's aegis. If

the physical educator coaches, he or she does not have time for this in addition to the regular teaching assignment. Furthermore, if we are not willing to provide some facilities at a reasonable time, perhaps we should ask community recreation to look after this phase of the boys' program.

8. Interscholastic Athletics - it would be helpful to find policy statements about this phase of the program in some sort of an administrative guide. Because of fine state leadership, and because this aspect of the total program is what the public usually sees, interscholastic athletics are in good condition, relatively speaking. We should make every effort, however, to offer competition in a greater number of sports, and we should give more boys a chance to participate in each sport through junior varsity and freshman schedules (where Grade 9 is included).

9. Voluntary Physical Recreation - this phase of the program can grow naturally from elective opportunities for upperclass students in the leisure, carry-over sports.

10. Evaluation and Measurement - more thought should be given to a "philosophy" of grading in a subject like physical education. I find that there is too great a variance between individual teachers and between schools. What is it that we are measuring? If we test and then classify at the outset, it follows that we should re-test at the end of the unit or semester to help with the determination of a fair grade.

Conclusion

Health, physical education, and recreation (including athletics) can and should play an important part in the life of the growing young man (or woman)--given fine leadership, adequate time, and adequate facilities. Much good work is being done, but it can be improved by energetic, imaginative leadership and by assistance from enlightened administrators. Certain deficiencies taken from a limited sampling have been noted. There is obviously much room for improvement in the many aspects of a total program. If we as adults haven't been wise enough to take care of our own bodies, haven't we the responsibility nevertheless to encourage our youngsters to take part in sports and games that will help them build strong, healthy bodies? Unless we act now to help our own children develop a way of life that includes regular participation in healthful physical activity, it won't be long before they will become adults who are victims of a wealthy economy that has provided them with flabby bellies, poked necks, weak arms, excessively curved backs, and pronated ankles. Certainly there is no single answer to the ever-present problem of "physical fitness" - fitness that is needed to help us work and play at our best. Each of us must act in our own community to insure our children and young people a program of health, physical education, and recreation that will give them the energy and stamina to offer leadership to the United States in a vital period--the last third of the twentieth century.

A BIASED VIEW OF HISTORY, HISTORIOGRAPHY AND PHYSICAL EDUCATION AND SPORT

The words chosen for the title of this presentation give the reader a working outline of the topics to be discussed, and this includes the order in which they will be presented as well.[1] It may be a little out of the ordinary for someone to declare his bias (or personal value system) in a scholarly paper. This would be much more legitimate, you might say, in a sermon from the pulpit. This is true enough in the Western world, and one can only hope that religion and philosophy will "cross swords" more often in the future. (The possibility of value-free judgment will be discussed further a bit later.)

After this brief introduction, this paper will be subdivided into four sections as follows: (1) some statements about the world in which we live; (2) some definitions that will hopefully clarify that which we are discussing: history, historiography, and physical education and sport; (3) some discussion about these three subjects based upon their current status; and (4) a short epilogue about "the good life" which should be in the same vein as the earlier remarks on related matters.

Statements About the World in Which We Live

Almost ten years ago (1961), Henry Steele Commager, the noted Amherst historian (Look, June 6, 1961), was asked to assess the significant advances made in the world in the twenty-five years prior to this date. He noted the presence of much evil, but he spoke optimistically implying that the forces of good had gone steadfastly ahead. As we consider his list of ten (!) advances, reflect over whether they still apply today, and whether any additional advances might be added to this listing. The major areas in which Commager felt progress had been made include:

1. the survival of civilization
2. the end of Western colonialism
3. the vast progress in natural sciences
4. the development of electronics
5. the formidable advances in medical science

---

[1] A paper presented to Section 1 of the First Canadian Symposium on the History of Sport and Physical Education on May 13, 1970 at the University of Alberta, Edmonton, Alberta, Canada. (Published in the Proceedings in 1972, 625-643.

6. the creation and growth of the United Nations
7. the acceptance of responsibility for the welfare of less fortunate nations
8. the rapid growth of Big Government
9. the unprecedented educational revolution, especially in America
10. the recognition of intellectual and material equality that eventually will destroy artificial inequalities of class, race, or color.

Commager's guarded optimism does not seem to be prevailing as we begin the 1970's, if we can put any trust in the thought of Albert Szent-Gyorgyi, Hungarian-born Nobel scientist who discovered Vitamin C. He expresses great fear that man will disappear because of his inability to adapt to changing conditions. In his book (The Crazy Ape, published in New York City by the Philosophical Library, Inc., in 1970), he explains that "the great change in human life came at the turn of the century" when man discovered the electron, X-rays, quanta and radioactivity, and relativity (reported in The New York Times, February 20, 1970). These discoveries showed man that there was a second world underneath the one visible to the naked eye. The world today is dominated by these new cosmic forces, and man has achieved control of them. Can America learn to use this great power for the good of the world? If we are "so deeply in a groove" because of the actions of our leaders in this gerontocracy, perhaps the only way out is to turn the future over to "idealistic youth." But Dr. Szent-Gyorgyi is not naive at the age of 76, and he can't envision such a development taking place.

This type of thinking has been duplicated many times. Dr. Glenn T. Seaborg, chairman of the Atomic Energy Commission of the U. S. A., told Congress (The New York Times, February 5, 1970) that "the age of triumphant science and technology was forcing man into a new philosophical era based on the 'why' of living." He expressed the belief (and hope) that the "despair and negativism of the time" would be followed by much greater concern for human values and goals. The expression of these ideas was part of his testimony in favor of increased Government aid to the humanities - hopefully an effort to improve the quality of man's life.

There does seem to be reason for the fears of these scientists. Who read without a shudder about the amazing neurobehavioral research of Dr. José Delgado at the Yale School of Medicine. Delgado believes that man can now take an evolutionary leap and become "master of his own mind" as he moves ahead to "the development of a psychocivilized society" (Yale Alumni Magazine, XXXIII, No. 4, January, 1970). Thus, through electrical stimulation of parts of the brain, it may be possible to cure mental disturbances, including epilepsy, and thereby to construct a better world for the future. Of course, it is immediately obvious to us that such power in the wrong hands could bring about a sort of Super-1984 in which the entire world would be controlled by an Electroligarchy - a situation in which about forty men and/or women would rule all others (whose brains would be controlled to varying degrees depending upon the role each was designated to play during his lifetime).

If these statements have not been enough to cause you to have increased fears for the future, hearken to Senator Samuel Ervin's words that the U.S.A. Congress is "so zealous in their efforts to enforce the law that they would emulate the example set by Samson in his blindness and destroy the pillars upon which the temple of justice itself rests" (The New York Times, February 1, 1970). This was part of an article in which Mr. Wicker asserts that our ideals are being made a fraud throughout our entire legal establishment.

This type of argument could go on indefinitely. The whole question of alienation from society - on the part of youth and others - bring statements from psychiatrists that Vietnam and civil rights are not the basic reasons for disturbance (The New York Times, February 20, 1970). The question of changing values has perplexed adults, and many of the former opportunities for character growth by "rebellion" are no longer available. Conversely, Joseph Adelson of Michigan denies that there is such a distinct "generation gap" between the young and the old (The New York Times Magazine, January 18, 1970). He asserts that this myth sprang up far too quickly to be true. Instead he points out that recent investigation has indicated that college youth are closer to their parents than ever before; that political attitudes are still acquired within the family; that the traditional middle-class values are still held by both generations; and that the mood of youth has changed simply because the mood of total America has changed.

Two further opinions are offered to point up the crisis of the times before we move ahead to the definitions of our task in history, historiography, and the history of physical education and sport. The first is offered by Samuel B. Gould, chancellor of the State University of New York. He finds serious faults with the universities and their faculties and students. He states, "the modern university has never been more necessary and central to our national life than it is today," but "we must also say in the next breath that no other major institution in this country is now so open to disbalance and in so precarious a state of health" (The New York Times, September 23, 1969). He believes that universities should be more democratic, more concerned with social problems, more alert to students' justified demands, and more critical of their own performances.

Fearing that needed change won't take place rapidly enough, the liberal Supreme Court Justice William O. Douglas states, "We must realize that today's Establishment is the new George the III [the King of England in 1776]. Thus, if the Establishment continues to adhere to its tactics of oppression, and is unwilling to change, "the redress," according to Douglas, "honored in tradition, is also revolution" (The New York Times, February 1, 1970, as taken from Points of Rebellion, New York: Random House, 1970).

Definitions to Clarify the Topics at Hand

History. In 1946, a definitive report of the Committee on Historiography of the Social Science Research Council was published. Chaired by Merle Curti, of the University of Wisconsin, this has proved to be a most useful statement during the past twenty-five years ("Theory and Practice in Historical Study," Bulletin 54, New York City, 1946). The term "history" is used "in at least five overlapping senses," and the meanings are offered below (arranged in a slightly different sequential order):

1. the past of mankind (or any part thereof) - as in "history as actuality" or "the totality of history."
2. the survivals and records (whether primary or secondary) of the past of mankind (or any part thereof) - as in "recorded history," "a history book," or "a case history."
3. the study, representation, and explanation of the past of mankind (or any part thereof) from the survival and records - as in "written or spoken history."
4. the systematic study of, or a treatise dealing with, natural phenomena - as in "natural history" or "life history."
5. the branch of knowledge that records, studies, represents, and explains the past of mankind (or any parts thereof) - as in "department of history" or "school of history."

To this fivefold series of "uses" for the term "history" can be added at least four other meanings of a supplementary nature that appear in The Random House Dictionary of the English Language (New York City: Random House, 1967, p. 674). These included the following: (1) a continuous, systematic narrative of past events as relating to a particular people, country, period, person, etc., usually written in chronological order: "a history of France"; (2) a past that is full of important, unusual or interesting events: "a ship with a history"; (3) acts, ideas or events that will or can shape the course of the future: first hand observers of our space program see "history in the beginning"; and (4) a drama representing historical events: "Shakespeare's comedies, histories, and tragedies." Obviously, one must be careful when he "talks about the dead."

Historiography. As if it were not difficult enough to keep the many definitions and uses of the term "history" straight, we are now faced with distinguishing among three ways of defining historiography. It means literally "what has been written about history," but let us turn once again to the 1946 Report mentioned above. Thus, the term "historiography" is used in the following three senses:

1. primarily as the intellectual processes, critical and constructive, by which history is written (in which sense it is often treated as equivalent to synthesis in historical work).
2. the results of these processes (in which sense it is largely equivalent to secondary historical literature).
3. the study and criticism of the sources and development of history (in which sense it is largely equivalent to the history and critique of history.

Physical Education and Sport. Inasmuch as these above definitions can be transferred directly to our area of concern, it would seem that we have only to define the terms "physical education" and "sport" in order to proceed to the main discussion. Would that the task were that simple! As might be expected, there is great ambiguity to the term "physical education." To the present it has been possible to identify some six different meanings as follows:

1. The subject-matter, or a part of it (e.g., tennis, or some other sport or active game; some type of physical activity involving exercise such as jogging or push-ups; a type of dance movement or activity; movement with purpose relating to these three types of activities).
2. The activity of physical educating carried on by teachers, schools, parents, or even by oneself.
3. The process of being physically educated (or learning) which goes on in the pupil or child (or person of any age).
4. The result, actual or intended, or (2) and (3) taking place through the employment of that which comprises (1).
5. The discipline, or field of enquiry, in which people study and reflect on all aspects of (1), (2), (3), and (4) above; that which is taught (the "body-of-knowledge") in departments, schools, and colleges of physical education.
6. The profession whose members employ (1) above, practice it (2), try to observe (3) taking place; attempt to measure or evaluate whether (4) has taken place, and base their professional practice on the body-of-knowledge developed by those undertaking scholarly and research effort in the discipline (5). (Adapted from

W. K. Frankena, <u>Three Historical Philosophies of Educa-tion</u>. Chicago: Scott, Foresman and Company, 1965, p. 6, with some modifications and two additional "meanings" added.) (See also E. F. Zeigler, <u>Physical Education: Progressivism or Essentialism?</u> Champaign, Illinois: Stipes Publishing Company, Revised edition, 1968, p. 8. Harold J. VanderZwaag is Co-author).

The term "sport" could be still more difficult to define, but a detailed analysis of the meanings will not be included at this point. In the 1967 <u>Random House Dictionary</u>, for example, the word "sport" is used thirteen ways as a noun, two ways as an adjective, six ways as an intransitive verb, and five ways as a transitive verb. Thus, we will offer here only two definitions which seem to be most applicable to the topic at hand:

1. an athletic activity requiring skill or physical prowess and often of a competitive nature, as racing, baseball, tennis, golf, etc.
2. diversion; recreation; pleasant pastime.

The reader can be thankful that play, game, and athletics aren't be-ing defined, as there are 74 ways in which the word "play" is used, and the terms "game" and "athletics" are employed in 23 and three ways, respectively.

Discussion of History, Historiography, and Physical Education and Sport

In this third subdivision of this paper, a relatively brief look will be taken at the subjects of history, historiography, and physical education and sport based on their current status. Not being certain whether relatively value-free analysis and synthesis is possible, an effort will be made to declare my "orientation" from time to time. Certain positive recommendations will be made later - ideas which if employed could improve the status of the history of physical education and sport greatly.

<u>History</u>. Writing recently in the <u>Saturday Review</u> (September 6, 1969), Richard L. Tobin decried certain activist professors who seem to be agreeing with Henry Ford. You will recall that he is purported to have said history was bunk, and that its study would serve no use-ful purpose. Marshall Fishwick (<u>Saturday Review</u>, May 13, 1967) puts this problem in excellent perspective for us by asking the question, "Is American History a Happening?" He explains that "men have long preferred to be hysterical to being historical" (p. 19). It is true that many of the "Now Generation" are seemingly cool and detached, and yet there is a real desire to be "tuned in" - to be "happening-oriented."

A "happening," of course, is a series of events that is spontaneous, often disconnected, and unstructured. If you are involved in a happening, this should be good for you and the others concerned. But don't plan it, don't evaluate it, and don't try to repeat it. The assumption, therefore, is that perhaps life on earth has been that way; that no purpose has been incorporated into the design of the Universe; and that in the final analysis history itself is nothing but a multitude of happenings. Thus, you - the reader - must ask yourself in which way you view history; it could have an effect on your work.

It is also quite possible to state that history has been a "conservative discipline"; by its very nature this is probably quite true. Yet even here significant changes are taking place. As Robert W. Heywood says, "history is necessarily an interdisciplinary discipline" (Social Education, May, 1964, p. 275). Referring to William Langer's presidential address to the American Historical Association in 1956, Heywood states that,

> The point is that the requirements of historical research, and of affective teaching as well, necessitate an understanding of statistics, perhaps even of cybernetics and the potential applicability of computers for the historian engaged in certain types of research. We also need an understanding of what the behaviorists (for lack of a more comprehensive word) regard as unconscious motives and irrational forces. (p. 275)

But we are getting ahead of our story, and should state a few more ideas about the meaning of history.

Erich Kahler offers assistance when he explains that the "concepts and representations of history merge with history itself." The very "fact that we can conceive of a 'study of history' gives sufficient evidence that history is to be understood as the happening itself, not the description or investigation of this happening" (The Meaning of History. New York: George Braziller, 1964, p. 16). What Kahler is affirming here is that happenings don't take place in a vacuum:

> Thus, to make even a simple story, three factors are indispensable: connection of events, relatedness of this connection to something, or somebody, which gives the events their specific coherence, and finally a comprehending mind which perceives this coherence and creates the concept which means a meaning. (p. 17).

As he states, " . . . there is no history without meaning" (p. 18). History, therefore, appears to be an ever-widening process of intercreation between conscious comprehension and material reality" (p. 22).

Bestor underscores "The Humaneness of History" when he postulates that "societies are even more purely the products of history than the human beings who compose them" (The Craft of American History, Vol. 1. New York: Harper and Row, Publishers, 1966, p. 8). He argues that the conservative and progressive historian should both embrace the study of history. It is history itself that investigates "the universal fact of change," and "it is history alone that reveals this as a changing world" (p. 9).

In concluding these few comments about history per se, I would like to offer you an interpretation of history that really strikes home with me. Perhaps it will mean that my "bias is showing" - that it shows by the very acceptance of this rationale for the meaning of history. But it is an honest assumption that I have made, and I encourage you to do the same in your own way. Nevins explains the function of history as follows:

> Although when we use the word history we instinctively think of the past, this is an error, for history is actually a bridge connecting the past with the present, and pointing the road to the future . . .

> This conception of history as a lantern carried by the side of man, moving forward with every step taken, is of course far ampler than the concept of a mere interesting tale to be told, a vivid scene to be described, or a group of picturesque characters to be delineated. It is essentially western and modern. (Allan Nevins, The Gateway to History. Garden City, New York: Anchor Books, 1962, p. 14).

Historiography. The discussion of this particular aspect of this paper - historiography - is most specifically to the point of the present assignment. It is most specifically with meanings #1 and #3 (see page 37) that we will direct our remarks. Thus, we will comment about the "intellectual processes, critical and constructive, by which history is written," and about "the history and critique of history."

The Harvard Guide to American History explains that the "process of choice from a mass of materials is the subjective element inherent in the historian's duty of analysis and synthesis" (Written by Oscar Handlin, et al., New York: Atheneum, 1967, p. 15). The facts can turn out to be right or wrong, we are told, but the "historical interpretations are far less determinate." Interpretations would be difficult, of course, even if we could be present at the actual happening. The historian, therefore, is faced with the fact that "theories of interpretation are peculiarly dependent on the needs and values of the age which produces them" (p. 15).

The approaches to historical interpretation in the twentieth century can be grouped in the following way:

1. interpretations assuming a plurality of separate civilizations and dealing with the reasons for their cyclical rise and decline, such as those of Toynbee and Spengler;
2. interpretations setting forth, in systematic rules, the general principles of continuous historical change applicable to all civilizations, such as those of Hegel and Marx;
3. interpretations, such as F. J. Turner's frontier thesis, which emphasize neglected factors in the historical development of a civilization, without claiming that these factors explain its whole development;
4. interpretations which deny the need for interpretation, asserting that objectivity is an attainable ideal, that the facts "speak for themselves," and that history is ultimately "scientific" (Ranke though not a member of this school, was its hero);
5. interpretations (such as those of Croce, Collingwood, and Beard) which assent that objectivity is an unattainable ideal and rest on the frank belief that all history is contemporary history;
6. interpretations which concede that perfect objectivity is unattainable but remain hostile to rigid or dogmatic historical theories. (This school is pragmatic and pluralistic, assuming always multiplicity of causation, and prepared to use ad hoc whatever general theories may illuminate a particular point.) (pp. 15-21).

While proclaiming an affinity to Interpretation #6 - the pragmatic and pluralistic school - I must confess further the great difficulty, if not the impossibility, of keeping history free from value judgments. As W. H. Dray reports, typically historical accounts "seem to be thoroughly value-impregnated." The question is whether such judgments necessarily enter into historical inquiry. The relativists maintain the great psychological difficulty of eliminating bias from conclusions, but the philosopher of history inquiries whether such value judgment isn't so much a part of the structure of historical investigation that the elimination of bias is logically impossible.

To make matters still worse, the historian doesn't have a special technical vocabulary like that of the scholars and scientists in other disciplines. He must use "ordinary language," and there is ample evidence from the field of philosophy that our everyday language is not purely descriptive (W. H. Dray, The Encyclopedia of Philosophy. New York: The Macmillan Company, 1967, pp. 26-30).

To draw an analogy, our ordinary language is "sick"; it needs "thera-py"; and then maybe it will be made "well" again. This is just one more vexing problem that the historian faces as he works on his craft. If history should ever become more scientific, then perhaps - as Kaplan states - the major task of philosophy (the analytic approach, that is) could be applied to history as well as the other sciences. This he explains as "a rational reconstruction of the language of sci-ence" (Abraham Kaplan, The New World of Philosophy. New York: Random House, 1961, p. 83).

Proof that there are indeed many approaches to and interpreta-tions of history is readily available from another source - the spate of paperbacks being issued on the subject of history. Leonard Krieger, Professor of History at The University of Chicago, attempt-ed to categorize all of this material and was able to "distinguish three different kinds of problems which are covered . . ." as follows:

> First, there is the philosophy of history which, properly
> so-called, should now be confined to questions of the valid-
> ity and value of historical knowledge.
> Secondly, there is what used also to be called the philoso-
> phy of history, but is now more properly denominated the
> theory of history - questions about the existence and
> identity of substantive laws, patterns, purpose or any other
> unifying constants in human history itself.
> Thirdly, there is universal or general history, which in
> our day calls into question the traditional assumptions of
> historical writing by emphasizing the relevance of other
> civilizations and of cross-cultural influences, thereby
> rendering parochial our standard Western criteria of histo-
> rical judgment.

There seems to be no question about the continued popularity of history, and also of the changing nature of the discipline. Barbara Tuchman, the author of The Guns of August who won a Pulitzer Prize in 1963, declares herself "a firm believer in the 'preposterous fal-lacy' of historical facts existing independently of the historian" (The New York Times Review of Books, March 8, 1964). She was re-sponding to an assertion by E. H. Carr of Cambridge University in his Trevelyan Lectures in 1962 ("What Is History" was also the title of a book by Professor Carr in the same year) that "the belief in a hard core of historical facts existing independently of the interpreta-tion of the historian is a preposterous fallacy but one that is hard to eradicate." Mrs. Tuchman goes on to take a firm stand against history "being served up hot." She would leave the dissection and a analysis of some contemporary life phenomenon to the field of socio-logy; in her opinion it is simply not possible for "compilers," "parti-cipants," "onlookers," or "axe-grinders" to gain any perspective on the story of man's past.

Writing in 1968, Allan Nevins reaffirms the idea that the discipline of history is going through a period of change. He states that "many powerful new forces are at work in the field of history as it is now being written and studied, and few men understand half of them" (Saturday Review, April 6, 1968). And then he proceeds to mention new studies from archaeology; advancements in epigraphy; development of the carbon-dating process; astronomical discoveries; opening up of new geographical units such as Antarctica and the reclaimed deserts; comparative ancient literature; new methods of dating Folsom points; the broadening of political and economic studies; the development of demography involving "a scientific study of all kinds of human tendencies and processes" relating to the growth and decline of populations; the latest studies in anthropology; the use of computers and statistics for a variety of purposes; and the role of psychology in history. To this ever-growing list of techniques can be added the use of the electron micro-analyzer in archaeological investigation - an invention employed originally by Robert E. Ogilvie to determine unerringly the composition and distribution of - say - paint on an early Egyptian coffin (John Lear, "Peering into Ancient Egypt Electronically," Saturday Review, February 3, 1968).

Then add to the above list a method developed by a Michigan chemist, Adon A. Gordus, whereby ancient counterfeiting of money may be detected. This process has been named neutron activation analysis, and it has been proved to be a reliable means of determining the metallic content of a coin. It has been possible to make such determinations earlier, but never before without destroying the coin itself (The New York Times, September 10, 1968).

Returning to the role of psychology - the entire behavioral area - in history, Barbara Tuchman sees definite possibilities for this approach, but she is most concerned that such a "Freudian method," for example, be applied by a responsible historian. To cite an example of its abuse, she discusses an analysis of Woodrow Wilson by Sigmund Freud and William Bullitt, the latter of these two being designated as "a Tom Jones of diplomacy" ("Can History Use Freud?" The Atlantic, February, 1967). She claims that both of these gentlemen entered upon this work with a significant bias (Woodrow Wilson: Twenty-Eighth President of the United States - a Psychological Study. Boston: Houghton-Mifflin Company, 1967). Such bias, she believes, led them to false conclusions; they gave a one-sided picture of the man and they have "twisted history."

C. Vann Woodward, Sterling Professor of History at Yale University, issues another warning because of the "New Immigrants" to the "arena" of history. In an essay entitled "Even Luther Is on the Couch," he complains that all of these immigrants into the historical arena from the social and/or behavioral sciences are being admitted to this province of learning "with no bother about passports and customs" (The New York Times Book Review, January 24, 1965). He states cynically also that "the underlying and complacent assumption has been that assimilation will eventually civilize all newcomers and invigorate the old stock" (p. 1). He does feel, however, that "under the influence of social sciences modern historian are becoming somewhat more analytical and somewhat less narrative." And it is true further that "individual historians differ in the degree to which they respond to the various social sciences" (p. 44). What Woodward is saying basically is that interdisciplinary effort can be most helpful - for example, in the debunking of the hallowed American Dream as "a land of opportunity for the common man" - but that the line must be drawn somewhere between the function of the historian and the function of the social scientist. Thus, Woodward believes essentially that "history presents," and "science synthesizes." To this, I would reply that both history and science are involved with analysis and synthesis, and I hope further that philosophers will become involved increasingly with "philosophizing" (although I certainly don't mean to put down the important function of language analysis).

Woodward makes his point well, but it is Nevins writing about "The Limits of Individualism" who really appeals to me (Saturday Review, November 25, 1967). He reveals how in his professional activity as both a journalist and a historian he was taught his "most forcible lessons in the superiority of cooperative effort to individualistic activity" (p. 27). Nevins emphasizes further that the countries of the world must work together to promote the highest interests of mankind. Thus, whether we are talking about history, any of the social sciences, or the family of man in general,

> What the world most needs today is the creation of a new battlefield of common endeavor and the rise of new heroes in the struggle to advance all mankind morally and spiritually as well as materially. (p. 78).

Unfortunately there are many forces at work in the world today which seem to be negating the ideal for which Nevins is striving. Barbara Tuchman stated her belief that "writers who dislike their fellowmen have taken over the literary world" (Saturday Review, February 25, 1967). She does not deny that much has happened since World War I that could well bring about "man's cumulative disillusionment in himself." The idea of man's progress "onward and upward" was harshly shattered through many examples of man's cruelty and inhumanity to other men. And now we see individual freedom being repressed at numerous points in the world, not to mention the spectres of unbelievably powerful bombs, overpopulation, and pollution of the environment. It is Mrs. Tuchman's sincere hope that historians will be able to explain what happened, why it happened -

and to communicate this information to the public in such a way that it will be understood and appreciated.

Most recently there have been a number of articles asking whether historians should concern themselves with what has been called "contemporary history." To many these two words together clash violently. Weighing carefully the pro's and con's of such historical endeavor, Henry Steele Commager comes to the conclusion that in a society such as ours "much must of necessity be left to the common sense, the intelligence, and the virtue" of the historian concerned. He claims that people who wish to censor overly much are "basically men of little faith" - "men who think the public is a great booby, easily misled." These are the folks, he asserts, who would impose all types of censorship in other realms as well (Saturday Review, February 12, 1966). Writing on his own behalf on this controversial subject in the following year, Arthur Schlesinger, Jr. contends that the writing of contemporary history can no longer be left to the passing whim of the occasional historian; he believes that it has now become an absolute necessity so that evidence will be preserved for future historians (The Atlantic Monthly, March, 1967). A final word on this subject indicates that "historians are growing increasingly critical of the Federal Government" because of the "protracted struggle we've been having with an unresponsive bureaucracy" (The New York Times, December 28, 1969).

I saved for next to last in this discussion of historiography several important points on the subject by Mrs. Tuchman again. In a fascinating paper ("History by the Ounce," Harper's Magazine, July, 1965) she makes a very strong point about a "major principle of historiography" - the fact that "corroborative detail is the great corrective" of history that tends to be invalid. The historian simply cannot afford the luxury of inventing his corroborative detail (as does the novelist). Such detail "will not produce a generalization every time but it will often reveal a historical truth, besides keeping one grounded in historical reality" (p. 66). In this highly informative essay, we find a talented historian going on record for the "gathering of history by the ounce rather than in gallon jugs." In her opinion, half of the historian's equipment is "the desire to find the significant detail plus the readiness to open his mind to it and let it report to him . . ." (p. 75).

Lastly, under this heading, I would like to insert an interesting idea about the professional responsibility of teaching history that was offered in 1966 by Elting E. Morison, Professor of Management at Massachusetts Institute of Technology (Ventures, Vol. VI, No. 2, Fall, 1966, Yale). He suggested "that one of the most profitable ways to learn historical meaning is through the intensive examination of the small situation - what is usually called today the case study." It was his thought that, the stuff of history, the stuff of the democratic process, the stuff of men trying to govern themselves can most usefully be got at from the reconstruction of a small situation in its totality . . . The nature of cause and effect, of process, can best be got at by the microscopic examination of the small particular case . . . In this way, more than from any other I can think of, he enters into an historical situation, can be made to discover for himself the complexity of any human experience, the feeling for past time and the social process in which he lives. (p. 44).

Physical Education and Sport. The matter of the "body-of-knowledge" in the history of physical education and sport is basic to us. The subject was considered as part of a development within the Big Ten Directors of Physical Education Meeting in 1964 (by E. F. Zeigler in Urbana, Ill. on December 10). At that time I stated that,

If we would answer this question honestly, we would be forced into the admission that the contribution of physical education historians is, relatively speaking, quite meagre indeed, and that the quality of our efforts leaves much to be desired. We have not come very far; we have a long way to go; and we ought to be about our business. This is not meant to be harsh and critical. We appreciate the contributions that have been made. Those of us who have contributed in small or larger measure to this "body-of-knowledge" realize full well the inadequacy of our efforts. Some have done much better than others, and much fine material exists in languages other than English. Our provinciality in this regard makes this material largely unavailable to us at the present. (This paper is available in E. F. Zeigler, Problems in the History and Philosophy of Physical Education and Sport. New Jersey: Prentice-Hall, Inc., 1968, pp. 3-7).

These opinions are, of course, not new to us. Dorothy Ainsworth had reported this in 1949 ("Historical Research Methods," in Research Methods in HPER. Washington, D. C.: AAHPER, 1949, pp. 125-135), and Marvin H. Eyler reiterated this opinion in 1960 when he referred to a "great dearth of credible historical studies in sports and physical education" (M. H. Eyler, "The Nature and Status of Historical Research Pertaining to Sports and Physical Education, in in W. Johnson, Science and Medicine of Exercise and Sports. New York: Harper and Row, Publishers, 1960).

But "the times, they are a 'changin'," as Peter Lindsay tells us us:

Such has been the existing state of history within physical education, but there are signs that things are changing. Physical education has entered a new era. Although teacher education still remains the primary concern of most departments of physical education, inroads into "academic" areas, as opposed to purely "practical" courses, have greatly increased . . . ("History Needs You," CAHPER Journal, Vol. 35, No. 2: 26, Dec., 1968-Jan., 1969).

Physical educators have written a significant number of ter's and doctoral theses on historical topics in physical education and sport. Recent surveys and analyses by Abernathy and Adelman have uncovered over 600 such studies in the United States since 1930. The quality of this work has not been too high typically, but who among us does not believe that historical studies of this nature are improving? It is true that a concerted effort is underway to remedy the situation that has been described. Certainly Bruce Bennett, AAHPER Historian, has been working to move this area ahead in a variety of ways. And Canada is making truly significant strides as well. The development at the University of Alberta through the herculean efforts of Professors Maxwell Howell, R. G. Glassford, and Ann Hall is well-known to us all. (And Dean M. L. Van Vliet should be commended for the support he gave the drive leading to Canada's first Ph.D. degree in physical education – two historical studies, incidentally, by Allan E. Cox and Peter L. Lindsay, respectively). We must moreover wish well to the new Journal of Canadian Sports History and Physical Education sparked by the enthusiasm of Professor Alan Metcalfe of the University of Windsor.

Further evidence – if it is needed – of the growing vitality of historical endeavor in our field in Canada is evidenced by the inclusion of some ten historical essays by Canadians in a new historical anthology of physical education and sport soon to be published (E. F. Zeigler, Ed., Selected Historical Topics in Physical Education and Sport. Pacific Palisades, Calif.: Goodyear Publishing Company, 1971, in press). Professor Howell's influence is felt in five of these studies, and a particularly noteworthy, interpretive essay by John R. Fairs of The University of Western Ontario, discusses the idea of physical education in Greek culture.

------

* Abernathy, Thomas D., "An Analysis of Master's and Doctoral Studies Related to the History of Physical Education Completed in the United States, 1930-1967."

Adelman, Melvin, "An Analysis of Master's and Doctoral Studies Related to the History of Sport and Athletics Completed in the United States, 1930-1967." Both studies were completed at the University of Illinois in 1969.

In concluding this subdivision of this essay, it now seems reasonable to ask ourselves rhetorically what we should do, and what we can do. The following recommendations and/or conclusions seem realistic at the present time:

1. Efforts should be made to assess and upgrade the quality of instruction in the history of physical education and sport at both the undergraduate and graduate levels. (This may be accomplished in a variety of ways, notably by in-service training techniques and by improvement of the professional program in which future history instructors are prepared.)

2. When the quality of instruction is reasonably high in a college or university, an effort should be made to have several of our history courses available to students in other disciplines on an elective basis.

3. Course experiences covering the history of physical education and sport should be offered early in the undergraduate professional preparation program. They should not be "diluted" by merger with orientation and principles courses.

4. Upper undergraduate elective courses on the history of sport and leisure activities should be offered as soon as qualified instructors are available.

5. Humanities and social science options should be developed in conjunction with physical education professional programs. Such options could offer the student an opportunity to select five or six full courses in history and closely related fields, and yet include an "irreducible minimum" of theory and practice course experiences in physical education.

6. Programs of specialization within M.A. and Ph.D. degree programs should be organized specifically in the history of physical education and sport. (Within these areas of concentration, there should be an opportunity to minor in closely related ancilliary fields such as sociology, philosophy, anthropology, social psychology, etc.)

7. Qualified instructors in the history of physical education and sport should be carrying on investigation and research of their own. Professors teaching in this area should have <u>some</u> time formally allotted in their workloads for scholarly endeavor.

8. Professors related to the history of physical education and sport should make efforts to gain at least Associate Member status in the various professional societies in the field of history - and the history of education as well.

9. Retrieval projects on historical literature in a variety of specialized topics can be developed at many different institutions (depending upon the interests of the particular professors concerned), and this could be coordinated by the professional association at the national level.

10. Museum exhibits of sport and physical education history should be organized in universities across the continent. In some instances, such exhibits could in time develop into full-fledged museums. Collaboration with directors and coaches of athletics should be explored to avoid duplication of effort.

Epilogue - "The Good Life"

We are all facing the 1970's with a good deal of fear. Behind us are all sorts of wars, depressions, and examples of man's inhumanity to man. We are in the middle of a "Cold War," as well as a very "Hot War," and these struggles could spell utter devastation for us, for our good neighbors - and for mankind itself. Yet we look ahead idealistically, realistically, pragmatically, existentially, materialistically, or what have you? (E. F. Zeigler, Philosophical Foundations for Physical, Health, and Recreation Education. Englewood Cliffs, New Jersey: Prentice-Hall, Inc., 1964). From our earlier discussion of the various interpretations of history, I think you may agree that your value orientation in all probability will influence your historical analysis and synthesis significantly. This should not frighten you so long as you are aware of your personal philosophical orientation. The "good life" quite obviously means many different things to many different people. Minority groups are clamoring for their share currently in America - and it could well be that the mirage they are seeking will turn out to be the highest standard of "low" living in the world! (E. F. Zeigler, "A Critique of Current Philosophies of Fitness, Sports, and Physical Recreation," Consultation of Physical Education, Toronto, November 24, 1969.)

For me, Barbara Tuchman has characterized the good life magnificently with some of the following ideas:

The good life is not an absolute; it is subjective and can be defined only in personal terms. Apart from private affections (mate, parents and children, friends) and a reasonable degree of material comfort, which I take it are axiomatic for everyone, the two fundamentals without which for me there could be no good life are freedom of the individual - and the enjoyment of art and nature.

The first means freedom of thought and expression, freedom to develop one's own capacities and find satisfaction in one's own function, whether it be writing a book or pitching a no-hitter or healing the sick, or cooking or teaching or selling or governing or contemplating one's navel.

The second - the esthetic value or, in a word, beauty - is a source of pleasure as important (notwithstanding the obsession of the 1960's) as sex. Art is the only thing that sustains faith in the human kind . . .

I am gloomy about the prospect for the '70s because it seems to me that these things I value are in the process of destruction. In the manipulated society which will be necessary to manage an overcrowded world - and which is already forming - freedom of the individual may not survive . . .

Art too is presently in decline. What is produced today in the name of art may be interesting or provocative or meaningful or relevant to some, but it is not primarily concerned with beauty . . . Nature, too, is suffering: the victim of pollutants . . .

Each of us has to fight for the things he holds dear, but the good life is not, I think, a likely prospect for society in general in the 1970's . . . (Barbara W. Tuchman, McCall's, January, 1970, p. 38).

Mrs. Tuchman may be right. Her two most important values - individual freedom and enjoyment of art and nature - may not be the same for you. As physical education and sport historians, you have a duty to tell mankind how sport, physical activity, and recreation have been related to man's development in the past. To the extent that you feel that it might be possible to write "contemporary history," the "rays from your historical lantern" will shine at the feet of man and show him how sport may be used for good or evil. The part that sport, dance, and exercise - man moving purposefully in this realm - may play in creating the good life has only been partially discovered. The history of physical education and sport can "point the road to the future."

Part II

PERSONALIZING PHYSICAL EDUCATION AND SPORT PHILOSOPHY

Selection #5

A CONSISTENT PHILOSOPHY IS THE SIGN OF A
TRUE PROFESSIONAL

A great many people have philosophical beliefs, but they are vague about them.[1] Unfortunately the man in the street still thinks of philosophy as something that is completely beyond him--a most difficult intellectual activity. Consequently, a subject-matter such as this is rarely, if ever, included in the high school curriculum. This means that most people make decisions based on common sense. This isn't necessarily bad, but it could be a lot better! The development of a philosophy would, however, help a man or woman fashion a better world for the future based on the past and the scientific discoveries of the present. Without philosophy--or philosophical thought --we may never know if we have the "correct goals" in life.

Some may ask immediately whether science might achieve an understanding of these goals of man by its everlasting probing into the unknown. This may be possible, but we should understand the relationship between philosophy and science. Both are most interested in knowledge; their exponents ask questions and want answers. Scientific investigators turn in facts; the philosopher must be cognizant of these advances in knowledge. Actually, philosophy as some view it starts where science leaves off by attempting to synthesize. What do these facts mean? When you become concerned about the ultimate meaning of these facts, it might be said that you are then philosophizing in the best sense.

A person striving to function intelligently in society needs a philosophy of life and/or religion. In addition, a physical educator and coach, a health educator, or a recreator should have a philosophy of education. To top this off, he should develop still further a philosophy of physical, health, and recreation education that, once again, does not clash with the rest of his beliefs about life and education. The achievement of such a total philosophy may well become a life-long task. The reflective thought required to accomplish this task, however, is a mightly cheap price to pay for a possible well-ordered life.

We have only to look at present programs with their shifting emphases to realize that we are to quite a degree vacillating practitioners. This is true both in the school and in public recreation.

---

[1] Published in The Physical Educator, Vol. 19, No. 1: 17-18, March, 1962.

Why is this happening? Probably because even many of our best and most experienced leaders have not worked out personal philosophies that are consistent and logical in the varied phases. So where does that leave the rest of us?

When a person assumes a role of leadership in the education profession in school health, physical education, or recreation education, or outside of the school in the recreation profession, he is implying that he has a life purpose. But, strangely enough, many leaders become hazy in their attempts at expressing a philosophy. To be sure, they have a lot of opinions, isolated, and often quite contradictory. It's generally a little like saying, "I'm for good and against evil!" The difficulty comes when we are asked to define what's "good" and what's "evil."

Where does physical, health, and recreation education fit into life's picture today? What is it? Why is it needed? What does the right kind of it do to a boy or girl, or to a man or woman? How can we prove that it does what we say it does? What is its future? What could its future be? What should its future be?

The Need for Determination of a Philosophy of Physical, Health and Recreation Education

The time has come for the true professional to adopt a basic or fundamental philosophy. Science and philosophy have complementary roles to play in aiding the field to find its place in the educational system and in society. For too long we have ignored the wisdom of both of these branches of learning in carrying out our program. Lately there has been a greatly increased interest in science with a corresponding lack of interest in philosophy--an imbalance which should be corrected.

Philosophy, employed normatively and analytically, can help us to attack the basic problems of physical, health, and recreation education in a systematic fashion. In the first place, philosophy will help the physical and health education teacher, or the director of recreation, to view their professions as a whole. They will not see themselves merely as athletic coaches, health education teachers, playground leaders, physical conditioners, sports skill teachers, community center supervisors, or corrective exercise specialists. In this sense, philosophy could help us to "criticize experience."

Philosophy can help the teacher of physical education and sport, for example, to fashion for himself a mental image of what physical education and sport ought to be in the light of his own personal philosophy of education. It will be prospective in the sense that it will form a vanguard leading practice in the field. It is true that there will be conflicting philosophies, but at least people will be considerably more logical and consistent in their approaches no matter which educational philosophy they accept.

A philosophy of physical, health, and recreation education--or however you may designate the field--would eventually have to be practical, or it would be worthless in the eyes of many. An instrumental philosophy would necessarily imitate science in part, but it would serve only as a plan for action. Science can describe physical education, and perhaps sport, as they exist; philosophy can help to picture the field as it ought to be. The same can be said for health education and for recreation education, of course. In addition, philosophy can fill in for science temporarily; its methods are faster. Eventually, when the facts are "in," decisions based on individual and societal norms and values will have to be made.

Methods employed by professional practitioners should be developed with a philosophical stance or position in mind. Actual philosophical differences can be tested in the practical execution of the program. It has rightfully been stated that aim and method should "go hand in hand."

Relationship between Sub-Philosophies and Parent Discipline

A philosophy of physical, health, and recreation education is considered by some to be a part of the sub-philosophy of education which has a direct relationship to the general field of philosophy. On this point there are varied and conflicting views. Most obvious is the position which holds a philosophy of life and/or religion basic and primary to a philosophy of education. To the former is assigned the establishment of fundamental principles (except for pragmatism and various techniques employed in what might be called "philosophical analysis" loosely). The application of these "principles" is often assigned to the philosophy of education with special attention to the educational process. If this viewpoint is acceptable, it obviously is of utmost importance that one's general philosophy be sound (i.e., defensible from the standpoint of logic).

The determination of at least progressivistic and/or essentialistic philosophical stances or positions--or an acceptance of an analytic approach that rejects either--should be helpful to both the practitioner and the practice even though conflicts will necessarily exist. At least professional practitioners will be able to determine for themselves under which banner they stand (if any). Knowing where one stands means that it is possible to work for consensus in practice with someone holding an opposing position. At present too many professionals are dilettantes, and hence are not able to present any solid arguments for many of the beliefs which they express. A professional person "knows which side of the fence he is on," and then he can decide "if he wants to stay there when someone tries to force or lure him to the other side."

Today there are many serious problems and conflicts evident within either of the professional fields being discussed or among them as possible interrelationships are considered. In some matters the allied fields should be able to present a united, determined, and powerful front at a time when the worth of programs within the community and educational system is being challenged in some way many times each year. The answers to the many controversial questions cannot be provided by the uninformed or the misinformed. The highest type of reflective thinking is needed so that a personal stand may be taken. Such an expression of opinion and belief should come only as a result of orderly thought that has resulted in a consistent philosophical stance developed as a result of knowledge and understanding consonant with societal norms and values.

Selection #6

PHILOSOPHICAL FOUNDATIONS AND EDUCATIONAL LEADERSHIP

It is a rare week that goes by when I do not talk to some young man (or woman) about his future in physical education and sport-- whether he wants to be a teacher, a coach, a performer, or even a professional in another field. When he asks what the future holds in store for him as a physical educator, I suppose that I should reply using the words of the late great American, "don't ask what physical education can do for you; ask what you can do for physical education!"

To make such a reply, however, is more easily said than done. Youth is typically realistic, and quite often materialistic as well. The average young man who is contemplating a major in physical education probably makes this decision because of his experience in athletics with a high school coach. He has admired his coach very much. He has assessed his own personal athletic ability and his liking of people. Then, often against the better judgment of his parents, he makes up his mind to be a coach and a physical educator --in that order. He sees himself coaching a successful high school football team and then possibly going on to bigger and better things as a college coach.

As a counselor, my task is to explain to this young man in a relatively few well-chosen words that the field of physical education is much more than simply being an athletic coach, as important a task as that is. This is very difficult to do, and I am not always certain just how much to say. So much depends upon his prior experiences. I usually tell him about the advantages and disadvantages, placing somewhat more emphasis on the former rather than the latter. I conclude by telling him that, even though he may have heard that the field is overcrowded for men at present, there is nevertheless ample room for a well-qualified, conscientious, devoted professional educator. Then we quite often shake hands as he is leaving. I tell him not to hesitate to contact me if he has a problem. Finally, I wish him good luck.

But after he leaves, I begin to wonder if I have said and done the right things. Of course, perhaps nothing I could have said or done would change his thinking radically. I do hope most sincerely that his

---

[1] A paper presented at the Leadership Workshop, Michigan Association for Health, Physical Education, and Recreation, Gull Lake, September 28, 1962. (Published in The Physical Educator, Vol. 20, No. 1: 15-18, March, 1963.)

university experience will be such that he will emerge upon graduation as a fine, competent young teacher of physical education ready to assume professional leadership of the highest type.

What happens to this young man? Many experiences affect his development, both good and bad. Eventually he acquires certain knowledge, competencies, and skills. He may be a good student, a fair student, or a poor student. Rarely is he an outstanding student. He develops a set of attitudes. Only very occasionally does he show an inclination after graduation to be active in at least one professional organization in his chosen field. I wonder where he has failed-- where we have failed. I think that I have one reasonably good answer.

Need for a Logical, Consistent Philosophy

I believe that the large majority of physical education haven't had the opportunity, or haven't taken the time, to work out their own personal philosophies. Granted that along the way there has been a great deal of discussion about aims and objectives, but it has usually been carried out in such a helter-skelter fashion that college seniors want no more of any such stultifying lists of objectives. "We have had our fill of that stuff," they say; "now give us some competencies and skills that we can use on the job next year." And so they leave the university not really knowing very well why they are doing anything and where they are going in the field.

Physical educators need exactly the same sort of progression in the area of aims and objectives as they usually get in anatomy and physiology and the applied aspects of these subjects. It is possible that they need it even more. Any person striving to function intelligently in society needs a philosophy of life and/or religion. Do our professional students ever take an introductory course in philosophy and a course in the philosophy of religion? Perhaps not one in a thousand had had this opportunity![1]

Furthermore, a teacher of health, physical education, and recreation should have a philosophy of education that is in harmony with his philosophy of life. But, strangely enough, even a subject like philosophy of education is often available only as an elective--and one that our students typically avoid like the plague because of the seemingly unfortunate experiences of their predecessors.

The culmination of this recommended sequence in the professional preparation of our "future leaders" should be an outstanding course in the philosophy of health, physical education, and recreation

---

[1] With apologies to Catholic universities.

--a course in which the prospective teacher begins to develop a personal philosophy of his specialized field that does not clash with the rest of his beliefs about life and education. The achievement of this total philosophy may well become a life-long task. The reflective thinking required to accomplish this task is a mighty cheap price to pay for a well-ordered life.

We have only to look at our present programs with their shifting emphases to realize that we are, to quite a degree, vacillating practitioners. This is true both within the school and in public recreation. Why is this happening? Probably because even many of our best and most experienced leaders have not worked out personal philosophies that are consistent and logical in their various phases. So where does that leave the rest of us!

If we ever hope to convince ourselves, our colleagues in education and the informed portion of the general public, we should as individual professionals at least determine whether we are progressivistic or essentialistic and then work from there. We simply shouldn't continue as dilettantes ready to jump in any direction when "the prevailing wind blows." For example, far too many physical educators were only too ready to subscribe automatically to the essentialistic and nationalistic banner that the late President Kennedy was waving at us. I am not stating unequivocally that he was wrong, but I do personally see a far greater role in education for the physical education field than I think he did. I believe sincerely that we should be fully aware of all of the implications of such an approach to the future of the field. Each presently "viable" philosophical stance or position has definite implications for the teacher of health, physical education, and recreation. Where do you stand?

Rungs on the "Philosophical Ladder"

I would like to offer for your consideration the concept of a philosophical ladder. You may find that you have been at the "Ostrich Stage"--the lowest rung--up to now. That is to say, you have had your head "buried in the sand" and have refused to allow yourself to become aware of the conflicting philosophies within education or within your specialized field.

Or perhaps you have climbed the ladder--in this instance a five-runged climbing device--a bit further and have arrived at what might be called the "Cafeteria Stage." At this stage one finds himself selecting some of this and some of that which looks "appetizing" for his "philosophical fare." This eclectic approach has a great deal of appeal initially, but there appears to be strong evidence that it is philosophical indefensible. It may be argued, of course, that it is but one stage in an individual's development. If this is true, let us hope that the devoted educator will soon make his way higher. An eclectic generally draws his ideas and principles loosely from many sources and, admittedly, there is every reason to believe that a person will be attracted by certain elements of each of the various philosophical stances or positions. However, the difficulty arises when people are somewhat careless and lift elements out of context and insert them elsewhere where they really don't belong. Following this practice means that one will end up with a "mixture" instead of the "compound" that we typically desire. In my opinion, the "mixture approach" is merely a resting place on the way up the ladder. If it is not followed by continued progress upward (personal growth), this may indeed prevent the individual from reaching his highest potential in the final analysis.

The third rung of the ladder is a popular place; there has to be a lot of room here to hold all of the people who have been stranded at this level seemingly indefinitely. We have designated this as the "Fence-Sitter Stage or Rung." Here we find people who have matured a bit more than those at the second stage and have found, perhaps unconsciously to a degree, that they are inclining in one direction or another. But beyond that they are unwilling to go! Why? Maybe they are too lazy intellectually, physically, or morally, if such distinction can be made in an indivisible organism. Perhaps they are afraid of the possible consequences resulting from a determined stand. We are told that all too many people today tend to be "organization men" who don't wish to "rock the boat" for fear of the consequences. Then, again, there are often other reasons not disclosed.

In time we fervently hope that you will rise to the fourth rung of this philosophical ladder. This we have chosen to call the "Stage of Early Maturity"--a stage where having the courage of one's convictions often comes into play. At this point the individual educator has wrestled with himself and his social environment and has achieved a quality of unity or harmony which is characteristic of a philosophical position that is reasonably logical and consistent in its various departments. He is able to justify his convictions (which may have earlier been only so-called persuasions) intellectually to the extent that scientific knowledge, and perhaps faith, can assist him. As a result he has developed strong attitudes (as psychologically defined) that are then reflected in the moral ardor of his personal and professional life in a particular society characterized by specific norms and values. It is probably not necessary to say that there is plenty of room on this rung (or stage) of the ladder! Also, one must beware of the strong possibility of intolerance and fanaticism at this point.

As we mature still further chronologically, it is to be hoped that we will mature concurrently in intellectual and social ways, also. If so, it is quite possible that we will achieve wisdom as well as mere knowledge. This may be called the "Stage of Later Maturity," or a time when wise people seek to achieve a certain amount of consensus on important issues where there is disagreement preventing social progress. This level of professional development can result from a sound experience, diligent study, and ordered reflection. It is at this point that we realize the supreme importance of, and need for agreement on, a national and international basis. Our world has reached a stage where the need for "peaceful strife" is infinitely greater than the horrible types of struggles that have taken place in the past. At this stage, or level of the ladder, we most certainly realize the unique aspects of our own positions and the importance of the continuing search for truth--however we may define it. And yet we should be tolerant of others and their beliefs, realizing that a sincere effort must be made to increase the boundaries of the presumed areas of consensus. After all, it is possible, and seemingly quite probable, that only one position may prove to be right or best.

Conclusion

No matter which stage of philosophical development you may be at presently, you may find it necessary to retrace the various steps necessary before the teacher of health, physical education, and recreation can truly build his own personal philosophy logically, consistently, and systematically. Obviously, there is no hard and fast progression to which you must adhere. You may discover that you are, philosophically speaking, quite pure already. Keep in mind that the philosophic quest is a never-ending one. You won't suddenly at some advanced stage of your development find all of the answers to the problems which have been perolexing you. But you will be leading a greatly enriched life that may truly be an "adventure of ideas," as Whitehead has so aptly expressed it. Each of you should earn the right to be an influential person in your chosen field at least within your own sphere of operation--and perhaps to a still greater extent. The allied fields of health, physical education, and recreation have a truly unique contribution to make in the lives of men. Whatever your philosophical position may be, understand it fully, and it may enable you to live up to the highest standards of your chosen profession. Ours can be a proud profession in the foreseeable future, if each of us strives to help people realize all of the values that life has to offer.

A CRITIQUE OF CURRENT PHILOSOPHIES OF FITNESS
SPORTS, AND PHYSICAL RECREATION: THEIR IMPLI-
CATIONS FOR PRIVATE AGENCIES

Every day in your life you express your values through statements of opinion and belief. How identical are the ideas and beliefs
that you express and those that you actually put into practice in your
work? Do you have a different image of yourself than others have of
you? Succinctly put, therefore, you live a philosophy of life, but you
and your agency are judged much more by your actions than by the
words that you speak--or by the words in the brochure that your
agency might publish annually.[1]

The assignment for this paper is to present a critique of current philosophies of fitness, sports, and physical recreation--and
their possible implications for private agencies. The implications
which I will suggest are based largely on my personal background and
experience with them over a period of some forty years. However,
you yourself will really have to work out the implications for yourself in conjunction with your associates in your own organization.

Actually I find it very difficult to tell you truly all that I have on
my mind and in my heart today. Maybe it's because I've reached
that magic time in life when you continue to say year after year, "I
am really only forty-nine" (I gave up on thirty-nine a long time ago.)
And why did I, a physical educator and an ex-coach, grow a mous-
tache this summer--and sideburns too? Is it because I want to create
a different image, and not look like an ex-football and wrestling coach
any more? Perhaps so.

It is true that I have been working most diligently recently to
develop what is usually designated as "mind," and also my interest in
and knowledge about the aesthetic, creative, social, communicative,
and so-called learning aspects of life. Nevertheless, I have also
been exercising quite vigorously in an attempt to preserve the image
of the young physical educator. This I have been doing mainly through
the employment of Arthur Steinhaus's Overload Principle and his
Reversibility Principle as well. By that I mean that I do specific
exercises to keep the large muscle groups strong, and then I also jog

---

[1] A paper presented at the Consultation on Physical Education,
Toronto, Ontario, November 23-26, 1969. (Published as "A Philoso-
phy for the Private Agency," Journal of Physical Education, Vol. 67,
No. 3: 67-71 (1970).

or swim middle distance to maintain a certain level of circulo-respiratory efficiency. Putting all of this together - the multi-faceted approach described - one ends up with a so-called "Renaissance Man Approach" that has been somewhat popular two or three times in the history of the world. I really do question how much it counts on North American continent today.

One thing is certain, and I can't emphasize this too much. I am doing everything possible back home to show my colleagues at the University, as well as my professional associates everywhere not necessarily in the field of physical education, that some people in physical education are truly concerned about being informed about current social events, as well as about present educational developments. Frankly, I find too much concern with rather narrow, so-called professional matters such as the <u>requirement</u> of physical education and how important the <u>winning</u> of athletic contests is--both of which are relatively small matters when the overall educational and recreational goals are seriously considered.

Let's face it; recent international, national, regional, and local occurrences do keep one's mind in a whirl these days. There are times when I think that a "news moratorium" might help - for a short while at least. Haven't you had that "stop the world I want to get off" feeling lately? I repeat myself, and maybe I am indeed getting old. There was a time when God was in the Heavens; when the flag wasn't used as the wrong kind of a political symbol; when my country really seemed to be sincere about wanting to make the world safe for demo-cracy - and Canada could get enthusiastic about helping us; and when I thought that I myself was indestructible and timeless. Now God is said to be dead; the flag is being used incorrectly by some who wish to throttle dissent; the question is being raised repeatedly that the United States might be engaged in "imperialistic meddling"; and per-sonally I find myself getting pessimistic and discouraged more than was the case previously. Thus, from a time when I fitted neatly into that picture of a world getting better day by day in every way as a happy, optimistic physical educator and coach doing my part in a relatively happy North America, I am now ever so much more sober, realistic, perplexed, and concerned. What has happened?

The Situation in Education

And what has happened to our schools and the learning process? We take that bright-eyed youngster at the age of six - almost invari-ably eager and ready to learn - and we quite thoroughly kill his or her desire within a few short years. We teach him the "modern" way: excessive drill, speed, winning, dull lectures, tests, quizzes, grades, competition, memorization, various types of overt and covert disci-pline - and "the work hard to get ahead' approach that makes money so

that he will eventually be able to buy all of the good things of life.
This includes new cars, color TV sets, new clothes, haircuts, winter
homes, summer homes, ornate churches, whiskey, tobacco,
divorces, stock and bonds ad infinitum. And all of this has added up
to the highest standard of living in the world; that's it: the highest
standard of <u>low</u> living in the world! The watchword is, "get an education so that you can make more money and try to achieve that 'high
standard' by keeping up with your friends and business associates."

I say to you today, try to tell a youngster, a high school student
or even a college man or woman that this pattern I've described is not
what education is all about in <u>your</u> world and <u>my</u> world. Is it any
wonder that this young person is telling us loudly and clearly - and
telling us in many countries on many continents around the world -
that such a world is <u>not</u> of <u>his</u> making, and that he wants to change it
so that there will be a difference tomorrow?

What has happened to me? Am I going off my rocker? Why am
I worrying about these kooky kids - these novices in the art of living
who are trying to tell me how they want things to be done? I've got it
made, and I can keep it that way without too much effort. I am part
of the nefarious "Educational Establishment" - probably the largest
single business in the country outside of the mushrooming military-
industrial complex. And you, too, are part of the establishment that
can keep things pretty much the way we want them (barring a revolution, of course).

And this statement seems to apply especially to us in the field
of physical education and sport. We are the squares who help keep
order and discipline. We are the conformists who never rock the
boat. We are the people who encourage the athletes to cut the hair off
the "long hairs" and to keep the blacks and other minority groups (including women and homosexuals) in their place in overt and covert
ways. We're big deals; haven't you heard? We know what's good for
kids. Haven't we lived through those immature years successfully?
Why just look at us--aren't we on top of the world really making things
happen?

But what is it that we want to make happen? Do we know? Can
we help to achieve it through the medium of physical education and
sport? What is it that the world is lacking today, and what can we do
about it anyhow? What is the purpose of education - and physical
education? Is it to cram knowledge, skills, competencies, win-at-
all-costs ideas, muscles, endurance, and discipline down their
throats. Must they respect us because we say so?

Physical Education's Blurred Image

To make matters worse, we in physical education and sport have one of the most blurred images in the entire educational system. This occurred because of individual confusion within the field, but it is nonetheless true because of the many conflicting educational philosophies in each of the sixty provincial and state educational systems extant on this North American continent. To understand how our field got itself into this situation, we must look both at our heritage and our present philosophical foundations. For the first time in the history of physical education, it can be reported that some scholars in our own field have become aware of the need to turn to philosophy as well as to history for assistance. (And an encouraging new development is the the interest in sociology as applied to this field as well.) Although it is true that such an approach is Western world oriented largely - and there is great need for the bringing-together of the East and West - at least we have begun to apply the techniques of normative and critical philosophizing to such analysis directed basically to physical education and sport. Such endeavor is long overdue when we think about our "bewildered public" trying to understand what we mean by a conglomerate term such as health, physical education, recreation, and athletics - not to mention safety education, driver education, dance, physical fitness, movement education, and park administration. Can you imagine how difficult it would be to put all of this on a sign in front of a building? And will you believe me when I say that some terms were omitted above, and some specialists within our field will undoubtedly be offended by such an omission.

Society Is More Value Conscious

One encouraging sign is the fact that our whole society does not seem to be more conscious than I can ever remember about the need for reassessment of the values by which we guide our lives. Such concern is heartening, but I have a deep-seated fear that it may be quite superficial because of the individual's basic lack of philosophical foundations. Of course, this is a failing that is typical throughout our entire society. Ask a person what he wants out of life, and you are apt to get a vague response such as "happiness" or "security," or some other such innocuous expression which reflects no deep reflection whatsoever. To make matters still worse, the gentle cynic would remind us that actions always speak louder than words, and that you can learn truly about the values that a person holds through careful observation of his daily practice.

Philosophy of Language

Strangely enough, just at the time that people have become more value conscious, the professional field of philosophy - in the English-speaking world at least - seems to have decided to cast the common man adrift into waters that are anything but calm and peaceful. Despite the fact that men have engaged in philosophical thought for many centuries, there is still a large amount of confusion over the exact nature of philosophy. Developing scientific method has for many of today's philosophers to ask themselves, "In what kind of activity am I engaging?" Many of them have decided that philosophical activity does not result in knowledge after all. And so - if true knowledge can only come from scientific experimentation - what is the justification for philosophy? A considerable group of influential people within the field feel that its primary function is to use ordinary and specialized language terms clearly and precisely.

The "Flavoring Influence" of Existentialism

In addition to the frontal attack on the more less traditional philosophies of idealism, realism, and pragmatism by the analytic movement in philosophy, another powerful group of troublesome and pessimistic ideas has permeated intellectual life on the North American continent. I am referring to the significant force known as existentialism which emanated from Europe. This approach may be said to have started as a revolt against Hegel's idealism in the latter half of the nineteenth century - a position that included the postulate that ethical and spiritual realities were accessible to man through reason. It developed to the position which included the idea that man's task was to create his own essence - his own ideals and values - inasmuch as science had shown, according to Nietzsche, that the transcendent ideals of the Church were nonsense. Thus, a man is on his own in a cold, cruel, world. Man, and this noun is spelled with a capital "M," has a responsibility therefore to give meaning and direction to a world essentially lacking in such qualities. The fundamental question for the future, according to this position, is whether man is capable of directing and guiding his own existence so that responsible action will result.

Where Can We Find The Answers?

It seems, therefore, that modern man is really at the cross-roads when it comes to the question of deciding which way he and his organizations shall turn in the years immediately ahead on the way to the hypothetical year 2000 A.D. How can we lead our lives effectively if we don't make decisions about such basic questions as the nature of the world, the problem of good and evil, the possibility of free will, whether God exists, if some values are more important than others, whether knowledge is really possible to man, and the possibility of an unchanging concept of beauty - just to name a few of life's enigmas? I believe it is quite safe to state that no one person or group has a corner on the market when it comes to answers to these fundamental questions.

Frankly, unless you are willing to proceed in a sloppy, haphazard manner, you are just going to have to be amateur philosophers. In fact, I would venture the opinion that your own personal life and the work of your private organization is so important that it may be worth the time for you to become semi-professional philosophers. After all, this is your life in your country that we are discussing, and you have simply got to make determinations for the last third of the twentieth century that will stand the test of time.

A Plan for Action

May I recommend plan of action for your consideration? It will relate primarily to the specified topic which you have delineated for this presentation, but it can also be applied to the total task of the private agency in an evolving democracy. Basically, it consists of an orderly progression through a series of steps which any effective organization needs to follow:

1. Re-examine your long range aims and specific objectives in the light of societal values, organizational values, and individuals' values.

2. Re-examine the relationships that exist, and which may develop, among the various units concerned (society, including public and private agencies; and the family and individuals involved).

3. Determine what your agency's persistent, recurring problems are (e.g., the influence of religion, economics, politics, values, nationalism, etc., and specific professional problems such as the healthy body, use of leisure, etc.).

4. Based on the aims and objectives accepted (see #1 above), make decisions as to how your organization will meet the persistent problems identified both generally and specifically (i.e., what effect your goals (and hierarchy of values) will have on the relationships established in #2 above, and how such acceptance and

understanding ought to influence the process of education, recreation education, and physical education your
organization may wish to implement).

5. Spell out specifically from the standpoint of your
    hierarchy of values what program features you will
    introduce and through what process (or method) you
    will implement your entire program.

6. After you have gained the final approval of your policy-
    making group and your professional, part-time, and
    volunteer staff (with possible staff changes where
    commitment is not present), implement the revised
    program vigorously reminding one and all regularly
    that this program (including the process employed to
    implement it) is theirs and merits full support.

7. Evaluate the revised program regularly from the stand
    standpoint of:

    a. Its effectiveness in achieving the stated objectives
        with particular emphasis on the realization of hu-
        man values in the lives of your constituents.

Conflicting Philosophies of Fitness, Sports, and Physical Recreation

Probably the best approach for you and your organization is to
designate your approach on an educational philosophy spectrum. This
can be done basically by distinguishing initially between a position of
essentialism or progressivism, or perhaps by declaring (at least)
"inclination" in the one direction or the other. In my opinion this is
the only way that you can put some logic and consistency in your approach and thereby steer clear of the mediocrity of what might be
termed middle-of-the-road eclecticism. This latter approach is the
"creeping cancer" of most private organizations that I have en-
countered. They are "limping along in a disabled condition on the
road to mediocrity and their eventual demise." I am absolutely convinced that this is because they are not truly living up to their ideals!

In attempting to find your organizational place on the spectrum,
keep in mind that progressivism is greatly concerned about such
attributes as youth's freedom, individual differences, student interest, individual growth, no permanently fixed values, and that the process by which the program is implemented means ideal living now.
The essentialist, conversely, believes typically that there are certain
educational, recreational, and physical educational values by which

the individual must be guided; that effort takes precedence over interest and that this tends to gird moral stamina; that the experience of
the past has powerful jurisdiction over the present; and the the cultivation of the intellect in most important in education. And some
essentialistic groups place even greater emphasis on the achievement
of a relationship with a Supreme Being.

Two major positions. Specifically, then, there appear to be
two major philosophies of fitness, sports, and physical recreation
(relating to the overall area of physical, health, and recreation education) in regard to personal and societal values in education, recreation, and physical education. The progressivists (which include the
experimentalists, reconstructionists, romantic naturalists, et al.)
emphasize the concept of total fitness rather than physical fitness
primarily. The essentialists (which include idealists, naturalistic
realists, rational humanists, and Catholic perennialists, et al.) have
two subdivisions: (1) the idealists who stress education of the physical
and yet who believe in education through the physical as well to a
degree; and (2) the naturalistic realists and Catholic perennialists who
typically accept education of the physical as the primary emphasis in
the field. (Note: idealists are typically Protestants and Jews, whereas realists are either naturalistically oriented or spiritualistically
oriented as the Catholics.)

Two variations on this theme. Then, to be completely up-to-
date, we must recognize the permeating influence of existentialism
(either atheistic, Protestant, or Catholic). In education, recreation,
and physical education we learn from this philosophical approach that
we ought to help the child who is "authentically eccentric" to feel at
home in our programs, and that self-actualization is vital in the entire
process. The question is how we can assist the person to become a
self-moving individual searching for truth in his own way.

Secondly, we should call attention to the fact that many philosophers have now turned to some type of philosophy of language in a developing twentieth century analytic tradition. Language analysis, for
example, can help us to distinguish ever so much more effectively
among such terms as play, recreation, fitness, sport, athletics, physical recreation, and physical education.

Conclusion: (Six) Possible Common Denominators

The very fact that this Consultation has been convened indicates
that there is an urgent need for the establishment of some specific
common denominators upon which all can agree minimally. Finding
areas of agreement, without destroying the unique qualities of your
particular private agencies, is most important. The following are
some common denominators in the matter of fitness, sports, and physical recreation upon which we can all agree:

1. Certain basic health knowledge should be taught in the school curriculum. This can be supplemented by the private agency. The home, the school, municipal recreation, and private agencies should work together cooperatively to help the child and young person develop certain attitudes toward his own health in particular and toward community hygiene in general.

2. All concerned should work together to help children, youth, adults, and the elderly to make worthy use of leisure. Physical recreation is important, but communicative, creative and aesthetic, social, and learning interests are very basic as well.

3. Physical vigor is fundamental, and activities designed to promote this as part of a pattern of total fitness should be encouraged and given a definite priority. We need to work continually to reach a higher level of agreement about the minimum amount of "physical" fitness required for total fitness as a citizen in our society.

4. Competitive sports for boys and girls are desirable at some stage of their development. The extent of involvement; the intensity of the actual experience; and the role of adults as coaches are aspects which need further clarification.

5. Remedial exercise for physical defects that may be corrected or conditions that may be alleviated is needed urgently. This is an area which the private agency should explore, because the school is not meeting its responsibility here.

6. Character and/or personality development has a relationship to participation in fitness activities, sports, and physical recreation, but substantive evidence as the effect on these activities on the individual is still negligible. (Research is needed here, as it is in each of the other five areas mentioned above.)

Recommendations of a General Nature

The need is still there for increased cooperation at the planning level among the various public and private agencies providing educational, recreational, and physical educational services. The private agencies should not be hesitant about taking the leadership in this matter. Private agencies should encourage the development of public education and recreation in every way. When the public agencies are meeting their responsibilities, private agencies should relinquish their <u>community</u> service (but not in such a way that service to their own clientele is diminished). Private agencies should provide as many opportunities as possible for their members to experience "closed group associations" of high <u>quality</u>, and these services should be available to all age groups with special emphasis on children and young people. Agency programs should be creative and innovative in keeping, of course, with designated aims and objectives.

In these most difficult and really trying times, I urge you to be the kind of professional people who look to your philosophical foundations. I believe this is absolutely necessary so that there will be greater consistency between your words and your actions. We must relate dynamically to people's lives, or we are not going to survive. As professional individuals we can't be the sort of person who watches things happening all around him, and who is not looked to by his constituents and community officials for dedicated leadership based on the wisdom of philosophical maturity developed through orderly reflection and discussion. I have every confidence that you will make significant progress toward your long range goals in the years immediately ahead.

NATURALISM IN PHYSICAL, HEALTH, AND RECREATION EDUCATION

Naturalism is probably the oldest philosophy in the Western World.[1] Its more basic concepts are not difficult to comprehend. In the late nineteenth and early twentieth centuries so-called unrefined or naive naturalism found its place usurped by realism and pragmatism. It remains, however, as a powerful pervasive influence which is diametrically opposed to idealistic philosophy in which the universe is characterized by a rational order and which regards mind or spirit as ultimate reality.

Naturalists feel that Nature is reliable and dependable--a process which exhibits continuity. Scientific investigation is recognized as the only true means of gaining knowledge about the world. Facts must be amassed carefully and painstakingly before generalizations about Nature become self-evident; such is the inductive approach which characterizes the logic of the modern naturalist. His system of values follows logically from a belief that they are inherent in Nature itself. Ethically, naturalism is hedonistic--the achievement of the highest type of abiding pleasure for all is basic. Experiences that are natural purely bring aesthetic pleasure. Religious value is identical with overall value realization; life now is what is significant. The relationship of the individual to the physical universe is paramount. The social system is accepted since it is better than anarchy.

The naturalist believes that each child has a natural growth and development. Education should be synchronized with the natural rhythm of this pattern. Thus, education may well serve as a "delaying action" while maturation (the natural rhythms of development) takes place. The teacher will be aided greatly by the inborn self-activity which each child possesses. The naturalist in education relies on scientific method and makes every effort to acquire all kinds of information and factual knowledge. Inductive methods of instruction are basic, and the experience should be interesting and pleasurable. Punishment and reward are part of this process, but they should come about "naturally" as consequences of the action. We should not be unduly harsh when the child makes a mistake. Lastly, it is very important that there be a balance between education for the mind and education for the body.

---

[1] This article appeared in the School of Education Bulletin (The University of Michigan), Vol. 34, No. 3: 42-46 (December, 1962).

The general aim of education is "complete living." Presumably in their order of importance, subsidiary objectives are: self-preservation, learning how to earn a livelihood, caring for one's family, understanding the pattern of the social structure, and learning how to use leisure wisely.

The naturalist is primarily concerned that man (and woman too!) be a rugged animal fit to withstand the excessive "wear and tear" that life's informal and formal activities may demand. The impact of this objective strikes to the heart of the problem as many physical educators see the situation today. For many reasons children and young adults on the North American Continent have "enjoyed" a way of life which has not been conducive to the achievement of the objective--a "rugged animal." A great many boys and girls cannot do one pull-up; regular, organized physical education classes in elementary schools are the exception rather than the rule, and when offered are not vigorous enough; high school programs in Michigan, for example, are typically limited to one year with only rare opportunities for further election; draft statistics showed almost unbelievable rejection rates; the average adult female is twenty pounds overweight. Objective physical performance tests indicate that many people twenty-seven years of age are old "physically."

Coincidentally, it was just about one hundred years ago that Herbert Spencer called the public's attention to this serious matter. He believed that a "nation of good animals" was a "first condition" before national prosperity could be achieved and maintained. Even in the "contests" of commerce he saw the need for workers with bodily endurance. His major thesis was that the findings of science should be applied to education. Rather critically he states pointedly that our children should be participating in the benefits that "sheep and oxen are deriving from the investigations of the laboratory."

From the standpoint of the naturalist it is only a short step forward to the conclusion that Nature "wants" men and women to have good physiques since the welfare of posterity is of the greatest importance. Spencer points out that a "cultivated intelligence" in a "bad physique" may die out in a few generations (advancing medical science has probably reversed any such trend to a degree). Conversely, he feels that a good physique is worth saving, because we may be able to improve the mental endowments of his descendants. At this point we may recall the statement of historians who felt that the barbarians who sacked Rome at least gave their superb bodies to posterity.

The unrefined naturalist is quite properly concerned about man's health habits and necessary instruction that should be offered to the child to protect him from ailments and diseases caused by infractions of Nature's physiologic law. In his native England, Spencer was concerned about under-eating on the part of city dwellers as a reaction to some of the past extremes in indulgence. He wondered why we should discourage something so natural as an individual's appetite. Today we encourage children to eat a balanced diet, and we like to see them have a healthy appetite, generally speaking. On the other hand, we find far too many overweight adults. They are now being encouraged to abstain while keeping balance in their diets. Vast quantities of vitamin tablets and liquid low-calorie dietary supplements are consumed in the United States every day. The role of exercise in weight control has not received enough attention.

Consistent with his naturalistic approach, Spencer disagreed with a then prevalent notion that sensations were to be disregarded. He postulated that this would indeed be a peculiar world if such were the case. It is not eating, drinking, breathing, or even exercising when we feel like it that is bad, it is doing these things when Nature indicates there is no need or urge to do so that causes all the difficulties. Our "physical conscience" can be a "faithful monitor."

The naturalist applies the standard of a "good animal" to girls as well as boys. He asks the question whether girls' constitutions are so different from those of boys that they don't need vigorous exercise. This question might well be asked today of women physical educators in North America who help to set a pattern of mild exercise for girls and young women. These "young animals" often do not have enough "natural" beauty as they advance into maturity and are forced all too frequently to become synthetic creatures--a sort of American ideal composed of unnatural padding in certain bodily areas and restrictive devices in others! Conversely, the adult male has many deficiencies as well.

There can be no doubt, however, that women are most concerned with their appearance. At the present time physical education courses which cater to "posture, figure, and carriage" have crowded sections at the university level at any rate. Television programs and magazine articles appear daily which encourage women to exercise regularly through the medium of a series of calisthenics. As fine as these efforts may be, they represent an artificial approach to a problem that can be met in a much more natural way through games and sports embodying the fundamental skills. Nor do these calisthenics give adequate emphasis to the need for circulo-respiratory efficiency in every vital animal, "human" or otherwise. The pale, angular fashion models in our magazine advertisements today are not natural or normal. Excessive study programs need to be relieved by vigorous sports participation:

Mammas anxious to make their daughters attractive, could scarcely choose a course more fatal than this, which sacrifices the body to the mind. Either they disregard the tastes of the

opposite sex, or else their conception of those tastes is erroneous. Men care little for erudition in women; but very much for
physical beauty, good nature, and common sense.[1]

Despite the efforts of the President's Council on Youth Fitness, we
find a disproportionate emphasis being placed on "intellectual development" and "so little for the body." In this manner would the naturalist
speak!

    The naturalist in physical education makes a strong plea for the
elimination of all types of artificial exercises insofar as possible. He
wants to see exercise patterns for boys and girls that develop naturally and spontaneously from play and sport activities. Artificial exercises negate the factor of amusement and a state of happiness that
should accompany a natural kind of exercise. A natural activity involving varied play can be a highly invigorating influence. The naturalist believes that the "riotous glee" accompanying sport is as
important as the strenuous exercise involved. Overemphasized athletics demanding businesslike attention to monotonous, routinized drill
would be quickly condemned. In regard to gymnastics, it seems
reasonable to assume that the introduction of a "play element" and
"freedom of choice" to all sorts of formalized gymnastics and calisthenics would go far toward making them more palatable to the naturalist.

    The naive naturalist can't help being disturbed by the imbalance
that he sees in operation in our "civilized society." He is vitally concerned with the child's growth and development pattern, and he believes that the years from six to sixteen are being increasingly
burdened from an "excess of mental application" as the tempo of civilization increases and the magnitude of "cultural heritage transmission"
increases proportionately. We are told that the Western world is engaged in a fierce struggle for its very existence, and that life is a
serious business. Our answer appears to be the encouragement of
intensive application to the "important subjects" in the curriculum.
Children are being forced to do hours of homework after sitting in
classrooms for the large part of the daylight hours. The child who is
gifted in motor capacity seems to be getting his share of attention, insofar as the boys are concerned, but the average youngster gets either
no regular physical education periods or else one or two inadequate
periods a week. The result is a child that is weak physically with
poor body mechanics and deficient play skills.

---

    [1] Herbert Spencer, Education, p. 226 in 1949 reprint. London:
Watts and Co., Ltd., 1861.

Everyone appears to give lip service to the glorious Greek ideal and to the more limited Roman "sound mind in a sound body" precept, but very few follow through and do anything about achieving this desirable state. We are warned that "Nature is a strict accountant; and if you demand of her in one direction more than she is prepared to lay out, she balances the account by making a deduction elsewhere." A civilization will continue to grow if it meets its challenges. America has a choice to make.

THE EDUCATIONAL PHILOSOPHY OF EXPERIMENTALISM: IMPLICATIONS FOR PHYSICAL, HEALTH, AND RECREATION EDUCATION

The Nature of Reality (Metaphysics)

Nature is an emergent evolution, and man's frame of reality is limited to nature as it functions. The world is characterized by activity and change. Rational man has developed through organic evolution, and the world is yet incomplete--a reality that is constantly undergoing change because of a theory of emergent novelty. Man enjoys freedom of will; freedom is achieved through continuous and developmental learning from experience.[1]

Educational Aims and Objectives

The general aim of education is more education. "Education in the broadest sense can be nothing less than the changes made in human beings by their experience." Participation by students in the formation of aims and objectives is absolutely essential to generate the all-important desired interest. Social efficiency can well be considered the general aim of education. Pupil growth is a paramount goal, as the individual is placed at the center of the educational experience.

The Educative Process (Epistemology)

Knowledge is the result of a process of thought with a useful purpose. Truth is not only to be tested by its correspondence with reality, but also its practical results. Knowledge is earned through experience and is an instrument of verification. Mind has evolved in the natural order as a more flexible means whereby man adapts himself to his world. Learning takes place when interest and effort unite to produce the desired result. A psychological order (problem-solving as explained through scientific method) is more useful than a logical arrangement (from the simple fact to the complex conclusion). There is always a social context to learning, and the curriculum must be adapted to the particular society for which it is intended.

---

[1] Published in The Physical Educator, Vol. 20, No. 4: 150-152 (December, 1963).

Physical, Health, and Recreation Education (Aims and Objectives)

I am much more interested in promoting the concept of total fitness rather than physical fitness alone. I believe that physical education should be an integral subject in the curriculum. Students should have the opportunity to select a wide variety of useful activities, many of which should help to develop "social intelligence." The activities offered should bring natural impulses into play. To me, physical education classes and intramural sports are more important to the large majority of students than interscholastic or intercollegiate sports and deserve priority if conflict arises over budgetary allotment, staff available, and use of facilities. I can, however, give full support to team experiences in competitive sports, because they can be vital educational experiences if properly conducted.

I believe that man should be a rugged animal, and this standard should apply generally to girls as well as boys. Health, as I see it, is a primary objective of education, and the child needs health instruction. The success of the school health education program depends upon the degree of cooperation among home, school, and community agencies. An educated person must understand the difference between health and disease, and he must know how to protect and improve his own health, that of his dependents, and that of the community. As I see it, the program of school health, physical education, and recreation may be administered as a unified program within a school system. I believe that natural types of exercise promote sound mental health. All these aspects of the total program may be coordinated because they are related in many ways. Through unity these subdivisions, which are basically related, could probably serve the needs of school children and youth much more effectively than is the case so often at the present. To be truly effective, school health education must be concerned with helping the individual to lead a rich, full life. This means more than providing a health service so that students can maintain minimum health needed to "pursue intellectual work with the least amount of strain." Health should be defined positively--as that quality which enables us "to live most and serve best."

I am inclined to favor the adoption of the name recreation education for the field. I see advantages in a unified approach whereby the three specialized areas of health, physical education, and recreation (in schools) would provide a variety of experiences that will enable the individual to live a richer, fuller life through superior adjustment to his environment. I believe that education for the worthy use of leisure is basic to the curriculum of the school--a curriculum in which pupil growth, as defined broadly, is all-important. Secondly, play shall be conducted in sucy a way that desirable moral growth will be fostered. Thirdly, overly-organized sport competition is not true recreation, since the welfare of the individual is often submerged in the extreme emphasis which is so frequently placed on winning. I believe it is a mistake to confuse the psychological distinction between work and play with the traditional economic distinction that is generally recognized. All citizens should have ample opportunity to use their free time in a creative and fruitful manner. I do not condemn a person who watches others perform with a high level of skill in any of our cultural recreational activities, including sport, so long as the individual kept such viewing in a balanced role in his entire life.

THE PRAGMATIC (EXPERIMENTALISTIC) ETHIC AS IT
RELATES TO SPORT AND PHYSICAL EDUCATION

The fundamental theme underlying this presentation is that the pragmatic (experimentalistic) ethic may be related to sport and physical education in Western culture in such a way that those holding this philosophical position will be enabled to employ these cultural forces as "socially useful servants."* The intent is to present these ideas in as logical and scientific a manner as possible, even though to some who embrace a different outlook and approach it may emerge as a polemic. The writer sees no way to avoid this dilemma because the discipline and sub-disciplines of philosophy seem to be presently incapable of "eschewing obfuscation."

With apologies to no one, therefore, the following sub-problems of the topic, phrased as questions, will be discussed in this order: (1) what is the essence of the ethical problem in sport and physical education in the present context? (2) what is the problem of the "good" and "bad" viewed in historical perspective? (3) what insight about values may be gained from an examination of Parsons's Action System? (4) what appear to be the problems of ethics today? (5) what answers are provided by pragmatic (naturalistic) ethics? (6) what seem to be the implications for experimentalism (pragmatic naturalism) as an educational philosophy? (7) what may be considered as the pragmatic (experimentalistic) ethic in sport and physical education? (8) what are the strengths and weaknesses of this position? (9) how may these ideas be summarized succinctly? (10) what reasonable conclusions may be drawn from this analysis and interpretation?

The Ethical Problem in Sport and Physical Education

The essence of the ethical problem in sport and physical education in present context cannot be delineated without an analysis of the social system and culture in which it is taking place. (The writer regrets his inability at present to separate the terms "sport" and "physical education," or at least the fact that for him no one term adequately describes this aspect of culture being considered. The following definition has merit currently: the art and science of human movement as related to the theory and practice of sport, dance, play, and exercise.)

---

* A paper presented at the Symposium on Sport and Ethics, State University College at Brockport, Brockport, New York, October 28, 1972. (Published in The Philosophy of Sport, R. G. Osterhoudt, ed. Springfield, Illinois: Charles C. Thomas, 1973, pp. 229-273.)

The problems in sport, dance, play, and exercise appear to be legion. The amateur ideal has long since been shattered in Olympic competition, and most recently we have witnessed a display of Canadian nationalism as a group of top professional, U. S.-oriented hockey players of Canadian origin barely won over a group of Russian "amateurs" who finished second to Czechoslovakia in the Olympic Winter Games. If dance may be classified as human movement with a purpose, it is obvious that all is not well here either. Certainly this form of aesthetic expression has not yet found its rightful place within the educational pattern of the culture, and one does not need to travel far to hear that freedom in various dance forms undermines the moral fibre of youth. The term "play" is one of the most ambiguous in the English language, the average unabridged dictionary offering about sixty-eight different definitions for the reader's consumption. Still further, at almost any age too much play in one's life in the eyes of many implies shiftlessness and lack of purpose and direction. As for the subject of exercise, some say it is excellent, others say it is beneficial in moderation, and a third group warns that too much of it is bad, that it is not essential or right in a school curriculum, and that an excess of exercise can cause very ill effects. Is it any wonder that the common man exhibits a large amount of confusion, and that there is a strong tendency to follow the line of least resistance and to do "what comes naturally" depending upon the exigencies of the moment?

It must be completely obvious that such diversity of opinion and belief could exist only in a social system within a culture characterized by pluralistic philosophies, philosophies of education, and philosophies of sport and physical education. Such a state is, of course, not necessarily bad, and it undoubtedly requires a political state in which a considerable amount of participatory democracy exists. And yet the opinion is often expressed that North America functions materialistically despite an overarching, inherent philosophical idealism. Many people are absolutely convinced that all of the old standards and morals have been completely negated, and that only a return to earlier halcyon days can prevent impending disaster. They decry what they believe are the prevailing "situation ethics," because they sense an uncharted course ahead on the way toward the year 2,000.

Oddly enough, at the very time when people seem to need guidance, a large percentage of the profession of philosophy - in the English-speaking world at least - seems to have abandoned them for a more strictly disciplinary approach to their work. (Of course, it is difficult to be too condemnatory when a similar phenomenon seems to have taken place in educational philosophy, and more recently a "similar infection seems to be spreading" within the philosophy of sport and physical education at an alarming rate.) To make matters worse, the general public has taken such words as pragmatism, idealism, realism, and now existentialism and given them other than their original philosophical meanings. The result is that correct use now requires extensive qualification.

All of this adds up to the conclusion that society has now "progressed" to the point where unanimity is largely lacking in regard to "what's good," "what's bad," and what lies somewhere in between. And this problem is present no matter what phase of life and/or society is under consideration. Writing somewhat editorially about these developments of recent years, Cogley (1972, p. 2) explains how in his opinion:

> every major institution in the land and most of the minor ones as well seemed to have been caught up in an identity crisis. Upheavals in the church were front-page news for almost a decade. The revolt against the prevailing idea of a university which began in Berkeley in 1964 kept erupting with dismaying frequency. Veteran army officers found themselves at a loss as to how to deal with rebellious troops. The Democratic debacle at the Chicago convention four years ago dramatized a widespread disillusionment with the political parties. The once sacrosanct public school system came under severe attack. Working newsmen who took to producing their own underground papers after hours voiced bitter disenchantment with the established press employing them. So prevalent was the discontent inside the academic and professional communities that the 'radical caucuses' within them were given semi-official status. Bishops, university presidents, military brass, publishers, politicians, school principals, and other established 'leaders,' it became increasingly clear, were no longer leading . . .

Thus, it should be obvious that values, morals, and ethical standards are undergoing an "identity crisis" from which they may never recover. If this be true, the implications for sport and physical education as a microcosm of the culture are that turmoil would inevitably be present there as well. This brings the reader directly back to the point made above that all is far from well in the realm of sport, dance, play and exercise.

The "Good" and the "Bad" in Historical Perspective

In a paper such as this, there is obviously not time to review the problem of the "good" and the "bad" in great detail so that the reader will have available even an outline history of that branch of philosophy known as "ethics." In a language where even the word "meaning" has eight different meanings, the term "ethics" is employed typically in three different ways (each of which has a relation to the other). First, it is used to classify a general pattern or "way of life" (e.g., Christian ethics). Second, it refers to a listing of rules of conduct or a so-called moral code (e.g., professional ethics). Lastly, it has come to be used when describing inquiry about ways of life or rules of conduct (e.g., that subdivision of philosophy now known as metaethics).

The primary focus here should be on metaethics and its central questions. What is meant when one searches for the "good" or the "bad"? What guarantee is there that any such intent is correct? Can there be right standards for use in judging actions or things to be good or bad? If such value judgments are made, how do they differ, if at all, from judgments that are value free (or value neutral) in nature? In any such search or investigation, it is also difficult to know whether to proceed from the general to the specific or vice versa (i.e., from the good in general to right conduct or justice in particular, or in the opposite direction).

Even a cursory examination of the history of ethics substantiates that it is a description of "irregular progress toward complete clarification of each type of ethical judgment." (Encyclopedia of Philosophy, III, p. 82.) It is indeed difficult to judge exactly, or even generally, how much "irregular progress" has been made since the development of Greek ethics starting with the fifth century B.C. contributions of Socrates. It could be argued presumably that the changing political, economic, and other social influences of the time required the development of a new way of conduct just as there is a need for altered standards of conduct today. The emergence of professional teachers of philosophy were in a sense the by-product of greater civilization. As Sidgwick stated,

> If bodily vigour was no longer to be left to nature and spontaneous exercise, but was to be attained by the systematic observance of rules laid down by professional trainers, it was natural to think that the same might be the case with excellences of the soul. (Outlines of the History of Ethics, p. 21).

Time and space do not permit a detailed consideration of the ideas of Socrates, Plato, and Aristotle, nor later Hellenistic, and Roman ethical tendencies that have come to be known as Epicureanism, Stoicism, and Neoplatonism. Socrates began the development of standards for the qualities of goodness, justice, and virtue. Plato gave a spiritual orientation to such thought as he believed that these timeless qualities or ideals had been defined in a world beyond the ken of man. Aristotle, conversely, sought his answers in what now have been designated as the sciences and social sciences. Plato's approach to goodness was through comparison with so-called universal ideals, while Aristotle's "happiness" resulted from the accomplishment of more natural goals. Individual good was related to social good, but the ideas of moral responsibility and free will were not viewed with the same importance as was to become the case later in Christian thought.

For the next two thousand years ethical thought was oriented much more to practice than to theory. This is why the meanings of the various ethical terms or concepts were not altered to any extent, even though moral codes and life purposes were viewed quite differently. The Hellenistic and Roman ideas were lacking in the necessary scientific insight required to advance beyond the intellectual genius of the earlier Greeks. It was during this period that the seedbed of later, all-encompassing Christian philosophy was established. As a result the Western world went into a long period during which time philosophy and religion were most closely interwoven. During this new period in the history of ethics there was one system in which man's reason and God's purpose for man were combined to produce one ultimate purpose for man - his eventual union with his Creator.

It was during this period of so-called medieval ethics that Thomas Aquinas brought together Aristotle's scientific and philosophic thought with the theology of St. Augustine. A highly significant and fundamental concept of the ethical system created by St. Thomas was his doctrine of natural law. Here he invented an accommodation of two different ethical systems so that there was a "natural domain" and a "theological realm." Reason and conscience were somehow fused inherently in man's nature; natural law contained God's ethical standards to which man could elevate himself by the application of God-given reason. The apparent weakness here is that religious dogmas, being infallible, could presumably negate valid scientific advances.

So-called modern ethics flourished during the marked period of social change of the sixteenth and seventeenth centuries. The philosophical watershed seems to be created immediately after a series of major social changes have occurred. Thus, when many considered the prevailing ethical system to be in a "state of disarray," various attempts at reconstruction began. Thomas Hobbes made a strong effort to release ethics from its complete servitude to theological law. He postulated that ethics was unreliable unless it was grounded on the objective laws of biology and psychology. If it turned out that the experimental analysis of nature was to be ethically neutral, then he argued that ethics should indeed be contrasted with science. Such thought brought reaction and counter-action from the early intuitionists (e.g., Henry More), Benedict Spinoza, John Locke, Bishop Butler, David Hume, and the so-called Common-sense Intuitionists (e.g., Thomas Reid). A similar "theoretical struggle" was being carried on in eighteenth century France through the efforts of Voltaire,

Jean-Jacques Rousseau and the Encyclopedists (e.g., Diderot), although some feel that their political orientation often distorted the objectivity of their arguments. Montesquieu did add to a more scientific approach, however, by viewing values more as sociological and historical facts.

Special mention must be made of the monumental role played by Immanuel Kant in the German Enlightenment. His complex and often perplexing nonutilitarian analysis based moral principles on a priori laws by which man's "practical reason" is guided. He postulated that man feels no obligation to obey laws of nature, but that he does sense subjectively a duty to respond to moral laws that are inherent in the universe. Kant's ethical system has three basic premises: (1) analysis of the evidence of moral experience, (2) consideration of the underlying logic, and (3) the construction of metaphysical principles undergirded or presupposed by ethical analysis that is in contradistinction to generalizations from science. He distinguished sharply between naturalistic ethics and moral law. His categorical imperative implied a moral code above and beyond any law of nature (e.g., man's strong desire for happiness). He postulated a universalizability criterion as the most fundamental moral principle ("Act only on that maxim which you can will to be a universal law"). This more precise statement of the "golden rule" represents perhaps Kant's greatest addition to the theory of ethics despite its apparent weakness. Lastly, he envisioned an autonomy of the will which placed man in a position to defy causal determinism grounded in regulative scientific principle. Man was conceived as part of, and yet distinct from, the laws of nature and science.

The nineteenth century in the Western world witnessed a sharp struggle between the two great traditions of utilitarianism and idealism, the former looming large in England and France and the latter predominant in Germany. So it is not surprising that both developing systems met with favorable responses from different quarters in the United States. Idealism was welcomed by certain philosophers and literary figures and, of course, the Christian Church. Utilitarianism blended with the drive for greater technological advancement, and then was joined or supplanted by the pragmatic ethics of Peirce, James, and Dewey. The developments in England, Germany, and the rest of the continent will not be catalogued here. They are quite well known, and the essential battle lines have already been drawn. The main concern in this paper is the pragmatic philosophy devised by James and Dewey in which ethical considerations relate to all of human knowledge. They were able to avoid the almost ageless, perennial distinction between value and fact by a type of reinterpretation that blurred the controversial issues for those who were willing to disavow Kantian ethics and the traditional outlook toward scientific knowledge as including only value-free facts. With this approach ethical judgment was simply a matter of applying human reason to the results of scientific (empirical) investigation by sscribing value to those human acts so designated as valuable.

At this point the historical thread will be broken and picked up later with a discussion of modern metaethical problems. In the meantime a short digression will be made to discuss the role of values in Parsons's Action System, thereby placing this problem in sociological perspective as well.

The Role of Values in Parsons's Action System

A student of the history of ethics, or the history of anything for that matter, soon realizes the importance of the major social forces as determinants of the direction a society may take at any given moment in its history. It is the opinion of the writer that both philosophers and historians would be well advised to avail themselves of the knowledge about cultures and social systems that is becoming available in a spiralling growth pattern through advancing sociological theory. Although it is current fashion in some quarters to debunk the complex "theory of action" developed by Talcott Parsons and others, it often appears that many of these critics have not even made a solid effort to understand his work. Because this theory is so firmly grounded in the descriptive and experimental methods of science, it seems both logical and consistent to review the role of values in Parsonian theory with an eye to any insights that may be gained for use in this analysis of ethics in pragmatism. It is also possible, of course, that the pragmatic outlook on values may in time strengthen the Parsonian theoretical structure.

Parsons's general action system may be regarded as a type of empirical system that is composed of four subsystems (culture, the social system, the personality, and the behavioral organism). The theory is that these subsystems compose a hierarchy of societal control and conditioning. (Harry M. Johnson, 1969, pp. 46-58; the writer is grateful to Professor Johnson, an authority on Parsons, for his generous willingness to assist in this interpretation of this theory; any errors or omissions, of course, rest with this writer.)

Culture as the first subsystem of the action theory provides the basic structure and its components "and, in a sense, the 'programming' for the action system as a whole." (Quotations in this section are from Dr. Johnson's paper.) The structure for the "social system," of course, "has to be more or less attuned to the functional problems" of social systems, and the same holds for the structure and functional problems of the personality and the behavioral organism, respectively. Further, the subsystem of culture exercises "control" over the social system, and so on up and down the scale. Legitimation is provided to the level below or "pressure to conform" if there is inconsistency. Thus, there is a "'strain toward consistency' among the system levels, led and controlled from above downward."

The terms "conditioning" and "strain" are used by Parsons to explain a hierarchy of conditioning. The higher systems depend on the lower ones, and the "strain" that may occur at the lower level "works" to change the very structure of the system above. Of course, "incipient strain" at the lower level may be resolved prior to the creation of such an effect that change takes place above. Generally speaking, a change in culture, is apt to take place when important scientific or religious beliefs are challenged or negated. This can, in fact, bring about structural change in larger social systems, while change in personality could well bring about change in somewhat smaller social systems.

Running the risk of inadequate treatment, it seems most important in this paper on ethics to consider the four levels of structure within the social system itself. Here we are referring to the United States or to Canada as social systems. Proceeding from the highest to the lowest level, from the general to the more specific, they are designated as: (1) values, (2) norms, (3) the structure of collectivities, and (4) the structure of roles. The reader should keep in mind that all of these levels are normative in that the social structure is composed of sanctioned cultural limits within which certain types of behavior are mandatory or acceptable.

Note that values are at the top - the highest level, and there are many categories of values (scientific, artistic, and values for personalities, etc.). "Social values are conceptions of the ideal general character of the type of social system in question." As Johnson explains,

> For the United States as a society, important societal values are the rule of law, the social-structural facilitation of individual achievement, and equality of opportunity. (p. 48).

It is most important to keep in mind the difference between values and the shared sanctioned norms that are the second level of the social structure. In the U. S. social system, for example, the basic norms are the institutions of private property, private enterprise, the monogamous conjugal family, and the separation of church and state. At this time no detailed discussion of collectivities or roles will be presented. The Democratic Party, or Liberal Party in Canada, would be examples of collectivities, and the fourth-level roles would in these instances would be the unique influence of a George McGovern or a Pierre Trudeau, respectively.

This brief abstract from sociological theory will cease at this point, hopefully after having whetted the appetite of the philosophically-oriented reader. Without going into detail about the interchange processes and the various subsystems of the larger social system, it can be stated that Parsons's action theory suggests that the most important cultural aspect of any society is its value system. In the United States, for example, there has been (according to Parsons) a remarkably stable value system with gradual value generalization such as that which accompanies structural differentiation.

Progress toward these so-called United States' values obviously has not been a straight-line movement, mainly because of various types of resistance that have arisen "along the way." Johnson (p. 55) outlines four of these obstacles as follows:

1. Many mistakenly identify norms with values and react indignantly to reform because to them this represents a subversion of values. Parsons calls this "fundamentalism."

2. Reform is most difficult because it comes into conflict with vested interests bent on preventing a redistribution of the benefits and burdens of the system.

3. So-called ideological distortion often develops, a situation in which many citizens hold a distorted view of the state of the system and of the probable effect of the proposed changes.

4. Because of the rapid change in the culture and the social systems of the United States, there exist a great many needs for change. Some of these needs are not being met, or are being met insufficiently at best. This is producing strain with a resultant "need" to restore solidarity (an integrative problem).

It is interesting to note that truly significant change can take place at the three lower levels without actually "doing violence" to the value level itself. The reason for this is the hierarchy of control and conditioning that prevails. It takes a "true" social revolution – in which a new value system becomes the source of legitimation, guidance, and control – to bring about a sufficient amount of disequilibrium to force the social system to adopt new or basically altered values.

Parsons's action system does not state that history is the unfolding of a predetermined cultural value system – the possible error of those who hold teleological beliefs, or who may even believe in some type of an idealistic philosophy of education. What is important for this paper is the evident relationship and actual identity of the scientific methodology underlying Parsonian theory and that of James and - particularly - John Dewey. Both Parsons and Dewey envision an actor-situation frame of reference in a world characterized by ever-present change and novelty. The crucial position and importance of values, and especially the approach to the determination of specific values, is paramount and undoubtedly lends strength to the case for pragmatic (naturalistic) ethical theory.

The Problems of Ethics

As anxious as the writer is to move ahead to a consideration of pragmatic (naturalistic) ethics, it is only reasonable that the problems of metaethics be put into perspective first. This brief treatment will include a very short discussion of what has gone before in the history of ethics and moral philosophy.

As has been indicated earlier, there are almost as many views of ethics and/or moral philosophy as there are philosophers - an obvious exaggeration, of course, but a definite indication that there is no single, non-controversial foundation stone upon which the whole structure of ethics can be built. In fact, it can even be argued that the nature and function of the subject are themselves topics upon which there is vigorous dispute. This is not to say that there are not some aspects of this branch of philosophy upon which there is fairly wide consensus. For example, in the past moral philosophers tried to offer general guidance as to (1) what to do, (2) what to seek, and (3) how to treat others. (Nowell-Smith, 1954).

Philosophers as a rule have not tried to "preach" to their adherents, although many have made strong efforts to offer fairly practical advice that included important pronouncements on the subject of good and evil. Many early philosophers believed that there was indeed a true moral code - a normative ethical system upon which people could and should base their conduct. In this sense, therefore, philosophers saw their task as the enunciation of basic principles of morality (usually with supporting justification). What is good? What is the good life? What are the limits of moral justification? How shall people live their lives? These were the types of questions to which philosophers spoke.

Others have offered such advice freely down through the years. Theologians, dramatists, novelists, poets, and even comedians have offered considerable insight into the question of good and evil, but such counsel was often viewed as dicta, and usually differed from distinctly philosophical accounts in that it was specific, unsystematic, and lacking in proof.

As was stated above, there is strong disagreement within the so-called traditional conception of the philosopher's task. Some believed that philosophers should not discover new truths (e.g., Kant), while others felt just the opposite to be the case (e.g., Bentham). There was an effort to systematize the knowledge that men already have and to demonstrate the ultimate rationale for these beliefs. Some were concerned with objective justification of any moral claims, whereas others (known as subjectivists) argued that true objectivity was simply not possible or reasonable. One group was extremely skeptical, therefore, about any body-of-knowledge which purported to tell men how they should live. Their opponents - the objectivists - worked away at the creation of a true moral code. In this struggle Nietzsche was a "true revolutionary" in that he contradicted previous objectivistic thought violently - even the common-sense moral principles unchallenged by most skeptics. In summary, therefore, the battle lines were drawn: one group of ethical theorists agreed with the traditional task (so-called) of the philosopher, and the "enemy" denied that moralists could every hope to achieve such an objective goal as a truly justifiable moral code.

It is very difficult if not impossible to gain historical perspective on the philosophical trends and developments of the past fifty to seventy-five years. So-called philosophical analysis has been a most interesting and important development during this period of time. Despite the fact that scholars in the Western world have been engaged in philosophical thought for more than two thousand years, there is still controversy over what the exact nature of philosophy is. And so into the struggle between the ethical objectivists and subjectivist came a third combatant - the contemporary analytic philosopher of the twentieth century who asked himself the question, "What kind of activity am I engaging in?" Searching for the answer, he began to develop three different analytic approaches that became known as (1) logical atomism, (2) logical positivism, and (3) ordinary language philosophy. Each looked at analysis somewhat differently, but there was agreement that philosophy must be approached through the medium of language analysis to a greater or lesser extent. Logical atomists struggled to rearrange our ambiguous language so that more logically arranged sentences would become crystal clear. Logical positivism's aim was to subject statements to a verifiability principle. This meant that ordinary language statements were to be arranged in logical, consistent form to see if they were empirically verifiable either through mathematical reasoning or scientific investigation. The main goal of so-called ordinary language philosophy was to decide what the basic philosophical terms were, and then to use them correctly and clearly so that all might understand. Obviously, these developments were a far cry from the efforts of the ethical subjectivists to get the objectivists on the run!

Thus, at the very time when the world is in such a turmoil full of "hot and cold" wars, at the very time when people of all ages are highly concerned about ethical values - about "what to do, what to seek, and how to treat others," brilliant philosophical scholars are relatively silent, avoid the rational justification of any type of moral system, and spend their time and energy analyzing the meaning and function of moral concepts and statements. The result is that there has developed a sharp distinction between the <u>normative ethics</u> of the moral philosophers and the analytic or critical or theoretical approach of that branch of philosophy now known as <u>metaethics</u>. Thus, it is possible to distinguish between a normative ethical statement and a metaethical statement as follows: "Harsh coaching methods have no place in amateur sport" would be an instance of the former, while "A coach knows through intuition whether his statements about sporting ethics are fundamentally true" is an example of the latter type of statement.

Obviously, it is of considerable concern to those of us interested in the philosophy of sport and physical education to ascertain in quite exact fashion what the relationship between normative ethics and metaethics should be. There are extremists on both sides, but a more reasonable approach would seem to be one in which a moral philosopher or ethical theorist engages in metaethical analysis, but at the same time works toward the elimination of irrational ethical beliefs while attempting to discover a truly sound ethical system. The one would not seem to be incompatible with the other so long as the scholar is fully aware of the interrelationships between the two research approaches or techniques.

It must be recognized, however, that the task of normative inquiry is most difficult, especially when complex issues and conclusions tend to stray into the realm of metaethics. For example, when a normative ethical theory such as hedonism includes a statement such as "Competitive sport is good because it brings pleasure," the nonhedonist might challenge this statement solely on the meaning of the terms "good" and "pleasure." The obvious difficulty of justifying a normative ethical theory brings to the four questions about metaethical relativism and subjectivism, questions which when pursued carefully point up the severity of the "subjectivistic threat."

Basically and fundamentally, then, justification of an ethical theory, or even an incomplete set of ethical statements about sport (or any other aspect of life), revolves around the ability of the theorist to state correctly, elucidate sufficiently, and defend adequately his moral and/or ethical claims and arguments. Is a moral judgment objective or subjectives? Does a moral judgment differ from a factual judgment? Is an ethical statement about correct conduct in sport, for example, "publicly warrantable?" In other words, is there some publicly acceptable procedure for verification which reasonable men would be willing to accept? Finally, then, ethical claims or judgments should be objectively verifiable; they should be universalizable, they should be practical for use in everyday life; and - ideally - they should be autonomous in that the structure or "fabric" of the theoretical statements does not rest on solely nonnormative statements.

Pragmatism (Ethical Naturalism)

The various metaethical theories are propounded, therefore, by philosophers who are striving to account as best possible for each of the four, so-called ideal features of sound moral or ethical discourse as listed immediately above (objectivity, universality, practicality, and autonomy). The reader will have to decide for himself to what extent the various ethical theories of the twentieth century satisfy the demands indicated for ideal ethical discourse. Since this paper is designed to focus on ethical naturalism or pragmatism, no effort can be made, other than incidental comments, to cover the nonnaturalism of G. E. Moore; the deontological nonnaturalists (e.g., C. D. Board) who are typically intuitionistic; the phenomenological intuitionists (e.g., Max Scheler); the noncognitive emotivists (e.g., A. J. Ayer); the noncognitivst existentialists who imply normative value theory through what has been called philosophical anthropology on the Continent (e.g., Albert Camus); the linguistic philosophical approach of a R. M. Hare which states that moral dicta are much like imperatives; and, finally, what has been called a "good-reasons approach" in that moral precepts should be justified on the basis of which resulting social practices would cause the least amount of suffering (e.g., Stephen Toulmin).

The focus in this section will be on the answers (or "answers") that seem to be provided by pragmatic (naturalistic) ethics. Space will not permit a detailed discussion of the various subdivisions of this philosophical position, although the broad outline will be presented. The point must be made immediately that Dewey's ethical theorizing was different that anything which had been heard of since the Greeks. As Rucker explains,

> . . . for Dewey there are no fixed ends, either psychological, sociological, or theological; no authoritatively decreed moral laws; and no externally specified virtues or vices . . . Dewey states in a variety of places that the job of philosophy is to restore the long-broken connection between the realms of science and value. Hence his insistence upon a science of ethics: the procedures of the natural sciences are the procedures of any search for knowledge and understanding. The analysis of the act of reflective thought yields the ground for science and for ethics, the distinction between them being one of the

primary interest at the time: knowledge or action, truth or goodness . . . (in Boydston, 1970, 116.)

Even before the turn of the century, therefore, Dewey realized that morality should not be compartmentalized and considered in a different way that other aspects of life. This point is a sine qua non which must be understood by any who would evaluate his efforts.

Interestingly enough, further substantiation of the "peculiar" approach comes from an analysis of the functions of the philosopher in American pragmatism written some twenty years ago by a young Catholic philosopher at the Catholic University of America in Washington, D. C. In an evident early effort to establish himself as a freethinker, Keating compared the function of the pragmatic philosopher with that of the philosopher in Thomism. His major findings help to set the stage for this present treatment:

1. It is the negative or critical function of the philosopher to dismiss make-believes, to clear the air of erroneous premises and attitudes.

2. The primary duty of the philosopher is to aid in the advancement of the common good.

3. The function of the philosopher is to provide the average man with a more rational conception of the framework of things and to aid in the creation and realization of human ideals.

4. The primary function of the philosopher is the application of the pragmatic test.. . . If a proposition has no practical meaning, what difference does it make whether we call it true or false?

5. It is the function of the philosopher to aid in the construction of a new science of human values.

Finally, in summary, he stressed that the philosopher "should organize and integrate the specialized results of the various sciences," and in the process he should take great care "to delineate fundamental concepts which, if left vague, inevitably cause unnecessary wrangling and dissension between the special sciences and philosophy." (1953, pp. 9-10).

Naturalism has been called the oldest philosophy in the Western world. It has been said further that it is the most elusive. Naive naturalism can be described quite accurately, but it tends to become either more pragmatic or realistic as it moves from questions about reality into theory about the acquisition of knowledge. For this reason many have felt that its place had been usurped in the twentieth century by these two major philosophical positions or tendencies. And yet it represents an attitude that we cannot escape even today, just as the philosophy of idealism is ever present to influence our thoughts and actions.

Nature is reliable and dependable according to naturalistic metaphysics. From an early belief that nature was composed of one substance, naturalistic philosophers later accepted the idea that energy was the "substance" out of which the universe was constructed. Now nature is viewed as a process exhibiting continuity. The epistemology of naturalism, starting with the idea that objects presented images of themselves in the mind, advanced to a greatly improved understanding of sensory knowledge. The observation of specifics in nature (induction) was suggested as complementary to the earlier idea of deduction. Still later, scientific investigation was recognized as the only true means of gaining knowledge about the world. The logic of naturalism relies heavily on induction - the "method of science." Generalizations about nature become self-evident when facts are amassed carefully and painstakingly. The axiology of naturalism is based on the many values inherent in Nature itself. Ethically, naturalism is hedonistic - the achievement of the highest type of abiding pleasure for all is basic. Experiences that are purely natural bring aesthetic pleasure. Religious value is identical with over-all value realization; life now is what is significant. Social goals are secondary values; the relationship of the individual to the physical universe is paramount. A social system is accepted since it is better than anarchy. (Zeigler, 1964, pp. 45-46, 52-53).

Moving ahead to a consideration of Deweyan pragmatism, which was subsequently designated by Dewey himself and others as "experimentalism," it should be kept in mind that other terms such as instrumentalism, pragmatic naturalism, and progressivism have been employed almost interchangeably by many educational philosophers (at least). General speaking, pragmatism proceeds on the assumption that it is possible to find out if something is worthwhile only after it has been tested in experience. Of course, this approach is not new to mankind, but Peirce, James, Dewey, Mead et al. were the first to organize this type of (or approach to) thinking to a philosophical position or tendency that has been accepted by many in both scientific and educational circles. It has been argued that epistemology looms so large in the consideration of pragmatism that this aspect of the total position - the study of how man acquires knowledge - should be considered first in any presentation. This approach will be followed here in keeping with an early statement by James that knowledge is the result of a process of thought with a useful purpose. According to pragmatism knowledge is wrought in the action of experience.

Epistemology. An adequate definition of knowledge has tried
the ingenuity and insight of scholars for many centuries. If knowledge
is fact, and fact is truth, then truth is knowledge. Knowledge has
been described as a "knowing about something," an "awareness," a
"comprehension," or an "understanding." Here it becomes a subjective matter, and it has to do with the "inner workings" of the mind.
Still others believe in a type of knowledge called objective - knowledge
existing in a world outside of the individual that is there to be known
(possibly) by man's intellect.

Modern scientific development, after Darwin's evolutionary
theory, opened the way for a new theory of knowledge - the pragmatic
or experimentalistic idea of knowledge and truth. Truth was to be
tested by its correspondence with reality and also by its practical
results. This pragmatic treatment of knowledge lies between the extremes of reason and sense perception with some ideas that are not
included in either rationalism or empiricism. This approach, interestingly enough, has quite a bit in common with a great deal of contemporary philosophy, because it revolves about those conditions
under which a statement does have meaning, and what specific meanings it has in the light of such conditions. Thus, if a proposition
truly has meaning, it must make a difference in people's lives. This
relates, of course, to the verifiability theory of meaning promulgated
by the logical positivists (and related so effectively to sport and physical education recently by Patrick). (1971).

The meaning develops, therefore, because such knowledge has
been earned through the experience of people for whom such knowledge serves repeatedly in their lives as an "instrument for verification." Viewed in this manner we can appreciate what James called
the "cash value" of an idea - the import that it has for the fulfillment
of human purpose. Knowledge is knowledge only if it works to help
man in the battle for survival.

Such an approach "naturalizes" mind and implies that intelligence is a "relatively later-comer" on earth. Such a function of mind
gives man a more flexible means of adapting himself to life. If his
mind were not functioning, man would lose control of his earth. Mind
serves to form knowledge or truth by undergoing experience. It must
be adaptable because of the possibility of novelty and the consequent
precariousness of man's relation with the world.

Pragmatism is based on a behavioral psychology which is now
conceived in a considerably different way than heretofore. This is
not the position which dispensed with consciousness on the assumption
that the mind and the central nervous system were identical. If the
mind is simply another bodily organ, man could simply stop thinking
and "do what comes naturally" according to impulse! That kind of

behaviorism simply did not take into account that meaning (and, therefore, mind) must have a social context in which to develop; it is a social phenomenon, and it "expands" when meaningful interaction occurs between organisms because of their identification with each other. Mind "is an abstraction derived from the concreta of intelligent behavior." (Kaplan, 1961, p. 26).

Mind, through evolution, has become part of the whole of man which enables him to cope with the surrounding world and all the creatures living in it (hopefully). Through experience, man's many problems have been, are, and will be solved as he encounters new ones in the future. An intelligent mind makes this possible. This theory of knowledge leads to Dewey's experimental method for the solving of problems, which is characterized by the following steps:

1. Life is characterized by movement, the smoothness of whose flow may be interrupted by an obstacle.

2. This obstacle creates a problem; the resultant tension must be resolved to allow further movement ot take place.

3. Man marshals all available and pertinent facts to help with the solution of the problem.

4. Data gathered falls into one or more patterns; subsequent analysis offers a working hypothesis.

5. This hypothesis must be tested to see if the problem may be solved through the application of the particular hypothesis. When the problem is solved, movement may begin again. A hypothesis which turns out to be true offers a frame of reference for organizing facts; subsequently, this results in a central meaning that may be called knowledge.

    Note: The experimentalistic (pragmatic) theory of knowledge acquisition merges with its value theory at this point, inasmuch as such knowledge acquired frees man to initiate subsequent action furthering the process of movement and change indefinitely into the "future." (reworked from Zeigler, 1964, pp. 72-74).

Logic. There is rather general agreement that logic is primarily concerned with the methods of reasoning that man employs in his search to find answers to the problems that confront him daily. As the reader might expect, pragmatism departs radically from traditional logic because ideas are viewed typically as instruments to be used for the solutions of problems. This is why the term "instrumentalism" was coined to explain an approach designed to meet the challenge of a universe which seemed to be boundless - and perhaps even expanding! Dewey calls this revised system "a unified theory of inquiry through which the authentic pattern of experimental and operational inquiry in science shall become available for regulation of the habitual methods by which inquiries in the field of common sense are carried on." (Dewey, 1938).

Such a pattern of logic bears a strong resemblance or relationship to the learning theory (experimental method for solving of problems) described above under epistemology. Again we see terms and phrases such as "indeterminate situation," "institution of a problem," "determination of a problem-solution," "reasoning," and "operational character of facts-meanings." Such a pattern of logic, of course, appears to bridge the gap between traditional logic and modern scientific inquiry, while at one and the same time providing an approach to reasoning that can be employed by any man with daily problem-situations. (Butler, 1957, p. 464). That such an approach is innovative hardly needs restatement. The typical patterns of thought peculiar to induction and deduction cannot be applied arbitrarily because of the uniqueness of each problem-situation. Secondly, there is a very close relationship between this pattern of logic and life on earth as we know it - "man and Nature are continuous." Thirdly, such a pattern of logic seems to fit man's sociological development as well as his biological progress. Lastly, it is important and interesting to note that pragmatic logic has application for individual as well as group and societal problems. (Ibid., pp. 264-266).

Axiology. The system of values of the philosophy of pragmatism is consistent with the other departments of this philosophical tendency and stems directly from the pattern of logic described above. A value is a fact which, when applied to life, becomes useful. An experience is adjudged as valuable by the human organism which is attempting to adapt itself to the environment in the best and most profitable manner. The comparison of values to determine the best ones is a problem of deciding which value or values will help achieve life's purposes in the best way ("the good life" that a man consciously or unconsciously chooses for himself). We should not forget, however, that these goals or human values may be (and, in many instances, will be) only temporary ones.

What are the main values? For the pragmatist, that depends on when, where, and how the individual is living. The pragmatist believes that "values must be closely related to the world in which man finds himself." (Geiger, 1955, p. 142). Man must choose which means and ends he will accept and which he will reject. His progress depends upon critical examination of values prior to intelligent selection. Our society has traditionally made the mistake of contrasting facts and values; the contrast that should be made is between old values and new ones! "The radical dualism which besets our culture is the institutionalization of a faulty philosophy. When we try to defend values by declaring them out of bounds to inquirers into fact, we succeed only in dehumanizing science and technology and in deranging politics, religion, morality, and art." (Kaplan, 1961, pp. 36-37). The pragmatist believes that man is perhaps dangerously unrealistic and romantic when he doesn't appreciate the instrumental quality of values lying on a "means-end continuum."

Ethically, the pragmatist (experimentalist) finds himself facing continually new situations in which he must exercise wise judgment in keeping with the apparent elements of the indeterminate situation. It is argued that pragmatism offers the possibility of avoiding a typically troublesome ethical problem - how to resolve a situation where one's motives are presumably pure, and yet his actions violate currently acceptable standards. When the pragmatic steps of logic are employed, it is possible to blend inner motives and outer behavior in planned, purposeful action to meet each new situation in a fresh, unbiased manner.

Aesthetically, men are concerned with experiences which convey beauty and meaning of an enduring nature to man. For the pragmatist, aesthetic appreciation is closely related to the nature of the experience. In life man fluctuates between tension and pleasure depending on whether indeterminate situations are resolved to our satisfaction. When the answers to problems are found, tensions are eased and enjoyment results. There is no state of aesthetic pleasure that may be designated as permanent for man, however, since life's rhythm of experience does not function ao as to make this possible. Thus, aesthetic satisfaction comes when close identification is maintained with the ebb and flow of life's indeterminate situations. We are all anxious to preserve a state of enjoyment and release; yet, if it is held too long and life's rhythm is disturbed, troublesome difficulties arise. The psychological problems arising from life in a dream world are only too well known. Fortunately, various types of artists help us to "freeze" many of these aesthetic values for possible subsequent enjoyment. The man who would achieve the greatest amount of aesthetic enjoyment for himself must possess and continue to develop those habits which promote keen insight. It should be mentioned that Dewey assigned a lesser role to values which are the opposite of beauty. Tragedy and horror, for example, may be preserved as art forms, so that man will be able to look back at these past experiences, still "feel" the experience but with some perspective, and perhaps accept it as a form of beauty despite its earlier impact.

Religiously, the pragmatist assumes a completely naturalistic approach. For him religion would not involve any worship of the supernatural, and hence would be considered unorthodox by many. The religious pragmatist would be a person who is most anxious to reach pragmatic values whenever and wherever possible by living purposefully. Man's task is to thrust himself into life's many experiences; only there will he find the opportunity to give his life true meaning.

Socially, the pragmatist (experimentalist) places great emphasis on this aspect of life. Social values are fundamental, since life (or society) is "an organic process upon which individuals depend and by which they live." (Butler, p. 475). Any person who would withdraw from relationships with his fellowman in order to devote himself to the realization of so-called other values in his life makes a drastic error. Recluses injure society by withdrawing from their responsibility to it, and it is quite possible that they do themselves still greater harm. Such social values as loyalty, cooperation, kindness, and generosity can hardly be achieved in a vacuum. The pragmatist envisions the relationship between the individual and the society as be being of the highest type, and this applies especially to life in a democracy. Pragmatic values are most in evidence when the individual has the opportunity to develop to the highest of his potentialities, so long as such development does not interfere with the good of the whole. It is impossible to develop social values in the same way in societies that are undemocratic, although to a degree such value realization may occur.

Metaphysics. The reader will understand now why it seemed legitimate to the writer to remove metaphysics from its usual position at "the head of the list." Followed through to its logical conclusion, the epistemological theory of pragmatism makes it clear that it is beyond man's power to speculate accurately about the infinite or to do anything about the fundamental course of the physical universe. Man's problem is to interpret what he finds. He looks at nature, and he asks questions about its interpretation. Is nature an inexorable process which is advancing according to a universal plan? Is the onward surge of nature a kind of emergent evolution? The pragmatists takes what he finds and functions from that point. He doesn't know whether nature is functioning inexorably. He tends to believe that nature is an emergent evolution, but he can't answer the question – emerging toward what? So this philosophy limits man's frame of reality to nature as it functions; any assumptions made are only hypotheses to be held tentatively. The future is always to be considered, because situations are continually changing. The ongoing process cannot be dealt with finally at any one time.

Even these preceding statements are not entirely free from inferences about the nature of reality. The world is characterized by activity and change. All that is known about the human response to nature can be known without first definitely making a final statement about the universe (multiverse?) as a whole. Thus, experience or interaction with the environment is all that the experimentalist has by which to live his life. If his environment doesn't give him an accurate account of reality, then he would conclude that humans could well be the victims of a fantastic hoax.

The pragmatist believes further in organic evolution, and that rational man has developed in this process. The logical conclusion to draw from this assumption is that the world is yet incomplete. This doesn't mean, of course, that everything is in a state of change. Some elements and structures appear to be relatively stable, but this quality of seeming stability is often deceiving. The experimentalist finds that he must look upon the world as a mixture of things relatively stable and yet incomplete. This makes all life a great experiment. It is the task of education to make this experiment an intelligent one.

A theory of emergent novelty makes great sense to the pragmatist if the universe (reality) is constantly undergoing change. An excellent example of novelty is explained by Brubacher:

> This is true about the individuality of any particular boy or girl. It is inescapably unique since any given offspring of bisexual reproduction is the only one of its kind. Such a child commences and lives his life at a juncture of space and time which simply cannot be duplicated for anyone else. (1939, p. 35).

The concept of freedom of will is a very strong point in favor of the pragmatic position. He can argue that man's future must allow for true freedom of will. He does not conceive of free will as a motiveless choice. His contention is that all beings are in process of interaction with other "existences." He inquires about the quality of this interaction and how great a role the individual can play in this process. Man should determine the character of this process from within (meaning through intense and intensive social intercourse in life experiences). Freedom developed in this manner is achieved through continuous and developmental learning from experience. As Childs states,

> In a changing world the only person who can become free and who can maintain his freedom is the one who has 'learned to learn.' A democratic society can hope to succeed only if it is composed of individuals who have developed the responsibility for intelligent self-direction in co-operation with others. (Childs, 1931, p. 168).

Implications from Pragmatism for Education

The possible implications from pragmatism (experimentalism) for education have been spelled out in such great detail by so many different people, educational philosophers included, that it hardly seems necessary to repeat this pattern ad nauseam for the reader at this point. Further, as the analysis movement in philosophy gathered strength on this continent, it began in the 1950's to influence educational philosophy to a great extent as well. Thus, it was only a matter of time before those interested in sport and physical education would "get the message and catch up." Well, this has indeed happened, and now the profession of physical education and sport is now beginning to reap the benefits of this "new wisdom" that is being made available to it. Fortunately or unfortunately, even though such effort was undoubtedly most worthwhile, the analytical "excursion" of educational philosophy in the fifties and sixties has certainly not influenced the conduct of education very much, and it can be argued also that the "structural analysis technique" and normative educational philosophizing may not have had the desired effect either. It seems quite safe to make exactly the same statement about the recent history of sport and physical educational philosophy as well.

The battlelines were quite clearly delineated in the presentations by Sterling McMurrin and B. Othaniel Smith at a symposium entitled "Philosophy of Education" held at the 59th Annual Meeting of the American Philosophical Association in December, 1962. Mr. McMurrin stated that "the chief deterrent to the advancement of the philosophy of education as a respectable discipline, beyond its identification with such a considerable number of persons lacking in adequate philosophic competence, is the obstinate assumption that from different metaphysical premises differing educational systems and methods can and should be logically derived." (1962). Mr. Smith in reply pointed out that McMurrin used the term "philosophy of education" in three of four different possible ways, and that such usage made it difficult to respond. Granting that "the path from the metaphysics of the system to the classroom is long and tenuous, and anyone who tries to travel it is apt to lose his way," Smith's response was that,

> any philosophical system will include a picture of man and society. Insofar as it deals with man's nature, his development, and his destiny, the system will necessarily have implications for the education of man . . . (1962, p. 639).

Then he went on to argue that McMurrin's latter two questions went to the heart of the matter: (1) should prospective teachers study the philosophy of education, and (2) if not, what philosophical pursuits are relevant to their preparation as teachers?

Obviously, this present paper cannot address these questions seriously, but it is important to note that Soltis has recently most strongly challenged "the efficacy of the analytic approach for both theorists and practicing educators alike who would realistically face problems concerning the proper description and adequate understanding of the learning process and the unescapable normative questions to be found in thinking deeply about education today." (1971, p. 29). A reply to Soltis by McClellan is most straightforward, even if arrogant, but it will serve to bring the present paper back to its purported progression. McClelland asserts that Soltis's historical analysis "ignores the overwhelming influence of John Dewey and his very talented collaborators and colleagues." Young educational philosophers were "impelled" to "abandon the Deweyan synthesis and start in pursuit of new ways of doing philosophy of education." Now there is a new generation upon us, so to speak, and educational philosophers may indeed not be ready to serve them either emotionally or intellectually. That the same may be said for sport and physical education philosophers ought to be apparent from the results of the last two symposia, and it is to be hoped that this present meeting will get them back on target. It is important to seek guidance from colleagues in related disciplines in an effort to gain strength, but it is even more important to avoid their mistakes in direction.

Thus, the position to be taken in the remainder of this paper regarding research methodology and technique is that of the Deweyan synthesis – the problems of ethics are problems of "developing the habits and skills to act intelligently." It is not being argued that educational philosophical systems – or sport and physical educational philosophical "systems" – should or can be slavishly and completely logically deduced from metaphysical positions. It is being argued that certain philosophical systems still extant do include "a picture of man and society," and that such systems "will necessarily have implications for the education of man." (Smith, 1962). The important point here, however, is that pragmatism (experimentalism) does not deduce educational aims from a metaphysical position; the tentative metaphysical outlook is a result of the application of the experimental method to the search for educational values. It is on this basis that some of the educational implications of pragmatism (experimentalism) are presented briefly prior to the offering of implications for sport and physical education.

Society, School and the Individual. There is no doubt but that pragmatism (experimentalism) has exercised influence on education on this continent, not to mention lesser influence elsewhere. An investigation would indicate, however, that it has not had nearly as much influence as its opponents would have educators and the public think it has. The reader is reminded that Parsons claims that the United States has had a remarkably stable value system over the years. (Cf. p. 87). The experimentalist views education as a social institution and, as a social phenomenon, education is presumably one of the basic means by which society progresses and regenerates itself. Further, according to this position, education is a moral affair - a value enterprise. To carry out its role best, there is no escaping the fact that the school, of necessity, must maintain an extremely close connection with society. (Zeigler, 1964, p. 78). Today there are many people who claim that such a "connection has all but severed!"

A belief in democracy (whatever that means!) as a way of life seems practical because of the opportunity for the free growth of the individual, as well as for the sharing of the cultural and social heritage. Furthermore, a democracy tends to have an economic system which allows children and young people to enjoy some form of so-called higher education.

In experimentalism, the school has a creative function - to guide the student as he develops understand of and ability to cope with the new and changing factors of his environment. Whether today's schools and universities are meeting this goal can be most vigorously debated; it is most difficult to preserve that which is useful from the social heritage, while at one and the same time to provide competencies, skills, and knowledge that will prepare youth for the uncertain future in the "new world" of tomorrow. The home and the school should play the leading roles in the education of most children, and the place of the private school in a democracy of an ideal nature is doubtful. Comparative religious education belongs in the public schools, and it deserves a place of importance. The church as a social institution appears to leave much to be desired at present, but religious freedom should be preserved so long as separation of church and state can be successfully maintained.

Process of Education. The individual not the subject-matter is placed at the center of the educational experience. Pupil growth through actual problem-solving in life experiences is the typical pattern employed to bring about learning. The unity of the human organism must be recognized, and mind is viewed as a function rather than as a structure. The "mind" reaches out to make its own knowledge from experience. Learning takes place when interest and effort combine to produce the desired result. The temporal order of the experimentalistic curriculum may follow both a logical arrangement (from the simple fact to the complex conclusion) and a psychological order (problem-solving as explained through scientific method). The latter approach is to be preferred, since it enables thinking to become actual problem-solving in a life experience. The pragmatic experimentalist has unusual difficulty in evaluating, because his aims and objectives are likely to change somewhat as experience indicates the need for such change. It can be determined partially when learning has taken place through the use of educational measurement. In the final analysis, the individual's ability to adjust to a changing environment is the best method of knowing whether learning has been effected. (Zeigler, p. 78 et ff.).

Educational Aims and Objectives. Aims and objectives (tentatively held) are the result of a meaningful educative process. Experimentalism suggests that "education in the broadest sense can be nothing less than the changes made in human beings by their experience." (Geiger, p. 144). For Dewey social efficiency - the competency, skill, and knowledge to adapt to a changing environment - was the general aim of education (1938, p. 90). If these instrumental educational goals are realized, the child will be prepared for present-day life, and future aims can and should grow out of continuing experience. The curriculum which develops from such an instrumentally-oriented, problem-solving approach to education cannot be gleaned from the traditional subject-matter approach of today. It should state which competencies, skills, and knowledge are needed to live life today (and looking toward the future). Dewey would agree with Alvin Toffler that "future shock" has already set in and that man is poorly prepared to counteract its effects.

The Pragmatic Ethic in Sport and Physical Education

Any analysis of the pragmatic ethic in sport and physical education must take cognizance to the longstanding fact vs. value dualism. Dewey's cognitive theory of value is one in which value judgments are determined experimentally in the light of experience. When an ethical problem, or moral dilemma, arises it is always within a social context. Wisdom accumulated from past experience is employed as an "intellectual instrumentality" or tool to aid in the verification of a moral hypothesis advanced to help in the solution of today's problem. In the process new definitions of ethical terms emerge as judgments are made in response to problematic situations that occur in unique social situations. Thus, problematic situations involving ethical theory in sport and physical education are resolved in this same fashion.

(It should be stated parenthetically at this juncture that the writer has been typically employing the term "physical education and sport" to describe the field as it exists today in educational institutions. He recognizes further that some wish to retain the term "physical education," while others are using "sport" or "sport sciences." Many will recall that much earlier Staley recommended the use of "sports education." At any rate, the writer recognizes the need for a new name for the profession, and also for the disciplinary aspect of the field. The art and science of human movement as applied to the theory and practice of sport, dance, play, and exercise seems to be a helpful definition presently. Furthermore, because of a tri-partite professional development within health, physical education, and recreation, health and recreational considerations per se will not be discussed here, even though the writer's pragmatic leanings over a thirty-year period caused him to use the term "physical, health, and recreation education" in earlier writings. Lastly, acknowledgment must be made to the careful and insightful analysis of Deweyan progressivism made recently by Francis Keenan, a study in which the writer shared slightly and which served to renew his conviction that experimental method applied to value theory in sport and physical education was being grossly neglected.)

Knowledge Acquisition in Sport and "Physical Education". The process of sport and physical education will be considered first because of the fundamental nature of this approach. It is vitally important that aims and methods go hand in hand. As Larkin stated decades ago, "Trading the drillmaster of calisthenics for the domineering coach of football does not appear to be enough." (p. 67). The salient qualities of the experimentalistic teacher of sport and physical education were further listed as follows:

> In restating the desirable methods in a physical education program the pattern appeared to be this: a broad social outlook, great consideration for the learner, well prepared teachers, and a minimum of inherited technique as such." (pp. 37-38).

The experimentalistic teacher and coach should aid the student and/or player in the development of skill for problem-solving. This skill is more than a conditioned reflex; the learner needs to develop insight into the nature of the anticipated outcome whether it be in the movement experience of sport, dance, play, or exercise. Keenan expresses it well as follows: "Man should not only learn to move, and learn about movement, he should also learn about himself and his culture through the medium of movement experience." (1971, p. 136). This implies that attitude development is most important along with the learning of competencies, skills, and knowledge.

Such an approach means that there will be a new conception of the curriculum (or of the "curricular or co-curricular" experience in sport). "As teachers we must make ourselves progressively unnecessary," says Kilpatrick, because "we face thus a new conception of the curriculum as consisting properly of such a succession of school experiences as will best bring and constitute the continuous reconstruction of experience." (1926, p. 123). It is important to start at the student's level and to give him "as much freedom as he can use wisely. And again the test is the learning that results." (p. 129). A coach who subscribed to this position could employ this line of reasoning quite nicely.

An experimentalistic educator has a responsibility to order the learning experience so that it is interesting and significant to the learner/performer. The idea here is that teachers and coaches will find a greatly different attitude if they involve the individual as "an agent or participant" rather than as a spectator. It could be argued that the coach has an advantage over the teacher in this regard because in competitive sport there is the possibility of quite complete psycho-physical integration for the player. This is true, but it fails to take into consideration the way that the coach involves the player in the total plan and operation. A quarterback who very rarely calls a play for his team seems to be expected to function as a "conditioned reflex." And then there are all those players on the squad who may never get in the game, or who play only a few moments, or who stand around even during practices and may indeed serve as "dummies" or members of the taxi squad.

The teacher/coach as the agent of the school or university should create an environment in which "play and work shall be conducted with reference to facilitating desirable mental and moral growth." Obviously, the mere introduction of games and sporting contests is not sufficient. "Everything depends on the way in which they are employed." (Dewey, 1916, p. 230). There must be an environment offering great opportunity for interaction between the individual and his "natural and social" surroundings. For Dewey it is the interaction that is vital, because it "will effect acquisition of those meanings which are so important that they become, in turn, instruments of further learnings." (p. 320).

Standardization of the curriculum or coaching plan from year to year is something that the pragmatic experimentalist is most anxious to avoid. There should be opportunities for changes in plan and program involving student choice. Morland, for example, explained that an experimentalistic curriculum should be flexible and not systematically arranged. The avoidance of direct prescription of - say - a syllabus in a course was recommended so that the student would have the chance to use and thereby develop his own judgment. How often is such an approach adopted in the coaching of an individual, dual, or team sport?

Too often today the teaching and coaching methods employed in overly commercialized varsity sports have brought criticism of a most sharp and intense nature against the entire athletics establishment. As Keenan forthrightly states,

> . . . the evils of athletics often receive more attention than the values. Athletics in some instances have been 'a cancer in the side of physical education.' This refers to the growing immorality which has its base in the individualism of coaches and athletes, and the effort to win at any

cost. Under such conditions, valid educational values have no chance for survival. There are those who think that the 'metastasis of this sort of educational disease' is too widespread; the cancer is incurable! This view must be avoided since it is this pessimism that allows perpetuation of immoral systems. Educators should speak out for removal of 'cancerous athletic growths' while physical education is still alive. If the malpractices cannot be discontinued, then athletics ought to go its own way as separate from physical education aimed at desirable educational practices. There is an optimum level of athletic activity which can serve educational priorities. Uninhibited quests for victory leave little time for reflection and evaluation of athletics in terms of educational objectives. (1971, pp. 139-140).

The recommendation is, therefore, that the best possible learning occurs when the student/player aids in the origination and planning of his own educational experience, when he has a fair share in the execution of the entrrprise, and when he has the opportunity to evaluate the success or failure of the whole venture. Measurement of individual growth by grades, term marks, testing, and other evaluative devices deserves most careful consideration. Is it more important to evaluate individual pupil growth than it is to measure whether an overweight, sensitive student comes up to a national norm in pull-ups for his age or grade? How does such objective testing take into account that there may be as much as a four-year difference in the physiological maturity of two students at the same age? Furthermore, there is evidence to support the position that certain students "go to pieces" in situations where the psycho-social factors are such that the performer feels unusual stress. It would seem much more sensible to consider the individual's body type, his continuing health record, and his past performances before testing him to determine whether individual pupil growth has taken place. Competitors in athletics learn to live with stress or they are confined to the bench. One wonders how much consideration is given to the question of whether young people can gradually learn to have so-called stress immunity.

There is an element of uncertainty with a considerable measure of contingency when an experimental problem-solving approach is employed in the teaching of a class. Dewey placed great emphasis on the idea of education as "life experience." Presented with a problem, the student, guided by the teacher, searches for ways and means to solve it. A desirable third stage is when the student - not the teacher! - comes up with a proposed solution which he proceeds to test by putting it into practice (a fourth stage). If the plan of action works, or it appears that it might work after a reasonable amount of practice, then learning is the result of the experience. This particular learning experience should enter upon a fifth stage when it is correlated with previous experiences to give broader meaning and perspective to the entire educational process. (Brubacher, 1950, pp. 255-256). During this process any disciplinary measures, if absolutely necessary, should arise from the actions of the class itself. The teacher's role is to be ready to help out in management; he should be "a responsible leader as well as a thoughtful follower upon occasion." (Williams, 1959, p. 273).

Lastly under this heading is the recognition that there may be a variety of learnings in a class or coaching experience. There is the technical learning of how to bring a man to the mat in wrestling, but there is also the associated learning that the wrestler will have to follow - a rigorous training routine and possible dieting in order to be fit and make his ideal weight. In addition, there are other important concomitant learnings that accompany the sport (e.g., no punishing holds are allowed, and a young man should "give the best" that is in him).

Sport and Physical Education Aims and Objectives. Very brief-ly, then, as this paper draws to a close, what meaning do people ob-tain as they understand what the learning process of experimentalism is supposed to do (i.e., how it works to fulfill its purpose)? The most fundamental goal for philosophy ought to help man "assimilate the impact of science on human affairs." Is man to be the "master of the machine?" As Kaplan states,

> The business of philosophy today is to provide a system of ideas that will make an integrated whole of our beliefs about the nature of the world and the values which we seek in the world in fulfillment of our human nature. (1961, p. 16).

Applied to sport and physical education, the experimentalist affirms the priority of man over athletics and physical activity. He is much more interested in promoting the concept of total fitness rather than physical fitness alone. Sport and physical education can provide excellent problem-solving experiences to children and young people. Students should have the opportunity to select a wide variety of useful activities, many of which should help to develop social intelligence. The activities offered should bring natural impulses in-to play. Physical education classes and intramural sports are more important to the large majority of students than interscholastic or intercollegiate athletics and deserve priority if conflict arises over budgetary allotment, staff available for guidance and instruction, and use of facilities. The experimentalist can, however, give full support to team (as well as to individual and dual) experiences in competitive sports, because they can be vital educational experiences if properly conducted.

Man should be a strong, healthy animal - a standard which can apply to girls as well as to boys in today's world. Health should be a primary objective of education; a child needs health instruction. Although the basic responsibility for health education and recreation education ideally should not rest with the physical educator - coach, he can give full support to a unified approach whereby the three specialized areas of health, physical education, and recreation would provide a variety of experiences that will enable the individual to live a richer, fuller, life through superior adjustment to his social environment.

The school program of health, phsyical, and recreation education may be administered as a unified program even though three separate professions are now emerging in society. The success of the school health-education program depends on the degree of cooperation among home, school, and community, and much the same can be said about the cooperation necessary for a successful physical education and sport program or a recreation education program. All these aspects of the total program may be coordinated because they are related in so many ways.

Education for the worthy use of leisure is basic to the curriculum of the school - a curriculum in which pupil growth, as defined broadly is all important. Play should be conducted in such a way that desirable moral growth will be fostered. Overly organized sport competition is not true recreation education, since the welfare of the individualsis often submerged to other more materialistic goals. It is a mistake to confuse the psychological distinction between work and play with the traditional economic distinction that is typically recognized. All citizens should have ample opportunity to use their free time in a creative and fruitful manner. A person who watches others with a high degree of skill perform should not be condemned for this recreational pursuit. The important point is that the individual keeps such viewing in a balanced role in his life pattern. (Zeigler, 1964, pp. 107-108; a more detailed discussion of this topic extends from pp. 88-89).

The Strengths and Weakness of Pragmatism (Experimentalism)

Generally speaking, experimentalism is strong because it encourages man to meet each daily experience fully - one step at a time. In an age when scientific discoveries are legion, emphasis on experimental method can accomplish much good more rapidly in the world. If it is indeed a changing world, experimentalism would appear to be a highly practical approach to life.

In education, experimentalism breaks down the distinction between life in the school and life outside the school by keeping teacher and student close to experience and by making every effort to eliminate much of what might be called "academic artificiality." The aim, as had been heard so often, is to place the student at the center of the educational process, not the teacher or the subject-matter. Freedom for the pupil - at least as much as can be used widely - is certainly appealing to the individual; yet in experimentalism there is undoubtedly great concern for society and the social implications of the educational process. If initiative and self-reliance are desirable educational goals, pupil freedom might well bring about these qualities more quickly and much more fully. This approach should have great appeal to a people presumably devoted to the concept of an evolving political democracy. Stress on interest as the basis for motivation of instruction should bring greater involvement on the part of the student and should, therefore, be a strength. Furthermore, as we move toward Asimov's concept of a "global village," a philosophy such as experimentalism is desirable because it promotes easy interchange of diverse cultural viewpoint; this is vital as man seeks to promote better understanding among various races and creeds at home and throughout the world.

The experimentalistic position offers a great deal of strength to the profession of physical education and sport. Physical education viewed in this context can become an integral subject in the curriculum if it realizes its educational potentialities. Secondly, despite present efforts toward separate professionalization by health education and recreation, experimentalism at least encourages these fields to remain allied and closely affiliated within education so that the needs and interests of the student may be met. Thirdly, a teaching method based on an effective combination of interest and effort affords strength for the educational task in today's schools.

From a general standpoint, many have argued that experimentalism is weak because it doesn't provide the stability that many people seem to need. Critics say that it is a house built on sand. The thought of no fixed aims in advance can be very disturbing to men who are fearful for the future. How does experimentalism speak to the decade of the 1960's during which time so many problems arose that experimental method does not seem equipped to solve? Many argue that progressivism in education has served its purpose and run its course. Such an approach may be helpful with certain types of youngsters, but we don't have enough good teachers equipped to use this approach. In addition, teachers are typically swamped with large numbers of students, and this approach can only work with small, select groups.

Other critics assert that the application of the experimental method in physical education classes would mean chaos and lowered physical fitness. Coaches, who tend to hold an essentialistic orientation in educational philosophy, would have to learn to be "good losers" if they adopted such an approach with their squads. Youth needs to be guided by "a strong hand"; experimental teaching is "soft," and indeed may be at least partially responsible for the general weakening of moral fibre of youth today. These ideas, critics say, arose from observation of experimentalism in action.

What Reasonable Conclusions May Be Drawn?

Drawing "reasonable" conclusions from a presentation such as this is probably the most difficult and risky phase of the entire project. One hesitates to be too bold; on the other hand, these appear to be unusual times. Certainly a type of world transformation is taking place as the tempo of civilization increases almost exponentially. People are frightened as they look to the future. Societies have become increasing complex, and sociologists until most recently were in great demand so that they might serve as "psychoanalysts" of society. The "dialogue of freedom," we are told, may go on indefinitely, but the "solutions to our problems are not primarily ideological but structural . . . They constitute a new political direction in the world, not left or right, but human and forward." (Platt, pp. 21-22). We are exhorted further to prepare for the continuing and advancing technological thrust, and that "the only indispensable human component is the mind component for design, redesign, complex evaluation, and control." (p. 26). If these predictions be even approximately true, then as Platt states,

> Yet millions of the older generation, alternately disgusted and terrified by these developments, will have to learn new values and a new language . . . (Ibid.).

In the same vein Callahan writes about searching for an ethic in a new culture that is on its way here, but that still does not yet exist. (1972, p. 4 et ff.). It will need to be "one in which human beings can live (and die) securely, harmoniously, and humanely in the presence of constant advances in the medical and biological sciences." (Ibid.).

The general conclusion of the writer is that pragmatism (experimentalism) offers the best and most humane approach to the problem of new values - and possibly a new culture - that is quite evidently being thrust upon us. Pragmatism has always been a philosophy of social protest from the moment of its conception; "a pragmatist is always dissatisfied, always striving for betterment." (Kaplan, p. 41). By its very nature and approach it is receptive to innovation and change. Its method relies upon the application of human intelligence to problems that arise in social planning for the future. It offers man not a philosophy of life, but a philosophy for the living of life today and tomorrow.

The reader is undoubtedly familiar with the general and specific conclusions that have been drawn on behalf of pragmatic philosophy applied to the educative process. Thus, only a few brief conclusions will be drawn. Basically, the writer concludes that social conditions are presently such that the school and society must maintain a very close connection. The pragmatic philosophy of education is founded upon this premise! Creative answers to life's problem now and in the future will most certainly be needed, and it is this experimentalistic position which is based on an educative process that provides pupil growth through actual problem solving in life experiences. If "future shock" has already set in, the provision of competency, skill, and knowledge is necessary to adapt to a continually changing environment.

Most important for this study are possible implications from pragmatic educational philosophy for sport and physical education. Early in this paper certain exemplar problems in sport, dance, play, and exercise were cited. In regard to the amateur-professional controversy, a pragmatist would most certainly search for alternatives based on a world situation that has changed sharply in the past one hundred years. The amateur ideal of Olympic competition has failed miserably; it is simply not adequate today. A pragmatic answer to the problem of dance in North American society would be to encourage its introduction into an articulated curriculum in such a way that the movement experience would relate to the child's growth and development pattern. It brings natural impulses into play and thereby can contribute to man's total fitness for life. Aesthetic experiences convey beauty and meaning to life's rhythm of experience - in the ebb and flow of its indeterminate situations.

The experimentalist has an answer to the traditional distinction between the concepts of work and play. Just because children and youth usually take part in play outside of school proper is no reason why educators should think that something completely different should take place when school is in session. The psychological distinction between work and play has been confused with the economic one. Thus, when the play instinct is introduced into school activities, the complete psycho-physical organism exhibits a type of integration not normally present in activities that have been typically designated as "work."

The question of exercise awaits some definitive answers as well. One great problem confronts many physical educators today who are armed with a seeming abundance of literature emphasizing the life-preserving qualities of regular exercise. The problem is how to motivate people to take part in this important aspect of the "life of an amphibian." The conclusion to be reached from pragmatic naturalism (experimentalism) is that the element of artificiality must be

reduced in proportion to the introduction of the play element and freedom of choice. People now appreciate that they should exercise, but
that is all too logical. The task is, therefore, to devise a psychological order of learning which will "lure the human animal into the
trap."

These are obviously only a very few of the conclusions that
might well be drawn. Many of the points made earlier (Cf. pp. 38-
47) could be reiterated, but the essence of these conclusions should
be clear by now. Sport and physical education must serve as "socially useful servants" to man in the world of today and tomorrow. Man
should use these activities for his own welfare, individually and collectively. The individual must not be "used" by anyone else. Sport
and physical education activities should provide excellent problem-
solving experiences for children, young people, and adults. Professional ethics and standards can be successfully developed with the
philosophical undergirding of the ethical naturalism of the pragmatist.

Selected References and Bibliography

Archambault, Reginald D. "The Philosophical Bases of the Experience Curriculum," Harvard Educational Review, Vol. 26,
No. 3:263-275 (Summer, 1956).

Bair, Donn E., "An Identification of Some Philosophical Beliefs Held
by Influential Professional Leaders in American Physical Education." Ph.D. dissertation, University of Southern California,
1956.

Barton, George E., Jr. "John Dewey: Too Soon a Period Piece,"
The School Review, Vol. 67, No. 2:128-138 (Summer, 1959).

Belth, Marc. Education as a Discipline. Boston: Allyn & Bacon,
Inc., 1965.

Berkson, I. B. Education Faces the Future. New York: Harper and
Row, Publishers, Inc., 1943.

_____. Preface to an Educational Philosophy. New York:
Columbia University Press, 1940.

Bode, Boyd H. Conflicting Psychologies of Learning. Boston:
D. C. Heath and Company, 1929.

_____. How We Learn. Boston: D. C. Heath and Co., 1940.

_____. Progressive Education at the Crossroads. New York:
Newson and Company, 1938.

Brameld, Theodore. Ends and Means in Education: A Mid-century Appraisal. New York: Harper and Row, Publishers, Inc., 1949.

_____, "Imperatives for a Reconstructed Philosophy of Education," School and Society, Vol. 87, Jan. 17, 1959, pp. 18-20.

_____. Patterns of Educational Philosophy: A Democratic Interpretation. New York: Harcourt, Brace and World, Inc., 1940.

_____. Philosophies of Education in Cultural Perspective. New York: The Dryden Press, Inc., 1955.

_____. Toward a Reconstructed Philosophy of Education. New York: The Dryden Press, Inc., 1959.

Brubacher, John S. (editor). Eclectic Philosophy of Education. 2nd edition. Englewood Cliffs, New Jersey: Prentice-Hall, Inc., 1962.

_____. Modern Philosophies of Education. 4th edition. New York: McGraw-Hill Book Company, 1969.

_____, et al. The Public School and Spiritual Values. New York: Harper and Row, Publishers, Inc., 1944.

Burke, Roger K., "Pragmatism in Physical Education," in Philosophies Fashion Physical Education. (E. C. Davis, editor). Dubuque, Iowa: Wm. C. Brown, 1963.

Burton, W. H. Introduction to Education. New York: Appleton-Century-Crofts, Inc., 1934.

Butler, J. D. Four Philosophies. Revised edition. New York: Harper and Row, Publishers, Inc., 1957.

Callahan, Daniel, "Search for an Ethic: Living with the New Biology," in The Center Magazine, Vol. V, No. 4:4-12 (July/August, 1972).

Cassidy, Rosalind. New Directions in Physical Education for the Adolescent Girl in High School and College. New York: A. S. Barnes and Co., 1938.

Childs, John L. American Pragmatism and Education. New York: Holt, Rinehart and Winston, Inc., 1956.

_____, "Boyd H. Bode and the Experimentalists," Teachers College Record, Vol. 55, No. 1:1-9 (October, 1953).

_____. Education and Morals: An Experimentalist Philosophy of Education. New York: Appleton-Century-Crofts, Inc., 1950.

_____. Education and the Philosophy of Experimentalism. New York: Appleton-Century-Crofts, Inc., 1931.

Clark, Margaret C., "A Program of Physical Education in a State Teachers College." Ph.D. dissertation, New York University, 1943.

Cobb, Louise Staples, "A Study of the Functions of Physical Education in Higher Education." Contributions to Education No. 876, Teachers College, Columbia University, 1944.

Cogley, John, "The Storm before the Calm," The Center Magazine, Vol. V, No. 4:2-3 (July/August, 1972).

Counts, George S. Education and the Promise of America. New York: The Macmillan Company, 1946.

Cowell, C. C. and France, W. L. Philosophy and Principles of Physical Education. Englewood Cliffs, New Jersey: Prentice-Hall, Inc., 1963.

Curti, Merle. The Social Ideas of American Education. New York: Chas. Scribner's Sons, 1935.

Davis, E. C. The Philosophical Process in Physical Education. Philadelphia: Lea and Febiger, 1961. (There is a second edition of this pioneering effort with Donna Mae Miller as co-author).

_____, (editor). Philosophies Fashion Physical Education. Dubuque, Iowa: Wm. C. Brown Co., Publishers, 1963.

Dewey, John. Art as Experience. New York: Minton, Balch and Company, 1934.

_____. A Common Faith. New Haven, Connecticut: Yale University Press, 1934.

_____. Democracy and Education. New York: The Macmillan Company, 1916.

_____. Education Today (Joseph Ratner, editor). New York: G. P. Putnam's Sons, 1940.

_____. Experience and Education. New York: The Macmillan Company, 1938.

_____. Experience and Nature. Chicago: The Open Court Publishing Company, 1925.

_____, "From Absolutism to Experimentalism," in Contemporary American Philosophy, Vol. II (G. P. Adams and W. P. Montague, editors). New York: The Macmillan Company, 1930, pp. 13-27).

_____. How We Think. (new edition). Boston: D. C. Heath and Company, 1933.

_____. Human Nature and Conduct. New York: Holt, Rinehart and Winston, Inc., 1922.

_____. Intelligence in the Modern World (Joseph Ratner, editor). New York: Modern Library, Inc., 1939.

_____. Logic, The Theory of Inquiry. New York: Holt, Rinehart and Winston, Inc., 1938.

_____. Problems of Men. New York: Philosophical Library, Inc., 1946.

_____. The Quest for Certainty. New York: Minton, Balch and Company, 1929.

_____. Reconstruction in Philosophy. London: University of London Press, Ltd., 1921.

_____, and Tufts, James H., (editors). Ethics. New York: Holt, Rinehart and Winston, Inc., 1908.

_____, et al. Creative Intelligence. New York: Holt, Rinehart and Winston, Inc., 1917.

Downey, Robert J., "An Identification of the Philosophical Beliefs of Educators in the Field of Health Education." Ph.D. dissertation, University of Southern California, 1956.

Edman, Irwin. John Dewey: His Contribution to the American Tradition. Indianapolis: Bobbs-Merrill Company, Inc., 1955.

Encyclopedia of Philosophy, The. (Paul Edwards, editor). New York: The Macmillan Company and The Free Press, 8 vols. 1967.

Esslinger, A. A., "A Philosophical Study of Principles for Selecting Activities in Physical Education." Ph.D. dissertation, State University of Iowa, 1938.

Feibleman, James. An Introduction to Peirce's Philosophy. New York: Harper and Row, Publishers, Inc., 1946.

Frederick, Mary Margaret, "Naturalism: The Philosophy of Jean-Jacques Rousseau and Its Implications for American Physical Education." D.P.E. dissertation, Springfield College, 1961.

Geiger, George R., "An Experimentalist Approach to Education," in Modern Philosophies and Education (N. B. Henry, editor). Chicago: University of Chicago Press, 1955.

Groos, Karl. The Play of Animals. New York: Appleton-Century-Crofts, Inc., 1898.

_____. The Play of Man. New York: Appleton-Century-Crofts, Inc., 1901.

Hansen, Kenneth H. Philosophy for American Education. Englewood Cliffs, New Jersey: Prentice-Hall, Inc., 1960.

Henry, N. B. Modern Philosophies and Education, Fifty-fourth Yearbook of the National Society for the Study of Education. Chicago: University of Chicago Press, 1955.

_____ (editor). Philosophy of Education, Forty-first Yearbook of the National Society for the Study of Education. Chicago: University of Chicago Press, 1942, Part I.

Hess, Ford A., "American Objectives of Physical Education from 1900-1957 Assessed in the Light of Certain Historical Events." Ph.D. dissertation, New York University, 1959.

Hetherington, Clark. School Programs in Physical Education. New York: Harcourt, Brace and World, Inc., 1922.

Hobbes, Thomas. The English Works of Thomas Hobbes (Sir William Molesworth, editor). London: John Bohn, 1889, Vols. I-X.

Hook, Sidney. Education for Modern Man. New York: The Dial Press, Inc., 1946.

_____. The Metaphysics of Pragmatism. Chicago: The Open Court Publishing Company, 1927.

Horne, Herman Harrell. The Democratic Philosophy of Education. New York: The Macmillan Company, 1932.

Huxley, Thomas Henry. Science and Education. New York: Appleton-Century-Crofts, Inc., 1896.

James, William. Essays in Radical Empiricism. New York: David McKay Co., Inc., 1912.

_____. The Philosophy of William James Drawn from His Own Works. New York: Modern Library, Inc., n.d.

_____. A Pluralistic Universe. New York: David McKay Co., Inc., 1909.

_____. Pragmatism. New York: David McKay Co., Inc., 1907.

_____. Talks to Teachers (new edition). New York: Holt, Rinehart and Winston, Inc., 1946.

_____. The Will to Believe. New York: David McKay Co., Inc., 1912.

Johnson, Glen. Some Ethical Implications of a Naturalistic Philosophy of Education. New York: Bureau of Publications, Teachers College, Columbia University, 1947.

Johnson, Harry M., "The Relevance of the Theory of Action to Historians," Social Science Quarterly, June, 1969, pp. 46-58.

Kaplan, Abraham. The New World of Philosophy. New York: Random House, 1961.

Keating, James, "The Function of the Philosopher in American Pragmatism." Ph.D. dissertation abstract published by The Catholic University of America Press, Washington, D. C., 1953.

Keenan, Francis W., "A Delineation of Deweyan Progressivism for Physical Education." Ph.D. dissertation, University of Illinois, Urbana, 1971.

Kilpatrick, William H. The Educational Frontier. New York: Appleton-Century-Crofts, Inc., 1933.

_____. *Education for a Changing Civilization*. New York: Appleton-Century-Crofts, Inc., 1926.

_____. *Philosophy of Education*. New York: The Macmillan Company, 1951.

Kozman, H. C. (editor). *Democratic Human Relations, First Yearbook of the American Association for Health, Physical Education, and Recreation*. Washington, D. C. AAHPER, 1951.

Krikorian, Yervant H. (editor). *Naturalism and the Human Spirit*. New York: Columbia University Press, 1944.

Lange, Frederick A. *History of Materialism* (trans. by E. C. Thomas). Boston: James R. Osgood and Co., 1877, Vols. I-III.

Larkin, Richard A., "The Influence of John Dewey on Physical Education." Master's thesis, The Ohio State University, 1936.

Lucretius. *Of the Nature of Things* (trans. by W. E. Leonard). London: J. M. Dent and Sons, Ltd., 1921.

Lynn, M. L., "Major Emphases in Physical Education." Ph.D. dissertation, The University of Pittsburgh, 1944.

Maccia, George S., "The Educational Aims of Charles Peirce," *Educational Theory*, Vol. 4, No. 3:206-212 (July, 1954).

Mayhew, K. C. and Edwards, A. C. *The Dewey School*. New York: Appleton-Century-Crofts, Inc., 1936.

McClellan, James E., "In Reply to Professor Soltis," in *Philosophy of Education 1971*. (Proceedings of the 27th Annual Meeting of the Philosophy of Education Society, Dallas, April 4-7, 1971). Edwardsville: Southern Illinois University, 1971, pp. 55-59.

McCloy, C. H., "A Half Century of Physical Education," *The Physical Educator*, Vol. XVII, No. 3:83-91 (October, 1960).

_____. *Philosophical Bases for Physical Education*. New York: Appleton-Century-Crofts, Inc., 1940.

_____. "Physical Education as Part of General Education," *Journal of Health and Physical Education*, XXXI, 45 (November, 1928).

McMurray, Foster, "The Present Status of Pragmatism in Education," *School and Society*, Vol. 87:14-17 (Jan. 17, 1959).

McMurrin, Sterling M., "What About the Philosophy of Education?" Journal of Philosophy, Vol. LIX, No. 22:629-637 (October, 1962).

Mills, C. Wright. Sociology and Pragmatism. New York: Oxford University Press, 1966.

Morland, Richard B., "A Philosophical Interpretation of the Educational Views Held by Leaders in American Physical Education." Ph.D. dissertation, New York University, 1958.

Mosier, Richard D., "School and Society in Experimentalism," School and Society, Vol. 89:106-109 (March 11, 1961).

Nash, Paul, "The Strange Death of Progressive Education," Educational Theory, Vol. 14, No. 2:65-75 (April, 1964).

Nowell-Smith, P. H. Ethics. Harmondsworth, England, 1954.

Patrick, George, "Verifiability of Physical Education Objectives." Ph.D. dissertation, University of Illinois, Urbana, 1971.

Platt, John, "What's Ahead for 1990," The Center Magazine, Vol. V, No. 4:21-28 (July/August, 1972).

Ratner, Joseph. The Philosophy of John Dewey. New York: Holt, Rinehart and Winston, Inc., 1929.

Raup, R. Bruce, et al. The Improvement of Practical Intelligence: The Central Task of Education. New York: Harper and Row, Publishers, Inc., 1950.

Rousseau, Jean-Jacques. Emile. London: J. M. Dent and Sons, Ltd., 1943.

_____, _____, "Social Contract," in Social Contract: Essays by Locke, Hume, and Rousseau (Sir Earnest Barker, editor). New York: Oxford University Press, Inc., 1948.

Rucker, Darnell, "Dewey's Ethics (Part Two)," in Guide to the Works of John Dewey (Jo Ann Boydston, editor). Carbondale and Edwardsville: Southern Illinois University Press, 1970, pp. 112-130.

Sayers, E. V. and Madden, W. Education and the Democratic Faith. New York: Appleton-Century-Crofts, Inc., 1959.

Schilpp, P. A. The Philosophy of John Dewey. Evanston and Chicago: Northwestern University Press, 1939.

Shepard, Natalie M., "Democracy in Physical Education: A Study of the Implications for Educating for Democracy Through Physical Education." Ed.D. dissertation, New York University, 1952.

Shivers, Jay S., "An Analysis of Theories of Recreation." Ph.D. dissertation, The University of Wisconsin, 1958.

Sidgwick, Henry. Outlines of the History of Ethics. London, 1886.

Smith, B. Othaniel, "Views on the Role of Philosophy in Teacher Education," Journal of Philosophy, Vol. LIX, No. 22:6 8-647 (October, 1962).

Spears, Betty M., "Philosophical Bases for Physical Education Experiences Consistent with the Goals of General Education for College Women." Ph.D. dissertation, New York University, 1956.

Spencer, Herbert. Education: Intellectual, Moral, and Physical. London: C. A. Watts and Co., Ltd., 1949. (Originally published in 1861.)

Tenenbaum, S. William Heard Kilpatrick. New York: Harper and Row, Publishers, Inc., 1951.

Van Dalen, D. B., "Philosophical Profiles for Physical Education," The Physical Educator, Vol. 21, No. 3 (October, 1964).

Wegener, Frank C., "The Philosophical Beliefs of Leaders in American Education." Ph.D. dissertation, University of Southern California, 1946.

White, Morton G. The Origin of Dewey's Instrumentalism. New York: Columbia University Press, 1943.

Williams, J. F. The Principles of Physical Education. 7th edition. Philadelphia: W. B. Saunders Co., 1959.

Wood, T. D. and Cassidy, Rosalind. The New Physical Education. New York: The Macmillan Company, 1927.

Wynne, John P. Philosophies of Education. Englewood Cliffs, New Jersey: Prentice-Hall, Inc., 1947.

Zeigler, Earle F., "The Implications of Experimentalism for Physical, Health, and Recreation Education." A paper presented to the American Association for Health, Physical Education, and Recreation Convention, May 3, 1963. (An abridged version appeared in The Physical Educator, Vol. 20, No. 4:150-152, December, 1963.)

_____ "Naturalism in Physical, Health, and Recreation Education." The University of Michigan School of Education Bulletin, Vol. 34, No. 2:42-46 (December, 1962).

_____. Philosophy of Physical, Health, and Recreation Education. Englewood Cliffs, New Jersey: Prentice-Hall, Inc., 1964.

_____. Problems in the History and Philosophy of Physical Education and Sport. Englewood Cliffs, New Jersey: Prentice-Hall, Inc., 1968.

_____ and VanderZwaag, H. J. Physical Education: Progressivism or Essentialism? Champaign, Illinois: Stipes Publishing Company, revised edition, 1968.

THE EDUCATIONAL PHILOSOPHY OF RECONSTRUCTIONISM: IMPLICATIONS FOR PHYSICAL, HEALTH, AND RECREATION EDUCATION

The Nature of Reality (Metaphysics)

Experience and nature "constitute both the form and content of the entire universe" (multiverse?). There is no such thing as a pre-established order of things in the world. Reality is evolving, and humanity appears to be a most important manifestation of the natural process. The impact of cultural forces upon man are fundamental, and every effort must be made to understand them as we strive to build the best type of a group-centered culture. In other words, "the structure of cultural reality" should be our foremost concern. Cultural determinants have shaped the hisotry of man, and he now has reached a crucial stage in the development of life on this planet. Our efforts should be focused on the building of a world culture.[1]

Educational Aims and Objectives

Social self-realization is the supreme value in education. The realization of this ideal is most important for the individual in his social setting - a world culture. Positive ideals must be molded toward the evolving democratic ideal by a general education which is group-centered and in which the majority determines the acceptable goals. Education by means of "hidden coercion" is to be avoided as much as possible. Learning is explained by the organismic principle of functional psychology. Social intelligence acquired teaches man to control and direct his urges as he concurs with or attempts to modify cultural purposes.

The Educative Process (Epistemology)

An organismic approach to the learning process is basic. Thought cannot be independent of certain aspects of the organism; it is related integrally with emotional and muscular functions. Man's mind enables him to cope with the problems of human life in a social environment. Social intelligence is closely related to scientific method. Certain operational concepts, inseparable from metaphysics

---

[1] This explication was published in Physical Education: Progressivism or Essentialism? (with H. J. VanderZwaag). Champaign, Illinois: Stipes Publishing Company, 1966.

and axiology (beliefs about reality and values), focus on the reflective thought, problem-solving, and social consensus necessary for the transformation of the culture.

Physical, Health, and Recreation Education (Aims and Objectives)

As I see it, there can be no such thing as a fixed or universal curriculum in physical, health, and recreation education. It should be developed through the employment of shared planning to determine what specific contributions our field might make to the program of general education. Education should be available for all through what is now called junior college, and this means that a greater amount of time would be available to us in the long run. If the "community school concept" were employed, we should certainly be able to offer about an hour and a half a day for recreation and relaxation alone. Instruction in motor skills would be employed to allow for a sufficient amount of "physical" fitness activity. "Carry-over" games and sports with opportunities for wholesome educational play would undoubtedly contribute to total fitness. Since my goal in education is social self-realization, mental hygiene and sex education are very important as are planned opportunities for leadership roles in a democratic social setting. Creative artistic expression through physical education and recreational activities such as dance should be emphasized. Essential also are intramural sports with the emphasis on team activities and a corresponding de-emphasis of the prevailing situation in interscholastic competitive athletics. I see the teacher employing democratic method to aid the group to bring to realization goals arrived at through democratic consensus. Self-expression is important for human development; the self can only rise within the group, and self-realization comes through the attainment of common purpose. Administrative policies are determined through "shared participation" by all concerned. The nation should play a constructive and integrative role in all phases of education including our specialized field.

UTOPIAN RECONSTRUCTIONISM AS ONE TYPE OF EDUCATIONAL PROGRESSIVISM: IMPLICATIONS FOR PHYSICAL, HEALTH, AND RECREATION EDUCATION

If we accept the premise that a number of educational philosophies are possible, and perhaps even desirable, in a diverse society such as ours, then a discussion of the implications of the educational philosophy known as reconstructionism for physical, health, and recreation education is perfectly appropriate at this juncture of the development of our evolving democracy.* An effort to delineate the characteristic aspects of this distinctive educational philosophy (an "off-shoot" or "flowering" of experimentalism) and the possible implications for our specialized field should be considered a worthwhile project even though this particular position is typically classified as utopian in nature.

At the risk of stressing what is to almost all quite obvious, mankind's obvious predicament in relation to the future of life on one minute planet in only one of the innumerable galaxies of the universe demands that educators do all in their power to ensure that the peoples of this planet continue to have a future ahead of them.

The United States, really so very young, has had a unique national purpose. As the leading power of the Western world, there is no doubt but that everything we do here is being scrutinized very carefully and very critically. The ideologies of democracy and communism should and must be understood by as many as possible on both sides of the Iron Curtain. The late President Kennedy understood the conflict between these political positions very clearly and warned that "we shall have to test anew whether a nation organized and governed such as ours can endure." The educational philosophy of reconstructionism recognizes fully the extreme urgency of the world situation and would have us get to work immediately on a

---

* The writer is pleased to recognize the help received from the publications of Theodore Brameld and from the excellent interpretation by Richard M. Morland; the implications drawn for this specialized field are original. This study was carried out during the 1963-64 academic year and was presented to a Research Section Meeting at the AAHPER Convention in Washington, D. C., May 7-11, 1964. This investigation was published in Physical Education: Progressivism or Essentialism? (Zeigler, E. F. and VanderZwaag, H. J.). Champaign, Illinois: Stipes Publishing Company, Second edition, 1968, pp. 41-65.

reconstruction of our entire way of life, including our educational system, so that the "American dream" may be realized in the best possible way by all peoples on earth.

A "Spectrum" for Educational Philosophy. In order to understand our philosophic foundations, it has been recommended that a professional educator should assess his philosophy of life and/or religion, his philosophy of education, and his philosophy of physical, health, and recreation education. Consistency among the various categories and departments of his examined position may mean that his life has become ordered to a considerable degree and that greater on-the-job effectiveness has been achieved. The belief is that individual should "find his place on a somewhat loosely-knit educational philosophy spectrum." (69) At this point, however, it seems necessary to warn the individual concerned about what Whitehead (67)

EDUCATIONAL PHILOSOPHY SPECTRUM

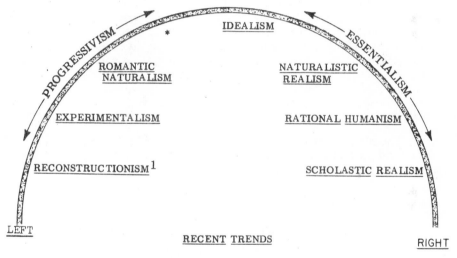

LINGUISTIC ANALYSIS — Philosophy "in a new key"

*EXISTENTIALISM (a permeating influence)

---

[1] It has been decided that Reconstructionism and Romantic Naturalism, although both are progressivistic, should be interchanged in this diagram. The reason for this change is the "doctrine of defensible partiality" espoused by Dr. Brameld for the reconstructionistic position.

designated as "the fallacy of misplaced concreteness" - that is, we must be careful not to mistake the abstract for the concrete and not to forget that we live in a world of abstract symbols and concepts. Furthermore, we must not forget to judge a man's philosophy by what he does, and not merely by what he says!

This spectrum, or continuum, may be subdivided broadly into progressivism, starting from the center and moving to the left, and essentialism, starting at the center and moving to the right. It ranges from left to right as follows: reconstructionism, experimentalism or pragmatic naturalism, romantic naturalism, idealism, naturalistic realism, rational humanism, and Catholic realism (70). Morland (42) categorizes these positions in educational philosophy broadly as reconstructionism, progressivism, essentialism, and aritomism.

Progressivism is greatly concerned about such things as pupil freedom, individual differences, pupil interest, pupil growth, no fixed values, and that education is life now. The essentialist stresses that there are certain educational values by which the individual must be guided, that effort takes precedence over interest and that this girds moral stamina, that the experience of the past has powerful jurisdiction over the present, and that the cultivation of the intellect is most important in education. These beliefs attributed to each broad position are, of course, only representative and not inclusive (69).

Purpose

The purpose of this study was to delineate through structural philosophical analysis a reconstructionist (utopian experimentalistic) philosophy of physical, health, and recreation education.

Procedure

The methodology of this study was as follows:

1. The metaphysics (inquiry into the nature of reality), epistemology (theory of learning), logic (exact relating of ideas), and axiology (system of values) of reconstructionism were reviewed. This included an examination of the philosophy of pragmatism, educational progressivism, and the educational philosophy of experimentalism (pragmatic naturalism).

2. The information obtained through this preliminary step served as a basis for the extraction of those elements

of reconstructionism which appear to have specific implications for physical, health, and recreation education.

3. Data of both an empirical and scientific nature were gathered which tended to support the implications drawn in the analysis phase of the study.

Results

Step One:

The Nature of Reality (Metaphysics) (70). Experience and nature "constitute both the form and content of the entire universe," which could actually be a multiverse. There is no such thing as a pre-established order of things in the world. Reality is evolving, and humanity appears to be a most important manifestation of the natural process. The impact of cultural forces upon man are fundamental, and every effort must be made to understand them as we strive to build the best type of a group-centered culture. In other words, "the structure of cultural reality" should be our foremost concern. Cultural determinants have shaped the history of man, and he has now reached a crucial stage in the development of life on this planet. Our efforts should be focused on the building of a world culture (11).

Theory of Learning (Epistemology). An organismic approach to the learning process is basic. Thought cannot be independent of certain aspects of the organism; it is related integrally with emotional and muscular functions. Man's mind enables him to cope with the problems of human life in a social environment. Social intelligence is closely related to scientific method. Certain operational concepts, inseparable from metaphysics and axiology (beliefs about reality and values), focus on reflective thought, problem-solving, and social consensus necessary for the transformation of the culture.

Exact Relating of Ideas (Logic). Reconstructionism, actually related structurally to pragmatism, has basically the same position in regard to logic, or the exact relating of ideas. Pragmatism is a philosophy in which there is a radical departure from the traditional logic of realism and idealism. The search is for a method of reasoning which will help man to solve his problems in the best possible way. Dewey, America's leading pragmatist, felt that Aristotelian logic was completely out of place in the twentieth century. Such a system, starting from a metaphysical position which views Nature as a fixed system, seemed completely wrong to him, inasmuch as he viewed the universe as boundless, "open-ended," and perhaps expanding. Dewey recommended, therefore, a completely revised system of logic--"a unified theory of inquiry through which the authentic pattern of experimental and operational inquiry in science shall become available for regulation of the habitual methods by which inquiries in the field of common sense are carried on." This problem-solving approach was his answer to the gap which he found between traditional logic and twentieth century scientific inquiry.

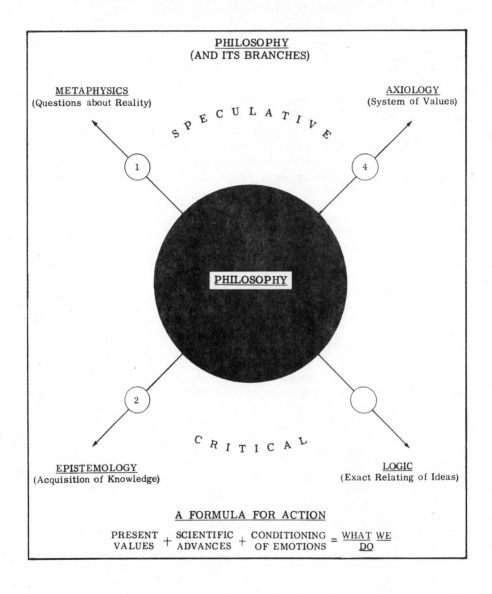

PHILOSOPHY
(AND ITS BRANCHES)

METAPHYSICS
(Questions about Reality)

AXIOLOGY
(System of Values)

SPECULATIVE

1

4

PHILOSOPHY

2

CRITICAL

EPISTEMOLOGY
(Acquisition of Knowledge)

LOGIC
(Exact Relating of Ideas)

A FORMULA FOR ACTION

$$\text{PRESENT VALUES} + \text{SCIENTIFIC ADVANCES} + \text{CONDITIONING OF EMOTIONS} = \underline{\text{WHAT WE DO}}$$

System of Values (Axiology). Values, for the reconstructionist, "are grounded in the reality of individual and group experience and are inseparable from the process of seeking truth through social consensus." The "grounding of reality in individual and group experience" points up the integral relationship between pragmatism and reconstructionism in regard to theory concerning ethical, aesthetic, religious, and social values. The differentiation between the two systems seems to arise from the emphasis placed on the fundamental need for social consensus and how this should be achieved. It is the wants of the group, not the individual, which are paramount in reconstructionism. Goals are determined by majority consensus after all relevant, available evidence is carefully weighed. The highest value for the reconstructionist is social self-realization, which he believes can be best realized through world democracy - an evolving concept. "Loyal" minorities would occupy an important place in such a system; they would criticize constructively, while acceding to the legally-sanctioned wishes of the majority, any and all established policies in an effort to convince the majority of the wisdom and necessity for change. The government would have the responsibility of converting these expressed wishes into a program of action based on experimental design. Such a design of democratic living, admittedly utopian, should and could hold great promise for the future of mankind.

The Implication for Education. Social self-realization is the highest value for the reconstructionist in education (11). The realization of this ideal is most important for the individual in his social setting - a world culture.

Some of the means whereby the reconstructionist's educational aim may be accomplished through the educative process are as follows:

1. All students should share equally in all phases of the program.

2. A citizenship emphasis is extremely important - the molding of positive attitudes toward the evolving democratic ideal.

3. Development of the group process and product should be stressed.

4. Education by means of "hidden coercion" is to be avoided as much as possible.

5. All classes should be coeducational.

6. Learning is based upon progressivism's functional psychology.

a. The reconstructionist believes that "prehension" in learning takes place. Prehension "precedes and succeeds the conscious analyses and syntheses (the apprehensions) of experience." In this theory the "body responds to stimuli as body rather than as mere brain and nervous system." With this organismic principle operating, the best kind of educative experiences contribute to the want-satisfactions of the individual.

b. The role of imagination and emotion is considered, especially as related to the unrational component in learning. "The ego is seen as the mediator between the id and superego" - that is, social intelligence acquired teaches us to control and direct our urges as we concur with or attempt to modify cultural purposes (42).

7. Thus, the following concepts would apply:

a. "Learning is a co-operative enterprise through which the individual achieves constituent values of social self-realization."

b. Social consensus should be applied to learning in every possible way; it is a self-correcting process in itself.

c. With committed group goals, "fact-teaching and skill-practicing are necessary but such inculcation should always be geared to maximum group learning a future-centered framework."

d. The problem-solving approach should be paramount with "explicit normative objectives in view." (42)

8. Interest and effort are interdependent. Interest is basically the true key to learning. The activity must be "fused" with purposeful goals. Such a philosophy as reconstructionism provides purpose to the individual and the group. Yet it should be understood that the schools should cultivate non-conformity as well as conformity.

9. Drill can be valuable if it is correlated with, and is a means to, attaining goals upon which there is consensus; a personal stake in the outcome will encourage the student to do what is necessary.

10. Transfer of learning does take place; values which are learned can be strengthened in other situations according to the group's willingness to accept them.

   a. The reconstructionist does not believe that so-called intellectual disciplines effect transfer of learning; valuable experiences do develop traits and abilities.

General speaking, there can be no such thing as a fixed or universal reconstructionist curriculum. Some consensus would undoubtedly result from experimental patterns of practice in accord with this utopian progressivist theory. An overall curriculum plan does have a goal by which experimental alternative curricula could be measured. The curriculum would be extended for all through what is now considered junior college. All aspects of the program would be developed through the employment of shared planning to determine what specific contributions they might make to general education.

Role of the Teacher - the teacher employs democratic method to aid the group to bring to realization goals arrived at through democratic consensus:

   1. Social consensus involves presentation of evidence, communication, agreement, and action.

   2. Instruction is designed to help the students cope with the many problems of human relations.

   3. A first name relationship between student and teacher seems desirable.

   4. The teacher has a mandate for action.

   5. The best type of group dynamics is free and uncoerced communication.

   6. The teacher should recognize the "unrational" component of the student's goals.

   7. The teacher's task is to help the student become a "life master." (42)

Role of the Individual - the individual works democratically with the group to realize his goals as follows:

   1. He is considered to be responsible.

2. Self-expression is important for human development; the individual has an obligation to express himself.

3. The self can only rise within the group.

4. Self-realization comes through attainment of common purpose.

Administration Overview - policies are determined through "shared participation" by all concerned. Values, policies, and plans are determined in the following order:

1. By the majority's wants.

2. Through policy formulation by the board.

3. By an all-school council.

4. By the administrator as he administers at this fourth level, executing specific operations according to policies determined through social consensus. The program should be financed by all agencies of government at the various levels; the people must be convinced that education is worthy of such support.

Role of the Administrator - the administrator executes policies agreed upon in such a way that a democratic atmosphere pervades the entire operation; co-operative endeavor should characterize the relationship existing between the administrator and the supervisor, as well as the relationship between the supervisor and the teacher.

Discipline - discipline is enforced by the group when it is necessary to facilitate the attainment of the group's goals. Some degree of inculcation and control is certainly necessary in the lower grades.

Grading - numerical grades are not used. The total aspects of the student's growth are appraised in conferences between teacher and student. Honor rolls and prizes are eliminated.

Tests - tests are used for the following purposes:

1. Tests should be designed to measure "social intelligence." The whole concept of failure is used with a different meaning; it means that the student's program needs change.

2. Students should take part in the development of the entire process of measurement. "Comprehensive"

examinations (which will measure true comprehension) should be used for guidance.

3. Tests should be "shared efforts designed to synthesize and evaluate the quality of the learning experience." (11) Tests are "progress checks"; objective examinations of contents and skills given in the traditional manner are decidedly inadequate. Tests are very helpful when they measure growth toward increased participation.

Indoctrination - freedom of inquiry is basic to reconstructionism. Indoctrination is opposed strongly. Debatable issues are approached inductively. Propaganda is fine, but it should be labelled as such. Reconstructionism emphasizes the position of "defensible partiality" as being justifiable; the idea is to "arrive at group decisions partial to those who hold them, because they've sustained examination . . ." (11)

Relationship Between School and Community

1. The schools are community-centered in reconstructionism. They are the hub of political and social activity. Education's main goal is to exert "a positive influence by serving as an integrating force in the reconstruction of the culture." The goal is democracy on a global scale. Human freedom, therefore, is a cultural goal. The primary objective for education in relation to the individual is social self-realization. (11)

2. Education should work closely with labor unions.

3. The nation should play a constructive and integrative role in all phases of education. A much stronger international emphasis is needed as well.

4. At the local level, education should reflect the ideals of the community.

Step Two:

The Implications for Physical, Health, and Recreation Education

1. General Comments. The teacher of physical, health, and recreation education should keep the educational level of social self-realization uppermost in his thinking when approaching his task.

It is difficult, and seemingly not desirable, to treat health, physical education, and recreation separately in the realization of the reconstructionist educational aim.

There can be no fixed or universal curriculum in this specialized field.

Our program should be group-centered, and it is developed through shared planning.

Reconstructionists will avoid "education by means of persuasion and hidden coercion. Progressive education has been thus debased. It has failed to become what it was intended to be and has never developed as it was meant to be." (46)

Education should be available to all through the junior (or community) college level. This should means that there will be considerably more time available for health, physical education, and especially recreation.

In the truly democratic society, all students should share equally in all phases of the program.

To the greatest extent possible, all activities will be conducted coeducationally.

Activities stressing co-operation and the learning of democratic attitudes should receive primary emphasis.

The nation (the federal government) will play a constructive and integrative role increasingly in educational enterprises.

Our field should continue to develop its international emphasis as we move toward the "one world" concept.

To the greatest extent possible, we should promote pure and applied research in our effort to gain greater knowledge about desirable educational theory and practice.

Reconstructionism stresses orientation to the future, which places our field in a position requiring the planning of programs for a changing society.

2. Aims and Objectives - Physical Education

    a.   Social self-realization, and the concept of "total fitness" implied in this aim, gives firm direction to all curriculum planning in the reconstructionist scheme of educational design.

    b.   In physical, health, and recreation education there should be an opportunity for all to select a wide variety of useful activities to promote the broad goals of this educational philosophy.

    c.   Instruction in motor skills is necessary to provide the individual with a sufficient amount of "physical" fitness activity. In this connection our research authorities will tell us what is "sufficient" as soon as possible.

    d.   Activities such as dance can contribute to man's creative expression. Moreover, the introduction of art into physical education will provide many opportunities for the creative expression of culture.

    e.   Intramural sports, and voluntary physical recreational activities, should be stressed. This applies especially to team competition with particular stress on cooperation and promotion of the concept of friendly competition.

    f.   Extramural sport competition can be introduced when there is a need. Striving for excellence is important in the development of an individual, but this aspect of the program must be kept in balance with the total curriculum.

    g.   During the period of education within the framework of so-called formal education, educators must guard zealously against the exploitation evident in many interscholastic and intercollegiate competitive athletic programs. "Sport was created for man," and we cannot permit materialistic influences in our society to win out over sound educational philosophy.

    h.   Relaxation techniques should be a legitimate phase of our instructional program in a society where stresses and tension are increasing steadily.

i. Instruction in carry-over games and sports (the whole concept of education for leisure) should have an important place in the curriculum.

3. Aims and Objectives - School Health Education

    a. Emerging from a naturalistic undergirding, re-constructionism includes the tenet that men and women were to be "rugged animals" - rugged in that they should be sturdy and possess vigorous health; this does not imply a need for huge, heavily-muscled creatures.

    b. Positive health, therefore, should be a primary educational aim in the sense implied by Jesse Feiring Williams - "to live most and to serve best."

    c. Such a program of school health education would necessitate the co-operative involvement of many agencies including the home, the school, and various groups concerned at different government-al levels.

    d. The learning of health knowledges, understandings, and attitudes should be realized through the pro-vision of experiences involving problem-solving. Such learning could take place through "direct" health instruction, but could also be acquired in-directly through learning experiences in the sci-ence curriculum. All teachers should instruct for technical, associated, and concomitant learnings to occur.

    e. Sex education and family relations instruction are very important in the curriculum, as such experi-ences are vital for full social self-realization. The status of women in the future social order is a most complex question and is closely related to this area of instruction.

    f. Mental hygiene instruction needs serious attention is our increasingly complex society.

4. Aims and Objectives - Recreation Education

    a. Because of the recommended unified approach for physical, health, and recreation education, it is difficult to separate the objectives of recreation education from physical education when physical activities are being considered.

b. In this presentation, only those recreational activities which are "physical" in nature are included. The reconstructionist would make leisure activities available to all on a year-round basis.

c. Wholesome educational play is important for moral growth.

d. Inasmuch as recreation education is a legitimate phase of the core curriculum, an opportunity to participate in physical recreational activities later in the day should be provided.

    i. Opportunity for creativity in the area of physical movement should be available to those who show capability and interest.

e. Educational benefits, as well as satisfaction and pleasure, can result from observation of others engaging actively and creatively in physical recreational pursuits.

5. <u>Methodology</u>

a. A great deal of the educational methodology of the experimentalist applies directly to reconstructionists as well. Methodology should go hand in hand with aims and objectives. Typically, it is characterized by "a broad social outlook, great consideration for the learner, well-prepared teachers, and a minimum of inherited technique as such." (70, quoting Larkin)

b. In keeping with the organismic principle of functional psychology, the best kind of education (educative experience) in our specialized field contributes to the want-satisfactions of the individual.

c. The reconstructionist position was outlined in considerable detail earlier in this paper when the educative process was described. For this reason it will be repeated at this point only under its subheadings with certain specific comments and/or implications for the teacher of physical, health, and recreation education.

d. <u>Sub-headings</u> - Methodology

    i.   <u>Discipline</u> - give student as much freedom as he can use widely; use group to help enforce.

    ii.   <u>Grading</u> - eliminate numerical grades; appraise student's growth and development through conference.

    iii.   <u>Tests</u> - designed to measure "social intelligence"; eliminate concept of failure by change of program pattern; involve student in evaluation of self and program; employ examinations of a comprehensive nature in keeping with educational ideal; tests are progress checks.

    iv.   <u>Indoctrination</u> - vigorously opposed; freedom of inquiry is vital.

    v.   <u>Propaganda</u> - is understood for what is; learn to analyze its techniques; can be used when necessary; has both "good" and "bad" connotations.

    vi.   <u>Role of teacher</u> - employs social consensus; emphasis on human relations; first name relationship with student desirable; employs free and uncoerced group dynamics; should encourage group to accomplishment; recognizes "unrational" component of student's goals; urges students to work independently as soon as possible.

    vii.   <u>Role of individual</u> - considered responsible; self-expression important for development; self can rise only within group; self-realization comes through attainment of common purpose.

    viii.   <u>Development of leadership</u> - planned opportunities for leadership roles whenever possible.

    ix.   <u>Interest and effort</u> - interest the true key to learning; interest and effort are interdependent; activity must be purposeful.

x.   <u>Transfer of learning</u> - transfer does take place; through valuable experiences attitudes are developed in keeping with values accepted by the group.

xi.   <u>Concepts of learning</u> - learning a co-operative enterprise; social consensus should be applied to learning (it is self-correcting); fact-teaching and skill-practicing are still necessary with committed group goals (should be geared to maximum group learning in a future-centered framework); problem-solving approach should be paramount.

x.   <u>Research findings</u> - as available should be introduced into learning process.

Step Three:

Presentation of Empirical and Scientific Data to Support These Implications

This step in the study appeared to be crucial and most appropriate in order to make the entire effort as meaningful as possible. The data was procured from certain available evidence in the behavioral sciences, notably psychology, sociology, and anthropology. A number of the studies which appeared to hold implications for this position were completed under the auspices of our own field of health, physical education, and recreation. It should be mentioned that no attempt has been made to incorporate the results obtained through research which would tend to bear out the positions of any of the other fairly definitive philosophies of education extant. When such studies are completed in the future, it will give us an excellent opportunity to make comparisons.

   1.   General Empirical Data.

       a.   There have been a number of publications in the past few decades which point the way for reconstructionism. Some of this material is empirical and perhaps unverifiable, at least to a certain degree. Other information is related definitely to the background research experience of the person or group concerned.

           Over thirty years ago, Counts (19) asked the question: "Dare the Schools Build a New Social Order?" This, of course, is the goal of the reconstructionist. Counts saw the need for rather militant organization of the teaching profession in order to bring about desired social changes.

Kilpatrick (35) was concerned at this time also about the need for "reconstruction of experience." In Education and the Social Crisis, he pointed out that teachers had too great a tendency to remain aloof from matters of emerging life in our society. He felt that they should attempt to promote a social philosophy that was much more explicit.

In the Social Ideas of American Educators, which appeared in 1935, Curti (24) denotes a concluding chapter to "Post-War Patterns" in which he makes an excellent assessment of the efforts of a "new breed" of educator who was concerned with needed social change. He explained how there "had been the same cleavage between fact and ideal in educational circles as in other groups in American life, the same tendency to discover achievement in the aspiration."

This pattern of thinking – this ideal regarding the function of education – was in evidence throughout this period before the Global War and has really never stopped. In The American Democracy, published in 1948, Laski (37) stated his belief that "what is wanted is a fundamental change in the spirit by which the present American system of education is permeated down to its very foundations."

Even twenty-five years ago when Becker's (2) Modern Democracy appeared (1941), forward-thinking individuals were concerned about "government of the people, by the politicians, for whatever pressure groups can get their interests taken care of." A careful examination of the underlying motives behind the sponsors of lobbyists in our nation's capital might be very enlightening as well as frightening.

Brameld has been in the forefront in developing reconstructionist thought. In his Design for America (9) (1945) he urged as basic the "projection of a concrete attainable goal." As he pointed out further in Patterns of Educational Philosophy (10) (1950), progressivism – really a transitional philosophy – doesn't give sufficient direction to

living since there is not enough commitment to
needed positive beliefs. He believes that progressivism did serve a valuable purpose, but that now
forthright commitment and even "radical audacity"
is needed.

Some of our leading anthropologists seem to be
giving us the same message - that man must do
something quite soon about molding our culture as
part of the evolutionary process. The late Professor Malinowski (39) in The Dynamics of Cultural
Change (1945) stresses that "culture is an instrumental reality." Recently in Culture Against
Man (1963), Henry (32) reiterates that "man shall
not wait 200 million years . . . until some organic
mutation determines his course; rather shall he
hunt, in anguish and perplexity, for a pattern of
decent relations with his fellows." It is in answer
to such exhortation that the reconstructionist
speaks about his plan for "future-centered education."

Berkson (4), who is said to have used the term
"reconstructionism" first in this context, explains
in The Ideal and the Community (1958) that "in the
favorable situation - as in the democratic society -
the opposition between tha actual and the ideal
creates a tension which impels toward the ever-
greater embodiment of the ideal in the life of the
individual and the nation." He sees philosophy of
education as an aspect of social philosophy.

Neill (46), in Summerhill: A Radical Approach to
Child Rearing (1960) tells about his highly unusual
educational experiment in England. There is great
concern in this unique school for the individual and
his development as a free person. Erich Fromm,
in his introduction to the book, criticizes progressive education for the "subtle manipulation" that
even it uses. As he explains, "the child is forced
to swallow the pill, but the pill is given a sugar
coating. Parents and teachers have confused true
non-authoritation education with education by
means of persuasion and hidden coercion." Neill,
it must be said, does not specifically support educational reconstructionism, but he certainly appears to be employing much of what it recommends.
He would no doubt wish to inquire most carefully
into reconstructionism's "doctrine of defensible

partiality" and the "indoctrination," which progressivists fear, that it seems to imply.

The former President of Sarah Lawrence College,
Harold Taylor (55), wrote just recently in a vein
which would have great appeal to the reconstructionist and which offers him seemingly very strong
support. He says:

> Yet this generation of students has come of
> age when the educational system has fallen be-
> hind them; they are ready for more than the
> schools, the colleges, or the society are
> ready to give. The social philosophy now
> dominant in America is not one that nourishes
> the young imagination in either its moral or
> its intellectual dimension. The direction of
> educational thinking is conservative, restric-
> tive, reactionary . . ."

Most recently, Gallup (27), in a highly stimulating
book The Miracle Ahead (1964) urges us to con-
trive "new ways to actualize our potential." He
inquires, "How can civilization be lifted to a new
level?" Proceeding from the premise that such
advancement is distinctly possible, he stresses
that a new educational philosophy is required - a
plan that embraces the entire life span. What
Gallup does not seem to appreciate is the urgent
need for much greater research emphasis on the
psychological order of learning - how to stimulate
the student's interest early and how to maintain it
through life. Gallup points out further that there
is a great opportunity for collective effort as yet
unexploited. Thirdly, he believes that we can use
the social sciences increasingly to solve social
problems. Lastly, he discusses the problem of
change and explains that we must teach future
generations how to understand change and to seek
it. He sees much of this progress becoming a
reality through better teaching, improved methods
of problem-solving and decision-making, and
through the much wiser and efficient use of committees to raise the calibre of collective effort.

In The Adolescent Society (1961), Coleman (18)
states that, "a boy or girl growing up never has a
chance to 'practice' with many of the difficult problems which will face him as an adult, because

these are not interpersonal problems. They are problems involving a more impersonal and more powerful environment - the large institutions with which he must cope if he is to survive in this complex society." He is looking for what he calls an "intangible quality" that is missing in the large majority of our educational institutions. The reconstructionist believes that he knows what this missing "intangible quality" is!

The late John Dewey knew what was needed to bring about the necessary reconstruction in education when he spoke about education as the "continuous reconstruction of experience." He believed further that philosophy had a vital role to play; to such a belief the reconstructionist would immediately assent. In the introduction to the revised edition of his Reconstruction in Philosophy (1948), Dewey (25) stated that,

> It must undertake to do for the development of inquiry into human affairs and hence into morals what the philosophers of the last few centuries did for promotion of scientific inquiry in physical and physiological conditions and aspects of human life.

To conclude, Muller (43) in The Uses of the Past (1923) outlined the path that must be followed if man wishes to learn from the past. He says that "we cannot ignore the human agency in history, cannot escape the implication that within limits it is a free agency." He explains further that historians have "tended to minimize the power of ideas and ideals, or even to deny this power" by implying that "man has no real freedom to make his history." The reconstructionist would concur fully with Muller's theme that "the problems we face are clearly of man's own making." Reconstructionism recognizes that "the gauntlet has been thrown down" and that it is up to man to rebuild his society so that "social self-realization" can become a reality for all.

2. Scientific Data (General)

a. It is more difficult to know just which data from the behavioral sciences has application to the matter at hand. The amount of evidence has multiplied to such an extent recently that it is almost impossible to keep abreast of it. Fortunately, Berelson and Steiner (3) recently completeted Human Behavior: An Inventory of Scientific Findings. These "findings" may also be called "important and verified generalizations" according to the authors. As they indicate, many of their findings perhaps ought to be preceded by "under certain circumstances," "other things equal," and "in our culture." At any rate, this writer has gleaned the following findings from the 1045 studies included in their inventory which seem to bear on the topic at hand - the opportunity for our society, and especially our educational system to promote social self-realization.

From the standpoint of behavioral development,

> The closer the correspondence between socializing agencies (home vis-à-vis school or parents vis-à-vis peers), the more securely and the more rapidly the socialization takes place. The more the conflicts between them, the slower and more uncertain the process. (3, p. 48)

From the standpoint of face-to-face relations, in small groups,

> The more people associate with one another under conditions of equality, the more they come to share values and norms and the more they come to like one another. (3, p. 327)

> The leader will be followed more faithfully, the more he makes it possible for the members to achieve their private goals, along with the group's goals. (3, p. 343)

> In a small group, authoritarian leadership is less effective than democratic leadership in holding a group together and getting its work done. Democratic leadership is more effective with respect to the durability of the group, the members' satisfaction with it, their independence vis-à-vis the leader, and their productivity on the task. (3, p. 344)

The amount of interaction among the members
of a small group varies with the following
conditions:

> .1 Interaction increases as the cohesive-
> ness of the group grows . . . (3,
> p. 346)

Both the effectiveness of the group and the
satisfaction of its members are increased
when the members see their goals as being
advanced by the group's goals, i.e., when the
two are perceived as being in harmony. When
members push their own needs, both satisfaction and effectiveness decline. (3, p. 352)

Active discussion by a small group to determine goals, to choose methods of work, to
reshape operations, or to solve other problems is more effective in changing group
practice than is separate instruction of the
individual members, external requests, or the
imposition of new practices by superior
authority - more effective, that is, in bringing
about better motivation and support for the
change and better implementation and produc-
tivity of the new practice. (3, p. 353)

From the standpoint of organizations,

> The more rigid or formal the hierarchy is,
> the less the upward flow of informal communi-
> cations. (3, p. 370)

The efficiency of a large formal organization
in sizably enhanced when its own chain of
command or decision or communication is tied
into the informal network of groups within the
organization, so that the network can be used
to support the organization's goals. (3,
p. 370)

The more friendly-helpful the boss,

> .1 the less the absenteeism.
> .2 the more the productivity (if that is the
> goal of the organization and the unit).

.3 the more likely the subordinates are to feel that the organization's requirements are reasonable, and the more willingly they accept changes in organizational practices.

.4 the better liked the leader is.

.5 the more strongly the subordinates identify with the organization.

.6 the less tension there is within the organizational unit, and the more the internal cohension.

.7 the higher the subordinate's morale (and this is especially so). (3, p. 374) p. 374)

The leader's style of leadership tends to be influenced by the style in which he himself is led." (3, p. 376)

From the standpoint of institutions,

Democratic political institutions are likely to be stable over a long period when the following social conditions are present:

a) some, but not great, differences in culture or standard of living among classes.

b) few sharp discontinuities due to such major historical movements as industrialization, urbanization, war, depression, or a shift out of feudalism or colonialism.

c) open leadership, accessible to various groups within the society (or at least perceived to be), and diversity of background of leaders.

d) substantial numbers of intermediate organizations, between the primary group or the family on the one hand and the society on the other, that tie the individual to the national scene, provide representation of his interests, and limit the power of the national government and of other organizations. Those sections of major social strata (e.g., classes) that are poorly integrated tend to support mass movements in disproportionate numbers.

e) cross-cutting, overlapping, pluralistic
identifications among parties and positions, rather than sharply clear and distinct associations.

f) predominantly secular ideologies. (3,
pp. 421-22)

From the standpoint of the society,

Social changes, however large, that are
desired by the people involved can be assimi-
lated with little social disruption. Changes
that are not desired, even quite small ones,
oan be put into effect only at considerable
social and personal cost. (3, pp. 613-14)

From the standpoint of opinions, attitudes, and
beliefs,

OAB's are more differentiated in more complex societies. (3, p. 559)

As a child grows up, he grows away from the
original parental influence to the extent that
he comes into contact with new ways of life,
new social groups, new community environments, and so on. (3, p. 566)

People hold OAB's in harmony with their
group memberships and identificiations.
(3, p. 663)

These findings, and possibly many others that will
be found in the near future, offer some substantiation to the position of the educational reconstructionist. Furthermore, they can well serve as
"guides for social action." Berelson and Steiner
conclude their monumental undertaking with a
description of the man of the behavioral sciences:

How, in a similar way, might we characterize
the man of the behavioral sciences? He is a
creature far removed from his animal origins
. . . a creature of enormous plasticity, able
to live in a wide range of physical environments and an even wider range of social or
cultural ones . . .

Perhaps the character of behavioral science man can best be grasped through his orientation to reality. He is a creature who adapts reality to his own ends, who transforms reality into a congenial form, who makes his own reality. (3, p. 663)

3. Scientific Data (Specific)

   a. The reconstructionist is firmly convinced that man's future life will be best to the extent that he "grows as a social animal" and learns to live with others in an evolving democratic society. What contributions can physical activity make to this social development? Cowell (23) completed a significant inventory of research findings relating to this question prior to his death.* Some of these findings were examined, inasmuch as they seemed to be specifically related to the goal of the reconstructionist:

   From the standpoint of social psychology,

      Baldwin (1) found that democratically raised children were more active, were more extroverted (friendly and hostile), and were favored in their group. They rated high in intellectual curiosity, originality and constructiveness. The variable "indulgence" seemed to produce the opposite effects of democracy.

      Symonds (54), studying normal adolescent boys and girls, concluded that the greatest need of these adolescents was opportunity for social participation and that the greatest personality handicap was social isolation. Physical education and recreation activities were indicated.

   From the standpoint of the school and teacher as social forces,

      Lewin and his associates (38) found that autocratic situations produced tension, individual

---

* Some of these findings overlap with the generalizations listed from Berelson and Steiner; these findings are specific.

hostility, and less stability in the group structure whereas in the democratic situation there was greater constructiveness and a stronger feeling of group property and group goals.

Pressey and Hanna (49) compared two classes, one operated in the traditional manner, the other in a more or less permissive manner which encouraged social interaction. Students in the social interaction class knew the names of more of their classmates than in the traditional class. Obviously, proper social atmosphere is essential for social contacts.

Nedelsky (45) indicates that the child's first social world is his family; he then shifts to a world in which his orientation grows out of being a part of a group of other children whom he accepts as equals. The school then becomes the social system which is an important setting in which children relate to one another.

Todd (58), in a sociometric study on the senior high level demonstrated the value of the democratic method of physical education class management by objective date showing greatly increased acquaintanceship and significant decrease in the number of unpopular and unwanted girls during a one-semester experimental period.

Witty (68) analyzed 12,000 letters from children and adolescents describing "the teacher who helped me most." All teacher personality attributes which tended to bolster the security and self-esteem of the pupils were valued highly. Praise and recognition, kindliness, fairness, sense of humor, interest in pupil's problems, and similar qualities were prominent, and these attributes markedly affected the personality development of pupils.

From the standpoint of social development,

Bunker (16) studied fifty male college students active in physical education and sports and fifty who tended to be inactive in these activities. Histories indicated that participation in team games by the "actives" was consistently greater through the upper grades than for the "inactives" . . . Bunker concluded that the bases for active participation must be laid in the elementary grades.

Shugart (53), while a psychiatric case worker in the receiving ward of a large neuropsychiatric service in a naval hospital, invariably found histories of meager play experiences in men being referred to the hospital. Patients experienced lack of interest in play as children, and deficiencies therein were evident in both quantity and quality.

Gough (28) used four high school senior classes in his study. Students who had a higher number of extra-curricular activities seemed to be characterized as: (a) frank, unpretentious; (b) self-disciplined, but tolerant of others; (c) broader cultural and intellectual interests; (d) identification with and acceptance by the group; (e) possessed effective social skills; and (f) optimistic, with higher levels of drive and energy.

Wells (66) administered a 38-item battery of physical fitness tests and Cattel's 16 Personality Factor Inventory to eight male college students. Dynamic strength related negatively to personality described as emotional, tense, and withdrawn; and positively with traits described as being less anxious, less emotional, more poised, and less unsure.

Rarick and McKee (50) selected for investigation twenty third graders from a larger group of normal children. Ten had a high level of motor achievement and the other ten a low level of motor achievement. Though a small number of cases were observed, those children who attained a high level of motor proficiency tended to be more frequently well adjusted in school and personal relationships.

From the standpoint of antisocial behavior,

Frank (26) stated that withdrawn children may "emerge with increasingly spontaneous participation" in a congenial play situation. "Similarly, an aggressive destructive child in a play situation offering little opportunity or provocation may discover new ways of relating himself to others through more cooperative play."

Chittenden (17) used play situations as a means of helping children get a better understanding of their own problems and as a means of finding whether they gained in understanding. Play was used also as a means of directing teaching of manners and techniques that would help children to avoid quarrels.

Shaw (52) found that an inconsistent or conflicting environment retards the development of socially sanctioned behavior. He showed quite dramatically the influence of the group, or small segment of society and its mores, upon the attitude and behavior of individuals.

Wattenberg (64) noted that in any group of full-fledged delinquents the first signs of behavior difficulties appear in later childhood, often before the age of ten. The author suggests that for those who failed in efforts to earn social recognition (in sports or scholarship), daring deeds of theft or bravado may have been a compensation.

From the standpoint of personal-social adjustment,

Cowell (22) found that social adjustment ratings by teachers and by classmates were positively and significantly related to physical education grades.

Biddulph (5) found that students ranking high in athletic achievement showed a significantly greater degree of personal and social adjustment than students ranking low in athletic achievements.

Bonney (6) found, at the sixth-grade level,
that among children frequently chosen as play
playmates there was more "in-group" feeling
whereas among children infrequently chosen
as playmates there was little acceptance of
each other. The rejected children were those
considered to be poor playmates.

From the standpoint of sociometrics (study of patterned relationships among members of groups),

Todd (59) stated that squads chosen on the
basis of sociometric information are likely to
produce happy, cooperative work and play.

Bretsch (13) stated that sports participation
is related to social skills and activities of
adolescents which distinguish socially accepted from unaccepted adolescents.

Wellman (65) found that differences in size,
strength, and health seemed to be more
important factors in social adjustment than
are moderate differences in intelligence.

Bower (8) pointed out that popularity was unrelated to intelligence, height, home ratings,
or school achievement but was significantly
related to strength and to physical ability.

Kuhlen and Collester (36) found that drop-out
was related to such factors as health, un-
happiness, and a sense of lack of status.

From the standpoint of social mobility,

Popp (48) had a small group of administrators
and teachers select ten boys "most nearly like
sons they would like to have" and ten boys
"least like sons they would like to have." Of
the boys who fell into the desirable category,
sixty-nine percent had high PFI's, of the boys
in the undesirable category, seventy-five percent had low PFI's.

Cowell (12), in a study of 1400 boys and girls
in grades seven to twelve, indicated that the
purposes students try to satisfy in physical

education change with the process of maturation, but "mastery of game skills," "to have
fun," and to "learn to control myself and be a
good sport," are strong in both sexes . . .
Social purposes related to submerging one's
ego for the good of the team, "to be with my
friends," and "to get along with and understand others" rated well up in the upper half.

From the standpoint of social integration,

Trapp (60) revealed in his study the evidence
of social integration possible in a college
football squad. The process of social integration in the team, as a whole, was positive and
continuous throughout the season . . .

Gustad (30), in summarizing the research
literature dealing with factors associated with
social adjustment and maladjustment, noted
that those participating in social activities
tended to have fewer significant scores on adjustment inventories and to exhibit less maladjustment . . .

Cowell (20) found that some of the outstanding
social traits which homeroom teachers,
physical education teachers, and special observers ascribed to actives and which differentiated between junior high school boys who
participated wholeheartedly in the activities
of the physical education program and those
who did not were "unembarrassed and at home
in a crowd," "talkative and active," "gave
considerable leadership to the group," "a
good mixer," "seems to like and seek social
contacts," and other social behaviors indica-
tive of satisfactory adjustment.

Walters (63) presented an analysis of the
change in social adjustment of motivated and
nonmotivated groups in a seven-week bowling
class. The results seem to indicate that
though both groups became more socially
adjusted as a result of group participation and
acquaintance, the motivated group became
better adjusted than the nonmotivated . . .

From the standpoint of aggression and competition,

May and Doob (41) related cooperation and competition to personality and culture. By the use of experimental problems, they came to certain theories or propositions. American children work more effectively in competitive than in cooperative situations. The individual will compete or cooperate in cooperative situations. The individual will compete or cooperate if he feels he can achieve his level of aspiration . . .

Greenburg (29) studied the growth of the competitive impulse in the use of building stones. A well-defined and orderly course seemed to be apparent. From four to six years of age, the child showed a desire to excel and thus compete. There was increased critical judgment along with the competitive spirit.

Johnson and Hutton (33) tested eight college wrestlers with a personality test under three conditions. The first was before a wrestling season, the second four to five hours before the first intercollegiate match of the season, and the third the day after the competition. Several group tendencies revealed were decrement of functioning intelligence, increased aggressive feelings, and increased neurotic signs in the before-match condition.

Conclusions

Social self-realization is the supreme value for the reconstructionist (utopian experimentalist) in education. To the extent that physical, health, and recreation education can contribute to the realization of this goal, it becomes an integral part of the core curriculum. There is a fairly substantive body of data of both an empirical and research nature which indicates that radical innovations in educational aims and educational process will be needed to cope with life in an evolving democracy. It could be that more, not less, progressive and reconstructionist tendencies in education are needed. Time will tell, but the reconstructionist wonders if there will be time in the face of such sharply conflicting ideologies as democracy and communism. The reconstructionist would support continuing pure and applied research to the greatest extent possible to prove his claims and to prove the claims of progressivist physical, health, and recreation educators. There appears to be evidence accumulating that physical, health, and recreation education can help the individual to realize the reconstructionist goal of social self-realization.

Recommendations

Continuing studies of this nature are needed to validate or reject, on the basis of scientific data, the various positions in educational philosophy. This specialized field has its role to play in such assessment.

References

1. Baldwin, Alfred L., "The Effect of Home Environment in Nursery School Behavior," Child Development 20:49-61; June 1949.

2. Becker, Carl. Modern Democracy. New Haven: Yale University Press, 1941.

3. Berelson, Bernard and Steiner, Gary A. Human Behavior, An Inventory of Scientific Findings. New York: Harcourt, Brace & World, Inc., 1964.

4. Berkson, Isaac B. The Ideal and the Community. New York: Harper and Row, Publishers, 1958.

5. Biddulph, Lowell G., "Athletic Achievement and the Personal and Social Adjustment of High School Boys," Research Quarterly 25:1-7; March 1954.

6. Bonney, Merl E., "Personality Traits of Successful and Unsuccessful Children," Journal of Educational Psychology 34:449-72; November 1943.

7. Bourne, R. Untimely Papers. New York: B. W. Heubsch, 1919.

8. Bower, Philip A., "The Relation of Physical, Mental, and Personality Factors to Popularity in Adolescent Boys." Doctoral dissertation, University of California at Berkeley, 1941.

9. Brameld, T. Design for America. New York: Hinds, Hayden, and Eldredge, 1945.

10. _____. Patterns of Educational Philosophy. Yonkers, New York: World Book Company, 1950.

11. _____. The Remaking of a Culture. New York: Harper and Row, Publishers, 1959.

12. _____. Toward a Reconstructed Philosophy of Education. New York: The Dryden Press, Inc., 1956.

13. Bretsch, Howard S., "Social Skills and Activities of Socially Accepted and Unaccepted Adolescents," Journal of Educational Psychology 43:449-58; December 1952.

14. Brubacher, John S. Eclectic Philosophy of Education. Englewood Cliffs, New Jersey: Prentice-Hall, Inc. Second edition, 1962.

15. _____. Modern Philosophies of Education. New York: McGraw-Hill Book Company, Inc. Third edition, 1962.

16. Bunker, Herbert., "The Selective Character of the Active and Non-active Student in Physical Education," Journal of American Association of College Registrars 20:350-66; April 1945.

17. Chittenden, G. E., "An Experimental Study in Measuring and Modifying Assertive Behavior in Young Children," Monographs of Society for Research in Child Development 2; 1942.

18. Coleman, James S. The Adolescent Society. New York: Crowell-Collier Publishing Company, 1961.

19. Counts, G. Dare the Schools Build a New Social Order? New York: John Day, 1932.

20. Cowell, Charles C., "The Contributions of Physical Activity to Social Development," Research Quarterly, Vol. 31, No. 2, Part II:286-306; May 1960.

21. _____, "Physical Education as Applied Social Science," Educational Research Bulletin (The Ohio State University) 1:147-55; September 1937.

22. _____, "Student Purposes in High School Physical Education," Educational Research Bulletin (The Ohio State University) 18:89-92; April 1939.

23. _____, "Validating an Index of Social Adjustment for High School Use," Research Quarterly 29:7-18; March 1958.

24. Curti, Merle. The Social Ideas of American Educators. New York: Charles Scribner's Sons, 1935.

25. Dewey, John. Reconstruction in Philosophy. New York: Henry Holt and Company, 1920. (Revised edition, 1948).

26. Frank, Lawrence K., "Play in Personality Development," American Journal of Orthopsychiatry 25:576-90; October 1955.

27. Gallup, George. The Miracle Ahead. New York: Harper & Row, Publishers, 1964.

28. Gough, Harrison G., "Predicting Social Participation," Journal of Social Psychology 35:227-33; May 1952.

29. Greenburg, P. J., "Competition in Children: An Experimental Study," American Journal of Psychology 44:221-48; April 1932.

30. Gustad, John W., "Factors Associated with Social Behavior and Adjustment - A Review of the Literature," Educational and Psychological Measurements 12:3-19; Spring 1952.

31. Hansen, Kenneth H. Philosophy for American Education. Englewood Cliffs, New Jersey: Prentice-Hall, Inc., 1960.

32. Henry, Jules. Culture Against Man. New York: Random House, 1963.

33. Johnson, Warren R. and Hutton, Daniel C., "Effects of a Combative Sport Upon Personality Dynamics as Measured by a Projective Test," Research Quarterly 26:49-53; March 1955.

34. Kilpatrick. W. H. Education and the Social Crisis. New York: Liveright Publishing Company, 1932.

35. _____. Education for a Changing Civilization. New York: The Macmillan Company, 1926.

36. Kuhlen, Raymond G. and Collester, E. G., "Sociometric Status of Sixth and Ninth Graders Who Fail to Finish High School," Educational and Psychological Measurements 12:632-37; Fall 1952.

37. Laski, H. The American Democracy. New York: Viking Press, 1948.

38. Lewin, Kurt., "Experiments on Autocratic and Democratic Atmospheres," Social Frontiers 4:316-19; July 1938.

39. Malinowski, B. The Dynamics of Cultural Change. New Haven: Yale University Press, 1945.

40. _____. Sex, Culture, and Myth. New York: Harcourt, Brace & World, Inc., 1962.

41. May, Mark A. and Doob, Leonard., "Competition and Co-operation," Washington, D. C., National Social Science Research Council, Bulletin No. 25; April 1937.

42. Morland, Richard B., "A Philosophical Interpretation of the Educational Views Held by Seven Leaders in American Physical Education." Ph.D. dissertation, New York University, 1958. (Available through Microcard Publications, University of Oregon, Eugene).

43. Muller, Herbert J. The Uses of the Past. New York: Mentor Books, 1954.

44. Mumford, L. The Conduct of Life. New York: Harcourt, Brace & World, Inc., 1951.

45. Nedelsky, Ruth, "The Teacher's Role in the Peer Group During Middle Childhood," Elementary School Journal 52:325-34; February 1951.

46. Neill, A. S. Summerhill: A Radical Approach to Child Rearing. New York: Hart Publishing Co., 1960.

47. Nelson, G. A., "Personality and Attitude Differences Associated with the Elective Substitution of R.O.T.C. for the Physical Education Requirement in High School," Research Quarterly 19:2-17; March 1948.

48. Popp, James, "Case Studies of Sophomore High School Boys with High and Low Fitness Indices." Master's thesis, University of Oregon, 1959.

49. Pressey, S. L. and Hanna, David, "The Class as a Socio-Psychological Unit," Journal of Psychology 16:13-19; 1943.

50. Rarick, Lawrence and McKee, Robert, "A Study of Twenty Third-Grade Children Exhibiting Extreme Levels of Achievement on Tests of Motor Proficiency," Research Quarterly 20:142-52; May 1949.

51. Sayers, E. V. and Madden, Ward. Education and the Democratic Faith. New York: Appleton-Century-Crofts, 1959.

52. Shaw, C. Delinquency Areas. Chicago: University of Chicago Press, 1929.

53. Shugart, George, "The Play History: Its Application and Significance," Journal of Psychiatric Social Work 24:204-09; September 1955.

54. Symonds, Percival M., "Education for the Development of Personality," Teachers College Record 50:163-169; December 1948.

55. Taylor, Harold, "Portrait of a New Generation," Saturday Review, December 8, 1962, 10-12.

56. "The Contributions of Physical Activity to Human Well-Being," (R. A. Weiss, Chairman), Research Quarterly 31, 2, Part II; May 1960.

57. Thune, John B., "Personality of Weightlifters," Research Quarterly 20:296-306; October 1949.

58. Todd, Frances E., "Democratic Methodology in Physical Education." Doctoral dissertation, Stanford University, 1951.

59. _____, "Sociometry in Physical Education," JOHPER 24:23-24; May 1953.

60. Trapp, William G., "A Study of Social Integration in a College Football Squad," 56th Annual Proceedings. Washington, D. C.: College Physical Education Association, 1953.

61. VanderZwaag, Harold J., "Delineation of an Essentialistic Philosophy of Physical Education." Ph.D. dissertation, The University of Michigan, 1962.

62. Veblen, Thorstein. <u>The Theory of the Leisure Class</u>. New York: Random House Modern Library, 1934.

63. Walters, C. Etta, "A Sociometric Study of Motivated and Non-motivated Bowling Groups," <u>Research Quarterly</u> 26:107-12; March 1955.

64. Wattenberg, William W., "Factors Associated with Repeating Among Preadolescent Delinquents," <u>Journal of Genetic Psychology</u> 4:189-95; June 1954.

65. Wellman, Beth, "The School Child's Choice of Companions," <u>Journal of Educational Research</u> 14:126-32; September 1926.

66. Wells, Harold P., "Relationships Between Physical Fitness and Psychological Variables." Ph.D. dissertation, University of Illinois, 1958.

67. Whitehead, Alfred North. <u>Science and the Modern World</u>. New York: The New American Library, 1948. (Published originally in 1925.)

68. Witty, Paul, "An Analysis of the Personality Traits of the Effective Teacher," <u>Journal of Educational Psychology</u> 40:663; April 1947.

69. Zeigler, Earle F., "Implications from Experimentalism for Physical, Health, and Recreation Education," <u>The Physical Educator</u>, Vol. 20, No. 4:150-152; December 1963.

70. _____. <u>Philosophical Foundations for Physical, Health, and Recreation Education</u>. Englewood Cliffs, New Jersey: Prentice-Hall, Inc., 1964.

THE EDUCATIONAL PHILOSOPHY OF REALISM: IMPLI-CATIONS FOR PHYSICAL, HEALTH, AND RECREATION EDUCATION

The Nature of Reality (Metaphysics)

"The world exists in itself, apart from our desires and knowl-edges." There is only one reality; that which we perceive is it.[1] "The universe is made up of real substantial entities, existing in themselves and ordered to one another by extramental relations . . . To be is not the same as to be known . . ." Some feel that there is a basic unity present, while others believe in a non-unified cosmos with two or more substances or processes at work. Things don't just happen; they happen because many interrelated forces make them occur in a particular way. Man lives within this world of cause and effect, and he simply cannot make things happen independent of it.

Educational Aims and Objectives

"A philosophy holding that the aim of education is the acquisition of verified knowledge of the environment; recognizes the value of con-tent as well as the activities involved in learning, and takes into ac-count the external determinants of human benavior . . . Education is the acquisition of the art of the utilization of knowledge." The pri-mary task of education is to transmit knowledge, without which civil-ization cannot continue to flourish. Whatever man has discovered to be true because it conforms to reality must be handed down to future generations as the social or cultural tradition. Some holding this philosophy believe that the good life emanates from co-operation with God's grace and that development of the Christian virtues is obviously of greater worth than learning or anything else.

The Educative Process (Epistemology)

There are two major epistemological theories of knowledge in this position. One states that the aim of knowledge "is to bring into awareness the object as it really is." The other emphasizes that ob-jects are "represented" in man's consciousness, not "presented." Students should develop habits and skills involved with acquiring

---

[1] This explication was published in Physical Education: Pro-gressivism or Essentialism? (with H. J. VanderZwaag). Champaign, Illinois: Stipes Publishing Company, 1966.

knowledge, with using knowledge practically to meet life's problems, and with realizing the enjoyment that life offers. A second variation of epistemological belief indicates that the child develops his intellect by employing reason to learn a subject. The principal educational aim here must be the same for all men at all times in all places. Others carry this further and state that education is the process by which man seeks to link himself ultimately with his Creator.

Health, Physical Education, and Recreation (Aims and Objectives)

I believe in the development of physical vigor and health. There is no question in my mind but that the school should provide "an atmosphere conducive to both emotional and physical health." Furthermore, "knowledge about the principles of physical and emotional health is a proper ingredient of the curriculum." I believe that the community does have a responsibility to provide "clinical facilities for therapy, but this does not mean that they are part of the school program or curriculum any more than are the boilers in heating systems." I assert that the home must have the complete responsibility for assisting youth to acquire desirable health habits--that is, unless we wish to establish some form of community youth organizations to accomplish this end. "The health of adolescents is for the most part too good and their sources of energy are too great to make health problems real to them." In similar vein, sex education is certainly not a proper function of the school. Is it not logical that teaching of the means for securing the health values would be incomplete anyhow until the perspective from which they are viewed is also taught; this perspective is found only in the humanities--in literature, art, religion, and philosophy. In summary, therefore, every person needs a basic core of knowledge in order to lead a human life, and this includes the learning of health knowledge. This is consistent with the central purpose of the school--the development of the individual's rational powers.

I believe that education "of the physical" should have primary emphasis in our field. I am concerned with the development of physical vigor, and such development should have priority over the recreational aspects of physical education. Many people, who believe in the same educational philosophy as I do, recommend that all students in public schools should have a daily period designed to strengthen their muscles and develop their bodily co-ordination. Physical education, of course, must yield precedence to intellectual education. I give "qualified approval" to interscholastic athletics since they do help with the learning of sportsmanship and desirable social conduct if properly conducted. But all these things, with the possible exception of physical training, are definitely extra-curricular and not part of the regular curriculum.

As I see it, work and play are typically sharply differentiated in life. Play serves a most useful purpose at recess or after school, but it should not be part of the regular curriculum. I believe that the use of leisure is significant to the development of our culture, but I realize today that "winning the Cold War" is going to take a lot more hard work and somewhat less leisure. I see leisure pursuits or experience as an opportunity to get relief from work while it serves a re-creative purpose in the life of man. The surplus energy theory of play and recreation makes sense to me. So does the more recent bio-social theory of play--the idea that play helps the organism to achieve balance. I feel that the "play attitude" is missing almost completely in many organized sports. Play (and recreation) is, therefore, very important to me; I believe it should be "liberating" to the individual. People can develop their potentialities for wholesome hobbies through recreation. Furthermore, recreation can serve as a "safety valve" by the reduction of the psychic tensions which are evidently caused by so many of life's typical stresses. Even though play should not be considered as a basic part of the curriculum, we should not forget that it provides an "indispensable seasoning" to the good life. Extra-curricular play and recreational activities and a sound general education should suffice to equip the student for leisure activities in our society.

THE EDUCATIONAL PHILOSOPHY OF IDEALISM: IMPLICATIONS FOR PHYSICAL, HEALTH, AND RECREATION EDUCATION

The Nature of Reality (Metaphysics)

Mind as experienced by all men is basic and real.[1] The entire universe is mind essentially. Man is more than just a body; he possesses a soul, and such possession makes him of a higher order than all other creatures on earth. "The order of the world is due to the manifestation in space and time of an eternal and spiritual reality." The individual is part of the whole, and it is man's task to learn as much about the Absolute as possible. There is divided opinion within this position regarding the problem of monism or pluralism. Man has freedom to determine which way he shall go in life; he can relate to the moral law in the universe, or he can turn against it.

Educational Aims and Objectives

Through education the developing organism becomes what it latently is. All education may be said to have a religious significance, which means that there is a "moral imperative" on education. As man's mind strives to realize itself, there is the possibility of realization of the Absolute within the individual mind. Education should aid the child to adjust to the basic realities (the spiritual ideals of truth, beauty, and goodness) that the history of the race has furnished us. The basic values of human living are health, character, social justice, skill, art, love, knowledge, philosophy, and religion.

The Educative Process (Epistemology)

Understanding the nature of knowledge will clarify the nature of reality. Nature is the medium by which God communicates to us. Basically, knowledge comes only from the mind--a mind which must offer and receive ideas. Mind and matter are qualitatively different. A finite mind emanates through heredity from another finite mind. All finite minds are "materializations" of an infinite mind. Thought is the standard by which all else in the world is judged. An individual attains truth for himself by examining the wisdom of the past through

---

[1] This explication was published in Physical Education: Progressivism or Essentialism? (with H. J. VanderZwaag). Champaign, Illinois: Stipes Publishing Company, 1966.

his own mind. Reality, viewed in this way, is a system of logic and order that has been established by the Universal Mind. Experimental testing helps to determine what the truth really is.

Health, Physical Education, and Recreation (Aims and Objectives)

I believe that health is a basic value of human living and that the truly educated individual should be "physically fit," should live "near the maximum of his efficiency," and should have "a body which is the ready servant of his will." But even though I believe health is a basic value for all the others, I would have to place it at the bottom of the hierarchy of educational values. Worship must be placed at the top, because through it man is brought "into conscious relation to the infinite spirit of the universe . . . ." Thus it would probably not be included in a listing of the "essential studies" of the curriculum except when it would be included incidentally under biology. I am interested, however, in "building wholeness of mind and body, the development of strong, healthy bodies, good habits of mental and physical health, and the right start in the teaching of health, safety, and physical education to children." There is no question in my mind but that educators should work for a larger measure of integration in the individual by promoting "more intensive study of the body, leading to scientific knowledge: anatomy, body chemistry, hygiene, physiology, etc.; and attention to sex characteristics and habits, leading to a greater understanding of the place of sex in human life, with implications for hygiene . . . ." But such knowledge is made available to boys and girls, and to young men and women, as a "service" program in the schools--a service to man, and through this contribution to his health he is enabled to pursue higher educational goals.

I am extremely interested in individual personality development. I believe in education "of the physical," and yet I believe in education "through the physical" as well. Nevertheless, I do see physical education as important but occupying a "lower rung on the educational ladder." I believe that desirable objectives for physical education would include the development of responsible citizenship and group participation. In competitive sport, I believe that the transfer of training theory is in operation in connection with the development of desirable personality traits, but sports participation should always be a means and not an end.

I believe that the role of play and recreation in the development of personality and the "perfectly integrated individual" is looming larger with each passing year and that it has not been fully understood or appreciated in the past. For this reason it seems quite logical to me that education should reassess the contributions that recreation and play do make in the education of man. The self-expression theory of play suggests that man's chief need in life is to achieve the satisfaction and accomplishment of self-expression of one's own personality. Here is an explanation that seems to consider quite fully the conception of man as an organic unity--a total organism. That there is a need for educational research along these lines is self-evident.

I believe that man is a purposive being who is striving to achieve those values which are embedded in reality itself. To the extent that we can realize the eternal values through the choice of the right kinds of play and recreation without flouting the moral order in the world, we should be progressive enough to disregard a dualistic theory of work and play. Another difficulty that confronts us is differentiating between physical education and recreation. Recreation has developed to the point where it is now one of our major social institutions. I believe that recreation can make a contribution to the development of an "integrated individual in an integrated society growing in the image of the integrated universe." Mankind today is actually faced with a "recreational imperative."

CHRISTIAN IDEALISM AT WORK IN Y.M.C.A. HEALTH AND PHYSICAL EDUCATION

In 1851, a mere seven years after the founding of the Young Men's Christian Association by George Williams in London, England, in 1844, the Boston Young Men's Christian Association was origi- nated.[1] Certain aims and objectives were expressed as follows:

> a social organization of those in whom the love of Christ has produced love to men; who shall meet the young stranger as he enters our city, take him by the hand, direct him to a boardinghouse where he may find a quiet home provided with Christian influence, introduce him to the church and Sabbath School, and in every way associate him with good influence.[2]

In 1965, over one hundred years later, there are undoubtedly many who would argue that any relationship between the goals of the origi- nal Y.M.C.A. and today's typical organization is purely coincidental. If this statement be true, or even partially true, we must ask our- selves about the realization of objectives of a Christian idealistic character in today's institution, and especially through the medium of the health and physical education program.

Characteristics of the Y.M.C.A.

Historically and constitutionally, of course, the Young Men's Christian Association has always proclaimed its intention to develop Christian character. We recognize further that it is primarily a pri- vate membership organization, which has been financed chiefly by private and subscription funds. It has been a layman's movement, a movement that has tradition and experience, and that has made exten- sive use of volunteer and lately part-time leadership. Furthermore, it has been quite democratic in that it is governed by a board of management or directors elected by members. A basic aim has been

---

[1] A paper delivered to the Illinois Area Congress on Health and Physical Education, Rockford, Illinois, May 15, 1965. (Published in the Journal of Physical Education as Part I, Vol. 64, No. 6:163- 165 (1967). Also, as Part II, in Vol. 64, No. 7:28-31 (1967). Dr. Zeigler was active in YMCA work for more than forty years.

[2] H. Hopkins. History of the Y.M.C.A. in America. (New York: The Association Press, 1951), p. 18.

to develop leadership through small group work. By its very nature, the Y.M.C.A. has been free to pioneer in new fields and directions. One of these directions has been to develop national and international committees to promote its general and specific goals.

With these statements serving as an introduction, we should now turn to the main theme of this paper--the background, status, and definition of Idealism, especially Christian Idealism, and the subsequent implications of this philosophical and theological position for life, education, and health, physical education, and recreation in the Western world. This is especially important, indeed vital, to all those who are concerned with the Y.M.C.A. Movement and the ways in which it can influence the lives of its members, and indirectly life in America today.

Brief Background of Idealism

The idealistic tradition in philosophy started with Plato (427-347 B.C.), developed with the Hebrew-Christian tradition in religion, and was consolidated through the efforts of Descartes, Spinoza, Leibniz, Berkeley, Kant, Hegel, and a host of nineteenth and twentieth century idealistic philosophers.[3]

There seems to be fairly general consensus on the belief that early Christianity had exerted a negative influence on sport and certain excesses. But there is considerable evidence that this situation began to change about one hundred years ago. Johnson points out that:

> Leaders in the Young Men's Christian Association movement just after the middle of the nineteenth century realized that physical education and athletics were very attractive to young men. Their objectives mentioned the improvement of physical status (as well as spiritual, mental, and social status). An idealistic concept of physical education became apparent as man was viewed as an organic unity. Athletic activity in YMCA gymnasia was believed to exert a definite influence on the development of Christian character.[4]

---

[3] Earle F. Zeigler, Philosophical Foundations for Physical, Health, and Recreation Education. (Englewood Cliffs, New Jersey: Prentice-Hall, Inc., 1964), pp. 30-36.

[4] Elmer Johnson, "A History of Physical Education in the Young Men's Christian Association." (Ph.D. dissertation, University of Southern California, 1954), pp. 47 and 89.

Down through the years of the twentieth century there is ample evidence that health and physical education programs in YMCA's has developed significantly. Johnson designated the period from 1870 to 1890 as "The Era of Gymnasium Building," the years from 1890 to 1910 as "The Age of Gulick," the period from 1910 to 1930 as the "Pre-War and Post War Eras," and from 1930 to the present as "The Modern Era."[5] In this last period he explains that "personality development replaced character education; the concept of transfer was challenged; and social dancing and group techniques were introduced . . ."[6] Evidently "progressive" thinkers sought to alter physical education to bring it more in line with democratic educational concepts. McCloy, the late professor of physical education at the State University of Iowa, believed that the YMCA got so educational that "it departed from the practice of emphasizing the physical in man," and thereby "was troubled with turnover and lack of interest."[7] Outstanding professional leaders like Dr. T. K. Cureton, Jr., of the University of Illinois, have reaffirmed the importance of physical fitness in the past few decades.

Idealism on the Wane?

Protestant Christian Idealism, although a certain percentage of our citizenry would deny this most vehemently, appears to be gradually declining as a major influence in our society today. Despite the fact that membership rosters of churches appear to be increasing in size, there are over eighty million people in the United States who don't even nominally belong to any religious organization. The results of the latest gallup survey show that an increasingly larger proportion of the nation's adults feel that religion is losing its influence, that average church attendance is falling off, that younger adults are more pessimistic about religion's influence on American society, and that there is an increasing trend toward secularization with religion's apparent inability to solve moral, social, and economic problems. Many students are saying that church participation is unnecessary for life fulfillment.[8] It may be said, therefore, with considerable accuracy that the powerful force of a realism that is strongly materialistic has threatened America's idealistic superstructure to such an extent that it has been said that "traditional philosophic idealism, in all of

---

[5] Ibid.

[6] Ibid., p. 497.

[7] Charles H. McCloy. Philosophical Bases for Physical Education. (New York: Appleton-Century-Crofts, Inc., 1940), p. 96.

[8] "Religious Influence Seen Waning," Champaign-Urbana Courier, April 20, 1965.

its numerous variants, is probably obsolescent if not already obsolete."[9] As profoundly disturbing as the above statement might be to a Christian Idealist in a Y.M.C.A. setting, he would probably concur in the belief that it is necessary for America to build (or rebuild) its spiritual core to meet this ominous challenge in the second half of the twentieth century.

Who would state forthrightly and assuredly that Y.M.C.A. health and physical education programs are of such calibre in this realm of Christian Idealism that they are making a significant contribution toward helping to "turn this tide" even with their own members? Why can this question be asked? Are the sociological influences so strong that Y.M.C.A.'s are powerless with their efforts? This may be true, but the answer will never be known unless something aggressively positive is planned, organized, directed, co-ordinated, and controlled in regard to Christian Idealistic influence in Association health and physical education programs.

The Nature of Reality (Metaphysics)

Initially, from the standpoint of metaphysics, idealists believe generally that mind (or spirit) as experienced by all men is basic and real; the entire universe is mind essentially. Man is more than just a body; he possesses a soul, and such possession makes him of a higher order than all other creatures on earth. "The order of the world is due to the manifestation in space and time of an eternal and spiritual reality." The individual is part of the whole, and it is man's task to learn as much about the Absolute as possible. There is divided opinion within this position regarding the problem of monism or pluralism. Man has freedom to determine which way he shall go in life, he can relate to the moral law in the universe, or he can turn against it.[10]

Educational Aims and Objectives

Through education the developing organism becomes what it latently is. All education may be said to have a religious significance, which means that there is a "moral imperative" on education. As man's mind strives to realize itself, there is the possibility of realization of the Absolute within the individual mind. Education should aid the child to adjust to the basic realities (the spiritual ideals of truth, beauty, and goodness) that the history of the race has

---

[9] Kenneth H. Hansen. Philosophy for American Education. (Englewood Cliffs, New Jersey: Prentice-Hall, Inc., 1960), p. 45.

[10] Zeigler, op. cit., pp. 311-316.

furnished us. The basic values of human living are health, character, social justice, skill, art, love, knowledge, philosophy, and religion.

The Educative Process (Epistemology)

Understanding the nature of knowledge will clarify the nature of reality. Nature is the medium by which the Absolute communicates to us. Basically, knowledge comes only from the mind--a mind which must offer and receive ideas. Mind and matter are qualitatively different. A finite mind emanates through heredity from another finite mind. Thought is the standard by which all else in the world is judged. An individual attains truth for himself by examining the wisdom of the past through his own mind. Reality, viewed in this way, is a system of logic and order that has been established by the Universal Mind. Experimental testing helps to determine what the truth really is.

Values in Health Education

The idealist believes that health is a basic value of human living and that the truly educated individual should be "physically fit," should live "near the maximum of his efficiency," and should have "a body which is the ready servant of his will." But even though he believes health is a basic value for all the others, he would have to place it at the bottom of the hierarchy of educational values. Worship must be placed at the top, because through it man is brought "into conscious relation to the infinite spirit of the universe. . . ." Thus, it would not be included in a listing of the "essential studies" of a program except where it would probably be included incidentally under biology. However, he is interested in "building wholeness of mind and body," "the development of strong, healthy bodies, good habits of mental and physical health," "and the right start in the teaching of health, safety, and physical education to children." There is no question in his mind but that educators should work for a larger measure of integration in the individual by promoting "more intensive study of the body, leading to scientific knowledge: anatomy, body chemistry, hygiene, physiology, etc.; and attention to sex characteristics and habits, leading to a greater understanding of the place of sex in human life, with implications for hygiene . . . ." But such knowledge is made available to boys and girls, and young men and women, as a "service" program in the schools--a service is provided to man, and through this contribution to this health he is enabled to pursue higher educational goals.

Values in Physical Education

The idealist is extremely interested in individual personality development. He believes in education "of the physical," and yet he believes in education "through the physical" as well. Nevertheless, he does see physical education as important but occupying a "lower rung on the educational ladder." He believes that desirable objectives for physical education would include the development or responsible citizenship and group participation. In competitive sport, he believes that the transfer of training theory is in operation in connection with the development of desirable personality traits, but sports participation should always be a means not an end.

Values in Recreation (Education)

The idealist believes that the role of play and recreation in the development of personality and the "perfectly integrated individual" is looming larger with each passing year and that it has not been fully understood or appreciated in the past. For this reason it seems quite logical to him that education should reassess the contributions that recreation and play do make in the education of man. That there is a need for educational research along these lines is self-evident. He believes further that we should examine very closely any theories of play and recreation which grant educational possibilities to these activities of man. The self-expression theory of play suggests that man's chief need in life is to achieve the satisfaction and accomplishment of self-expression of one's own personality. Here is an explanation that seems to consider quite fully the conception of man as an organic unity--a total organism. He believes that man is a purposive being who is striving to achieve those values which are embedded in reality itself. To the extent that we can realize the eternal values through the choice of the right kinds of play and recreation without flouting the moral order in the world, we should be progressive enough to disregard a dualistic theory of work and play. Another difficulty that confronts us is differentiating between physical education and recreation. Recreation has developed to the point where it is now clearly one of our major social institutions. He believes that recreation can make a contribution to the development of an "integrated individual in an integrated society growing in the image of the integrated universe." Mankind today is actually faced with a "recreational imperative."

The Physical Director's Responsibility

But let us shift our focus to the individual YMCA physical director. This person, it would appear, has a responsibility to become fully aware of the implications of Christian idealism and then to examine himself and to construct his own personal philosophy so that he may become an effective professional person within this framework. At first glance the average physical director may not see the need for such a disciplined approach. He may well argue that he hasn't got time to be bothered with any sort of a detailed analysis, and that he is already serving the YMCA Movement quite effectively. His argument quite often is that he possesses a certain amount of common sense and that this has proven quite satisfactory. This is a fairly difficult argument to overcome, especially if the individual has achieved considerable success through his efforts. The method is actually fairly sound, because problems of an everyday nature in the association can be met by using this common sense. He is operating, along with his fellow secretaries, on the basis of certain underlying beliefs--a sort of a "theoretical group bias" toward organized Christianity. To this extent, therefore, it may be said that YMCA secretaries do have a philosophy of Christian education.[11]

The premise here, of course, is that any such person may increase his influence and effectiveness by the achievement of a Christian idealistic philosophy--one that is as consistent and logical as possible in keeping with the individual's background and experience. So, the rebuttal is that the common sense system of deciding problems breaks down when extended planning is necessary, and certainly planning of an idealistic nature appears to be vital as we face the many persistent and recurring problems of the second half of the twentieth century. We might through analogy liken the YMCA physical director using the common sense approach to an automobile moving along in second gear with the attendant stresses caused by continual progress in such a manner. In fact, a careful analysis of such "progress" might even indicate that the car is swaying from side to side all over the road. The question is how we can get the car to shift into high gear, or possibly into overdrive, and follow a straight course. We contend that YMCA health and physical education needs a great many more people who are truly operating in "high gear" rather than in "second" or even, as occasionally appears to be the case, in "low."

Conservative versus Liberal Positions

Another extremely important consideration is that there is a range of belief existing even within Christian idealistic philosophy of education--from the extremely conservative to the extremely liberal position, or from the philosophy of the educational traditionalist to that of the educational progressivist. Keep in mind that the educational traditionalist believes that there are certain educational values by which the individual must be guided, that effort takes precedence

---

[11] Ibid., pp. 247-253.

over interest and that this girds moral stamina, that the experience of the past has powerful jurisdiction over the present, and that the cultivation of the intellect is most important in education. The progressivistic idealist, although he does believe in the idealistic tenets of truth, beauty, and goodness relative to realization of the good life, is greatly concerned about individual personality development, the opportunity for the member to be free and to follow his interests, and that health and physical education should be strongly related to life in the present. The more conservative and traditional individual in the YMCA would tend to relegate health and physical education to lower status in the hierarchy of values, whereas the liberal and progressivistic secretary or layman would emphasize the absolute necessity of health and physical education assuming an integral role in the YMCA program.

International Influence of the YMCA

The Young Men's Christian Association has exerted a significant influence throughout the world on health, physical education, and recreation. This influence has emanated from an idealistic base, the tenets of which were expressed clearly:

> The conceptions of the various faiths and philosophies regarding the human body are as numerous as sand is plentiful on the beach. There are all shades of opinions-- from the cenception 'the body is divine' to the other extreme, 'the body is evil.' The YMCA is neither a religion nor a philosophy. It is a movement which from the very beginning has left no doubt as to how it regarded the human body: as a living reality, as a part of the great whole-- mind, body, spirit. Just as the Movement itself has achieved such success in the age of urban civilization, so also this conception was so sound that it has proved and maintained its value right up to the middle of our own century.[12]

In 1960 the theme of the World YMCA Consultation on Health and Physical Education, held at Rome in connection with the Olympic games, was "Health and Physical Education--YMCA Practice and Purpose." At this important meeting, delegates from twenty-one national YMCA's in all five continents heard discussions from outstanding leaders of the movement concerning purpose and practice. Steinhaus explained that "the concept of the mind-body-spirit unity of

---

[12] "Physical Education, Sport, and Recreation," World Communiqué (January-February 1961), p. 3.

man is today a basic tenet of all sciences dealing with man, and also on education." Because of this, he stated his belief that "every impact of man on man or of programme on man invariably does influence in some way man's body, man's mind, man's spirit."[13] Steinhaus means in this statement that a physical activity leaves its influence on the whole man, and there is a strong inference that the leader has a great deal to do with whether this influence is for good or for bad.

Limbert Explains Central Emphases

Paul Limbert, Secretary General of the World Alliance of YMCA's, speaking at the Rome consultation clarified the reason for the hierarchy of values in Christian idealism in the following statement:

> The central emphasis of Christian faith is not on development of the individual as such but on equipment for service, both to God and man. Focus on the development of physical strength or athletic prowess runs the risk of self-centeredness; that which should be a means to an end becomes an end in itself, an 'idol.' Too much attention to personal development as such tends toward pride and self-righteousness.[14]

He pointed out that "the YMCA's emphasis on health and physical education is rooted in a Christian understanding of man and his world." He asked the question, "How could the objectives of health and physical education in the YMCA be rephrased to show more clearly how this programme is grounded in Christian faith?" He continued by asking YMCA leaders to work for a larger measure of integration in the individual by promoting "more intensive study of the body, leading to scientific knowledge: anatomy, body chemistry, hygiene, physiology, etc.; and attention to sex characteristics and habits, leading to a greater understanding of the place of sex in human life, with implications for hygiene."[15]

---

[13] Ibid., p. 9.

[14] Paul M. Limbert, "Physical Education as an Integral Part of YMCA Programme." A paper presented at the Fifth World YMCA Consultation on Health and Physical Education, Rome, September 12-14, 1960. Summarized in World Communiqué (January-February 1961).

[15] Ibid.

Friermood Lists Five Objectives

In another important paper presented at Rome, Harold T. Friermood, U. S. National YMCA Secretary for Physical Education, assessed the role of physical education as an integral part of the YMCA program. He listed the five objectives for physical education which appeared in a publication resulting from a two-year study in the United States:

1. Development of health and physical fitness
2. Education for leisure
3. Personality adjustment (learning to live with self and others)
4. Development of responsible citizenship and group participation
5. Development of a philosophy of life based on Christian ideals.[16]

Pointing out that "people are more important than the program tools," he explained that "things can happen in the life of a person that are just as significant for him in the gymnasium, in the locker room, or on a hike as in a bible clas."[17]

Avoid Overemphasis Says Jones

R. W. Jones of the United Kingdom, director of the UNESCO Youth Institute, sounded a warning at Rome concerning "growing specialization" in sport. He explained his feeling that overemphasis in international sport would tend to have deleterious effects on personality growth as follows:

The growing specialization tends to reduce the interest of people who aee concerned for the whole personality of the participant. The mechanics become more important than the competitors. The rules are beoming more important than the participant. More notice is being taken of making sport a spectacle for the spectator than the effect of the play on the player.[18]

---

[16] A New Look at YMCA Physical Education. (New York: Association Press, 1959). As mentioned in Friermood's mimeographed articles.

[17] World Communiqué (January-February 1961), p. 9. Quoting H. T. Friermood.

[18] Ibid., p. 10.

Teaching Method in Christian Idealism

At this juncture we shall turn to a brief consideration of teaching with more of a Christian idealistic emphasis. Limbert felt that the leader should emphasize the concept of "equipment for service, both to God and man."[19] Jones was troubled by "the growing specialization that tends to reduce the interest of people who are concerned for the whole personality of the participant. The mechanics become more important than the competitors."[20] Steinhaus stressed the idea that "every impact of man on man or of programme on man invariably does influence in some way man's body, man's mind, man's spirit. This is the most important truth which I would bring to your attention."[21] Friermood continued with this idealistic emphasis when he postulated that "the chief considerations are how the tools are used in serving human needs and in helping persons see clearly and be guided in the Christian principles fostered by the organization."[22] This concept of the importance of the leader in developing individual personality growth was reiterated further by Limbert as he explained how method must be broadened and widened as follows:

> The leader must not only be able to teach specific skills
> and impart technical knowledge, he must be alert to oppor-
> tunities for developing related interests, leading into deep-
> er understandings which involve a wide range of human
> experience.[23]

Christian education definitely places firm emphasis on the need for the Christian physical educator and coach to so arrange his teaching and/or coaching that ethical conduct is fostered:

> The development of ethical conduct is more easily taught at
> the elementary and secondary levels but is part of the
> value of physical education in college. The attributes of
> team work, perseverance, courage, respect for law and
> order are all part of all Christian education, but games and
> sports contribute to their development through direct and
> dramatic means.[24]

---

[19] Ibid.

[20] Ibid.

[21] Ibid.

[22] Ibid.

[23] Ibid.

[24] Barney Steen, "Physical Education at Calvin College," The Banner, XCVI, No. 35 (September 1, 1961), 11.

Five Possible Stages of Development

That there is a need within the field of health, physical education, and recreation for some common denominators seems self-evident. YMCA physical directors have used common sense, to be sure, but have used philosophical analysis only rarely. Finding areas of agreement, without destroying the unique qualities of Christian idealism, can do much to sharpen the image of our field in the minds of many of the members of our associations.

You may find that you have been in the "ostrich stage" up to now --that is, you may have "buried your head in the sand" and refused to allow yourself to become aware of the conflicting philosophies within education or within your specialized field.[25]

Or perhaps you have climbed the ladder a bit further and are at the "cafeteria stage," which involves selecting some of this and some of that which looks "appetizing" for your "philosophical fare." This eclectic approach has a great deal of appeal initially, but there is strong evidence that it is generally regarded as philosophically indefensible. It may, of course, be one stage on the way up the ladder.

The third rung of the ladder is a popular place. This may be called the "fence-sitter stage" or level. Here we find people who have matured a bit more and are inclining in one direction or another. But beyond that they seem unwilling to go. Are they lazy, afraid of the consequences of a determined stand, or "organization men"?

Perhaps you will rise, or have risen, to the fourth rung on this "philosophical ladder." This we may call the "stage of early maturity." At this point the individual educator has wrestled with himself and his environment and has achieved a quality of unity or harmony which is characteristic of a philosophical position that is reasonably logical and consistent in its various departments. He is able to justify his convictions intellectually to the extent that scientific knowledge, and perhaps faith, can assist him. As a result he has developed strong attitudes that are reflected in the moral ardor of his personal and professional life.

Hopefully, as we mature still further, we will achieve wisdom as well as mere knowledge. If we do, we may arrive at a "stage of philosophical maturity." This level of professional development can come from a broad, sound experience, diligent study, and ordered reflection. At this level on the ladder, we most certainly realize the unique aspects of our own position and the importance of a continuing

---

[25] Zeigler, op. cit., pp. 292-293.

search for truth, however we may define it. And yet we should be tolerant of others and their beliefs, realizing that a sincere effort should be made to increase the boundaries of the areas of consensus if possible.

The philosophic quest is a never-ending one. You won't suddenly find, at some advanced stage of your development, all of the answers to the problems which have been perplexing you. But you will be leading a greatly enriched life that may truly be an "adventure of ideas." The field of physical, health, and recreation education has a truly unique contribution to make in the lives of men. Your philosophical position will enable you to live up to the highest standards of your profession. A career in YMCA health and physical education can be a true vocation, if each of us strives to help people realize all values that a life of Christian idealism has to offer.

THE EDUCATIONAL PHILOSOPHY OF EXISTENTIALISM:
IMPLICATIONS FOR PHYSICAL, HEALTH, AND RECREATION
EDUCATION

The Nature of Reality (Metaphysics)

The world of material objects extended in mathematical space
with only quantitative and measurable properties is not the world we
live in as human beings; our world is a human world not a world of
science.[1] From the context of the human world all the abstractions
of science derive their meaning ultimately. Man is first and foremost a concrete involvement within the world, and we distinguish the
opposed poles of body and mind. Existence precedes essence; man
decides his own fate. His self-transcendence distinguishes him from
all other animals, and he cannot be understood in his totality by the
natural sciences. Truth is expressed in art and religion, as well as
in science. Time and history are fundamental dimensions of human
existence. The basic human task is for man to become an authentic
individual in his own right. Life's present conditions can be transformed by man, an animal, who stands open to the future. (Quoted
material by W. Barrett)

Educational Aims and Objectives

The existentialist is cognizant of the fact that the socialization
of the child has become equally as important as his intellectual development as a key educational aim in this century. He is concerned,
however, because the leading educational theories "see" the young as
"things to be worked over in some fashion to bring them into alignment with a prior notion of what they should be." Even the Experimentalists seem to have failed in their effort to bring "the learner
into a self-determining posture." Also, if there is general agreement
that a set of fundamental dispositions is to be formed, should the
criterion used for the evaluation of the worth of individual dispositions
be "public rather than a personal and private criterion?" "If education is to be truly human, it must somehow awaken awareness in the
learner - existential awareness of himself as a single subjectivity in
the world." Students should "constantly, freely, baselessly, and
creatively" choose their individual pattern of education. The subjectivity of the existentialistic learner should thrive in the arts (music,

---

[1] Published in the Illinois News Health, Physical Education, and
Recreation, Vol. 14, No. 1:9-10 (1966).

painting, poetry, and creative writing, etc.), but similar possibilities to study human motivation are available in the social sciences as well. (Quoted material by Van Cleve Morris)

The Educative Process (Epistemology)

Childhood is viewed as a "pre-Existential phase of human life." About the time of puberty in the individual, there is an "Existential Moment" in the young person's subjective life. It is the time of the "onset of the self's awareness of its own existing." For the first time, the "individual sees himself as responsible for his own conduct." Then, and only then, "education must become an act of discovery." The learner's experience must be such that he gets "personally implicated in the subject-matter and in the situation around him." Knowledge must be "chosen, i.e., appropriated, before it can be true for that consciousness." It isn't something that is objective purely, nor is it merely purposeful in the person's life. Knowledge "becomes knowledge only when a subjectivity takes hold of it and puts it into his own life." It could be argued that "the Existentialist has little to offer in the way of a method of knowing." Whether we are considering logic, scientific evidence, sense perception, intuition, or revelation, "it is the individual self which must make the ultimate decision as to what is, as a matter of fact, true." Perceptually and cognitiviely, the individual is aware of the objects of existence, but there is something more--an "internal, subjective awareness"-- which enables him to know that he knows. Psychology seems to have given very few answers about this latter phase of the epistemological process to-date. (Quoted material by Van Cleve Morris)

Physical, Health, and Recreation Education (Aims and Objectives)

This field ahould strive to fulfill a role in the general educational pattern of arts and sciences. The goal is total fitness--not just physical fitness--with a balance between activities emphasizing competition and cooperation. The concept of "universal man" is paramount, but we must allow the individual the opportunity to choose for himself based on self-evaluation knowledge, skills, and attitudes. We should help the child who is "authentically eccentric" feel at home in the physical education activities program. We should further devise opportunities for youth to commit themselves to values and people. An important question in sport and athletics is how may we preserve the individual's authenticity in individual, dual, and team sports where winning is so often overemphasized. In sport, as opposed to competitive athletics, a person may personally select the values he derives from activity. We should play, therefore, for actualization of self--an attempt to use the sport for our own purposes. Physical activities such as modern dance, in which the opportunity for creativity is so important, should be stressed.

The educational process itself should be natural--a give-and-take situation. The student should be allowed to observe and to inquire freely. Freedom is most important, but the teacher is needed as the student can't teach himself. A good teacher should show passion, but he should not be egocentric nor too biased about a system or a point of view. He should be completely dedicated to the search for truth and to the need to develop a "self-moving" individual. Typically, the search for truth is an individual matter, but majority opinion should be tested when action is needed in a group situation. The student should develop an "orderly mind"; he should be willing to debate issues; and he should strive to be creative. Education has not been successful, it the student becomes a "carbon copy" of his teacher. This methodology should characterize the physical educator's teaching and coaching.

In regard to health and recreation education, much of which has been stated above should apply. The child must develop an awareness of the need for self-education about the various aspects of personal and community health. Controversial issues should never be avoided. All types of recreational needs and interests should be met through recreation education. One function of play is personal liberation and release. All sorts of group recreational activities are fine, and have a place, but opportunities for individual expression should not be downgraded. (A few ideas here have been borrowed from R. Harper.)

THE PERSISTENT PROBLEMS OF SPORT AND PHYSICAL ACTIVITY IN EDUCATION: AN AGNOSTIC, EXISTENTIALISTIC INTERPRETATION

Introduction*

This analysis and interpretation of some of the persistent prob-lems of sport and physical activity in education in the light of an "ag-nostic, existentialistic interpretation" has been carried out sincerely, optimistically, and humbly. This writer has undoubtedly exhibited a strong pragmatic orientation and inclination over the years--a phi-losophical stance that has been satisfying to him, and which includes the belief that the search for truth involves never-ending scientific investigation as it is "wrought through experience." It has become in-creasingly obvious to him, however, that what is perhaps best called existential philosophy has something truly worthwhile to offer to edu-cation in these most difficult times.

The results of this investigation are offered cautiously (1) be-cause it is dangerous to state unequivocally that "a metaphysical and/or epistemological position has logical implications for educational theory and practice" (Hook, 1956, p. 145); (2) because it has been stated that "Existentialism is not a philosophy but a label for several widely different revolts against traditional philosophy" (Kaufmann, 1956, p. 1); and (3) because the writer always approaches his work keeping firmly in mind what C. S. Peirce has designated as an atti-tude of "fallibilism"--the underlying belief that knowledge is never absolute.

It would serve no purpose here to dwell at length on the world's ills. Those persistent and devastating problems of mankind repre-sented by The Four Horsemen of the Apocalypse are still present in the 1970's despite the high hopes expressed earlier in this century by some who encouraged involvement in the "war to end all wars." A "Fifth Horseman" now plaguing most nations in the world may be designated as "galloping" inflation, a vital issue with which countries and their leaders seem unable to cope successfully. The "clock won't turn back," but who is ready to "face the morrow" and the many high-ly serious problems that it will bring?

---

* A paper presented to the Eighth Annual Meeting of the Cana-dian Association of Sport Sciences, Edmonton, Alberta, October 2, 1974.

In this difficult and trying period, there is an uneasy mood prevailing in education at all levels on this continent and, for that matter, throughout the entire West as well. The importance of a sound general or liberal education has been decried, and its ideals have seemingly been deserted by the young. The revolutionary mood of the 1960's may have subsided to a considerable extent, but the relatively placid, "cud-chewing contentment" of the 1970's is equally as frightening to those who ponder over the frightening apparitions hazily delineated by the naysayers for the future. Today's students seem imbued with a sense of urgency regarding the transmission of types of professional knowledge that will bring about quick assimilation into the community and at least a reasonably high standard of living.

The West, with its increasing emphasis on participatory democracy, is struggling for its very existence and future against very large world cultures in which the schools are providing a type of historic dynamism based on dictatorial and didactic philosophic and/ or religious thought that prescribes the exact route and all of the signposts to the establishment of a broad integrating culture that in due time would literally rule the world. Kaplan, in the face of these present juggernauts with supporting authoritarian ideologies (such as Russia and China), counters by stating that he has, on the basis of examination, discovered certain recurring "themes" of rationality, activism, humanism, and preoccupation with values in the leading world philosophies today (1961, pp. 7-10). In the 1970's, however, it does appear to be increasingly difficult to make a case for a strong, vital "integrating ideological unity" in the West (Wild, 1956, pp. 180-181). Somehow people in the West--if they truly wish to preserve the vaunted "individual freedom" about which they boast with regularity--will need to devise educational methods and techniques consistent with democracy's way of life that will result in marked improvement of the inculcation of such a value orientation indelibly in the minds and hearts of their youth.

Could a carefully planned, serious, but yet spontaneous encounter with the stark challenge of existential philosophy serve to engender a brightly burning desire for the preservation of individual freedom within the society? Would it be possible to provide some guarantee of a resultant ideal societal mix providing just the right amount of opportunity for self-realization with the necessary social constraints of evolving participatory democracy? Whether it would ever be possible to plan systematically to overcome the problem of "the uncommitted" and the alienation of a goodly percentage of intellectual youth has been the object of sociological investigation by various social scientists (e.g., Keniston, 1965), but formal education has never been the testing ground for the serious introduction of this type of social planning. Far too often it has merely reflected the status quo orientation of the cultural heritage, and change has been forced upon the educational system from the outside. Of course, the serious problem of such alienation does not apply to the majority of youth who have fair success in adapting to the values, norms, and constraints of society. Nevertheless, who would not agree that only a very small percentage of youth today has a deep commitment to work faithfully throughout their lives for the realization of the prevailing values and norms of Western culture? As a matter of fact, most intelligent people would experience some difficulty in identifying the major values and norms; so, where does that leave the vast percentage of the population who never have given the problem the slightest bit of thought?

With this brief introduction, it is now possible to restate the main problem of this paper and to enumerate the sub-problems or sub-headings by which the topic will be approached. Basically, therefore, this will be an analysis and preliminary interpretation of the persistent problems of sport and physical activity in education--with very brief reference to the concepts of health and leisure--based on ideas which may be called agnostic and existentialistic. In an effort to finally draw a few reasonable conclusions, the writer will (1) consider the background and present status of existential philosophy; (2) describe what seems to be the nature of reality (metaphysics) of this philosophical stance; (3) delineate what appear to be appropriate educational aims and objectives in the light of certain "recurrent themes" of existentialism; (4) designate what might be considered a consonant educative process with the educational goals that have been stated; (5) set forth the aims, objectives, and educational process of sport, physical activity, health, and recreation that might flow from existential philosophy; (6) trace and describe very briefly and preliminarily how selected persistent problems might be viewed by the individual with an agnostic, existential orientation; and (7) draw a few reasonable conclusions based on the discussion.

Background and Present Status

To write about the background and present status of so-called existentialism is not a simple task because it has not been one of the long-standing, mainstay philosophic positions or schools replete in its many ramifications. In fact two writers, who would admit to being existentialistic in their orientation--or who might be included in someone's historical summary of this approach to philosophizing--might well be in rather complete disagreement on the majority of the main tenets of a philosophical stance. Thus, one so-called existentialist is never a "direct descendant" of another, and it is often almost impossible to place them anywhere in what might be identified as a "philosophical family tree."

Certainly somewhere in the tradition of social philosophy, however, one can find specific ideas in the writings of the great philosophers of the West which have been echoed by advocates of existential philosophy, but the typical precursors within the modern era have been important men like Pascal, Kierkegaard, and Ortega y Gassett. As Kaufmann indicates (1956, p. 11), "The three writers who appear invariably on every list of "existentialists"--Jaspers, Heidegger, and Sartre--are not in agreement on essentials." He goes on to name others such as Rilke, Kafka, and Camus and explains that the "one essential feature shared by all these men is their perfervid individualism." How can this approach, therefore, be characterized as a philosophy?

MacIntyre (1967, pp. 147-149) provides one answer to this rhetorical question by relating all of these people on the same family tree, so to speak, because he can identify six recurrent themes that are typically associated in a number of different ways. Firstly, reality for the existentialist cannot be comprehended within a conceptual system. A second theme is that of a "doctrine of intentionality"--the idea that "the object of belief or emotion is internal to the belief or emotion" and cannot be explained in the naturalistic terms of the associationist psychologist. Thirdly, one encounters time and again the thought that man's existence is fundamentally absurd in a flawed universe that seems to be lacking basic purpose--although it is true that such a flaw does give man a guarantee of freedom of action. A fourth theme of existential philosophy is that "the possibility of choice is the central fact of human nature," and that man makes choices through action or inaction (p. 149). Such choices are often controlled by criteria irrationally selected. Fifthly, in man's existence the concepts of "anxiety," "dread," and "death" loom very large because of this freedom and the "fragility" of man's existence in the universe. Lastly, dialogue and communication involving argument between reader and author that involves deductive logic will serve no purpose unless there is agreement on basic premises. Thus, plays and novels are often best employed as viable forms of expression by existentially oriented philosophers or authors.

As helpful as knowledge and comprehension of these six recurrent themes may be, the reader will still find it necessary to remain exceptionally alert whenever this term is employed in an article or conversation. Unfortunately the term "existentialism" seems to have gone the way of other unfortunate philosophical terms such as "idealism," "realism," "pragmatism," "naturalism," etc. In other words, it, like they, has been the victim of bastardization, and wherever it appears in popular literature care should be taken to examine the source and usage for authenticity. As DeMott says, "a foreign entry, heavy, hard to pronounce, fast in the forties, faded in the fifties . . . Despite the handicaps, though, 'existential' is breaking through.

Improving its place steadily, unfazed by cheapening, inflation, or technical correction, it's closing once again on high fashion . . ." (1969, p. 4)

Despite the above difficulties--once that any such words from philosophy seem to encounter when they become jargon--it is relatively simple to explain a few basic "truths" about existential philosophy to teachers and to reasonably intelligent laymen. Many people recognize quite fully the long list of unanswered questions of the day. Churchmen have had increasing difficulty in answering many of these questions satisfactorily, and most college students have discovered that in the past few decades many philosophy professors haven't been trying to answer them in acceptable and interesting ways. Thus, it seems really important when a philosopher such as William Barrett of New York University explains that,

> Existentialism is a philosophy that confronts the human situation in its totality to ask what the basic conditions of human existence are and how man can establish his own meaning out of these conditions. . . Here philosophy itself--no longer a mere game for technicians or an obsolete discipline superseded by science--becomes a fundamental dimension of human existence. For man is the one animal who not only can, but must ask himself what his life means (Barrett, 1959, p. 126).

Such an approach quite obviously makes this type of philosophizing potentially absolutely vital in the life of man because he is actually offered a way of life. This is in contrast to other leading philosophical positions in which man is confronted with a depersonalized Nature, a transcendent Deity, or a State seemingly possessing both of these qualities. As Kaplan explains, "The meaning of life lies in the values which we can find in it, and values are the product of choice" (1961, p. 105). Thus, the direction of movement within selected concepts is from existence to choice to freedom!

Unfortunately (or fortunately--depending upon one's perspective) such seemingly wonderful freedom is not what it might appear to be at first glance. This opportunity for choice and freedom places an awesome responsibility upon individual man or woman: he or she is ultimately responsible for what happens to others too! In a sense "I am determining through my choice what all mankind everywhere is forever to become" (Ibid., p. 108). Kaplan, in describing Sartre's position, explains that there are two kinds of people in the world (other than true existentialists, of course): "those who try to escape from freedom and those who try to deny responsibility--cowards and stinkers" (Ibid., p. 109).

Such an outlook or life philosophy postulates no bed of roses for those who subscribe to it fully. Accordingly, man should choose his life pattern freely and with integrity; then he can become an "authentic" person only by accepting full responsibility for his choices. The beatnik blunder was to think that authenticity required freakish individuality that was absolutely unique. Actually, what is being offered is that man should responsibly choose one world or another for tomorrow; that man will have to be shaped so that he can somehow cope with such a world; and that each of us adhering to this process of living defines his own being and his own humanity--and this is the only way that this absurd world can acquire meaning!

The Nature of Reality (Metaphysics)

The world of material objects extended in mathematical space with only quantitative and measurable properties is not the world we live in as human beings; our world is a human world, not a world of science. From the context of the human world all the abstractions of science derive their meaning ultimately. Man is first and foremost a concrete involvement within the world, and we distinguish the opposed poles of body and mind. Existence precedes essence; man decides his own fate. His self-transcendence distinguishes him from all other animals, and he cannot be understood in his totality by the natural sciences. Truth is expressed in art and religion, as well as in science. Time and history are fundamental dimensions of human existence. Man's basic task is to blend the past, present, and future together so that the world--the human world--assumes meaning and direction. In this way man can be authentic. He stands open to the future, and the future stands open to him. Life's present conditions can be transformed so that responsible social action will result. (This basic material has been paraphrased from William Barrett, Irrational Man: A Study in Existential Philosophy. New York: Doubleday and Company, 1959.)

Educational Aims and Objectives

It does not seem possible to refute the position that existential philosophy raises most serious questions about man and his life on earth. Consequently, considering the importance of education as a social institution, the problems raised typically by existential though relate almost inevitably to schools and universities and the programs and experiences that are provided. As Langer has indicated, "In philosophy this disposition of problems is the most important thing that a school, a movement, or an age contributes. This is the 'genius' of a great philosophy; in its light, systems arise and rule and die. Therefore a philosophy is characterized more by the formulation of its problems than by its solution of them . . ." (Langer, 1964, p. 16). Existential philosophy has most certainly confronted

- 188 -

the problems of the age which man is facing generally and which he meets specifically in his educational institutions at all levels. Many of these problems were critical thirty or forty years ago on a national basis at least, but now they must be resolved internationally--that is, if solution is still possible (e.g., overpopulation, pollution, etc.). "Designs for the education of man living on the planet earth ought to produce diversity, for there must be many paths to this goal" (Redefer, 1974).

Proceeding from the above statements, does existential philosophy offer any implications of a positive and optimistic nature for education? If educators can bring themselves to accept Bedford's interpretations and conclusions regarding existentialism's implications, it would seem to be wise to give this philosophical stance most serious consideration:

1. Man can always turn, reform, or rechoose.
2. Man has worth . . . either derived from God or he makes his own worth (value).
3. Each new person plays a decisive role in history.
4. Man is never permanently degraded.
5. Man can create meaning out of his existence no matter what its circumstances.
6. Man has everything to gain and nothing to lose by risking himself in life (Bedford, 1961, p. 47).

Thus, an existentially oriented teacher and coach would be cognizant of the fact that the socialization of the student has become equally as important as a key educational aim (in this country) as his purely intellectual development. He is most concerned because many of the educational theorists see men as "things to be worked over in some fashion to bring them into alignment with a prior notion of what they should be." Even the Experimentalists could be challenged for their seeming failure with their effort to bring "the learner into a self-determining posture." Even if there is general agreement that a set of fundamental dispositions is to be formed as a result of the educational process, the existentially oriented teacher would inquire whether the criterion used for the evaluation of the worth of individual dispositions should be "public rather than a personal and private criterion." As Morris states, "If education is to be truly human, it must somehow awaken awareness in the learner--existential awareness of himself as a single subjectivity in the world." Students should "constantly, freely, baselessly, and creatively" choose their own individual pattersn of education. The subjectivity of the existentialistically oriented learner can and should thrive in the arts (music, painting, poetry, and creative writing, etc.), but it should not be forgotten that similar possibilities to study human motivation are available in the social sciences as well (and probably to a lesser extent in the natural sciences). (This basic material has been paraphrased

from Van Cleve Morris, <u>Philosophy and the American School</u>.
Boston: Houghton-Mifflin Company, 1961.)

The Educative Process (Epistemology)

Great emphasis has been placed on the teaching - learning process, but it is indeed extremely difficult to describe the essential ingredients of the educative process. The language analyst would inquire whether (1) the subject-matter was being considered; (2) the teacher's actions were being analyzed; (3) that which takes place within the student was being assessed; or perhaps (4) the end result was being evaluated.

The existentially oriented teacher would view his task in a less systematic manner and from a different perspective. For him childhood is characterized as a "pre-Existential phase of human life." About the time of puberty in the individual, there is an "Existential Moment" in the young person's subjective life. This is the time of the "onset of the self's awareness of its own existing." For the first time, the "individual sees himself as responsible for his own conduct." Then, and only then, "education must become an act of discovery." The learner's experience should be such that he gets "personally implicated in the subject-matter and in the situation around him." Knowledge must be "chosen, i.e., appropriated, before it can be true for that consciousness." It is never something that is objective purely, nor is it somewhat purposeful in the person's life. Knowledge "becomes knowledge only when a subjectivity takes hold of it and puts it into his own life."

It could be argued, of course, that "the Existentialist has little to offer in the way of a method of knowing." And yet, whether logic, scientific evidence, sense perception, intuition, or revelation is being considered, "it is the individual self which must make the ultimate decision as to what is, as a matter of fact, true." Perceptually and cognitively, the individual is aware of the objects of existence, but there is something more--an "internal, subjective awareness"-- which enables him to know that he knows. To the present time a case could be made for the position that psychology has given very few answers about this latter phase of the epistemological process. (Some of this material has been paraphrased from Morris, 1961, and also from Van Cleve Morris, <u>Existentialism in Education</u>. New York: Harper & Row, Publishers, 1966, pp. 150-154.)

Sport, Physical Activity, Health, and Recreation

What does all of the above mean for sport and physical education, not to mention health and recreation? Obviously, it is quite dangerous and possibly somewhat illogical to draw highly specific implication in this manner. On the other hand, it would be ridiculous to refrain from any consideration of possible implications whatsoever. The field of physical education and sport--and the allied professions of health education and recreation--should strive to fulfill a significant role in the general educational pattern of the arts, social sciences, and natural sciences. The goal postulated for the individual should be total fitness--not just physical fitness, as important as this may be--with a balance between activities emphasizing competition and cooperation. The concept of "universal man" should be most highly regarded as an educational aim, but it is absolutely necessary for the person to have the opportunity to choose for himself based on his knowledge, skills, and attitudes as determined by self-evaluation. Somehow the child who is "authentically eccentric" should be made to "feel at home" in the physical activities program. Further, there should be opportunities for youth to commit themselves to values and people in sport. An important question in sport and athletics, of course, is how to help preserve the individual's authenticity in individual, dual, and team sports where winning is so often overemphasized. It should be possible to aid the young man or woman athlete to personally select the values that are being sought in the activity. The young person is playing and taking part for actualization of self--that is, he is attempting to use sport for his own purposes. Because the opportunity for creativity is so important and should therefore be made available wherever possible to young people, physical activities such as modern dance should be included in the program prominently.

The educational process employed by the physical education teacher and sport coach should be as natural as possible under the circumstances; a give-and-take situation would be ideal. The student should be allowed to observe and to inquire freely. Freedom is very important, of course, but the teacher is needed since the student cannot teach himself competencies and skills especially as effectively as when he is under the guidance of an excellent teacher. A good teacher should show passion, but he should not be strongly egocentric nor too biased about a system or a point of view. If the aim of the program is a student who is able to move his body with purpose and meaning in such activities as sport, play, dance, and exercise, the teacher should be absolutely dedicated to the search for truth in these aspects of life. It is vitally important that the end result be a "self-moving" individual both literally and figuratively. In existential philosophy the search for truth is typically an individual matter, but majority opinion should be tested when action is needed in a group situation. The student should strive to develop an "orderly mind" within an organism that seeks to move purposefully and with definite meaning. The student should be willing to debate issues, and he should be encouraged to strive for creativity. A physical education program--as is the case similarly with the entire educational program--should not be considered successful if the student becomes a "carbon copy" of his teacher. Such an inclusive methodology with

accompanying specific techniques should characterize the existentially oriented physical educator's teaching and coaching.

In regard to health education and recreation education, professions which have been allied with physical education in the past, much
of which has just been stated above should apply in these fields as
well. For example, the child must develop an awareness of the need
for self-education about the various aspects of personal and community health. Controversial issues should never be avoided. All types
of recreational needs--social, aesthetic and creative, communicative,
learning, and physical--should be met through a program of recreation education in the schools during the day and in the evening community school offerings. One function of play is most certainly personal liberation and release. All sorts of group recreational activities are important, and most certainly have a place, but opportunities
for individual expression should not be downgraded and should be
made available regularly. (Some of this material has been paraphrased from E. F. Zeigler, 1966, pp. 9-10.)

Some Persistent Historical Problems

In addition to the question of values which has been discussed
above both generally and also specifically in relation to general education, the writer has identified a number of other persistent problems which have been treated both historically and philosophically by
him elsewhere (Zeigler, 1968). For example, there is the question
about the influence of politics--the type of political state, that is--on
the educational system of a country, and also on the pattern of physical education and sport that might prevail either within the educational system or in the society generally. Of course, it should be
pointed out that existentially oriented writers have usually not turned
their attention to the social question of the ideal political state. The
existentialist philosopher would characterize twentieth century man
as a "homeless creature" seeking new and different kinds of recognition since the earlier so-called stability existing for men within
society seems to have vanished. There is no question, therefore, but
that the existentialist would feel completely out of place within a
totalitarian regime. Obviously, any authoritarian situation demanding obedience requires blind allegiance, and this would inevitably
negate the development of individual personality and rights.

Life in the variety of so-called democratic states leaves much
to be desired as well. The dangerous problem of an exploding population in so many countries, democratically oriented or otherwise,
tends to make man more lonely than ever--even though he may be
"rubbing shoulders" with the masses daily. The era of "organization
man" within democratic, capitalistic society has further destroyed
man's identity as an individual. The democratic ideal within a republic does offer him an opportunity to be a vocal, enlightened citizen,

but somehow so few seem to take advantage of this chance for individual expression which almost guarantees anyone a certain amount of immediate recognition and resultant identity.

Transposed to the educational system, the existential philosopher would tend to be disturbed by the failures of present day programs to produce a sufficient quantity of young men and women who show evidences of "self-determining posture." How can educators "awaken the awareness" of the learner so that he will demand a more individualized pattern of education? This should be possible with the pluralistic philosophies of education that are in existence on the North American continent. Carried one step further into physical education and sport the task becomes that of helping the child who is "authentically eccentric" to feel at least somewhat "at home" in the typical physical activity. Certainly standardized class routines and insistence upon measuring up to physical fitness norms or standards are not the way to enhance the "quality of individual freedom" in an evolving, democratic country.

A second persistent historical problem in education and in physical education and sport is the extent to which nationalism may be employed by government officials in a democratic country. At the present there is a strong current of nationalism evident in Canada, for example, and the basic question, of course, is which agency-- the school, the family, the private agency, or the state--should exert the greatest amount of influence on the young person. The answer to this question would seem to be more obvious the more totalitarian the state becomes. The existential philosopher would not be particularly disturbed by the presence of what might be called a "healthy" type of nationalism in a society, but he would be violently opposed to overriding nationalism that destroys individual human aspirations. He would argue that it is up to individual man to make something out of himself, of course, but that man himself must choose his own values in order to give his life meaning. However, the existentialist would not wish man to shirk from the responsibility of making decisions that might affect the final outcome of civilization for all mankind.

The profession of physical education should evaluate continually the extent to which the federal government, or even the provincial or state governments, are attempting to employ athletic competition and physical fitness activities to promote what might be designated as "unhealthy" nationalism or an excessive amount of chauvinism. The Olympic Games have been criticized in the past for allowing violations of its rules in this regard. Of course, it is very difficult to prevent the news media from keeping track of how many gold, silver, and bronze medals are won by such-and-such a nation from the so-called free world, etc., but who is it that allows national anthems to be played every time award ceremonies are conducted? In the Western world any one of a number of news media or others groups can and do criticize a particular government for the promotion of excessive nationalism. Within the Communist Bloc, on the other hand, such criticism would undoubtedly be quelled at the very source.

Within the space at hand for this discussion, it is not possible to consider each and every one of the persistent historical problems that have been identified in the light of existential philosophy. In addition to the question of values that was discussed above the influence of politics and the influence of nationalism have been sketched very briefly. Each of these problem areas could be the subject for a monograph, as could other such persistent problems--or social forces--as the influence of economics or religion, for example. Now several persistent problems of a professional nature for physical educators will be treated concisely so that the "flavor" of existential philosophy in such matters may be identified.

The place or role of dance of all types in the field of physical education has been of concern to the profession for some time. What are the possible implications from this philosophical stance in this regard? Keep in mind that the existentialist views man as a unique historical animal; that this philosophical tendency emphasizes that man should involve himself concretely in the human world; and that man is urged to obtain the truth from life in whatever way that he can. Further the existentially oriented teacher would have man search himself as he becomes involved with the finite world prior to choosing his values freely in an attempt to transform himself and the world in the wide-open future ahead of him. Such a personal involvement and free choice of educational values implies automatically that there should be a solid foundation in the arts or humanities where there is subjectivity and an opportunity to explore the human world more than the scientific world extending into mathematical space.

If the education of the young man or woman should be generally liberal, and based on experience in such arts as poetry, painting, music and creative writing, it seems consistent and logical to state that modern dance could contribute in an unusually fine way to the growth of creativity in the individual. The student receives the opportunity here to explore his movement patterns fully in an attempt to experience the feeling of "being at home in his own body." As he becomes aware that he is truly free in this medium, he is able to use dance activity as play of the finest type. Such dancing can provide a sense of release and personal liberation along with creative self-expression. True artistic creation provides the possibility of conveying one's innermost feelings in patterns of creative movement. Kinesthetic awareness is enhanced; one tends to "find himself" through this medium; and "appropriation" through dance occurs.

Two other persistent historical problems of what can be called a "professional nature" for physical educators are the use of leisure for physical recreation and sport activities and the perennial issue of amateurism and professionalism. What might be some of the basic implications from existential philosophy? Basically, the type of play in which personal liberation is a fundamental characteristic would be viewed most favorably. In sport the individual can be free only as he selects his own values and achieves self-expression. At an earlier age it is obvious that the child creates his own world of play and thereby--through a number of such experiences during the formative years--eventually realizes his true identity. Conversely, unless more planning in this direction is undertaken by varsity coaches, the typical varsity athletics experience in Canada could well move in the direction of U. S. intercollegiate athletics with its misdirected emphases and resultant dehumanizing effects. This writer is not against excellence in sport at the university level, but he is dedicated to the preservation of the person's "authenticity" and under no circumstances could he accept the exhortations of the crowd to "win at any cost." Thus, the sport coach is confronted with a dilemma of truly great complexity--how to encourage excellence; how to preserve the athlete's authenticity; and how to satisfy the spectators who have come to accept victory as the only desirable outcome for the home team.

The above persistent problem is almost necessarily closely linked with the seemingly ever-present issue of amateurism and professionalism--a question that somehow has become linked with sport more than any other area of so-called cultural endeavor. As these words are being written, the Russian amateurs are playing hockey with the Canadian professionals on an equal basis. Obviously, the terms "amateur" and "professional" must have different meanings in the area of sport for both countries. The use of new and different criteria for the determination of amateur or professional status must be explored; the former idea that the taking of money of small or large denomination--or any article that is worth money--immediately disqualifies the participant from being considered as an amateur has been so riddled with varying interpretations by a multitude of sports-governing bodies around the world as to become a travesty.

Summary and Conclusions

This paper represents an attempt to present an analysis and preliminary interpretation of some of the persistent problems of sport and physical activity in education based on an agnostic, existentialistic position within philosophy. The writer has considered the background and status of existential philosophy with special reference to the nature of reality of this philosophical position, as well as the delineation of the possible educational aims and objectives and educative process implied by such a stance. Then, in similar fashion, the aims, objectives, and educative process of sport, physical activity, health, and recreation were delineated from this existential position. Finally, several persistent historical problems of sport and physical education were examined in the light of the teacher and coach holding an agnostic, existential orientation.

Everything considered, while recognizing the fact that this examination of the agnostic, existentialistic philosophic stance in regard to sport and physical activity in education has been somewhat limited in scope, the writer cannot escape the conclusion that physical education teachers and sport coaches would be well advised to seriously consider the strong implications from this powerful and yet somewhat curious philosophical position for their professional endeavors. The future is too uncertain and frightening, and the "warning and red lights are flashing too strongly and too regularly" against so many prevailing educational practices to be ignored by the continuance of a "business as usual" approach.

The above statements are made with the full recognition of the fact that "there is not one philosophy called existentialism . . . There is no set of principles common to the [many] beliefs of the various existentially oriented philosophers . . . Though their answers are not identical . . . the term 'existential' points to a certain state of mind . . . a spiritual movement . . . which is alive" (Heinemann, 1958, p. 165).

The position of physical education and sport in the educational hierarchy is not so strong that it dares ignore the implications of existential philosophy. What dedicated professional person in any field would not attempt to answer the absolutely vital questions raised by this philosophic stance as he faces the serious challenges of the 1970's and thereafter?

Selected References

Barrett, William. Irrational Man: A Study in Existential Philosophy. New York: Doubleday and Company, 1959.

Bedford, Charles M., "The Concept of the Authentic Individual and Its Implications for Building a Framework for an Existential Philosophy of Education." Unpublished doctoral dissertation, University of Southern California, 1961.

Brubacher, John S. Modern Philosophies of Education. New York: McGraw-Hill Book Company, Fourth edition, 1969.

Cumming, Robert D. The Philosophy of Jean-Paul Sartre. New York: Random House, 1965.

DeMott, Benjamin, "How Existential Can You Get?" The New York Times Magazine, March 23, 1969, pp. 4, 6, 12, 14.

Harper, William A., "Man Alone," Quest, XII, May 1969, 57-60.

Heinemann, F. H. Existentialism and the Modern Predicament. New York: Harper Torchbooks, 1958.

Hook, Sidney, "The Scope of Philosophy of Education," Harvard Educational Review, Vol. 26, No. 2:145-148, Spring 1956.

Kaplan, Abraham. The New World of Philosophy. New York: Random House, 1961.

Kaufmann, Walter. Existentialism from Dostoevski to Sartre. Cleveland: The World Publishing Company, 1956.

Keating, James W., "Sartre on Sport and Play." An unpublished paper.

Keniston, Kenneth. The Uncommitted: Alienated Youth in American Society. New York: Harcourt, Brace & World, 1965.

Kleinman, Seymour, "Phenomenology - The Body - Physical Education." A paper presented to the History and Philosophy Section, A.A.H.P.E.R. Convention, March 21, 1966.

Kneller, George F. Existentialism and Education. New York: Philosophical Library, Inc., 1958.

Langer, Susanne. Philosophy in a New Key. New York: New American Library of World Literature, 1964.

MacIntyre, Alasdair, "Existentialism," in The Encyclopedia of Philosophy. New York: The Macmillan Company, 1967, Vol. 3, 147-154.

Morris, Van Cleve. Existentialism in Education. New York: Harper & Row, Publishers, 1956.

_____. Philosophy and The American School. Boston: Houghton-Mifflin Company, 1961.

Redefer, Frederick L., "A Call to the Educators of America," Saturday Review-World, July 27, 1974, 49-50.

Sartre, Jean-Paul, on "Play" in The Philosophy of Jean-Paul Sartre (R. D. Cumming, editor). New York: Random House, 1965, pp. 310-316.

VanderZwaag, Harold J., "Sport: Existential or Essential," Quest, XII, May 1969, 47-56.

Wilson, Colin. Introduction to the New Existentialism. Boston: Houghton-Mifflin Company, 1967.

Zeigler, Earle F., "The Educational Philosophy of Existentialism," Illinois News Health, Physical Education, and Recreation, 14, No. 1, 1966, 9-10. (A very concise treatment of the subject).

_____. History and Philosophy of the Problems of Physical Education and Sport. Englewood Cliffs, New Jersey: Prentice-Hall, Inc., 1968.

NOTE: Although he did not quote from this source directly, the writer feels it is appropriate to give recognition to the first comprehensive treatment of the relationship between man and sport written in the tradition of existential philosophy. It is Howard Slusher's Man, Sport and Existence. Philadelphia: Lea & Febiger, 1967.

THE RATIONALE FOR PHILOSOPHICAL ANALYSIS (LANGUAGE ANALYSIS): IMPLICATIONS FOR PHYSICAL EDUCATION AND SPORT

The analytic movement in philosophy (including the philosophy of language) has become an extremely important and influential approach in the English-speaking world.[1] This is not to say that philosophers and others were not concerned with the analysis of concepts for many centuries; it is simply that such a sharp contrast between this method of philosophizing and the more traditional approaches did not become apparent until the twentieth century. Thus, despite the fact that various citizens of the Western world have been engaged in philosophical thought for more than two thousand years, there is still controversy about the exact nature of philosophy.

Early Greek philosophers thought that philosophy should serve a function not unlike that which we attribute to contemporary science. Today, of course, we employ scientific method which involves reflective thought and hypothesis, long-term observation, and experimentation prior to subsequent generalization. Thus, many of today's philosophers have asked themselves, "what kind of activity am I engaging in?" The implication is that the older type of philosophizing has lost its basis of justification since scientific method has demonstrated its power as a "producer of true knowledge."

There have been three developments in this century that have sought to answer the above question, and all have tried this through the medium of what might be called language analysis or philosophy of language: (1) logical atomism; (2) logical positivism; and (3) ordinary language philosophy. Each of these approaches is characterized by a different view of analysis, with the last position being held by those who assume that the immediate goal of the philosopher is to explain the use, the function, and the actual workings of man's language. The eventual goal would, therefore, be one of "language therapy," or the making of ordinary language "well" again. Some went so far as to state that the actual reconstruction of ordinary language was necessary. Whatever the approach here, it is obvious that philosophy was in a sense relegated to the role of "servant" of science, and philosophers were to assist in the exact formulation of scientific propositions. As Kaplan states, the major task of analytic philosophy is to

---

[1] Published in the Illinois Journal of Health, Physical Education and Recreation, Vol. 18, No. 1:17-18 (1970). Examples of this approach to philosophizing may be read in this book; see Selections #30 and #48.

provide "a rational reconstruction of the language of science"
(Abraham Kaplan, The New World of Philosophy, p. 83).

How can language analysis help us in physical education and
sport? For one thing it may help the physical education philosopher
to clarify the meaning of certain terms, which have been used synono-
mously for years (albeit incorrectly); for example, a more careful
definition of the terms "sport" and "athletics." Professor James W.
Keating, in "Sportsmanship as a Moral Category" (Ethics, Oct.,
1964, pp. 25-35), states that we have been using these terms interchangeably and incorrectly. Sport is a diversion that brings fun, but
athletics is a competitive activity in which winning and the prize is
most important. Now Keating has come to believe that he might win
the argument, but that such a distinction will never be accepted again.
So he has tended to distinguish between "philosophy of play" and "philosophy of conflict," and athletics is subsumed under the latter category. This is one example of how language and/or conceptual analy-
can help us to communicate more effectively.

(Self-Evaluation Check List)[1]

PHILOSOPHY OF LIFE, EDUCATION, AND

(1) Physical Education and Sport

(2) Health and Safety Education

(3) Recreation (Education)

Instructions: Read the statements below carefully – section by section – and indicate by an (X) that statement in each section which seems closest to your own personal belief. Check your answers only after all six sections have been completed. Then complete the summarizing tally on the answer sheet prior to checking your position on the Philosophy of Education Spectrum at the end.

---

[1] This self-evaluation check list has been developed by the author over a period of years. The concept of "individual freedom" as proposed by Herbert J. Muller is basic to an understanding of the Philosophy of Education Spectrum located at the end of this check list. The author is grateful for advice received from associates and students. Earlier versions appear in Zeigler, Earle F., Philosophical Foundations for Physical, Health, and Recreation Education. Englewood Cliffs, New Jersey: Prentice-Hall, Inc., 1964, as well as in Zeigler, Earle F. and VanderZwaag, Harold J., Physical Education: Progressivism or Essentialism? Champaign, Ill.: Stipes Publishing Company, Revised edition, 1968.

I. The Nature of Reality (Metaphysics)

a. _____Experience and nature "constitute both the form and content of the entire universe" (multiverse?). There is no such thing as a pre-established order of things in the world. Reality is evolving, and humanity appears to be a most important manifestation of the natural process. The impact of cultural forces upon man are fundamental, and every effort must be made to understand them as we strive to build the best type of a group-centered culture. In other words, "the structure of cultural reality" should be our foremost concern. Cultural determinants have shaped the history of man, and he has now reached a crucial stage in the development of life on this planet. Our efforts should be focused on the building of a world culture.

b. _____Man's world is a human one, and it is from the context of this human world that all the abstractions of science derive their meaning ultimately. There is, of course, the world of material objects extended in mathematical space with only quantitative and measurable properties, but we humans are first and foremost "concrete involvements" within the world. Existence precedes essence, and it is up to man to decide his own fate. This makes man different from all other creatures on earth. It appears true that man can actually transform life's present condition, and thus the future may well stand open to this unusual being.

c. _____Nature is an emergent evolution, and man's frame of reality is limited to nature as it functions. The world is characterized by activity and change. Rational man has developed through organic evolution, and the world is yet incomplete--a reality that is constantly undergoing change because of a theory of emergent novelty. Man enjoys freedom of will; freedom is achieved through continuous and developmental learning from experience.

d. _____Mind as experienced by all men is basic and real. The entire universe is mind essentially. Man is more than just a body; he possesses a soul, and such possession makes him of a higher order than all other creatures on earth. "The order of the world is due to the manifestation in space and time of an eternal and spiritual reality." The individual is part of the whole, and it is man's task to learn as much about the Absolute as possible. There is divided opinion within this position regarding the problem of monism or pluralism. Man has freedom to determine which way he shall go in life; he can relate to the moral law in the universe, or he can turn against it.

e. _____ "The world exists in itself, apart from our desires and knowledges." There is only one reality; that which we perceive is it. "The universe is made up of real substantial entities, existing in themselves and ordered to one another by extramental relations . . ." Some feel that there is a basic unity present, while others believe in a non-unified cosmos with two or more substances or processes at work. Things don't just happen; they happen because many interrelated forces make them occur in a particular way. Man lives within this world of cause and effect, and he simply cannot make things happen independent of it.

II. Educational Aims and Objectives

a. _____ Socialization of the child has become equally as important as his intellectual development as a key educational aim in this century. There should be concern, however, because many educational philosophers seem to assume the position that children are to be fashioned so that they will conform to a prior notion of what they should be. Even the progressivists seem to have failed in their effort to help the learner "posture himself." And if it does become possible to get general agreement on a set of fundamental dispositions to be formed, should the criterion employed for such evaluation be a public one (rather than personal and private)? Education should seek to "awaken awareness" in the learner--awareness of himself as a single subjectivity in the world. Increased emphasis is needed on the arts and social sciences, and the student should "constantly, freely, baselessly, and creatively" choose his own pattern of education.

b. _____ Social self-realization is the supreme value in education. The realization of this ideal is most important for the individual in his social setting--a world culture. Positive ideals should be molded toward the evolving democratic ideal by a general education which is group-centered and in which the majority determines the acceptable goals. Education by means of "hidden coercion" is to be scrupulously avoided. Learning is explained by the organismic principle of functional psychology. Social intelligence acquired teaches man to control and direct his urges as he concurs with or attempts to modify cultural purposes.

c. _____ The general aim of education is more education. "Education in the broadest sense can be nothing else than the changes made in human beings by their experience." Participation by students in the formation of aims and objectives is absolutely essential to generate the all-important desired interest. Social efficiency can well be considered the general aim of education. Pupil growth is a paramount goal, as the individual is placed at the center of the educational experience.

d. _____ "A philosophy holding that the aim of education is the acquisition of verified knowledge of the environment; recognizes the value of content as well as the activities involved in learning, and takes into account the ties involved in learning, and takes into account the external determinants of human behavior . . . Education is the acquisition of the art of the utilization of knowledge." The primary task of education is to transmit knowledge, without which civilization cannot continue to flourish. Whatever man has discovered to be true because it conforms to reality must be handed down to future generations as the social or cultural tradition. Some holding this philosophy believe that the good life emanates from co-operation with God's grace and that development of the Christian virtues is obviously of greater worth than learning or anything else.

e. _____ Through education the developing organism becomes what is latently is. All education may be said to have a religious significance, which means that there is a "moral imperative" on education. As man's mind strives to realize itself, there is the possibility of realization of the Absolute within the individual mind. Education should aid the child to adjust to the basic realities (the spiritual ideals of truth, beauty, and goodness) that the history of the race has furnished us. The basic values of human living are health, character, social justice, skill, art, love, knowledge, philosophy, and religion.

III. The Educative Process (Epistemology)

a. _____ Understanding the nature of knowledge will clarify the nature of reality. Nature is the medium by which the Absolute communicates to us. Basically, knowledge comes only from the mind--a mind which must offer and receive ideas. Mind and matter are qualitatively different. A finite mind emanates through heredity from another finite mind. Thought is the standard by which all else in the world is judged. An individual attains truth for himself by examining the wisdom of the past through his own mind. Reality, viewed in this way, is a system of logic and order that has been established by the Universal Mind. Experimental testing helps to determine what the truth really is.

b. _____ About the time of puberty, the child experiences an "existential moment" in his subjective life--and is never the same thereafter. He becomes truly aware of his own existence, and of the fact that he has become responsible for his own conduct. After this point of life, education must be an "act of discovery" to be truly effective. Somehow the teacher should help the young person to become involved personally with his education and with the world situation in which such an education is taking place. Objective or subjective knowledge must be personally selected and "appropriated" by the youth unto himself, or else it will be relatively meaningless in that particular life. Thus, it matters not whether logic, scientific evidence, sense perception, intuition, or revelation is claimed as the basis of knowledge-acquisition, no learning will take place for that individual self until he decides that such learning is "true" for him in his life. Therefore, he knows when he knows.

c. _____Knowledge is the result of a process of thought with a useful purpose. Truth is not only to be tested by its correspondence with reality, but also its practical results. Knowledge is earned through experience and is an instrument of verification. Mind has evolved in the natural order as a more flexible means whereby man adapts himself to his world. Learning takes place when interest and effort unite to produce the desired result. A psychological order (problem-solving as explained through scientific method) is more useful than a logical arrangement (from the simple fact to the complex conclusion). There is always a social context to learning, and the curriculum must be adapted to the particular society for which it is intended.

d. _____An organismic approach to the learning process is basic. Thought cannot be independent of certain aspects of the organism; it (thought) is related integrally with emotional and muscular functions. Man's mind enables him to cope with the problems of human life in a social environment. Social intelligence is closely related to scientific method. Certain operational concepts, inseparable from metaphysics and axiology (beliefs about reality and values), focus on the reflective thought, problem-solving, and social consensus necessary for the transformation of the culture.

e. _____There are two major epistemological theories of knowledge in this position. One states that the aim of knowledge "is to bring into awareness the object as it really is." The other emphasizes that objects are "represented" in man's consciousness, not "presented." Students should develop habits and skills involved with acquiring knowledge, with using knowledge practically to meet life's problems, and with realizing the enjoyment that life offers. A second variation of epistemological belief indicates that the child develops his intellect by employing reason to learn a subject. The principal educational aims here must be the same for all men at all times in all places. Others carry this further and state that education is the process by which man seeks to link himself ultimately with his Creator.

IV. Values in Specialized Field (Physical Education)

a. _____ I believe in the concept of "total fitness" implies in an educational design pointed toward the individual's self-realization as a social being. In our field there should be opportunity for selection of a wide variety of useful activities. Instruction in motor skills is necessary to provide a sufficient amount of "physical" fitness activity. The introduction of dance and art into physical education can contribute to man's creative expression. Intramural sports and voluntary recreational activities should be stressed. This applies especially to team competition with particular stress on co-operation and promotion of friendly competition. Extramural sport competition can be introduced when there is a need; striving for excellence is important, but it is urgent that materialistic influence be kept out of educational programs. Relaxation techniques should have a place, as should the whole concept of education for leisure.

b. _____ I believe that the field of physical education should strive to fulfill a role in the general educational pattern of arts and sciences. The goal is total fitness--not only physical fitness--with a balance between activities emphasizing competition and cooperation. The concept of "universal man" is paramount, but we must allow the individual to choose his physical education and sport activities for himself based on knowledge of self--what knowledge and skills he would like to possess. We should help the child who is "authentically eccentric" feel at home in the physical education program, and also to find ways for youth to commit themselves to values and people. A person should be able to select a sport according to the values which he wishes to derive from it. This is often difficult because of the extreme overemphasis on winning in this culture. Creative physical activities such as modern dance should be stressed, also.

c. _____ I believe that education "of the physical" should have primary emphasis in our field. I am concerned with the development of physical vigor, and such development should have priority over the recreational aspects of physical education. Many people, who believe in the same educational philosophy as I do, recommend that all students in public schools should have a daily period designed to strengthen their muscles and develop their bodily co-ordination. Physical education, of course, must yield precedence to intellectual education. I give "qualified approval" to interscholastic athletics since they do help with the learning of sportsmanship and desirable social conduct if properly conducted. But all these things, with the possible exception of physical training, are definitely extra-curricular and not part of the regular curriculum.

d. _____ I am much more interested in promoting the concept of total fitness rather than physical fitness alone. I believe that physical education should be an integral subject in the curriculum. Students should have the opportunity to select a wide variety of useful activities, many of which should help to develop "social intelligence." The activities offered should bring natural impulses into play. To me, physical education classes and intramural sports are more important to the large majority of students then interscholastic or intercollegiate sports and deserve priority if conflict arises over budgetary allotment, staff available, and use of facilities. I can, however, give full support to team experiences in competitive sports, because they can be vital educational experiences if properly conducted.

e. _____ I am extremely interested in individual personality development. I believe in education "of the physical," and yet I believe in education "through the physical" as well. Nevertheless, I see physical education as important, but also occupying a "lower rung on the educational ladder." I believe that desirable objectives for physical education would include the development of responsible citizenship and group participation. In competitive sport, I believe that the transfer to training theory is in operation in connection with the development of desirable personality traits, but sports participation should always be a means not an end.

V. Values in Specialized Field (School Health Education)

a. _____ I believe that health is a basic value of human living and that the truly educated individual should be "physically fit," should live "near the maximum of his efficiency," and should have "a body which is the ready servant of his will." But even though I believe health is a basic value for all the others, I would have to place it at the bottom of the hierarchy of educational values. Worship must be placed at the top, because through it man is brought "into conscious relation to the infinite spirit of the universe . . ." Thus, it would not be included in a listing of the "essential studies" of the curriculum except where it would probably be included incidentally under biology. However, I am interested in "building wholeness of mind and

body," "the development of strong, healthy bodies, good habits
of mental and physical health," "and the right start in the
teaching of health, safety, and physical education to children."
There is no question in my mind but that educators should work
for a larger measure of integration in the individual by promoting "more intensive study of the body, leading to scientific
knowledge: anatomy, body chemistry, hygiene, physiology,
etc.; and attention to sex characteristics and habits, leading to
a greater understanding of the place of sex in human life, with
implications for hygiene . . ." But such knowledge is made
available to boys and girls, and young men and women, as a
"service" program in the schools--a service is provided to
man, and through this contribution to this health he is enabled
to pursue higher educational goals.

b. _____I believe strongly that the child must develop an
awareness of the need for self-education about the various aspects of personal and community health. Such educational experiences will not take place, of course, unless the educational
process itself is a natural one--a give-and-take situation in
which the student is allowed to observe and inquire freely.
Obviously, controversial issues should never be avoided with
such an approach. Typically, the search for truth is an individual matter, but it is most important to test majority opinion
when action is needed in a group situation. The debating of
issues relating to health knowledge and practice will help the
student decide what is most important for him in this society at
this time. In this way he will be able to commit himself to personal and community health values.

c. _____I believe in the development of physical vigor and
health. There is no question in my mind but that the school
should provide "an atmosphere conductive to both emotional and
physical health." Furthermore, "knowledge about the principles of physical and emotional health is a proper ingredient of
the curriculum." I believe that the community does have a
responsibility to provide clinical facilities for therapy," "but
this does not mean that they are part of the school program or
curriculum any more than are boilers in heating systems." I
assert that the home must have the complete responsibility for
assisting youth to acquire desirable health habits--that is, unless we wish to establish some form of community youth organizations to accomplish this end. "The health of adolescents is
for the most part too good and their sources of energy are too
great to make health problems real to them." In similar vein,
sex education is certainly not a proper function of the school.
Is it logical that teaching of the means for securing the health
values would be incomplete anyhow until the perspective from
which they are viewed is also taught; this perspective is found

only in the humanities--in literature, art, religion, and philosophy. In summary, therefore, every person needs a basic core of knowledge in order to lead a human life, and this includes the learning of health knowledge. This is consistent with the central purpose of the school--the development of the individual's rational powers.

d. _____ As I see it, there can be no such thing as a fixed or universal curriculum in physical, health, and recreation education. Men and women should be sturdy and possess vigorous health. Positive health should be a primary educational aim. Such a program would necessitate the co-operative involvement of many agencies. Health knowledge and attitudes should be realized through the provision of experiences involving problem-solving. "Direct" health instruction should be offered, but such learning can take place indirectly in the science curriculum. Sex education and family relations instruction are very important. Instruction in mental hygiene needs serious attention in our highly complex society.

e. _____ I believe that man should be a strong yet agile creature, and this standard should apply to girls as well as boys. Health, as I see it, is a primary objective of education, and the child needs health instruction. The success of the school health education program depends upon the degree of cooperation a among home, school, and community agencies. An educated person must understand the difference between health and disease, and he must know how to protect and improve his own health, that of his dependents, and that of the community. As I see it, the program of school health, physical education, and recreation may be administered as a unified program within a school system. I believe that natural types of exercise promote sound mental health. All these aspects of the total program may be co-ordinated because they are related in many ways. Through unity these subdivisions, which are basically related, could probably serve the needs of school children and youth much more effectively than is the case so often at the present. To be truly effective, school health education must be concerned with helping the individual to lead a rich, full life. This means more than providing a health service so that students can maintain minimum health needed to "pursue intellectual work with the least amount of strain." Health should be defined positively--as that quality which enables us "to live most and serve best."

VI. Values in Recreation (Education)

a. _____As I see it, work and play are typically sharply
differentiated in life. Play serves a most useful purpose at
recess or after school, but it should not be part of the regular
curriculum. I believe that the use of leisure is significant to
the development of our culture, but I realize today that "winning
the Cold War" is going to take a lot more hard work and somewhat less leisure. I see leisure pursuits or experience as an
opportunity to get relief from work while it serves a re-
creative purpose in the life of man. The surplus energy theory
of play and recreation makes sense to me. So does the more
recent bio-social theory of play--the idea that play helps the
organism to achieve balance. I feel that the "play attitude" is
missing almost completely in many organized sports. Play
(and recreation) is, therefore, very important to me; I believe
it should be "liberating" to the individual. People can develop
their potentialities for wholesome hobbies through recreation.
Furthermore, recreation can serve as a "safety valve" by the
reduction of the psychic tensions which are evidently caused by
so many of life's typical stresses. Even though play should
not be considered as a basic part of the curriculum, we should
not forget that it provides an "indispensable seasoning" to the
good life. Extra-curricular play and recreational activities
and a sound general education should suffice to equip the student for leisure activities in our society.

b. _____I believe that all types of recreational needs and
interests should be met through recreation education. The
individual should have an opportunity to choose from among
social, aesthetic and creative, communicative, learning, and
physical recreational activities within the offerings of what
might be called a "community school" in the broadest sense of
the word. It is absolutely imperative, of course, that these
choices be made according to the person's sense of personal
values and in accord with his desire to relate to people. All
are striving for self-realization, and the recreation education
program can provide opportunities for both individual expression, as well as for group recreational undertakings. Play
seems necessary for people of all ages, and it assumes many
different forms. We should not forget that one of its functions
is simply personal liberation and release.

c. _____I believe it is difficult to separate the objectives of
recreation education from physical education when physical
activities are being considered. Within the schools I recom-
recommend a unified approach for physical, health, and recreation education. In this discussion I am only including those
recreational activities which are "physical" in nature. All

these leisure activities should be available to all on a year-round basis. I see recreation education as a legitimate phase of the core curriculum, but would include further recreational opportunities as well as opportunity for relaxation later in the day. My core curriculum is adapted from progressivism, and the extracurricular activities are quite as integral as "spoke and hub activities." In fact, the word "extra" is now most misleading.

d. _____I am inclined to favor the adoption of the name recreation education for the field. I see advantages in a unified approach whereby the three specialized areas of health, physical education, and recreation (in schools) would provide a variety of experiences that will enable the individual to live a richer, fuller life through superior adjustment to his environment. I believe that education for the worthy use of leisure is basic to the curriculum of the school--a curriculum in which pupil growth, as defined broadly, is all-important. Secondly, play shall be conducted in such a way that desirable moral growth will be fostered. Thirdly, over-organized sport competition is not true recreation, since the welfare of the individual is often submerged in the extreme emphasis which is so frequently placed on winning. I believe it is a mistake to confuse the psychological distinction between work and play with the traditional economic distinction that is generally recognized. All citizens should have ample opportunity to use their free time in a creative and fruitful manner. I do not condemn a person who watches others perform with a high level of skill in any of our cultural recreational activities, including sport, so long as the individual kept such viewing in a balanced role in his entire life.

e. _____I believe that the role of play and recreation in the development of personality and the "perfectly integrated indidivual" is looming larger with each passing year and that it has not been fully understood or appreciated in the past. For this reason it seems quite logical to me that education should reassess the contributions that recreation and play do make in the education of man. That there is a need for educational research along these lines is self-evident. I believe further that we should examine very closely any theories of play and recreation which grant educational possibilities to these activities of man. The self-expression theory of play suggests that man's chief need in life is to achieve the satisfaction and accomplishment of self-expression of one's own personality. Here is an explanation that seems to consider quite fully the conception of man as an organic unity--a total organism. I believe that man is a purposive being who is striving to achieve those values which are embedded in reality itself. To the extent that we can realize the eternal values through the choice of the right kinds of play and recreation without flouting the moral order in the world, we should be progressive enough to disregard a dualistic theory of work and play. Another difficulty that confronts us is differentiating between physical education and recreation. Recreation has developed to the point where it is now clearly one of our major social institutions. I believe that recreation can make a contribution to the development of an "integrated individual in an integrated society growing in the image of the integrated universe." Mankind today is actually faced with a "recreational imperative."

(Please turn to the next page.)

Answers: (Read only after all six questions are completed, and then complete the summarizing tally underneath.)

I. The Nature of Reality (Metaphysics)
    a. Reconstructionism
    b. Existentialism
    c. Experimentalism (Pragmatic Naturalism)
    d. Idealism
    e. Realism (basically essentialistic with elements of naturalistic realism, rational humanism, and positions within Catholic educational philosophy)

II. Educational Aims and Objectives
    a. Existentialism
    b. Reconstructionism
    c. Experimentalism
    d. Realism
    e. Idealism

III. The Educative Process (Epistemology)
    a. Idealism
    b. Existentialism
    c. Experimentalism
    d. Reconstructionism
    e. Realism

IV. Physical Education
    a. Reconstructionism
    b. Existentialism
    c. Realism
    d. Experimentalism
    e. Idealism

V. School Health Education
    a. Idealism
    b. Existentialism
    c. Realism
    d. Reconstructionism
    e. Experimentalism

VI. Recreation (Education)
    a. Realism
    b. Existentialism
    c. Reconstructionism
    d. Experimentalism
    e. Idealism

SUMMARIZING TALLY

	Experimentalism (Pragmatic Naturalism)	Reconstructionism	Existentialism (atheistic and agnostic and theistic)	Idealism	Realism (varying positions)
I					
II					
III					
IV					
V					
VI					

— — — — —   Totals

<u>Note</u>: It should now be possible to determine your position based on the answers given in the various categories. At least you should be able to tell if you are largely progressivistic or essentialistic in your educational philosophy (see Spectrum on next page). If you discover considerable eclecticism in your overall position, closer analysis may be necessary to determine if your beliefs are philosophically defensible. Continued self-examination of aims and objectives should make you a better professional person.

<u>Finally</u>, after tallying the answers, and keeping in mind the subjectivity of such a check list as this, did the self-evaluation show you to be:

Strongly Progressivistic	( )	
Progressivistic	( )	
Eclectic (checks in <u>3 or more</u> positions)	( )	?????????
Essentialistic	( )	
Strongly Essentialistic	( )	
<u>or</u>		
Existentialistic (and probably somewhat	( )	?????????

PHILOSOPHY OF EDUCATION
SPECTRUM

<u>Note</u>: The reader may wish to examine himself - his personal phi-
losophy of education - based on this spectrum analysis. Keep
in mind that the <u>primary</u> criterion on which this is based is the
concept of "individual freedom."

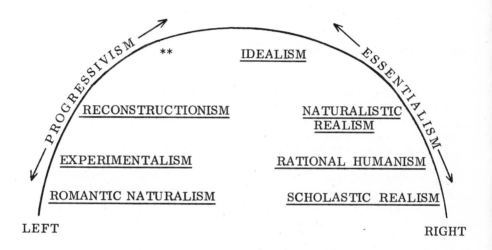

RECENT TRENDS

** <u>EXISTENTIALISM</u> - a <u>permeating</u> influence; individualistic, with
atheistic, agnostic, and Christian "branches."

LINGUISTIC ANALYSIS - philosophy in "a new key"; the assumption here is that man's ordinary language has many defects that
need to be corrected. Another objective here is the "rational reconstruction of the language of science" (Abraham Kaplan).

Selection #20

YOU LIVE A PHILOSOPHY OF LIFE!

Despite all that you have read and heard, it is quite probable that "you live a philosophy of life more than you express it in words! This is most certainly true for the student major in the fields of health, physical education, and recreation! Physical educators are more active in sports and games than most others, but physical recreation is only one aspect or phase of the recreational kaleidoscope which is available for selection in America today. As the prospective physical educator thinks of his own life pattern, he should ask himself to what extent he engages in social, communicative, creative and aesthetic, and learning recreational interests (hobbies). To what extent are you availing yourself of all of these aspects of campus life presently available to you?

We hear all the time that physical educators should change their image within university walls and out in the community at large. This may well be true. Some say you "can't make a leopard changes its spots," or "make a silk purse out of a sow's ear." However, the point would best seem to be that we should not change our image, but build upon it. This may seem to be a play on words, but let's examine it more closely. There is much that is fine about the image of the man and woman physical educator--much that many people admire and would like to emulate! Physical educators are typically healthy, vigorous and energetic, reasonably extroverted, personable, and anxious to succeed. If this is true, what needs to be changed? Well --we need to be more "cultured" in the best sense of Webster's definition of the word--that is, we need to become more intellectually curious about all aspects of our society and of the world in which we live. Is this so difficult to do? Perhaps so; perhaps not. Is it worth the effort? Yes!

An important point in this connection is that the world is changing so rapidly. Knowledge is multiplying at a prodigious rate. It may be that our fathers, and our father's fathers, could afford to enjoy a four-year hiatus during which the amassing of factual knowledge supposedly took place, but the persistence of such practice today means, quite simply, that the world will pass one by. Can prospective educators afford this type of luxury today? I think not.

---

[1] Published as "Be Curious about Life," in JOHPER, Vol. 35, No. 9:47 (September 1964).

Of course, we are faced with the fact that grade point averages must be maintained, and that instructors are marking tests and papers as stringently as ever. Yet much of this is not education in the best sense. A pragmatic definition of education explains it as those changes which take place in the individual as a result of his experiences. Such an education can be good, bad, or indifferent--depending on the experiences that we have. It is at this point that instructors and students need to plan together so that the best type of experiences are realized through the learning process.

Broad, active recreational interests can insure, in many instances, the achievement of knowledge, competencies, and skills so essential to the educator who wishes to devote his life to the truly exciting fields of health, physical education, and recreation--individually or collectively. However, so much more is needed than "passive and vicarious" participation. Not that such is completely devoid of desirable human values for the individual; the point is that "active and creative" participation brings us so much more value in our lives.

The average physical educator, male or female, is not very interesting to talk to unless the subject revolves around the current sports' scores and certain of life's rather monotonous banalities. His knowledge of politics and other current affairs is typically superficial. His philosophy of religion is often stereotyped or unintelligible. Art and music are "things" about which other people talk, and he doesn't usually have time for hobbies other than keeping his own scrapbook of newspaper clippings.

Physical educators are not necessarily more stupid than others, although they are often what may be described as "culturally disadvantaged"--and here I am not referring to the color of their skin necessarily! The case so often is that they--and many of their instructors too!--have never been provided with interesting and stimulating educational experiences that would challenge anyone's intellect. This means that both teacher and student should make an effort to relate to other teachers and students in other departments on campus. Additionally, there is a need for teacher and student to interact more effectively in the office, in the classroom, and in the gymnasium. What is life about? What role should the young physical educator play on the campus and then in the community when he gets his first job? To be most effective, he simply must be more than just a "gym teacher" and a coach. We can be satisfied with nothing less than the title of "educator" and "scholar," in the best meanings of the terms.

Broad recreational interests involving the use of "intellectual curiosity" can do much to build upon the image that was discussed above. See a new play. Attend a lecture or a concert. Inquire deeply into your religious beliefs, whether you be theist, agnostic, or atheist. Take time to read The New York Times (and most certainly do this on Sundays). Read one or two editorial pages, daily if possible. Cultivate the friendship of a wide variety of people on campus. Don't be afraid to ask a question because you may seem ignorant. Challenge your instructors' views if you find yourself in violent disagreement. Force him to defend his position if it seems unreasonable. "Drink of life" more fully day in and day out. Know how to express your philosophy of life--and then live it!

Part III
SPORT AND ATHLETICS

THE ROLE OF THE SPONSORING AGENCY IN SPORTS LEADERSHIP

Over thirty years ago Ryan re-emphasized a study of twenty thousand young people by psychologists which showed conclusively that group games and sports made a most important contribution to wholesome personality development (Ryan, 1929, xi).[1] This concept has now gained recognition by most informed people.

When young people take part in sports and games, we find a type of psycho-physical integration that is rarely present in many of life's other activities (and this is particularly true in the usual educational environment). They concentrate on the task at hand, which may be to shoot the basket or to drive the puck into the net. (This point was stressed often by the late Arthur Steinhaus.)

In many sports, especially contact team sports, opponents face situations where the emotions are aroused to a high pitch. Game rules and traditions have developed to such an extent that the actions of the players are controlled. Here we have one example of an ideal learning situation. However, the sport itself does not insure that good personality traits will be developed. The quality of leadership shown by the coach may be the deciding factor.

When we talk about the role of the sponsoring agency in sports leadership, we must know something about the aims and objectives of the particular agency involved. Are we talking about junior high school football, semi-professional baseball, recreation midget hockey, employee recreation softball, or professional hockey? No matter which type of sport competition we are considering, one principle stands out above all else. Sport was made for man, not man for sport! Unfortunately there are times when we wonder if this thought is uppermost in the minds of the directors of the sponsoring agency. Should this principle still hold in semi-professional and professional sport?

In recreation and in education there are at least three basic questions which the public or private sponsoring agency should ask about the competitive sports program it is financing:

---

[1] Published in the School of Education Bulletin (The University of Michigan), Vol. 29, No. 6:92-93 (March 1958).

1. Are we planning cooperatively with all concerned? (This includes the participant, the parents, the family doctor, the principal, the physical educator and coach, and the recreation director.)

2. What values are we seeking for children and young people through the medium of sports and games? (That is, are we placing sufficient emphasis on the achievement of skills, cooperation, sportsmanship, and the enjoyment of game?)

3. Will the promotion of this activity result in the neglect of other boys and girls not sufficiently skilled to participate at this level? (Here we must bear in mind the fact that in a democracy we want to give each person the opportunity to develop to the maximum of his or her development, so long as this development does not impede the progress of the whole community.)

If we can say that we are planning cooperatively; that we are placing sufficient emphasis on the important values; and that we are not going against the fundamental principles of democracy, then we know that the sponsoring agency is living up to its responsibility.

One last thought seems imperative. Nothing but the highest type of leadership can carry out these broad aims and specific objectives most effectively.

References

Ryan, W. Carson, Jr. The Literature of American School and College Athletics. New York: The Carnegie Foundation for the Advancement of Teaching, Bulletin 24, 1929, xi.

A PHILOSOPHICAL ANALYSIS OF AMATEURISM IN
COMPETITIVE ATHLETICS

Certainly one of the most persistent problems facing higher education is that of amateur, semi-professional, and professional sport
and its relationship to our educational system as well as our entire
culture.[1] Comprehending the ramifications of this enormous problem
has seemed almost impossible at times, and many educational administrators have eventually given up and "drifted with the tide." Many
teachers and coaches do not understand much of the underlying rationale behind the conflict between the N.C.A.A. and the A.A.U. from
the standpoint of educational philosophy. Sport is part of the very
"life blood" of the field of health, physical education, and recreation
and offers the possibility of great benefits and satisfaction to the participant and the coach alike. It is a great cultural influence which
offers the possibility of good or bad to our society. How we allow or
help it to develop depends to a considerable extent on us--on how we
use it for the service of man.

Why People Play Games

It is really quite difficult to say why people take part in games
and sport. The motivation behind such participation is so complex
that there is really no general agreement on the matter. Over and
above this, you can't always believe the answers that many might give
as to their motivation, because they really don't fully comprehend the
situation. Many might not tell you if they did. Do we take part in
games and sport for fun, for re-creation, for self-expression, for
health, for exercise, for competition, or perhaps because of the
money or other benefits it might bring us? Or do we do it for a variety of reasons, some stronger at times than another? Or perhaps we
rarely ever give it much thought at all!

Primitive and pre-literate man undoubtedly felt the urge to play;
so, he did. Often he took part in games as part of his religious observances. And there is no denying that sport served a very practical
purpose as well. It gave him the opportunity to practice skills upon
which he relied for his very survival.

---

[1] For a fuller discussion see the introductory chapter by
E. F. Zeigler in A. W. Flath's, A History of the Relations between
the N.C.A.A. and the A.A.U. Champaign, Illinois: Stipes Publishing Co., 1964.

The urge to play is probably older than any so-called human culture since animals play in the same ways that men do. It has been stated that civilization has contributed no significant aspect to the general concept of play, although we must admit that considerable thought and investigation has been devoted to the matter. It is possible that scientific investigation will eventually give us the answer to the question, or perhaps we may never really know the reason. Did God give man a play instinct, or did Nature give us play--play the very essence of which defies all analysis; play which appears to be completely irrational; play which is both beautiful and ridiculous at one and the same time. It is free and voluntary and seemingly not concerned with the serious business of life. Yet it can be and often is completely absorbing; it starts and stops at a given moment; and it has rules.

Excellence in Sport

It is the so-called higher forms of play with which we will concern ourselves primarily, and especially those types which eventually became semi-professional and professional in the Graeco-Roman Period. The very nature of sport has made it difficult to regulate both then and now. The goal of excellence in a number of sports as part of overall harmony of development of all aspects of man's nature seemed to be an unattainable objective. If a man wanted to win, he specialized. The more he specialized, the more time he spent in one particular phase of sport, and the less time he had for the other aspects of his cultural development and for his livelihood. If he were wealthy enough, of course, at least he didn't have to worry about where his next meal was coming from--often a serious concern for our "amateur" athletes today in certain "non-gate-receipt" sports!

The period since 1930 in the United States has been one in which interest in competitive sport and physical recreation has continued on unabated, and has, in fact, grown. The use of leisure has become an urgent concern. High school athletics have attained new heights, as have college athletics and international competition. Competition in sport has helped to promote a concept of internationalism, but who can deny the undercurrents of nationalism present in the Cold War athletic contests between the U. S. and the U.S.S.R. Furthermore, usually behind the scenes as far as the public is concerned, the gnawing, persistent problem of amateurism has plagued us and made a mockery of the high ideals for which we strive. The words of that cynic haunt us: "Amateurs? There ain't none!"

A Titanic Struggle

In the 1960's the United States finds itself the scene of a titanic struggle between the Amateur Athletic Union and the National Collegiate Athletic Association for control of what is still called "amateur sport," although an attempt by anyone to offer a blanket definition that would cover all "amateur" athletes in the U.S. is an absolute impossibility. A dictionary, of course, goes along with the norm, explaining that an amateur is one who is not rated as a professional, and that a professional is one, generally, who has competed in sport for a stake or purse, or gate money, or with a professional for a prize, or who has taught or trained in sports or athletics for pay. Which brings us back to that cynic again, who says that "an amateur is a guy who won't take a check!"

Some one group is going to win this struggle, but not before the United States is terribly embarrassed or before many fine young athletes are hurt in one way or another. What appears to be needed is some frank, straightforward thinking which takes into consideration the fact that the United States has entered the second half of the twentieth century, and that history may seem to be repeating itself but but not in the same way.

Two Opposing Positions

There are, broadly speaking, two opposing positions: an essentialistic position, and a progressivistic position. Subsequently, we will examine the positions of the three leading positions in educational philosophy (experimentalism, realism, and idealism) regarding the role of competitive athletics in education. Initially, we must recognize that the essentialist will look at past history and will tend to believe that the classic definition of amateurism has considerable merit. He will be apt to wish to retain the good from the past and to change the status quo very slowly if at all. If, for example, it can be proved scientifically that a change is needed, certain people holding philosophical positions within educational essentialism would be willing to accept change. Others within this position are skeptical about so-called scientific proof in certain areas of human life; these people believe typically that "right is right, and wrong is wrong."

The progressivist (the second broad category of opposing positions) believes that there are no fixed values and that changing times demand new methods. He appreciates the contributions of the past, but doesn't regard them as sacrosanct and hopes that we can learn lessons from past mistakes. He would be willing to accept a new approach to this perennial problem in sport if it worked; his attitude would be that we will never know the answer to this problem unless we try out some of the proposed solutions using a problem-solving approach.

Further Delineation of Positions in Educational Philosophy

The experimentalist (a progressivistic position) believes that physical education classes and intramural sports are more important to the large majority of students than interscholastic and intercollegiate sports and deserve priority if conflict arises over budgetary allotment, staff allotment, and use of facilities. He can give full support to team experiences in competitive aports, because they can be vital educational experiences if properly conducted. He believes further that "physical" educational, athletic, or "physical" recreational activity at a reasonable level of skill (at the least!) can be an esthetic experience of a fine type. If stress is placed on the continuous development of standards to guide conduct, a significant contribution may be made to "moral training" through laboratory experiences. Thus, the planned occurrence of educational situations within sports competition is important to the experimentalist.

The realist (an essentialistic position) might find that he holds a similar but not identical position with other realists in regard to the place of competitive athletics in education; such, of course, would be the case with experimentalists. Typically, the realist is concerned with the adequate training and development of the body itself. He gives "qualified approval" to competitive sport, because he believes that it contributes to the learning of sportsmanship and desirable social conduct. Competitive athletics, however, is extracurricular and should come after the official school day is over. One "classical realist" goes so far as to state that every child should be required to learn one team game and two individual sports that can be played as an adult before graduation, but this should not be considered as part of the regular curriculum. The underlying reasoning, therefore, is that work and play cannot be identified under the same psychological rubric. The use of leisure is significant to the development of our culture, but "winning the Cold War" is going to take a lot more hard work and somewhat less leisure--especially in the classroom and the laboratory. Play for young adults is "carefree activity performed for its own sake" and for the sake of re-creation. Unfortunately, this "play attitude" is quite often missing from organized sport.

The idealist (an essentialist position with a progressivistic wing) definitely favors physical education and sport because of the atatus accorded such activity in Greek idealism. He believes in the transfer of training theory which implies that attitudes of sportsmanship and fair play learned through desirable athletic competition can and do transfer to life situations. The Christian idealist believes that a coach should fulfill the moral and ethical demands of his calling by setting a good example for his charges to emulate; the athlete, therefore, should strive "for that same perfection that we seek on our athletic teams" in his individual life. The desired moral and social values that sport can yield must be made realities. The teacher of

- 225 -

sports is actually in a unique position, because he can be one of the most influential members of the school community in the shaping of these values. But he must be careful not to let his boys to become too self-centered; sport should be a means to an end, not an end in itself. Extreme specialization may warp the personalities of all concerned. As Oberteuffer of Ohio State has emphasized time and again, we cannot be satisfied with scores instead of character. Idealism believes in "giving the game back to the boys." It seems reasonable to state that educators subscribing to idealistic philosophy of education should reassess the contribution that the right kind of recreation and play can and do make in the education of man.

The Role of the Educator

As we can see from these very brief summaries of the place of competitive sport in American education, athletic competition is accepted to a greater or lesser degree as an integral or ancillary phase of that process. But no one can deny that vigorous, competitive sport has become a vital phase of our American way of life! This means that a persistent problem in this important area must eventually be resolved in a way that the majority of our citizens will accept. It is for this reason that the following comments are offered for your consideration. There are some basic questions to be answered, and educators have a great stake in the answers that are given in the near future. Many teachers are coaches of one or more sports at the different levels of public education, and there is no question but that they can make their influence felt as to the direction that we believe athletic competition should take in the future. Such influence as they may have in the future determination of policy will achieve the results we desire only as we are articulate, logical, and consistent in the arguments that we present to our colleagues. These good folk are quite often not convinced of the worth of the enterprise; hence, the task is to make a case for athletics based on a carefully-conceived philosophy of education. This had not been done very effectively in the past. There has been a tendency to rely on the great interest which competitive sport generates in the student population and in the community-at-large.

What influence educators can have at the conference level, at the district and national level in the various sports-governing bodies, and at the international level depends largely upon the degree of "enlightened participation" which we are willing to assume whenever and wherever the opportunity presents itself. The truly professional person who is dedicated to the promotion of the highest and finest type of sport competition cannot be satisfied with doing his own work well at home (however important that may be); he must fight off any lethargy "to let George do it" in the professional associations and the sports-governing bodies where the policies for the future are being formulated. The average coach typically feels that he, as merely one individual, doesn't have much to say about this persistent problem of the amateur, semi-professional, and professional in sport. He fails to realize that united with other like-minded coaches in, for example, the Men's Athletic Division of the American Association for Health, Physical Education, and Recreation, this Division could have a strong influence on the future of American sport. It is true that any such progress will necessarily involve cooperative effort with the N.C.A.A., the A.A.U., the National Association of Intercollegiate Athletics, the National Federation of State High Schools Athletic Associations, and other similar groups, but has it not been characteristic of our American democratic way of life to work things out amicably for the good of all?

Is Re-evaluation Necessary?

It may well be that we will have to re-evaluate some of our treasured, basic assumptions about the amateur code in sport. What are the reasons today for the continuation of such a sharp distinction between the amateur and the professional? History tells us where the ideal originated, but it tells us also that the conditions which brought it about do not exist in America today. It is quite possible that we are trying desperately to perpetuate a concept which served its purpose well in the era for which it was designated, but which simply does not apply to the situation as we know it today. Why must we persist with the ideology that in sport it is a question of "black" or "white"--the professional being the "black" one, and the amateur being the "white"? Can't we recognize and identify the many shades of "gray" that inevitably exist in-between?

And what is so wrong with a young sportsman being classified as "gray," or a semi-professional? Do we brand the musician, the artist, or the sculptor in our society who develops his talent sufficiently to receive some remuneration for his efforts as being a "dirty pro"? Why must this idea persist in sport--a legitimate phase of our culture? The answer to these questions may well lie in the fact that we are not willing, almost subconsciously, to accept sport as a legitimate and worthwhile aspect of our culture.

A New Role for the Professional Athlete

The materialistic image of today's professional in sport does not help very much either. Granted he is a "different breed" than his predecessor, especially in such sports as basketball and football, but even here he is a "professional" in the limited sense of the word. He is usually after all the money that his physical talent can bring him on the open market. He sees sport as a means to an end--his security and ultimate happiness in life. Not that there is anything

basically wrong with using a talent in this way, if it is honest. But it
could be so much more, if he would attempt to make himself a professional in the broader and finer sense of the word. Everything considered, this man has an unusual talent which he has developed to a
high degree in a cultural activity that has proved itself to be important in our society. Furthermore, it is probably true that a particular professional who has reached his peak of attainment is better-
qualified in this sphere of activity than he will ever be in any other
phase of life. What would be more natural than to expect this man to
become a true professional and to devote the rest of his life to the
promotion of his sport with the youth and adults of his country?
There is absolutely no reason why the professional sportsman--a man
who typically loves his sport--cannot devote his life to a social ideal
and become a really fine professional individual--one whose primary
aim in life is to serve his fellowman through his contributions to his
own sport and to the highest ideals of sportsmanship. Such an approach can work; the country is dotted with men and women who have
made it work. It is not as idealistic as it may sound. It would do
much to help us look at the "amateur controversy" in a new light.

A New Approach?

We cannot agree either with the cynic who says that there are
no more amateurs in sport. This is not true. There are, and ever
will be, amateurs in the only logical sense of the word today. The
amateur is the beginner, the dabbler, the dilettante. This is not
saying that he "loves" the activity any more or less than the semi-
professional or professional. As a matter of fact, he isn't well
enough acquainted with it to "love" it. When the business man goes
out to the local golf course early on a Sunday morning and turns in a
neat score of one hundred and twenty-five for eighteen holes, he is
displaying all of the traits of an amateur in what should be today's
parlance.

Proficiency in the chosen sport, and the amount of time spent
practicing it, should certainly be considered when we feel that we
must classify some sportsmen for the protection of others. The boy
who plays the trumpet in the high school band is an amateur. If he
qualified to play in his college dance band on Saturday nights, and receives fifteen dollars weekly for his efforts (which helps him to earn
his way through college), he is a semi-professional. Who would
criticize him for this? Let us assume that this young man is majoring in music and goes on after college to become either a professional
musician or a professional teacher. We find that this is perfectly
commendable in our society, also. But there are a great many people in the United States who don't believe that this should be an accepted practice in sport. The first time that an athlete takes fifteen
dollars for playing his favorite sport, he is a professional and,

presumably, could be barred from any attempt to participate in the Olympic Games. Obviously, such a stand is ridiculous today.

The Problem of Athletic Scholarships

It is, of course, the excesses and overemphasis that are feared. The United States is committed to a great educational experiment on a grand scale. We are the only country in the world where thirty-five to forty percent of our young people go on to some form of higher education in the more than 2,000 junior colleges, community colleges, colleges, and universities. Semi-professionalism to a fairly high degree in college sport can possibly only be justified for physical education majors and those who might wish to become professionals in those sports which bring in substantial gate receipts. Because of the desire to have winning teams in college sports for the prestige and gate receipts that they bring, competition for fine athletes is keen. The N.C.A.A. and the N.A.I.A. have made athletic scholarships legitimate with certain stipulations. Many people felt that the Western Conference (Big Ten) was only being realistic when it removed the "need factor" from its athletic tender plan; others felt this was a serious mistake, agreeing with the stand of those institutions who retain this factor. Other important colleges and universities admit students on the basis of their intellectual attainment and many other factors, of which athletic accomplishment is one. Then scholarship aid is given on the basis of the parents' total financial position--their ability to pay for their son's college education. No matter which approach is used, the athlete is still being subsidized to a greater or lesser extent. It is extremely difficult to say which approach is right and best for the individual and for society. One thing is certain; whatever help the young man receives should be known by all and should be in conformity with established rules and regulations that work in today's world.

PUTTING THE GREEK IDEAL IN PERSPECTIVE IN NORTH AMERICAN ATHLETICS TODAY

How can we put the Greek ideal of Periclean times in perspective today? Obviously it can be done only with difficulty and with perhaps only reasonable adequacy. In this paper we shall discuss (1) the Greek ideal in Periclean Athens; (2) role differentiation in the social system; (3) the objectives of Greek physical activity and athletics; (4) some critical analyses of the Greek system of physical education and sport; (5) the concept of freedom in our transitional society; (6) the "future shock" that is confronting North American education; (7) the situation in athletics and sport today; (8) five different, chronologically overlapping, definitions of man; (9) man viewed as a problem-solving organism; and (10) how the individual should make his own assessment of the relevancy of the Greek ideal today.[*]

Periclean Athens (463-431 B.C.) was a period designated as "the most memorable in the history of the world." (6, p. 245 et ff.). Muller refers to "the phenomenal achievement of Greece," and states, "My concern is the Greek spirit - the spirit that led them to embark, without maps, charts, or guides, on the adventure of freedom and the life of reason." (21, p. 107). Followers of Herbert J. Muller will, of course, recognize immediately his great concern for the evolution of the concept of "freedom" throughout the history of man. It was during the public career of Pericles that men for a "fleeing moment" evolved a democratic ideal which they were able to put into practice with consieerable success. Can it be said that "at the heart of our civilization there is still the naturalistic, humanistic faith of Greece?" (p. 142).

The Greek Ideal in Periclean Athens

North Americans must ponder the term "freedom" deeply today as they face an uncertain future. Here freedom is defined as "the condition of being able to choose and carry out purposes." (20, ix). Periclean Greeks considered themselves to be free men capable of choosing and carrying out their own purposes. They demanded of the ideal citizen perfection of body, extensive mental activity and culture, and irreproachable taste. (9, p. 276). And, as Freeman indicates

---

[*] A paper prepared specially (but adapted from a 1971 talk) for the Symposium on "Athletics in America," Oregon State University, Corvallis, February 14-17, 1972. This paper was published in Athletics in America (A. W. Flath, editor). Corvallis, Oregon: Oregon State University Press, 1972, pp. 79-90.

further, "the object of education was to make symmetrical, all-around men, sound alike in body, mind, character, and taste, not profession- al athletes who were mentally vacuous and without any appreciation of art, nor great thinkers of stunted physique, nor celebrated musicians who lacked brains." (p. 287)

Two Different Social Systems

This was a magnificent ideal, but we must not forget for a min- ute that it applied to some 43,000 citizens of a total Attic population of some 315,000. Moreover, the role of Athenian women is not revered by the "Women's Lib" Movement today. We are dealing with a social system whose structure was such that it would have to be character- ized as relatively undifferentiated in comparison with our differen- tiated society of today. This statement can be made despite the fact that "Greece, then, like the people of Israel, developed a highly dis- tinctive cultural system by a process which involved the radical dif- ferentiation of the whole societal unit from other societal types." (22, p. 107) Still further, it must be granted, as Johnson explains,

> . . . . every "permanent" social system, even one smaller than a total society, has its division of labor. For the pro- duction of goods and services, role differentiation seems to be necessary. Even if every person could acquire the knowledge and skill necessary for the performance of di- verse tasks, there would still have to be role differentia- tion, for no one person could perform simultaneously all the tasks that have to be so performed . . . . (15, p. 53).

Thus, it becomes obvious to us that in our highly complex society there is a great deal of role differentiation, which makes possible the extremely high degrees of knowledge, skill, and competency possess- ed by many men and women fulfilling an infinite variety of roles.

Greek Physical Activity and Athletics

The Greek experience, especially as it related to physical ac- tivity and athletics, has been explained by scholars at considerable length. Gardiner points out that "the idea of effort is the very es- sence of athletics," and that "Pindar describes the athlete as one 'who delights in the toil and the cost.'" (11, p. 1). Woody asserts that "Athenian ideals and attainments in physical culture form an im- pressive chapter of the past, a past which is, for all its antiquity, a living presence. These were significant not only in themselves, but for their bearing on the aesthetic achievements of Athens." (31, p. 467) Thompson, in "The Grecian View of Athletic Competition," discusses how such competition contributed to the educational ideal of "kalós kai agathós" (kalokagathia), which means the "beautiful and good" in a broader sense as achieved through "gymnastiké" and "mousiké." (27, p. 8) Siedentop, while analyzing the "Differences between Hebrew and Greek Views of Man," lauds the heroic ideal of the Greeks while explaining that the Greek position "is much more easily discernible in the concept of 'areté' than in any relationships among mind, body, and spirit." (26, pp. 11-18) It remained for Diem to grant Greece the supreme accolade when he stated,

> We thank the Greeks for the lesson; no education without sport, no beauty without sport; only the well-forced human has been educated; only he is really beautiful. And beauty is, as we know from Socrates, of the same essence as is the good. (3, p. 129, as translated by E. F. Zeigler)

By this time there should be absolutely no doubt but that "to the Greeks, sport was not merely a pleasant form of relaxation; it was a highly serious business, involving a whole complex of affairs concerned with hygiene and medicine, aesthetics and ethics." (18, p. 165) The spirit of this influence can be felt in the plea for harmonius development made by Socrates in Plato's Republic:

> And as there are two principles of human nature, one the spirited and the other the philosophical, some God, as I should say, has given two arts to mankind answering to them (and only indirectly to the soul and body), in order that these two principles (like the strings of an instrument) may be relaxed or drawn tighter until they are duly harmonized. (25, p. 129, as translated by Robinson)

A More Critical View of Greek Physical Education and Sport

The time has come in our analysis to become somewhat more critical and a bit less irrationally idealistic. Harris has stated that "it is generally believed, and it is probably true, that some of the Greeks at some periods of their history came nearer to achieving this balance than any other people of whom we know. But the tendency to idealize the Greeks can easily be carried too far." (12, 187) Still further, it remained for Fairs to point out to the field of physical education and sport that Plato, "as the progenitor of metaphysical dualism, is the symbol of 'the betrayal of the body' in Western Culture." This means that we have Plato to thank for the mind-body characterization of man. (7, p. 22) But then, despite Fairs' "exposé" of Plato, he somewhat later identified Periclean Athens as "The Golden Age of the Body" - as a period in the history of man when "the Periclean vision of individual and social perfection was intimately intertwined with the perfection of the body. In other words, the blue print to the realization of the good life was via the bodily dimension." (8, p. 18) What Fairs is explaining further is that "the essential core of ideals of the Athenian body mentality . . . all made the body the focal point in the achievement of the good life." (Ibid.)

Freedom in a Transitional Society

Our task here is not explain what went wrong with ancient Athens - or even to ponder over the loss of individual freedom in present-day Athens. And we can only refer fleetingly to the concept of "Renaissance Man" which was presented to the world in the humanistic educational pattern prescribed for the courtier of the Renaissance period - an aim of education which represented a revival of the Greco-Roman prescription for liberal education. (2, pp. 7-8) We must move forward about 500 years to take a look at the North American educational ideal today, and where our specialized field fits into the educational pattern. Moreover, we must not forget the earlier consideration of freedom and the extent to which all people are "able to choose and carry out" their own purposes today.

Even though much progress has been made in the achievement of civil rights for man on this continent in the twentieth century, there have been developments recently in both the United States and Canada which make a reflective individual realize how precarious a commodity an individual's freedom really is. Muller outlines a series of occurrences and changes that have taken place just since the end of World War II, most of which are too well known to repeat. (20, pp. pp. 516-517) He points out further that many "Americans themselves evidently did not trust their free institutions or their fellow Americans" during the Joe McCarthy era. (p. 520) Thus, despite the tremendous advances that the United States, for example, has made in many areas, one cannot help but be brought up very sharply by the devastating description of our problems as explained by Reich in the best-selling The Greening of America. (24) Even granting the fact that many scholars in a variety of fields have been highly critical of this Yale law professor who dares to cut across many fields of knowledge with his analysis, and admitting further that his prescription the bloodless revolution that is coming may be a bit naive, there is obviously a lot of trouble, strife, poverty, and anger in the United States today. Reich's request for understanding of the plea of many of today's younger generation should be considered seriously by all fairminded people. On a similar theme Boulding makes it abundantly clear that The Meaning of the Twentieth Century is that we are in the midst of a great transition, and that now "we must learn to master ourselves as we are learning to master nature." (1, p. 24) Hence we must learn to avoid a "number of traps" along the way, or it is quite possible that life on this planet will cease - at least in the form that we have known it up to this point. (Ibid.)

Future Shock Confronts North American Education

The plight of people on earth in the decades immediately ahead has been brought home to us in a most penetrating fashion by Alvin Toffler in Future Shock, another best-selling publication which is as well-documented as such a future-oriented book could be. Toffler explains how we are on a "collision course" with the future because the tempo of civilization is increasing so rapidly that a great many people aren't going to be able to adjust satisfactorily to the new demands that are being made of them. In addition to his presentation of a highly detailed analysis of the present situation, and the "future shock" which many people are already finding overwhelming from both physical and psychological standpoints, we are fortunately offered a series of "strategies for survival." Of significance to this paper is the discussion of "education in the future sense." (28, pp. 353-378) Toffler states that "one of our most critical subsystems - education - is dangerously malfunctioning." "Our schools face backwards toward a dying system, rather than forward to the emerging new society." (pp. 353-354) The people preparing for tomorrow's world, those "who must live in super-industrial societies . . . . will need new skills in three crucial areas: learning, relating, and choosing."* (p. 367)

The Situation in Education Today

The story of education with its successes and its many failures looms large in our minds at present. Somehow there has been great difficulty in maintaining motivation on the part of children and young people. We are told that our schools are "on the whole doing a poor job in training students to think clearly, critically, independently about fundamental issues. In this country the race against catastrophe has called out chiefly for more scientists and engineers; a broad liberal education is not generally considered a vital need." (20, p. 536) The watchword seems to be to get an education so that you can make more money and try to achieve the optimum of America's high standard of material living by keeping up with your friends and business associates.

---

* Oddly enough, despite the threats which many of us see on the horizon for man's freedom and his opportunity to make choices about his life and purposes, Toffler envisions the eventual dissolution of this present threat as we move into the world of tomorrow. "The Super-industrial Revolution also demands a new conception of freedom - a recognition that freedom, pressed to its ultimate, negates itself . . . this is why, despite 'backlash' and temporary reversals, the line of social advance carries us toward a wider tolerance, a more easy acceptance of more and more diverse human types." (p. 282)

The field of athletics and sport seems to be at least as poorly prepared as any in the educational system to help young people to get ready for the future. In our pluralistic, highly differentiated society we appear to be so torn by "internecine warfare" that we would undoubtedly find it almost impossible to even determine where ancient Athens was situated geographically, much less to reach some agreement about the relevancy of the Greek ideal in physical education and sport today. Most men in the profession don't want anything to do with the women, and the women are not overly impressed with the image of the male coach or physical educator either. Excesses and poor educational practices abound in interscholastic and intercollegiate athletics, and many physical educators rightfully "quake in their boots" at the thought of a confrontation with the "athletics establishment." Educational administrators are generally of no help in the struggle and conveniently manage to "look the other way or speak platitudes" to avoid displeasing the press, alumni, or legislators.

And what do the students at all levels think of us in athletics and physical education? They certainly don't look to us for creative educational plans. We are the conformists who want to preserve the status quo at almost any cost. We are anxious to keep order and discipline. We are the people who have encouraged the athletes to beat up the "long hairs" or to cut off their hair on occasion - and to keep the Blacks and other minority groups (including women and homosexuals) in their place in a variety of overt and covert ways. We continue to feel that our mission on earth is to cram skills, win-at-all costs ideas, muscles, endurance, and discipline down the throats of our young people.

At present I fear that we would have a lot of nerve to talk about transplanting the Greek ideal anywhere. How can we transplant some ideas from an educational ideal that the large majority of our profession doesn't even understand? And if they do understand it, they certainly haven't given much evidence that they truly appreciate it. Moreover, we should appreciate that the Greek ideal was outstanding for its time, but that we in all probability need a different ideal for today that is based upon a conception of man on earh moving into the twenty-first century.

Five Definitions of Man

Throughout history the primary business of philosophy has been to answer the question: "What is a man?" Morris has categorized five definitions of man's basic nature as follows: (1) the Platonic conception of man as a rational animal dichotomized into a body and a mind; (2) the Aritomistic three-dimensional man including mind, body, and soul; (3) the Renaissance man with a great need for knowledge to

improve man's lot on earth; (4) the redefinition of the Platonic-Aris-
totelean man divided into mind and body with emphasis on the development of intellectual qualities with "lip service" to bodily exercise; and
(5) the Deweyan man who is a problem-solving animal in the process
of evolution on earth. (19, pp. 21-22, 30-31)

One Recommended Position

Thus, with the problems that we are facing today - and those
that are most assuredly going to confront us tomorrow - the definition
of man which views him as a problem-solving organism in the process
of evolution on earth seems to make the most sense to me. This is
my "Greek ideal" for today's differentiated society. I believe along
with Morris and many others that man's capabilities have developed
because he has struggled with and overcome the problems which have
confronted him down through the centuries. We make sense out of
our experience, and then we adapt and reconstruct it to help us cope
with problems as they arise during our lives. It is not a question
here, therefore, of the dual nature of man, or a three-dimensional
man, or a "knowing creature" absorbing knowledge, or even the
Roman "sound mind in a sound body" with much greater stress on the
development of the intellect. In this pragmatic naturalistic definition
of man, the organism is unified, and we are concerned with the education of an amphibian in which "mind and body are instrumental
extensions of one another." (Ibid., p. 22) Athletics' and physical
education's task within this pattern is to teach man to move efficiently
and with meaning in sport, dance, exercise, and expressive activities
within the context of man's socialization in an evolving world.

What is Your Position?

But this is my ideal of athletics and sport for today, and not
necessarily yours. This you must work out for yourself, of course,
and it will probably change during your lifetime. Your beliefs about
the aims and objectives of athletics will necessarily be based on what
Charles Reich has called your "configuration," or on what Ayn Rand
has designated as your "sense of life." I don't believe, however,
that you can escape an in-depth self-analysis through which you
assess your philosophical foundations as they may relate to the values
and norms of North American society. In your personal life Weiss
postulates that you have "two main choices: to try to partake of all
that is good, but at the price of not being able to master anything, or
to be in full possession of a limited number of excellences while
benefitting from the presence of what other men produce." (30,
p. 142). Thus, you should decide upon your own hierarchy of educational values in this pluralistic society, and then attempt to bring
them to pass for yourself, for your family and friends, and most

definitely for all citizens within the framework of our evolving democratic society on this continent in a rapidly changing world.

What would it mean, therefore, if agreement could be reached on this definition? I believe that the following conditions would exist:

1. That educators and coaches alike would challenge the materialistic influences that are dominating athletics today almost insuperably.

2. That men _and_ women would work _together_ in our colleges and universities to provide opportunities in athletics of a sound educational nature for both sexes.

3. That coaches would become more professionally and disciplinarily oriented. Because it today is not developing a body of scientific knowledge, coaching is a trade unworthy of professional status.

4. That athletics and sport would acquire increased recognition as bonafide forces within our culture which can serve good or evil depending upon the leadership provided.

5. That recruiting student-athletes to attend a particular college or university to attain a legitimate education is not in itself a practice which can be condemned as bad or evil. The difficulty arises when the actual recruiting involves unnecessary, disproportionate, or illegal factors designed to induce a young athlete to attend one particular college or university. Problems arise because of hypocrisy and pressures to cheat. Life is too short - and the goal is not worth the involvement - to be dishonest with the life of a malleable young man or woman.

6. That competitive sports for boys and girls are desirable at some stage of their development. To encourage beneficial results, the extent of involvement, the intensity of the actual experience, and the role of coaches need much deeper scientific analysis.

7. That all concerned should work together to help children, youth, adults, and the elderly make worthy use of leisure. Physical recreation in lifetime sports can be one important part of this use of leisure.

8. That temporarily or permanently handicapped people can find enjoyable and profitable experiences in sports designed for their level of competency.

9. That we must relate dynamically to young people's lives or we are not going to survive. We must be dedicated, but relevant. In a free society our goal should be one in which young people have the opportunity to think and make decisions for themselves under wise guidance.

10. That, above all, we should work diligently to correct the prevailing situation in which the typical athlete arrives at the college door both educationally and culturally disadvantaged. When the minority group athlete becomes part of this mix, the urgency of the matter is doubled. We have seen evidence that black athletes are often knowingly and unknowingly exploited, but it would be the worst type of exploitation if black scholarship athletes did not obtain degrees from the institution they attend. Each of us must re-dedicate himself or herself to positive, sustained action toward the realization of "the Good Life" for all of our citizens. In the final analysis, "gradualism" may in the long run be fatal to us all.

Conclusion

Most assuredly, only you can decide to what extent you will help others to freely choose their own values and ideals--and to what extent you will help to provide a society where all men and women can develop their potentialities based on freedom of choice leading to a democratic social ideal. Finally, I think we can now see why some of the Greek ideal is out of phase in the late twentieth century, but that certain aspects of it still do have meaning today. You alone can decide for yourself what the "Greek ideal" should mean to you--today and tomorrow.

Footnotes and References

1. Boulding, Kenneth E. The Meaning of the Twentieth Century. New York: Harper & Row, Publishers, 1964.

2. Brubacher, John S. A History of the Problems of Education. New York: McGraw-Hill Company, Second edition, 1966.

3. Diem, Carl. Weltgeschichte des Sports und der Leibeserziehung. Stuttgart: J. G. Cotta'sche Buchhandlung, 1960.

4. Dimont, Max I. Jews, God, and History. New York: Simon and Schuster, 1962.

5. Drees, Ludwig. Olympia: Gods, Artists, and Athletes. New York: Frederick A. Praeger, Publishers, 1968.

6. Durant, Will. The Life of Greece. New York: Simon and Schuster, 1939.

7. Fairs, John R., "The Influence of Plato and Platonism on the Development of Physical Education in Western Culture," Quest, XI (December, 1968), 14-23.

8. _____, "When Was the Golden Age of the Body?", Journal of the Canadian Association for Health, Physical Education, and Recreation, Vol. 37, No. 1:11-24 (September-October, 1970).

9. Freeman, Kenneth J. (M. J. Rendall, editor). Schools of Hellas. London: Macmillan and Co., Ltd., 1922.

10. Galasso, P. J. and Duthie, J. H., "Escape to Opus," Journal of the CAHPER Vol. 37, No. 3:3-4 (January-February, 1971).

11. Gardiner, E. Norman. Athletics of the Ancient World. Oxford: Clarendon Press, 1930.

12. Hardy, W. G. The Greek and Roman World. Canada: McClelland and Stewart, Ltd., Revised edition, 1962.

13. Harris, Harold A. Greek Athletes and Athletics. London: Hutchinson & Co., Publishers, Ltd., 1964.

14. Janson, H. W. History of Art. Englewood Cliffs, New Jersey: Prentice-Hall, Inc., 1962.

15. Johnson, Harry M. Sociology: A Systematic Introduction. New York: Harcourt, Brace & World, Inc., 1960.

16. Kateb, George, "Utopia and the Good Life," in Daedalus, Vol. 94, No. 2:454-473 (Spring 1965).

17. Lindsay, Jack. The Ancient World. New York: G. F. Putnam's Sons, 1968.

18. Marrou, H. I. A History of Education in Antiquity. New York: Mentor Books, 1964.

19. Morris, Van Cleve, "Physical Education and the Philosophy of Education," JOHPER, 27, 3:21-22, 30-31 (March 1956).

20. Muller, Herbert J. Freedom in the Modern World. New York: Harper & Row, Publishers, 1966.

21. _____. The Uses of the Past. New York: Mentor Books, 1954.

22. Talcott, Parsons. Societies: Evolutionary and Comparative Perspectives. Englewood Cliffs, New Jersey: Prentice-Hall, Inc., 1966.

23. Quennell, Peter. The Colosseum. New York: Newsweek Book Division, 1971.

24. Reich, Charles A. The Greening of America. New York: Random House, Inc., 1970.

25. Robinson, Rachel S. Sources for the History of Greek Athletics. Cincinnati: Published by the author, 1955.

26. Siedentop, Daryl, "Differences between Hebrew and Greek Views of Man," a paper presented at the History of Sport Section, AAHPER Convention, Detroit, March 5, 1971.

27. Thompson, James G., "The Grecian View of Athletic Competition," a paper presented at the History of Sport Section, AAHPER Convention, Detroit, March 5, 1971.

28. Toffler, Alvin. Future Shock. New York: Random House, Inc., 1970.

29. Toynbee, Arnold J. Change and Habit: The Challenge of Our Time. New York: Oxford University Press, 1966.

30. Weiss, Paul. The Making of Men. Carbondale: Southern Illinois University Press, 1967.

31. Woody, Thomas. Life and Education in Early Societies. New York: The Macmillan Company, 1949.

32. Young, Alexander J., "Ancient Coaching Techniques, a paper presented at the Sports Science Symposium, APHPERA Convention, Halifax, Nova Scotia, 1970.

33.   Earle F. Zeigler. <u>Problems in the History and Philosophy of</u>
      <u>Physical Education and Sport</u>. Englewood Cliffs, New
      Jersey: Prentice-Hall, Inc., 1968.

34.   _____., "A Riddle for Tomorrow's World: How to
      Lead a Good Life," <u>Journal of the CAHPER</u>, Vol. 34,
      No. 2:3-8 (January 1968).

"BEYOND FREEDOM AND DIGNITY" FOR WOMEN IN SPORT

The values and norms of North American society have been preventing women from the achievement of their potential for excellence in athletics.[1] This denial of opportunity is definitely contrary to the idea of freedom which is espoused in democratic societies.

Of course, there is a world-wide idealogical struggle occurring that revolves around the concept of freedom. North Americans should become "incandescent" about this concept, if they would prevent the erosion of personal freedom in their lives. Absolute freedom for a person to do anything at any time would result in a truly anarchic state of affairs. The opposite extreme is well understood by millions in the world today. The "crunch" comes in democratic society when the group dictates to an individual "for his or her own good" - and presumably for the group's own good as well.

B. F. Skinner, in both Walden Two and his best-selling Beyond Freedom and Dignity, outlines a society in which the problems of men and women are solved by a scientific technology designed for human conduct. With this approach such prevailing values as freedom and dignity are reinterpreted to help bring about an utopian society. In sport it would appear that almost all women in our society have achieved Skinner's presumed halcyon state in which winning over another woman or man in high level athletic competition is not considered to be a laudable act. He states that the group can never really gain through the individual glory of any of its members in any competitive activity.

If a democratic society wishes to keep its ideals from being a mockery, women should be encouraged to reach their potential in all phases of life. Athletics is a significant cultural force, and women should not be prevented from competing or cooperating in individual, dual, and team sports with any other person - male or female. Only one reminder seems necessary - one of Arthur Steinhaus's principal principles - and it is that "sport was made for man" - and not vice versa. This means that no person should ever be exploited in a noneducational way in athletics. The individual's welfare - female or male - must never be sacrificed in the area. This we dare not forget.

---

[1] Prepared for presentation to the American Academy of Physical Education, Houston, Texas, March 22, 1972. Published as "Should Females Compete with Males in Non-Contact Sports?" The above was a reactor paper that appeared in The Academy Papers, Number 6, Iowa City, Iowa, September, 1972, pp. 16-17.

FITNESS AND AMATEUR SPORT ATHLETIC SCHOLARSHIPS
IN CANADA

My first reaction to the announcement of Fitness and Amateur Sport Athletic Scholarships in Canada was one of mild horror.* Then I realized that I was now a foreigner, and that I should mind my own business. After all, I reasoned, there is no doubt but that Canadians won't repeat all of the terrible mistakes made in the States; they're too smart to do that. And so I figured that the formula or format that you will follow must necessarily have been so designed as to carry out the plan in accordance with the highest of educational standards.

As this short reaction is being prepared, I have the benefit of a series of declarative statements prepared by Dean M. L. Van Vliet of the University of Alberta. I find myself in complete agreement with his position generally, and we would probably agree on most of the "specifics" as well. However, pluralistic philosophies of education – and of athletics, of course – are permitted on this continent, and each unique individual is entitled to his own beliefs.

The recruitment of athletes has a long and interesting history dating back at least to the ancient Greeks. "Recruiting" student-athletes to attend a particular college or university to obtain a bona-fide education is not in itself a practice which can be condemned as bad or evil. The difficulty arises when the actual recruiting involves unnecessary, disproportionate, or illegal factors designed to induce a young athlete, man or woman, to attend one particular college of university.

Basically, therefore, I feel that university personnel might even have a duty to encourage qualified young people to attend an institution of higher education, so long as any offers of assistance are consonant with the educational aims of the college or university, and are not restricted to some group whose purposes are subsidiary or actually contrary to these stated aims and objectives.

In my opinion we get into difficulty because of hypocrisy. Competitive athletics has not been officially accepted as an integral

---

* A reactor statement prepared for a meeting at the Convention of the Canadian Association for Health, Physical Education and Recreation, Inc., Waterloo, Ontario, June 7, 1971. The proceedings of this meeting were printed and distributed by the Faculty of Physical and Health Education, University of Windsor, 1971.

phase of a democratic educational system. Thus, even though athletics has great spectator appeal to those in all walks of life, and even though anthropologists tell us that star athletes from all educational levels serve as our "cultural maximizers," the social institution of competitive sport is fundamentally not considered to be fully respectable in our society. To this can be added immediately the most unfortunate distinction that has somehow developed between the amateur and the professional in sport - a distinction that is not applied in the same way to similar aspects of the culture such as music, dance, sculpture, painting, or any other performing art.

It is difficult to draw any comparison between the Canadian and the American scene. A large number of American colleges and universities have been recruiting and subsidizing legally and illegally for so many decades that athletes and their parents now accept the entire sordid affair as part of the way of life in the States. The obtaining of a number of "offers" has now become a status symbol which, if not received, is seemingly to the discredit of the athlete concerned. Further, there are so many souls of American educational administrators resting uneasily in limbo because of misfeasance or malfeasance in office in the area of intercollegiate athletics that there probably won't be any room left for ordinary sinners like you and me.

What advice can we possibly offer to Canada based on past experience? We can say with certainty that to recruit, subsidize, and/or proselyte athletes in what has come to be regarded as either the legal or illegal American way will only make a travesty of your espoused educational ideals. Canada should avoid like "the plague" the concept of the "tendered athlete." A certain amount of under-the-table help to "needy" athletes by alumni or misguided businessmen is impossible to control. Absolutely fundamental in this regard is that officials of colleges or universities cannot be involved with such practices either directly or indirectly. At present Canadian intercollegiate athletics is so close to the ideal that the Federal Government, even in a sincere attempt to improve Canada's international image in sport, should venture into this area only with the greatest amount of caution. If "warning signals" appear, withdrawal from the scene should be so rapid that most people won't even know that the idea was contemplated and implemented to any degree. Talented, worthwhile young men and women must have the opportunity for higher education in Canada regardless of their family's economic stratum, if the country is to continue to move ahead. In the area of athletics and sport, the primary concern should be to provide the finest type of coaches who will follow the highest standards in making competitive sport the force for good that it has the potential to be in our society. No other goal is worthy of Canada at this time.

IS OUR PHILOSOPHY OF COACHING SHOWING?

The answer to the question "Is our philosophy of coaching showing?" must be an unqualified affirmative.[1] If philosophy may be defined as "practical wisdom," and if coaching is the teaching and otherwise preparing of athletes for competition, it is immediately obvious that we have a considerable way to go before efforts will be crowned with success at an international level. This statement is not meant to be harsh in any way. It is designed to be constructively critical, however, and it is based on the belief that Canadian sport is indeed "at the crossroads."

Because of increased interest and emphasis on athletics and coaching recently at both the provincial and national levels, Professors Wendy Jerome of Laurentian, Pat Lawson of Saskatchewan, and John Pooley of Dalhousie were each asked to prepare personal statements embodying their philosophy of coaching for presentation at Calgary. Wendy Jerome saw "philosophy as being a basic set of beliefs which affects the way in which an individual views things, events, and relationships, and which determines the value that he places upon these aspects." Pat Lawson, recognizing that "some interaction and some incompatibility between 'conceived' and 'operative' values is the common state in most individuals," felt that the role of sport in society and the role of the coach (i.e., how he viewed or went about his task) are fundamental and "basic to a philosophy of coaching." John Pooley, stressing that "the sum of values and attitudes an individual possesses which are reflected in his opinions and actions" is basic to the process of philosophizing, offered a listing of qualities which a coach should possess if he would hope to be truly effective. These are all fine statements and most important to the understanding of the topic at hand.

Above it was stated that Canadian sport is at the crossroads. This is undoubtedly true as we move toward the 1976 Olympics in Montreal. Oddly enough, however, the writer had an article published just about twenty years ago with this identical theme (Zeigler, 1954, p. 24). It was just as true then as it is now. Another article prepared by the writer at that point was entitled "Should Canada Drop Out of the Olympic Games?" The response to this question today is exactly the same new as it was then: "Given the opportunity Canada can do

---

[1] A paper presented at the CAHPER Convention, Calgary, Alberta, July, 1973. It was published in slightly modified form in the Coaching Association of Canada Bulletin, No. 4:17-18 (1974).

as well as any other country its size in the world. Let's give our youth the chance to become better athletes by providing them with improved leadership and facilities in school physical education and community recreation!" (Zeigler, 1952, p. 9).

This might be somewhat discouraging to today's coaches and athletes, not to mention governmental officials, to be reminded that the situation today is quite similar to the way things were twenty years ago. As a matter of fact, the situation has improved immeasurably from an objective standpoint; relatively speaking, however, there does not seem to be a great deal to choose in most sports between then and now.

The reason for the "at the crossroads" statement at that time was that the negative aspects of U. S. intercollegiate sport were somewhat of a problem here too. These have been controlled largely in Canada, although certain "trouble spots" are still with us and will require vigilance. The cry to drop out of the Olympic Games came as a result of the 1952 experience in Finland. Athletes from Canada were eliminated in the trials of the various events with quite monotonous regularity, and articles were written expressing the belief that we shouldn't bother with the Games unless we could do considerably better when it came to winning medals.

At that time the writer admitted that Canada was a small country in terms of population. Further, it was stated that many of our young men and women came from relatively small communities where opportunities for athletic participation under sound coaching were few. Then the status and existence of gymnasia, pools, and other athletic facilities was considered. For example, the lack of indoor track and field facilities in the East was cited. Despite these difficulties of the early 1950s, and one wonders what an accurate survey would indicate as to the status of these problems in the early 1970s, some hope was expressed for the future of instruction and coaching in athletic skills because of the inauguration of many programs of professional preparation in Canadian universities. Certainly the level of athletic coaching must have been improved, but the introduction of the "disciplinary trend" in the 1960s - with seemingly lessening of emphasis on the theory and practice of athletic skills - may have brought about a "levelling-off" of the "improvement of coaching ability curve" (a condition which should be carefully examined and rectified through greatly improved cooperation with departments of education if such has been the case).

The greatest stumbling block on the road toward success in world sport competition has been the Canadian philosophy toward sport and games - actually a series of beliefs about what is important in life which should be examined with great care and wisdom before a concerted effort is made to change them. Obviously, it would be sheer folly to attempt to become a carbon copy of the methods and techniques that are followed typically in the United States. You can sell your soul to the Devil, but there comes a day of reckoning when you are inevitably confronted with the stark reality of the situation when moral standards and/or educational standards are so defiled that intelligent, sensitive people cannot help but be ashamed of the result.

In a free country such as Canada, one that is characterized by a concept of evolving democracy, certain basic values such as freedom and the influence of such social forces as the type of political state, nationalism, economics, and religion are so strong that any effort to truly dictate the lives of young athletes from the federal level would be doomed to failure. On the other hand, we want to show the world that the Canadian way of life is capable of producing outstanding, fine sportsmen and sportswomen who can win their share of medals in international competition. Bringing this ideal to fruition will not be a simple matter. In fact, it may be impossible, but it is certainly worth the effort! This we should never forget.

Despite some errors of commission and omission, we must be proud of, and we should support, provincial and national efforts to improve the quality and quantity of athletic participation on the part of a steadily increasing percentage of young men and young women. For those who are fearful, let them remember that there are "checks and balances" in this society that will temper the few ridiculous fanatics who may wander into our midst.

There is one thought that should be left with our men and women involved in sport coaching. Some of you are amateurs; some of you are semi-professionals; and some of you are professionals. You all have a place and a contribution to make. What seems to be lacking at present is tenable sport theory and a solid, growing body of knowledge about the task at hand. Such knowledge can only be obtained through the efforts of dedicated scholars and researchers who will conduct both pure and applied research about the many coaching problems and questions which demand answers. Then we will need to devise administrative patterns whereby teaches of coaches will convey this knowledge to the three groupings listed above. Such a plan will require cooperation at all levels of our society, but it can be done by men and women of good will working together for the best interests of Canada and the world! Speaking as an administrator and professor, and as a former coach of three sports, I pledge myself to work for a more comprehensive and improved level of sporting competition. We should all make a similar pledge to do our part - and a bit more - in the development of the finest type of competitive sport in Canadian life.

Selected References

Zeigler, Earle F., "The Challenge of Sports in Today's World." Journal of CAHPER, Vol. 20, No. 7, March, 1954, pp. 23-25.

_____ ., "Should Canada Drop Out of the Olympic Games?" Journal of the Canadian Association for Health, Physical Education, and Recreation, Vol. 18, No. 2, October, 1952, pp. 7-9.

FREEDOM IN COMPETIVE SPORT

The concept of freedom within the framework of competitive sport is the major concern or problem of this paper.* The consideration of such a topic, and especially as it might relate to so-called educational sport, is absolutely vital at this time in North American sport and/or athletics. Some people might not immediately see the rationale for such a presentation, but the American Council on Education, the Carnegie Corporation, and the Ford Foundation would not have paid out "hard cash" for an exploratory study in this area of education if they had not been convinced that a searching look at the phenomenon of competitive sport was warranted at this time. It is hypothesized here that enough evidence and opinion can be marshalled to convince others that many, if not most, sports (or experiences in sports by individuals) may need to be modified by the injection of opportunities for the participants to make individual choices and decisions that will enhance the quality of life for all concerned.

Freedom is used here to describe the "condition of being able to choose and to carry out purposes" (Muller, 1961, xiiii). This concept will be discussed much more fully below, but for now it will simply be stated that the problem of individual freedom in what has been identified as a transitional society (the twentieth century) cannot be safely placed aside for future reference. Even though much progress has been made in the achievement of civil rights for man on this continent in this century, there have been a number of developments recently in both Canada and the United States which force a reflective person to realize how precarious a commodity an individual's freedom really is.

If it is indeed true that the present society is in the midst of a great transition, and that now "we must learn to master ourselves as we are learning to master nature," then along the way it will be necessary to avoid certain traps. If man is not able to steer his course around these traps, it is quite possible that life as it is presently known on this planet will cease (Boulding, 1964, p. 24). If sport has become an important part of culture—a culture that is in jeopardy in the years immediately ahead—it should be employed as a "socially useful servant." Such a purpose for sport is indeed justified for "individual man" and for "social man," whether its place in the

---

* A paper presented at the Fourth Annual Meeting of the Philosophic Society for the Study of Sport, London, Ontario, Canada, November 16, 1974. (This paper is being considered for publication at the time this book was being prepared.)

formal educational system is being considered or whether its role in society at large is the question.

The terms "sport" and "athletics" will be used here interchangeably, because that appears to be the accepted general practice on the continent. This is not to say that James Keating is not etymologically correct in his earlier distinction between these two terms, only that the public doesn't tend to recognize the former as the involvement of a "gentleman sportsman seeking to maximize the pleasure of the occasion for himself and his opponent" and the latter as the "prize-hunting athlete with a win-at-all-costs attitude."

The main problem of this analysis is, therefore, to posit a workable definition of the concept of "freedom" for an evolving democratic society today--one that may be adapted to the experience of men in competitive sport in such a way that they may live fuller lives while at the same time strengthening the position of democracy as a system of government. Obviously, this is a tall task that can only be considered in an exploratory way in such a relatively short paper. Further, this discussion for now will be limited to men's sport, although the problem is equally as important for women (and will be treated in a separate paper later).

The broad outline of this paper will, therefore, revolve around preliminary answers to the following questions: (1) what is the present status of man in regard to the future, and especially to the concept of freedom; (2) how has the concept of freedom been viewed in philosophy; (3) how has the idea of freedom been treated in philosophy of education; (4) what is the status of "freedom" in men's sport and/ or athletics in North America; (5) what are some of the prospects for individual freedom in the future; and (6) what conclusions may reasonably be drawn about the need for, and the possibility of, introducing more freedom into competitive sport in North America in the near future?

Man's Status and Its Relationship to Freedom

It was the best of time, it was the worst of times;
It was the age of wisdom, it was the age of foolishness;
It was the epoch of belief, it was the epoch of incredulity;
It was the season of light, it was the season of darkness;
It was the spring of hope, it was the winter of despair;
We had everything before us, we had nothing before us;
We were all going direct to heaven, we were all going direct the other way.

When Charles Dickens wrote these opening lines for his novel, A Tale of Two Cities, he hardly knew that he would also be describing conditions in the last quarter of the twentieth century. Of course, some had much more optimism than is expressed in this passage, while others are preaching a doctrine of despair. For example, the Nobel prize winner, biologist Albert Szent-Gyorgi, feels that mankind is moving inexorably toward calamity because society now has a "death orientation" rather than a "life orientation"--a condition which he felt was present only forty years ago (approximately 1937). Dr. Szent-Gyorgi believes that only youth can turn the world around and ward off the "terrible strain of the idiots who govern the world." (Of course, one could argue that these "idiots" are the only ones that appear to be available at the moment!) He describes the government as a gerontocracy that "cannot really assimilate new ideas" (Reinhold, Feb. 20, 1970).

Everything that is published is not so pessimistic. Writing in the early 1960's, Henry Steele Commager explained how "never before in a mere quarter century has the world seen so many revolutionary developments in society, politics, science, and technology" (1961, p. 80). He did point out, nevertheless, that these "were staggering possibilities for good or evil opened up to mankind." Lest too much optimism is exhibited, consider some of the cities' problems for just a moment: pollution of air and water; exodus of high-wage industries; flight to the suburbs of those earning higher incomes; influx of those with lower incomes to slum areas; shortage of recreation areas and leadership; sharp increase in the rate of crime of all types; rise in the population of juveniles and the aged; housing ghettos with unbelievable filth; overcrowded schools with almost built-in discrimination present; and transportation jams which daily try the patience and increase the tensions of the citizenry on the North American continent (Sullivan, May 12, 1967).

In the 1970's inflation and the energy crisis cause despair even as scientists and pundits discuss what mankind must do while there is yet time to keep accelerating technology from becoming the master rather than the servant of earth creatures. Julian Huxley describes the present situation as the crisis in man's destiny (January, 1967). Banesh Hoffman in Flatland (Abbott, 1952) says,

> We are like hapless passengers on a crowded escalator, carried relentlessly forward till our particular floor arrives, and we step off into a place where there is no time, while the material composing our bodies continues its journey on the inexorable escalator--perhaps forever.

In the same vein Loren Eiseley offering "reflections on man's uncompleted journey through time" describes him as the "cosmic orphan" (SR/World, Feb. 23, 1974). He explains how man is an evolutionary "changeling" whose final problem might be to "escape himself, or, if not that, to reconcile his devastating intellect with his heart" (p. 24).

An urgent need for prompt action usually accompanies such gloomy forecasts. One different but interesting analysis of the plight of the modern Western world is offered by Clarke as he reviews the work of Joseph Campbell. The claim is that myths tell as much about men in a society as a man's dreams tell him individually. Campbell believes that the former myths held by men have not been replaced by newer, equally vital myths today in the West. The resultant period of radical reorientation required to develop a modern mythology that will give men stability in cultural attitudes through "veiled explanations of the truth" has been forced upon the West almost too rapidly. Thus, in the opinion of Campbell, there hasn't yet developed an adequately functioning mythology for today's world in which man has acquired what he feels to be a sufficient explanation of the mysterious universe and man's place in such a vast enterprise. The rites and rituals which support the social order have been vanishing. As a result people haven't been receiving the necessary guidance available in the past to assuage the psychological crises that inevitably appear in the individual's birth to death cycle. Also, because of society's pluralism the former grand scale myths may have to be individualized and perhaps small-group oriented. Some political leaders may help, but the individual will have to conduct his own personal search in keeping to a degree with the social system's dominant values (Clarke, Jan. 17, 1972).

The concept of freedom--the "free man living in a free country" --is a dream or myth that means a great deal on this continent and to countless millions elsewhere. Even before Watergate and the almost unbelievable subsequent disclosures, Leonard Fein had urged his fellow Americans "to try to dream again"--and this time in a more modest manner (Fein, Feb. 11, 1973). The old dream, he stated, was about America's "innate goodness and bestness." It is now generally recognized that technological superiority does not mean that the United States has a charter to lead all people everywhere to a "word of peace, good will, and prosperity." This is not a put-down by someone expatriated; it is an exhortation to all to develop the capacity to dream again, to promote the ideal of individual freedom in a free society--and to so analyse sport and/or athletics philosophically that all concerned will work toward the inclusion of a greater amount of freedom in competitive sport as it is functioning today.

Turn where one will, there is a continuing flow of informed opinion in recent years pointing out man's dilemma or predicament in regard to the amount of freedom available in his life. These authors and scholars have examined the situation in the Western world, not the so-called Iron Curtain countries where very little real, individual freedom is available to the average man. As far back as 1941, Erich Fromm asserted that "modern man, freed from the bonds of pre-individualistic society, which simultaneously gave him security and

limited him, has not gained freedom in the positive sense of the realization of the individual self; that is the expression of his intellectual,
emotional, and sensuous potentialities . . ." His thesis is that even
though man may indeed have achieved a certain amount of indepen-
dence and rationality, he has still found himself anxious and powerless because of isolation. Somehow man is not ready for this isolation, and he therefore finds it unbearable. His alternatives are either
to discover new varieties of submission or to move forward, accepting his new status and potential, with "the full realization of positive
freedom which is based on the uniqueness and individuality of man"
(Fromm, 1969, viii).

There is no doubt but that various social forces and developments are truly forcing this issue of individual freedom as a potential
human value. War upon war, the cold war, and internal strife, along
with "the age of triumphant science and technology" is "forcing man
into a new philosophical era based on the 'why' of living" (Robertson,
quoting Seaborg, Feb. 5, 1970). Can it be that these "troubled times"
are "a prelude to deeper and more positive thinking in which man
would examine human values and goals?" (Ibid.)

Seaborg's wishful thinking may come true; in the meantime,
however, writers analyzing freedom in society have developed a variety of misgivings. Someone like Richard Rovere, the author of Waist
Deep in the Big Muddy, has expressed himself in an article entitled
"Freedom: Who Needs It?" Writing in 1968, he found something new
--"a disenchantment not only with the society in which individual
liberty thrives as it seldom has in the past but with the idea of liberty
itself"--and this may be considered to be most disturbing, because it
means that many of the young radicals, and a number of their elders
are losing faith in the usefulness of seemingly free institutions.
Rovere tends to think that such feelings are without precedent in
American history. He does go on to assert, nevertheless, that many
have been "mistaken as to the nature and value of individual liberty
and have even turned inside out the classic defenses of it." Basically,
he maintains that the famous and stirring appeals for freedom and
liberty have been mixed in their intent; to be sure people did want
self-expression fervently, but the great freedom crusades were cam-
paigns for collective freedom, so to speak (p. 41).

Distinguished historians like Henry Steele Commager may ask
a serious question like "Is Freedom Dying in America?" because he
seems that most people are "equating dissent with lawlessness" and
"nonconformity with treason," and in the process there is arising a
"popular indifference toward the loss of liberty" (Commager, 1970,
p. 17). Is it possible that this represents a failure to comprehend
what is at stake, or have a great many people of all ages decided that
it doesn't make any difference in the final analysis? Is even the "free

world" moving inexorably toward Skinner's "beyond freedom and dignity" concept as is embodied in his <u>Walden Two</u>? One hopes not.

Finally, Charles Reich, the author of <u>The Greening of America</u>, has told anyone who would listen that "what the times urgently demand, what our survival demands, is a new consciousness that will reassert rational control over the industrial system and the Corporate State, and transform them into a way of life that protects and advances human values" (<u>The New York Times</u>, October 21, 1970). Conversely, George Kennan, the noted historian and diplomat, who admits readily "the reality of the seriousness of the various evils to which Reich calls attention," describes Reich's proposed solution to the many evils of modern society as romantic, utopian, illusory, and hysterical. He concludes by stating that "there is, in short, plenty to do. But it is clear that if Mr. Reich's philosophy prevails, that will not happen" (<u>The New York Times</u>, October 28, 1970).

Freedom in Philosophy

This, then, in necessarily abbreviated fashion, is the situation. Times are exceedingly difficult, and man's freedom is being challenged and delimited for a variety of reasons. Keep in mind Muller's definition of freedom as "the condition of being able to choose and carry out purposes" (see page 1), but observe also Richard Goodwin's qualifying clause which states "to the outer limits fixed by the material conditions and capacity of the time" (<u>The American Condition</u>, 1974, p. 24). To this Goodwin adds further a "social dimension" that some might reject: "Not only does the free individual establish his own purposes, but they are consistent with the purposes of his fellows. He seeks his own wants and to cultivate his own faculties in a manner which is consistent with the well-being of others" (p. 28). One can just see Thoreau shaking his head vigorously from right to left because of the constraints imposed by Mr. Goodwin.

Despite the many outcries that are heard about the loss of, or the <u>possible</u> loss of--or even the <u>denial</u> of certain individual freedoms in North America--Walter Kaufmann has recently postulated that the large majority of people really "crave a life without choice." In fact, he has coined a name for the "malady" that seems to afflict most men. He calls it <u>Decidophobia</u> or the fear of autonomy or personal decision-making that affects a great many people. In his <u>Without Guilt and Justice</u> (Kaufmann, 1973), he delineates ten strategies by which modern man avoids making serious life decisions that would lift him from a decidophobic state to one of personal autonomy. These strategies (1) allegiance to a religion; (2) drifting by either adopting a stance of "statusquoism" or by "dropping out"; (3) commitment or allegiance to a movement; (4) allegiance to a school of thought--less politically active than #3; (5) exegetical thinking, a "text is God" approach; (6) Manichaeism, or an elementary "good and evil" battle-ground approach to the world; (7) moral rationalism, or a position which claims that correct reasoning alone can demonstrate what a person ought to do in all difficult or fateful situations; (8) pedantry, which involves continued concern with minute or microscopic details "while Rome is burning"; (9) "riding the wave of the future," a short-sighted position or faith assumed by some to give support to the aceeptance of dogmatic political ideologies (a belief often connected with a religious faith or similar movement); and (10) interestintly enough, is marriage--an extremely popular strategy for women in many societies that delimits very sharply thereafter their potential for autonomous decisions in their lives (a fate that often befalls men similarly). Of course, a number of these strategies can be combined in any one life with perhaps even more devastating effect on the possibility of a person leading an autonomous life. A truly autonomous person would strive successfully to avoid employing all of these ten strategies, or at the very most adopt only one or two of these strategies--and to a limited extent!

It is now the time in this discussion to examine the concept of "freedom" more carefully from a philosophical standpoint. In the history of philosophy this concept has typically been employed in such a way that it has related to events that occur in the everyday relations of men, or it has involved particular aspects or conditions of social life. Despite this delimitation, significant differences of usage are still available, more or less legitimate and convenient to a greater or lesser extent. For example, the traditional, liberal meaning of freedom relates to the absence of constraint or coercion. Thus, in Partridge's words--actually a position similar to that defined by J. S. Mills as "negative" freedom or "freedom from"--the following definition has been typically considered first in the Western world:

> "A man is said to be free to the extent that he can choose his own goals or course of conduct, can choose between alternatives available to him, and is not compelled to act as he himself would not choose to act, or prevented from acting as he would otherwise choose to act, by the will of another man, of the state, or of any other authority" (Partridge, 1967, Vol. 3, p. 222).

Obviously, this appears to be a carefully worded definition and quite complete, but some wonder if it should be broadened still further. For example, there are often natural conditions that limit man's freedom by preventing him from achieving his personal goals. Others would carry the definition one step further by the insertion of a stipulation that a man is not truly free unless he has the where-withal to achieve his life goals. This means that he should be provided with the means or power to attain a freely selected objective. Partridge complains at this point that this is stretching the definition far too much, and that indeed the ordinary language of this assumption has been distorted. Being free, in his opinion, is most certainly not the same as the ways and means that one employs to achieve the goals that he has set for his life!

Proceeding from the above premises--that is, the opportunity for uncoerced action--any definition of the term "coercion" must take into consideration the matter of indirect control of an individual's life style, as well as those obstacles or hurdles which are overtly placed in his path. For example, a rich man might covertly employ gifts of money and other valued articles so as to deprive another an opportunity to be selected as a candidate for some private or public office. Such a tactic could be carried out in a most subtle manner--or perhaps even unconsciously in certain cases--by the person with the large amount of assets. Still further, a person might not know enough to select the best possible alternative action leading toward a more successful future for himself and his family, no matter whether direct or indirect methods of control or coercion had been employed to limit his freedom by another person or group of people. The only conclusion to be drawn here is that a high degree of education becomes increasingly important for each individual in a society steadily growing more complex if we wish to guarantee citizens what might be called "full" freedom.

Up to this point this discussion about freedom has been limited to the idea or concept of freedom from certain impositions or controls in life, but obviously it is vitally important that the concept of freedom for certain opportunities or alternative actions be introduced hree as being more positive (as opposed to negative) aspects of freedom. Throughout the history of philosophy, for example, a number of different possibilities for, or approaches to, "the good life" have been postulated. Without becoming too specific at this point about what these approaches to the good life might be, certainly in political and social matters--or even so-called moral matters--the free person should look forward to a variety of freedom of, to, in, and from as he moves through life. Here are being suggested such freedoms as freedom of thought, speech, association; freedom to assemble, worship, move about; freedom in the use or sale of property, or the choice of occupation or employer; and freedom from want, fear, etc. Obviously, these ideas are tremendously important in education and, as is being contended in this paper, the ramifications of the concept of individual freedom have only vaguely and occasionally been considered seriously in North American competitive sport. When some individuals and/or groups become too powerful, other people's freedom is often curtailed. This situation can and does occur in both a negative and positive way in the various types of political states. Granted that pluralistic philosophical positions or stances are permitted in evolving democratic societies, what then can and should the concept of freedom mean in education and in competitive sport (within education primarily, but also in professional circles)? The remainder of the paper will be devoted to a relatively brief description of, and the recommendation of a few possible answers to, this very thorny problem that exists here and throughout the world at the present time.

Freedom in Philosophy of Education

In his book, Future Shock, which assuredly has exerted a considerable influence on North American thought in the early 1970's, Toffler devotes a chapter to "education in the future sense" as one of his "strategies for survival" (1970, pp. 353-378). He states that "one of our most critical subsystems--education--is dangerously malfunctioning." His analysis has indicated that "our schools face backwards toward a dying system, rather than forward to the new emerging society" (pp. 353-354). His assumption is that the people preparing for tomorrow's world, those "who must live in super-industrial societies . . . . will need new skills in three crucial areas: learning, relating, and choosing" (p. 367). Curiously enough, despite the threats which many see on the horizon for man's freedom and his opportunity to make choices about his life, Toffler envisions the eventual dissolution of this present threat to individual freedom in the world of tomorrow. He explains that,

> The Super-industrial Revolution also demands a new conception of freedom--a recognition that freedom, pressed to its ultimate, negates itself . . . this is why, despite 'backlash' and temporary reversals, the line of social advance carries us toward a wider tolerance, a more easy acceptance of more and more diverse human types (p. 282).

Despite this precious bit of optimism for the future, the story of education with its successes and yet its many failures looms large in the minds of a large number of people at present. Perhaps it has ever been thus, but there certainly has been great difficulty recently in maintaining motivation on the part of children and young people. People on all sides question whether young men and women are being prepared to think clearly, critically, and independently about fundamental issues. There is definitely an uneasy mood prevailing in education at all levels on this continent and, for that matter, throughout the entire West as well. The importance of a sound general or liberal education has been decried with regularity, and its ideals have seemingly been deserted by the young. The revolutionary mood of the 1960's, brought on to a large extent by the disastrous Vietnam involvement, may have subsided to a large extent, but the relatively placid, "cud-chewing contentment of the semi-drug and -alcohol culture" of the 1970's is equally as frightening to those who ponder over the scary apparitions hazily delineated by the naysayers for the future.

Today's students seem imbued with a sense of urgency regarding the transmission of varying types of professional knowledge that will bring about quick assimilation into the community and at least a reasonably high standard of living in the present inflationary economy.

In the opinion of the writer, the field of educational philosophy, with its present disciplinary emphasis, is "shedding very little light" for the average professional education student. It seems that there was a time, in the late 1800's and early 1900's, when a combined "common sense and rational thought approach, coupled with the occasional dash of theological fervor" stirred thought about educational aims and objectives. Such educational philosophy could possibly be identified as "normative philosophizing about education based on metaphysical speculation." This gradually brought about the advent of a philosophy of education "systems approach" based on the leading philosophical schools of thought. During this period it was relatively simple to understand what was meant by educational freedom. So-called educational progressivism, "sired" by the great John Dewey, involved the concepts of pupil freedom, individual differences, pupil interest, pupil growth, no absolutely fixed values, and that "education is life now." Conversely, educational essentialism, championed by such stalwarts as H. H. Horne, believed that there were certain educational values by which the individual must be guided; that effort takes precedence over interest and that this girds moral stamina; that the experience of the past has powerful jurisdiction over the present; and that the cultivation of the intellect is most important in education. Such beliefs attributed to each broad position were, of course, only representative and not inclusive. It was felt, however, that a person should be able to delineate his own position generally under one broad category or the other--and then base his professional practice on such delineation. Oh for the good old days!

Commencing in the 1950's philosophy of education on this continent began its own "Drang nach Disziplin" with a resultant "miasma" that tends to leave the average mortal in a bewildered state. Some have become theory-builders, while others analyzed language or various portions thereof. Those who espoused pragmatism have maintained their interest to a considerable degree, while others have adopted a phenomenological-existentialistic approach that in some quarters has seriously challenged the microscopic approach of the language analysts. With the possible exception of the occasional effort to analyze the term "freedom" conceptually, it has remained for those with a pragmatic leaning or those with an existential orientation to give present-day meaning to the urgent present-day need for a new type of "human education" theory that could possibly help man obviate the effects of "bureautechnocracy" and become something more than a "trivialized man."

Such a theory which serves to revitalize the concept of individual freedom in a jaded educational setting on this continent has been postulated by Charles Tesconi and Van Cleve Morris (1972, p. 161 et ff.). Tesconi and Morris characterize the developing social culture of the past few generations as a bureautechnocracy. Possibly as a result of the managerial revolution that has taken place in this century as well, man on this continent is now faced with an "ecological problem" of enormous proportions. The prevailing environment is homogenizing man:

> Bureautechnocracy may be defined as the pattern of social organization in which a pyramidal hierarchy of operational control is linked with rationalized and standardized means for reaching predetermined ends, with the overall aim of achieving systematization, efficiency, and economy (p. 161).

Such a bureautechnocratic state has certainly become characteristic of the educational system and, as a result, young people consistently have the feeling that they are being used by the system. As their self-esteem is being wounded, they are finding different techniques for striking back at the system. The end result of this scientific liberalism is that education has become steadily and increasingly anti-human while the "juggernaut of science rolls on"--as prophesied by John Dewey as a method to eventually resolve all of the affairs of man (p. 163).

Tesconi and Morris explain further their theory about how a "new conservatism" has set in:

> The old conservatives wanted to hold on to a set of transsocial values: hard work, saving for a rainy day, personal freedom, economic self-interest. The scientific liberals wanted to reexamine these values in light of social consequences, that is, apply the method of science to determine their social adequacy. But now, the liberals have grown conservative about the method; they want to hold on to it at all costs. Thus, the scientific liberals are now learning what the old conservatives have been trying to tell them for a hundred years: there is need for some sort of stability, an allegiance to some transsocial principle. The liberals have found it in science. Moreover, the liberals are quietly accepting another old conservative insight--there is need for an elite to make sure that the method of science is used correctly and protected from Philistine demands for harsh, unthinking "solutions" to social problems.
>
> Now the New Left, rejecting both stability and elitism but adopting a little from each ethic--hatred of government from the conservatives, concern for the weak from the

liberals--is bugging both right and left with its iconoclasm
and demand for change and reform (1972, p. 164).

The great concern is, therefore, that "in the bureautechnocratic
shuffle, men began to lose some of their humanness; they grew resis-
tant to the difficult task of thinking about life, content to go on believing in the sacredness of science as applied to both things and men and
willing to accept a system which indeed turns men into things as the
necessary order of the human world" (p. 166). All of this has both
immediate and direct application to the state of education today. For
many the present compromise between "the Aristotelian rationalists
and the Deweyan pragmatists"--the idea that mastery of knowledge
which leads to problem-solving ability--is breaking down because it
doesn't provide humaneness and a concern for fellowman--true personal significance. "If an experience expands awareness and intensifies personal significance, it is educational" (p. 208). The upshot of
this undoubtedly most insightful analysis of the plight of education in
North America today is that drastic change is needed, and that such
change revolves around the concept of individual freedom. People
must be free to make choices about their own life plans and professional careers; this has been known for some time. This "education
for personal significance" involves a reordering of priorities and an
alteration of educational methodology.

All of this seemingly utopian argument demands practical application to the situation at hand in education, and most particularly to
the question of freedom in competitive sport. The student (or student-
athlete as he--not she--has been typically designated) needs "to make
an assessment of his own feelings and attitudes, and then to compare
those with the feelings and attitudes of others" (p. 209). In this way
one will truly see the real world through his own eyes and perspective.
From this can follow--and, indeed, must follow--the opportunity to
make a personal choice that will result in much more of a "personal
contract" than the typical "social contract" with which youth is confronted on all sides at present. The third stage of this educational
process should follow up immediately on the idea that the "personal
encounter" allows a personal choice that can soon result in a "gut-
level passion" to know--what Tesconi and Morris call "affective
curiosity" (p. 211). Such an educational approach in the classroom,
in the gymnasium, or on the field would do much to bring about a
"personification of knowledge"; to establish a "joyful Socratic relationship" between teacher/coach and student in which the student "discovers knowledge" and explores his own feelings; and to start the student down the road to the establishment of a personal identity with a
significant amount of self-esteem. What is needed desperately is the
opportunity to make choices about the educational process that will
result in a "self-posturing" experience characterized by a developing
feeling of authenticity within the so-called anti-man culture.

- 260 -

Freedom in Competitive Sport

After a brief introduction, this paper considered the present status of man facing an uncertain future in which the amount of freedom available to him may be sharply curtailed. Then the concept of freedom was placed in philosophical perspective--that is, how the term is defined or conceived in typical philosophical discussions. In addition to the idea or concept of freedom from certain controls in life, it was stressed further that there should be freedom for certain opportunities and choices among alternative courses of action--a definitely more positive kind of freedom in the latter instance. It was obvious that the various "kinds" of freedom deserved most serious consideration in the educational system of an evolving democratic state.

Now the present pattern operative in competitive sport will be described with specific reference to the situation in intercollegiate athletics. Selected references to interscholastic athletics and professional sport will be introduced in certain instances where deemed pertinent. The concept of freedom as described above will be brought into the discussion whenever it seems necessary. The underlying hypothesis is that coaches of competitive sport in only very rare instances consider the concept of freedom to be an important aspect of the sport which they coach, the methodology which they employ to carry out their duties, or, for that matter, of the total educational experience being provided to their charges within the university or college concerned. It is believed that the prevailing competitive sport situation in Canadian universities is quite different than that of most universities in the United States, but no effort will be made to prove both this and the previous underlying hypothesis from the standpoint of historical, descriptive, or experimental group method research (although such investigations would undoubtedly bring out most interesting results). This is an effort to explore the prevailing situation tentatively using a philosophical orientation in which the concepts of freedom from (a negative approach) and freedom of, to, and/or in are considered. The idea of direct or indirect methods of control will be kept in mind also, but the definition of the term "freedom" will not be stretched to include all of the ways and means needed to realize all of one's life goals. The concept of "education for personal significance" will be kept in focus to determine whether competitive sport typically provides a "personal encounter" resulting in a subsequent personal choice that eventually leads to the "affective curiosity" that Tesconi and Morris also refer to as a "gut-level passion" to know.

U. S. Intercollegiate Athletics--1929 and 1974. In 1929 the Carnegie Report entitled American College Athletics explained that "the defects of American college athletics are two: commercialism, and a negligent attitude toward the educational opportunity for which the American college exists." Additionally, the Report stressed that

the so-called amateur code was violated continually; that recruiting
and subsidizing was "the darkest blot upon American college sport";
that athletic training and hygiene practices were deplorable and actually jeopardized health in many instances; that athletes are not poorer
academically, but that hard training for long hours impaired scholastic standing; that athletics as conducted fail in many cases "to utilize
and strengthen such desirable social traits as honesty and the sense of
fair play"; that few of the sports which are most popular contributed
to physical recreation after college; that many head coaches were receiving higher pay than full professors, but that their positions were
dependent upon successful win-loss records; that the athletic conferences were not abiding by the letter, much less the spirit of the established rules and regulations; and that athletes were not receiving the
opportunity to "mature under responsibility."

In 1974, some forty-five years later, there seems to be every
indication that the only one of the above-mentioned areas of criticism
showing improvement would be that of athletic training and hygiene
practices! Even on this point a cynic would be quick to point out that
improved athletic training could be expected because of the desire to
keep expensive athletic talent healthy enough to "earn its keep." At
any rate, in 1974 the American Council on Education discovered that
"there's a moral problem in college athletics," and that "the pressure
to win is enormous" (Cady, The New York Times, March 10, 1974)--
facts which have been known to cognoscenti in educational circles for
decades. For example, The New York Times commissioned a survey
of some forty colleges and universities and reported in 1951 that the
flagrant abuses of athletic subsidization in many colleges and universities "promoted the establishment of false values"; "are the bane of
existence in American education"; "lower educational standards
generally"; force educators "to lose out to politicians"; and "do further injury to democracy in education" (Grutzner, 1951). Obviously,
it serves no purpose to enumerate such statements endlessly, because
volumes could be filled with them before 1929 and up to the present.
Thus, the emphasis in this paper will be placed on exactly how these
various abuses impinge on the freedom of those who are often identified as "student-athletes."

Relationship to Concepts of "Negative Freedom" or "Freedom
from". The contention here is that in the United States the talented
young athlete is "caught up by the system" which in the final analysis
negates just about every aspect of the philosopher's definition of
"freedom from" as explained by Partridge earlier. The young athlete
is pressured inordinately to accept the society's goals and thereby his
course of conduct is limited. The truly gifted athlete is so besieged
by forceful, hypocritical recruiting that it is not possible for him to
choose intelligently between alternatives available to him. In the
final analysis he is compelled to act as "he himself would not choose
to act" or, to continue with phrases taken from Partridge's definition,

he "is prevented from acting as he would otherwise choose to act."
Lastly, all of this typically takes place or is forced upon him by
"the will of another man, of the state, or of any other authority"
(Partridge, 1967, Vol. 3, p. 222). Translated to the realm of competitive sport in the U.S., this becomes the will of the coach or members of his staff, the president of the university or even the governor
of the state; and "any other authority" could be well-intentioned, but
basically extremely shortsighted, parents, alumni, secondary school
coaches, or friends.

To place these assertions in better perspective by some docu-
mentation, recall the recent statement by Moses Malone, the outstanding high school basketball star drafted by the pros: "They drag-
ged me to as many as 24 schools; sometimes they brought me in to
meet the president of the university, who talked to me like he wanted
to be my father . . . they fixed me up with dates. Then when I got
home those girls called me long distance and pretended they were in
love with me" (Putnam, Sports Illustrated, Nov. 4, 1974, p. 20). If
the above isn't bad enough, and it most certainly is not atypical,
Putnam reports that:

> Perhaps the strangest of these episodes occurred when
> Oral Roberts showed up at Malone's home in Petersburg,
> Virginia and offered to cure his mother of her bleeding
> ulcer. Roberts left the Malones in no doubt that his univer-
> sity would be a fine place for Moses to play basketball.
> (Ibid.)

This sort of ridiculous information will be supplemented by only one
other comment, this by the great basketball player and former coach,
Bob Cousy:

> You get a kid to come to your school nowadays by licking
> his boots. It's an unhealthy situation. Once you have
> committed yourself to begging him to come, there can
> never be a player-coach relationship. The kid is the boss.
> There are plenty of rules that govern recruiting, yet there
> are no rules because there is no one really to enforce them.
> (Goldaper, The New York Times, March 9, 1969).

In addition to the pressure exerted upon the prospective athlete
to attend a particular institution, the freedom of the athlete to "choose
between alternatives available to him," or not to be "compelled to act
as he himself would not choose to act" is typified by the now famous
statement of Illinois' football great, Dick Butkus: "I wanted medicine,
but they put me in p.e.!" The situation in Butkus' case is simply one
of an endless string of infringements upon the individual's freedom of
choice by coaches eager to--and undoubtedly pressured to--win at almost any cost. The writer has experienced this problem first hand at

three major U.S. universities to varying extents. Once to his amazement while serving as a physical education department chairman at a large university that was desirous of status as a football power, he discovered that the athletic association was paying an undergraduate counselor in his department "under the table" to help delinquent student-athletes to substitute courses in a way contrary to regulations and to perform other "needed services" to athletes who had either arrived on campus as dubious scholars or who were in scholastic difficulty for a variety of reasons. The point of this present discussion in regard to the concept of freedom is that other people were invariably "leading the student-athletes around almost as if they had rings in their noses." The "life decisions" are being made to a large extent by men whose very positions depend upon keeping the athlete eligible in order to win games and thereby to bring in higher gate receipts! As Tee Moorman, 1960 Look All-American, said at the award ceremonies: "After you find out the cold facts, that you're all just there for the same reason, the fun wears off" (The New York Times, Dec. 11, 1960).

It is extremely difficult, if not impossible, to separate the various aspects of individual freedom from that of man as a social animal in a social setting. Careful analysis appears to verify the assertion that the situation has gradually and steadily developed in such a way that the social influences now almost completely envelop the individual in the gate receipt sports in the United States, and that he is confronted typically by competitive sport's own particular brand of "Decidophobia" as postulated by Kaufmann (1973). In other words, the financially tendered student-athlete, largely because of social influences that negate his opportunity for autonomy and personal decision-making, is almost forced to choose one or more of the "strategies" described by Kaufmann (but which has been specifically adapted to the world of competitive sport). The problem is not so acute in most of the sports that do not have a direct gate receipt relationship to the rise or fall of the program, although there is no doubt but that "the system" takes away the individual's autonomy in a number of highly important aspects of human existence at the very time that the athlete is in the formative stages insofar as the development of his personality and character is concerned. A tendered athlete must not think or speak too much about social and/or controversial issues. He should always be dressed neatly when he takes a trip with the team. Certain specific regulations apply in regard to hair length, beards, moustaches, sideburns, etc. The athlete must be careful about the people with whom he associates on campus. He must be especially careful not to appear nonconformist in regard to relations with members of the opposite sex of a different race and ethnic background. He should study very diligently so as to remain eligible for competition. He should take the courses that the coaches recommend, or even recommended major and minor programs, because the coaches know which professors are "soft touches" and favorable to athletics. This

list of commandments could be lengthened further, but it will be best
perhaps to conclude this aspect of the analysis by referring to the
famous "ABC" professor of the Big Ten--A for athletes; B for boys,
and C for coeds. Woe to the small, insignificant golf player on
scholarship who didn't alert this professor about his status and found
himself with a neat D at mid-term! Of course, such a difficulty could
perhaps be rectified by a coach in one sport talking to a coach in another sport, both of whom were on the physical education roster part-
time, and who happened to have this lad with excellent motor ability
in their physical education activity classes.

This section will be concluded by the presentation of several
"isolated voices" selected at random which point up various positions
and attitudes on this subject of competitive sport for men in U.S. colleges and universities. The reader should keep in mind the concept
of freedom under discussion and also the matter of so-called direct
or indirect control of the athlete concerned. On the one hand, professors like Michael Shaara speak out about how "Colleges Short-Change
Their Football Players" (The Saturday Evening Post, Nov. 5, 1966),
while on the other hand constructive organizations like the American
Alliance for Health, Physical Education, and Recreation hold a Conference on Personal Values in Sports that recommends "re-evaluation
of the relative emphasis that personal values receive in our programs"
(Letter of April 10, 1963 by Jennings Davis, Jr. to Members of the
National College Physical Education Association for Men). On April
12, 1967 this writer sent a letter to the Chairman of the Department
of Physical Education in a sister institution within the same state in
which he stated:

> All of us in physical education like to think that ideally we
> can function happily and satisfactorily with intercollegiate
> athletics in one unit. In fact last year I convinced our
> Dean to allow me to make a presentation recommending
> such a union to a committee studying this proposition . . .
> Since that time, I have discovered that I was completely
> wrong to even consider such a possibility. The involve-
> ment of the Governor, State Legislature, alumni, and local
> business men, and the unbelievable extent of this involve-
> ment, has convinced me that these individuals and the units
> which they represent are so powerful that it would be abso-
> lutely ridiculous to include intercollegiate athletics with
> physical education and other related fields into one profes-
> sional unit on a campus such as yours or ours in this State
> at the present time.

It is sad to relate, but such a statement can be made about most of
the fifty states in the United States insofar as the publicly-supported
universities are concerned. The interdependence of sport and culture

is now such that our citizens view the athletes as "cultural maximizers," and there seems to be almost nothing that educators can do to keep intercollegiate (and often interscholastic) athletics in proper perspective. Thus, last year at a professional meeting the writer was forced to smile sadly when a number of physical education administrators told him in effect: "Oh, we don't have any serious problems with athletics. You see, we are completely separate from them." This statement would be distressing even if it were made by a German professor, but the fact that it was made by a number of physical education professors in whose departments athletes are majoring in physical education, tells more than mere words can relate. It tells the informed educator that, in addition to the student-athletes involved with tenders and whose individual rights are continually being denied, the physical educators and the coaches themselves are caught up in the system and are being denied their own academic freedom to a greater or lesser extent. Obviously, the situation should be changed radically, but who is going to be able to accomplish this and when? To make matters worse, just last week (late 1974) it was announced by the new President very quietly that the football programs of the various academies would be stepped up so as to be competitive . . .

Freedom Available to Some on the Continent. It is not the intention of the writer to convey the impression here that all college and university athletes in the United States are having their individual freedom denied to them any more than the general run of the population is facing such curtailment. Of course, many citizens are truly worried about the level of individual freedom available to all regardless of race, creed, and financial status. Kaufmann's theory of prevailing Decidophobia with people choosing one or more strategies to avoid individual autonomy in their lives deserves careful study also. Additionally, Skinner's future-oriented, behavioristic approach implying a concept of "beyond freedom and dignity" has many wondering about what the future might hold in store for them and their descendants. But in the field of competitive sport there are some colleges and universities where wise leadership has somehow prevailed with resultant opportunity for athletes to be relatively free from undue coercion and to make choices among alternatives courses of action regarding their individual lives. One has to go no further than the Little Three in New England, most Ivy League institutions, a large university like Wayne State in Detroit, and the University of Illinois at Chicago Circle, to name just a few. There are, of course, a number of non-gate receipt sports where the amount of athletic scholarship help is relatively low (and is indeed declining) in the larger universities where revenues from football, basketball, hockey, etc. must be upheld to keep the entire program operational. Despite the hue and cry of many that educational progressivism has taken over the schools, competitive sport at both the university and high school levels is typically regarded as extracurricular. It must fend for itself largely because of this shortsighted educational philosophy, and thereby are planted the seeds for a great many of the serious ills that prevail.

Canada has been most fortunate in the realm of university competitive sport, and the prevailing "amateur spirit" has definitely influenced the secondary school outlook as well. This is not to say that there aren't warning signs on the horizon. One university in the Far West (Simon Fraser) has declared itself for the scholarship pattern of the United States, and therefore does not take part in the Canadian Intercollegiate Athletic Union schedules. The Association of Universities and Colleges of Canada, in cooperation with the Canadian Intercollegiate Athletic Union, recently engaged A. W. Matthews to conduct a study of athletics throughout the country. After careful analysis Dr. Matthews was able to report that intercollegiate athletics in Canada has been able to maintain its amateur spirit and educational balance, generally speaking, but that there are warning signs on the horizon that will need to be watched carefully. He states that,

> The rather wide divergences of opinion regarding intercollegiate athletics in particular, undoubtedly is an outgrowth of differing educational philosophies underlying our educational system. However, it is very evident that many persons see in U. S. college sport today much that they consider to be undesirable and foreign to the purpose of a university and see our intercollegiates inevitably being tarred with the same brush . . . Canadian universities appear to be in a position to strive for a very high level of athletic and recreational development in international comparison. University athletic programs must be seen as a need of the people--of individuals, of groups, and of the entire university community. This is particularly true in a cultural environment that is as heterogeneous and fast-changing as the one confronting today's university. In such context, "Canadianization" can take on a much-desired and a more positive meaning for university athletic programs. (Matthews, 1974, p. 3).

> (Editor's note: It should be pointed out that Dr. Matthews was requested to include the intramural, recreational, and instructional service programs in the above report. As he explained, "In this connection it is significant to observe that the discipline of physical education in Canada has developed and is maintaining its own distinctive characteristics . . ." (p. 3).

The above comments about certain institutions of higher education in the United States, and about the fact that a similar statement can be made on the Canadian scene generally, were made mostly in the context of this paper about freedom in competitive sport to point out that there may still be <u>some</u> hope for a return to sanity in competitive sport. This statement is made despite what to many is the seeming inevitability that the concept of individual freedom for the person holding an athletic scholarship in the United States today has been hopelessly destroyed. Those people who are vitally interested in the future of competitive sport in educational institutions must work their way out of the prevailing situation. The goal of a "free man living the good life in a free society"--an aim which in itself offers certain guarantees to the student-athlete, cannot be cast aside as hopelessly idealistic and impractical.

Freedom in the Future

What is the hope for individual freedom in the future in an over-populated world? This is obviously an impossible question to answer here, and perhaps anywhere for that matter, but it is a query that has direct implications for the question of freedom in competitive sport in Canada and the United States--and, of course, throughout the world eventually. Gallup, in <u>The Miracle Ahead</u>, addressed the question as to how civilization can be lifted to a new level. In reporting "new ways to actualize our potential," he suggests a new educational philosophy of individual effort that embraces a plan covering the entire life span. Secondly, he points out that man hasn't truly taken advantage of the great opportunity for collective effort. Further, he looks to the social sciences for assistance in the solution of social problems presently causing slow progress or institutional failure. Lastly, he explains that man must develop means whereby the new generation understands the concept of change and develops ways to overcome the various "resistances" to change (Gallup, p. 24). Approaching his subject from a quite different standpoint than Tesconi and Morris with their "anti-man culture," Gallup nevertheless sees a vital role for the education profession. He asks for an educational system that will arouse the intellectual curiosity of the students and that, in the final analysis, will cause them to become dedicated to the cause of self-education and informed political activity (p. 40). It appears to this writer that this comes right back again to the fact that present-day education is not providing a sufficient quantity of humanness and a concern for fellow man--true personal significance. "If an experience expands awareness and intensifies personal significance, it is educational" (Tesconi and Morris, p. 208). This <u>is</u> the plight of education in North America, and it is most certainly the plight of overly-organized sport in educational institutions. Is individual freedom a hopeless dream?

The answer to this rhetorical question must be in the affirmative unless a re-ordering of educational priorities can somehow take place. Such a dream is difficult enough for those aspects of the educational program that are indeed deemed educational, but what does such a goal mean to competitive sport that is so often automatically designated as extracurricular? One needs to at least make the squad, before he will be allowed to play the educational game!

The intent here is not to spread "gloom and doom" even though many aspects of the present situation could easily drive a concerned person to despair. This assertion is made despite Etzioni's recent statement that social scientists are beginning to re-examine their core assumption "that man can be taught almost anything and quite readily." He continues by stating that, "We are not confronting the uncomfortable possibility that human beings are not very easily changed after all" (Etzioni, SR, June 3, 1972, p. 45).

As described earlier, there are indeed a number of schools, colleges, and universities in the United States where programs of competitive sport have been kept in educational perspective with a resultant modicum of individual freedom for the athlete. Further, this situation or condition of "educational sport" does actually still exist throughout Canadian education. Still further, there are many so-called "individual sports" functioning reasonably well even in those universities where the "Big Business" approach to competitive sport has taken control out of the hands of the educators. Thus, there are indeed many athletes today who still believe that they are "self-posturing" individuals--and this ranges from the body-builders seeking perfectly developed physiques, to the long distance runner who trains himself, to the skier, the mountain climbers, the surfer, the parachutist--and, of course, the tough-minded athlete who despite the outcome still makes many key decisions for himself.

Not to be forgotten in this discussion is the intelligent, sensitive, hard-working coach who appreciates this problem of freedom in competitive sport, and who makes every effort to encourage the athletes on his teams to think for themselves, to plan their efforts, to pursue their self-chosen curricula successfully, and to feel that "joy of effort" that comes from a truly fine individual or team experience in competitive sport. These athletes can be called "self-posturing" individuals. These people have made "an assessment of their own feelings and attitudes" and also compared them "with the feelings and attitudes of others." As a result they have then made a personal choice that is a wholesome blending of a "personal contract" with a "social contract." Finally, these lucky, and unfortunately all too rare, athletes have acquired a "gut-level passion" or "affective curiosity" to know more about themselves and their sport; a desire to achieve a "personification" of knowledge; and an opportunity to receive guidance along the path toward the establishment of a personal identity with a significant amount of self-esteem. (Tesconi and Morris, 1972, p. 208 et ff.).

Summary and Conclusions

In the statement immediately above, the writer has spelled out for himself the only acceptable workable definition in which a concept of individual freedom can be carried out for athletes in competitive sport situations in education within an evolving democracy. This is the only way that competitive sport can assist athletes to live full, rich lives while at the same time strengthening the fabric and position of democracy as the best theory of government. This paper has examined the present status of man in regard to a precarious future. It has explained how the concept of freedom has been viewed in philosophy. There was a brief discussion of this same concept as it has related to the philosophy of education, and a stand was taken on the side of Tesconi and Morris' "personification of knowledge" approach to combat modern bureautechnocracy. It was explained how almost all of the aspects of individual freedom as defined are negated in far too many competitive sport situations on this continent today. Lastly, it pointed out that there are still some programs of educational, competitive sport in the United States, and that such is the prevailing pattern of competitive sport in Canadian education still.

Earlier in this paper it was pointed out that there hasn't yet developed an adequately functioning mythology for today's world in which man has acquired what he feels to be a sufficient explanation of the mysterious universe and man's place in such a vast enterprise. As a result Campbell claims that people haven't been receiving the necessary guidance available in the past to assuage the psychological crises that inevitably appear during the life cycle. If it is true the men need new myths, perhaps even more individualized and small-group oriented myths, then it seems logical that sport—which must be recognized as a vital force in culture today—needs to contribute positively to the creation of a new myth in the Western world. To this end a new myth is being recommended—that of free man molding the future in competitive sport according to his personal values, but in keeping with the values and norms of an evolving, democratic society. In the writer's opinion, this can, and indeed must, be the new myth promulgated by those guiding competitive sport in education. There can be no compromise if competitive sport is to serve as a "socially useful" force leading to the educational ideal described.

Selected References and Bibliography

Abbott, Edwin A. Flatland. New York: Dover Publications, Inc., Sixth edition, Revised, 1952. (Introduction by Banesh Hoffman).

Adler, M. J. The Idea of Freedom. Westport, Conn.: Greenwood Press, 1973.

Amdur, Neil, "The Linebacker Who Lose His Mean," San Francisco Chronicle, July 24, 1970. (Syndicated column by The New York Times).

_____, "Track Athletes Ask 'Liberation'," The New York Times, December 1, 1970.

Anderson, Dave, "The Redskin Connection," The New York Times, Nov. 18, 1973.

Anshen, Ruth N. (editor). Freedom: Its Meaning. New York: Harcourt, Brace & Co., 1940.

Babbidge, Homer D., Jr. An address by the President of the University of Connecticut to the National Association of Collegiate Directors of Athletics, Cleveland, Ohio, June 24, 1968.

Bay, Christian. The Structure of Freedom. Stanford, Calif.: Stanford University Press, 1958.

Bennis, Warren and Slater, Philip. "Organizational Democracy: Towards Work by Consent of the Employed," in The Future of Work (Fred Best, editor). Englewood Cliffs, N. J.: Hall, Inc., 1973.

Berlin, Isaiah. Two Concepts of Liberty. Oxford: Oxford University Press, 1958.

Boulding, Kenneth E. The Meaning of the Twentieth Century. New York: Harper & Row, Publishers, 1964.

Carnegie Foundation for the Advancement of Teaching, The. American College Athletics (Edited by Howard J. Savage, et al.). New York: The Foundation, Bulletin #23, 1929.

Chapin, Dwight, "College Athletics Vulnerable; Must Change to Survive," The News Gazette (Champaign-Urbana, Ill.), Aug. 8, 1969.

Clarke, Gerald, "The Need for New Myths," Time, Jan. 17, 1972.

Commager, Henry Steele, "Is Freedom Dying in America?" Look, Vol. 34, No. 14:16-21, July 14, 1970.

Cranston, Maurice. Freedom: A New Analysis. London: Longmans, Green, 1953.

Davis, Jennings, Jr., "Implications of the Interlochen Conference for the Division of Men's Athletics." A report from the Implementation Committee of the Conference on Personal Values in Sport held at Interlochen, Michigan in 1962. It was sent to the members of the College Physical Education Association on April 10, 1963.

Eiseley, Loren, "The Cosmic Orphan," Saturday Review/World, Feb. 23, 1974, 16-19.

Etzioni, Amitai, "Human Beings Are Not Very Easy to Change After All," Saturday Review, June 3, 1972, 45-47.

Fein, Leonard J., "To Try to Dream Again," The New York Times, February 11, 1973.

Friedrich, C. J. Man and His Government. New York: McGraw-Hill Publishing Co., 1963.

Fromm, Erich. Escape from Freedom. New York: Avon Books, 1969. (Originally published in 1941).

Fuller, Lon, "Freedom: A Suggested Analysis," Harvard Law Review, Vol. 68 (1955), 1305-1325.

Gallup, George. The Miracle Ahead. New York: Harper & Row, Publishers, 1964.

Goldaper, Sam. "N.I.T. Rings Down Curtain for Cousy," The New York Times, March 9, 1969, S3.

Goodwin, Richard N. The American Condition. Garden City, N. Y.: Doubleday & Co., Inc., 1974.

Grutzner, Charles., The Impact of Athletics on Education." Washington, D.C.: Babe Ruth Sportsmanship Awards Committee, 1951. (This pamphlet was reprinted with the permission of The New York Times.)

Hansen, Willard, "In Perspective: The Familiar Eliot Answer," The New Gazette (Champaign-Urbana, Ill.), March 7, 1971.

Hayek, F. A. The Constitution of Liberty. Chicago: University of Chicago Press, 1960.

Huxley, Aldous. Brave New World Revisited. New York: Bantam Books, Inc., 1960.

Huxley, Julian, "The Crisis in Man's Destiny," Playboy, January, 1967, 93-94, 212-217.

Jauss, Bill, "NCAA President: Change Recruiting Tactics," Chicago Daily News, Nov. 1, 1968, 39.

Johnson, Harry M. Sociology: A Systematic Introduction. New York: Harcourt, Brace & World, Inc., 1960.

Johnston, Richard W., "The Men and the Myth," Sports Illustrated, October 14, 1974, 106-111, 115-116, 118, 120.

Kateb, George, "Utopia and the Good Life," Daedalus, Vol. 94, No. 2:454-473 (Spring 1965).

Kaufmann, Walter. Without Guilt and Justice. New York: Peter H. Wyden, Inc., 1973.

Knight, Frank H. Freedom and Reform. New York: Harper & Row, Publishers, 1947.

Lipsyte, Robert, "Out of Their League--II," The New York Times, December 24, 1970.

London Free Press, The, "Minor Puck Players Claimed in Bondage," October 4, 1974.

Malinowski, Bronislaw. Freedom and Civilization. Bloomington, Indiana: Indiana University Press, 1960. (Originally published in London in 1947.)

Mandell, Arnold J., "A Psychiatric Study of Professional Football," Saturday Review/World, Oct. 5, 1974.

Matthews, A. W. Athletics in Canadian Universities. Ottawa: Association of Universities and Colleges of Canada, 1974.

Mill, J. S. On Liberty. London: Longmans, Green, 1865.

Morris, Van Cleve, "Physical Education and the Philosophy of Education," JOHPER, 27, 3:21-22, 39-31 (March, 1956).

Muller, Herbert J. Freedom in the Ancient World. New York: Harper & Row, Publishers, 1961.

_____. Freedom in the Modern World. New York: Harper & Row, Publishers, 1966.

_____. The Uses of the Past. New York: Mentor Books, 1954.

Nash, Paul. History and Education: The Educational Uses of the Past. New York: Random House, 1970.

Oppenheim, F. E. Dimensions of Freedom. New York: St. Martin's Press, 1961.

Owen, Lyle, "Equality on the Gridiron, Opportunity on the Court," AAUP Bulletin, Spring, 1971, 8-9.

Putnam, Pat, "Don't Send My Boy to Harvard . . ." Sports Illustrated, Nov. 4, 1974, 20-21.

Rand, Ayn. The Romantic Manifesto. New York and Cleveland: The World Publishing Company, 1969.

Ribeiro, Darcy. The Civilization Process. Washington, D.C.: Smithsonian Institution Press, 1968.

Rovere, Richard, "Freedom: Who Needs It?" The Atlantic, Vol. 221, No. 5 (May, 1968), 39-44.

Shaara, Michael, "Colleges Short-Change Their Football Players," The Saturday Evening Post, Nov. 5, 1966.

Toffler, Alvin. Future Shock. New York: Random House, Inc., 1970.

Tuckner, Howard M., "All-American Stalwarts Still Love Football, But . . .," The New York Times, Dec. 11, 1960.

Zeigler, Earle F., "Putting the Greek Ideal in Perspective in North American Athletics Today," in Symposium on Athletics in America (A. W. Flath, editor). Corvallis, Oregon: Oregon State University Bookstore, 1972.

_____., "A Riddle for Tomorrow's World: How to Lead a Good Life," Journal of the Canadian Association for HPER, Vol. 34, No. 2:3-8 (January, 1968).

ADDENDUM

Partridge, P. H., "Freedom," in Encyclopedia of Philosophy (Paul Edwards, Editor). New York: The Macmillan Company and The Free Press, 1967, Vol. 3, pp. 221-225.

Part IV

PROFESSIONAL PREPARATION

Selection #28

HOW DO WE EVALUATE PEOPLE IN PHYSICAL EDUCATION AND SPORT?

Recently a Commission on Tests established by the College Entrance Examination Board "pronounced the Board's tests insensitive, narrowly conceived, and inimical to the interests of many youths."[1] (The New York Times, 11/2/70) This type of judgment about the tests given annually to two million high school students in the U.S.A. is truly a remarkable indictment of our entire American system of education as well. This group of twenty-one leading educators has "said that the program had focused on the rather specialized needs of institutions, the colleges, while failing to serve the diverse interests of many individuals, the students."

The difficulty seems to lie in the very nature of the tests themselves. These "intelligence tests" are typically standardized tests on "mental ability and accomplishment" and purport to measure so-called "verbal factor" and "quantitative factor" in the students being examined. Thus, there is a determination being made of qualities "essentially rooted in the ability to speak, read, and write standard English and to handle quantitative or mathematical concepts." Because so many of our "better" young people eventually take tests offered by the CEEB, it is quite understandable what a profound effect these types of tests have on the educational offerings of the large majority of our public and private elementary and secondary schools.

You may ask, "what is so wrong with this established approach?" The Commission is telling us that there is ever so much more to "mental excellence" then verbal and mathematical ability. Still further, it must be stated that such tests foster an extremely narrow "intellectualistic approach" that denies any worth or validity to what might be called the non-verbal arts and sciences. Here we are referring to the indivisible psycho-physical instrument known as the body. Huxley in "The Education of an Amphibian" explains that education should include (1) training of the kinesthetic sense; (2) training of the special sense; (3) training of memory; (4) training on control of the autonomic system; and (5) training for spiritual insight. (Aldous Huxley, Tomorrow, Tomorrow, and Tomorrow. New York: Signet Books, 1964, p. 17 et ff.) The present system of examinations in effect penalizes literally tens of thousands of young

---

[1] Published in The Australian Journal of Physical Education, 53 (1971), 10-11. Also published in the Illinois Journal of HPER, 3 (Fall, 1971), 5.

men and women who don't fit into the traditional pattern of individuals for whom the tests are currently designed. It was pointed out that actually only a relatively small percentage of students go on to be become professional scholars and scientists.

A fundamental recommendation for change involved what was seen as an urgent need to reconstitute the examinations so that they would "assess not only verbal and quantitative but also such dimensions of excellence as musical and artistic talent; sensitivity and commitment to social responsibility; political and social leadership; vocational, technical, and mechanical skills; styles of analysis and synthesis; ability to express one's self through oral, non-verbal, or graphic means; ability to organize and manage information; ability to adapt to new situations; and characteristics of temperament and work habit under varying conditions of demand."

Implications for Physical Education and Sport

Interestingly enough, knowledge, skills, and competencies relative to sport, dance, and other movement (expressive) activities are nowhere stressed in this otherwise excellent listing. Perhaps it is erroneously concluded that the offering of athletic scholarships to the gifted covers this point, but such an assumption denies the role of our type of non-verbal humanities as educational experiences and should not go unchallenged. Actually, the recommendations of the Commission would appear to represent exactly the sort of measurement and evaluation that we have been talking about in our profession for a number of years. Thus, the implementation of these recommended changes may well have great implications for the profession of physical education and sport. We should attempt to determine, for example, whether the experiences we provide contribute to the "humanities and social science aspects" of a person's development, as well as to the "bio-scientific aspects." More specifically, for example, do sport, dance, and/or play experiences contribute to the development of "sensitivity and commitment to social responsibility" as well as to the improvement of circulo-respiratory efficiency?

Of course, what we do measure or evaluate depends mostly on what we want to determine--and our ability at this time in the history of science to measure validly and reliably these various items, characteristics, and traits. As we face the future in physical education and sport, we should undoubtedly become even more interested and concerned about the development of the attitudes, knowledge, competencies, and skills required for successful fulfillment of a professional career in any field, not to mention the still more fundamental attributes required for leading a "good life" in the newly described "global village."

Even more specifically, we should concern ourselves with the attributes and traits required for successful fulfillment of one of a variety of careers available in physical education and sport. Here we will need continued and continual assistance for measurement and evaluation experts in all related sub-disciplinary aspects of the field --humanities, social sciences, and bio-sciences (or natural sciences).

The following questions may serve to give us some direction as we seek to bring into specific focus the whole question as to why we evaluate anyhow. As we look to the future in a popular and seeming overcrowded field, what specific requirements (competencies, skills, attitudes, and knowledge) should we establish as guidelines for those who express an interest in entering our profession? More specifically, then, we should seek answers to the following four questions:

1. What are the requirements for successful motor performance in selected sport, dance, exercise, and other movement activities?

2. What are the requirements for a successful teacher of physical education and sport?

3. What are the requirements for a successful teacher of teachers in this field?

4. What are the requirements for a successful scholar and researcher in either the humanities, social science, or natural science aspects of a developing discipline as part of the total profession of physical education and sport? (Here we are referring to those who engage in what might be called "reflective inquiry," as well as to that which is identified usually as "frontier research." See Quest for the Optimum: Research Policy in the Universities of Canada, prepared by L. Bonneau and J. A. Corry. Ottawa: Association of Universities and Colleges of Canada, Volume 1, 1972, pp. 30-31).

THE IMPROVEMENT OF UNDERGRADUATE PROFESSIONAL PREPARATION FOR PHYSICAL EDUCATION THROUGH THE COMPETENCY APPROACH

In the United States the first program for the "training" of physical education teachers was begun by Dioclesian Lewis in 1861. It extended over a period of ten weeks. Today, the professional student of physical education can earn the Doctor of Philosophy degree or the Doctor of Education degree upon successful completion of a program extending over at least a seven-year period after high school graduation.[1] (Zeigler, 1951)

The curricula offered in the early period from 1860 to 1890 varied a great deal. The aim was to provide as much knowledge of the body as an early physician would know. The specific training in physical education theory and practice depended upon which foreign system of gymnastic was propounded by the organizer of the normal school being considered.

In the middle period from 1890 to 1920, the subject-matter of the curricula continued to expand. About 1910 certain professional programs began to include a fair distribution over the liberal arts, basic science, professional education, and professional physical education courses.

The modern period from 1920 to the present saw a continuation of this broadening outlook. It is interesting to note, however, that the most prevalent specialized curriculum in physical education in 1927 was that of athletic coaching. Because curricula were so heterogeneous, a national committee presented a standardized curriculum in 1935. A bit earlier, a futile attempt had been made to bring about a standardized course nomenclature.

By the middle of the 1930's the demand from the field had shifted so that a coach, an "academic" teacher, and a physical educator were desired in that order. The reason for this change was perhaps partly economic; yet, it might have occurred because the high schools were emphasizing the naturalized or "play" program in required physical education with a continued emphasis on strong interscholastic athletic teams.

---

[1] Published in the Illinois News HPER, Vol. XII, No. 3:13-14, 17-18 (March, 1965).

It had become apparent by the 1940's that the standards of the average professional program would have to be raised if the field hoped to consolidate gains made during the previous decade. Today a five-year program seems absolutely necessary if it is expected that the prospective teacher in this field will be qualified to teach health education, physical education, athletics, recreation, an "academic" subject, driver education, and others, just to mention some of his responsibilities. Some states have this five-year requirement, or are moving toward it by requiring further professional preparation above the bachelor's degree prior to permanent certification.

A Present Serious Problem

One serious problem that we are facing at the present is that we haven't come to grips with the traditional subject-matter approach to learning that has stifled initiative at every turn. As matters stand now, the student takes a certain number of courses while attending college for a required number of years. (Zeigler, 1955, 14-16) Upon graduation the "teacher" receives a provisional teaching certificate and is presumed to be a competent, educated person able to teach the youth of the country. The question is how can we be certain, or even reasonably certain, that our graduating students will be able to function satisfactorily as intelligent citizens and competent professional teachers of physical education. Do we not need a more effective way of measuring their ability as determined by specific competencies developed through selected experiences with the so-called subject-matters as resource areas?

It has been said that "it takes fifty years to get an idea across." If this is true, we can look for this development to take place about 1985. For it was about twenty-five years ago that certain professional leaders in our field began to suggest "the competency approach" in professional education for physical education. The late Harry A. Scott of Columbia Teachers College made a strong effort to gear professional preparation in this direction when he assumed the departmental chairmanship at The Rice Institute about a quarter of a century ago. Subsequent national conferences on undergraduate and graduate professional preparation for health, physical education, and recreation have echoed and re-echoed the "competency approach." We have even seen the development of evaluative criteria for professional staffs to employ locally or in connection with accreditation visits. Now we must ask ourselves to answer honestly in reply to this question, "Why haven't these evaluative criteria been used?" Are we afraid of the results? I'm afraid this is only too true!

Snyder and Scott have spelled these competencies out for us in great detail in their chapter entitled, "A Functional Program of Professional Preparation" in their text completely devoted to the subject of professional preparation in health, physical education, and recreation. (Snyder and Scott, 1954, Chapter 4.) Here are comprehensive charts which subdivide professional preparation into three areas: (1) General Education; (2) General Professional Education, and (3) Specialized Professional Education - Physical Education. Under each of these areas are listed one or more broad functions. For example, the function listed under General Education is "To participate as an enlightened person and cultured citizen in our democracy." Following this, each page is subdivided into four sections under four headings as follows: (1) Problems to be met by the student; (2) Selected competencies needed to meet the problem; (3) Selected experiences to develop the competencies; and (4) Resource areas.

To clarify this approach, let us consider several headings under one of the functions listed beneath Area of Specialized Professional Education - Physical Education.[2]

Perfection Is A Long Way Off

As matters stand now, we know that our professional programs are far from perfect. From time to time we make curriculum changes often based on the unscientific opinions of staff members. Far too often, also, we are not truly aware of what our neighboring institutions are doing, what the demands of the job are, what the alumni feel that the strengths and weaknesses were, what the professional students think about their experiences, and what a study of contemporary society indicates.

Through our own personal experiences we form certain opinions about present undergraduate professional preparation and the resultant products of these programs. We are disturbed because many students are weak in the skills of communication. We believe further that they are not being equipped generally to meet the many human relations problems which will beset them. They don't appear to have formed a philosophy that is carefully devised. They are rarely "cultured" individuals in the best sense of the word. Often their coaching skills appear to be weak, and they are certainly not "exercise specialists," insofar as the individual adapted program and sports developmental exercises are concerned.

There are too many male students and too few women in the field. The power structure within colleges and universities makes

---

[2] Under health, physical education, and recreation in the three areas mentioned above are given fifty-two functions, 107 problems, and many more competencies to be developed by selected experiences through the resource areas of the curriculum.

Function: Teaching (coaching) one or more competitive sports in the secondary school.

Problems to be met by student	Selected competencies needed to meet the problem	Selected experiences to develop the competencies	Resource areas
To make a vital contribution to the objectives of physical education and to the goals of general education.	Believes firmly that competitive athletics properly conducted contributes to the welfare of the student. Understands that athletics is a part of the broad program of physical education. Is skilled in developing the personal and social qualities through the athletic program. Provides for indivudal growth in activities directed toward increasing responsibility and self-direction. Evaluates the program of athletics on the basis of the objectives of the broad physical education program.	Participates in a broad program of physical education, including athletics. Outlines a total program of physical education and shows how athletics grows out of the intramural program. Traces the history of competitive athletics in American life and discovers its place in American culture. Assists a competent coach of athletics and attempts to develop the necessary personal and social qualities. Evaluates his skills, ability to teach, and attitudes toward athletics.	Methods of teaching physical education. Organization of physical education. Laboratory and field experiences. Administration of physical education.
To provide for wide participation in the athletic program.	Promotes wide participation in the athletic program. Develops a broad intramural program seeking a high percentage of student participation. Provides a sound basic program where students develop the basic skills early. Enlists student participation in organizing, planning, and conducting the athletic program. Conducts a safe and sane program which is interested in the total health of the individual.	Engages in several activities in the intercollegiate program. Assists and participates in the intramural program. Assists the instructor in teaching skills in the physical education program. Works with an experienced director of a physical education program in classifying students and arranging schedules. Officiates various sports activities on the secondary school level.	Organization of physical education. Administration of physical education. Materials of physical education.

intercollegiate athletics overly strong and physical education weak; professional students recognize this situation and its implications. Teachers and administrators need to clarify the concept of "democratic administrative process" for all to see. The articulation between undergraduate and graduate programs is not good.

We must take a hard look at our current methods of curriculum evaluation. Measurement techniques are weak and do not promote the concept of democracy in action. The areas, functions, problems to be solved, needed competencies, selected experiences and resource areas have been spelled out for us in great detail by Snyder and Scott. What are we waiting for?

Selected References

1. Snyder, R. A. and Scott, H. A. Professional Preparation in Health, Physical Education, and Recreation. New York: McGraw-Hill Book Company, 1954.

2. Zeigler, Earle F., "A History of Professional Preparation for Physical Education in the United States, 1861-1948." Ph.D. dissertation, Yale University, 1951. 506 pp. (Published through the Microcard Project - originally, School of Health, Physical Education, and Recreation, University of Oregon, Eugene, Oregon.)

3. _____., "Undergraduate Preparation in Physical Education," The Physical Educator, Vol. XII, No. 1:14-16 (March, 1955).

A BRIEF ANALYSIS OF THE ORDINARY LANGUAGE EMPLOYED IN THE PROFESSIONAL PREPARATION OF SPORT COACHES AND TEACHERS OF PHYSICAL EDUCATION

The analysis of concepts undoubtedly started before Socrates, but it wasn't until the twentieth century that there was such a sharp contrast drawn between analysis and other methods of philosophical endeavor.[1] Interestingly enough, it wasn't until the mid-1950's that educational philosophers became involved to a degree with so-called philosophical analysis, and then not until the latter half of the next decade that any philosophers of sport and physical education began to show even the slightest bit of interest or inclination to move in this direction as well. Whether this influence will be a lasting one remains to be seen.

To the uninitiated at least it can all be most confusing. Despite the fact that various scholars of the Western world have been engaged in philosophical thought for more than 2,000 years, there is still heated disputation over the exact nature of philosophy. Early Greek philosophers thought that philosophy should serve a function not unlike that which we attribute to contemporary science. Today, scientific method is employed, of course, and it involves reflective thought and hypotheses, long-term observation, and experimentation prior to subsequent generalization and theory-building. This is how new knowledge is developed and, unless today's philosophers engage in this sort of activity, there is serious doubt whether they can claim that their investigation results in any knowledge at all. If not, what is the justification for philosophy?

In the twentieth century there have been three major developments, and several sub-developments, within philosophy that have sought to answer this question through the medium of what might be called philosophical analysis: (1) logical atomism, which was preceded at the beginning of the twentieth century by the "realist analysis" of Russell, Moore, and Bradley; (2) logical positivism, which was followed by "therapeutic" positivism or "Neo-Wittgenstein-ianism"; and (3) ordinary language philosophy. The main idea behind these approaches - those under categories #1 and #2 at least - is that philosophy's function is analysis. The last category (#3), ordinary language philosophy or linguistic analysis, or the related group of pursuits now known as "philosophy of language," assumes that the immediate goal of the philosopher is to explain the use, the function,

---

[1] Published in the International Journal of Physical Education, Vol. XI, No. 4:9-13, Winter Edition, 1974.

or the actual workings of man's language. Within this third major category, one faction argues that a philosopher should help man refrain from misuses of his ordinary language, while another group believes that they as philosophers should assist with the reconstruction of man's ordinary language.

It is this third approach that will be employed in this present investigation in an experimental fashion. The investigator is quick to use the word "experimental," mainly because he has not employed it previously, and also because he views this type of philosophizing as important but definitely as a "handmaiden" to philosophy as it engages in its major tasks.

The reader should keep in mind that it was during the period between 1930 and 1952 that Wittgenstein decided that it would not be possible to devise a language so perfect that the world would be accurately reflected. He came to believe that much of the confusion and disagreement over philosophy emanated from the misuse of language in several ways. He believed that it was necessary to decide what the basic philosophical terms were, and then it would be possible to use these terms correctly and clearly so that all might understand. With this approach it may be possible for the philosopher to solve some problems through clarification of the meaning of certain terms which have been used synonymously (albeit often incorrectly). In this way man may be able to truly achieve <u>certain</u> knowledge about the world. Philosophy practiced in this way becomes a sort of logico-linguistic analysis, and most certainly not a set of scientific truths or moral exhortations about "the good life."

<u>Statement of the Problem</u>. The main problem of this investigation was to apply the Austinian technique of analyzing ordinary language to the terms that are typically employed in the professional preparation of coaches and teachers. The basic assumption is that these words (e.g., knowledge, experience, skills, etc.) are typically employed loosely and often completely improperly.

In order that the basic problem posited may be answered in a reasonably comprehensive and satisfactory manner, the following sub-problems, phrased as questions, will be considered initially:

  a. What particular area of the language will be considered for study? (The terms that are typically employed in the professional preparation of coaches and teachers.)

  b. What terms will be recommended by a team using free association as a technique after the reading of relevant documents has been completed? (At this point use of a good dictionary is essential.)

c. How does the term or group decide whether the terms included are appropriate? (By describing circumstances and conducting dialogues.)

d. What results may be formulated that are correct and adequate in relation to the terms which have been chosen initially; have been described clearly and in reasonable detail; and which have been accepted eventually as correct in the circumstances in which they are typically employed? (The terms selected are defined clearly, checked carefully on the basis of the experiences of the team members, and employed in a sequential fashion to describe accurately the total experience under consideration.)

Need for the Study. The need for this particular study became most apparent to the investigator while serving as a member of an Experimental Undergraduate Physical Education Committee in the 1963-64 academic year at the University of Illinois, Champaign-Urbana under the chairmanship of Professors L. J. Huelster and C. O. Jackson. The group realized very soon that their discussions were accomplishing very little because of a "language problem." They were using the same terms or words to describe the professional preparation experience of coaches and teachers of physical education, but they were using these terms differently (i.e., with different meanings). It became obvious that certain basic or fundamental terms would have to be selected, defined, used in descriptive statements, re-defined (perhaps), and then related in a sequential narrative of some type.

Limitations and De-limitations. Obviously, there is a very real possibility that the personal biases of the investigator and others involved in this early committee (team) may have affected the way in which the terms were chosen, defined, and employed. As a matter of fact, the group was not aware that the Austinian technique was being employed to the "T," so to speak; the steps of the technique as described simply "made good sense," and they were adopted. Thus, there was inevitably a certain amount of subjectivity present in the analysis that was made, and the results that were adopted unanimously by the committee for further use. One definite de-limitation, of course, is that the terms to be collected were only those that are used commonly in the professional preparation of teachers and coaches.

Related Literature

In a brief presentation such as this, no effort will be made to document the related literature from the field of philosophy per se that might be otherwise included. Certainly philosophy is at present in the midst of an "Age of Analysis," although no one would claim for a moment that this approach should be classified as a homogeneous school of thought (White, 1955). This present study seems to be "hovering" at some point in a category that Weitz has defined as "Linguistic, Ordinary Language, or Conceptual Analysis" (1966, p. 1).

Those who concern themselves with the history of philosophy will endeavor to determine as accurately as possible Russell's influence on his student, Wittgenstein, but none can deny the originality of the latter's Tractatus Logico-Philosophicus, first published in 1921. The language of philosophical discourse must be phrased so that its propositions are meaningful and empirical in nature. If one hopes to understand and solve problems, language must be used correctly.

Since they were contemporaries and involved with the same "movement," one would think that Austin would almost of necessity be influenced by such a powerful and seminal thrust in philosophy as that engendered by Wittgenstein. It is true further that "Austin is sometimes counted among the group of philosophers vaguely labeled 'Wittgensteinians'." (Furberg, 1963, p. 62). Despite this, however, the burden of proof of any strong relationship still remains open for some future scholar. They were approaching philosophy in a very similar fashion, but their emphases do seem to have been different.

John Langshaw Austin was a classical scholar who turned to philosophy after taking a degree in classics at Oxford. He was undoubtedly influenced by Moore indirectly and more directly by Pritchard (Hampshire, 1959-60, xii). "Doing" philosophy for Moore, however, was definitely in the direction of analysis, while for Austin the question of classifying distinctions within language was uppermost. In the process Austin was what might be called a "team man," since he believed in the necessity of working in groups to define distinctions among the language expressions employed by those whose language was being "purified."

Language Analysis Within the Field of Physical Education.
There has been very little ordinary language philosophy or conceptual analysis within the field of physical education. In 1970 when Fraleigh presented his definitive account and analysis of types of philosophic research that had been carried out in the 1960's, he included "three types of research labeled as theory-building, structural analysis, and phenomenology" (Fraleigh, 1971, pp. 29-30, in NCPEAM Proceedings). He did not exclude this methodology necessarily because of the lack of published material in physical education literature, but he might as well have taken such a stand. During that time James Keating of DePaul was beginning to make his case for the distinction between the terms "sport" and "athletics" in philosophical journals, but he has never agreed to classify himself as a philosopher of language (Keating, 1963, 201-210).

To the best of this writer's knowledge, the only physical education philosopher to consider the application of Austin's "linguistic
phenomenology" to sport and physical education was the late Peter
Spencer-Kraus, a student of this investigator at the University of
Illinois in Champaign-Urbana (1970). (As a matter of fact, it should
be stated parenthetically that one of the reasons for this paper is to
give this interesting and valuable technique of investigation a bit more
"mileage" in the hope that others will consider employing it further.)

Other approaches of this nature to the philosophy of language,
generally speaking, were made by two other former graduate students
working with the writer - George Patrick and Kathleen Pearson. The
study by Patrick was entitled "Verifiability (Meaningfulness) of
Selected Physical Education Objectives," and it is important to understand that the purpose of this investigation was not to show that any
such objectives were justified. An analytic description in terms of
form and function of the stated objectives was made, and the normative part of the study was based on the descriptive analysis of the objectives and the kind of knowledge provided by logic, ethics, philosophy of science, and philosophy of education. Positivism's "principle
of verifiability" was subdivided into two forms: weak or logical possibility of confirmation, and strong or operationally testable. Objective statements were viewed as informative, expressive, directive,
and performative. Three functions of objectives were stated (1) as a
slogan, (2) as a guide to the educative process, and (3) as a test. It
was found that objectives functioning as slogans were likely to be
meaningless or verifiable in the second degree (weak); that objectives
functioning as guides using informative-directive language were
verifiable in the first or second degree; and that objectives functioning as a test must use the informative-directive mode of language before they could be considered verifiable in the first degree. Thus,
"if physical educators wish to act responsibly, they should be able to
state that for which they are accountable" (Patrick, 1971, p. 94).

Pearson's study was analytic in nature and certainly related to
conceptual analysis within what has been called "philosophy of language" by many. She examined (1) the structure of the multi-concept
"integration-segregation" as it pertained to male and female participants in physical education classes, and (2) the functional aspects of
this multi-concept in the intentional, purposive, and responsible
actions of persons engaged in the professional endeavor called physical education (Pearson, 1971, p. 2). After extracting the various
meanings attached to the concept and describing their extensional
features in the "structural analysis" phase, Pearson proceeded to a
"functional analysis" stage in which she delineated the reasons set
forth for advocating the various "structures" or positions relative to
the usage of the concept by writers in the available literature. She
considered the assumptions implicit within each of the reasons and

the empirical evidence available to support or cast doubt on the validity of the hypotheses underlying these reasons. Lastly, the question was asked, "How might one be guided in making responsible decisions concerning the multi-concept in question?"

After carrying out the above steps, Pearson concluded specifically that physical educators attach many and varied meanings to the word "coeducation"; that the reasons set forth for this practice indicate a wide variety of objectives; that these claims or objectives have not been subjected to empirical research techniques; and that many contemporary physical educators still hold the dubious belief that jumping activities for girls and women cause injury to the pelvic organs. Generally speaking, she concluded that "the field is almost barren of empirical research to support or cast doubt on the advisability of integration-segregation of male and female participants in physical education classes" (pp. 213-214).

Methodology and Technique

J. L. Austin's technique was not spelled out in great length in innumerable papers as is sometimes the case with investigators, but the essence of it may be gleaned from his paper entitled, "A Plea for Excuses," as well as from his "Ifs and Cans" and from some notes called "Something About One Way of Possibly Doing One Part of Philosophy." (See Philosophical Papers published by The University Press in Oxford.) He himself coined the name "linguistic phenomenology" in connection with the technique (p. 130). In Austin's opinion there was hope in analyzing,

> . . . our common stock of words [which] embodies all the distinctions men have found worth drawing, and the connexions they have found worth marking, in the lifetimes of many generations: these surely are likely to be more numerous, more sound, since they have stood up to the long test of the survival of the fittest, and more subtle, at least in all ordinary and reasonably practical matters, than any that you or I are likely to think up in our armchairs of an afternoon--the most favoured alternative method. (Ibid., p. 130)

Initially, the Committee at Illinois, after a series of meetings during which time it became apparent to all that they were not "talking the same language," decided which words and terms were relevant to the topic at hand--the professional preparation of teachers and coaches. Even though they employed common sense and their professional judgment, they found that it was necessary to read the available literature on professional preparation in both so-called general professional education and also in the specialized professional education area of physical education. Then through the process of free association, they were able to eliminate words and also to begin to delineate shades and nuances of meaning of the words that were left. When disagreements developed, or when fine distinctions were not known, the group referred to a dictionary.

Referral to a dictionary was not the final answer, because it was discovered that still other terms – synonyms – were typically available for consideration as well. Early corroboration of this type was most helpful since it provided a helpful cross-check. As a result of this "field work" stage, the Committee decided to employ a minimum of twelve words (terms) and accompanying definitions to be used in the final statement that was to be framed to explain the professional preparation process as carefully and as precisely as possible.

The Committee proceeded to the second stage by attempting to relate clear and detailed examples of instances or circumstances in which a particular term or word was preferred to another. Then, too, the members of the group made an effort to explain those times when the use of the word would not be appropriate. During this stage it is important that any and all theorizing be excluded. Achieving unanimity at this juncture may be somewhat difficult, but it is certainly less time-consuming if there are no unusual "personalities" in the group and if the members of the team are relatively inexperienced.

Finally, in the third stage, an effort is made to formulate the various terms under consideration into a coherent account that will stand close scrutiny. There will undoubtedly be changes and modifications in the preliminary account that is developed. The final account can be double-checked with some of the literature examined earlier to see to what extent changes have been made that will seemingly stand up under very close examination. After this was done in the Illinois situation, the final statements including the terms adopted were presented to a graduate seminar for the disinterested examination and evaluation that such a group of people would provide.

Findings

As a result of the "field work" stage, the Committee decided to employ the following words and definitions:

1. Fact – a real event, occurrence, quality, or relation based on evidence.

2. Knowledge – acquaintance with fact; hence, scope of information.

3. <u>Understanding</u> - comprehension of the meaning or interpretation of knowledge.

4. <u>Ability</u> - quality or state of being able; capability; aptitude.

5. <u>Competency</u> - sufficiency without excess; adequacy.

6. <u>Skill</u> - expertness in execution of performance; a "quality of expertness"; a developed ability.

7. <u>Appreciation</u> - a recognition of the worth of something.

8. <u>Attitude</u> - position assumed or studied to serve a purpose.

9. <u>Experience</u> - the actual living through an event(s) which may result in skill, understanding, ability, competency, appreciation, attitudes, etc.

10. <u>Problem</u> - a question proposed or difficult situation presented which may be met and/or solved by experience(s).

11. <u>Resource Areas</u> - those subject-matters (disciplinary areas) referred to for facts.

12. <u>Functions</u> - the special duties or performances carried out by a person (or persons) in the course of assigned work.

The formulation of the various terms into a coherent account that describes what might actually occur in an experimental undergraduate curriculum for teachers and coaches resulted in the following statement:

A student is offered educational <u>experiences</u> in a classroom and/or laboratory setting. Through the employment of various types of educational methodology (lectures, discussions, problem-solving situations in theory and practice, etc.), he/she hears <u>facts</u>, increases the scope of information (<u>knowledge</u>), and learns to comprehend and interpret the material (<u>understanding</u>). Possessing various amounts of <u>ability</u> or <u>aptitude</u>, the student gradually develops <u>competency</u> and a certain degree or level of <u>skill</u>. It is hoped that certain <u>appreciations</u> about the worth of his/her profession will be developed, and that he/she will form certain _attitudes_ about the work that lies ahead in his/her chosen field.

In summary, there are certain special duties or perform-ances which the student preparing for the teaching/coaching profession should fulfill (functions). Through the profes-sional curriculum, he or she is exposed to both general and specific problems which must be met successfully. Through planned experiences, with a wide variety of re-source areas to serve as "depositories" of facts, the pro-fessional student develops competencies, skills, knowledge, understandings, appreciations, and attitudes which enable him/her to be an effective physical educator-coach.

Conclusion and Discussion

Based on this limited experience with the Austinian technique applied to ordinary language--in this case some of the terms employ-ed typically in the professional preparation of teachers and coaches--this investigator was able to conclude that certain problems that have typically beset those concerned with professional preparation are very definitely caused by linguistic confusion. This linguistic confusion is present because of the equivocal use of many of the key words and terms.

This is not to say, however, that more detailed investigation of a similar nature would remove basic conflicts in educational philoso-phy that have plagued those concerned with the transmission to others of the art and science of the teaching/learning process. What consti-tutes education and teacher education ideally will not, in the opinion of this writer at least, be resolved by the possible prevention of fur-ther ambiguous usage of terms and idioms. These difficulties and differences of opinion are far too deep-rooted and steeped in hoary tradition to vanish within the space of a few decades if ever.

There is absolutely no doubt, however, but that highly signifi-cant strides can be made in the near future if those interested in sport and physical education philosophy will labor to decrease the prevailing difficulties with language usage that exist at the present time. The late Peter Spencer-Kraus was preparing himself for this task, but his life was cut very short in a tragic car accident. Patrick and Pearson have shown interest and ability along a similar, if not identical, line, and hopefully they will continue with this inter-est in the future. Others are urged to experiment with Austin's ap-proach as well. It is relatively simple in design, but it may be difficult to bring together a team of investigators to carry out similar studies in the specialized area of sport and physical education. Such investigation would appear to be a necessary cornerstone for any fur-ther study in the years immediately ahead.

Selected References

Austin, J. L. _Philosophical Papers_. London: Oxford University Press, 1961.

Fraleigh, W. P., "Theory and Design of Philosophic Research in Physical Education," _Proceedings_ of the National College Physical Education Association for Men, Minneapolis, Minn. 55455, 1971.

Furberg, Mats. _Locutionary and Illocutionary Acts_. Stockholm: Almquist and Wiksell, 1963.

Hampshire, S., "J. L. Austin, 1911-1860," _Proceedings_ of the Aristotelean Society, N.S. LX (1959-1960).

Keating, J. W., "Winning in Sport and Athletics," _Thought_, 38:201-210, Summer 1963.

Patrick, G. D., "Verifiability (Meaningfulness) of Selected Physical Education Objectives," Ph.D. dissertation, University of Illinois, Urbana, 1971.

Pearson, K. M., "A Structural and Functional Analysis of the Multiconcept of Integration-Segregation (Male and/or Female) in Physical Education Classes," Ph.D. dissertation, University of Illinois, Urbana, 1971.

Spencer-Kraus, P., "The Application of 'Linguistic Phenomenology' to the Philosophy of Physical Education and Sport," M.S. thesis, University of Illinois, Urbana, 1969.

Weitz, M. (editor). _Twentieth Century Philosophy: The Analytic Tradition_. New York: The Free Press, 1966.

White, M. G. _The Age of Analysis_. Boston: Houghton-Mifflin, 1955.

Wittgenstein, L. _Tractatus Logico-Philosophicus_. London: Routledge and Kegan Paul, 1961.

Selection #31

THE BLACK ATHLETE'S NON-ATHLETIC PROBLEMS

It is basically deplorable that a discussion of the "problems of
the black athlete" - or those of any other so-called minority group for
that matter - even seems to be necessary in the United States of
America.* But the hard fact of the matter is that the "land of freedom and opportunity" has a long way to go yet; the black athlete still
faces a variety of non-athletic problems which most of his white bre-
brethren don't even recognize.

Athletes in educational circles typically cause enough problems
for all concerned, including themselves, no matter what their color,
ethnic background or creed might be. In fact, our society does its
level best to see to it that the athlete arrives at the college door both
educationally and culturally disadvantaged. Thus, when the disadvan-
tage of minority group status is added to the mix, the urgency of the
matter is doubled.

The separation of "athletic" from "non-athletic" problems is
almost impossible. We should be thinking of the "total individual" and
and his relationship with his fellow man in society. To be fair, some
of our attention should be directed to the plight of the black woman in
sport as well. Certainly a strong case can be made to show that the
woman is a second class citizen in the United States, and this fact has
often been devastating for the black woman athlete.

The former Chief Justice Earl Warren gets to the heart of the
matter. He believes that the American people can eventually get out
of war, can stop inflation and prevent depressions, can feed its people and care for them medically, can wipe out illiteracy, and can
defeat pollution. "But the problem which hovers over all these . . .
is whether we can achieve the plural society with freedom for everyone as envisioned by our Founding Fathers."[1] (This is the man the
far right wanted to impeach!) I believe that Mr. Warren has assessed the situation most accurately, and I support further Bayard
Rustin's analysis that "the basic problem is man's inhumanity to man
and must be fought from that basic principle regardless of race or
creed."[2]

Black America is telling the people of this country loudly and
clearly that it is very angry, but that basically it still "has a dream."
But attitudes are changing rapidly. We must ask ourselves how we

* Presented at the Indiana Association for Health, Physical
Education, and Recreation, Terre Haute, December 5, 1970. (Published in Educational Theory, Vol. 22, No. 4:14-16 (1972).

can continue when only 25% of our Blacks feel that the current Federal government is helpful to Negro rights.[3] The attitudes of Americans who feel culturally deprived - to a greater or lesser extent - is hardening, and it is rightful that it should.[4]

As we consider this problem, we must also understand the school segregation problem. About 80% of our white students attend schools that are at least 90% white, while 65% of Negro students go to schools that are more than 90% Negro.[5] We all recognize that the desegregation decision of the Supreme Court in 1954 made it very clear that separate schools are unequal; now what are we going to do about it?

Proceeding from these introductory remarks, I will (1) make some general observations about Blacks in American education; (2) some specific observations about the problems that black athletes face apart from the athletic situation;[6] and (3) some concluding statements.

Some General Observations

The first observation which I have - and one which tends to bear out my introductory remarks - is that the evidence seems to indicate that the reasons why nonwhite students seem to learn less than white students probably lie outside of the classroom and school itself. Christopher Jencks assessed this finding from the widely heralded "Coleman Report," which was presumably going to show that the nonwhites attended inferior schools, and therefore received inferior educations.[7] But the final conclusions was that the entire social environment needed alteration if we hoped to improve student achievement. Of course, the question must be asked further as to what is meant by "student achievement" - achievement of what specific educational objectives? Fortunately, the College Board's Commission on Tests has very recently recommended that the scope of the C.E.E.B.'s system of testing be broadened to include the evaluation and measurement of many other dimensions of excellence that a student might possess other than the traditional "verbal and quantitative factors."[8]

A second, highly significant study was completed under the auspices of the Carnegie Corporation very recently as well. This comprehensive, three-and-one-half-year study reported that schools not only were not educating students adequately, but that they were also "oppressive," "grim," and "joyless." And Charles Silberman concluded, "The tragedy is that the great majority of students do not rebel; they accept the stultifying rules, the lack of privacy, the authoritarianism, the abuse of power - indeed, virtually every aspect of school life - as The Way Things Are."[9]

And so it is within this framework that the black athlete is functioning - whether he is in the minority group in a white school, or in the majority in a black school. But no matter which environment he happens to encounter, he is faced with another great problem - that young people in American schools seemed to be "programmed for social class" in American schools. We seem to be vulnerable to the criticism that, despite the educational opportunity that we are offering ing to so many, we are also widening the gap between what may seem to be the bright and the not-so-bright youngsters in our society. Administrators, counselors, and teachers must be ever so careful about what they "do" to young people in this regard.[10]

At this point a word must be stated also for the Afro-American studies' emphasis that we are seeing around us at all educational levels. Whites have consciously or unconsciously deprived American Blacks of a good deal of their heritage, and we must now be understanding and supportive of efforts whereby Blacks are seeking to develop and understand their own culture within the United States of America and elsewhere. It must be done, and that's all there is to it; we can only hope that "it may help to rebuild the self-concept, positive group identification, and wholesale intergroup attitudes of the minority group members of this society, of which black people form the largest segment."[11]

One last "general observation" will be made that has to do with the matter of degree achievement. We have heard accusation that black athletes are exploited in a variety of ways,[12] but it seems to me that the worst type of exploitation would be if the black scholarship athlete did not eventually obtain the college degree from the institution where he enrolled. A thoroughgoing investigation of this matter should most definitely be instigated, keeping in mind the general statistics available on this subject. They show that of 100 students who enter college, 47% of them leave before graduation. Of the 53 students who graduate, thirty go on for the Master's degree, but only nineteen of this number finish their programs. Finally, eight of the nineteen students completing the master's program enroll for a doctoral degree, and only four of them finish the program.[13] In the light of these statistics, we must ask how black men and women fare in this process and, still further, what happens to black athletes? Lastly, we need to know accurately what are the "early warning signals" which can help us to meet the problem of the high school or college dropout.[14]

Some Specific Observations

The specific observations offered here are based on the opinions and beliefs of a number of people - mostly black and some white - who have been involved with the question at hand on a first hand, practical

or theoretical basis.[15] The problems have been classified as
(1) General Social Problems; and (2) Educational Problems, both general
and specific. (Note: the reader should keep in mind that the extent to which certain of these problems exist will vary within a school,
college, or university depending upon whether the particular institution is populated by a majority of white or black students.)

General Social Problems. The black athlete _may_ encounter any
or all of the following general social problems:

1. Cultural deprivation in both the community and the
   home from which he comes.

2. A different Value System which may be very materialistically oriented, and which undoubtedly will be at
   variance at important points with that of the majority
   group within the culture.

3. Poor Economic Status resulting from an unsettled
   home and early job discrimination (or lack of employment whatsoever).

4. Racist or Racialist Attitudes on the part of the majority group when the boy or girl, or young man or
   woman, relates to the "larger world."

5. Relationship to Government (an extension of #4 above)
   has often been marred by an unpleasant and unsatisfactory experience with some branch of local, state,
   or Federal government (police, draft board, protests
   to various governmental agencies, etc.).

Educational Problems. The black athlete _may_ encounter any or
all of the following educational problems:

General

1. He may be confronted typically with the stereotype that
   society has of athletes - that they are numbskull jocks!

2. He may acquire an "inflated" sense of his own importance, and sooner or later an inevitable "deflation"
   must follow.

3. He will receive no real opportunity to get involved with
   the decision-making process of the school or the college, either in an advisory or official capacity.

4. He may give evidence of a lack of fundamental educational skills – a lack that is due typically to present high school environments and the continuing presence of interscholastic-athletic pressure in a commercialized program.

Specific

1. The athlete may have difficulty adjusting to his new status as "celebrity" gracefully, inasmuch as such status has been so foreign to him, and it is often thrust upon him so rapidly.

2. Despite such newly acquired status, the black athlete may find that he is <u>still</u> the victim of overt or covert social discrimination by the majority group members.

3. The athlete is encouraged to go on to a college or university that offers the "best deal," but well-intentioned academic advisement and counseling may urge some supposedly "easy curriculum" upon the young man (or woman) despite his expressed interests and abilities.

4. The athlete is frequently placed at a distinct handicap, because in all probability he has not had the chance earlier to "internalize" a realistic standard of intellectual achievement.

5. Social cliques formed in interpersonal relationships <u>off</u> the field may have definite relevance for the team's cohesiveness and ultimate successful performance as a unit.

Summary Statement and Conclusion

It should be quite obvious to any reasonably intelligent citizen that changes in "The American Way of Life" will have to be made very, very soon. In a recent issue of <u>Look</u>, it was pointed out that "weapons, pollutants, and reproduction make it pretty clear that the old ways will kill us all."[16] The premise being made is that the world will make it to 1980, but that some basic values and norms are going to have to be altered by that time before it is too late. Sociologist Harry M. Johnson has pointed out that for the United States "important societal values are the rule of law, the socio-structural facilitation of individual achievement, and equality of opportunity."[17] Granting his further statement that "progress is no straight-line affair," one can only wonder whether the minority groups in our society are going to be willing to accept the correction of inequities "an inch at a time." In the advance copy of the (Kerner) <u>Report of the National Advisory Commission on Civil Disorders</u>, Wicker tells us in a "Special Introduction" that "only a commitment to national action on an unprecedented scale can shape a future compatible with the historic ideals of American society."[18]

As I see it, the solution to this problem lies in the "hearts and minds" of the white man in America. You, me, all of us must commit and re-commit ourselves to the realization of our accepted societal values.

To a considerable extent, the black athlete - and all Blacks - are running into "gut prejudice" and ignorance on a daily basis. A perfect example of this from several standpoints emanated recently from the writing of a white graduate professor of physical education at a large Midwestern university. Even though he would be astounded that his remarks are viewed thusly, I will let his printed words speak for themselves:

> All levels of athletics from the grades to postgraduate have taken on a more dusky hue progressively to the point where white students are being culturally deprived if athletics as presently conducted have any educational benefit. If Black Power advocates insist on 10 percent of everything as justifiable equality, then 90 percent of the athletic cake should be non-chocolate. I also favor desegregating Negro colleges. My final words of wisdom are that intelligent, responsible, respectable, energetic, and able people have never been culturally deprived regardless of how economically impoverished their parents were or how humble their abode.[19]

Jonathan Kozol, whose book Death at an Early Age characterizes the plight of the child in the "ghetto" school, states that "perhaps by the time another generation comes around a certain modest number of these things will have begun to be corrected. But if I were the parent of a Negro child, I know that I would not willingly accept a calendar of improvements scaled so slowly."[20] Please understand that I am not advocating rioting and "taking to the streets" to accomplish the realization of our declared and legalized American values for all citizens. I am firmly convinced that to follow such a course would be counter-productive (despite some modest gains that may have been made recently by these means). I am urging "full speed ahead," however, to all legal, non-violent types of pressures that can be brought to bear on the "Corporate State" and its agents. Charles Reich, in <u>The Greening of America</u>, has characterized extremely well the "technology-organization-efficiency-growth-pro-progress" orientation of Consciousness II (the Corporate State).[21] Granting that it may be wishful thinking on his part that the large majority of Americans will be willing to move from Consciousnesses I and II to Consciousness III "tomorrow," it is exactly this sort of social psychological attitude that is needed most urgently.

Of one thing we can be certain, as it was so well stated by Martin Luther King in Where Do We Go from Here?, and that is that "we will be greatly misled if we feel that the problem will work itself out . . . evil is recalcitrant and determined, and never voluntarily relinquishes its hold short of an almost fanatical resistance."[22]

The answer would seem to be simple and straightforward - and yet we know its complexity - to the problem of the black athlete in our society. Each of us must re-dedicate himself or herself to positive, sustained action toward the realization of "the Good Life" and "the American Dream" for all of our citizens. And it cannot be postponed until some future date, it must take place tomorrow, and tomorrow, and tomorrow.

Footnotes and References

1. The New York Times, November 23, 1970.

2. Bayard Rustin, "The Anatomy of Frustration." A pamphlet published by the Anti-Defamation League of B'nai B'rith, 315 Lexington Ave., New York, N. Y. 10016. (15¢)

3. "Report on Black America," in Newsweek, June 30, 1969.

4. The New York Times, October 26, 1969. (Reports an updated analysis by Dr. Gary T. Marx, Harvard sociologist.)

5. "Education in the Ghetto." A report and analysis made available in Saturday Review, January 11, 1969, 48.

6. It seemed necessary to put some of the specific problems faced by black athletes in perspective with problems faced by all athletes and all Blacks in our society.

7. Christopher Jencks, "A Reappraisal of the Most Controversial Educational Document of Our Time," The New York Times Magazine, August 10, 1969.

8. The New York Times, November 2, 1970.

9. From "Crisis in the Classroom" by Charles E. Silberman, as quoted in The New York Times, September 20, 1970.

10. Walter E. Schafer, Carol Olexa, and Kenneth Polk, "Programmed for Social Class: Tracking in High School," Trans-Action, October, 1970, 39-45, 63.

11. Adelaide Jablonsky, "Media for Teaching Afro-American Studies," in IRCD Bulletin, VI:1 and 2, Spring, Summer, 1970, 1.

12. Starting with July 1, 1968, Sports Illustrated magazine ran a five-part series extending through the July 29 issue.

13. The New York Times, November 24, 1970.

14. Ann P. Eliasberg, "How to Stop a Dropout," The New York Times Magazine, November 10, 1968.

15. So that there would be both direct and indirect input to the writer of this paper, ten Blacks, a white sociologist, and a white social psychologist, were asked to react to the basic issue raised in this paper. The Blacks included men and women at the various educational levels, as well as coaches and former professional athletes.

16. John Poppy, "Mankind's Last, Best Chance," Look, 34:1, January 13, 1970, 17.

17. Harry M. Johnson, "The Relevance of the Theory of Action to Historians," Social Science Quarterly, June, 1969, 48, 57.

18. Tom Wicker, "Introduction," in Report of the National Advisory Commission on Civil Disorders. New York: Bantam Books, 1968, ix.

19. It was deemed best to keep this quotation anonymous.

20. Jonathan Kozol, "Where Ghetto Schools Fail," The Atlantic, October, 1967, 110.

21. Charles A. Reich, The Greening of America. New York: Random House, 1970.

22. Martin Luther King, Jr. Where Do We Go from Here: Chaos or Community? New York: Harper & Row, Publishers, 1967.

Note: Just in case progress isn't as rapid as we would like to see, a new manual has been made available for those who would counsel minority group young men and women regarding college opportunities. In this guide, entitled "College Bound," is a listing of some 176 colleges that are actively seeking minority group students. This softbound book sells for $2.75, and may be obtained from the Urban League of Westchester, 2 Grand Street, White Plains, New York 10601.

Addendum

The Black Athlete - Female

Some very informative comments about the black woman in sport were given to me by an outstanding black woman coach after this article had been completed. They tend to bear out the statements made about the non-athletic problems of the black male in regard to home background and school background as well.

But over and above this, there seems to be an indication that some black males tend to "berate their girl friends" for excelling in a sport - especially when the male does not have such talent himself. (Of course, this could also occur with whites as well, but perhaps for a slightly different reason.). Then, too, the female athlete finds that she must curtail her social life just at the age when she is becoming attractive to the other sex.

At the college level, if the young lady should by chance be considered for a scholarship, the coach tends to ignore the overall educational program of the athlete. For example, still further, these young ladies might travel to many interesting places for athletic competition, but it is rare that opportunities are taken to visit places which could enrich the cultural background of the young women concerned.

ONE APPROACH TO THE TEACHING OF PHILOSOPHY
OF PHYSICAL EDUCATION AND SPORT

My ideas about the teaching of philosophy of physical education and sport will of necessity appear to be somewhat of a confessional-booth presentation.* I feel a little embarrassed appearing with this group, because I hold no degree in philosophy itself. I am a product of a small liberal arts and science institution (Bates College) with subsequent undergraduate and graduate minors in physical education from Arnold College and Columbia Teachers College, respectively. Along the way I earned the Master's degree in German from Yale University. It was then that I decided to retrace my steps a bit, and I spent the equivalent of three years relating to the Department of Education at Yale. Thus, my final degree was the Ph.D. in Education with specialization in the history and philosophy of education.

Past Development

As I see it, there is a mother discipline - philosophy, and then a sub-discipline called the philosophy of education developed that seemed to have only a tangential relationship with philosophy itself. At this juncture, I came on the scene and learned about the latter sub-discipline in the mid- and late forties. About 1953 I began to realize that there should also be a sub-discipline of philosophy concerned with physical education and sport. As I recall, however, I subsumed this largely under philosophy of education (perhaps not realizing fully at the time that this could develop independently under philosophy itself to the extent that sport and athletics are considered independent of the educational process at any rate.)

Just about the time that I began to understand philosophy of education and its possible implications for physical education, philosophy of education scholars decided that they were carrying out their function improperly, and a large number of them began to ape the parent discipline. At that point, therefore, I, working at The University of Michigan, was developing a text on the subject of physical education

---

* This presentation was made by Professor Zeigler as part of a panel of philosophers discussing teaching methodology in philosophy at the First Canadian Symposium on the Philosophy of Sport and Physical Activity, University of Windsor, May 3-4, 1972. (Published in the Proceedings. Distributed and produced under the editorship of P. J. Galasso by the Sport Canada Directorate, Department of National Health and Welfare, Ottawa, Canada, 1972, pp. 73-85.)

and sport philosophy, and I discovered to my amazement one day in 1962 that E. C. Davis had been doing the same thing at the University of Southern California. So his book appeared, and mine followed shortly after.

So there I was, and presumably there was Craig Davis, too (and others as well by this time), looking at a parent discipline (philosophy) that had gone largely "analytic" and a philosophy of education sub-discipline that had done largely the same thing. I think this puts the physical education quasi-philosopher in a bit of perspective (up to about 1964 at any rate). It has been a sort of coattail operation, and yet it has been very exciting and a lot of fun. I can say further that I have found this line of endeavour to be more of a challenge than anything I've run into within the total field. This is a value judgment on my part, of course, colored largely I'm certain because of the great personal <u>and</u> professional satisfaction I've received through such an involvement.

Present Status

Now we find that the field of physical education is assuming more of a disciplinary orientation, and I think that this is good - and absolutely necessary. In the earlier days we were, of course, such generalists that we really didn't speak too knowledgably about specific subjects such as philosophy, history, or sociology with possible relationships to the profession of physical education. Now I am a Fellow of the Philosophy of Education Society, and also a full member of the American Philosophical Association. Despite the many philosophic approaches extent, I find that I still have a largely pragmatic orientation developed no doubt because of my earlier, and then continuing, association with Professor John S. Brubacher of Yale and Michigan. He had employed a "persistent problems" approach with both the history and philosophy of education, and I found that this could be adapted admirably to the history and philosophy of physical education and sport. So this is exactly what I did with additions and modifications here and there as I saw fit. Now my thinking, with the help of a number of colleagues and graduate students, has "progressed" to the point where I have identified some fifteen of these persistent problems. Some of these are social forces affecting all aspects of a society, and some - such as amateurism in sport - are more peculiarly <u>our</u> problems.

The "Persistent Problems"

After tracing these problems historically, and they <u>are</u> brought right down to the present day, we attempt to examine these same problems in the light of the leading philosophical tendencies present on this continent. Still further, we are currently beginning the examination of these "problems" on a cross-cultural basis. This would seem to be absolutly necessary because of the "communications revolution" taking place at lightning speed in our "one world."

These problems are then at one and the same time both current and controversial. It's at this point where my pragmatic orientation comes in as far as sport and physical activity are concerned. I attempt to relate to students in such a way that they can begin to put these problems in perspective for themselves in their own lives. I try to teach them how to make their own decisions in a reasonably logical and consistent manner based upon their freely chosen philosophical foundations. There's one thing that I really feel strongly about, and it relates to a point made earlier by Jim Keating - this is, the question of indoctrination. And, despite this effort to allow individual freedom of choice to the greatest possible extent, I found out recently that people don't want me to be quite so neutral about everything (i.e., about my personal views). So I am now beginning to be somewhat more assertive, and I say, "Look, this is really what I stand for, and this is why I believe such-and-such. I'm not ashamed of it, and I don't mind telling you." But I do want to be very careful about such an approach early in the course, because I don't want to indoctrinate and to seem too dogmatic. There are some people whose temperaments seem to be ever so much more malleable than others, and it would be a shameful thing to try to indoctrinate them each term.

One of the persistent problems which I've identified happens to be the role of the administrator as he relates to sport and physical activity. Depending upon your world orientation, and how you approach matters which have philosophical import, you will find that this gives you a direction insofar as being an administrator is concerned. That's giving it quite a pragmatic orientation, and I confess to this freely. Consequently, I must say that I am quite appalled by the fact that so many courses that students elect nowadays do not have "relevance, accountability, and involvement."

Course Specifics

As far as a few specifics of the course are concerned, over a period of time I've developed a rather extensive course outline. I have devised further certain devices or techniques which I attempt to employ. I create a rather large reserve shelf in the library, and I encourage students to "get involved" with it. I spell out a tentative schedule of classes: typically we have three 50-minute sessions in a two and one-half hour period. We can deviate from this at any time, and we do on occasion. So I outline the sessions carefully, and there is a definite progression. So you see, this is where I've gotten away a little bit from the so-called pragmatic approach which I mentioned

- 305 -

earlier. For each of the series of three weekly sessions I have readings that people can get involved with, and then I have tried also to keep a running account of the scholarly work on the philosophy of sport and physical education (which I will soon refer to as well). I've developed - although I don't think that it's absolutely vital or urgent that people categorize themselves - a self-evaluation checklist which I ask students to fill out at the outset of the course. It involves them with a delineation and assessment of their philosophy of life and/or religion, their philosophy of education, and their philosophy of physical education, including sport, health education, and recreation (these latter two areas being ancillary to us).

In addition, because I see it as being part of the total picture, I developed with my son a type of political spectrum analytic device. I believe that we have to be informed about, and seriously concerned with, the influence of the more important social forces - type of political system, economic pattern, system of values, nationalism, religion - on our sport and physical activity patterns.

During the course experience I have students relate to completed research (see above), and they develop abstracts of theses, books, and major articles, etc. These are reported to class sessions and exchanged with the others in either dittoed or mimeographed form.

Certain Major Assignments

I ask for the completion of certain major assignments. One such assignment is the preparation of a personal philosophy as a culminating experience in the course. Another project, often carried out in cooperation with one or more classmates, involves the delineation of the living world philosophies and the way in which people imbued with one or another of the positions might react to the persistent problems that have been delineated. I have devised a spectrum based on the concept of freedom and authoritarianism in our society. I believe thare are certain leading ideologies in existence in the world, and I feel that we in the Western world have to become absolutely "incandescent" about the promulgation of the concept of individual freedom as opposed to a tyrannical, authoritarian concept. This is probably the greatest and most important struggle or conflict going on in the entire world - the effort to control men's minds (and thus their entire lives).

And so I've developed almost everything around these opposites. Absolute freedom, or anarchy, is at the one extreme, and at the other extreme would be absolute authoritarianism or dictatorship. I see many of these philosophical positions or tendencies, these living world philosophies, falling somewhere on this spectrum of freedom and authoritarianism. I happen to believe that in a democratic society

the most desirable position on this spectrum falls somewhere to the
left of center. This represents my own value orientation, of course,
and I don't insist that people agree with me. I do urge them to find
their own places based on their background and experience.

Students are then given an opportunity to look at these fifteen
different persistent problems in the light of the world positions, the
living world philosophies. For an example of a problem designated as
a social force - say the influence of economics - they determine for
themselves (based on the freedom/authoritarianism spectrum) how
they feel that economics should be treated and viewed in a society,
with particular regard for the implications of this stance as it might
affect education and physical education.

Then there are a number of persistent problems which are definitely of a professional nature, and which apply quite specifically to
the field of physical education and sport. For example, there are
"problems" like the use of leisure, the concept of the body, amateurism and professionalism, the role of women, and others.

Delineation of a Personal Philosophy

Perhaps the most important thing I try to get people to do is the
delineation of their own personal philosophies. I want them to get involved and to be held accountable. In my opinion philosophy serves as
the vehicle by which people can accomplish these objectives. As the
outset because of the difficulties that people have with terminology,
I involve students with definitions in a competitive game. Those who
attain a certain standard win an ice cream cone, a cup of coffee, or a
dime. If people don't have a reasonable mastery of the terms that
are being used, obviously they won't know in any precise way what is
going on. So I use this little essentialistic teaching device, but I do
my best to assure people that the scores won't be held against them.

I receive some interesting term papers embodying people's
personal philosophy of life, education, and physical education. Last
year one completed by a man from Great Britain was a "classic." I
brought it with me for anyone to examine. This person was a bit of
an artist as well, and some of the diagrams and sketches included
were worth thousands of words. This picture I am holding up is of a
crew-cut fellow, and he's got a red, white, and blue key sticking out
just above his left ear. He was called the "Clockwork Jock," and it
says, "will switch to an electric model sometime in the next 100
years - maybe!" This paper, written just within this past year, was
most insightful, and actually involves what might be designated as
"patterned eclecticism."

A Final Examination?

I do throw in a quite essentialistic final examination where I go back to some of those "original statements" referred to earlier. I select those quotations directly from all kinds of literature, and then I ask the students to give me the "flavor" of each of the quotations. There are typically phrases and ideas embodied here which are characteristic of the different philosophical tendencies which have been discussed during the course experience. It is sometimes amazing the "flavors" that you get back. I'll cite just one example from the examination before I conclude this presentation. Oddly enough, very few people have "caught the flavor" of this passage, which goes something like this:

> What has suddenly happened is that the white race has lost its heroes; worse, its heroes have been revealed as villains, and its greatest heroes are the arch villains. The new generation of whites appalled by the sanguine and despicable record carved over the face of the globe by their race in the last 500 years is rejecting the panoply of white heroes whose heroism consisted in directing the inglorious edifice of colonialism and imperialism. Their careers rested on a system of foreign and domestic exploitation rooted in the myth of white supremacy in the Manifest Destiny of the white race's emerging shape of a new world order and the requisites for survival in such a world are fostering in young whites a new outlook. They recoil in shame from the spectacle of cowboys and pioneers, the heroic forefathers whose exploits filled earlier generations with pride galloping across a movie screen shooting down Indians like Coke bottles. Even Winston Churchill who was looked upon by older whites as perhaps the greatest hero of the twentieth century, even he, because of the system of which he was a creature in which he served, is an arch villain in the eyes of the young white rebel. The sins of the fathers are visited upon the heads of the children, but only if the children contend with the evil deeds of their fathers.

What is the "flavor" of that passage? Give up? Well, that's Eldredge Cleaver's Soul on Ice. It bespeaks black militantism, a truly living philosophical position in the United States today. Let's face it: it's having an impact on our culture. To the extent that this "position" is held by people in that society, it will have greater or lesser influence on the educational system – and also on sport and physical activity. So that's the sort of identification that I give as a final "wrap-up" to a course experience in the philosophy of sport and physical education.

Concluding Statement

So there you have it - one teacher's approach embodying an
"eclectic methodology" and a variety of teaching techniques. It has
progressivistic techniques in it and essentialistic ones as well. Maybe it's a course with so many elements of either approach that it must
be classified as eclectic in nature basically. All I can safely say is
that it has seemed to meet students' needs very well. They enjoy it; I
enjoy it; and I believe that they - and I - learn and grow from the experience together. I believe that such a teaching approach employs
problem-solving at its best.

A RECOMMENDED IRREDUCIBLE MINIMUM FOR GRADUATE STUDY IN PHYSICAL EDUCATION AND SPORT

In the future the profession of physical education will probably find an increasing number of applicants for graduate study possessing academic backgrounds other than that of the typical physical education major.[1] This type of individual needs specialized professional preparation in physical education, and perhaps also general professional education courses depending upon which type of graduate program he plans to enter (i.e., Master of Science or Master of Science in Teaching).

From another standpoint, the physical education major applying for graduate work in those universities offering the Ph.D. program often finds that his undergraduate program has not included a sufficiently strong emphasis in either the humanities or the social sciences - and perhaps even in the natural sciences. The physical education major may find, therefore, that he is quite weak in those subject-matters which now are emphasized in the current "disciplinary approach" to the development of a body-of-knowledge for our profession.

Obviously, an undergraduate professional program in physical education cannot be "all things to all people." Even a carefully designed, five-year curriculum could not produce graduates prepared to study profitably in all types of graduate study presently offered in our field. Thus, directors of graduate programs are faced with the problem of deciding just what is an irreducible minimum of course experiences that will be considered acceptable for psospective graduate students with different backgrounds applying for admission into several types of graduate programs in physical education.

Generally speaking, the applicant for graduate study should have had a broadly based general education including a variety of course experiences in the humanities, social sciences, and natural

---

[1] Published in the Journal of Health, Physical Education and Recreation, Vol. 42, No. 2:85-86 (1971).

sciences.* In recent years there has been general agreement that at least <u>one half</u> of the undergraduate program ought to be able to be classified as "general education."** Realizing the impossibility of including all subject-matters in the undergraduate curriculum, the following listing of courses (or <u>the knowledge, competencies, or skills</u> represented by these course experiences) ought to be represented in the general education background of the prospective graduate students:

Humanities (Incl. Mathematics)	Social Sciences	Natural Sciences
English Composition	Psychology	Biology
American Literature	Social Psychology	Chemistry
Foreign Language	Abnormal Psychology	Zoölogy
Philosophy	Sociology	Geology
History	Cultural Anthropology	Physics
The Arts	Economics	Human Anatomy
College Algebra	Political Science	Human Physiology

Note: There could be a "great debate" on whether <u>any</u> subject should be included or excluded. Further, some of these course experiences might necessarily have to come at the high school level.

The General Professional Education Dilemma

If a student wishes eventually to teach or coach in the public schools (and this often includes teaching at the junior college level), he is faced with meeting state certification requirements for teachers. A college or university teacher is not required to show evidence of such certification to his prospective employer. This is not to imply, however, that course experiences in general professional education are not needed by most prospective teachers and coaches. The implication here is that teachers should possess certain knowledge, competencies, and skills about <u>the teaching and coaching act</u> itself!

---

* These recommendations are grounded to a considerable extent on <u>Professional Preparation in Health Education, Physical Education and Recreation Education</u>. Washington, D. C.: American Association for Health, Physical Education, and Recreation, 1962. Professor Zeigler was a participant in this Conference and prepared the background paper on the history of professional preparation in physical education (pp. 116-133).

** The traditional subject-matter approach needs modification as soon as possible in the direction of one in which stress is placed on the development of <u>competencies</u> and <u>knowledge</u> through a planned sequence of problem-solving experiences of a laboratory nature. This comment applies to all phases of education.

It seems most reasonable, therefore, to recommend that prospective teachers and coaches should have fine course experiences in the following areas:

1. Social Foundations of Education (history, philosophy, sociology, and comparative education).
2. Educational Psychology (man's equipment for learning and the learning process).
3. Educational Administration (organization and administration of the public schools).
4. Methods of Teaching (generally and specifically as applied to physical education and sport).
5. Student Teaching and Coaching.

Specialized Professional Preparation

Exactly how much specialized professional preparation should be required prior to the granting of "regular standing" to a graduate student in physical education and sport is a really thorny problem. (The writer faced this problem personally once, and found himself confronted with professional, ethical, university, and practical considerations.) Obviously, a university should not be so restrictive that people are automatically scared away; on the other hand, it would not be fair to the profession or the individual to downgrade the undergraduate specialized professional preparation within the field by assuming that the graduate student from another field has nothing to "make up" so long as he is reasonably skilled in motor and athletic performance and has some fine personality traits. Somewhere between these two extremes there must be a "happy medium" - and irreducible minimum of course experiences in physical education and sport. (And it must be stressed strongly at this point that a prospective graduate student should be given every opportunity to proficiency as much undergraduate professional theory and practice as possible. We should not ask a man or woman to "spin wheels" making up course work in subjects where we know they have reasonable proficiency.)

Everything considered, then, what should be required of the prospective graduate student in professional physical education and sport? The following recommendations seem reasonable:

Introduction to Health, Physical Education, and Recreation
History of Physical Education and Sport
Philosophy of Physical Education and Sport

Administration of Physical Education and Sport
Sociology of Sport
Social Psychology of Sport (and Physical Education)
Physiology of Exercise
Kinesiology (Biomechanics)

Measurement and Evaluation
in Physical Education and
Sport
Psychology of Sport (motor
learning)
Therapeutic Exercise

Professional activities courses
in exercise, team sports,
individual sports and dance
(approximately the equivalent
of 12 semester hours)

The above listing of course experiences may seem overly long
and stringent; so, for this reason three statements of opinion are
offered for the consideration of all concerned:

1. The admissions officer in the graduate department
    should assess the total background of each applicant on
    an individual basis. The faculty member fulfilling this
    role should make every effort to become a "credentials
    analyst," relating to admissions officers and person-
    nel of the larger graduate unit on the campus. He
    should develop a routine and format whereby prospec-
    tive graduate students can demonstrate to the depart-
    ment that they do indeed have varying amounts of
    proficiency (acquired formally or informally) in speci-
    fic aspects of physical education and sport.

2. The admissions officer should attempt to determine as
    soon as possible whether the student has strong inclin-
    ations to pursue one track or the other at the Master's
    level (i.e., the teaching-coaching, professional degree
    path, or the scholar-researcher-teacher, more
    disciplinary degree pattern). On the basis of such
    determination, he should be ready to suggest an indi-
    vidualized pattern of course experiences that should be
    followed by the prospect student. Such a program
    might often include undergraduate, "make-up" course
    experiences depending upon the student's ultimate goal
    (and, of course, any absolutely fixed requirements of
    the graduate school or college that cannot or should not
    be bypassed).

3. The school or college of education has an important
    place in a university, and has presumably a key role to
    play in the preparation and certification of teachers and
    coaches (practitioners) in the various publicly-support-
    ed schools of a state. This statement is true whether
    the professional physical education unit is under such a
    school or college or separately constituted. In the
    larger state universities especially, preparing teach-
    ers to teach should be the function of the school or col-
    lege of education as an entity on campus and in the

state. It should <u>not</u> be the function ideally of departments of physical education and sport. Blind continuance of an "automatic" teacher-education function for departments of physical education is simply a vestigial remnant from the field's earlier history.

CONSOLIDATION AND INNOVATION IN GRADUATE STUDY IN PHYSICAL EDUCATION AND SPORT (with Garth A. Paton)

The main idea behind this paper is that there is a definite need for both consolidation and innovation in graduate study in physical education and sport at the present time.* (The terms "consolidation" and "innovation" may seem to be somewhat contradictory, but a case will be made for the appropriateness of the inclusion of them both.) In some quarters graduate programs in the field are being challenged, while in others their expansion in a reasonably controlled manner is being encouraged. Those that are developing do not typically seem to be following a plan in which the aims and objectives have been clearly delineated. Thus, the hypothesis is that there is not a completely rational explanation for developing programs based on the significant change that has taken place in the past decade.

In an effort to place this development in perspective and to offer some positive recommendations for the immediate and long range future, the authors will seek to answer the following questions within the limited space and time allotted: (1) What is the present status of graduate study in physical education and sport? (2) What needs to be done? (3) How should we go about the task? and (4) What will we have then? (a concluding statement).

What Is The Present Status?

The present status of graduate study in physical education and sport, considered on a North American basis, is difficult to ascertain without the benefit of a comprehensive investigation. Quite obviously it is not "going great," nor does it appear to be "on the way out." No one was making any great claims for the quality of graduate study and research programs in physical education in the 1950's, but there was a general feeling that programs were gradually improving. Thus, it was a distinct shock when James Conant in 1963 recommended that graduate programs in physical education should be abolished.[3] McCloy had warned us in 1957 that graduate study was of a poor quality. Specifically he deplored the all too frequent elimination of the thesis requirement; the lack of prerequisites for graduate study in the field; the fact that many graduate faculty members were themselves

---

* A paper prepared for the Division of Professional Preparation, National College Physical Education Association for Men, Kansas City, Missouri, December 27, 1973. (Published in Proceedings of the Association, Minneapolis, Minn., 1974, pp. 101-107.)

not engaged in scholarly work; and the gradual elimination of reading competency in foreign languages as a definite requirement.[4]

Whether one agrees with Conant's recommendation or the specifics of McCloy's criticism is no longer particularly important, but factors such as these, including the knowledge that a national conference on graduate study hadn't been held since 1950,[5] were undoubtedly somewhat responsible for the Conference on Graduate Education sponsored by the American Association for Health, Physical Education, and Recreation that was held in Washington, D. C. from January 8-13, 1967.[2] The Report of this Conference designated the following five purposes of graduate study:

1. To add to the store of human knowledge through basic research.
2. To extend the range of nonverbal expression (dance, games, sports, etc.) through encouragement of human invention and imagination.
3. To prepare scientific research workers and humanistic scholars.
4. To provide advanced preparation for practitioners (teachers, coaches, supervisors, activity specialists, and administrators) at various levels of competency.
5. To develop leaders who have the ability to think and to employ their rational powers in gaining understanding, aesthetic sensitivity, and moral responsibility.
   (2, p. 21)

It would certainly be difficult to argue too strenuously against any or all of these five excellent purposes. The problem facing us, or course, is the extent to which we are achieving any of these purposes adequately in the early 1970's!

Quite obviously the 1960's was a decade in which a disciplinary emphasis became a prominent influence in physical education. The Big Ten Body-of-Knowledge Project, which was spearheaded by the late Arthur Daniels of Indiana and King McCristal of Illinois, was an example illustrating the importance of such a trend.[9] The 1967 Conference on Graduate Education includes similar areas as central to the scholarly study and research of physical educators:

1. Meaning and significance of physical education including philosophical and historical considerations.
2. Social, cultural, and aesthetic aspects of physical education.
3. Behavioral aspects of physical education.
4. Motor learning and motor development.
5. Biomechanics.
6. Exercise physiology.

7. Administration.
8. Curricular aspects of physical education including supervision, instruction, and curriculum development.
9. Evaluative aspects of physical education. (2, p. 62)

Unfortunately just at the time when physical education appeared ready to add more of a "disciplinary thrust" including the humanities and social science aspects of the field to an already heavily professional-preparation-oriented graduate curriculum, the financial outlook began to darken considerably. Research funds from Washington were cut drastically. Legislatures faced with ever-mounting budgets found that educational spending at the college and university level could be cut without fear of political reprisal. Further, in many instances higher boards of education were created to keep a check rein on the universities, and it soon became apparent that political influences were pressuring these boards to exert a leveling influence on previous institutional profiles. On the other hand, it is undoubtedly fortunate that some controls were instituted to prevent just about every university going from establishing Ph.D. degree programs in a multitude of subjects (including physical education). Concurrently it suddenly became apparent that a "Ph.D. glut" was developing in many different fields--a situation which practically no one had predicted.

What Needs To Be Done?

The authors believe that there is an urgent need for both consolidation and innovation, and this must be preceded by self-evaluation on a local, state (provincial), regional, national, and continental basis.[1] Many of us know particular universities that have recently taken a hard look at their graduate programs. Of course, there are institutions where physical education is being forced to do just that. Some states (e.g., Illinois) have professional organizations which are devoted exclusively to professional preparation matters, and quite recently the IAPPHPER zeroed in on the master's degree program and managed to achieve rather remarkable consensus among the participants.[8] Most recently the voluntarily organized Council of Universities in Ontario directed each discipline to form a planning group composed of representatives from interested universities in order to plan for the next ten years at both the master's and doctoral levels.[6] Earlier in this paper the 1967 Conference on Graduate Education in Physical Education was alluded to, and this represents planning at the national level. And recently the State University College at Brockport invited Canadian representation to a graduate study planning conference held at the upper New York State institution.

Recently Zeigler and Penny offered a number of generalizations about developing graduate programs in physical education.[10] These thoughts were directed primarily at the master's level programs, but they have direct implications for doctoral degree programs also. In the first place the development of a master plan for the program was urged in cooperation with all concerned. There is considerable merit in seeking advice from a highly competent, outside resource person. This person should be selected only after it has been ascertained initially just which type or pattern of program is contemplated (e.g., discipline-oriented). It is recommended strongly that any advisory person should be broadly based in orientation with one highly specialized area of competency as a minimum.

Graduate faculty members should be added slowly keeping in mind the type of program for which they may be qualified. In the past there has been a tendency to elevate people to graduate level work too soon; thus, it would be wise to "re-certify" graduate faculty members each five years to make certain such status is still warranted. A reasonable balance between the numbers of men and women is important, but decisions must be made on the basis of qualification to serve according to the demands of the type of program being offered.

Local and regional needs must be served by universities within that geographical areas, but no one will ultimately thank an institution that becomes a "diploma mill for tired teachers and coaches." Demands of school boards for upgrading notwithstanding, universities should resist the impulse to help with the creation of a glut because more bodies seem to increase financial leverage for larger budgets.

Whether one or more types of degree program patterns are implemented, it seems highly desirable to preserve a common core experience of physical education knowledge which all must have prior to elective course experiences. There should be a reasonable amount of articulation among the competencies, skills, and knowledges required at the undergraduate program level and the common core experience of physical education and sport knowledge required at the master's level. This common core should include from twelve to fifteen semester hours of course work involving (1) research methods (including statistics), (2) history and philosophy of physical education (from a persistent problems standpoint); (3) human motor behavior; and (4) thesis or project seminar (credit or no credit).[8]

In addition to consolidation - i.e., a graduate program where a disciplinary-oriented program combines its various offerings into two options (e.g., humanities and social science option and bioscience option) - a need is seen for at least three different types of master's programs being offered (or available) at universities situated in one region of a state or province. The greatest demand would naturally be for a master's program to prepare a more qualified teacher and/or coach (the M.A.T. program or the M.S.T. program). A second type of program or degree pattern that should be available to a considerably smaller group within a state or a province typically

would be the disciplinary-oriented master's program leading to the
M.A. or M.S. degree. A third type of program deserves early consideration as well--a master's degree program where the student
could specialize in the theory and practice of some type of human
motor performance (e.g., dance, gymnastics, aquatics, etc.).[7] This
idea is recommended on the assumption that it is time that we move
positively to establish sport as a legitimate part of our culture which
merits scholarly study at the university level. What should we call
the degree? How about a master's degree in human motor performance (M.H.M.P.) with specialization in the theory and practice of
gymnastics, aquatics, or racquet sports? If one is worried about
these unusual letters, forget it. The letters M.P.E. (or D.P.E.) are
as strange and lowly as they come in the academic world; the fundamental question is whether the student graduates with a sound body-of-
knowledge about human motor performance theory and competency and
skill in human motor performance practice! At present one might
guess that seventy percent of the students would be interested in the
teaching-coaching degree program, while approximately fifteen percent each would get involved with each of the other two program patterns (i.e., the disciplinary-oriented program and the human motor
performance program, respectively).

Graduate programs in North American universities have traditionally been superimposed gradually on undergraduate programs.
As a result they have grown organizationally in a relatively haphazard manner. The deans and assistant deans of graduate schools
are usually "here today and gone tomorrow" - the assumption being
that Professor Such-and-Such ought to be offered the post because of
his scholarly achievements and ability to garner large research
grants for the institution. As a result of this practice in many institutions, management policies and procedures have developed slowly
in graduate schools. Typically the best way to find out how a problem
should be handled was to ask "good, old Miss Murgatroyd" who knew
six times as much about traditional practice as Dean Such-and-Such
anyhow. All of this adds up to the firm belief that administrators of
graduate physical education programs are well advised to develop
their own policies and procedures manuals. Such a loose-leaf document should include (1) those policies and procedures which the
graduate school insists on; (2) those policies and procedures which
the physical education graduate faculty have decided upon - over and
above those of the graduate school; and (3) those policies and procedures which the graduate chairman implements because they seem to
be in the best interest of all concerned. In passing, it is recommended that whenever possible graduate programs should be constituted
with a separate budget so that one and all will know just how much it
costs to finance such a venture.

Moving from the assumption that both consolidation and innovation are necessary which involve both new program emphases and

combination of former options, administrators and their executive committees should be most careful to see to it that money for equipment and facilities for scholarly endeavor and research should be made available to those who give every evidence of possession of the necessary knowledge, competency, and skill to carry out investigation. A "proven track record"--not promises to talk about what is underway--is undoubtedly the best recommendation as to where to put your money. There are far too many young men and women who are "just about ready to get set to go" in this regard. (This is not to say, of course, that a promising newcomer should not be offered the opportunity to make a modest beginning.) Along these lines administrators would be very wise to encourage young scholars with a humanities and social science orientation. For far too long the secret password of one of our favorite fraternities has conveyed a rather one-sided opinion as to the importance of the sciences in our outlook. It is now time to present our students with a comprehensive and balanced pattern of offerings in the humanities, social sciences, and sciences at both the undergraduate and graduate levels.

Still further, the graduate programs of recreation and park administration and of health and safety education need and should have their own autonomous status so that these professions may develop fully in their own right. This is not to state that physical education and sport should not remain "allied" to these emerging professions, nor that the three programs cannot continue to function alongside each other in one overall administrative unit such as a school, college, or faculty. A similar position seems possible for the field of dance and dance education, if it is possible to somehow make dance personnel "feel at home" in a physical education/athletics environment.

No matter where one turns, problems and difficulties confront those who would improve graduate study and research in physical education and sport. The focus of the various degree programs needs to be sharpened. The scholarly experience needs to be strengthened for some, while the internship experience necessary for others needs to be improved immeasurably (or in many cases begun for the first time). No matter in which direction one looks, there is an obvious need for quality control. "A better mouse trap can be built," if the field will simply set itself to the task!

The following incomplete listing of questions that can be raised bristles with unanswered needs that should be met as soon as possible in the 1970's:

1. What are the long range aims and the specifically realizable objectives of the graduate department?
2. How do these aims and objectives correlate with the development plan of the university concerned?

3. How do these aims and objectives fit into the overall educational scheme for the state or province in which the institution is located?
4. How can the status of the graduate program in physical education be raised within the graduate school or faculty of the university?
5. Is it advisable for some qualified person to be made available - either within physical education or through the agency of the graduate school - who can assist professors to prepare excellent research grant applications?
6. Should there be a separate graduate department of physical education and sport with a separate budget? (What are the possible advantages and disadvantages of this type of arrangement?)
7. How can better qualified students be encouraged to apply for admission to the graduate program?
8. Has an admission quota been imposed on the graduate program in physical education? (What are the implications of the presence or absence of such a quota?)
9. How is the workload of graduate faculty members determined? (Is credit given for writing and research? Is thesis advisement considered as a factor in the faculty member's workload? Are there limitations as to the number of master's and doctoral students that a faculty member may accept or be assigned? How is it determined whether a faculty member is qualified to advise at either level in a specific sub-disciplinary area?)

How Should We Go About The Task?

If we are serious about improving our graduate study and research programs from the standpoint of both quality and breadth, the authors urge again the need for both consolidation and innovation. For example, a university may decide that it should consolidate its present conglomerate master's program into one specialized master's program that produces excellent coaches in one or more sports. Or it may be decided that a master's program at X University will be known for the outstanding elementary school teachers that it graduates. How about one university in a given state really specializing in the social psychology of sport and physical activity (most certainly an area of study which would seem to warrant "positive reinforcement" at the present time)? The idea here is to innovate through consolidation, while at the same time making certain that various needs and interests of graduate students are met in a particular geographical region. An extremely important point to make in this connection is that each and every student should be guaranteed a fine core experience in those sub-disciplinary areas of the field that emanate from the humanities, social sciences, and bio-sciences.

Obviously, we are going to have to obtain most of our help from "within ourselves"--from people already in the field or at some stage in the educational training process. The important point to remember here is that graduate professors cannot and should not "be all things to all people." It is an extremely rare person who is qualified to assist graduate students in thesis development in more than one or two sub-disciplinary areas of research endeavor, not to mention helping advise research and/or scholarly projects relating to the teaching or coaching process. When to this is added the creativity and the understanding of human motor performance theory and practice in - say - dance, gymnastics, aquatics, or basketball that is needed for a degree program for the performer, it can readily be seen that a variety of professors with often different knowledge, competencies, and skills will be needed to fulfill the curricular aims and objectives of three different types of graduate programs. Obviously, any one university would be extremely hard pressed to offer the three types of programs unless there was a most unusual commitment on the part of the institution concerned. Still further, the faculty needs required to staff these programs would of necessity have to be met by recruitment of truly scholarly physical educator/coaches from all levels and aspects of professional endeavor. We would need to seek out those men and women with potential and desire for knowledge, skill, and competency development -- and even retrain them if need be!

As a field such as physical education seeks recognition within scholarly circles, there is always an effort to draw personnel from related disciplines. This is unfortunately more easily said than done. In the first place the sincerity of the commitment of the related discipline professor being lured to relate to the physical education field must be examined most carefully. Quite often the professor may "at heart" feel that he is "slumming" when he goes over to the P. E. department. Or it may well be that he isn't doing so well in his own discipline for any one of a number of reasons, and he decides therefore to bolster his morale with a cross-appointment. Based on considerable experience along these lines, it is recommended that the appointment in physical education not exceed twenty-five percent for the first few years, and an identical percentage proportion is recommended for a physical educator with a cross-appointment to a related department. The idea of a 50-50 split is really not workable because of too many committee involvements, voting jurisdiction problems, etc. Appointments committees are well advised to search carefully for strong "physical educators' hearts beating within the breasts" of those proposed for cross-disciplinary responsibilities and duties.

A Concluding Statement - What Will We Have Then?

Considering the present status of graduate study and research programs in physical education and sport, this statement has offered a variety of ideas about what needs to be done as we look to the future. Recommendations have been made for consolidation and innovation as part of the implementation of three or more different types of graduate programs. The question of where we can get assistance - and how we should go about it - has been considered as well. Professors with a variety of talents are needed, and they must have a deep commitment to this field.

The internal and external environments in which we operate are, of course, most important and cannot be neglected in any future plans. However, a profession such as ours will develop properly only if it is based on a sound fund of knowledge provided by scholars and researchers. Then men and women will be able to perform, teach, coach, administer, and supervise fine programs of physical education and sport according to the highest tradition of a respected profession.

Selected References

1. American Association for Health, Physical Education, and Recreation, Evaluation Standards and Guide in Health Education, Physical Education, Recreation Education. (Washington, D. C.: AAHPER, 1959).

2. _____, Graduate Education in Health Education, Physical Education, Recreation Education, Safety Education, and Dance. (Washington, D. C.: AAHPER, 1967).

3. Conant, James B. The Education of American Teachers. (New York: McGraw-Hill Book Company, 1963).

4. McCloy, C. H., "Current Trends in Graduate Study," Journal of Health, Physical Education, and Recreation, 28 (November, 1957), 33-34.

5. National Conference on Graduate Study in Health Education, Physical Education, and Recreation, The, Report on Graduate Study in Health Education, Physical Education and Recreation. (Chicago, Illinois: The Athletic Institute, 1950).

6. Ontario Council on Graduate Studies, "The First Three Years of Appraisal of Graduate Programmes" (Toronto, Ontario: Committee of Presidents of Universities of Ontario, 1970). (Pamphlet).

7.   Zeigler, Earle F., "A Model for Optimum Professional Development in a Field Called 'X'," in Proceedings of the First Canadian Symposium on the Philosophy of Sport and Physical Activity (Ottawa, Canada: Sport Canada Directorate, Department of Health and Welfare, 1972). (P. J. Galasso, editor).

8.   _____ and Jones, Margaret L., "Common Denominators in Physical Education Graduate Study in Illinois," Journal of Health, Physical Education, and Recreation, 40, 3 (March, 1969), 85-87.

9.   _____ and McCristal, King J., "A History of the Big Ten Body-of-Knowledge," Quest, IX (December, 1967), 79-84.

10.   _____ and Penny, William J., "Generalizations about Developing Graduate Programs in Physical Education," The Physical Educator, 26 (December, 1969), 169-170.

Selection #35

HISTORICAL PERSPECTIVE ON CONTRASTING PHILOSOPHIES OF PROFESSIONAL PREPARATION FOR PHYSICAL EDUCATION IN THE UNITED STATES

Historical research and so-called philosophical research are carried out in a wide variety of ways.* This brief paper represents an effort to combine one technique of historical method--a "persistent problems" approach--with two techniques of philosophical method--a combination of "structural analysis" and ordinary language" approaches. The underlying hypothesis is that there have indeed been contrasting philosophies of professional preparation for physical education in the United States. More specifically, it has been hypothesized that these contrasting philosophies or positions can be classified roughly as "progressivistic," "essentialistic," or "neither" with the departmental or sub-disciplinary entity known as educational philosophy.

(As background experiences which served to give the writer some insight into these methods and techniques, a history of professional preparation for physical education in the United States from 1861 to 1961 was prepared (Zeigler, 1962, pp. 115-133). Further, a comprehensive analysis was made of physical education philosophy based on the structural analysis technique (Zeigler, 1964). A brief history and philosophical analysis of the persistent problems of physical education and sport was published subsequently (Zeigler, 1968). Most recently a paper on the ordinarly language analysis of typical professional preparation terms was completed for presentation at Ottawa in May (Zeigler, 1974).)

The remainder of this paper will be subdivided into five parts as follows: (1) a brief historical review of professions in general, and teaching in particular; (2) a summary of professional preparation for physical education in the United States, with emphasis on selected persistent problems; (3) an enumeration of selected problem areas in teacher education in physical education that seem to imply adherence to specific stances within educational philosophy; (4) a comparative analysis of the philosophical stances underlying the contrasting positions within professional preparation for physical education; and (5) six recommended criteria for a philosophy of professional preparation for physical education.

---

* A paper presented at the Convention of the North American Society for Sport History, The University of Western Ontario, London, Ontario, Canada, May 11, 1974. (Published in 1975 in the Canadian Journal of History of Sport and Physical Education; accepted by the Editors in December, 1974.)

Historical Review of Professions (including the Teaching Profession)

Even though the idea of professions and rudimentary preparation for this type of work originated in the very early societies, it seems that the term "profession" was not used commonly until relatively recently (Brubacher, 1962, p. 47). However, centers for a type of professional instruction were developed in Greece and Rome a as bodies of knowledge became available. In medieval times universities were organized when the various professional faculties banded together for convenience, power, and protection. The degree granted at that time was in itself a license to practice whatever it was that the graduate "professed." This practiced continued in the Renaissance, at which time instruction became increasingly secularized. Further, in England especially, training for certain professions (e.g., law) gradually became disassociated from universities themselves (Brubacher, 1962, pp. 42-56).

An unabridged dictionary offers a number of different meanings for the term "profession," but it is usually described as a vocation which requires specific knowledge of some aspect of learning in order to have the practitioner accepted as a professional person. The now legendary Abraham Flexner recommended six criteria as being characteristic of a profession as far back as 1915 in an address to a group of social workers. A professional person's activity was (1) fundamentally intellectual, and the individual bears significant personal responsibility; (2) undoubtedly learned, because it is based on a wealth of knowledge; (3) definitely practical, rather than theoretical; (4) grounded in technique that could be taught, and this is the basis of professional education; (5) strongly organized internally; and (6) largely motivated by altruism, since its goal is the improvement of society (Flexner, 1915, pp. 578-581). The crucial aspect of this analysis was, however, "the unselfish devotion of those who have chosen to give themselves to making the world a fitter place to live in (Ibid., p. 590) and the presence or lack of this "unselfish devotion" will tend to elevate a doubtful activity to professional status or lower an acknowledged profession to a venal trade.

Professional preparation of teachers, at least to any considerable extent, is a fairly recent innovation. In early times the most important qualification for the position of teacher was a sound knowledge of the subject. If the subject-matter was deemed important, the status of the teacher rose accordingly. For example, when a larger percentage of the populace (recognized citizens) acquired a knowledge of reading and writing in the later years of the Greek period and in the Roman Era, the status of children's teachers declined, but those who taught the more complex subjects were highly respected (although not rewarded highly with money) (Brubacher, 1966, pp. 466 et ff.). Over the centuries public esteem accorded teachers has been highest when they have prepared students for what were considered to be the more important demands of life.

The medieval university, with its emphasis on the learned professions of theology, law, arts, and medicine, elevated the function of the teacher in the eyes of the public. Teachers who possessed background knowledge in the seven liberal arts--knowledge that laymen could not comprehend--were considered qualified to carry on with this art. At this time there was no such thing as professional education prior to becoming a teacher, at least in the sense that state or provincial certification is needed today on this continent in order to teach in the publicly-supported institutions at certain levels. During this period there was, however, a type of professional teacher organization similar to that of the medieval guild. Butts has explained that, "In the thirteenth century a career in university life became so important that it began to challenge a career in church or state as an outlet for the energies of able young men" (Butts, 1947, p. 179).

There were evidently not enough good teachers at the secondary level up through the period of the Renaissance. Despite this fact the status of teachers remained very low up through the eighteenth century, and this can probably be attributed to a considerable degree to no type of development that might be classified as a science of education. It was generally recognized that teaching was an art (a belief that prevails in many circles yet today), and this belief led to the position that the individual either had this ability inherently or not. During this period the Catholic Church made some progeess in turning out good secondary teachers, but competent instructors were in very short supply, and conditions were even worse at the elementary level (Brubacher, 1966, p. 472 in quoting from Edmund Coote's English Schoolmaster).

In the late eighteenth and early nineteenth centuries, it was Prussia where the most headway was made in improving teacher education. The government gave strong support to this development under Frederick the Great. The teaching methods of Pestalozzi were later introduced to strengthen this program still further, and the system was copied extensively in America. The advancements made in the theory of pedagogy based on his approach to the child's nature were truly significant. These developments were "the product of the reform movement in education which tended toward realism and away from classicism--an effort which had for its object the practical education of the masses, the fitting of youth for citizenship and the practical duties of life" (Luckey, 1903, pp. 27-28).

The United States. The status of teachers in the Colonial Period in the United States depended largely upon whether a teacher taught at the college level or in the lower branches of education. Once again it was a question of knowledge of subject-matter with no emphasis on theory of pedagogy. The advancement that was made in the nineteenth century came in the type of professional education offered to elementary school teachers through the rise and growth of the normal school idea. Gordy reports that elements of the German pattern were adopted in the first normal schools in the United States, but that much originality on the part of the early advocates was also evident (1891, pp. 20-21).

The years between 1830 and 1860 witnessed the struggle for state-supported schools, and by the end of this "architectural period" the American educational ladder as a one-way system was fairly complete. Once the various types of schools were amalgamated into state systems, attention was turned to the quality of teacher engaged for the educational task. Although there was a steadily larger number of state normal schools, improvement in the status of teachers came slowly in the period from 1860 to 1890. By the end of the nineteenth century, the normal school was a well-established part of the American educational system. However, the transformation of this type of institution from secondary status to college-level rank has occurred since the beginning of the twentieth century. With the tremendous growth of the number of public high schools, it became absolutely imperative for the normal schools to become normal colleges and to graduate men and women with degrees that would be accepted by accrediting associations as being roughly comparable to university degrees. (Interestingly enough, colleges and universities were uncertain about the role they should play in the technical phases of teaching in the nineteenth century; thus, so-called professional education for teachers was quite often no better than normal school training.)

The Twentieth Century. This century has witnessed a number of significant developments in teacher education, but primarily for elementary and secondary school teachers. Normal schools became normal "colleges" and were subsequently designated as teachers' colleges. During the 1950's and 1960's most of these institutions were elevated to university status by the proclamation of state legislatures. In a number of cases such declaration was undoubtedly premature, be because the "scholarly writing and research" component of many of these universities has been very slim indeed. Also, a full component of schools and colleges representing the many disciplines and professions has been lacking.

Education as a professional area of study has gradually made an inroad into most of the well-established, leading colleges and universities, but it has yet to justify the disciplinary status that is claimed by many. Yet there was such a demand for secondary school teachers that it seemed unreasonable for these institutions not to make some provision for such programs in their educational offerings. Thus, despite the fact that colleges and universities did not require that their professors present evidence of course work in professional education leading to certification, more than 500 institutions of higher education added such programs between 1900 and 1930 to help prospective teachers meet the teacher certification requirements imposed in the various states.

Professional Preparation for Physical Education

Professional preparation for physical education in the United States began in 1861 when Dio Lewis started the first ten-week diploma course (Lewis in Barnard's American Journal of Education). The Normal School of the North American Turnerbund began in 1866 in New York City (North American Turnerbund Proceedings, 1866). In many instances these early schools were owned by the individual or society sponsoring them, but eventually these normal schools underwent a distinct transformation. Names were changed; curricular were expanded; staffs were increased in number greatly; degrees were offered; and eventually affiliation with colleges and universities took place (Zeigler, 1962, pp. 116-133).

The field has been influenced by a variety of societal forces as the American scene changed. Foreign traditions and customs held sway initially, but gradually a fairly distinct American philosophy of physical education emerged. If there was indeed a "fairly distinct" image, it has since become blurred as it became possible to delineate the various educational philosophical trends (Zeigler, 1964, Chapters 5, 7, 9, 11). Such occurrences as wars and periods of economic depression and prosperity have typically brought about sweeping changes.

In the period from 1900 to 1920 educators began to take the place of physicians as directors of professional programs (Elliott, 1927, p. 21). In addition, many publicly-supported colleges and universities had entered the field and were awarding baccalaureate degrees upon the completion of programs with majors in physical education. Specialized curricula were developed in schools of education, but they were organized independent of professional education schools as well in several other organizational patterns. The subsequent establishment of separate schools and colleges of physical education within universities has had a truly notable influence on professional preparation and on the status of the field as a whole (Zeigler, 1972, p. 48).

In the twentieth century many leaders have urged that a stronger "cultural" education be provided for prospective physical teachers. A need was expressed further for an improved background in the foundation sciences. Until recently there was a definite trend toward increasing the so-called general professional education course requirement. A number of studies have indicated a lack of standardization in course terminology within the specialized professional education area (as it was typically designated) of health, physical education, and recreation (for example, see Professional Training in Physical Education, 1972, p. 41).

In the decade after World War I--a conflict which exerted a tremendous influence upon the field forcing a flood of state health and physical education laws, some 137 colleges and universities joined those already in existence to offer professional education in health and physical education (Zeigler, 1950, p. 326). As a result, school health education and physical education were interwoven in a somewhat confusing manner in the curriculum. In addition, courses in recreation, camping, and outdoor education were often introduced. Gradually separate curricula in school health and safety education and recreation leadership were developed in many of the leading universities functioning in the field. A series of national conferences helped to bring the various curriculum objectives into focus (for example, see the National Conference on Undergraduate Professional Preparation in Physical Education and Recreation, 1948). Presently there is a strong trend toward specialization of function which may take the present three areas still further apart (and this seems to include dance and athletics as well). The American Association for Health, Physical Education, and Recreation, the largest single department of the National Education Association, has been a great unifying force in the total movement, but nevertheless the various philosophies of education are almost impossible to overcome as consensus is sought.

There have been many attempts to improve the quality of professional preparation through studies, surveys, research projects, national conferences, and accreditation plans. Snyder and Scott recommended careful consideration of the "competency approach" in the 1950's as a means of improving the entire professional preparation process in physical education (1954). Influences such as the need for a disciplinary approach and economic pressures (accompanied by the introduction of higher educational boards at the state level) have had a marked effect on colleges and universities offering professional programs in the field. The leaders in the field are currently moving most carefully, often with great introspection, as they look to the future. The current "shake-down" taking place in higher education may yet prove to be beneficial to physical education, but only if wise leadership and dedicated professional effort is able to influence the rank and file of the profession to raise their standards higher than they appear to be at the present.

Selected Problem Areas in Professional Preparation History

Since the early development of teacher education in physical education, a great number of developments have taken place which, in many instances, either solved specific problems or created new areas of concern. In a study published in the late 1920's, five "outstanding developments in professional training" were listed as follows: (1) the philosophy of physical education has undergone a change; (2) educators take the place of physicians as directors; (3) academic degrees are granted for major units in physical education; (4) specialized curricula in physical education are offered in schools of education; and (5) the organization has become very complex (Elliott, 1927, pp. 16-23). In the process of this investigation, however, Elliott found that many "interesting problems" presented themselves for further study as follows:

1. An investigation of the qualifications and functions of the physical educator.
2. The need of a selective process in the admission of students to professional curricula which will not only determine mental and physical fitness, but personality and leadership qualifications.
3. The organization of a professional curriculum, with a greater freedom of election than is now in practice, which will provide the necessary and desirable professional preparation in physical education, as well as the cultural background.
4. The organization of courses, especially in the foundation sciences, anatomy, physiology, etc., that are adapted to satisfactorily meet the needs of students majoring in physical education.
5. A standardized nomenclature in physical education.
6. Means of coordinating the several departments, schools and colleges which contribute to the professional curriculum . . .
7. The determination of the minimum essentials for the preparation of teachers . . .
8. The organization of graduate work in physical education for specialists, administrators, and directors of physical education (Ibid., pp. 56-57).

The present author, in undertaking a comprehensive history of professional preparation for physical education in the mid-1940's, subdivided his investigation into a number of persistent problems, or areas of concern, which confronted those concerned with teacher education in physical education since it began in 1861 in the United States (Zeigler, 1950). Thus, he was concerned with describing the historical development in each of the following topical headings that are enumerated briefly:

Selective Admission, Placement and Guidance. The first school had no entrance requirements, but by 1948 complicated routines were involved. The trend in the 1950's was toward generalization of entrance requirements, working toward a continuous, long-range program of selection.

Curriculum--Aims and Methods. The aims and methods of the early schools varied greatly, but toward the end of the 1800's some leaders were taking an eclectic and fairly scientific approach. In the period from 1920 to 1950, a unique American philosophy of physical education developed, and the physical educator was conceived as a person of more professional stature. Although many still think primarily of "courses taken," the curriculum is also being conceived as all the experiences provided for the development of the professional student.

Curriculum--Length of Course and Types of Degrees. The first course for training teachers of physical education extended for a ten-week period, and the successful student received a diploma. Now the professional student in physical education may be awarded the doctor of philosophy degree, or the doctor of education degree, upon successful completion of a program extending over a seven-year period at least.

Curriculum--Specific Courses and Trends. Early curricula in the field varied greatly with some including about as much knowledge of the body as an early medical doctor would be expected to know. The program varied depending upon which foreign system of gymnastics was being propounded. In the twentieth century there was a gradually broadening outlook including a fair distribution over the general academic, basic science, professional education, and professional physical education courses. In the 1920's the more prevalent specialized curriculum was that of athletic coaching, but in the 1930's the emphasis shifted so that a coach, an academic teacher, and a gymnasium instructor were desired in that order.

In-Service Training of Teachers--Summer Schools, Professional Organizations, Professional Periodicals. In the late 1800's and the early 1900's a number of summer training programs in physical education began (e.g., the Harvard Summer School of Physical Education under Dr. Sargent). This movement really expanded in the 1920's, so that by 1931 the total number of summer sessions was 654, or approximately twenty-eight and six-tenths percent of the total number of teachers (273,148 enrolled) (National Education Association, Research Division, 1931). In addition, a number of professional associations have been organized by people with special professional interests in the field (e.g., The National College Physical Education Association for Men in 1897). Still further, either as organs of these associations or separately, a number of professional periodicals were started (e.g., Mind and Body of The North American Gymnastic Union).

Administrative Problems of Teacher Training. Four other "administrative problems" were delineated as follows: (1) staff evolution; (2) growth in the number of training programs; (3) teacher certification and state laws involving a steady trend toward centralization of certification in state departments of education along with a progressive raising of minimum requirements; and (4) professional status and ethics, an area in which there has been some development within the so-called education profession (but not for the various individuals relating to physical activity professionally in the public sector).

Contrasting Philosophical Positions Within Professional Preparation

Broadly speaking, it is possible to delineate among educational progressivism, educational essentialism, and a philosophy of language approach to educational philosophy in relation to professional preparation for physical education. In any attempt to do this, the "teacher of teachers" should keep in mind that progressivism is greatly concerned about such elements as pupil freedom, individual differences, student interest, pupil growth, no fixed values, and that "education is life now." The essentialist believes that there are certain educational values by which the student must be guided; that effort takes precedence over interest and that this gir s "moral stamina"; that the experience of the past has powerful jurisdiction over the present; and that the cultivation of the intellect is most important in education. These beliefs attributed to each broad position are, of course, only representative and not inclusive (Zeigler, 1963, p. 10). Existentialist "flavoring" in educational philosophy may typically be viewed as somewhat progressivistic in nature, mainly because it is individualistic and quite often fundamentally atheistic or agnostic. A philosophy of language approach may be regarded as neither--neither progressivistic or essentialistic. It is basically concerned with language and/or conceptual analysis--the former being based on the belief that much of the confusion and disagreement over philosophy emanates from misuse of language in various ways, while the latter seems to incline a bit more toward a technique which seeks to define a term or concept (as opposed to how it is used). Somewhat broader analytic philosophy provides "a rational reconstruction of the language of science" (Kaplan, 1961, p. 83).

An attempt will now be made to enumerate some eleven aspects of teacher education about which there has been sharp divisions of opinion historically. It has been possible to achieve some consensus on these problems from time to time through the medium of a number

of national conferences on teacher preparation that have been held in
the United States since the late 1800's. All factions are in agreement,
of course, on a statement that qualified teachers are the most important determinant of the status of the profession; yet, there are many
areas of disagreement in which consensus is a long way off--or indeed
may never be found. Such disagreement will not necessarily be resolved through democratic employment of the ballot box at national
conferences; however, such a technique is fundamental in a democratic society, and the influence of a majority on a contentious issue
should be helpful but not "overwhelming to the undecided or recalcitrant individual."

Course Emphasis--Technique or Content? The first of the
eleven problem areas to be discussed briefly is the question of
whether the prospective teacher/coach needs more or less time spent
on courses emphasizing technique rather than content. Historically
the essentialist is typically suspicious of the value of the so-called
general professional education courses; he tend to believe that teaching is much more an art than a science. The idealistically oriented
essentialist would be inclined to stress the need for the physical educator to have somewhat more of a background in the humanities, while
the essentialist with a natural realistic orientation has usually wished
to place increased emphasis on the foundation science courses
(Zeigler, 1964, pp. 263-265).

"Competency Approach" vs. "Courses and Credits Approach".
The previous discussion leads to a further problem that has plagued
teacher education historically and still has not been resolved. This
is the possible use of the "competency approach" (Cf. p. 330) as
opposed to the "courses and credits approach" that has been with the
field traditionally since the first professional program was introduced
in 1861. As matters stand now, the student takes a certain number of
courses while attending college for a required number of years. Upon
graduation the "teacher" receives his degree for the successful completion of 132 semester hours, more or less, and a provincial teaching certificate--a certificate which informs local school boards that
the recipient is presumably a competent, educated person able to
teach physical education to the youth of the state. The problem is that
there is no guarantee that graduating seniors will be able to function
well as intelligent citizens and competent professionals, unless there
is developed a more effective means of assessing their abilities as
determined by specific competencies developed through selected experiences with subject-matters as resource areas.

Over the years the essentialistic teacher educator has not been
disturbed at all about the pattern in which the students take a certain
number of specified courses for a required number of years; earns
the required number of credit hours with approximately a C plus
grade point average; and then goes out to teach if he can find a job.

The education progressivist, conversely, has seemed to be more concerned about what is happening to this individual as this process goes on, especially insofar as his knowledge, skills, and competencies are concerned--and specifically as these may be related directly and evaluatively to excellent teaching performance.

Relating Language Analysis to the Competency Approach. When a special committee at Illinois related a language analysis approach to teacher education in physical education in 1963, the author was charged with preliminary preparation of a statement employing this ordinary language terminology. The members of the committee were not approaching their task in either an essentialistic or progressivistic manner; they were merely attempting to define the terms that are typically employed and then to place them in proper perspective. Thus, after this process had been completed, when a specific term (e.g., "competency") was employed, they knew where it fit into the pattern being developed and how the term was being used. (For purposes of this presentation, therefore, this philosophy of language approach is clearly understood as possessing no value orientation such as is the case with either progressivism or essentialism.)

The results of this deliberation was as follows: the student enrolled in a professional preparation program in physical education and sport is afforded educational experiences in a classroom, laboratory, gymnasium, pool, field, or field work setting. Through various types of educational methodology (lectures, discussions, problem-solving situations in theory and practice, etc.), he hears facts, increases his scope of information (knowledge), and learns to comprehend and interpret this material (understanding). Possessing various amounts of ability or aptitude, the student gradually develops competency and a certain degree of skill. It is to be hoped that certain appreciations about the worth of his profession will be developed, and that he will form certain attitudes about the work that lies ahead in his chosen field. To sum it up, there are certain special duties or performances which the student preparing for the teaching profession should fulfill (functions). Through the professional curriculum, he is exposed to specific problems which he must face successfully. Through planned experiences, with a wide variety of resource areas to serve him as "depositories" of facts, he develops competencies, skills, knowledge, understanding, appreciations, and attitudes which will enable him to be an effective educator (his chosen profession) (Zeigler, 1974, pp. 11-13).

Specialization or Generalization in the Curriculum? A fourth problem that has been faced by the field in this century has been the question of whether there should be a specialized curriculum or a generalized program that might include health and safety education (including driver education) and recreation education. Those with an essentialistic orientation have felt typically that the trend toward

generalization of function must be halted; many professional educators with such an orientation would prefer that attention be devoted toward turning out a good _physical_ education teacher or gymnasium in-
structor--an exercise specialist. The essentialist tends to believe
that the field has "spawned" many of these allied fields, but that they
have now "grown up" and should be allowed (urged) to "try out their
own wings." Some with an essentialistic orientation believe that _phy-
sical_ education can be considered curricular, but there is almost
unanimous agreement that all of these other areas are really _extra-
curricular_. The educational progressivist, conversely, believed--at
least until the disciplinary emphasis of the 1960's arrived--that we
should include any and all of these areas (e.g., health and safety education) within a department or school _and_ as a part of the physical
education major curriculum.

Election versus Requirement in the Curriculum. The pendulum
has been swinging surely and steadily back and forth in connection
problem area #5 from generation to generation over the past 100
years. The writer recalls a professional curriculum of twenty-five
years ago in which a student was allowed one elective course in the
senior year--and even with this "elective" the young man or woman
was urged to selected a basic geography course. Now twenty-five
years later there is almost complete freedom of election in the same
university, and a student could graduate without taking anatomy and
physiology! it is true that the "elective promiscuity" of the 1960's is
now being changed, however, and a modified or basic core of courses
is being established as a requirement in both the humanities and social
science aspect of the curriculum and the bio-science division as well.

Influence of Competitive Athletics. Most women in the field of
physical education have been appalled by the strongly materialistic
influences that have beset men's athletics since the early years of the
twentieth century. In making every effort to set "proper standards"
for women in this regard, it is quite possible that women physical
educators in the United States tended to "throw out the baby with the
bath water." During the decades when interscholastic and intercollegiate athletics for women were zealously kept under control and at
a very low level, Canadian women physical educators maintained
competitive sport for women in educational perspective and at a
slightly higher level of competition in the colleges and universities.
Now the situation has very definitely changed, however, and the social
influence of "women's rights" is bringing about a new emphasis on
women's competitive sport throughout the land. Recent Title IX legis-
lation clearly means that women should have exactly the same opportunities as men in competitive sport, and one conjectures in horror
whether the women's program will inevitably lose almost all sight of
sound educational perspective in the process. The almost plaintive
statement of the American physical educator which maintains that "we

don't have any problems with intercollegiate athletics; we are completely separate from them" is almost as frightening as the rationalization of the politicians caught in the Watergate fiasco. Both educational essentialists and educational progressivists decry the materialistic excesses operating within competitive sport in education, but they seem almost powerless to combat these abuses successfully. The essentialist is typically probably a little less disturbed, because he may see this activity as extracurricular, whereas the progressivist, who sees this experience as potentially curricular in nature, is disturbed greatly by such an evil.

Discipline Emphasis versus "Professional Preparation". It is now recognized by almost all that the need for a disciplinary orientation to a body-of-knowledge for physical education that became evident in the early 1960's has somehow challenged or threatened those who felt that the field's primary mission was to prepare teachers and coaches of physical education and sport primarily for the secondary schools. This would not seem to be an "either-or" decision that must be made, because most certainly any true profession needs enough supporting scholars and researchers providing the necessary knowledge required for successful functioning. For a variety of reasons the field of physical education has not attracted a sufficient quantity of scholars in the past, although fortunately the situation has improved in the past ten years. This previous deficiency has resulted in physical education as a field "acquiring a rather massive inferiority complex," and is it any wonder, therefore, that the theory and practice of human motor performance (or human movement) has not been considered acceptable for introduction into the educational curriculum at any level?

The Bio-science versus the Humanities-Social Science Conflict. An eighth problem that has come into sharp focus recently--although it has surfaced on occasion in the past--is the actual conflict that has developed between those in the field who feel that a bio-science approach is sufficient for its fullest development. Thus, their efforts are devoted fully in this direction, and they decry any expenditures for the development of the humanities and social science aspects of the profession. Of course, this is not the first time in education or elsewhere when "haves" became worried about "have-nots" wanting to get support for their work, and the present financial cutbacks in university support may make this problem more acute. Still further incidents of this type, such as isolated efforts by social scientists to downgrade the humanities aspects of the field, represent the type of internecine conflict that will inevitably be self-defeating for the entire field of physical education and sport (and even here there is often unreasonable hostility against those who would retain or discard the term "physical education").

The Accreditation of Teacher-Preparing Institutions. Efforts to improve the level of teacher education generally, and physical education specifically, have resulted in several approaches to the matter of accreditation. Over the past forty years or so, a number of attempts have been made to standardize professional curricula with some positive results. Many national conferences in both general professional education and in this specialized field have been held in an attempt to determine desirable practices for teacher education institutions. From this movement have evolved standards to be used by teams of professionals serving under accrediting agency auspices. The first step was the establishment of evaluative criteria for the rating of professional programs, and at this time individual departments were encouraged to undertake self-evaluation of major programs. More recently, however, the National Council on Accreditation of Teacher Education began conducting institutional surveys as rapidly and as carefully as possible. The entire field of teacher education is involved in this effort, and accreditation is being withheld from institutions that do not meet the prescribed standards. There is a considerable amount of consensus between the essentialists and the progressivists about this development, even if their agreement is not always based upon the same reasoning for backing this move by NCATE. The progressivist typically supports the concept of self-evaluation and believes that standards should allow room for flexibility, while the essentialist would generally vote to eliminate substandard institutions from the teacher education field if their programs' standards are not elevated within a fixed period of time.

Involvement of Students in Evaluation Process. A tenth problem has been the extent to which students are allowed or encouraged to share in the evaluation of the professional program's progress. Typically, the progressivist has seen a great deal of merit in such a process, whereas the essentialist has avoided the employment of such an evaluative technique. The student unrest of the 1960's and public disenchantment with colleges and universities have forced essentialistic professors and administrators to accept course evaluations by students as a "necessary evil." The publication of course evaluation manuals by student organizations has met with considerable hostility on the part of segments of the faculty. Still further, demands that such evaluations be employed by committees on promotion and tenure have brought strong reactions by professors on the assumption that "the immature cannot possibly evaluate correctly what they do not fully understand."

Patterns of Administrative Control. The final problem (#11) to be discussed at this time relates to the question whether the approach to the administrative function within education has a vital part to play in the achievement of the objectives of the professional preparation program in physical education. The educational essentialist tend to see administration as an art, while the progressivist views it as a developing social science--that is, all evidence should be brought to bear in the administrative process, while the program is being administered artfully. An educational progressivist serving as an administrator would seek to conduct the affairs of the department in a truly democratic manner and would encourage faculty members to share in policy formation. The chairperson would encourage faculty, staff, and students to offer constructive criticism in a variety of ways. The essentialistic administrator tends to function on the basis of his ascribed authority which has been centralized through a line-staff pattern of control. He has the ultimate responsibility and, although he may ask for opinions of faculty members--and indeed there are aspects of the university situation now where faculty and even students vote on important matters--he would not hesitate to overrule majority opinion if he were convinved that some incorrect decisions had been made. In the final analysis there is still no firm understanding in an evolving democratic society as to what constitutes the best type of "democratic process" within a college or university's pattern of administrative control. Thus, because man is an imitator, and professional students will not be exceptions to this generalization, it is most important that undergraduate students observe (and take part in?) the finest pattern of administrative control consistent with representative democracy.

Six Recommended Criteria--Summary and Conclusions

The main objective of this paper was to offer some historical perspective on contrasting philosophies of professional preparation for physical education in the United States. It was hypothesized that there were contrasting philosophical positions or stances, and that they could be classified roughly as "progressivistic," "essentialistic," or based on a "philosophy of language approach." To accomplish his objective, the writer combined one technique of historical method--a "persistent problems" approach--with two techniques of philosophical method--a combination of "structural analysis" and "ordinary language" approaches.

The history of professions in general was reviewed very briefly, with teaching singled out for special attention. Then a brief summary of the history of professional preparation for physical education in the United States was discussed, with emphasis on certain types of problems that have occurred. The third part of this presentation involved an enumeration of selected historical problem areas in teacher education in physical education, and this was followed by a comparative analysis of the philosophical stances that seemed to underly the contrasting positions. The following eleven problem areas were identified on the basis of the writer's ongoing historical assessment of professional preparation for physical education:

1. Course Emphasis--Technique or Content?
2. "Competency Approach" vs. "Courses and Credits Approach".
3. Relating Language Analysis to the Competency Approach.
4. Specialization or Generalization in the Curriculum?
5. Election versus Requirement in the Curriculum.
6. Influence of Competitive Athletics.
7. Discipline Emphasis versus "Professional Preparation".
8. The Bio-Science versus the Humanities-Social Science Conflict.
9. The Accreditation of Teacher-Preparing Institutions.
10. Involvement of Students in Evaluation Process.
11. Patterns of Administrative Control.

Conclusions. On the basis of ongoing historical investigation and philosophical analysis of professional preparation for physical education in the United States, it seems possible and reasonable to draw the following conclusions:

1. That physical education is considered typically to be part of the teaching profession, a field of endeavor that has many of the earmarks of a true profession (although its internal organizational structure could be strengthened considerably).

2. That professional preparation for physical education has undergone a process of emergent evolution over the past 113 years, during which time it has been influenced by a variety of societal forces.

3. That greater progress may have been made in the United States in the area of professional preparation for physical education, but that there are strong influences evident at present that may retard the field's progress seriously.

4. That the most serious problems confronting professional preparation for physical education in the United States at present are as follows:

   a. The need to graduate competent, well-educated, fully professional physical educators and coaches.

   b. The need to develop sound options within the professional curriculum in which specialization is encouraged.

c. The need to <u>control</u> competitive athletics for both men and women in such a way that the entire educational process is <u>strengthened</u>--rather than <u>distorted</u> as it is at present.

d. The need to develop <u>a sound body-of-knowledge</u> in the <u>humanities, social science, and bio-science</u> aspects of physical education and sport.

e. The need to <u>fully</u> implement patterns of administrative control within educational institutions that are fully consonant with a desirable amount of <u>freedom</u> in an evolving democratic society.

<u>Recommended Criteria for a Philosophy of Professional Education</u>. At the end of a paper such as this--one that has reviewed its topic historically; delineated its historical "persistent problems"; and attempted to place them in some sort of educational philosophical perspective; it was considered reasonable to draw some conclusions based on the investigation and analysis carried out for the past twenty-five years, and which was reviewed here briefly in respect to professional preparation for physical education in the United States. Finally, one last step will be taken--the recommendation of six criteria whereby a philosophy of professional education might be develveloped by any sincere, reasonably intelligent individual practicing in the field. The position taken here is that a philosophy of professional education should--to be most effective--include the following:

1. The expression of a position concerning the nature of the universe (<u>metaphysics</u>). (To the extent that such position is possible, it should be founded on knowledge that is systematically verifiable--or at least recognition of non-verifiability should be admitted.)

2. A statement about the possibility of the acquisition of knowledge (<u>epistemology</u>). (Such a statement should be <u>logical and consistent</u> in its several divisions.)

3. A determination of educational aims and objectives in relation to societal aims or values (<u>axiology</u>). (Such aims should be both broad and inclusive in scope.)

4. A <u>design of action</u> for education. (Education should be <u>meaningful and enjoyable</u>, as well as practical and attainable.)

5. A design for implementation of <u>general</u> professional education. (This should be based on the achievement of of knowledge, competencies, and skills through planned experiences.)

6. A design for implementation of <u>specialized</u> professional education. (This should also be achieved through the acquisition of knowledge, competencies, and skills as a result of carefully planned experiences.)

Selected References and Bibliography

1. Abernathy, Ruth and Waltz, Maryann. "Toward a Discipline: First Steps First," <u>Quest</u>, 2, 1-7, April, 1964.

2. American Association for Health, Physical Education, and Recreation. <u>Evaluation Standards and Guide in Health Education, Physical Education, Recreation Education.</u> Washington, D. C.: American Association for H.P.E.R., 1959.

3. American Association for Health, Physical Education, and Recreation. <u>Professional Preparation in Health Education, Physical Education, Recreation Education</u>. Washington, D. C.: The Association, 1962.

4. American Association of Colleges for Teacher Education, The. <u>Standards and Evaluative Criteria for the Accreditation of Teacher Education</u>. Washington, D. C.: The Association, 1967.

5. Bramwell, Amy B. and Hughes, H. M. <u>The Training of Teachers in the United States of America</u>. New York: Macmillan and Co., 1894.

6. Brubacher, John S., "The Evolution of Professional Education," in <u>Education for the Professions</u> (edited by Nelson B. Henry). <u>Proceedings</u> (Part II) of the National Society for the Study of Education, Chicago, Illinois, 1962.

7. Brubacher, John S. <u>A History of the Problems of Education</u>. New York: McGraw-Hill Book Co., Second edition, 1966.

8. Brubacher, John S. <u>Modern Philosophies of Education</u>. New York: McGraw-Hill Book Co., Fourth edition, 1969.

9. Brubacher, John S. and Rudy, W. <u>Higher Education in Transition</u>. New York: Harper & Row, Publishers, Inc., 1958.

10. Butts, R. Freeman. A Cultural History of Education. New York: McGraw-Hill Book Company, 1947.

11. Conant, James B. The Education of American Teachers. New York: McGraw-Hill Book Company, 1963.

12. Daniels, A., "The Potential of Physical Education as an Area of Research and Scholarly Effort," Journal of Health, Physical Education, and Recreation, 36, 1:32-33, 74, January, 1965.

13. Doggett, Laurence L. Man and a School. New York: Association Press, 1943.

14. Elliott, Ruth. The Organization of Professional Training in Physical Education in State Universities. New York: Teachers College, Columbia University, 1927.

15. Esslinger, A. A. "Undergraduate versus Graduate Study," in Journal of Health, Physical Education, and Recreation, 37, 9:63-64, September, 1966.

16. Flexner, Abraham. "Is Social Work a Profession?" in Proceedings of the National Conference of Charities and Correction. Chicago, Illinois: Hildmann Printing Co., 1915, pp. 576-590.

17. Gordy, J. P. Rise and Growth of the Normal School Idea in the United States. Washington, D. C.: U. S. Bureau of Education Circular of Information 8, 1891.

18. Hartwell, E. M., "On Physical Training," in Report of the Commissioner of Education. Washington, D.C.: Government Printing Office, 1903, Chapter XVII.

19. Henry, Franklin H., "Physical Education: An Academic Discipline," Journal of Health, Physical Education, and Recreation, 35, 7:32-33, 69, September, 1964.

20. Hofstadter, R. Anti-intellectualism in American Life. New York: Alfred A. Knopf, Inc., 1963.

21. Hubbell, L. G. The Development of University Departments of Education. Washington, D. C.: The Catholic University of American Press, 1924.

22. Kaplan, Abraham. The New World of Philosophy. New York: Random House, 1961.

23. Knight, Edgar W. Twenty Centuries of Education. Boston:
    Ginn and Company, 1940.

24. Lee, E. A. The Development of Professional Programs of
    Education. New York: Columbia University Press, 1925.

25. Lewis, Dio., "New Gymnastics," Barnard's American Journal
    of Education, 12:665.

26. Luckey, G. W. A. The Professional Training of Secondary
    Teachers in the United States. New York: The Macmillan
    Co., 1903.

27. National Commission on Teacher Education and Professional
    Standards. New Horizons: The Becoming Journey.
    Washington, D. C.: NCTEPS, National Education Associ-
    ation of the United States, September, 1961.

28. National Conference on Undergraduate Professional Preparation
    in Physical Education, Health Education, and Recreation.
    Weston, West Virginia: Jackson's Mill, May 16-27, 1948.

29. National Education Association (Research Division). "Growth
    of Summer-School Attendance," Journal of the National
    Education Association, 20:298, November, 1931.

30. National Survey of the Education of Teachers. Washington,
    D. C.: U. S. Office of Education Bulletin 10, Volume 5,
    Chaps. 1-4. (Further bibliographical references on the
    history of teacher training are in Volume 1, pp. 56-61

31. Nordly, Carl L., "Teacher Education," in Proceedings of the
    50th Annual Meeting of the College Physical Education
    Association, 1947.

32. North American Turnerbund. Proceedings of the Convention,
    St. Louis, Missouri, April 1-4, 1866.

33. Pangburn, J. M. The Evolution of the American Teachers
    College. New York: Teachers College, Columbia Uni-
    versity, 1932.

34. Professional Preparation in Health Education, Physical Edu-
    cation, Recreation Education. Washington, D. C.:
    American Association for Health, Physical Education,
    and Recreation, 1962. (This is a report of a national
    conference held in January, 1962 in Washington, D. C.)

35. _Professional Training in Physical Education_. Washington,
       D. C.: U. S. Bureau of Education, Physical Education
       Series, No. 9, 1928. 45 p. (This is a report of a confer-
       ence arranged by the U. S. Bureau of Education on March
       30, 1927.)

36. Snyder, R. A. and Scott, Harry A. _Professional Preparation
       in Health Education, Physical Education, and Recreation_.
       New York: McGraw-Hill Book Company, 1954.

37. Stish, Eugene E., "Anthropokinetics," _Journal of Health,
       Physical Education, and Recreation_, 35, 9:33, 60-62,
       November-December, 1964.

38. Wilson, D. M., "Next Problem of Articulation: The Under-
       graduate College and the Professional and Graduate
       Schools," _Educational Record_, 39:124-128, April, 1958.

39. Zeigler, Earle F., "A Brief Analysis of the Ordinary Language
       Employed in the Professional Preparation of Sport Coach-
       es and Teachers of Physical Education." A paper pre-
       sented to the Annual Convention of the Canadian Associ-
       ation for Health, Physical Education and Recreation,
       Ottawa, Canada, May 27, 1974.

40. Zeigler, Earle F., "An Historical Analysis of the Professional
       Master's Degree in Physical Education in the United
       States," _Canadian Journal of the History of Sport and Phy-
       sical Education_, 3, 2:44-68, 1972.

41. Zeigler, Earle F., "A History of Professional Preparation for
       Physical Education (1861-1961)," in _Professional Pre-
       paration in Health Education, Physical Education, and
       Recreation Education_. Washington, D. C.: The Ameri-
       can Association for Health, Physical Education, and Re-
       creation, 1972, pp. 116-133.

42. Zeigler, Earle F., "A History of Professional Preparation for
       Physical Education in the United States, 1861-1948."
       Ph.D. dissertation, Yale University, 1950. (Published in
       microcard form through the University of Oregon.)

43. Zeigler, Earle F., "A Model for Optimum Professional De-
       velopment in a Field Called 'X'." _Proceedings_ of the
       First Canadian Symposium on the Philosophy of Sport and
       Physical Activity, Windsor, Ontario, 1972, 16-28.

44. Zeigler, Earle F. Philosophical Foundations for Physical, Health, and Recreation Education. Englewood Cliffs, New Jersey: Prentice-Hall, Inc., 1964.

45. Zeigler, Earle F. Problems in the History and Philosophy of Physical Education and Sport. Englewood Cliffs, New Jersey: Prentice-Hall, Inc., 1968.

46. Zeigler, Earle F., "A Recommended Irreducible Minimum for Graduate Study in Physical Education and Sport," Journal of Health, Physical Education, and Recreation, 42, 2:85-86, February, 1971.

47. Zeigler, Earle F., "Values in Physical, Health, and Recreation Education," Journal of the Canadian Association for Health, Physical Education, and Recreation, 29, 3:10-12, February-March, 1963.

48. Zeigler, Earle F. and McCristal, King J., "A History of the Big Ten Body-of-Knowledge Project," Quest, IX, 79-84, December, 1967.

Part V
THE DISCIPLINARY APPROACH

A MODEL FOR OPTIMUM PROFESSIONAL DEVELOPMENT
IN A FIELD CALLED 'X'

It is a truism that a profession of necessity rises or falls depending upon the extent and validity of the body-of-knowledge under-girding it. Because of disenchantment with the name of "physical education,"[2,12] and because the field has not yet truly re-adjusted its sights to bring about more rapid achievement of needed scientific knowledge,[14] this paper will attempt to describe to a seemingly short-sighted professional population a model for optimum professional development in a field called 'X'.* (Please note that the term 'X' was coined temporarily by Professor Galasso of Windsor.)

Mankind is said to be on a "collision course" with the future, because the tempo of civilization is increasing so rapidly that people may not be able to adjust satisfactorily to the new demands that are being made of them. (9) This has been called a "century of transition," and men must learn to master themselves along with their effort to master nature. (1, p. 24) Further, it remains to be seen whether Canada can escape the terrible effects of the devastating problems outlined as the cause of trouble, poverty, and anger in the United States today. (8)

As might be expected, all of education - including higher education - has not been able to escape the influence of a variety of social forces. School and university appear to many to be malfunctioning badly. They are challenged for not providing new skills in "learning, relating, and choosing" that will help men and women life fully in the emerging society of super-industrial civilization. (9, p. 367) Even though education doesn't seem to be doing very well in helping students to think clearly and forthrightly about the basic problems besetting North American society, and despite the fact that a great many people have expressed considerable concern about the realization of personal values in their lives, there still doesn't appear to be a great concern on the part of most young people for the achievement of a well-rounded education embodying arts and science courses that bespeak a broad general education. The idea is to get the necessary education for a job that will provide enough money to cope with the high standard of material living available in the culture on this continent.

---

* A paper presented to the First Canadian Symposium on The Philosophy of Sport and Physical Activity, The University of Windsor, Windsor, Ontario, May 3-4, 1972. (Published in the Proceedings, Ottawa, Ontario (P. J. Galasso), pp. 16-28.)

Physical Education and Athletics Caught in the Middle

Physical education and athletics, typically promoted by leaders committed to the advocacy of conservative cultural forces, is caught right in the middle of the societal transformation taking place. Professional leaders are gradually being forced to make an effort to understand what idealistic youth means when they use such terms as "relevance," "accountability," and "involvement." Past evidence lends credence to the prevailing belief held by some that the physical education profession will give ground grudgingly to the demands of the future. Furthermore, over and above those professionals and citizens who see increasingly more exercise as life's panacea and who will always be with us (God bless them!), the large majority of professional thought is so rudderless that almost any seemingly legitimate Messiah with a "palatable" doctrine could lead us to the "ideal program."

Once again physical education and athletics finds itself (or themselves, depending upon whether you are referring to Canada or the United States, respectively) in a mildly or strongly defensive posture. In Canada higher education is facing greater financial expenses with seemingly stead-state or declining legislative allotments; this means, quite naturally, that some subject-matters and professional faculties on campus have higher priorities than others. In the United States a similar situation prevails, and the problem is compounded even further by possibly indefensible required p.e. programs; overcrowded, academically inferior teacher education curricula; and intercollegiate athletics programs which seem to have lost - except in selected instances - what might be called sound educational perspective.

Five Internal Problems

Speaking to the American Academy of Physical Education at Detroit in 1971, this writer called for a concerted professional effort to "put our house in order" by sharpening the issues, by placing them in some order of priority, and by urging the field to "get in step" with with the demands of changing times. (15) Five internal problems of a major nature were postulated:

1. "Specific Focus Approach" vs. "Shotgun Approach" - should the profession attempt to unite behind the idea that the professional task within formal and informal education is to teach humans to move efficiently and with purpose in sport, dance, exercise, and play within the context of man's socialization in an evolving world?

2. "The Physical Education vs. Athletics Encounter" - does the profession in the United State dare to speak out in a statesman-like, forcible manner against poor education practices in competitive athletics, or are the tenured positions really not impregnable?

3. "The Male-Female Dichotomy in Physical Education" - can men's and women's departments in the United States be amalgamated equitably so that greater professional strength will be gained at the same time that money for operation is being saved? In Canada, even though university departments are typically combined, can women become "first-class citizens?"

4. "Professional Preparation Wing vs. Disciplinary Wing" - can the field of physical education make the adaptation to the newer disciplinary approach - that is, can we successfully provide opportunities for undergraduate students to choose options within their curricula that will enable them to move eventually in any one of number of professional directions?

5. "The Bio-science vs. The Humanities-Social Science Controversy" - is it possible for faculty members teaching and researching in the bio-sciences to live in peace with colleagues forming undergraduate and graduate options in the humanities and social science aspects of physical education and sport?

A Disciplinary Approach in Physical Education

Perhaps the first of a number of articles characterizing physical education as an incipient discipline was that presented by Franklin Henry at the 1964 conference of the National College Physical Education Association for Men. Significant contributions to thought on this subject have been made by other theorists (Fraleigh, Kenyon, Metheny, and others). This writer recalls that Henry's statement made great sense to him when first presented, but that Henry himself expressed difficulty when it came to conceptualizing about the borderline "between a field such as physiology and the field of physical education." (5) He implied further that physical education would gradually become more differentiated from other disciplines as it became more "specialized, complex, and detailed" in the investigation of those phenomena occurring in the life of man which were of central interest to the scholar in this field and of peripheral interest to scholars and researchers in other disciplines.

This subject became much clearer to the writer after a series of seminar discussions at the University of Illinois, Urbana, and the resultant contribution made by Cyril White, a sport sociologist, now in Dublin, Ireland. White argued that physical education had many of the characteristics of a multidiscipline and some of a crossdiscipline.

He postulated that physical education's "future development to inter-disciplinary level will require a far greater degree of sophisticated research abilities and orientations than the field at present possesses." (10: see Figure 1.)

Even before this type of conceptualizing about the composition of a discipline took place, a great deal of effort had been expended by many in an attempt to define what constituted the "discipline of physical education." One such effort was the Big Ten Body-of-Knowledge Project promoted largely by the late Arthur Daniels (Indiana) and King McCristal (Illinois). (16) At the very least this helped to fill in the "circles of the diagram" depicting the projected stages of development outlined above.

Recommended Composition of the Discipline

The composition of the physical education discipline will in all probability be an "evolving entity" over the years. This writer has tentatively accepted the following definition of the discipline of physical education: "the study of human motor performance in sport, dance, play, and exercise." For purposes of curriculum development and discussion, the discipline is viewed as containing arts and social science aspects and bio-science aspects. (See Table 1.) A further discipline definition has been organized on the basis of the descriptive aspects of the sub-areas of study within physical education (with accompanying related discipline affiliation). (See Table 2.)

A Model for Optimum Professional Development

In an effort to clarify for himself, and perhaps for others, what has been a muddled matter during the 1960's, a model for optimum professional development in a field called "X" (physical education) has been conceived. (See Figure 2.) It is a model which can in all probability be applied to other professions as well (e.g., law or medicine). It includes the following five subdivisions: (1) professional practice; (2) professional preparation; (3) disciplinary research; (4) a theory embodying assumptions and testable hypotheses; and (5) operational philosophy.

Professional practice can be characterized as (1) public; (2) semi-public; and (3) private. Professional preparation should be designed to educate (1) the performer; (2) the teacher-coach; (3) the teacher of teachers; and (4) the scholar and researcher. Disciplinary research includes (1) the physiological; (2) the sociological; (3) the psychological; (4) the biomechanical; and (5) the historical, philosophical, and comparative aspects of human motor performance in sport, dance, play, and exercise.

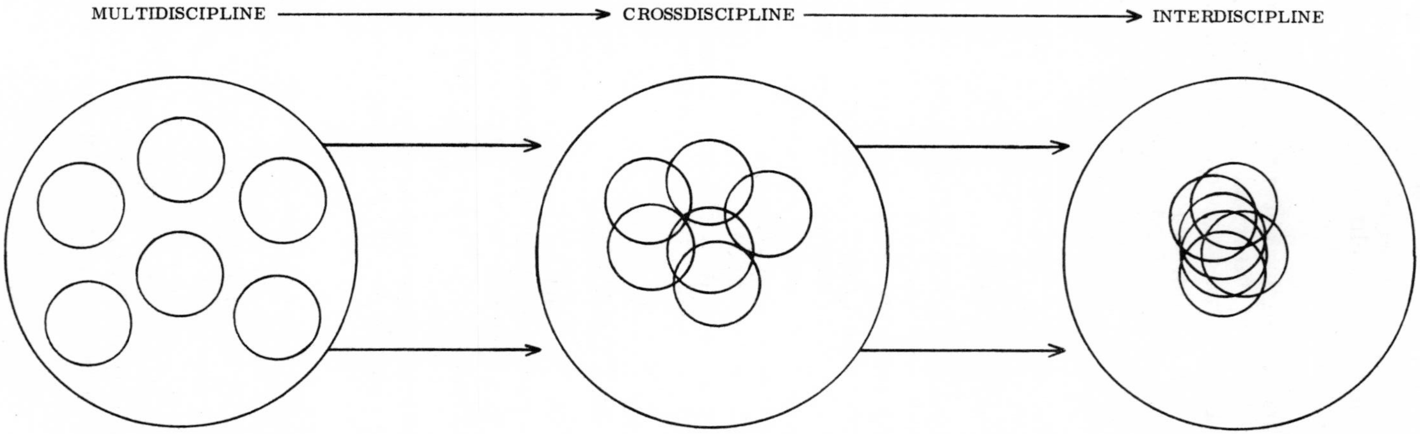

MULTIDISCIPLINE ————➤ CROSSDISCIPLINE ————➤ INTERDISCIPLINE

Figure 1. Physical Education--A Crossdiscipline on the
Way Toward Becoming an Interdiscipline?

Courtesy of
Cyril M. White, Ph.D.
Dublin, Ireland

Table 1. The Composition of the Physical Education Discipline.

(1) <u>Humanities and Social Science Aspects</u>

Sub-Area 1

History, Philosophy and Comparative and International Physical Education and Sport

Sub-Area 2

Sociology, Social Psychology and Anthropology of Sport, Leisure and Physical Acvitity

Sub-Area 3

Administrative Theory and Practice of Physical Education and Athletics

(2) <u>Bio-Science Aspects</u>

Sub-Area 4

Exercise, Physiology, Anthropometry and Scientific Training in Sport and Exercise

Sub-Area 5

Motor Learning and Performance; Growth and Development Related to Sport and Physical Activity

Sub-Area 6

Anatomy, Kinesiology and Analysis of Movement in Sport and Physical Activity

Sub-Area 7

Health Problems Related to Sport and Exercise

Table 2. A Discipline Definition Based on Descriptive Aspects of the Sub-Areas of Study within Physical Education (with Accompanying Related Discipline Affiliation)

Humanities and Social Science Division		Bio-Science Division	
Description	Related Discipline	Description	Related Discipline
Meaning and Significance	Philosophy, History International, etc.	Biomechanical Analysis	Physics Anatomy
Social and Cultural Aspects	Sociology Anthropology	Anthropometry	Anthropology Physical Medicine
Aesthetic Aspects	Fine Arts	Motor Learning and Development	Psychology Medicine
Behavioral Aspects	Social Psychology	Physiological Aspects	Physiology Medicine
Administration and Management; Curriculum Development and Instruction	Administrative Science (and Related Disciplines) Education	Health Aspects (including injuries and rehabilitation through exercise)	Physiology Medicine (Physical) Psychology Public Health
Measurement and Evaluation (through research techniques employed in related disciplines as well as in physical education)	Mathematics	Measurement and Evaluation	Mathematics

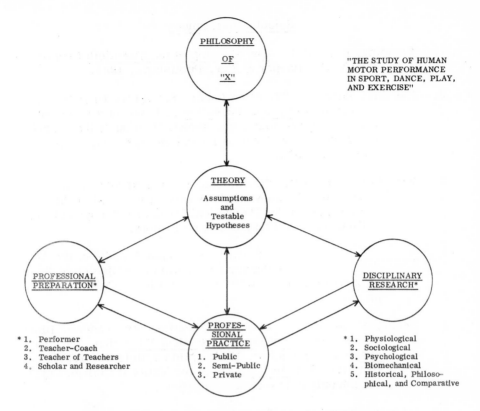

Figure 2. A Model for Optimum Professional Development in a Field Called "X".

The assumptions and testable hypotheses of <u>theory</u> should comprise a "coherent group of general propositions used as principles of explanation for the phenomena" (7) exhibited in human motor performance in sport, dance, play, and exercise.

Finally, inclusion of the <u>philosophy of "X"</u> as an "overarching entity" in the model propounded is based on the belief that the value system of a society will in the final analysis be gradually realized within a social system. (6) For the purposes of this presentation, this means simply that decisions regarding the development of a profession are based on the prevailing social values over and above any scientific evidence that may become available.

Selected References

1. Boulding, Kenneth E. The Meaning of the Twentieth Century. New York: Harper & Row, Publishers, 1964.

2. Cassidy, Rosalind, "Position Paper: Should We Drop the Designation Physical Education in Favor of a Different Name?" Presented at the Annual Meeting of the American Academy of Physical Education, Houston, Texas, March 22, 1972.

3. Fraleigh, Warren P., "Developing a Physical Education Theoretical Framework." A paper presented at the Conference on the Theoretical Structure of Physical Education, June 3, 1969, Chicago, Illinois.

4. _____., "Toward a Conceptual Model of the Academic Subject of Physical Education as a Discipline," Proceedings of the NCPEAM, San Diego, Calif., 1967, pp. 31-39.

5. Henry, Franklin M., "Physical Education: An Academic Discipline," Journal of Health, Physical Education, and Recreation, September, 1964. (This article was reprinted from the 1964 Proceedings of the National College Physical Education Association for Men.)

6. Johnson, Harry M., "The Relevance of the Theory of Action to Historians," Social Science Quarterly, June, 1969, 46-58.

7. Random House Dictionary of the English Language, The. (Jess Stein, editor). New York: Random House, 1967, p. 1471.

8. Reich, Charles A. The Greening of America. New York: Random House, Inc., 1970.

9. Toffler, Alvin. Future Shock. New York: Random House, Inc., 1970.

10. White, Cyril M., "Some Theoretical Considerations Regarding Disciplinary Development." An unpublished paper presented at a graduate seminar, University of Illinois, Urbana, 1968.

11. Zeigler, Earle F., "Discipline Definition Should Precede Curriculum Development." A paper submitted for publication to The Physical Educator in early 1972.

12. _____., "How Do We Evaluate People in Physical
Education and Sport?" The Australian Journal of Physical Education, No. 53, September, 1971, pp. 10-11.
(Appeared also in Illinois Journal of HPER, Vol. 3:5,
Fall, 1971.)

13. _____., "Putting the Greek Ideal in Perspective in
North American Athletics Today." A paper presented at
the Symposium on Athletics in America, Oregon State
University, Corvallis, February 14-17, 1972. (Published
through the Division of Health, Physical Education, and
Recreation there and the Oregon State University Press.)

14. _____., "A Tale of Two Titles," JOHPER, Vol. 39,
No. 5:53, May, 1968. (Appeared also as "The Basic Nature of Physical Education" - the author's title - in
Health and Physical Education Council Bulletin (Alberta),
Vol. VII, No. 2, Spring, 1968, 6-10.)

15. _____., "United We Stand - Divided We Falter!"
A paper presented at the Annual Meeting of the American
Academy of Physical Education, Detroit, Michigan,
March 31, 1971.

16. _____ and McCristal, King J., "A History of the
Big Ten Body-of-Knowledge Project," Quest, Monograph
IX, Winter Issue, December, 1967, 79-84.

A HISTORY OF THE BIG TEN BODY-OF-KNOWLEDGE PROJECT IN PHYSICAL EDUCATION, 1963-1967 (with King J. McCristal, University of Illinois, Urbana-Champaign)

In 1930 the first meeting of the Big Ten (Western Conference) Physical Education Directors was called by Seward C. Staley of the University of Illinois.[1] This originally all-male group, now composed of deans, directors, and department heads--three official representatives from each institution--has met annually ever since for the past thirty-six years. The organization has no official status nor constitution, dues, or officers. Responsibility for calling the meetings is simply rotated alphabetically among the universities starting with Illinois and continuing through Indiana, Iowa, Michigan, Michigan State, Minnesota, Northwestern, Ohio State, Purdue, and Wisconsin.

The 1964 Western Conference Physical Education Meetings

The program for the annual meetings is in the hands of a different chairman each year--usually the chief administrative officer of the institution whose turn it is to organize the meetings. Typically the members have gathered to discuss common problems, assess trends, and compare techniques for furthering the advancement of physical education in all of its aspects within the Western Conference.

In 1964 the sessions were held on the Urbana campus of the University of Illinois. King J. McCristal, as Dean of the College of Physical Education at the host institution, was therefore responsible for the planning of the program and discussed the matter at length with Arthur S. Daniels (now deceased), who was Dean at Indiana University. The "body-of-knowledge" topic had received some attention at the two previous annual meetings, and it was obvious to both of them that the theme held great interest for professors from the Big

---

[1] The junior author of this article (EFZ) suggested this topic to Dr. Marvin H. Eyler, Editor of Quest, in early 1967. Because of Dean McCristal's active involvement with this project since its inception, he hesitated to undertake the article. Editor Eyler and E. F. Zeigler stressed the importance of this development in the history of physical education, however, and thus it was prepared for the December, 1967 issue. Dr. McCristal provided much of the basic material and insight, and Dr. Zeigler, a member of the original Steering Committee of the Project, developed this brief narrative statement with him. (Published in Quest, Monograph IX, Winter Issue, December, 1967, pp. 79-84.)

Ten institutions. The fact that the American Academy of Physical Education had also conducted sessions on this topic presented additional evidence of the importance of this topic to everyone in the profession.

Thus, as a result of a meeting between McCristal and Daniels in Champaign in July of 1964, the program was outlined for the December meeting. The conference theme was "The Body of Knowledge in Physical Education," and the following people were selected to make presentations at the second, third, and fourth general sessions, respectively:

1. Arthur Daniels (Indiana) - "Recent Efforts at Definitions and Boundary Lines: Current Status of the Profession."
2. Earle Zeigler (Illinois) - "History of Physical Education and Sport."
3. T. K. Cureton (Illinois) - "Exercise Physiology."
4. John Lawther (Penn State) - "Motor Learning."
5. Coleman Griffith (Illinois) - "Sport and the Culture (or Cultural Anthropology)."
6. Lawrence Rarick (Wisconsin) - "Human Growth and Development."
7. James Counsilman (Indiana) - "Biomechanics of Human Movement."
8. Arthur Daniels (Indiana) - "Implications These Reports Hold for Undergraduate Professional Preparation."

In his opening remarks at the Second General Session, Professor Daniels said,

> If we are to gain greater recognition in the academic world, we must follow pathways similar to that traversed by other disciplines. This means a greatly expanded program of scholarly research and development in which the body-of-knowledge in physical education is defined as nearly as possible in terms of its fundamental nature, and in its relationships with other disciplines.

The Fifth General Session of the 1964 Meetings, chaired by Professor McCristal, was devoted to "Future Planning." The delegates agreed to appoint a steering committee to insure the continuity of program planning. Arthur Daniels, as the administrative head of physical education at Indiana University (the next institution in alphabetical order after Illinois), was named Chairman, and other committee members were Louis Alley (Iowa), Wellman France (Purdue), and King McCristal (Illinois). The plan was that each year a representative from the next host institution would be added to the Steering Committee, and thus would become responsible for the arrangements for the next annual meeting. The following year the pattern was changed. The representative of the host institution was still to be placed on the Steering Committee, but it was felt that the original nucleus of members should continue to function in order to keep the project aligned with the original plan.

In January of 1965 the first of a number of "on-call" meetings was held during the Annual Meetings of the National College Physical Education Association for Men in Minneapolis. A second meeting was held in July in Chicago at which time the plans for the 1965 meetings in Iowa City were completed. Dr. Stanley Salwak, Director of the Committee on Institutional Cooperation,[2] was invited to attend this meeting. When the development was explained to him, he agreed to provide a seeding grant of fifteen hundred dollars so that the developmental plans for the Body-of-Knowledge Project might be continued.

The 1965 Western Conference Physical Education Meetings

In 1965 the Western Conference Physical Education meetings at Iowa City, chaired by Louis Alley, followed a similar format but with certain changes in regard to the subject-matters or sub-areas under consideration. Initially, Arthur Daniels (Indiana) presented a "Progress Report on Developing a Blueprint for an Academic Discipline in Physical Education." Then King McCristal (Illinois) spoke to the subject "On Becoming an Academic Discipline." He explained that many established academic disciplines had rather modest origins, and he pointed out that,

> . . . it wasn't easy for the 'old guard' to achieve the coveted positions they now hold in the academic community. The road to unquestioned status as a discipline is far from being all down hill with a tail wind. The present interest of Physical Education in disciplinary status closely parallels the historical controversy which accompanied admission to other areas to the charmed circle of academic disciplines.

After these two presentations which oriented the members present to the task at hand, five papers were presented which explained the status of the "body-of-knowledge" in additional sub-areas:

---

[2] The Committee on Institutional Cooperation was formed in 1958 to encourage voluntary cooperation within a variety of programs in a federation of midwestern universities composed of Big Ten institutions and the University of Chicago.

1. Louis Alley (Iowa) - "Biomechanics."
2. Bruno Balke (Wisconsin) - "Exercise Physiology."
3. Leon Smith (Iowa) - "Psychology and Motor Learning."
4. Earle Zeigler (Illinois) - "Philosophical Research in Physical Education and Sport."
5. Arthur Daniels (Indiana) - "Sport and the Culture."

Upon the conclusion of presentations, Stanley Salwak, Director of the Committee on Institutional Cooperation, spoke on the topic "The C.I.C. and Developmental Plans for Physical Education."

Papers and both formal and informal discussions at both the 1964 and 1965 meetings tended to substantiate the belief that there is a body of knowledge--and a potential body-of-knowledge--that may well comprise the academic discipline of physical education, sport, human movement, kinesiology, human motor performance, or what have you? Portions of this body-of-knowledge are in related disciplines, and portions of it are unquestionably, uniquely "physical education" in character. We are not completely certain what is "pure" and what is "applied."

Delegates at Urbana in 1964 and Iowa City in 1965 agreed to retain the "body-of-knowledge" format for future meetings. No time limit was specified, and it was presumed that such a declaration meant a period of at least five years to insure continuity. In fact, there is no reason why a portion of the time allotment at future annual meetings cannot be allotted to a continuation of the project indefinitely.

Following the untimely death of Arthur Daniels in July of 1966, the Steering Committee decided that the C.I.C. seed grant funds should be transferred to the University of Illinois. King McCristal, then the senior member of the committee, was to administer them as the project developed. The 1966 meetings were planned in late August during a two-day meeting in Chicago. The University of Michigan, through Paul Hunsicker, was the host institution, but the actual meetings were held through the cooperation of Sheldon Fordham at the Chicago Circle Campus of the University of Illinois. At the August meeting of the Committee, it was decided to organize the academic content--at least initially--into six specific areas of specialization as follows: (1) Exercise Physiology; (2) Biomechanics; (2) Motor Learning and Sports Psychology; (4) Sociology of Sport Education; (5) History, Philosophy, and Comparative Physical Education and Sport; and (6) Administrative Theory. There has been considerable debate as to what these areas are--or should be. For example, it can well be argued that Administrative Theory as a topic is not basic to our discipline--if it is indeed a discipline and whatever it may be named. Conversely, it can be stated that the managing of organizations within our field is becoming so complex that pure and applied research in this developing social science may be warranted.

The 1966 Western Conference Physical Education Meeting

At the August 1966 meeting it was decided to bring together work groups of two or three Big Ten faculty members in each of the six areas of specialization designated. Instructions were prepared and distributed to the chairmen and members of each of these groups, and each group was asked to be responsible for the presentation of a paper by one member, the leading of a discussion by a second member, and the third member would be expected to serve as recorder. More specifically, each group was to undertake the following definite assignments:

1. Identify the related disciplines in its work areas
2. List in topical form the primary concepts in each related discipline (those that comprise what might be regarded as the body-of-knowledge for physical education in this area).
3. Supplement the primary concepts from the related disciplines with any additional primary concepts that seem unique to physical education.
4. State the prerequisites to the study of these concepts.

Thus, from a long-term standpoint, the intention was that any such concepts would be integrated where deemed necessary and desirable into all levels of our curricula (basic instruction, undergraduate professional, and graduate programs). During October and November of 1966 the work groups met in Chicago and elsewhere at their convenience and distributed the work load in what seemed to be the best manner in relation to the specific sub-area concerned. For example, inasmuch as Professor Zeigler had presented earlier papers (in 1964 and 1965) on history and philosophy, respectively, it was decided that Professors Bruce Bennett (Ohio State), Harold VanderZwaag (Illinois - Now Massachusetts), and William Johnson (Illinois) would present aspects of history, philosophy, and comparative physical education in that order.

At the December annual meeting the first presentation was a progress report on the C.I.C. project by King McCristal (Illinois). The committee reports were then presented, and the presentation of each paper by the respective chairman elicited animated discussion. The titles of the topics presented and the names of those who made presentations, chaired the ensuing discussion periods, and served as recorders are as follows:

1. Sociology of Sport and Physical Education
(G. Kenyon, Chairman - Wisconsin; G. Lüschen - Illinois; H. Webb - Michigan State)

2. Administrative Theory
   (K. McCristal, Chairman - Illinois; R. Donnelly -
   Minnesota; W. Helms - Michigan)
3. History, Philosophy, and Comparative Physical Educa-
   tion and Sport
   (E. Zeigler, Chairman - Illinois; B. Bennett - Ohio
   State; H. VanderZwaag - Illinois; W. Johnson -
   Illinois)
4. Exercise Physiology
   (J. Faulkner, Chairman - Michigan; F. Nagle -
   Wisconsin; C. Tipton - Iowa)
5. Biomechanics
   (L. Alley, Chairman - Iowa; J. Cooper - Indiana;
   J. Counsilman - Indiana)
6. Motor Learning and Sports Psychology
   (L. Smith, Chairman - Iowa; R. Herron - Illinois;
   A. Slater-Hammel - Indiana)

Present Status and Future Plans

Immediately following the Big Ten meetings in Chicago, the
augmented Steering Committee--now consisting of the chairmen of all
six areas--met to lay plans for further development of the Project.
On January 28, 1967, the Committee assembled in Iowa City, and
after a two-day series of sessions a "symposium project" was outlined. The purpose of this proposed project was to develop and clarify still further the basic philosophic and scientific concepts of Physical Education. Still further, the Committee felt that it would be
desirable to enrich the quality of the present Physical Education
graduate programs in C.I.C. institutions (except Chicago) by providing selected faculty members with opportunities to exchange ideas
about our developing discipline with recognized authorities from
related disciplines. This continuing project seemed to be absolutely
necessary, because the three-year effort had carried the Steering
Committee's original plans about as far as they could progress--
without active involvement in the process of attempting to discover
avenues and approaches that might lead to the creation of new knowledge.

All members of the Steering Committee now believe that the
success of the Symposium Project will hinge on the ability of the
group to secure a sizeable monetary grant from a foundation or public
agency. King McCristal, as Chairman of the Steering Committee,
has explored many sources of grants. The Dean of the College of
Education at Illinois feels that the greatest opportunity for support of
the proposal seems to rest with the United States Office of Education.
Changes are now being made in the research proposal to conform to
the usual specifications of the U. S. Office of Education. A telephone

conference was held on September 27, 1967 to discuss the final format of the research proposal. This material has now been forwarded to Dr. Salwak at the office of the Committee on Institutional Cooperation in Lafayette, Indiana. He may be willing to co-sponsor the project with the members of the Steering Committee, and an approach will be made shortly to prospective sponsoring agencies.

The Steering Committee does not believe that the Western Conference Physical Education Directors are "trespassing upon territory" that ought to be the particular province of the American Association for Health, Physical Education, and Recreation or the American Academy of Physical Education. There would be some overlapping of personnel; this is granted. The Big Ten Body-of-Knowledge Project, which has been underway for more than three years already, would seem to be a "natural" by virtue of the long-standing association of the the institutions concerned, as well as the means for mutual cooperation that is provided through the structure of the Committee on Institutional Cooperation. It is quite possible that multiple approaches to this matter of a body-of-knowledge and a possible discipline are desirable. Obviously, too great proliferation of such ventures would dissipate readily available "strengths." At present a certain amount of consensus has been reached--a level of agreement which might not be possible at the national level--and the present Symposium Project is distinctly an effort to provide high level opportunities for our graduate professors to improve their understandings and sharpen their research techniques in relation to our developing body-of-knowledge.

Selection #38

THE BEHAVIORAL SCIENCES AND PHYSICAL EDUCATION

The assigned topic for this presentation - "supporting evidence from sociology" - soon forced the writer to seek permission to expand the paper to include a discussion of "the behavioral sciences and physical education" (as opposed to those fields that are typically identified as the social sciences).* There were three reasons why such a request was made: (1) the concept of the behavioral sciences, of which sociology is a subdivision, was not included in the overall projection for this program and seemed necessary; (2) most of those who have a sociological orientation: (a) seem unwilling to identify themselves with physical education, (b) have carried out very little investigation relative to physical education that can be recognized as evidence, and (c) have yet been unable to postulate even fairly elementary theories about the origins, structures, and functions of the various elements of sport within social life; and (3) the limitation of this paper to "evidence from sociology" would have made it difficult for the writer to place the topic into some philosophical perspective.

By the behavioral sciences here is meant the following:

> the disciplines of anthropology, psychology, and sociology --minus and plus: Minus such specialized sectors as physiological psychology, archaeology, technical linguistics, and most of physical anthropology; Plus social geography, some psychiatry, and the behavioral parts of economics, political science, and law (Berelson and Steiner, 1964, pp. 10-11).

The social sciences, of course, typically include the six disciplines of anthropology, economics, history, political science, psychology, and sociology.

Well, then, do the behavioral sciences as defined tend to support the work of the physical education profession? Is there evidence to prove or disprove the claims usually made by physical educators as to the objectives of the field? We are told that it is vital to consider these questions right now (1) because "education is in a period of turmoil at practically every level; (2) because "financial support

---

* A paper prepared for presentation to the American Academy of Physical Education, Anaheim, California, March 27, 1974. (Published in The Academy Papers, No. 8 entitled "The New Focus on Physical Education." Iowa City, Iowa: The American Academy of Physical Education, 1974, pp. 35-44.)

has grown tighter"; (3) because "administrators are talking about program accountability"; (4) because "reallocation of resources is being directed toward the support of more relevant and efficient programs"; and (5) because "physical education, among other subjects, will probably continue to be one of education's 'whipping boys' " (McCristal, "Program Suggestions for 1974," p. 1).

Recent Developments

Space limitations prevent definitive treatment of this subject in a similar manner to either Cowell's "The Contributions of Physical Activity to Social Development" (1960, pp. 286-306) or Scott's "The Contributions of Physical Activity to Psychological Development" (1960, pp. 307-320). Cowell explained that:

> Culture consists of the things that we have learned to do, to make, to believe, to value, and to enjoy in our lifetime. Our culture expresses the basic values of our society. The forces which interact on the playing fields, in the gymnasium, and elsewhere provide for children a steady flow of motivations and feelings which gradually shape the personality. In the sense that we as teachers have a part in controlling or influencing to some extent these factors in our culture, we become guardians and developers of personality by influencing the dominant attitudes and goals of that part of our culture related to games, sports, and recreation in general (1960, p. 287).

At this same time, Scott substantiated with the best available evidence of the time certain claims being made for physical education in regard to: (1) changing attitudes (2) improving social efficiency; (3) improving sensory perception and responses; (4) developing sense of well-being--mental health; (5) promoting relaxation; (5) providing psychosomatic relief; and (7) acquiring skill (1960, p. 308). She concluded that "there is perhaps no area of our professional background that offers more challenge to us than psychological development" (p. 317).

It may be asked, of course, if anyone really foresaw the disciplinary thrust that was to take place during the 1960's and thereafter --a development undoubtedly occasioned by a variety of social forces. We can all recall McCloy's warning about the quality of graduate study, Sputnik, Conant's condemnation, Esslinger's efforts with others to marshall our forces in response, and Henry's early effort to define the discipline in 1964. Somehow, however, there was not comparable "ten years later" publication updating the 1960 A.A.H.P.E.R.'s Research Council effort entitled The Contributions of Physical Activity to Human Well-Being that was alluded to above.

Individual scholars did begin to develop their own retrieval systems with particular subdisciplinary areas, and there has been the annual publication of completed research by the Research Council. Fortunately, there may soon be an Encyclopedia of Physical Education published through the efforts of members of the Research Council with Professor T. K. Cureton as Chief Editor. However, it does seem that a second volume will be necessary to include all of the evidence regarding physical education that has been assembled. Further, much of this material is of a bio-science orientation, and we should be alert also to the evidence which is accruing from the social science and humanities aspects of the field.

An example of the increasing number of subdisciplinary areas that are impinging on--or being included within - the field of physical education, kinesiology, and related areas has recently been made available by the Physical Education Discipline Group in Ontario which includes representatives from eleven universities planning for the next decade in graduate study and research. The following subdisciplinary areas or subdivisions were listed as being "viable" at the present time:

1. Sport and physical activity history
2. Sport and physical activity philosophy
3. Sport and physical activity sociology
4. Sport and physical activity social psychology
5. Sport psychology and psycho-motor learning
6. Administrative theory
7. Sport and exercise physiology
8. Growth and development (related to physical activity)
9. Biomechanics and kinesiology

Note: A tenth category was included under the heading of "Professional Studies." (Taken from Reponse of the Physical Education Discipline Group to the Consultants' Report on Graduate Programmes in Physical Education, Kinesiology, and Related Areas, 1974.)

In a 1971 submission to the Committee to Study the Rationalization of University Research (Association of Universities and Colleges of Canada), the following were included as additional sub-areas of specialization: (1) Comparative and international physical education and sport; (2) Sport and games anthropology; (3) Anthropometry applied to physical education and sport; (4) Scientific sport training; (5) (5) Health problems in sport and physical education; and (6) Research in dance (Faculty of Physical Education, The University of Western Ontario, 1971).

Evidence from the Behavioral Sciences

Keeping in mind, therefore, those disciplines which have been included under the heading of behavioral sciences (Cf. p. 487), a few selected observations will be made regarding (1) behavioral development; (2) learning and thinking; (3) motivation; (4) small group relations; (5) organizations; (6) institutions; (7) social stratification; (8) ethnic relations; (9) mass communication; (10) opinions, attitudes, and beliefs; (11) the society; and (12) the culture. Statements about other possible topics will not be included (e.g., "perceiving" or "the family") because they did not appear to be specifically pertinent (see Berelson and Steiner, 1964).

Behavioral Development. Man employs adaptive behavior to satisfy his own needs and to cope with the problems with which his environment confronts him. Some of these responses are instinctual, whereas certain adaptation is for the purpose of fulfilling subjective desires. Maturation is the term employed to describe bodily development, whereas the term development is more general in nature applying to normal, orderly change that may occur between birth and death. Socialization is the means by which a society prepares an individual for membership.

Support for physical activity and physical education as an integral aspect of this development is both implicit and explicit. The behavior of humans shows greater variability than that of all other creatures on earth and may be regarded as quite unpredictable. Lower animals rely greatly on "innate behavioral predispositions," of course, whereas human behavior is strongly dependent upon an improved learning process. Adaptive human behavior resulting from learning depends upon communication, and such learning is fortunately cumulative. For better or worse, modern man has reached the point where much of his daily striving is clearly unrelated to physical welfare and survival. Obviously, this has direct implications for the field of physical education and sport--implications which are not readily perceived by a majority of people on this continent.

The sequence of development within children is quite general to the species of man. Some children do develop faster than others, but this does not mean that the sequence of development is different. It is now well-established that bright children are--and remain--superior to others more average in such attributes as health, physique, personality and character traits, etc. As the child grows older, his behavior typically becomes more differentiated. It should be kept in mind that encouragement of a child to perform a skill prior to physical readiness may indeed slow down the development of the desired ability. Interestingly, the correlation between verbal aptitude and many other capacities is quite high, and mental growth through adolescence shows similarity to physical growth (i.e., rapid initially with a decline at puberty). (See Martin and Stendler, 1959.)

Various types of physical, mental, and social contact are vital for what is considered to be normal development in humans. Socialization will probably take place more erratically if conflicts exist among the usual socializing agencies; however, even though cultures differ markedly, there are similarities in the socialization processes cross-culturally. General personality development needs an environment in which there is affection and satisfaction of dependence. Punishment as a technique is not recommended, although it is true that isolated traumatic events typically do not damage personality permanently. To be effective, moral values should be taught consistently and definitely by example. If a child identifies favorably with his or her parents, and has an opportunity for early and regular success, a higher need for achievement tends to result after maturity. Quite obviously, almost every one of the above statements has strong implications for physical activity, physical education, and physical recreation! (Space and time do not permit a careful discussion of each of the remaining eleven sub-headings outlined above, but representative statements will be made to indicate where strong evidence in support of physical education could be provided--and also where applied research should be undertaken.)

Learning and Thinking. Learning usually refers to the changes that take place in individuals based on their experiences. Somehow the "human motor performance" or "movement experience" aspect of education has been slighted. Huxley has designated this as the "education of the non-verbal humanities"--the education of the "psychophysical instrument of an evolving amphibian." (1964, p. 31.) If man's kinesthetic sense were prepared more efficiently through the educational process, the effects of such experience will inevitably influence subsequent behavior for better or for worse. Thinking, and who can deny that we "think with our whole body," so to speak, has most generally been characterized best as "symbolic experience," the assumption being that the formation of habits results from direct experience. An interesting finding is that thinking tends to be facilitated when there is a general increase in muscle tone. In addition, as thought becomes more concentrated, general muscle tension becomes even greater.

Motivation. This term is employed usually to describe the various inner strivings of man. Such a state tends to activate an individual and channel his behavior so that objectives are realized. A sample finding here which helps individuals achieve goals is that a moderate level of tension is necessary for efficient performance, but that a person's physical performance in a context will probably deteriorate rapidly when motivation becomes too high.

Relations in Small Groups. A small group is a cluster of people that varies from two to a larger--but not too large--number (of perhaps twenty). An example of a finding here that is useful to physical education is that the small group may be used by the teacher or coach to set and to help enforce norms or standards of desired behavior. The group provides individual members with security and encouragement.

Organizations. It is difficult to define the term organization, but it means typically that a group of people have joined together and that through the execution of certain functions a stated goal can be achieved. A finding of importance here to the physical educator is that his approach to leadership usually is influenced by the leadership techniques that move him to follow a leader. People tend to model themselves, of course, after those who are rated higher within the social system.

Institutions. The term "institution" as employed here refers to a complex normative pattern or matrix that tends to govern the behavior of people in a recurring fashion in fundamental matters. The typical institutions within modern societies are religious, economic, political, educational, and military in nature. In referring to educational institutions, an important finding for physical education is that the effect of teaching style on teacher-student relations and on teaching effectiveness is still an open subject. There is some evidence that teaching method and curriculum content (presumably based on objectives) go hand in hand, so to speak.

Social Stratification. There is stratification within a society when people rank others socially according to some standard based on the possession of certain attributes, goods, or other possessions. It is important for the physical educator-coach to stress to a young man or woman that a college education can provide an opportunity for a higher-class position and, accordingly, that an individual's evaluation of himself is strongly influenced by the class status which he is able to achieve (e.g., according to one poll a used car salesman may now feel more proud of himself than a politician).

Ethnic Relations. Ethnic origin usually relates to the individual's generic background and it therefore cannot be changed. Major ethnic groups are differentiated typically according to race, religion, or nationality. The question of possible ethnic differences is a most difficult one to attack, and probably should be deemphasized at the present because of its relative unimportance and tendency to inflame emotions in a tense society. The question of inherent differences in temperament by virtue of race or body type cannot be resolved without testing instruments that are much more refined than those available at present, and statistical techniques will seemingly need to be improved as well. Physical educators and coaches should understand clearly that prejudice and discrimination are usually learned early in life, but that they are not innate. Further, it is the quality of personal contact between ethnic groups that may reduce social tensions. This evidence imposes a great leadership burden upon the physical educator-coach.

Mass Communication. One person communicates to another in a variety of ways (e.g., by expression of emotions, ideas, etc.). The mass media, including television, books, newspapers, radio, movies, etc., have steadily and perhaps permanently influenced the quality of life on earth (and the stratospheric satellite is becoming an enormous influence). The effect of such communication on the audience depends upon the predisposition of those receiving messages, as well as upon the quality and quantity of the information provided. Teacher-coaches need to become "Communications Pro's" in all possible ways in order to maximize their influence on children and young people. Physical educators must understand better the predispositions held by their students and should include subject-matter that is perceived as interesting and vital. People misperceive and/or misinterpret various types of communication if they are not psychologically ready to receive it; yet, attitudes tend to change quite readily when the majority of their peer group seems to be in agreement with a different position or stance. If students themselves are actively involved in the communication process, retention of information and attitudes is promoted. The involvement of opinion leaders serves as a mechanism for the dissemination of information and influence.

Opinions, Attitudes and Beliefs. Opinions, attitudes and beliefs may be either emotional or rational judgments (or both), and usually refer to the position a person assumes in regard to a controversial issue. The more complex the society involved, the more such beliefs and opinions are differentiated (i.e., acquire special or discriminating characteristics). The beliefs held by people are acquired early in life and tend to change slowly depending upon subsequent group memberships. The potential of the team or sports club is immediately obvious insofar as attitude development is concerned, and such influence may be exercised particularly by the respected members of the group. Obviously, the social strata in which these experiences occur condition a young person's outlook greatly (e.g., the urban, suburban, or rural location of the larger geographical region). For better or worse, it is extremely difficult, if not impossible, to change opinions and beliefs significantly if steady support has been received throughout life from parental, peer, and other social groups. In fact, the beliefs tend to change more slowly than actual behavior, although certain change may occur when patterns of beliefs seem to be illogical or inconsistent to those holding them. Considering the often intense psycho-physical involvement of the young man or woman in a sport or physical education experience, the potential for change in attitudes and beliefs should be an ever-present factor in the mind of the physical educator-coach.

The Society. A group of people living together in a particular location for a fairly long period of time may eventually become able to sustain themselves and develop a "way of life." At that point in time such a group may rightly be called a "society." Of concern to those in physical education is that the profession may employ its influence to help bring about desirable social change. However, social changes in a society have rarely been the result of influence brought to bear by any group, or part of a group, that has traditionally been in control (e.g., the physical educator-coach). The members of the profession of physical education could consider whether social conflict in the United States seems to be challenging the value structure of the society. If so, the profession should decide whether it feels that a crisis situation exists, and whether it is advisable to intensity the crisis with the hope of changing the value structure or whether it (the profession) wishes to alleviate the crisis as best possible in the belief that the present value structure should remain.

The Culture. Everything discussed to this point has been influenced by the culture in which we live. A precise, yet encompassing definition of culture is extremely difficult, if not impossible. When a group of people within a social order achieves certain changes in their way of life, the resultant social characteristics may be loosely identified by the term "culture." Culture may be viewed implicitly or explicitly based upon its "conscious or unconscious" manifestations. It is shared; it is cohesive; and it is behavior that is learned. Physical education and sport develop within a culture; they are inevitably influenced by the culture, and yet they also help to shape the culture in which the profession exists. We should now seek to discover whether "cultural universals" exist within physical education and sport--and if, so, to what extent. Such investigation could be carried out with the understanding that--even though specific cultures have differed significantly--man's culture viewed as a whole has undergone various stages of development.

Summary and Conclusions

In this brief presentation the behavioral sciences of anthropology, psychology, and sociology--plus and minus--were considered by a physical education and sport philosopher in regard to their possible support for the field of physical education. It was pointed out that Cowell and Scott, in separate papers, had considered the contributions of physical activity to social development and psychological development, respectively, in 1960, but that the many social changes a and professional developments of the 1960's have quite probably altered our idea of "behavioral science man" since that time. A number of subdisciplinary areas are in the process of formation within physical education and its affiliated fields.

The behavioral sciences tend to provide substantive support for physical activity and sport conducted with an eye to a "physical education outcome," but the obvious need for the finest type of leadership is everywhere apparent. This statement would appear to be true whether the topic of motivation, of organizations, of ethnic relations, of attitudes and beliefs, or what have you are being considered. From all indications it seems that the profession of physical education is not greatly concerned about making provision for scientific investigation in the behavioral aspects of its disciplinary thrust, although many unproven claims are made regularly regarding the social and psychological benefits to be derived from such activity. To make matters worse, the younger, still relatively unproven social scientists within the field typically avoid identification with the term "physical education" whenever possible. For example, what university specializes in graduating men and women with a behavioral scientist orientation in the sociological, social psychological, or cultural anthropological aspects of physical education and sport? (By specialization is meant that there are two or three productive scholars in each of these areas functioning with the physical education unit.)

The final conclusion should be obvious: quite a few in the field pay lip service to the importance of behavioral science investigation within physical education, but very few have accomplished anything tangible to improve the present situation. What is the difficulty that is holding back reasonably rapid and substantive development in the behavioral science, subdisciplinary areas of the physical education field? Dare we answer this question honestly?

Selected References

1. Alderman, R. B. Psychological Behavior in Sport. Philadelphia: W. B. Saunders Company, 1974.

2. Beals, A. R., Spindler, G. D. and Spindler, L. S. Culture in Process. New York: Holt, Rinehart and Winston, 1966.

3. Berelson, Bernard and Steiner, Gary A. Human Behavior: An Inventory of Scientific Findings. New York: Harcourt, Brace and World, Inc., 1964.

4. "Contributions of Physical Activity to Human Well-Being, The," Research Quarterly, Vol. 31, No. 2, Part II, May 1960.

5. Cowell, Charles C., "The Contributions of Physical Activity to Social Development," in Research Quarterly, Vol. 31, No. 2:286-306, May 1960 (Part II).

6. Huxley, Aldous. Tomorrow and Tomorrow and Tomorrow. New York: The New American Library of World Literature, Inc., 1964.

7. Kneller, George F. Educational Anthropology: An Introduction. New York: John Wiley & Sons, Inc., 1965.

8. Martin, W. E. and Stendler, C. B. Child Behavior and Development. New York: Harcourt, Brace and World, Inc., Revised edition, 1959.

9. McCristal, King J. American Academy of Physical Education unpublished statement to program participants for Anaheim meeting, 1973.

10. Physical Education Discipline Group (Ontario Universities). "Response of the Discipline Group to the Consultants' Report on Graduate Programmes in Physical Education, Kinesiology and Related Areas." Toronto, Ontario: Council of Universities, 1974.

11. Rose, Peter I. (editor). The Study of Society. New York: Random House, 1967.

12. Scott, M. Gladys, "The Contributions of Physical Activity to Psychological Development," in Research Quarterly, Vol. 31, No. 2:307-320, May 1960 (Part II).

13. Western Ontario, University of. Faculty of Physical Education "Submission to Commission to Study the Rationalization of Research (A.U.C.C.)," December, 1971.

THE HISTORICAL ROLE OF SPORT IN SELECTED SOCIETIES: AN APPROACH TO DESCRIPTION, EXPLANATION, AND EVALUATION

The description, explanation and evaluation of the historical role of sport in selected societies could readily consume a lifetime of endeavor for a considerable number of qualified scholars.* It is for this reason that the writer wishes to quickly dispel any thought that he may be unwarrantedly presumptuous in implying that this preliminary paper will be definitive in regard to findings and conclusions. Its aim is to show some progress, and also to alert fellow historians about some possible opportunities for enlightenment through cooperation with scholars in related disciplines - and, of course, through the employment of some of their research techniques and/or findings.

This paper is, therefore, a follow-up of a proposal made at the International Relations Meeting of the National College Physical Education Association for Men Meeting at Portland, Oregon, December 28, 1970. The plan was for the establishment of a long-term comparative analysis of educational values in selected countries with their implications for sport and physical education. (31) The basic assumption is that the need is most urgent to make our earth sort of a "global village" in which the level of personal communication among people of all countries will be increased tremendously. The achievement of such status would be more than a mere "opportunity to promote international relations and goodwill"; it would, rather, be mandatory if civilization as we know it is to survive. As Asimov has predicted, mankind is fast reaching the point where "signs of breakdown are everywhere, for the problems introduced by our contemporary level of technology seem insuperable." His dire prediction is that we are as a result faced with a race "between the coming of the true fourth revolution [in man's ability to communicate with his fellow man everywhere!] and the death of civilization that will inevitably occur through growth past the limits of the third." The message here is simply that all men on earth must learn to communicate more efficiently and effectively very soon! (1)

Why, therefore, should anyone be concerned with the historical role of sport in society? The answer would appear to be obvious and

---

* A paper presented at the Second World Symposium on the History of Sport and Physical Education, Banff, Alberta, Canada, June 1, 1971. (Published in Proceedings of the Second World Symposium on the History of Sport and Physical Education, Ottawa, Canada, pp. 115-126.)

straightforward - "history is actually a bridge connecting the past with the present, and pointing - the road to the future." History, thus conceived, is "a lantern carried by the side of man, moving forward with every step taken . . ." (24) And we simply cannot forget the importance of the rays from the lantern that shine to the <u>rear</u>, to our <u>side</u>, and on the road <u>ahead</u>!

How may such a comparative analysis and interpretation of the historical role of sport in society be made in the best possible way? What knowledge is needed before any assessment can be made even tentatively? The remainder of this paper will consist of certain steps recommended by one fallible person who has been working at the subject. It will soon be obvious that much assistance and collaboration is indicated. To approach the task at hand, the following topics will be considered: (1) the disciplines through which men have gained knowledge about the individual and group values held by past societies; (2) the research methods and techniques available for investigation, and which have special relevance for this problem; (3) the chronology of civilizations considered in this delimited paper; (4) the discipline of history, and the persistent problems approach adopted by this investigator; (5) the discipline of sociology, and the relevance of one broad theory to historical investigation; (6) the discipline of anthropology, and how some of the theories of cultural anthropology shed light on the topic at hand; (7) the discipline of psychology, and how social psychology may explain how man has made certain emotional and social adaptation to his environment through sport and physical activity; (8) the discipline of philosophy, and how a type of language analysis may assist with the understanding of the meaning of sport terms both in the past and the present; (9) the theories of sport and play propounded by scholars from a variety of disciplines; (10) a persistent historical problems approach based on the analysis of the social institutions of a society and the influence of values and norms on education, including sport and physical education; and (11) a brief summary including some tentative findings and conclusions based on the relatively limited perspective of this preliminary analysis and interpretation.

Related Disciplines

Men have employed a variety of psychological or learning processes to gain knowledge about the present and the past, notably (1) thinking (rationalism); (2) feeling (intuitionism); (3) sensing (empiricism); and (4) believing (authoritarianism). (28) As a discipline has become more scientific, and has therefore placed increased emphasis on research techniques involving a more empirical approach, there has been a marked tendency to turn to a variety of related disciplines for assistance. The late Allan Nevins, writing in 1968, reaffirmed the idea that the discipline of history was employing "many powerful new forces . . . and few men understand half of them." (25) He was referring to such aspects as new studies from archeology; advancements in epigraphy; development of the carbon-dating process; comparative ancient literature, etc. (25) With the present topic, however, the need is to turn to those disciplines through which men have gained knowledge about the individual and group values held by past societies. Thus, in addition to history, brief reference will be made to direction and knowledge that may be gained from sociology, cultural anthropology, social psychology, and philosophy.

Research Methods and Techniques

There have been many types of historical investigation embodying both critical and constructive intellectual processes. Basically, the historian is confronted initially with a mass of data which he must organize, analyze, interpret, evaluate, and synthesize in such a way that his efforts enable him to write history that reflects man's past as accurately as possible. As Kahler tells us, "there is no history without meaning." (16) And if the meaning is "teased out" of the data, there is no doubt but that the question of values will arise.

Historians are now confronted with a need to understand the research methods and techniques of the related disciplines described above. The other two broad methods are typically designated as descriptive and experimental group method, each offering a multitude of techniques and variations for the eager researcher to employ in his effort to investigate his problem in the most adequate fashion. "Philosophical method" has often been considered a fourth broad method of research, but it is difficult to claim that much of the earlier philosophical endeavor produced new knowledge in a scientific sense, and much of present philosophical investigation is highly scientific in nature and approach. This brings the discussion full circle back to the employment of descriptive techniques, mathematical logic, or experimental investigations in which a control group is employed. (11)

History - Chronology of Selected Societies

It is to history that the investigator turns for the main subdivisions of this preliminary analysis. The analysis and interpretation will be limited to (1) Primitive and Early Societies; (2) Greece and Rome; (3) The Middle Ages; (4) The Enlightenment and 19th Century Europe; and (5) North America. (32) It is granted immediately that such a presentation is definitely provincial (Western world) when it arrives at the modern period especially. This deficiency must be remedied just as soon as possible by the combined efforts of many of us, and there is no doubt but that this will be done soon. As we work together for further understanding, the maxim- "neither a borrower nor a lender be" - most certainly should not apply to the matter at hand.

It is literally frightening today if one reflects deeply in the area of historical interpretation, and the investigator must keep in mind further that historical theories of interpretation are almost inescapably attached to the needs that people have and the values that they hold at the time that the history of any era is being written. (37) For example, the writer does not subscribe to the cyclical rise and fall of civilizations, nor does he believe that there are certain systematic rules or principles which describe historical change in a way applicable to all societies. Nor is he convinced that history is ever completely objective or subjective. He is pragmatic and pluralistic in his approach, and accepts always the idea of multiplicity of causation. An ad hoc theory may well offer a very sound reason for a particular historical development. Thus, because it is not possible to repeat historical events, historians will probably never be able to attain complete objectivity. They should remain openminded in a world characterized by evolutionary humanistic change. (12)

As this topic is approached, it will be possible to obtain considerable help from the earlier work of Marvin H. Eyler entitled "Origins of Some Modern Sports." (8) From a methodogolical standpoint, the writer has, over a period of several decades, been identifying and collecting data about some fifteen persistent historical problems that have had a relation to sport and physical education. (39) The first six of these so-called problems have been identified as social forces which have influenced sport and physical education significantly in the societies being considered. These forces or influences are (1) values and norms; (2) type of political state; (3) nationalism; (4) economics; (5) religion; and most recently (6) ecology, or man's use of his environment. The remaining nine of these problems may be considered as professional problems for the person who practices in the field of physical education and sport, although most certainly each one of these problems is of somewhat greater or lesser concern to the general public in all of our societies. These "persistent problems" are (1) professional preparation, including curriculum; (2) methods of instruction; (3) the role of administration; (4) the concept of health; (5) the use of leisure; (6) amateurism, semi-professionalism, and professionalism in sport; (7) dance in physical education and recreation; (8) physical education and sport for women; and (9) the concept of progress. (32) The investigator has adapted an approach to educational problems which is employed also by John S. Brubacher in his historical and philosophical investigations. (4,5) (Professor Brubacher was recently selected as one of eleven leaders in American education in the twentieth century.) (23)

Sociology - Parsons' Theory of Action

The discipline of sociology can be extremely helpful to the sport and physical education historian, and especially so when the concern is for an analysis and interpretation of the values and norms of various social systems. Parsons' theory of action, a structural-functional theory, has been described by Johnson as "a type of empirical system." (14) Four levels of social structure are postulated as (1) values; (2) norms; (3) the structure of collectivities; and (4) the structure of roles. These proceed from highest to lowest, with the higher levels being more general than the lower ones. Values, for example, are categorized, and values in sport would of necessity reinforce the important societal values and shared sanctioned norms of a particular social system.

To get at the historical role of sport in a society, there would appear to be a prior need to achieve an acceptable synthesis of the history of the social system being considered. The functional interchanges between and among the subsystems of the social system should be understood (e.g., how its economy serves as an effective adaptive subsystem), as should the means whereby a social system maintains its equilibrium (e.g., the social processes whereby a society maintains a given structure or changes it). (35) If, as is typically postulated, sport, games, and physical activity exert significant social force within a society (and vice versa), a knowledge of these factors will offer increased "explanatory power." Just recently, Lüschen has reported that there is a "strong relationship" between sport and society, and he cites for evidence analyses of American football, the running races of Hopi Indians, three Illinois frontier subcultures, and the log races of the Timbira tribe in Brazil. (20) It can only be hoped that in the future an increasingly greater number of sociologists will concern themselves with sport as an important social institution. Thus, the function it fulfills in the total system of social integration would be gradually much better understood.

Anthropology - a "Giant" of a Discipline

The fields of anthropology include the study of the physical, cultural, and social development and the behavior of men and women since they appeared in the evolutionary development of the planet that has been designated as Earth. For this reason anthropology can readily be called a "giant" of a discipline! The human animal has a culture or a social heritage, and this subdivision of the total field has been named cultural or social anthropology. As man's various social units are traced, the interrelationship of cultural values and human behavior is a perennial concern for the members of a particular society.

Cultural anthropology has only recently been recognized as a science, and anthropological theories about sport and games as dynamic processes of social life have not been given the attention that perhaps ought to have been the case. Of course, the work of the cultural anthropologist would often not even be sufficiently exact to warrant the employment of complex statistical procedures - and may never be when one is studying the processes that occasion the development or change of cultural patterns. This is not to say, however, that games and sporting patterns of early cultures cannot or should not be described with care, or that ad hoc theories may not be applied to them wherever possible. It seems reasonable to assume that certain types of games and sports will appear as identifiable cultural elements in the culture complex of a society (e.g., the idea of sportsmanship and fair play in the games of a democratic society). (13)

An example of a recent effort to relate game theory to cultural complexes is an investigation completed by Glassford in 1970. He traced sporadic attempts to prove that an interrelationship exists between a culture and its game forms. He postulated that the nature of sport and games would undergo changes depending upon the possible changes in values and norms of a culture undergoing transition. Based on a theory of games and economic behavior outlined by Von Neumann and Morgenstern (30), Glassford developed a game classification model which he then tested on a culture (Eskimo) which was undergoing a marked transition. Basically, he hypothesized that "the orientation of the traditional generation toward the values of reciprocity and sharing would be reflected in their game preferences," and that "the new-era generation would express a stronger preference for competitive games." The findings enabled Glassford to verify his postulations (at least tentatively), and also confirmed the hypotheses that the traditional generation seems to prefer self-testing games more, and also preferred a game strategy which afforded "tolerable satisfactions" with minimum risk. (10)

Social Psychology - Emotional and Social Adaptation to Environment

There is no doubt but that the historian will need to keep the investigation of social psychologists increasingly in mind in the future as he hypothesizes about the historical role of sport and games in various civilizations. Fundamentally, the present concern is with "the development of the social phases of personality, attitudes, and values by means of" these activities. (6) The challenge of explaining how personality is developed and maintained in a culture is such that fully adequate explanations may not be available for some time to come. The many variables involved complicate the possibility of investigation greatly. And yet society readily accepts the hypothesis that physical activity in competitive sport situations does lead to social development. It seems true further that social behavior and personality growth can be influenced positively or negatively according to a society's values and depending upon the quality of the leadership and the opportunities for participation afforded. Thus, the profession of sport and physical education has a responsibility to provide practitioners exhibiting the finest type of leadership consonant with the highest values of the social system.

An inventory of findings about human behavior is now available (3), which serves as a foundation "layer" of knowledge for investigators in sport and physical education. The 1960 project of the Research Council of the American Association for Health, Physical Education, and Recreation, entitled The Contributions of Physical Activity to Human Well-Being, includes the late Charles Cowell's "The Contributions of Physical Activity to Social Development." (This particular section is to be up-dated as soon as possible.) One cannot help but feel, however, that this highly important aspect of the disciplinary ap-approach to sport and physical education is not receiving sufficient support and encouragement from the many people who hade made such strong but unsupported claims for the social values of sport and games in the past. (Can it be that they fear the results of such investigations because they suspect that current leadership is of such a calibre that positive benefits may be at a low level?) At any rate, the classification of games based on socio-psychological phenomena should go on (e.g., 27 and 18), as should the "people experiments" discussed by Martens (21) and broadened in his plea for "a social psychology of physical activity." (22)

Philosophy - Definitions and Value Theories

The field of philosophy offers a storehouse of data to the sport and physical education historian; the difficulty is how and on what basis the historian can or should approach all of this information. Philosophy has traditionally been subdivided into four subdivisions with axiology (system of values) as the end result of philosophical endeavor. Thus, fundamental beliefs about values - whether in life generally, or in education, or in sport - would tend to be as consistent as possible with a person's beliefs in regard to the other three subdivisions of the total discipline or subject-matter. Metaphysics (questions about the nature of reality) is combined with axiology to form what has been called speculative philosophy. Epistemology (acquisition of knowledge) and logic (exact relating of ideas) are designated typically as critical philosophy.

How a particular historian employs philosophy to serve his purposes as a historian depends almost completely on his background and experience within the culture in which he is living. Pragmatists would tend to be concerned about learning theory prior to questions about the nature of reality. Another philosopher might wish to study the many histories of philosophy in which certain theories about the various branches would be presented chronologically. (Some of these treatments might be in the form of biographies of great philosophers of the past.) A third approach might be to read progressively from the actual works of the philosophers themselves (often through the location of the best translations available). Another method would be useful - the determination of the major recurring issues or problems with which philosophers have concerned themselves over the centuries. It was this approach that Brubacher used with the departmental philosophy of education, and was also employed by this investigator because of its seemingly effective application to sport and physical education (3) through the application of a structural analysis research technique (9).

Strangely enough, just at the time that people all over the world seem to have become more "value conscious," so to speak, the professional field of philosophy - in the English speaking world at least - seems to have "cast the common man adrift in waters that are anything but calm and peaceful." The main reason why many philosophers seem to be devoting less time to the "service" aspects of the general education of students is undoubtedly that they have taken more of a "disciplinary approach" by the adoption of research techniques which are more effective in the achievement of the goals of the philosophical analysis movement. As Kaplan has indicated in describing this twentieth century movement, "philosophy is a kind of logico-linguistic analysis, not a set of super-scientific truths about man and nature, nor a sustained exhortation to live one's life in a particular way." (17) He clarifies this explanation further by intimating that the professional activity of the philosopher is a type of "linguistic therapy" directed toward restoring both ordinary language and scientific propositions to a state of "semantic well-being" through a "rational reconstruction of the language of science." For example, the philosopher would be asking, "what makes sense, and what is nonsense?" He does not determine whether theoretical propositions are true or false - that is the scientist's realm - but he does try to see to it that they are expressed clearly, precisely, and logically.

Returning to the task of the historian, it is possible to conclude with some confidence that a philosopher may approach his work speculatively, normatively, or analytically - or through some combination of these approaches with the employment of several techniques. The historian may, therefore, look to the language analyst for a more careful delineation of the terms "sport," "play," and "athletics," for example, or he may be guided by the normative philosophizing of some outstanding person who evolves a systematic, coherent plan of a society and explains how sport and the culture displayed greater or lesser interdependence. (40)

One last suggestion may be made in the delineation of possible approaches to the task accepted for this present paper. It is a type of normative and analytic philosophizing applied to comparative and international education, which may be adapted to the social institution of sport. Lauwerys recommends that an investigator should make an effort to understand the dominant philosophy and philosophy of education in a culture undergoing study. The assumption is that such an assessment will provide true insight concerning the reasons why a definitive pattern of education is carried out by those responsible for policy formulation and execution in the educational system of a culture. (19)

Theories of Play, Sport, Athletics - from Various Disciplines

As soon as one attempts a reasonably careful analysis of the literature on play theory, he realizes that there are in existence a plethora of theories emanating from a variety of disciplines. In the past most people have tended to use the words "play," "sport," and "athletics" with the blithe assurance that they would not be seriously challenged. Because this statement could typically applied to scholars as well as laymen, the situation is now such that an un-abridged dictionary includes the word "sport" thirteen different ways as a noun, two ways as an adjective, six as an intransitive verb, and five ways as a transitive verb. "Play" is employed in 74 different ways, and the terms "game" and "athletics" are used in twenty-three and three ways, respectively. (26) For the purpose of this paper, the appropriate definition of sport can be "an athletic activity requiring skill or physical prowess, usually of a competitive nature (e.g., wrestling, racing, tennis, rugby, etc.). But does this definition apply to the past?

Most recently, Ellis at Illinois' Motor Performance and Play Research Laboratory has accomplished some fine analytical and inte-grative theorizing about play theory. (7) After a precise recapitula-tion of the so-called "classical" theories of play, he continues with an analysis, interpretation, and evaluation of the more recent theo-ries that have been presented since the end of World War II - theories typically postulating homeostatic behavior patterns. Accepting the basic premise that man is the most neophilic (novelty-liking) of all animals, Ellis takes a stand that man's non-utilitarian behavior (play) is largely arousal-seeking in nature. Thus, he is saying that man plays competitive sport because he as an individual (and probably as a social animal) has a need "to generate interactions with the environ-ment or self that elevate arousal towards the optimal for the indi-vidual."

It seems obvious to this investigator that the historian needs to keep the above-mentioned definitions of terms in mind as he approaches his work. Further, he should have as comprehensive an understanding of play theory as is needed to help him comprehend as best possible the true role of sport in the society which he is analyzing.*

Persistent Historical Problems Approach - Comparison and Interpretation

The persistent or perennial historical problems approach employed by this investigator has been explained earlier in this paper and, as was indicated, values in sport and physical education has been selected as first in a list of some fifteen problem areas. Further, the matter of amateurism, semi-professionalism, and professionalism in sport was condidered important enough to warrant inclusion in this tabulation of historical problems. (It is admitted readily, of course, that this organization of problems is contemporary, and that it must necessarily have an "American bias" to a degree.) (33) (34) (36)

The following, then, is a recommended step-by-step approach for the description, explanation, and evaluation of the historical role of sport in selected societies. It is an approach that is multi-disciplinary in nature and which also rests upon findings that are available - and which will become increasingly available - from all research methods and techniques known to man.

1. Review the best evidence available concerning the sofical foundations of the society, culture, or social system being considered (e.g., values, norms, type of political structure, economic system, leading religions, etc.).

2. Assess the available evidence in regard to the educational foundations of the society (e.g., educational values in some hierarchical order; the curriculum and the process of education; and the relationship among the school, society and the individual).

3. Describe, interpret, and assess tentatively - based on tentative hypotheses - the sport and physical education practices of the society available through historical sources of both a primary and secondary nature. Categorize according to (1) aims and objectives; (2) methods of instruction; and (3) possible strengths and weaknesses.

---

* Because of space limitations, economics as a pivotal social institution with highly significant implications for sport and physical education was not included, nor was the developing subdiscipline of comparative education.

4. Based on the literature of sociology, and available sociological analyses of the society being investigated, attempt to discover whether the functionally necessary processes of the social system (e.g., according to Parsons' theory of action) are operating in such a fashion that a hierarchy of control and conditioning is present that enables functional interchanges to take place in order to maintain equilibrium or to promote change. (The aim here, of course, is to learn whether an acceptable synthesis of the social system under investigation has been determined; whether there has been a realization to at least a certain extent of the society's value system; and the extent to which the social institution of sport and physical education has facilitated the achievement of the society's values.) (15)

5. Based on the literature of anthropology, and available anthropological theories of the culture being examined, attempt to discover to what extent games and sporting patterns have been assessed as dynamic processes within that specific culture. If careful ethnographical descriptions have been carried out, it is possible that an ad hoc theory such as Glassford's (10) may be applied, and at least compared with the evidence from sociological analysis available.

6. Based on the literature of social psychology and closely related aspects of the other behavioral sciences, attempt to learn if currently tenable theories about social behavior and personality growth may have been applicable in the social system being investigated. And, further, is it possible that such behavior and growth were influenced markedly by the society's value system as leaders sought to employ sport and physical activity to develop the desired individual and social values?

7. Based on the literature of the history of philosophy, it should be possible for the historian to correlate still further his earlier findings relative to the values considered important in the social system involved, and to relate the concerns ("persistent problems!") of the philosophers of a particular society to "value determinations" that have been postulated in the findings from other disciplines. In this way a type of "normative philosophizing" might be carried out in which the dominant philosophy and philosophy of education could be postulated and substantiated (perhaps) through "verification" by means of knowledge available from the related disciplines. Further, philosophical language analysis techniques may be providing means of determining inadequacies in the language of the people within the system.

8. At this point - and there is no doubt but that further evidence will become available from subdisciplines not yet "invented" - the sport historian and philosopher should be able to "proclaim the 'validity and reliability' " of his earlier tentative hypotheses about the

historical role of sport in a particular social system at a much higher "level of confidence" than previously.

9. At least one more possibility is available for <u>cross-cultural comparison</u> of the role of sport and physical education in society. This is the <u>comparative method</u> as developed by Bereday as a type of descriptive investigation. (2) Here the stages or steps are (1) <u>description</u>, in which descriptive data will be obtained about the plan of sport and physical education in each of the countries being studied; (2) <u>explanation</u>, in which an attempt will be made to explain the theory and practice in sport and physical education based upon the prevailing educational philosophy in each of the countries; (3) <u>juxtaposition</u>, in which the patterns of sport and physical education in the countries being compared cross-culturally will be <u>related</u> on the basis of the implications for sport and physical activity from the hierarchy of educational values existing in each of the countries; and (4) <u>comparison</u>, in which the findings and some reasonable conclusions will be presented based on the similarities and differences - with the final comparison taking into consideration the economic and educational status of the countries being considered.

Conclusions and a Final Word

In essence the writer hopes that the reader will conclude that it has now become possible for the sport historian to become ever so much more sophisticated in his work. The historian is being urged to become increasingly aware of the literature and evidence that is being provided steadily by sociology, cultural anthropology, social psychology, philosophy, and comparative education. Still further, the sport historian should consider the advisability of adopting at least certain of the research techniques available through the other disciplines. Much sport history has been written on the basis of common sense and simple description, which are, of course, necessary steps in the early development of a discipline. The time has come, however, for the sport historian to make apparent his underlying theory of history. He may wish further to apply his own ad hoc theory to his evaluation of the history of sport. It is only in this way that the field can look forward to the future development of "theories of the middle range" and ultimately far more complex theories about sport in the history of man. (39)

Lastly, it seems important at this particular moment to mention that scholars have been identifying "recurrent elements in the various world philosophies." (17) Kaplan asserts that there are four themes displaying a strong "family resemblance" in the living philosophies of the world today. The first is a theme of <u>rationality</u> displaying either causal or historical systematic unity. Secondly, there is a theme of <u>activism</u> which implies that understanding is a guide to positive action.

Thirdly, he has detected a theme of <u>humanism</u>, a pervading belief that there is a continuity of man and nature in both the East and the West. Lastly, there is a preoccupation with values - a view that the life of man should be strongly related to values, and that his highest aspiration is to fulfill moral and spiritual values in his life. (38)

The sport historian, by identifying the historical role of sport in all societies and cultures, can help to make <u>internationalism</u> in sport and physical education one of the highest professional goals.

Footnotes and References

1. Asimov, Isaac, "The Fourth Revolution," <u>Saturday Review</u> (October 24, 1970), 17-20.

2. Bereday, G. Z. F. <u>Comparative Method in Education</u>. New York: Holt, Rinehart and Winston, 1964, p. 19 et ff.

3. Berelson, Bernard and Steiner, G. A. <u>Human Behavior: An Inventory of Scientific Findings</u>. New York: Harcourt, Brace and World, Inc., 1964.

4. Brubacher, John S. <u>A History of the Problems of Education</u>. New York: McGraw-Hill Book Company, Second edition, 1966.

5. _____. <u>Modern Philosophies of Education</u>. New York: McGraw-Hill Book Company, Fourth edition, 1969.

6. Cowell, Charles C., "The Contributions of Physical Activity to Social Development," in <u>Research Quarterly</u>, Vol. 31, No. 2:286-306 (Part II), May, 1960.

7. Ellis, M. J., "Play and its Theories Re-examined," in <u>America's Leisure</u>, Yearbook of the National Recreation and Park Association, 1971.

8. Eyler, Marvin H., "Origins of Some Modern Sports." Unpublished Ph.D. thesis, University of Illinois, Urbana, 1956.

9. Fraleigh, Warren P., "Theory and Design of Philosophic Research," in <u>Proceedings</u> of the 74th Annual Meeting of the National College Physical Education Association for Men, Portland, Oregon, Dec. 27, 1970.

10. Glassford, R. G., "Application of a Theory of Games to the Transitional Eskimo Culture." Unpublished Ph.D. thesis, University of Illinois, Urbana, 1970.

11. Good, Carter V. and Scates, D. E. Methods of Research. New York: Appleton-Century-Crofts, Inc., 1954.

12. Harvard Guide to American History (Written by Oscard Handlin et al.). New York: Atheneum, 1967, pp. 15-21.

13. Hershkovits, M. J. Cultural Anthropology. New York: Alfred Knopf, 1955, pp. 33-85.

14. Johnson, Harry M., "The Relevance of the Theory of Action to Historians," Social Science Quarterly, June, 1969, 46-58.

15. _____. Sociology: A Systematic Introduction. New York: Harcourt, Brace and World, Inc., 1960.

16. Kahler, Erich. The Meaning of History. New York: George Braziller, 1964.

17. Kaplan, Abraham. The New World of Philosophy. New York: Random House, 1961, pp. 3-12.

18. Kenyon, Gerald S., "A Conceptual Model for Characterizing Physical Activity," in Research Quarterly, Vol. 39, No. 1:97-105, March, 1968.

19. Lauwerys, Joseph A., "The Philosophical Approach to Comparative Education," International Review of Education, Vol. V, 1959, 283-290.

20. Lüschen, Günther, "The Interdependence of Sport and Culture," International Review of Sport Sociology (Poland), 2:127-141, 1967.

21. Martens, Rainer, "Demand Characteristics and Experimenter Bias." A paper presented at the Research Methodology Symposium, Research Council, AAHPER Convention, Detroit, April 5, 1971.

22. _____, "A Social Psychology of Physical Activity," Quest, 14:8-17, June, 1970.

23. National Society for the Study of Education (Seventieth Yearbook). Leaders in American Education (editor, R. J. Havighurst). Chicago: The University of Chicago Press, 1971, 17-64.

24. Nevins, Allan, "The Explosive Excitement of History," Saturday Review, April 6, 1968.

25. _____. The Gateway to History. New York: Doubleday & Co., Inc., 1962, p. 14.

26. Random House Dictionary of the English Language, The. New York: Random House, 1967.

27. Roberts, J. M. and Sutton-Smith, B., "Child Training and Game Involvement," Ethnology, Vol. I, 1962. (The reader might wish to review also "Games in Culture," which appeared in 1959 in American Anthropologist (Vol. 61) by Roberts, Arth and Bush.)

28. Royce, J. R., "Paths to Knowledge," in The Encapsulated Man. Princeton, New Jersey: Van Nostrand, 1964.

29. Toffler, Alvin. Future Shock. New York: Random House, Inc., 1970.

30. Von Neumann, J. and Morgenstern. O. The Theory of Games and Economic Behavior. Princeton, New Jersey: Princeton University Press, Second edition, 1947.

31. Zeigler, Earle F., "Amateurism, Semi-Professionalism, and Professionalism in Sport - a Persistent Educational Problem," in Arnold W. Flath's A History of Relations between the National Collegiate Athletic Association and the Amateur Athletic Union of the United States, 1905-1963. Champaign, Illinois: Stipes Publishing Co., 1964.

32. _____., "A Comparative Analysis of Educational Values in Selected Countries: Their Implications for Physical Education and Sport," in Proceedings of the 74th Annual Meeting of the National College Physical Education Association for Men, Portland, Oregon, Dec. 27, 1970.

33. _____, "Foreword," in Physical Education Around the World (editor, William Johnson). Indianapolis, Indiana: Phi Epsilon Kappa Fraternity, Monograph #4, 1970.

34. _____, "Persistent Historical Problems of Physical Education and Sport," in Proceedings of the First International Seminar on the History of Physical Education and Sport, Wingate Institute for Physical Education, Netanya, Israel, April 9-11, 1968, 1-13. (Published in March, 1969 by the Institute, editor, Uriel Simri.)

35. _____. *Philosophical Foundations for Physical, Health, and Recreation Education.* Englewood Cliffs, New Jersey: Prentice-Hall, Inc., 1964.

36. _____. *Problems in the History and Philosophy of Physical Education and Sport.* Englewood Cliffs, New Jersey: Prentice-Hall, Inc., 1968.

37. _____, "Putting the Greek Ideal in Perspective," A paper presented to the History of Sport Section, AAHPER Convention, Detroit, April 5, 1971.

38. _____, Howell, M. L. and Trekell, Marianna. *Research in the History, Philosophy and International Aspects of Physical Education and Sport.* Champaign, Illinois: Stipes Publishing Company, 1971, 350 p.

39. _____ and VanderZwaag, H. J. *Physical Education: Progressivism or Essentialism?* Champaign, Illinois: Stipes Publishing Co., 1966. (Second edition in 1968.)

INTRAMURALS: PROFESSION, DISCIPLINE, OR PART THEREOF?

The main objective of this paper is to present to the field of physical education and sport, and specifically to those who are related primarily to the promotion of intramural athletics, some ideas about the past, present, and possible future of that aspect of sport that has commonly been designated simply as "intramurals."* Interestingly enough, this term is just about as common as the term "P.E." on the North American continent. These ideas about intramurals ask the fundamental question: "Is intramurals a profession, a discipline, or part thereof?"

To meet this paper's objectives, the following questions or topics will be considered in order: (1) definition of the terms "profession" and "discipline"; (2) the fractionating influences in physical education today; (3) intramural athletics - then, now, and in the future; (4) a model for the profession; (5) implications from the proposed model for intramurals; and (6) a summary with recommendations for the future.

The ideas about to be expressed in this paper are the result of long observation of programs of intramural athletics; close personal association with several of the field's leading intramural directors; a recent relationship as administrator of a faculty of physical education in which both physical recreation and intramurals and intercollegiate athletics programs are included; and the writer's study of the philosophy of physical education and sport, which includes a pragmatic orientation and recent disciplinary concern.

Definition of the Terms "Profession" and "Discipline"

The current controversy or problem within the field of physical education and sport about whether it is a profession or a discipline of necessity applies to intramurals, itself presumably a subdivision of physical education. One simple definition of a profession is an occupation or a vocation requiring knowledge and understanding of some department or field of learning. Traditionally a professional person serves mankind; follows a code of ethics; is licensed or certificated

---

* A paper presented to the Intramural Athletics Section of the National College Physical Education Association for Men, 76th Annual Conference, Pittsburgh, Pennsylvania, January 8, 1973. (Published in Proceedings of the NCPEAM, edited by C. E. Mueller, Minneapolis, Minnesota, 1973, pp. 85-90.)

to practice; considers his work a lifetime career; and does not consider the amount of money he earns to be of primary importance. Of course there are other criteria that could be added to this list.

A discipline is, on the other hand, a branch of instruction or learning. Thus, a professional person bases his practice upon the knowledge and understanding provided by the disciplinary investigator in one or more fields of instruction or learning.

Based on a preliminary analysis of intramural athletics up to this point in the discussion, intramurals would have to be categorized as a subdivision or subunit within the profession of physical education (which itself is typically thought to be a subdivision of the teaching profession). In responding to the question, "Is your professional practice based on undergirding disciplinary knowledge," the intramural director would probably indicate some hesitancy before responding relatively weakly that the field was moving in that direction. By such an answer he would be basing his case on physical education's effort to orient itself disciplinarily, but he would be hesitant about making any significant claims for the scholarly body-of-knowledge developed by "intramurals people" for use in the professional practice of intramural directors. Does this imply that intramurals directors need only to be personable organizers with a broad, but possibly superficial, background in sports? No attempt will be made to answer this rhetorical question definitvely, but there is a definite problem here.

The Fractionating Influences in Physical Education Today

Before proceeding further with the "intramurals case," it is imperative that a look be taken at the field of physical education as it presently exists. (Parenthetically it must be stated that this exposition assumes that the 1960's has been a traumatic experience for most of the population, and that the impact of this past decade has been such that the critical subsystem of education is malfunctioning to a most serious degree.)

Whether or not mankind is on a collision course with the future because the tempo of civilization is increasing so fast that many people are unable to adjust satisfactorily, there seems to be ample evidence that the field of physical education is on a "collision course" with itself! Its professional leaders are gradually being forced to make an effort to understand what idealistic youth mean when they use such terms as "relevance," "accountability," and "involvement." At the same time higher education is facing greater financial expenses with seemingly steady-state or declining legislative allotments. This means that certain subject-matters and professional faculties on campus will inevitably have higher priorities than others. This problem is compounded further by possibly indefensible required p.e. programs, academically inferior teacher education curricula, and intercollegiate athletics programs that have typically lost sound educational perspective in almost all regards.

Still further, there are internal problems of a truly major character within what has been loosely called "the field" or "the profession." These are explained as follows:

1. "Specific Focus Approach" vs. "Shotgun Approach" - should the profession now attempt to unite behind the idea that the professional task within formal and informal education is to teach humans to move efficiently and with purpose in sport, dance, play, and exercise within the context of man's socialization in an evolving world?

2. "The Physical Education" vs. "Athletics Encounter" - does the profession in the United States dare to speak out time and again in a statesmanlike, forcible manner against practices in competitive athletics which don't even have a rightful place at any educational level or in society?

3. "The Male-Female Dichotomy in Physical Education" - can men's and women's departments at all educational levels be amalgamated equitably, efficiently, and rapidly so that greater professional strength will be gained at the same time that money for the total operation is being saved?

4. "Professional Preparation Wing" vs. "Disciplinary Wing" - can the field of physical education make the adaptation to the newer professional-disciplinary approach? This implies that all who teach in the various undergraduate curricula will be scholars (with all that this implies).

5. "The Bio-Science" vs. "The Humanities-Social Science Conflict" - is it possible for faculty members teaching in the natural and bio-scientific aspects of the field to live in peace with colleagues forming undergraduate and graduate options in the humanities and social science aspects of physical education and sport?

As if these problems aren't enough, the profession is additionally confronted with a situation in which the field of health and safety education and the field of recreation are successfully earning separate professional status (and would rather not have the term "physical education" on their letterheads). Moreover, the field of physical education can't even decide what to call itself; required physical education is in trouble in a great many places; and intercollegiate athletics "rolls on" in "lofty contempt" of so-called physical education (possibly the subject held in least regard traditionally in academic circles). It must be mentioned in passing also that intercollegiate athletics is "running on a financial treadmill that is set at an impossible angle" for it to survive in the form which is now generally recognized. This brings the discussion around again to the topic at hand - intramural athletics. What is its state of health?

Intramural Athletics - Then, Now, and in the Future

Strangely enough with all of the woes that seem to be plaguing the field at present, it is intramural athletics that seems to be healthy and thriving both ideologically and practically. No matter which educational philosophy is held by the evaluator, intramurals tends to emerge as a program of "sport for all" which defies the onslaughts of campus critics. Since its beginning early in the twentieth century as an organized entity, it is safe to say that its popularity has never been higher. The various theories of play that are extant seem to allow at least a significant place for individual, dual, and team experiences in a form of competitive athletics that is fairly well organized but not overemphasized. Even the use of public funds for the promotion of intramurals meets with general approval, because people sense intuitively that there's room potentially in the program for all students, male and female alike.

After painting such a rosy picture of intramurals, however, somehow or other there is a dark side to the representation. The intramurals function has been taken for granted in the past, and this seems to be true even today. Intramurals is regarded as a service program and not as an educational one. There is still the feeling both within the field and without that intramurals can "make do" with inferior facilities and equipment. The officials in intramurals contests, for example, can be at the same level as the players according to the opinion of many--fairly good, that is. After all it's all for fun anyhow; so what if the official makes a few poor calls? Students just take part in intramural athletics to "let off steam," and such "emission tends to provide a safety valve" for campuses that otherwise might even be more troublesome were it not for strenuous physical activity provided by the "establishment" for the aggressive mesomorphs.

And what about the status of the intramural director and his associates in the athletics or physical education hierarchy? Here we tend to find a similar situation - at least in the eyes of colleagues.

Certainly intercollegiate athletic coaches and officials rarely provide more than lip service to the present "intramurals ideal," while often using the provision of such service as a good excuse for the continued drive to keep up gate receipts. Intramurals organizers don't fare much better with their presumably academic colleagues in physical education departments. Promotions and comparable salary levels are somewhat more difficult to achieve because the intramural director is usually so busy managing his program that truly scholarly efforts on his part are a rarity indeed. Thus, when the higher administrative posts within physical education and/or intercollegiate athletics are filled, it is almost self-evident that the good old "missionary" running a fine intramurals program is passed by for the proven scholar or the successful coach.

It is at this low point that the main thesis of this presentation emerges. The idea is simply this: the development of physical education and sport on this continent has reached the time when intramural's supposed inferiority can be overcome through the use of a revised definition that can guarantee at least equality of status within the very near future to all properly conceived, well-organized, and adequately financed programs. An explanation about how to arrive at this halcyon state must begin with the presentation of a conceptual model for the entire field.

A Model for the Profession

A model for optimum professional development in a field called "X" has been developed. This model can serve for any given field based on its broad outline, but here it is designed to encompass that which at the present time probably ought to be called "physical education and sport." Such a designation for the field undoubtedly only represents a "holding action" for the next period immediately ahead. For purposes of this discussion, the following definition of the disciplinary aspect of the field is conceived as follows: "the art and science of human movement as related to the theory and practice of sport, dance, play, and exercise." The position taken here is what it is logical and in the best interest of intramurals to adopt a similar disciplinary definition immediately and to begin the conduct of its professional practice on the basis of the body-of-knowledge available.

This model (see Figure 1) includes the following five subdivisions, all of which are applicable to what is presently called intramural athletics: (1) professional practice; (2) professional preparation; (3) disciplinary research; (4) a theory embodying assumptions and testable hypotheses; and (5) operational philosophy.

Professional practice can be characterized as (1) public; (2) semi-public; and (3) private. Professional preparation should be

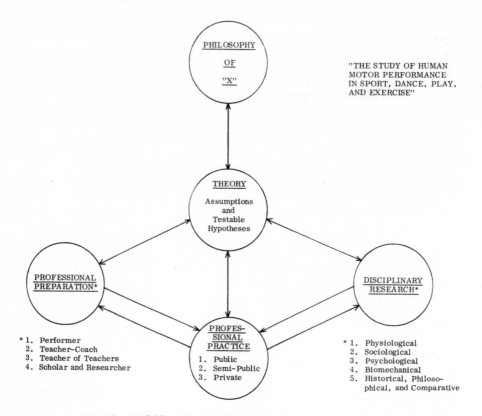

Figure 1. A Model for Optimum Professional Development in a Field Called "X".

designed to educate (1) the performer; (2) the teacher-coach; (3) the teacher of teachers; and (4) the scholar and researcher. Disciplinary research includes (1) the physiological; (2) the sociological; (3) the psychological; (4) the biomechanical; and (5) the historical, philosophical, and international aspects of human motor performance in sport, dance, play, and exercise. The assumptions and testable hypotheses of theory should comprise a "coherent group of general propositions used as principles of explanation for the phenomena" (Random House Dictionary, 1967) exhibited in human motor performance in sport, dance, play, and exercise. Lastly, inclusion of the philosophy of "X" as an overarching entity in the model propounded is based on the belief that the value system of a society will in the final analysis gradually be realized within a developing social system.

Implications from the Proposed Model for Intramurals

Are there certain implications for intramurals that might be drawn from the discussion to this point? It could be argued that intramurals is popular and is making headway--good reasons for "leaving well enough alone." On the other hand, the way that the world is going today, mere maintenance of a "low profile" in a period of turmoil is certainly not sufficient planning for the future. With the current decline in the growth curve of higher education, it is inevitable that all programs will be undergoing continuous evaluation. Those programs on campus which can stand close scrutiny will be supported increasingly, but those programs which can't present evidence that certain educational objectives are being achieved will be challenged. The mere statement that such-and-such a percentage of the student population is taking part, or that so many teams are in various basketball leagues, will no longer suffice. Evidence might also be mustered to claim that a certain percentage of the student population masturbates, but on what basis can the case be made that one activity is better than the other?

The argument is, therefore, that it is high time for intramural directors to become thoroughgoing, highly competent professional people whose professional practice is based on disciplinary investigation resulting in a sound body-of-knowledge. Up to now the approach has been that of the evangelist ever exhorting his "sheep" to greater involvement with the "flock" in an amalgam of physical recreational activities. What does it all add up to? Who knows?

The essence of this position is, then, that intramurals has the wrong name and the wrong emphasis; that the old physical educationa triangle is now terribly dated; and that the intramurals subdivision of the field of physical education is somewhat like "the headless horseman ever ready and willing to ride off in any one of a number of directions at the same time." The recommendation is that intramurals should probably call itself something like "Physical Recreation and Intramural Sport," and the entire area should direct itself immediately to the matter of "hammering out" in joint session an acceptable definition for the disciplinary undergirding of the profession that individual professionals are seeking to practice all across the land at all educational levels. Acceptance of new instructional and physical recreational objectives immediately realizable, as well as long range goals of a more intangible nature, must become a reality soon. A disciplinary-professional approach stressing the art and science of human movement in sport and play would serve notice to the entire field - and to those outside of profession itself - that "second class citizen days" for intramural directors and their associates are on the schedule for relegation to history's trashheap.

Educational institutions can no longer justify the concept that public funds should be used for low-organizational, intramural sports programs that serve as "recess periods" for those men and women students who are presumably not suited or capable of acceptable human motor performance. Educators do have the responsibility to provide instructional and physical recreational programs of the highest calibre for the ninety-five percent of the student population who should have the opportunity to learn about "the art and science of human movement as related to the theory and practice of sport, dance, play, and exercise." Such achievement for all young people - the learning of sound physical recreational skills - is being recommended as a part of "the good life" for all to be used whenever desired in their later lives. Up to now the finest instruction, facilities, and equipment - and the prime time - have been available to the people who needed it least! Obviously the needs and interests of the larger majority must be met. This is not to say that the program for the gifted or accelerated man or woman should be eliminated, but it is obvious that better balance is needed.

A Summary with Recommendations for the Future

Looking to the future, the profession of physical education and sport - a name for the field that is being recommended for the immediate future - should emphasize that human movement undergirds sport, dance, play, and exercise. Understanding the theory and practice of such movement - actually the "non-verbal humanities" - can only come from knowledge, skill, and understanding of a basic disciplinary core. A division or department of physical recreation and intramural sport can relatively soon demonstrate scientifically that active and creative physical recreation should be a part of a way of life during school and college years - and thereafter! Thus, its program can be either instructional or recreational in regard to physical recreation and sport.

A realistic assessment of the current situation will show that there is a need for improved cost-benefit analysis. Those concerned with the administration of these programs should explain clearly to all concerned what the realizable objectives of the program are; how these objectives can be achieved by those taking part; and how the results will be evaluated to demonstrated conclusively that further - and possible increased - financial support is justifiable.

With such an approach it would be possible to respond to the opening question about the possible disciplinary or professional status of intramurals. Physical recreation and intramural sport are important, integral aspects of the profession of physical education and sport. This emerging profession operates in public, semi-public, and private agencies, and it includes performers, teachers and coaches, teachers of teachers, and scholars and researchers. Professional practice is based on a disciplinary core of knowledge developed through scholarly and scientific investigation. The field is developing a theory of human motor performance in sport, dance, play, and exercise based on study of the physiological, sociological, psychological, biomechanical, and historical, philosophical, and international aspects of the phenomena being investigated.

Based on this analysis of the original question, physical recreation and intramural sport programs are potentially integral parts of the educational program offered to all in the department, school, or college of physical education and sport. Whether those concerned with this phase of the program truly achieve such professional status based on a core of sound disciplinary knowledge will depend on many factors in the years immediately ahead. The long range goals would most certainly seem to warrant a "good old college try" on the part of us all.

Part VI
THE MEANING OF PHYSICAL EDUCATION

PHILOSOPHY AND DEFINITION OF PHYSICAL EDUCATION

Physical education could be exemplified by a child bouncing a ball on a school playground, an overweight businessman doing a sit-up, or a high school girl taking part in modern dance.* From an other standpoint physical education could be explained by a halfback scampering for the goal line in the Rose Bowl, boys and girls playing coeducational volleyball in a church recreation room, or a high school boy pinning his opponent in an interscholastic wrestling match. A doctor of philosophy candidate might be analyzing the contents of a Douglas gas bag full of a runner's expired air in a physical education laboratory, or a housewife might be trying out rhythmic exercises-- any of these activities could well be designated as aspects of <u>physical education</u>.

Until most recently the term "physical education" has generally been employed as a broad, inclusive term comprising the fields of physical education, health education, safety education, athletics, re-creation, and dance education. After an extensive study of physical education literature, Cobb (6, p. 6) stated that there were four basic beliefs about the place of physical education in education: (1) there is no place for physical education in education; (2) physical education is for the maintenance of health in order that students may carry on their intellectual work with the least strain; (3) physical education should develop students physically, mentally, and morally (mind-body dichotomy implied); and (4) physical education should contribute to the growth of the individual as an integrated personality by discovering the health, recreation, and personality needs of each student, and helping him to meet those needs through the program.

With beliefs #3 and #4 above a "total fitness" concept is perhaps implied. It is true that modern man has been much more successful than his uncivilized, prehistoric brother in making an adjustment to his evvironment. He has had the experience of his forefathers upon which to base his judgments underlying his actions. His "adjustment" is dependent, however, upon complicated procedures. His teeth de-spend upon the services of competent dentists. His eyes very often must be aided through the competency of highly trained ophthalmolo-gists, optometrists, and opticians. Highly qualified medical doctors

---

* An article prepared for the forthcoming <u>Encyclopedia of Phy-sical Education</u> that will be published by the American Alliance for Health, Physical Education, and Recreation on behalf of the Research Council, Prof. T. K. Cureton, Chief Editor. (To be published also in <u>Proceedings</u> of Singapore Physical Education Seminar, 1975.)

and surgeons preserve the health of his heart, lungs, and other vital organs (even with transplants when necessary). Protruding neck, round shoulders, sagging abdomen, pronated ankles, and weak feet are the results of modern society with its advanced technology. Muscles become weak, and the constant force of gravity upon vertical man exacts a toll. A sedentary man's heart pounds wildly when he runs fifty yards after a departing bus, or to catch a subway train, or even when he climbs a flight of stairs fairly rapidly.

Still further, modern man often has difficulty adjusting his elemental emotions to the habit pattern of "do's and don'ts" that represents today's civilization. When this occurs, and it seems to be happening with increased regularity, man cracks under the strain and is referred to a physician, and perhaps a hospital, as another victim of what has been designated as psychosomatic illness. The field of physical education, and those sub-fields which are related to it within the educational pattern, has an important role to fulfill. It can provide the health knowledge, the physical activity, and the recreational outlets whereby the boy and girl, and young man and woman, will learn how to take care of their bodies, how to use them effectively, and how to provide themselves with healthful recreational activities.

Five Meanings of Physical Education

The ambiguity of the term "physical education" may be clarified by approaching it from another direction. An extension of Frankena's categorization (9, p. 6) transposed from an analysis of the meanings of education indicates that physical education may mean any of five things:

1. The activity of physical educating carried on by teachers, schools, and parents (or by oneself);

2. The process of being physically educated (or learning) which goes on in the pupil or child (or person of any age);

3. The result, actual or intended, of (1) and (2);

4. The discipline or field of enquiry that studies or reflects on (1), (2), and (3) and is taught in departments, schools, and colleges as the theory of physical education;

5. The profession whose members practice (1) above; try to observe (2) taking place; attempt to measure and/or evaluate whether (3) has occurred; and base their professional practice on the body-of-knowledge developed by those undertaking scholarly effort in the discipline (4). (34, p. 8)

A Plethora of Objectives

However the field is designated or defined, there can be no argument with the statement that its leaders have made a great many --often unverifiable--educational claims for it over the years. Notable among these leaders who have defined a variety of objectives, starting in the early 1920's, have been Hetherington (1), Bowen and Mitchell (1), Wood and Cassidy (27), Williams (25), Hughes (26), Nash (18), Sharman (21), Wayman (24), Esslinger (8), Staley (23), McCloy (14), Clark (5), Cobb (6), Lynn (13), Brownell and Hagman (2), Scott (20), Bucher (4), and Oberteuffer (19).

Hess (10) assessed the objectives of American physical education from 1900 to 1957 in the light of certain historical events. These were: (1) the hygiene or health objectives (1900-1919); (2) the socio-educational objectives (1920-1928); (3) the socio-recreative objectives, including the worthy use of leisure (1929-1938); (4) the physical fitness and health objective (1939-1945); and (5) a total fitness objective, including the broader objectives of international understanding (1946 1957).

It appears that the profession should take positive steps to plan for the possible achievement of a significant amount of consensus among the various philosophies of physical education extant in the Western world. This seems especially important, because the field is increasing its efforts to relate to other countries in all parts of the world.

Possible common denominators are as follows:

1. That regular physical education periods should be required for all school children through sixteen years of age (approximately).

2. That a child should develop certain positive attitudes toward his own health in particular and toward community hygiene in general. Basic health knowledge should be taught in the school curriculum.

3. That physical education and interscholastic athletics can make a contribution to the worthy use of leisure.

4. That physical vigor is important for people of all ages.

5. That boys and girls at some stage of their development should have an experience in competitive athletics.

6. That therapeutic exercise should be employed to correct remediable physical defects.

7. That character and/or personality development may be fostered through physical education and athletics. (30)

Historical Background and Perspective

To achieve a better understanding of physical education, it may be possible to gain truer perspective by viewing the question historically. If one of the primary functions of philosophy is to help us decide what a man is or should be, the fivefold classification provided by Morris (16) should be very helpful. Throughout history he explains that man has been defined as follows:

1. Man is a rational animal.

2. Man is a spiritual being. St. Augustine in the 5th century set the stage for a man consisting of mind, body, and soul--a three-dimensional man. With this came a hierarchy of values with the "animal nature" assuming the lowest position. (Excesses in athletics were roundly condemned.)

3. Man is a receptacle of knowledge, a "knowing creature" who should absorb as much knowledge as possible.

4. Man has a mind which can be trained by exercise. It was decided that education should exercise both mind and body. After all, man was an organic unity.

5. Man is a problem-solving organism. Dewey redefined man as a problem-solving animal in the process of evolution on earth. All of his capabilities had come, however, from his developing capacity to solve the problems which confronted him. Thus, man tried to make sense out of his experience, and he reconstructed it to improve future experience. Physical education's task within this pattern is to teach man to move efficiently and with meaning and purpose within the context of man's socialization in an evolving world.

Those who have written about history, including education, appear to have slighted "physical culture" through bias. Woody (28) tells us that "lip-service has been paid increasingly to the dictum 'a sound mind in a sound body,' ever since western Europe began to revive the educational concepts of the Graeco-Roman world," but that "there is still a lack of balance between physical and mental culture."

Primitive Physical Education

It is true that physical activity has been a basic part of the fundamental pattern of living of every creature of any type that has ever lived on earth. For this reason the condition of his body must have always been of concern to him. In primitive society there appears to have been very little organized, purposive instruction in physical education, although early man knew that a certain type of fitness was necessary for survival. The usual activities of labor, searching for food, dancing, and games were essential to the development of superior bodies. With physical efficiency as a basic survival need, man's muscles, including his heart, had to be strong; his vision had to be keen; and he had to be able to run fast and to lift heavy loads.

Even if it were an objective, it would not have been possible to separate completely the physical and mental education of primitive youth. The boy underwent an informal apprenticeship which prepared him for life's various physical duties. A great deal of learning occurred through trial and error and through imitation. Tradition and custom were highly regarded, and the importance of precept and proper example were important aspects of both physical and mental culture.

Testing in early societies was carried out through various initiatory ceremonies designed to give the young man (and occasionally the young woman) the opportunity to test himself in the presence of his peers and his elders. Although most of the education was informal, the educational pattern followed the same traditions and customs from generation to generation. The practical aspects of life were learned by doing them repeatedly, and strict discipline was often employed if the child was lazy or recalcitrant.

There was, of course, a great deal of ignorance about sound health practices. Vigorous exercise undoubtedly did much to help early man remain healthy. The health care in infancy and in early youth was probably even more deficient typically than health practices followed by adults in the society.

In preliterate societies, there does not appear to have been as sharp a division between work and play (or labor and leisure) as is found later in civilized societies. Children had many play activities, because they weren't ready for the serious business of living. Their parents had very little leisure in a subsistence economy.

Persistent Forces

There were at least four significant social forces that have influenced the field during the various periods of history. (3, 32)

1. The influence of politics, or the type of political state. Throughout history the kind and amount of education has varied depending upon whether a particular country was a monarchy, an aristocratic oligarchy, or a type of democracy. A philosophically

progressivistic educational approach, and this applied to the field of school health, physical education, and recreation (including athletics), can flourish only in a type of democratic society. Conversely, a philosophically essentialistic or traditionalistic type of education, with its very definite implications for this field, may be promoted successfully in any of the three types of political system.

2. The influence of patriotism or nationalism on physical education throughout history is obvious. If a strong state is desired, the need for a strong, healthy people is paramount. There have been many examples of this type of influence as far back as the Medes and Spartans, and as recently as some twentieth century European and Asian powers.

3. The influence of economics has been most significant in that throughout history education has prospered when there was a surplus economy, and declined when the economic structure weakened. Educational aims have tended to vary depending upon how people made their money and created such surplus economies. Advancing industrial civilization has brought uneven distribution of wealth, which meant educational advantages of a superior quality to some. Education "of the physical" can be promoted under any type of economic system. In largely agrarian societies much physical fitness can be gained through manual labor. In industrial societies some means has to be developed whereby all will maintain a minimum level of physical fitness and health. The more individual freedom is encouraged in a society, the more difficult a government will find it to demand that all citizens be physically fit.

4. The influence of organized religion on education throughout history has been very strong, but there is evidence that the power of the church over the individual is continuing to decline in the twentieth century. In the Western world the Christian religion sould be recognized for the promulgation of principles in which man was considered valuable as an individual. Today a society needs to decide to what extent it can, or should, inculcate moral and/or religious values in its public schools.

Nine more persistent historical problems or social forces will be mentioned and described extremely briefly. These will be viewed as professional "problems" (a problem used in this sense, according to its Greek derivation, would be "something thrown forward" for man to understand or resolve).

5. Values (aims and objectives). Throughout history there have been innumerable statements of educational aims, and almost invariably there was a direct relationship with a hierarchy of educational values present in the society under consideration. Physical

education and athletics has been viewed as curricular, co-curricular, or extracurricular.

6. The healthy body. A study of past civilizations indicates that the states of war or peace, as social influences, have had a direct bearing on the emphases placed on personal and/or community health.

7. The use of leisure. This persistent problem has a relationship to the influence of economics on a society. Both education and recreation prospered in times past when there was a surplus economy. Many civilized nations have reached the time when education for the worthy use of leisure warrants serious consideration.

8. The role of administration (management). Social organizations, of one type of another, are inextricably related to man's history as a human and social animal. Superior-subordinate relationships evolved according to the very nature of things.

9. Professional preparation. Professional preparation of teachers to any considerable extent began in the late nineteenth century. Starting with the normal school, this organization has progressed in the twentieth century to college and/or university status. Throughout the world, generally speaking, professional preparation for physical education is included at the normal and/or technical school level. University recognition has been achieved at a relatively few institutions in England, Japan, Germany, and, to a considerable extent, in the United States and Canada.

10. Methods of instruction. The educational curriculum has been influenced strongly by a variety of political, economic, philosophic, religious, and scientific factors. A primary task is to determine which subjects should be included because of the recurring interest that has been shown in them.

11. Physical education and recreation for women. Throughout history women's physical education has been hampered not only by the concept of the place of physical education in a particular society, but also by the place that women themselves held in most societies. One of the significant social trends of the twentieth century has been women's emancipation. Many people feel that men's and women's physical education programs should more nearly approximate each other in scope and intensity.

12. Dance in physical education and recreation. In all ages people have danced for personal pleasure, for religious purposes, for expression of the gamut of emotions, and for the pleasure of others. An analysis of the dance forms of a civilization can tell a qualified observer much about the total life therein. The twentieth

century has witnessed a truly remarkable development in the dance, since the body is being gradually rediscovered as a means of communication through the dance medium. As both an art and as a social function, dance will probably always be with us, and will reflect the dominant influence of the age in which it is taking place.

13. The concept of progress. A criterion must be considered by which progress may be judged. It is true that man has made progress in adaptability and can cope with a variety of environments. Education has been based largely on the transmission of the cultural heritage. Following a traditional educational pattern has typically prevented the school from becoming an agent of social reconstruction.

Historical Philosophical Foundations

Philosophy had its beginning in Greece over 2,500 years ago where the word originally meant knowledge or love of wisdom. The main method used by philosophers then was speculation, and practical knowledge gained through experience and observation was differentiated from speculative knowledge.

Idealism, which may be traced through Plato, the Hebrew-Christian tradition in religion, Descartes, Spinoza, Leibniz, Berkeley, Kant, and Hegel, indicates that man is a real, existent being with a soul; that in each man is a spirit or mind which is basically real--and that the essence of the entire universe is in some way mind or spirit; and that a man is a son of God, who was the Creator of the universe. Education should aid the child to adjust to the basic realities (the spiritual ideals of truth, goodness, and beauty) that the history of the race has furnished us.

The idealist is extremely interested in individual personality development. He believes in education "of the physical" and yet he believes in education "through the physical" as well. He sees physical education as important, but essentially it must be on one of the lower rungs of the educational ladder. He believes that desirable objectives for physical education would include the development of responsible citizenship and group participation. In competitive athletics the transfer of training theory is in operation working toward the development of personality traits.

Realism, which began with Aristotle and developed through the thought of St. Thomas Aquinas, Descartes, Comenius, Spinoza, Locke, Kane, Herbart, James, and the various trends of the twentieth century, implies that man lives in a world which is undoubtedly real; that things actually happen exactly the way man experiences them.

Realistic philosophy holds that the aim of education should be to acquire verified knowledge about the environment. It recognizes the value of content, as well as the activities involved in learning. Such knowledge acquisition will help man to adjust to his environment.

The realist believes typically that education "of the physical" should have primary emphasis. Development of the maximum physical vigor has priority over the recreational aspects of physical education. The realist could well recommend that all students in public schools should have a daily period designed to strengthen their muscles and develop their bodily coordination. Under a philosophy of realism, "there would be continuing enlargement of systematic teaching which would lead to measurable results." (7, pp. 32-33) Physical education must yield precedence to intellectual education. The realist gives qualified approval to interscholastic athletics; they can help youth to learn sportsmanship and desirable social conduct (if properly conducted). But all of these aspects of the program, with the exception of physical training for the naturalistic realist, are definitely extracurricular.

Pragmatism may be said to have begun with Heraclitus, gathered momentum with Francis Bacon and John Locke, gained strangth through the many early scientists of the sixteenth and seventeenth centuries, and blossomed into fruition through Comte, Peirce, James, and Dewey. Its position is (1) that the world is constantly undergoing change; (2) that an idea is not true until it has been tested through experience; (3) that we can only learn what an idea really means by putting it into practice; and (5) that we can't really find out what the basic nature of the universe is.

The experimentalist (pragmatic naturalist) is much more interested in promoting the concept of total fitness rather than physical fitness alone. He believes that so-called physical education can and should be an integral part of the curriculum. Students should have the opportunity to select a wide variety of useful activities, many of which should help to develop what Dewey called "social intelligence." The activities offered should bring natural impulses into play. Physical education classes and intramural sports are more important to the large majority of students than interscholastic or intercollegiate athletics and deserve priority if conflict arises over budgetary allotment, available staff, and use of facilities. Full support can be given to team experiences in athletics; they can be vital educational experiences in both cooperation and competition if properly conducted.

These traditional positions have been under sharp attack in this century. Prior to World War I, idealism had lost some of the prestige that it had enjoyed in the late 1800's. The defense of scientific investigation by Spencer and Darwin was a tremendously powerful influence. Pragmatism continued to be influential, especially in the

United States, and has influenced all aspects of education quite considerably. It gathers much strength from underlying naturalism and from the overwhelming influence of scientific inquiry.

Philosophical analysis has been a most interesting and important development in this century, and in the English-speaking world it has left an indelible mark on philosophy already. In the past few years physical education and sport philosophers have been experimenting with certain of the techniques for language analysis that have been made available. Further, existentialism, as a "flavoring influence" rather than full-blown philosophy, has emerged as a significant force both in Europe and on the North American continent as well. This approach began as a revolt against Hegelian idealism, and developed to the position (Sartrean) which affirmed that man's task was to give meaning and direction to his world. The existentially oriented person recognizes the importance of the child's socialization as over against his intellectual development. Education's goal should be to awaken the child's awareness of himself as a "single subjectivity," and with this approach education can become an "act of discovery." In physical education and sport, therefore, the goal should be total fitness, not just so-called physical fitness. The individual should choose his sports and physical activities based on self-evaluation of his knowledge, skills, and attitudes. It is especially important further that the individual's authenticity be preserved in both individual and team athletic encounters.

The Reason for Sport and Physical Education Philosophy

No matter where you may travel on the North American continent, teachers and parents, both individually and collectively, often express sharply divided opinions as to what should be included in the curriculum. Health, physical education, and recreation (including compeittive athletics) is right in the middle of this controversy. How shall children be educated for the prevailing social conditions? Shall education--and hence physical education--be "progressive," "somewhat progressive," or should it deal exclusively with the "essential studies" that are time-proven? Thus, physical education and sport may be viewed as "curricular," "co-curricular," or "extracurricular." A possible desirable plan is to work for an acceptable consensus that brings common sense and tradition into alignment with the results of available scientific knowledge. Then the philosophic process could be employed by philosophers and those functioning within subdivisions of this discipline. In the final analysis the people will make what they feel to be the necessary decisions within a democratic society. These judgments will be based on the prevailing system of values and norms.

A Suggested Program for Health, Physical Education, and
Recreation in Junior and Senior High Schools

If a person were to examine and/or evaluate the physical education and athletics program of a junior or senior high school, he might
consider asking questions about the following categories or subdivisions:

(1) Aims and Objectives

Physical education--a way of education through vigorous,
muscular activities selected with concern for the student's growth and
development pattern.

Health education--includes experiences which contribute to
student's health knowledge, habits, and attitudes.

Recreation--all those activities students engage in for enjoyment during their leisure; the activities should be reasonably consistent with socially accepted values.

(2) The Medical Examination

Assignment for physical education should be made on the
basis of a medical examination initially.

(3) The Classification of Students

This serves individual needs; promotes fair competition between individuals and groups; facilitates instruction; assembles students of like interests as well as like abilities; and insures program
continuity from year to year.

(4) The Individual (Therapeutic) Program

Those with remediable physical defects should receive
help in improving their condition if possible; some form of interesting
modified sport activity should be provided where possible.

(5) Health Instruction

Aside from specific classes designed for health instruction,
indirect instruction through example and practice can do much to influence sound health practices.

(6) The Conditioning Program

It a student has not met the minimum standards of the physical education classification test, the general level of physical conditioning should be raised and maintained.

(7) The Sports Instructional Program

Students who pass the various aspects of a classification test should be encouraged to elect some sports or physical recreational activity (of both an indoor and outdoor nature) in which they will receive instruction within the physical education and/or intramurals department.

(8) The Elective Program

Election of course experiences should in all probability be introduced at some point in the latter half of the high school years in keeping with the findings of earlier classification tests; there should be definite instruction, supervision, and guidance if credit is to be granted for courses taken on an elective basis.

(9) Physical Recreation and Intramurals

The assumption here is that every student should have an opportunity to take part in competitive sport and physical recreation on a voluntary basis.

(10) Interscholastic Athletics

As many young men and women as possible should be included in this phase of the program; participation gives an opportunity for "physical, mental, and social" development; skilled coaches with a sound educational background are absolutely necessary.

(11) Evaluation and Measurement

Evaluation based on personal improvement primarily is highly important. Such measurement should be closely related to stated aims and objectives.

Possible Disciplinary Status for Physical Education

Physical educators have realized the need for development of a "body-of-knowledge" through a greatly expanded program of scholarly and research endeavor in a variety of related disciplines. (33) Some of the field's scientists had realized this earlier, especially in the physiological area and certain aspects of psychology. Relationships are gradually being strengthened with such fields as anatomy, sociology, history, philosophy, comparative and international education, anthropology, and organizational theory within the behavioral science and educational administration.

The definition of the field as a discipline, as part of an effort to provide a body-of-knowledge upon which the profession may practice, may well assist man quite substantially to realize a "wondrous future" both on this planet and in space. The kinesiologists, exercise physiologists, psychologists, and sociologists within physical education should be able to discover how man moves, what happens to him when he moves in certain ways, and how this influences his social relations, but it will be the province largely of those interested in the historical, philosophical, and comparative aspects of physical education and athletics to assist the profession to "contemplate the trajectory" of this field in the Space Age.

As the body-of-knowledge within physical education increases, and inventories of scientific findings from the various related disciplines improve in both quantity and quality, it will become increasingly possible to verify whether a planned program of physical education does actually result in the achievement of the many objectives which have been claimed over the years. Maybe then the field will be able to achieve consensus on certain "common denominators" in the "education of an amphibian" (12) or a "naked ape" (17). What seems to be really important in the classification of a "relatively hairless ape," in addition to the obviously still prevailing legacy from ancestors, is that man has now become almost non-apelike. Still further, there remains ample opportunity for all sorts of differential development in the eons which lie ahead. (22) Physical education may eventually be called <u>human movement</u>, human motor performance, kinesiology, anthropokineticology, homokinetics, sport, or what have you. The important point is that the field has a significant role to play in man's education and future development.

References

1. Bowen, W. P. and Mitchell, E. D. <u>The Theory of Organized Play</u>. New York: A. S. Barnes and Co., 1923.

2. Brownell, Clifford L. and Hagman, E. P. <u>Physical Education --Foundations and Principles</u>. New York: McGraw-Hill Book Co., Inc., 1951.

3. Brubacher, John S. <u>A History of the Problems of Education</u>. Second edition. New York: McGraw-Hill Book Co., 1966.

4. Bucher, Charles A. Foundations of Physical Education.
    St. Louis: The C. V. Mosby Company, 1952.

5. Clark, Margaret C., "A Philosophical Interpretation of a Program of Physical Education in a State Teachers College."
    Ph.D. dissertation, New York University, 1943.

6. Cobb, Louise S., "A Study of the Functions of Physical Education in Higher Education." Ph.D. dissertation, Teachers
    College, Columbia University, 1943.

7. Davis, E. C. and Miller, D. M. The Philosophic Process in
    Physical Education. Second edition. Philadelphia: Lea
    & Febiger, 1966.

8. Esslinger, A. A., "A Philosophical Study of Principles for
    Selecting Activities in Physical Education." Ph.D.
    dissertation, State University of Iowa, 1938.

9. Frankena, William K. Three Historical Philosophies of Education. Chicago: Scott, Foresman and Company, 1965.

10. Hess, Ford A., "American Objectives of Physical Education
    from 1900-1957 Assessed in the Light of Certain Historical Events." Ed.D. dissertation, New York University, 1959.

11. Hetherington, Clark. School Program in Physical Education.
    New York: Harcourt, Brace & World, Inc., 1922.

12. Huxley, Aldous. Tomorrow and Tomorrow and Tomorrow.
    New York: The New American Library of World Literature, Inc., 1964.

13. Lynn, Minnie L., "Major Emphases of Physical Education in
    the United States." Ph.D. dissertation, University
    of Pittsburgh, 1944.

14. McCloy, C. H. Philosophical Bases for Physical Education.
    New York: Appleton-Century-Crofts, Inc., 1940.

15. Morris, Desmond. The Naked Ape. New York: McGraw-Hill
    Book Company, 1967.

16. Morris, Van Cleve. Existentialism in Education. New York:
    Harper & Row, 1966.

17. _____, "Physical Education and the Philosophy of Education," JOHPER, 27(3):21-22, 30-31, March, 1956.

18. Nash, Jay B. (editor). Mind-Body Relationships (Vol. I). New York: A. S. Barnes and Co., Inc., 1931.

19. Oberteuffer, Delbert. Physical Education. New York: Harper & Row, 1951. (The Second edition in 1962 was in collaboration with Celeste Ulrich.)

20. Scott, Harry A. Competitive Sports in Schools and Colleges. New York: Harper & Row, 1951.

21. Sharman, Jackson R. Modern Principles of Physical Education. New York: A. S. Barnes and Co., Inc., 1937.

22. Simpson, George Gaylord, "What Is Man?", The New York Times Book Review, February 11, 1968.

23. Staley, Seward C. Sports Education. New York: A. S. Barnes and Co., Inc., 1939.

24. Wayman, Agnes R. A Modern Philosophy of Education. Philadelphia: W. B. Saunders Co., 1938.

25. Williams, Jesse F. The Principles of Physical Education. Philadelphia: W. B. Saunders Company, 1927.

26. _____ and Hughes, W. L. Athletics in Education. Philadelphia: W. B. Saunders Company, 1930.

27. Wood, Thomas D. and Cassidy, R. The New Physical Education. New York: The Macmillan Company, 1927.

28. Woody, Thomas. Life and Education in Early Societies. New York: The Macmillan Company, 1949.

29. Zeigler, Earle F. Administration of Physical Education and Athletics. Englewood Cliffs, N. J.: Prentice-Hall, Inc., 1959.

30. _____, "The Need for Consensus and Research," The Physical Educator, 24(3):107-109, 1967.

31. _____. Philosophical Foundations for Physical, Health, and Recreation Education. Englewood Cliffs, N. J.: Prentice-Hall, Inc., 1964.

32. _____. Problems in the History and Philosophy of Physical Education and Sport. Englewood Cliffs, N. J.: Prentice-Hall, Inc., 1968.

33. _____ and McCristal, King J., "A History of the Big Ten Body-of-Knowledge Project in Physical Education," Quest, IX:79-84, December, 1967.

34. _____ and VanderZwaag, Harold J. Physical Education: Progressivism or Essentialism? (Second edition). Champaign, Ill.: Stipes Publishing Company, 1968.

AN ANALYSIS OF THE CLAIM THAT "PHYSICAL EDUCATION" HAS BECOME A "FAMILY RESEMBLANCE" TERM

This investigation was designed to discover the different meanings – not objectives or aims – that are currently being applied to the term "physical education" in the English language.* It was based generally on Wittgenstein's idea that a "family resemblance" term is radically different than a word or term which may be said to have an essential definition. The traditional way of analyzing a term has been to attempt to find those conditions or characteristics which apply to any given term in all cases. This new idea is based on the assumption that there are some words or terms for which there are no definite lists or sets of characteristics, even though the term may be relatively correctly employed in a number of different circumstances. In other words, two persons using this term – "physical education" – may have similar but fundamentally different concepts in mind, but both uses do have a "family resemblance" inasmuch as there is some overlapping of characteristics. And thereby hangs the tale of this presentation . . .

Such an approach to doing philosophy is part of a twentieth century development that has become known as "philosophical analysis." In fact, White has said that this is the "Age of Analysis" for philosophy (1955), and Weitz has written about "the analytic tradition" in twentieth century philosophy (1966). This is not meant to imply that there is no longer debate about the exact nature of philosophy – far from it. Many seem to worry about the justification for philosophy since scientific method has been used to demonstrate that true knowledge can only come through controlled experimentation. If science is becoming the "be all and end all" of scholarly endeavor, one might well ask what is the justification for an area of study treating such matters as values, truths, ethics, and related matters?

In a brief effort to place this present study in perspective, it should be recalled that there have been three developments in this century that have sought to provide answers to this quite crucial question: (1) logical atomism; (2) logical positivism; and (3) ordinary language philosophy. The underlying tenet behind these approaches was that philosophy's function is analysis, but each one tended to view

---

* A paper presented to the First Canadian Congress for the Multi-Disciplinary Study of Sport and Physical Activity, Montreal, Canada, October 14, 1973. (To be published in the Proceedings of a Seminar on Concepts in Physical Education held at the Wingate Institute of Physical Education in the spring of 1974.)

analysis somewhat differently. There was general agreement, however, that philosophy was to be approached through the medium of so-called language analysis to a greater or lesser extent (Zeigler, 1968, pp. 39-44).

Logical atomism involved a new approach to logic as devised by Bertrand Russell (1872-1970) and Alfred North Whitehead (1861-1947) called mathematical logic. It had been thought that Aristotle had said the last word on this subject, but these two great philosophers developed a logic that was much broader in scope because of its inclusion of propositions rather than with classes only. This more inclusive logical system involved the recommended greater relationship of mathematics to logic--ideas which were to a considerable degree brought to Russell's attention by the work of Peano whom he met at the International Congress of Philosophy in Paris in July of 1900 (Russell, 1968, p. 191).

Russell's next step was to show that a language like English has essentially the same structure as mathematics. Because the language was not exact enough, however, it was thought that mathematical logic would help man explain the components of language through sentences designed to offer "world facts." Carried through to its presumably logical conclusion, the philosopher would then be in a position tion to find out everything about the structure of the world by using this type of philosophical analysis to rearrange an ambiguous language so that the newly arranged, logical sentences would become crystal clear. This approach, which flourished for twenty years or more in some quarters, was thought to offer a new metaphysical system, but it was eventually superseded by logical positivism which carried mathematical logic a step further.

In the 1920's a group subsequently known as the Vienna Circle came to believe that it was not possible for logical atomism to provide the world with a system of metaphysics. Their answer was logical positivism which presented philosophy as an activity--not as theories about the universe. They felt that philosophy s task was to analyze and explain what statements meant. Some statements would be able to "withstand being subjected" to the verifiability principle. This means that a sentence might be factually significant to a given person, if he understands those observations which would enable him to accept or reject the proposition therein contained. However, a logically valid, factual sentence must be "confirmable" or "disconfirmable" if one really wishes to say that "he knows what he is talking about." A statement's meaning is inextricably involved with the verification method (Feigl, 1949, p. 9 et ff.).

Thus, some sentences may be significant factually; others are not directly applicable to this world, although they appear to be analytically true; and a third group are nonsensical or nonsignificant.

It can readily be seen how devastating such an approach to philosophical activity would be to traditional philosophical approaches. The usual philosophical statement of the past was definitely not empirically verifiable, which means--at least in the eyes of those employing this new approach--that the older efforts were typically mere conjecture and not really important to man! Philosophy was thereby awarded a new role--analysis of ordinary language statements into logical, consistent form. As a result it could be told quite quickly whether a problematical question could be answered either through mathematical reasoning or scientific investigation. The philosopher does not therefore provide the answers; he <u>analyzes</u> the questions to see what they mean.

<u>Ordinary language philosophy</u> is the third approach to philosophy which involves a type of language analysis - but in a slightly different way. It was started in the 1930's by Ludwig Wittgenstein (? -1952) who has earlier been one of the originators and developers of logical atomism. In the period between the 1930's and 1952 (when Wittgenstein died), he decided that it would not be possible to devise a language so perfect that the world would be reflected accurately. Accordingly, he came to believe that much of the confusion and disagreement over philosophy emanated from misuse of language in various ways. With this approach the task of the philosopher was not to transpose the problems of philosophy into certain language terms; rather, it was to decide what the basic words and terms were and then to use them correctly and clearly so that all might understand. This is, of course, closer to semantics, the science of meanings. Wittgenstein was more anxious to learn how the term was used than he was to discover how people defined it. With such an approach it may be possible for philosophy to solve some problems through clarification of the meaning of certain terms which have been used synonymously (albeit often incorrectly). In this way man might gradually achieve certain knowledge, at least about man's reaction to the world and how he describes it, through the medium of ordinary language philosophy--the newest of the three types of philosophical analysis (sometimes called "philosophy of language").

In concluding this introductory section, it must be granted that analytic philosophy has become most influential in the English-speaking world. Where these many achievements will lead philosophy - and man! - remains open to question. Obviously, it is now clear that the philosopher can use any language that he wishes, but he is obligagated to make very clear the language rules that he is employing (Carnap's "principle of tolerance"). Further, the newer mathematical logic with its scientific inference offers infinitely greater possibility of relating logic more completely to the technology of the computer, not to mention the development of an ideal language for philosophical endeavor based on synthetic statements (symbolic or mathematical logic). As Kaplan indicates, this may provide man with a "rational reconstruction of the language of science," but where will he then find a philosophy to live by (1961, p. 83)?

Related Literature and Background

To return directly to the topic at hand--whether "physical education" has become a "family resemblance" term--the writer is quick to admit that this problem had never occurred to him in exactly this way until relatively recently. For some thirty years the field of physical education has been stumbling along in what might be called, not too gently, "philosophical confusion." This investigator, in the 1940's and early 1950's, was as fully imbued and confused by the so-called "objectives of physical education" propounded through the normative philosophizing of so many of the strong, dedicated leaders of the field between the years from 1920 to 1950.

Because of a highly important experience in a doctoral program at Yale with the eminent historian and philosopher of education, John S. Brubacher, the writer began to understand in the mid-1950's the implications for physical education that the various "schools" of educational philosophy seemed to possess. At this point he and a few others began the slow and tedious "conversion" of this type of philosophizing to physical education--a move which this writer does not regret even though at that very time many within the field of educational philosophy began to feel the influence of the movement toward analytic philosophy that was developing so strongly on this continent. In addition, existential philosophy of varying types--atheistic, agnostic, Christian--had been "transported" in various ways from the European continent, and it too was having a considerable influence (in quite sharp contrast to philosophical analysis).

It was roughly in the mid-1960's that existential philosophy was called to the attention of the field of physical education, and this emphasis is certainly still evident today. (It should be pointed out in passing that some of Metheny's "theory of physical education approach" and the "movement" emphasis must have undoubtedly reflected the emphases toward philosophical analysis that had taken place in philosophy and which was changing the educational philosophy "scene" as well.)

In the late 1960's and early 1970's, this writer was privileged to serve as thesis committee chairman for four men and women specializing in the philosophy of sport and physical education, all of whom used a different variation of "philosophical analysis" in an attempt to answer the requirements of their main problems and sub-problems. Each of these investigations - in one way or another - was concerned with the meaning of some aspect of the term "physical education." The first was an attempt by the late Peter Spencer-Kraus to consider the possibility of the application of Austin's "linguistic phenomenology" to sport and physical education (1970). Spencer-Kraus found "that many of the problems recurring in that area [the philosophy of physical education and sport literature] were steeped in a confusion resulting directly from the equivocal use of the terms and idioms employed." He concluded that there was "a great need for consensus" in the matter of precise definitions of terms employed in sport and physical education, and he believed strongly that "the application of the Austinian technique might greatly improve the chances of arriving at that consensus" (pp. 56-57).

George Patrick's study was the second of the four projects, and it was entitled "Verifiability (Meaningfulness) of Selected Physical Education Objectives." An _analytic_ description in terms of form and function of the stated objectives was made, and the _normative_ part of the study was based on the descriptive analysis of the objectives and the kind of knowledge provided by logic, ethics, philosophy, and philosophy of education. Positivism's "principle of verifiability" was subdivided into two forms: _weak_ or logical possibility of confirmation, and _strong_ or operationally testable. Objective statements were viewed as informative, expressive, directive, and performative. Three functions of objectives were stated (1) as a slogan, (2) as a guide to the educative process, and (3) as a test. It was found that objectives functioning as slogans were likely to be meaningless or verifiable in the second degree (weak); that objectives functioning as guides using informative-directive language were verifiable in the first or second degree; and that objectives functioning as a test must use the informative-directive mode of language before they could be considered verifiable in the first degree. Thus, "if physical educators wish to act responsibly, they should be able to state that for which they are accountable" (Patrick, 1971, p. 94).

The third investigation that was analytic in nature was carried out by Kathleen Pearson. It related to so-called conceptual analysis within what has more recently been called "philosophy of language" by many. She examined (1) the structure of the multi-concept "integration-segregation" as it pertained to male and female participants in physical education classes, and (2) the functional aspects of this multi-concept in the intentional, purposive, and responsible actions of persons engaged in the professional endeavor called physical education (Pearson, 1971, p. 2). After extracting the various meanings attached to the concept and describing their extensional features in the "structural analysis" phase, Pearson proceeded to a "functional analyais" stage in which she delineated the reasons set forth for advocating the various "structures" or positions relative to the usage of the concept by writers in the available literature. She considered the assumptions implicit within each of the reasons and the empirical evidence available to support or cast doubt on the validity of the hypotheses underlying these reasons. Lastly, the question was asked,

"How might one be guided in making responsible decisions concerning the multi-concept in question?"

Pearson concluded specifically that physical educators attach many and varied meanings to the word "coeducation"; that the reasons set forth for this practice indicate a wide variety of objectives; that these claims or objectives have not been subjected to empirical research techniques; and that many contemporary physical educators still hold the dubious belief that jumping activities for girls and women cause injury to the pelvic organs. Generally speaking, she concluded that "the field is almost barren of empirical research to support or cast doubt on the advisability of integration-segregation of male and female participants in physical education classes" (pp. 213-214).

The final of the four thesis investigations was Robert Osterhoudt's encyclopedic study entitled "A Descriptive Analysis of Research Concerning the Philosophy of Physical Education and Sport" (1971). Building upon - and, in certain instances, subtracting from - a selected bibliography on sport and physical education developed by this writer, Osterhoudt's efforts resulted in an organization of the body-of-knowledge in this area, and it also offered "a reference for the classification and treatment of future works" (p. 227). He analyzed descriptively the selected literature of the twentieth century and, very importantly, reviewed major taxonomies for research prior to the development of a specific one for this particular investigation. The broad outline of this taxonomy had been suggested earlier in a paper by Pearson entitled "Inquiry Into Inquiry" (unpublished) that had been investigated as a special project while studying with the writer at Illinois (Urbana). Once again, Osterhoudt built most effectively on this taxonomy when his detailed study of the literature warranted the institution of certain modifications. Basically, the literature was divided into three categories as follows: (1) construct analysis; (2) system analysis; and (3) concept analysis. Interestingly enough - and this finding of Osterhoudt points up the significance of this present paper inquiring into "family resemblance" status for the term "physical education," he found one hundred and thirty-eight (138) studies which he was able to classify as "the analysis of concept construction!" In his "Discussion" section Osterhoudt pointed out gently that "a more abiding consultation with the mother discipline, with philosophy proper, is required, so as to avoid the dogmatic espousals, with which the philosophy of physical education and sport has all too long been preoccupied" (p. 235).

Methodology and Findings

The various aspects of the "Age of Analysis" are undoubtedly leaving their marks on all of us to a greater or lesser extent. (The reader is referred to the excellent publications embodying a type of conceptual analysis which were authored by Harold VanderZwaag and Daryl Siedentop in 1972.) This writer had long been concerned with the multitude of objectives propounded by the normative physical education philosophers of yesteryear, but it was only in the late 1960's that he became truly familiar with the efforts of William K. Frankena in the area of educational philosophy. In this Michigan philosopher's work entitled <u>Three Historical Philosophies of Education</u> (1965, p. 6), he explained that the term "education" was indeed ambiguous inasmuch as it could mean "any one of four things" as follows:

(1) the <u>activity</u> of <u>educating</u> carried on by teachers, schools, and parents (or by oneself);

(2) the <u>process of being educated</u> (or learning) which goes on in the pupil or child;

(3) the <u>result</u>, actual or intended, of (1) and (2);

(4) the <u>discipline</u> or field of enquiry that studies on or reflects on (1), (2), and (3) and is taught in schools of education.

Somehow this type of analysis of the term "education" had simply never occurred to the writer before and it didn't seem very important at the time. After giving the matter some thought, however, the matter became more intriguing especially when it became apparant that there might indeed be a <u>fifth</u> meaning that had been somehow overlooked. This was envisioned as the profession of education. Still further, it soon became evident further that a similar approach could be employed with the term "physical education," no matter whether the term was still considered acceptable by the intelligentsia of the field.

Correspondence was initiated with Professor Frankena and, on May 21, 1968, he stated in a letter that:

. . . you suggest that there is a fifth sense of 'education' in which it refers to a 'profession.' This did not occur to me. I guess I don't much use 'education' that way. But I suppose it does get used in that way, and that one can add this fifth definition, as you do.

Well, the reader can appreciate that at this point the writer was at least "partially hooked" by virtue of his great discovery that had been conceded by the Chairman of the Department of Philosophy at The University of Michigan!

The next step, of course, was to adapt this approach to the definition of the term "physical education," and in the process - Eureka - somehow a <u>sixth</u> meaning of the term "physical education" emerged. In addition to the basic four meanings outlined by

Frankena, the fifth one "discovered" by Zeigler, it became quite obvious that "physical education" also meant the subject-matter (e.g., tennis, or some other physical involvement that was considered to be part of the physical education program). Now what to do - write Professor Frankena again? The decision - absolutely not!

The next problem faced by the writer was how to announce this great discovery to the unsuspecting world of physical education. One could just feel the thrill that would run through the audience when these six distinctions or definitions were offered to the assembled multitude.

Such an occasion presented itself quite soon in a formal paper prepared for presentation at the First Canadian Symposium on the History of Sport and Physical Education held at the University of Alberta in Edmonton on May 13, 1970 (where this investigator was given the opportunity to make the opening presentation). At the beginning of the paper it was stated, "As might be expected, there is great ambiguity to the term "physical education." To the present it has been possible to identify some six different meanings as follows:

1. The subject-matter, or a part of it (e.g., tennis, or some other sport or active game; some type of physical activity involving exercise such as jogging or push-ups; a type of dance movement or activity; movement with purpose relating to these three types of activities);
2. The activity of physical education carried on by teachers, schools, parents, or even by oneself;
3. The process of being physical educated (or learning) which goes on in the pupil or child (or person of any age);
4. The result, actual or intended, of (2) and (3) taking place through the employment of that which comprises (1);
5. The discipline, or field of enquiry, in which people study and reflect on all aspects of (1), (2), (3), and (4) above; that which is taught (the "body-of-knowledge") in departments, schools, and colleges of physical education; and
6. The profession whose members employ (1) above; practice it (2); try to observe (3) taking place; attempt to measure or evaluate whether (4) has taken place; and base their professional practice on the body-of-knowledge developed by those undertaking scholarly and research effort in the discipline (5).

(Adapted from W. K. Frankena, 1965, p. 6, and the reader should see also Zeigler and VanderZwaag, 1968, p. 8.)

The writer can still hear that hall echoing with thunderous applause on that important morning. Seriously, and to be quite truthful, no one has ever mentioned that bit of language analysis to its "perpetrator since that fateful day!" This very fact would seem to be reasonable evidence that this type of philosophical analysis has in no sense yet "arrived" in the field of physical education despite the relative importance which the present investigator feels should be accorded to such inquiry now and in the future.

One further development must be reported at this time, and it revolved around the writer's subsequent realization that "physical education" might indeed be a "family resemblance" term à la Wittgenstein. This was an idea propounded as a theory of meaning for certain general terms such as "see," "know," "reason," and "free." Such general terms have been used in many seemingly different ways - that is, the conditions for the accurate use of the word vary in different circumstances. (This was, of course, basically at variance with the traditional method of analyzing a term in which it was necessary to discover the specific conditions or characteristics which appeared in all cases in which the term was employed. It was thus possible to determine what might be considered to be the "essential definition" of that term under discussion.)

With the "family resemblance approach" the idea of determining requisite properties for employment in the definition of a specific term is discarded. This is done because it has been shown that the term may be employed correctly in different situations even though no one essential property (or set of properties) appears each and every time that the term is used. But all of the uses do indeed bear a "family resemblance" to each other (i.e., to a certain extent elements of characteristics overlap so that every use has something "in common with every other use," even though "there is no property which it holds in common with all of these other uses" (Gochnauer, 1973, p. 216).

The question then is, "Can this "family resemblance approach" be applied to the term "physical education?" Fortunately (or unfortunately) the answer at present appears to be a resounding "yes" and "no." Generally speaking, the answer must be in the negative, but for many individual groups within the profession an affirmative might be possible because they individually see "physical education" as either sport or play, or exercise, or dance. If there were agreement almost unanimously that "human movement" or "human motor performance" in these areas is the essential definition, then it would be possible to dispense with the "family resemblance term" idea, but quite obviously those in the field are far from consensus on this important point. Thus, the answer to this question must be "yes" and "no," or at the very best it can possibly be shown that the term "physical education" is a family resemblance term partially or it is such a term to a greater or lesser extent.

Would that it were possible to leave you with such clarity and precision! However, the analysis must in all fairness to the reader be pursued further. As the presentation of a diagram is considered, keep in mind the following definitions of the uses or meanings of the term "physical education" as postulated on page 13 above:

A = Subject-Matter (Theory and Practice) of Field X (what is presently called Physical Education by many)

Thus, $A = SM(T+P)$ of $X(PE)$
$A_1 = SM(T)$
$A_2 = SM(P)$

B = Teaching of Subject-Matter (Theory and Practice) of Field X (Physical Education) by Instructor

Thus, $B = T$ of $SMX(T+P)$ by I
$B_1 = T$ of $SMX(T)$ by I
$B_2 = T$ of $SMX(P)$ by I

C = Process of Learning of Subject-Matter (Theory and Practice of Field X (Physical Education)

Thus, $C = P$ of L of $SMX(T+P)$
$C_1 = P$ of L of $SMX(T)$
$C_2 = P$ of L of $SMX(P)$

D = Result of Teaching of Subject-Matter (Theory and Practice) of Field X (Physical Education) by Instructor so that the Process of Learning (Knowledge, Skill, and Competency) occurs in Student

Thus, $D = R$ of T of $SMX(T+P)$ by I so that P of L (K, S, and Co) occurs in S
$D_1 = R$ of T of $SMX(T)$, etc.
$D_2 = R$ of T of $SMX(P)$, etc.

E = The Discipline of Subject-Matter (Theory and Practice) of Field X in which Scholars and Researchers investigate all Aspects of the Subject-Matter (Theory and Practice) of Field X; its Teaching by Instructor; the Process of Learning by Student; and the Result of its Teaching by Instructor which results in a Body-of-Knowledge and Theory of the Subject-Matter

Thus, E = The Di of SMX(T+P) in which Scholars and Researchers investigate all Aspects of the SMX(T+P); its T by I; the P of L by S; and the R of its T by I which results in a B of K and Th of the SM

E_1 = The Di of SMX(T), etc.

E_2 = The Di of SMX(P), etc.

Note: Subject-Matter of the Discipline of "X" (Physical Education) includes currently (1) the History, Philosophy, and International Aspcets; (2) the Sociological and Social Psychological Aspects; (3) the Motor Learning and Performance Aspects; (4) the Physiological Aspects; (5) the Biomechanical Aspects; and others (such as Anthropometrical, Cultural Anthropological, and Growth Aspects, etc.)

F = The Profession of "X" (Physical Education) whose Members employ Subject-Matter (Theory and Practice); practice its Teaching; try to observe the Process of Learning take place; attempt to measure or evaluate whether the Result has occurred; and base their professional practice on the Body-of-Knowledge developed by Scholars and Researchers in the Discipline and Related Fields

Thus, F = The Profession of X(PE) whose Members employ SM(T+P); practice its Teaching(T+P); try to observe the P of L take place; attempt to measure whether R has occurred; and base their professional practice on the B of K developed by Scholars and Researchers in the Di and Related Fields

F_1 = The Teachers and Coaches of the Profession of X(PE), etc.

F_2 = The Performers, etc.

F_3 = The Teachers of Teachers, etc.

F_4 = The Scholars and Researchers.

Now that definitions have been offered, and an attempt made to establish certain formulas describing the six different meanings or uses of the term "physical education" (and its several variations), the reader is asked to recall that a family resemblance term is one in which the term may be employed correctly in different situations even though no one essential property (or set of properties) appears each and every time that the term is used. All of the uses do have at least elements of characteristics that overlap. An example of this might be as follows:

Q: F, H
R: F, G
S: G, H
T: G, F

In this example Q has F in common with R and T, and H in common with S; R has F in common with Q and T, and G in common with S and T, etc. Note that there is no one characteristic (or set of characteristics) which can be found in all of the cases (Q, R, S, and T).

The analysis has progressed to the point where a similar analysis can be made of the claim that "physical education" is a family resemblance term based on the above example and on the definitions and the formulas prior to that which explain that the term is currently being allotted six meanings or uses--and also keeping in mind that the term physical education is being employed to cover such "sub-meanings" as sport, play, exercise, and dance. Consider therefore uses U, V, W, X, Y, and Z which do have a distribution of overlapping characteristics - but which also have an "essential definition" if a person, or group of people, within the profession is willing to allot the field of "X" such an essential definition (e.g., sport, play, dance, or exercise):

The Field of "X" (Physical Education) Analyzed as a Possible Family Resemblance Term

U: A   Subject-Matter (Theory and Practice)

V: B (A)   The Teaching of the Subject-Matter

W: C (A via   The Process of Learning the Subject-
        B)   Matter through the Efforts of the Teacher

X: D (A via   The Result of the Subject-Matter Being
        B in C)   Taught by the Teacher so that the Process
                  of Learning Takes Place in the Student

Y: E (A, B,   The Discipline Includes Knowledge of the
    C, D)   Subject-Matter, its Teaching, the Process
              of Learning, and the Result

Z: F (A, B,   The Profession Includes Teachers and
    C, D   Coaches, Performers, Teachers of Teach-
    used   ers, and Scholars and Researchers who
    by   Employ the Subject-Matter; may Practice
    F_{1-4} its Teaching; Observe whether the Process
               of Learning Takes Place; and Evaluate
               whether the proper Result Occurs.

Specific Findings. As a result of this preliminary analysis, the following specific findings may be stated:

1. Each use has <u>something</u> in common with the other five uses.

2. This <u>something</u> can and does vary greatly, however, depending upon whether theory or practice is being considered, and also upon whether the term "physical education" is viewed and/or defined as sport, play, exercise, <u>or</u> dance, etc.

3. Each use has a distinct characteristic separate from each of the other five uses even though there is general agreement that the term is being used correctly in each each of the six instances described. A particular use typically includes a combination of one or more of the meanings and/or characteristics of a different one.

Conclusions

As a result of this investigation or analysis of the claim that "physical education" has become a family resemblance term," it is not possible to state definitively and in a clear-cut fashion that physical education <u>is</u> such a type of term or it <u>isn't</u>! The following conclusions appear to be possible:

1. "Physical education" <u>is</u> a family resemblance term by virtue of the fact (1) that the term is relatively correctly employed in connection with each of the uses and/or meanings enumerated; (2) that two persons using this term at present may have similar but fundamentally different concepts in mind; and (3) that there is some overlapping of characteristics from meaning to meaning. (See Specific Finding #3 above.)

2. "Physical education" <u>could be</u> a family resemblance
   term if there is variance in the meaning from use to
   use as explained in Conclusion #1 above, but it might
   not be if there was complete agreement by those concerned about the meaning A (A_1, A_2) or SMX. (Specific
   Finding #2 above.)

3. "Physical education" <u>is not</u> a family resemblance
   term if (1) the literal meaning of the words "physical"
   and "education" is accepted as the "essential definition" which applies to all cases in which the term is
   employed; or (2) if there is general consensus that
   "human movement" is at the core of the definition of
   the term whenever it is used, no matter whether human movement is viewed in a narrow sense (as related only to sport, play, exercise, and/or dance), or
   in a broad sense (as related to man's movement under
   all conditions). (Specific Finding #1 above.)

Recommendations

The investigator believes that he has demonstrated quite conclusively that there is great confusion in connection with the use of
the term "physical education," so much in fact that it seems to test
sorely a "philosophy of language" approach of philosophical analysis.
Further study is needed of each of the three conclusions offered above
in the hope that further light may be shed on what has been a vexing
problem to so many people in the field of physical education and sport.
In the meantime, if the term "physical education" is still employed by
those whose philosophical persuasion is not offended by such usage,
its use should be sharply delimited and care should be taken to employ qualifying and descriptive terms precisely in this connection.

Selected References

Feigl, H., "Logical Empiricism," in H. Feigl and W. Sellars,
Readings in Philosophical Analysis. New York: Appleton-
Century-Crofts, 1949.

Frankena, W. K. Three Historical Philosophies of Education.
Chicago, Illinois: Scott, Foresman and Company, 1965.

Gochnauer, M. L., "Analysis of Knowledge." Unpublished Ph.D.
dissertation, The University of Western Ontario, 1973.

Kaplan, A. The New World of Philosophy. New York: Random
House, 1961.

Metheny, E. and Ellfeldt, L. E., "Movement and Meaning: Development of a General Theory," Research Quarterly, 29:264-273, October, 1958.

Osterhoudt, R. G., "A Descriptive Analysis of Research Concerning the Philosophy of Physical Education and Sport." Unpublished Ph.D. dissertation, University of Illinois, 1971.

Patrick, G. D., "Verifiability (Meaningfulness) of Selected Physical Education Objectives." Unpublished Ph.D. dissertation, University of Illinois, 1971.

Pearson, K. M., "Inquiry into Inquiry." A Special Report carried out in the Graduate Department of Physical Education, University of Illinois, 1970. (Unpublished).

_____., "A Structural and Functional Analysis of the Multi-Concept of Integration-Segregation (Male and/or Female) in Physical Education Classes." Unpublished Ph.D. dissertation, University of Illinois, 1971.

Russell, B. The Autobiography of Bertrand Russell. New York: Bantam Books, Inc., 1968 (Vol. I).

Siedentop, Daryl. Physical Education: Introductory Analysis. Dubuque, Iowa: Wm. C. Brown Co., 1972.

Spencer-Kraus, P., "The Application of 'Linguistic Phenomenology' to Physical Education and Sport." Unpublished M.S. Thesis, University of Illinois, 1969.

VanderZwaag, H. J. Toward a Philosophy of Sport. Reading, Mass.: Addison-Wesley, 1972.

Weitz, M. (editor). Twentieth Century Philosophy: The Analytic Tradition. New York: The Free Press, 1966.

White, M. G. The Age of Analysis. Boston: Houghton-Mifflin, 1955.

Zeigler, E. F., "A Biased View of History, Historiography, and Physical Education and Sport," in Proceedings of the First Canadian Symposium on the History of Sport and Physical Education, University of Alberta, Edmonton, Canada, May 13, 1970. Published by the Fitness and Amateur Sport Directorate, Ottawa, Canada.

_____. Philosophical Foundations for Physical, Health, and Recreation Education. Englewood Cliffs, New Jersey: Prentice Prentice-Hall, Inc., 1964.

_____ and VanderZwaag, H. J. Physical Education: Progressivism or Essentialism. Champaign, Illinois: Stipes Publishing Company, Revised edition, 1968.

Part VII
THE FUTURE

Selection #43

A POINT OF VIEW: THE NEED FOR CONSENSUS
AND RESEARCH

Recent historical occurrences, social influences, scientific discoveries, and inventional all hold greater or lesser implications for education and hence have similar meaning for physical education.* They have caused leaders in physical education, for example, to become concerned about the body-of-knowledge upon which our developing profession is based. The "knowledge explosion" has caught up with us, as it has our colleagues in other areas of education, and this increase in knowledge (not wisdom!) in a geometric ratio threatens to engulf us. We are faced with the absolute necessity of "re-tooling" and upgrading our research efforts radically. We can no longer feel complacent about our university research programs in physical education that have typically and largely been related to the physiological aspects of physical fitness (as truly important as these efforts have been). In the process we will need to structure our graduate teaching and research programs in such a way that we will be able to cope with the need for highly competent research workers who can understand and assess the knowledge which is available to us in a multitude of disciplines. Many of these disciplines, some of which we are only dimly aware, are truly our related fields or foundation arts and sciences. We will be successful as a profession only to the extent that we are able to assimilate this knowledge and the resultant ordered generalizations that have meaning for us in physical education. It will then be necessary for researchers and scholars in our field to set up tentative hypotheses, based on these findings of scholars and scientists in related fields and our own, and to apply all known methods and accompanying techniques of research carefully and painstakingly to problems which appear to belong uniquely to physical education. This task belongs to us alone, and we must accomplish this goal primarily through our own efforts if we hope to survive! No other discipline will do this for us, except in a secondary way and belatedly. It may sound trite to say, but no other generation of physical educators has ever faced such an enormous problem. It is fortunate that we are aware of it, but at present we are poorly prepared to meet it--and the time is short.

---

* A paper originally presented to The Design Conference, Sherman House, Chicago, Illinois, October 13-16, 1965. (Published in The Physical Educator, Vol. 24, No. 3:107-109, 1967.)

The Need for Consensus

Philosophical investigation of a normative and analytical nature over the past fifteen years has convinced the writer of the vital importance of a continuing search for, and the possibility of, consensus among the conflicting philosophies of physical education in the Western world. We in this field have been floundering around for so long with our own biased and eclectic statements of philosophical position that even the current attempt to delineate our own individual positions represents a vast improvement. These words are not meant to be derogatory of any one individual, or group of individuals; such philosophical ineptitude is actually characteristic of the large majority of practitioners in the educational world.

But the delineation of one's own philosophy that is being recommended, as truly basic as it is to one's own professional advancement, is not enough in the light of the world situation today. We cannot, and dare not, be an island unto ourselves as we seemingly tried to be in the past. Educators, both here and abroad, will have to be capable of rising above their divisions in educational philosophy if we ever hope to establish attitudes truly desirous of world peace. (1)

The Difficulty of Achieving Consensus

The difficulty of achieving consensus is, of course, exactly the problem that we are facing in physical education in North America today. It is really questionable, although this writer is sufficiently reconstructionistic in his philosophy to believe in such approaches strongly, whether the American Association for Health, Physical Education, and Recreation, for example, can hope to achieve true consensus by the typical conferences that are held periodically. With such a careful effort being made to have both sexes, all educational levels, the various educational agencies, and other related groups represented, such meetings usually result in a group in which progressive Christian idealists and pragmatic experimentalists (including reconstructionists) predominate and only a sprinkling of naturalistic realists, rational humanists, and moderate (Catholic) realists is evident. The outcome of any such deliberations is consequently predetermined. If a vote is taken, the realists are hopelessly outnumbered. When the conference report is published, "complete loyalty to God, mother, and country" is proclaimed resoundingly, the "progressivist banner" is gallantly waved, and there is just enough of an "eclectic taint" to the entire document that the realist, who figures the whole affair was simply a matter of "pooled ignorance" anyhow, acts blithely disinterested and somewhat "sullen but not actively mutinous" about the end result. Is this an overstatement of the situation? I think not.

We are fortunate, of course, that there is more agreement in practice than there is in theory. Strangely enough, a certain amount of agreement is necessary in order to disagree. To make any progress we must agree on the issues and on an interpretation of the rules for debate. Furthermore, we realize that we aren't striving for complete agreement on all issues anyhow.

Methods for Achieving Greater Consensus

There are actually a number of methods available by which greater consensus can be achieved. A formidable, but perhaps not impossible task, is to attempt to break down communications barriers. The study of semantics, the language analysis movement in philosophy, and the developing social science of human relations in administration will make significant contributions toward the improvement of communication in the years to come. The development of a truly international language, which could be taught in all countries in conjunction with the mother tongue, would be an enormous aid to such a development as well (2).

Common Denominators in Education

It is interesting and important to note that there are some common presuppositions or denominators among the different educational philosophies. Greene makes this quite clear as follows:

> In the first place, different philosophical points of view, 'schools,' or positions are not mutually exclusive in all respects. On the contrary, all of necessity share some common presuppositions, and each finds itself in considerable agreement with one or more of its presumptive rivals. More significant, then, than any specifiable type or types of philosophy is the larger pattern of partly contrasting, partly overlapping, emphases and trends of contemporary belief on ultimate matters. (4)

Some of these areas of practical agreement are that (1) the safety of the child is basic; (2) the school has a responsibility to provide a health-service unit; (3) that boys and girls must be educated for a certain period of time; (4) that teachers need a certain educational background and experience; and (5) that there are certain "cardinal principles" of education. A recent statement of the Educational Policies Commission reflects current social influences and, after reaffirming earlier statements of 1918 and 1938, states a central purpose--the development of the ability to think, which is not meant to be thought of as exclusive. (4)

Then there are some additional areas of agreement or consensus, but the "ice is getting rather thin in spots". The extent of class involvement in the discussion of controversial issues, for example, is one area where there is difference of opinion. Many would say further that the student should be free to arrive at a solution, but we all recognize that he'll have to be quite careful about how he expresses himself in certain areas of politices, religion, or problems of a social nature. We could argue further that there is general agreement that the race heritage ought to be the common heritage of all, but the rub comes when we get down to the specifics of how it shall be taught. And so it goes as increasingly less consensus becomes apparent. (5)

Common Denominators in Physical, Health, and Recreation Education

What common denominators do we find in our specialized field of physical education and sport, or in health and safety education, or in recreation education? The fact that health and recreation people, for example, aren't in attendance at this meeting reflects a consensus (or perhaps a philosophical bias) on the part of the conference planners. Can we really discuss knowledge based on research? It would be absolutely necessary to re-affirm immediately that research knows no such thing as disciplinary boundaries--that we will be crossing the seeming boundaries daily of any and all related disciplines where we can uncover a relationship. It seems highly improbable that we will be able to find a completely "specifiable scope of inquiry and a structured subject-matter," although there is every likelihood that we will make steady improvement toward "a recognized set of procedures for acquiring, validating and ordering new knowledge," and toward the development of truly "accepted techniques and tools for applying knowledge in specific cases to specified practical ends."

The common denominators that we seem to have accepted currently are:

1. The belief of the large majority of physical educators that <u>regular</u> physical education periods should be <u>required</u> for all school children through grade ten or eleven at least.
2. That it is vitally important that a child develops certain attitudes toward his own health in particular and toward community hygiene in general. Furthermore, certain basic health knowledges should be taught somewhere and at some time in the curriculum.
3. Leisure should be put to worthy use; it is understood that in North America many people are presumably enjoying a greater amount of leisure than has ever been available before.

4. Physical vigor is extremely important, but there is no general agreement among the men, or between men and and women, about what really constitutes physical fitness. There are national norms, but no national standards.
5. There is general agreement that boys and girls at some stage of their development should have an experience in competitive sport. This is a somewhat meaningless statement, however, unless we clarify it very carefully.
6. It is generally agreed that something should be done about the youngster who needs therapeutic exercise for remedial physical defects. But there is evidently no general agreement across the country about who should look after this, or when or where.
7. We know that character and personality development is important; we have the belief generally that our specialized field can make an unusual contribution to this area; and we don't know how much this should be stressed.

Having stated these common denominators, it would appear that the time is long overdue when the field should be able to present to the North American public concrete evidence of far greater agreement on what it is that we do. It would appear that our discipline should be built around those areas upon which we have been able to achieve a minimum of consensus. The Contribution of Physical Activity to Human Well-Being (Research Quarterly, Vol. 31, No. 2, Pt. II, May, 1960) was seemingly as important a project as the AAHPER's Research Council, or the Association itself has ever undertaken. This now needs to be up-dated, "sharpened," and clarified with a format similar to that of the recent publication of Human Behavior; An Inventory of Scientific Findings by Berelson and Steiner (New York: Harcourt, Brace & World, Inc., 1964).

The Present Need

The potentialities for pure and applied research in physical education and sport (or however else you may wish to designate what it is that we do) are limitless. The unique nature of the field and its role in the "education of an amphibian," (6) relates us quite obviously to physiology, anatomy, psychology, sociology, history, philosophy, anthropology, chemistry, medicine, and administrative theory at least. If we will be completely honest, we will have to admit that we have only a miniscule quantity of qualified researchers possessing "physical educator's hearts" (i.e., people with professional preparation for physical education, with sound backgrounds in related fields, who are really interested in the future of the field). Many more bright, idealistic young people are on the way to help us accomplish the task, but the quality of our graduate teaching and research programs, with accompanying post-doctoral research opportunities, must be improved immeasurably. Time is running short!

References

1. Brubacher, John S. Modern Philosophies of Education, Third edition. New York: McGraw-Hill Book Company, Inc., 1962, pp. 348-349.

2. Brubacher, op. cit., pp. 350-354.

3. The Educational Policies Commission, The Central Purpose of American Education. Washington, D. C.: National Education Association, 1961, p. 12.

4. Greene, Theodore M., "A Liberal Christian Idealist Philosophy of Education," Fifty-Fourth Yearbook of the National Society for the Study of Education. Chicago: University of Press, 1955, Part I, p. 91.

5. Huxley, Aldous. Tomorrow and Tomorrow and Tomorrow. New York: Signet Books, The New American Library of World Literature, Inc., 1964, pp. 9-31.

6. Zeigler, Earle F. Philosophical Foundations for Physical, Health, and Recreation Education. Englewood Cliffs, New Jersey: Prentice-Hall, Inc., 1964, p. 284.

PHYSICAL EDUCATION HAS "DECIDOPHOBIA": FIVE "STANCES" THAT "HAVE GOT TO GO!"

The profession of physical education is suffering from what Walter Kaufmann has recently identified as "Decidophobia"* - the fear of making autonomous decisions without the aid of "crutches" such as religions, political ideologies, philosophical positions, microscopic deviational maneuvers, and other "band-aids of life." (1)

The urgent need to make decisions has developed because of societal change which is taking place, and which has created what Alvin Toffler has described as "future shock." (3) Simply put, this describes a condition that affects an individual or a group when life confronts him or it with a situation that is (1) beyond control; (2) almost beyond control; or (3) is at least stressful enough that the ingenuity and energies of the person(s) concerned are significantly taxed. Indeed, if the "shock" is sufficiently strong, the man or woman affected may suffer a breakdown and lose touch with reality.

Most people can recognize that change is taking place all around them, and many for one or more reasons are fighting to hold it back wherever possible. What is not recognized so readily is that the rate of change is increasing sharply, and it is this fact that should force just about everybody to plan for the future much more carefully than has typically been the case in the past. Curiously enough, when one attempts to cope with so many of life's problems today, it is not a question of being "traditional" or "liberal" as was so often the situation heretofore. It is more a matter of resolving a problem or issue "pragmatically" and/or "realistically," and thereby allowing society to move "forward."

Despite the fact that the field of "physical education and sport" - a term used to describe the field at present as a "holding pattern" until the decidophobic state is overcome - is caught right in the middle of this societal transformation, unfortunately "many of us in physical education are seemingly so rigid in our outlooks that we don't give evidence of recognition that something is indeed taking place."(4) Of course, this syndrome is not limited to the physical education field field; indeed it appears to characterize a rather large percentage of

---

* An adaptation of a position statement prepared for the Annual Meeting of the American Academy of Physical Education, Detroit, Michigan, March 31, 1971. (Published in JOHPER, Vol. 44, No. 7: 48-49, September, 1973.)

the population, and makes one fear for the very survival of the culture ultimately. Youth appears to be ready to modify its stance, if the experience of the White House Conference on Youth held in Colorado in 1971 can be accepted as any indication. Despite the fact that this group of young people was selected to represent a much broader spectrum of opinion that one would get typically from college and university men and women, "the discussion showed that youth as a whole is far less conservative - far more in agreement with the activist collegians - than conservative adults tend to claim and believe." (2) Physical educators and coaches take note!

Thus, the question is how are we going to display "accountability," "relevance," and "involvement" when practically our entire field is out of step with the large majority of the younger generation in the country. If this is a reasonable assumption - and I believe that our social scientists should help us to determine what the prevailing attitude and opinions are - it is incumbent upon the American Academy of Physical Education; the American Association for Health, Physical Education, and Recreation; the National College Physical Education Association for Men, and the National Association of Physical Education for College Women to direct all of their efforts to help us "put our house in order." We simply must (1) sharpen the issues; (2) place them in some order of priority; and (3) tell professional colleagues how our field can once again "get in step" with the demands of changing times.

This brief paper points up as succinctly and precisely as possible five "internal" problems and/or issues of major import. In the opinion of the writer, these represent five prevailing "stances" of the field of physical education and sport that HAVE GOT TO GO! If we as professionals will do something truly positive and tangible toward rectifying these unfortunate stances, our profession would very soon be in an infinitely better position to exert "outward" influence based on the elimination of the present credibility gap that exists between us and so many of the children and young people whom we wish to serve.

The Five "Stances" That Have Got to Go!

Stance #1 - "The Shotgun Approach to Professional Preparation." Our "bewildered public" seems to be having some difficulty keeping up with the image that our profession seeks to project. Does the profession seek to perpetuate the idea that physical education includes health, physical education, recreation, and athletics--not to mention safety education, driver education, dance, physical fitness, movement education, and park administration? Or can we possibly agree that our task within formal and informal education is to teach humans to move efficiently and with meaning in sport, dance, exercise, and expressive activities within the context of man's socialization in an evolving world?

Stance #2 - "The Athletics Über Alles Approach in Education."
The perennial struggle between physical education-oriented and athle-
tics-oriented people in the educational system, both public and private, is continuing along unabated with just about everybody condemn-
ing excesses that appear almost daily in programs for children and
young men especially. Are most of us going to allow poor educational
practices in competitive sport to multiply almost unchallenged because materialistic influences and general inertia seem well nigh insuperable? Does the profession dare to speak out on this problem in
a statesmanlike, forcible manner, or are our tenured (continuing contract) positions really not impregnable?

Stance #3 - "The Women Are All Right in Their Place Approach." Ever since the heyday of Mabel Lee, who served as first
woman president of the American Association in 1931-32, there has
seemingly been no need for a Women's Lib Movement within the ranks
of the AAHPER. This condition of "equal opportunity" has been present at the District and State levels within AAHPER as well, even
though its operation on an arbitrary basis often leaves something to
be desired as far as the "spontaneity" of elections is concerned. And
yet ample evidence has been gathered by HEW that professional women in universities, for example, have often been rewarded as
"second-class citizens." From another standpoint many women in
physical education at the college and university level are highly fearful about any amalgamation of men's and women's departments where
they are outnumbered by men, or where the top administrative officer
would almost inevitably be a man. Physical education at all educational levels is undoubtedly weaker because of the frequent separation
of men's and women's units. Furthermore, separate national associations at the university level simply perpetuate this problem.

Stance #4 - "The Body-of-Knowledge Approach and Its Implications." For some as yet not fully explained reason, the current
battle seems to be on between those who feel that the field's mission
is to prepare "teachers and coaches of physical education" primarily
for the secondary school level, and those who are saying "how can
we have a true profession unless we prepare scholars and researchers in sufficient quantity to give us a body-of-knowledge with which to
function to our optimum?" This would not seem to be an "either-or"
decision that must be made; as a matter of fact, both approaches are
needed, but some can't help but feel that they are being challenged
by the newer "disciplinary approach." This has often resulted in a
downgrading of scholarship in various ways and a concerted offort to
keep undergraduates from being "defiled" by scholarly effort. Conversely, it has often resulted in a "let's keep up with the Jones's approach," because many departments in the relatively smaller state
universities presently offering master's degrees in our field are attempting to move Ph.D. programs without adequate staffs, facilities,
and equipment.

Stance #5 - "The Password Is 'Treadmill" Approach." As if we don't have problems enough to contend with, there is a struggle going on within many universities between faculty members teaching and researching in the bio-science aspects of our work and faculty members attempting to form undergraduate and graduate options in the humanities and social science aspects of physical education and sport. Of course, this is far from the first time in education, or in other aspects of life for that matter, when "haves" became worried about "have-nots" wanting to get support for their work. Even though scholars in the humanities and social sciences have traditionally received far less financial support than their counterparts in the natural sciences, the present recession in financial support to universities may make this problem more acute. Physical education and sport, a field which is largely concerned with the non-verbal arts and sciences, seems to have unique relational possibilities in so many directions. For this reason it is very shortsighted for those in fairly well-established research units to attempt to thwart even limited developments in the humanities and social science aspects of physical education and sport. In the final analysis such efforts could well be self defeating and would lead to lowering of overall status in the educational hierarchy.

Conclusion

In this brief presentation a straightforward case has been made to point out five "stances" or "problems" that characterize the present situation in which the field of physical education and sport finds itself. This writer believes that these five prevailing "stances" are so detrimental to the profession that they simply "have to go" and very soon. Physical education's decidophobia is not limited to these issues alone, but these five urgently warrant continuing analysis and assessment--and then direct action on the part of a united profession. Mature members of the field should be offering their opinions and beliefs regularly about what it means to be a deeply committed professional person. This can be done by speaking out persistently and often regarding issues, values, and purposes in physical education and sport. Professional action should be taken democratically through established professional associations. We must work to strike a balance in order to avoid both "tyranny of the majority" and "tyranny of the minority."

The field of physical education and sport is not in the vanguard in North American education. Why are we so completely alienated from so many intelligent young people--teachers and students alike--in our society? Certainly we need to ask ourselves why we seem to be so far removed from "governance circles" in public and private education. Is it because we are too far removed intellectually and philosophically from our colleagues, or are we too busy to get involved in issues and problems that affect us all?

As important as the matter of ecology is, for example, I have a fear that we are tending to use this along with other "escape hatches" to avoid the painful solutions to perhaps even more basic problems in our country and the world. We know that very positive steps are being taken to improve man's use of his environment, but will we do what is absolutely necessary soon enough in regard to man's relationship to his fellow man? Physical educators may look "inward" or "outward" in regard to their professional problems, but all of us need to search our hearts and minds to discover why there continues to be an unwillingness to accord so-called minority groups full equality in all phases of our society and profession. At this moment in American history, perhaps as never before, many leaders must speak out and persuade their colleagues to make decisions that will eliminate prevailing stances that are negating the best possible future development of physical education and sport. We must convince the public that we are functioning in the highest tradition of a fine profession.

Selected References

1. Kaufmann, Walter. Without Guilt or Justice. New York: Peter H. Wyden, Inc./Publisher, 1973, pp. 1-35.

2. New York Times, The, "Education Section," April 25, 1971.

3. Toffler, Alvin. Future Shock. New York: Random House, Inc., 1970.

4. Zeigler, Earle F., "Focus on the Future: Planning Ahead to Prevent 'Future Shock' in Physical Education and Sport." A paper presented to the North York (Ontario) Physical and Health Education Association, May 5, 1973.

Selection #45

PLANNING AHEAD TO PREVENT "FUTURE SHOCK" IN PHYSICAL EDUCATION AND SPORT

The field of education has been noted historically for its great reliance on the wisdom of the ages--a stance which most recently can be characterized as a "marked inclination to the rear."* It seems quite safe to state further that the field of physical education and sport has not been regarded typically as one which has led the way within educational circles. Where this leaves "poor old PE" in the hierarchy of educational values typically becomes immediately obvious. The big question for us, however, is whether this lowly, defensive position is fully warranted. The thrust of this paper is not to make a number of value-laden claims for the numerous accomplishments possible through the implementation of a fine program of physical education and sport. This paper does represent an effort to offer a means whereby you can plan ahead in order to lessen the impact of the future on our entire profession.

At the outset I want to say that these ideas do not in any way add up to a prescription to physical educators and/or coaches at any educational level as to what they must or even should do to improve their programs. These plans for improvement on the "home front" must be developed by those closest to the scene, perhaps with some advice from others--if such counsel is needed and sought by those who are professionally concerned. In the final analysis, of course, we all have to answer to some advisory board and legislative body if it is found that we are not performing our professional duties well.

We all know that change is taking place around us in so many different aspects of life, but what is often not understood is that even the rate of change is increasing sharply. Such a development seems to leave us no recourse but to develop a readiness or awareness that will enable us to "modify our posture by a considerable number of degrees" if such modification seems necessary as we plan for the future. The "future shock" described so aptly by Alvin Toffler is not something that our grandchildren will be the first to face. Education at all levels is facing such "shock" right now, and the educational structure may be in for a remodeling that is in no way anticipated by any of us. And, unfortunately, many of us in physical education and

---

* A paper presented to the Tennessee Association for Health, Physical Education, and Recreation, Memphis, Tennessee, December 2, 1973. (Published in the Journal of the Canadian Association for HPER, Vol. 40, No. 5:14-20, May-June, 1974.)

sport are seemingly so rigid in our outlooks that we don't give evidence of recognition that something is taking place! And often, even if we do recognize the outlines of such evolution, there seems to be a pitiful plea for a return to the good old days of Reich's Consciousness One - or even Two.

The emphasis in the remainder of this paper will focus back and forth from the profession to the individual (and vice versa). Every day in your life you express your values through statements of opinion and belief. How identical are the ideas and beliefs that you express and those that you actually put into practice in your work? Do you by chance have a different image of yourself than others have of you? Succinctly put - you live a philosophy of life, and you are judged much more by your actions than by the words (or platitudes) that you speak.

Personally, I believe that we all try to create an image within our social system, large or small. I'm frank to say that I don't want to look like the proverbial clock-work jock any more with the red, white, and blue key in his head; you know, the one with the brush cut, the aggressive leadership traits, and the coaching jacket that was worn whatever the occasion. Yes, I have been attempting to create a different image by the development of what is perhaps falsely designated as "mind." I have been expanding my interest in and knowledge about the aesthetic, creative, social, communicative, and so-called learning aspects of life. Nevertheless, I have also been exercising quite vigorously in an effort to preserve the image of a person that is physically fit. This involves specific exercises to stretch and strengthen the large muscle groups, and then I also jog or swim middle distance to maintain a minimum level of circulo-respiratory efficiency. This is supplemented several times a week by paddleball or handball. Putting all of this together - the multi-faceted approach described - creates what might be called a "Renaissance Man Approach" - one that has been somewhat popular two or maybe three times in the history of the world. However, I really do question how much it impresses or convinces most people on the North American continent today.

One thing is certain, and I can't emphasize this too much. I am doing everything possible back home to show my colleagues at the University, as well as my professional associates everywhere including those in physical education, that some people in physical education are truly concerned about what is going on in the world, and they want to be involved as equal partners in the evolving democratic venture that is taking place. Make no mistake about it; there is an ideological struggle going on in the world, and the freedom of the individual to make his or her own decision is at stake.

Let's face it; recent international, national, regional, and local occurrences do keep the minds of all but ostriches in a whirl these days. Periodically I feel that a news moratorium would help very much, at least one that lasted for a few weeks (or even days). Haven't you had that "stop the world I want to get off" feeling lately? Maybe I am getting old, and I'm simply telling you that I will never see forty-nine years of age again. There was a time when God was in the Heavens; when flags weren't often used as the wrong kind of political symbols; when the U. S. really seemed to be sincere about wanting to make the world safe for democracy - and Canada could get enthusiastic about getting involved in the whole enterprise; and when I saw myself as indestructible and timeless. Now God is said to be dead (if indeed He ever did live); flags are often used incorrectly by those who wish to throttle dissent; the United States forces many to question her motives; and personally I find myself more introspective and pessimistic quite often - at least distinctly more than was the case previously. Thus, from a time when I fitted neatly into that picture of a world getting better day by day in every way as a happy, optimistic physical educator and coach doing my part in a relatively happy North America, I now find myself so much more sober, realistic, perplexed, and concerned. One is forced to inquire: what happened?

The Situation in Education

And what has happened to our schools and the learning process? We take that bright-eyed youngster at the age of six or sooner - almost invariably eager and ready to learn - and we quite thoroughly kill his or her desire within a few short years. We indoctrinate the child into what is - for the lack of a better or more apt term - called "the modern way." This involves excessive drill, speed, competing, dull lectures, tests, quizzes, grades, memorization, various types of overt and covert discipline - and the "work hard to get ahead" approach that makes money so that the young adult who emerges from the system will eventually be able to buy all of the good things that presumably characterize good living. This includes new cars, color TV sets, new clothes involving changing fashions, special hair styling, winter homes, summer homes, ornate churches, whiskey and other alcoholic depressants, tobacco and pot, divorces, supplemental sex, stocks and bonds, etc. All of this has added up to the highest standard of living in the world; that's it: the highest standard of low living in the world! The motto is, "get an education so that you can make more money and try to achieve that "high standard" by keeping up with your friends and business associates.

I say to you today: try to tell a youngster, a high school student, or even a college man or woman that this pattern I've described is not what education is all about in the eyes of the layman in your world and my world. Is it any wonder that so many of these young people are telling us loudly and clearly - and telling us in many

- 449 -

countries on many continents around the world - that such a world is not of their making, and that they want to change it so that there will be a different tomorrow.

And this statement seems to apply especially to us in the field of physical education and sport. We are typically the squares who help keep order and discipline. We are the conformists who rarely if ever rock the boat. We are the people who frown on odd hair styles, and who help to keep minority groups (including women and homosexuals) in their place. We know what's good for kids; haven't we lived through those immature years and become successes? Just look at us - aren't we on top of the world making things happen?

But the question now seems to revolve around what we want to make happen. How do we know that it is best in this changing world? What is it that the world is lacking today, and what can we do about it anyhow? Can we help to achieve any such goals through the medium of physical education and sport? What is the purpose of education - of physical education? Is it to cram knowledge, skills, competencies, win-at-all-costs ideas, muscles, endurance, and discipline down the throats of young people? Must they respect us because we say so?

Physical Education's Blurred Image

To make matters worse, we in physical education and sport have one of the most blurred images in the entire educational system. This occurred originally probably because of the many conflicting educational philosophies in each of the sixty provincial and state educational systems extant on this North American continent. The image with its fuzzy boundaries continues today for this same reason and, of course, because of a considerable amount of individual confusion within the field. To understand the origins of this dilemma with reasonable accuracy, we must look, therefore, at both our heritage and our present philosophical foundations.

For the first time in the history of the profession of physical education, at least some scholars in the field have become aware of the need to turn to philosophy and sociology as well as to history for assistance. Although it is true that such an approach is Western world-oriented largely, there is assuredly great need for the techniques of normative and critical philosophical analysis to be directed basically to physical education and sport. Such endeavor is long overdue when we consider our "bewildered public" trying to understand what we mean by a conglomerate term such as health, physical education, recreation, and athletics - not to mention safety education, dance, driver education, physical fitness, movement education, human kinetics, leisure studies, kinanthropology, human motor performance, kinesiology, park administration, and sport, to name just a few. Can you imagine how difficult it would be to put all of this on a sign in front of a building in order to keep almost everyone happy?

Society Is More Value Conscious

Fortunately there are at least some signs on the horizon which give some hope that this mishmash of names for the field will eventually be untangled. Some people are beginning to realize that we are actually attempting to describe a number of different professions. Further, we are making a term such as "physical education" bear too much strain by having it contain literally six different meanings. More important, however, is the fact that our whole society seems to be more conscious than I can ever remember about the need for reassessment of the values by which we guide our lives. Such concern is heartening, although I do have a fear that such concern may be quite superficial because of the individual's basic lack of philosophical foundation in his life. This failing does appear throughout our entire society. Ask a person what he wants out of life, and you are bound to get a vague response such as "happiness" or "security" or some other innocuous expression which reflects no deep reflection whatsoever. Moreover, we are reminded immediately by the skeptic that you can only learn truly about the values that a person holds through careful observation of his daily practice.

The Dilemma of Professional Philosophy

Curiously enough, just at the time that people have become more value conscious, the professional field of philosophy - in the English-speaking world at least - seems to have decided to cast the common man adrift in waters that are anything but calm and peaceful. The field of philosophy has incurred its own "Drang nach Diziplin," and the assumption of this posture has left an indelible mark on philosophers of education and sport and physical education philosophers in that order chronologically.

Thus, despite the fact that men have engaged in philosophical thought for many centuries, there is still a large amount of confusion over the exact nature of philosophy. Developing scientific method has forced many of today's philosophers to ask themselves, "In what kind of activity am I engaging?" Many of them have decided that philosophical activity of any type does not result in knowledge after all. And so - if knowledge can only come from carefully controlled scientific experimentation - what is the justification for philosophy? A considerable group of influential philosophers have therefore turned to various types of so-called philosophical analysis. A good share of this effort involves philosophy of language, such aspects of conceptual analysis and using ordinary and specialized language terms more clearly and precisely than heretofore.

The "Flavoring Influence" of Existential Philosophy

In addition to the massive frontal attack on the traditional philosophies of idealism, realism, and pragmatism by the entire analytic movement in philosophy, another powerful group of troublesome and often pessimistic ideas has gradually emanated from the European continent to become a significant, permeating force on the North American scene. I am referring to existential philosophy – an approach which many say began as a revolt against Hegel's idealism in the latter half of the nineteenth century. Hegelian idealism was a position that included the postulate that ethical and spiritual realities were accessible to man through reason. Atheistic and agnostic existentitalism include the tenet that man's task on earth is to create his own essence – his own ideals and values – inasmuch as science had shown (as explained by Nietzsche) that the transcendent ideals of the Church were actually non-sense. Thus, man – spelled with a capital "M" – is really on his own in a cold, cruel world. He has a responsibility to give meaning and direction to a world essentially lacking in such qualities. The fundamental question for the future, according to this position – and one which has great implications for education including physical education and sport – is whether man is capable of directing and guiding his own existence so that responsible individual and social action will result.

Where Can We Find the Answers?

A great deal of evidence can be mustered to support the position that modern man is really at the crossroads when it comes to the question of deciding which way he and his associates on this globe should turn in the years immediately ahead on the way to the hypothetical year 2,000 A.D. How can we truly lead effective and purposeful lives if we don't make decisions for ourselves about the basic questions which are confronting us? This, as I see it, confronts man with the predicament of overcoming what Walter Kaufmann has recent recently identified as "Decidophobia" – the fear of making autonomous decisions without the aid of "crutches" such as religions, political ideologies, philosophical positions, and other "band-aids of life." Thus, persistent philosophical problems such as the nature of the world, the problem of good and evil, the possibility of free will, whether God exists, if some values are more important than others, whether knowledge is really possible to man, and the possibility of an unchanging concept of beauty – just to name a few of life's enigmas – need to be answered by each individual man and woman as he and she wend their respective ways through life. It is safe to say, of course, that no one person or group has a corner on the market when it comes to answering these fundamental questions.

Frankly, my recommendation is that you become at least <u>amateur</u> philosophers, because the present haphazard approach of most won't do. Actually, I would venture the opinion that your personal life and the work of the organization in which your work is so important that it may well be worth the time for you to become <u>semi-professional</u> philosophers. After all, this is <u>your</u> life in <u>your</u> country on <u>your</u> continent in <u>your</u> world that we are discussing. Unless you intend to follow the approach of the proverbial ostrich, you have simply got to make determinations for the years ahead that will hopefully stand the test of time.

A Plan for Action

May I recommend a plan of action for your consideration? Basically, it consists of an orderly progression through a series of steps which you and your colleagues can follow:

1. Re-examine your long range aims and specific objectives in the light of societal values, educational values, and the values of the individuals concerned.

    In attempting to find a position on an educational philosophy spectrum or continuum, keep in mind that <u>progressivism</u> is greatly concerned about such attributes as personal freedom, individual differences, student interest, individual growth, no permanently fixed values, and that the process by which the program is implemented is problem-solving in nature and means ideal living <u>now</u>.

    Conversely, the position of <u>essentialism</u> implies typically that there are certain educational, recreational, and physical educational values by which the individual <u>must</u> be guided; that effort takes precedence over interest and that this tends to gird moral stamina; that the experience of the past has powerful jurisdiction over the present; and that the cultivation of the intellect is most important in education.

2. Re-examine the relationships that exist, and which may develop among the various units concerned (society, including public and private agencies; the school; and the family and individuals involved).

3. Determine what your institution's persistent, recurring problems are (e.g., the influence of nationalism, politicis, economics, religion, values, ecology, etc. - and the specific professional problems such as curriculum content, teaching methodology, the healthy body, use of leisure, etc.).

4. Based on the aims and objectives accepted (in #1 above), make decisions as to how your school will meet the persistent problems identified both generally and specifically (i.e., what effect your goals - and hierarchy of values - will have on the relationships that are established and maintained in #2 above, and how such acceptance and understanding ought to influence the process of education and, specifically, the program of physical education and sport which your school may wish to implement.)

5. Spell out specifically from the standpoint of the agreed-upon hierarchy of societal and educational values accepted what program features you will introduce and through what process (or method) you will implement your entire program.

6. After you have gained the final approval of your policy-making group, including your professional and non-professional staff (with possible staff changes where commitment is not present), implement the revised program vigorously reminding one and all regularly that this program (including the process employed to implement it) is theirs and merits full support.

7. Evaluate the revised program regularly from the standpoint of its effectiveness in achieving the stated objectives with particular emphasis on the realization of human values in the lives of your constituents.

Conclusion

Who will argue that these are not most difficult and really trying times in all phases of our lives? I urge you to be the kind of professional people who look to your philosophical foundations. I believe that this is absolutely imperative so that there will be greater consistency between your words and your actions. We simply must relate dynamically to people's lives if we hope to see our programs survive. As professional teachers of physical education and sport, we can't be the sort of person who watches things happening all around us. We should be looked to by our colleagues, students, and the community for dedicated leadership that is based on the wisdom of philosophical maturity - sound ideas developed through orderly reflection and discussion. I have every confidence that you as part of a truly important profession at this time will make significant progress toward both your immediate objectives and your long range goals in the years ahead.

A RIDDLE FOR TOMORROW'S WORLD: HOW TO LEAD
A GOOD LIFE

There is no doubt but that the good life does beckon us all, but
there is also the distinct possibility that we may "be dashed on the
rocks below."* With this rather cryptic remark, I am making reference to the famous German poem by Heinrich Heine, "Die Lorelei."
Heine describes a cliff high on the right bank of the Rhine River. At
this point the river runs through a very dangerous narrows. According to German legend a beautiful, feminine creature lived up on this
cliff, and her singing lured unsuspecting sailors to their death on
dangerous rocks below. Such would appear to be the situation today,
as the human race looks longingly at a coming age of leisure and yet
is unable to cope with the many problems of urban communities today.

The question of "the coming age of leisure and its effect on the
community" can become really disconcerting to us personally, because those of us working in the fields of health, physical education,
or recreation are finding increasingly that we have less, not more,
time on our hands. In addition to the lack of leisure that most of us
find, there lies before us the frightening possibility that we may not
be anywhere nearly fully prepared to truly help people cope with the
North America of tomorrow. To do this, it is vitally important that
we know ourselves, our society, and the world in which we live. We
could well ask ourselves the question, "How can we get people ready
to lead a good life tomorrow, when we don't know what tomorrow will
be like?" Still further, Julian Huxley (8) informs us that we are
entering a new stage in the history of mankind--a stage in which we
must recognize "the oneness of all mankind."

Some Basic Assumptions

In looking ahead we can, as Michael (11, p. 5) has done, make
certain basic assumptions as follows:

> (1) international relations will derive from the same gener-
> al conditions that pertain today; (2) the weapons systems
> industries will continue to support a major share of our
> economy; (3) major discoveries will be made and applied in
> other technologies, including psychology and medicine;

---

* A paper presented to the Canadian Symposium of Recreation
(Symposium Canadien de la Récréation), Montreal, Quebec, June 12,
1967. (Published in Parks and Recreation, Vol. 11, No. 9:28, 47-
49, 1967.)

(4) trends in megalopolis living and in population growth will continue; (5) no major shifts in underlying social attitudes and in public and private goals will take place.

Definitions

A few brief definitions seem to be in order as well. Leisure will be used to explain the time that a person has free from his work and does not need for his sleep and basic survival activities. For our purposes here, it is not necessary to delineate the various meanings of play too carefully; so, we will accept the definition that play is an instinctive form of self-expression through pleasurable activity which seems to be aimless in nature. Note that the term recreation, often used interchangeably for play by the layman, seems to have developed a broader meaning. Typically, recreation embodies those experiences or activities that people have or engage in during their leisure for the purposes of pleasure, satisfaction, or education. Recreation is a human experience or activity; it is not necessarily instinctive; and it may be considered as purposeful - but probably not for its survival value.

Leisure Came Slowly for the Average Man

One may well ask why it took so long--that is, so many hundreds of years, before the possibility of earning and using leisure became a reality for the average man. This is not a simple question to answer. In the first place, we might argue that this possibility has really come quite rapidly considering the length of time that man has been developing on earth. For one thing, there have been many wars, and nothing is so devastating to an economy. We can't escape the fact that a surplus economy is absolutely necessary if men are to have a high standard of education and leisure (2, p. 76 et ff.). Secondly, the truism that times change slowly must be mentioned. It is extremely difficult to change the traditions and mores of a civilization. The existing political system continued to prevail, and it took finally revolutions to overthrow them before the concept of political democracy had an opportunity to grow. Thirdly, the power of the Church-- an almost absolute power--had to be weakened, before the concept of separation of church and state could become a reality. Fourthly, the beginnings of the natural sciences had to be consolidated into very real gains before the advanced technology could lead men into an industrial revolution, the outcomes of which we possibly still cannot foresee, and which in certain countries at least have lowered man's working hours down to what seems to be a relatively low figure.

Not the least of these changes by any means was the idea of naturalism which has its rebirth in the classical humanism of the early Renaissance. Actually, unrefined naturalism has been considered by some to be the oldest philosophy in the Western World dating back to five hundred years or more before Christ. Thales, who lived in Miletus in Asia Minor, believed that he had found the final stuff of the universe within nature. He and his contemporaries believed that nature exhibited order, and that this order could be relied upon by man. They believed that man should live simply and in harmony with nature. Both their intuition and their reason told them that man should allow nature to take its course.

This was a philosophy, then, which had a close relationship with the individual humanism of the twelfth and thirteenth centuries. Its educational aims included development of the individual personality through a liberal education based on classical literature and art with the "humanities" replacing the "divinities." The world of nature should be studied; the real life of the past should be examined; and the joys of living should be extolled. Physical education and sport were considered to be natural activities for man and should be encouraged. For these reasons, as well as those mentioned above, naturalism emerged in the eighteenth century as a full-blown philosophy of life with obvious educational implications. These implications were expressed magnificently by Jean Jacques Rousseau, who encouraged educators to study the child carefully and then to devise an educational plan based on this examination. The results of this approach became evident in the educational innovations of the next two centuries both in Europe and North America, not to mention certain other regions of the world. For the first time, play was recognized as a factor of considerable importance in the development of the child. The aftermath of these new ideas has been of untold value to health, physical education, and recreation.

North America

Before leisure could be used in North America, it had to be earned. The land mass had to be actually conquered and mastered by the various settlers. When Jacques Cartier looked at Canada, for example, he is purported to have said, "This must be the land that God gave Cain." (15) Furthermore, certain prevailing ideas about idleness had to be broken down. (7) From an economic standpoint we must realize that there is more to the question of leisure for the average man than the fact that some people had a lot of money, and he had very little of the same commodity. A more fundamental issue was that the level of production was not high enough to support our population at more than a subsistence level. The advance of industrial technology appears to have changed this imbalance; and in the past one hundred years the average worker has produced five times as much as he had done previously. While the man-hours that men worked were increasing only five times, the value of their production was growing twenty-five times. In addition, the population increase

did not offset this development. Now we find ourselves in a much
more favorable situation, because the average work week has been almost cut in half. Many people are now choosing leisure instead of
more work, because they want to "enjoy life." Many others are being
forced to accept an increased amount of leisure, although they do not
have all the material possessions of life that they might wish to have
(11, pp. 14-24). Of course, acceptance of a concept of education for
leisure depends a great deal on the prevailing educational philosophy.
Will the people--the taxpayers--make available sufficient financial
support so that education for leisure could be part of the program
offered by the schools?

A Unique Phenomenon in World History

Along with this great surplus economy, which is absolutely
necessary if education and recreation are to prosper, we have
witnessed the occurrence of a unique phenomenon in world history--
an organized pattern of community recreation embodying a wide variety of cultural opportunities. The outlines of this pattern had been
barely discernible toward the end of the nineteenth century, but in the
past fifty years the development of public and voluntary agency recreation has been absolutely phenomenal. Further social and economic
changes have taken place; professional associations have developed;
professional preparation for recreational leadership has mushroom-
ed; and city-supported recreation and park programs, along with
community centers - both within schools and separately--form a network across the United States and Canada.

Advancing industrial civilization has brought many advantages
to man, but it has created many problems as well. One of these has
to do with specialization in function--some people manage and other
people labor, and this results in an uneven distribution of wealth.
Of course, there has always been specialization of function of one
sort of another in societies, and the leaders have invariably seemed
to end up with the lion's share of the "good things of life." The people with more money have as a result been able to afford longer
periods and different types of education and recreation for themselves
and their children. (2) The labor movement is striving mightily to
reverse this trend to a degree, and this has had a definite effect on
the educational structure and recreational opportunities of our society. It is not difficult to understand why the social welfare state concept has been popular with the middle and lower economic classes.

Philosophical Analysis

Now we face the last one-third of the twentieth century with a
good deal of fear. Behind us are all sorts of wars, depressions, and
examples of man's inhumanity to man, as well as much that gives us

hope for the future. We are in the middle of a "Cold War," as well as a very "Hot War," and these struggles could spell utter devastation for mankind. Yet we look ahead idealistically, realistically, pragmatically, existentially, materialistically, or what have you? (19) On the home front we watch the rises and declines of the economy apprehensively. We try to comprehend the "peaceful" and the shooting revolutions going on all about us. We hear that automation is here and may bring about a situation where people will be paid not to work. Education for leisure would seem to warrant serious consideration in the face of such a development. History shows that no civilization has survived for long when the people had too much free time. Can we continue our unprecedented development as a continent where most people will find happiness and satisfaction, despite the fact that we are increasingly crowding people together in heavily-populated cities and suburbs?

Ponder over these problems for just a moment--pollution of air and water; an exodus of high-wage industries; a flight to the suburbs of those earning the higher incomes; a corresponding influx of those with lower incomes to the cities; a shortage of recreation areas and leadership; a frightening increase in the rate of crime of all types; a rise in the population of juveniles and the aged; housing ghettos with unbelievable filth; overcrowded schools with almost built-in discrimination present; and transportation jams which daily try the patience and increase the tensions of millions of our citizenry on the North American Continent. (4) Not a very pretty picture, is it?

Despite all of these seemingly almost insuperable problems Prime Minister Lester B. Pearson (17) recently asked Canada's Parliament to devote its new session to improving "the quality of Canadian life" as the country celebrates her 100th anniversary as a confederation. At the same time Campau (4), writing in the Saturday Review, asks such questions as whether Canada has a national identity, and whether the country is "cultured." Still further, a relatively few miles to the south, President Johnson is exhorting his fellow countrymen to build "a great society" and to fight a grueling war many thousands of miles away--and to carry on both of these tasks at one and the same time.

Happiness is said to be the "natural effect" of a good life. (12) If we are ever able to decide what "the good life" is, and if we are then able to bring its benefits to all in the world--provided that we don't blow ourselves to bits along the way--what sort of a prospect will we face? Paradoxically, making privileges available to all which are now only accessible to a relatively few, well-to-do people may afford us a type of life which we never anticipated. Is it not possible that, if all privileges are available to all people, no one will have any --or at least relatively few--of these "good things of life?" The only

hope here is that everything--but everything--will be completely auto-
mated.

Thus, as the work week gets shorter and shorter, there will be
fewer people to "keep the wheels turning." Who will want to perform
the million and one tasks necessary to keep the society active? Who
will "mind the store," repair the plumbing, clean up the garbage,
put heels on battered children's shoes (or will we just throw them
away?), and even teach schools, coach teams, and lead children in
recreation? Will you do it, if everyone else is being paid by the
Government not to work?

We are told by Michael (11, p. 29) that cybernation, with its
automation and computers, will bring additional leisure to practically
all of us on this Continent, but thus far we recognize but dimly the
problems that will be created. Presumably there will be a transitional stage that will extend over several decades before the supposedly
relatively stable future "sets in," so to speak. Naturally, it's this
transitional period which must be considered most carefully. The
four different leisure classes are postulated as follows:

1. Leisure Class One - the unemployed.

2. Leisure Class Two - the low-salaried employees working short hours.

3. Leisure Class Three - the adequately paid to high-
salaried group working short hours.

4. Leisure Class Four - those with no more leisure than
they now have (i.e., very few hours of leisure indeed).
(11, pp. 29-33)

Of course, the interesting thing about this development on the horizon
is that our countries don't have to cybernate. "Cybernation is by nature that sort of process that will be introduced selectively by organization, industry, and locality." (11, p. 28) It could "sneak up" on a
community, and the general population might not even recognize it.
And, I suppose, if its effects are too harsh, it would always be possible to "decybernate." To sum up this point, it appears that the
Shakespeare of the future is apt to say: "To cybernate, or not to
cybernate, that is the question!"

But what about our people--both individually and collectively?
The Old World countries all seem to have a character; it is almost
something that they take for granted. Citizens of the United States
are supposed to have a character too, although it is undoubtedly true
that Americans--as opposed to Canadians--are heterogeneous and
individualistic as a people. Recently, Henry Steele Commager, the

- 461 -

noted Amherst historian, enumerated "some common denominators in the American character." (pp. 246-254) These, he says, are (1) carelessness; (2) openhandedness, generosity, and hospitality; (3) self-indulgence; (4) sentimentality, and even romanticism; (5) gregariousness; (6) materialism; (7) confidence and self-confidence; (8) complacency--bordering occasionally on arrogance; (9) cultivation of the competitive spirit; (10) indifference to, and exasperation with laws, rules, and regulations; (11) equalitarianism; and (12) resourcefulness. This is an interesting list, don't you think? Were you Canadians perhaps chuckling just a bit at the American foibles? But lest you become too smug, remember that the American Goliath represents a force which you can hardly escape--even if you wanted to! How many of those traits which were mentioned above apply to you, your family, your friends and associates, or are characteristic of Canada for that matter?

Interestingly enough, the United States thinks that it enjoys the highest standard of living in the world. It is possibly true, however, that Canada and the Scandinavian countries have a still higher standard. Someone remarked recently, not altogether facetiously I'm certain, that the United States has "the highest standard of low living in the world." Statements such as this should cause all of us to take stock, as we conjure the "spirit and tone" of life on this continent between now and the year 2000.

We will need to think very seriously about the character and traits for which Americans and Canadians will educate in the years immediately ahead. What attitudes will we seek to develop toward work, use of leisure, participation in government, and the various types of consumption? Recreation education, as a part of general education, will definitely have a unique role to play.

Kateb, writing about "Utopia and the Good Life," considers the problem of increased leisure and abundance very carefully. (9, pp. 454-473) He sees no fixed pattern of future perfection such as that foreseen by others. While engaging in such speculation, he asserts that he is entering the realm of philosophical anthropology--perhaps a new combination of disciplines for some of us. Professor Kateb considers a progression of possibilities or definitions regarding the good life. There are, in fact, six of them as follows: the good life, (1) as laissez faire; (2) as the greatest amount of pleasure; (3) as play; (4) as craft; (5) as political action; and (6) as the life of the mind. His final conclusion, and this could perhaps have been predicted from a scholar, is that the life of the mind offers the greatest potential in the world as we know it--or may know it in the future. Kateb concludes, "that the man possessed of the higher faculties in their perfection is the model for utopia and already exists outside it . . ." (1, p. 472).

Having progressed this far in our discussion, it will undoubtedly be obvious to all that we need to plan, and that we must prepare our youth to learn how to adapt to change itself. All types of recreation education, including physical, social, aesthetic and creative, communicative, and learning interests, will need to be introduced into the educational system earlier. These activities cannot be considered ancillary and auxiliary even today. Having made this statement, we do not wish to convey the impression that a sound general education, including command of the language (two in Canada!), should receive less emphasis.

The statement "life can be beautiful" has become trite, but it should really describe a characteristic that will be increasingly present in the life of man. There are so many aspects of life that can be truly beautiful, and through careful development and "nurture" they can make unique contributions to the good life. We must make every effort as individuals to decide what the true end of man is. Is it ultimate union with his God? Is it hedonistic materialism characterized by a life in which one searches boldly for sensual pleasures? Or is it the life of the mind--the development of the higher faculties--as Kateb has stated it. (9, p. 462). We must ask ourselves further whether following a particular philosophical position or tendency logically and consistently will help us achieve our goals more effectively. Commager has maintained that "if there is an American philosophy, it is pragmatism, which looks to conduct, function, processes." (6, p. 253). Yet it would seem that our society is too pluralistic to be correctly characterized in this way.

Whatever your personal philosophy may be at present, and there is some evidence that this has a tendency to relate closely to one's particular stage of growth and development, the "good life" of the truly cultivated man in the future will probably be one in which the higher types of creative recreation will play a most important part. Our task is to guide man "a bit further down the path" through the highest type of professional endeavor on our part. The final choice belongs to each individual, of course, even if a "black box approach," similar to that now being employed with computers for diagnosis by the medical profession, were ever available to assist prople in making decisions relative to their best "avenues" to follow in the search for the highest or best type of living. Our children should not be faced with a future in which the life they find will come to them by default through the poor planning and lack of prescience of their parents. Mankind can, and must, do better than that to prepare future North Americans in the best possible way for the coming "Age of Leisure."

Selected References

1. Bliven, Bruce, "Using Our Leisure Is No Easy Job," The New York Times Magazine, April 26, 1965, pp. 18-19, 114-115.

2. Brubacher, J. S. A History of the Problems of Education. New York: McGraw-Hill Book Company, Second edition, 1966.

3. Campau, DuBarry, "Is Canada Cultured?", Saturday Review, April 29, 1967, pp. 58-60.

4. Campbell, Roald F., "Tomorrow's Teacher," Saturday Review, January 14, 1967, pp. 60-64, 73.

5. Chase, Stuart, "Can We Stay Prosperous?", Saturday Review, February 11, 1967, pp. 20-22.

6. Commager, Henry Steele. Freedom and Order. New York: George Braziller, 1966.

7. Holiday (Editorial), March, 1956.

8. Huxley, Julian, "The Crisis in Man's Destiny," Playboy, January, 1967, pp. 93-94, 212-217.

9. Kateb, George, "Utopia and the Good Life," Daedalus, 94, No. 2 (Spring, 1965), 454-473.

10. Leisure (Supplement), "The American Weekly", The Detroit News, March 19, 1961.

11. Michael, Donald N. Cybernation: The Silent Conquest (Pamphlet). Santa Barbara, California: Center for the Study of Democratic Institutions, 1962.

12. Royal Bank of Canada Monthly Letter, The. "In Search of a Happy Life," Vol. 42, No. 3, 4 pp.

13. Sullivan, Walter, "Can Science Be Curbed to Serve Man's Real Needs?", The Globe and Mail (Toronto), March 30, 1967.

14. _____, "Challenge of the City," The New York Times, Times, May 12, 1967.

15. Time Essay, "Canada Discovers Itself," May 5, 1967.

16. Toynbee, Arnold J. _Change and Habit: The Challenge of Our Time_. New York and London: Oxford University Press, 1966.

17. Walz, Hay, "Ambitious Tasks Set by Pearson," _The New York Times_, May 7, 1967.

18. Wolk, Ronald A., "The Challenge of Change." An unpublished paper presented at the 19th National Conference on Higher Education, Chicago, Illinois, April 19-22, 1964.

19. Zeigler, Earle F. _Philosophical Foundations for Physical, Health, and Recreation Education_. Englewood Cliffs, New Jersey: Prentice-Hall, Inc., 1964.

COMMUNICATION, DIVERSITY, AND COOPERATION IN INTERNATIONAL RELATIONS

Over the past two decades the affiliated professions of health, physical education, and recreation have gradually and steadily placed greater emphasis on international relations. Most people within the professions would say that this is a good thing; yet, the basis for their opinions would undoubtedly vary considerably. Only time will tell whether we are moving rapidly enough to promote the dissemination of knowledge, opinions, and understanding. In this brief presentations the concepts of "communication," "diversity," and "cooperation" will be considered as fundamentally important in the years immediately ahead - and perhaps to a greater extent than ever before.[1]

William Glaser, in his new book The Identity Society (New York: Harper and Row, 1972), theorizes that mankind is moving toward a role-dominated society, which he identifies as "Civilized Identity Society," in which the concern of humans will again focus on such concepts as "self-identity," "self-expression," and "cooperation." Glasser envisions this as the fourth phase of man's development, the first three of which are "Primitive Survival Society," "Primitive Identity Society," and "Civilized Survival Society." He explains how man, after struggling to survive for three and one-half million years in a most difficult environment, entered a second stage about 500,000 years ago in which he lived relatively peacefully in a somewhat abundant, much less stressful situation. Then, during the past several thousand years, primitive identity societies ended in a great many areas in the world as populations increased sharply. Certain societies found it necessary to take essential resources from neighboring societies, and this aggression and conflict returned mankind to a survival situation - even though many societies could be identified as relatively civilized. Glasser views this third period as a distortion of an earlier evolutionary heritage, one which has extended for the past ten thousand years. Now he postulates that it may become possible for mankind to enter a fourth phase. He claims that many men and women in the Western world, and to a certain extent in the Eastern world as well, are either clamoring or working quietly and resolutely for a role-dominated society in which each person can have an opportunity to seek his own identity and then to express it as he sees fit.

---

[1] A paper presented at the AAHPER International Relations Breakfast, Houston, Texas, March 26, 1972. (Published in Gymnasion, Vol. IX, No. 4:14-16, Winter, 1972.)

Communication

As the world moves into the last third of the twentieth century, the concept of "communication" has now risen in importance to the point where its significance is paramount if world society as we know it is to continue. Asimov tells us that, along with the increasing tempo of civilization, the "fourth revolution" is now upon us, and it is a different sort of revolution than we have been hearing about lately. What is referred to here is the fourth revolution in the area of communications that will in certain specific ways make our earth sort of a "global village." (Isaac Asimov, "The Fourth Revolution," Saturday Review, Oct. 24, 1970, 17-20.) Moving from the invention of speech, to the invention of writing, to the mechanical reproduction of the printed word, and now to relay stations in space, all people on earth will very soon be confronted with a blanketing communications network that will make possible personal relationships hitherto undreamed of by man. This development will have fantastic implications for physical education and sport, and it is highly urgent that we view comparative analysis of international physical education and sport in a new light. This is true because the world is now faced with a sort of "race" - a race that is on "between the coming of the true fourth revolution and the death of civilization that will inevitably occur through growth past the limits of the third." The basic idea behind this theory is that we must have vastly improved means of communication and put them into use so effectively that the signs of present breakdown will be alleviated.

Diversity

Diversity may be defined as the state or fact of being different, unlike, or diverse. Such a concept should be very important to all people on earth, and it would seem to be especially significant to men and women in the Western world where freedom and dignity for the individual is a basic aspect of a world-wide ideological struggle.

B. F. Skinner, in both Walden Two (New York: The Macmillan Co., 1948) and his recent best-selling Beyond Freedom and Dignity (New York: Alfred A. Knopf, 1971), outlines a society in which the problems of men and women are solved by a scientific technology designed for human conduct. With this approach such prevailing values as freedom and dignity are reinterpreted to help bring about a utopian society. Skinner's "operant conditioning" involves a type of behavior modification that would bring about a new variation or kind of social and political environment in which man's actions would be regulated more reasonably than heretofore on earth. Thus, this technique is available to improve the lot of humans on earth, and it is being recommended for implementation no matter what effect is might have on the possibility of diversity within man's life in a democratic society.

Cooperation

Cooperation implies working or acting together for a common purpose or benefit. Although healthy competition most certainly should have a place in our North American society and in the world at large, the field of international relations must increasingly give attention to the concept of cooperation among individuals, groups, and societies on earth. It is fortunate as we look ahead that there are certain "recurring elements in the various world philosophies." (A. Kaplan, The New World of Philosophy. Boston: Houghton-Mifflin, 1961, pp. 7-10.) If it is true, as Kaplan postulates, that these recurring "themes" of rationality, activism, humanism, and preoccupation with values are present in the leading world philosophies today, it does offer greater hope for an increased amount of world cooperation in the future.

Summary and Conclusions

Greater understanding and the implementation of the concepts of communication, diversity, and cooperation in international relations seem absolutely necessary if we are to create a better life on earth. One does not have to be too wide-awake today to know that a significant minority of our youth all around the world is telling the "establishment" that the world situation is not of their making. It is clear that youth wants to change things so that there will indeed be a better world tomorrow. It seems very clear further that the profession of physical education and sport have a unique opportunity to relate to youth on an international scale through the medium of sport and physical activity (as expressed in human movement in dance, play, and exercise).

The large majority of men and women in this profession have so little knowledge about what really takes place in physical education and sport in other countries. This is true even though many colleges and universities are adding comparative and international course experiences at both the undergraduate and graduate levels. There is now an urgent need for a sound body-of-knowledge about this aspect of the broader disciplinary approach to the profession. This can be gained through quality graduate study and research based on the employment of the variety of research methods and techniques available.

Finally, the words of the late Lord Bertrand Russell (The Autobiography of Bertrand Russell, Volume 3. New York: Simon and Schuster, 1969, pp. 318 et ff.) offer a basis unparalleled for the continuation of a superior effort in international relations:

> I wanted on the one hand to find out whether anything could be known; and, on the other hand, to do whatever

might be possible toward creating a happier world . . . as
I have grown older, my optimism has grown more sober
and the happy issue more distant . . .   The causes of un-
happiness in the past and in the present are not difficult to
ascertain. There have been poverty, pestilence, and
famine, which were due to man's inadequate mastery of
nature. There have been wars, oppressions, and tortures
which have been due to men's hostility to their fellow men.
And there have been morbid miseries fostered by gloomy
creeds, which have led men into profound inner discords
. . . I may have thought the road to a world of free and
happy human beings shorter than it is proving to be, but I
was not wrong in thinking that such a world is possible,
and that it is worthwhile to live with a view to bringing it
nearer. I have lived in the pursuit of a vision, both
personal and social . . .   These things I believe, and the
world, for all its horrors, has left me unshaken.

Appendix
SELECTED REFERENCES AND BIBLIOGRAPHY

A CHRONOLOGICAL LISTING OF SELECTED STUDIES ON THE PHILOSOPHY OF PHYSICAL EDUCATION AND SPORT

Compiled by
Earle F. Zeigler*
The University of Western Ontario
1974

1922

1. Hetherington, Clark. School Program in Physical Education. New York: Harcourt, Brace & World, Inc., 1922. 132 p.

1927

2. Williams, J. F. The Principles of Physical Education. Philadelphia: W. B. Saunders Co., 1964 (First edition, 1927).

3. Wood, T. D. and Cassidy, Rosalind. The New Physical Education. New York: The Macmillan Company, 1927. 457 p.

* Professor Zeigler developed this bibliography over a period of twenty years, and especially in connection with a body-of-knowledge report presented to the Western Conference (Big Ten) Directors' Meeting at Iowa City, Iowa, December 9, 1965. Since then it has been updated regularly, notably quite recently by Sue Cook and Debbie Shogan while working cooperatively with EFZ as graduate research assistants. The reader is encouraged to call any notable omissions to Prof. Zeigler's attention. The bibliography has been employed in connection with related literature chapters of various master's and doctoral theses and dissertations. In the early 1970's, for example, Dr. Robert G. Osterhoudt, now at Minnesota, completed a definitive study in which he described and briefly evaluated this material and other efforts as well. (See his "A Descriptive Analysis of Research Concerning the Philosophy of Physical Education and Sport." University of Illinois, Urbana, 1971.) The 1922 date was selected arbitrarily by Professor Zeigler as a starting point. (This bibliography was published in Physical Education: Progressivism or Essentialism? with H. J. VanderZwaag. Champaign, Illinois: Stipes Publishing Company, 1966.)

1929

4. Savage, H. J. et al. <u>American College Athletics</u>. New York: The Carnegie Foundation for the Advancement of Teaching, 1929. 383 p.

1930

5. Williams, J. F. and Hughes, W. L. <u>Athletics in Education</u>. Philadelphia: W. B. Saunders Co., 1930. (Second edition in 1937, 472 p.)

1931

6. Nash, Jay B. (editor). <u>Mind-Body Relationships</u> (Vol. I). New York: A. S. Barnes and Company, Inc., 1931. (This was the first volume of the Interpretations of Physical Education Series.)

1934

7. Nash, Jay B. (editor). <u>Character Education Through Physical Education</u> (Vol. III). New York: A. S. Barnes and Company, Inc., 1934. (This was the third volume of the Interpretations of Physical Education Series.)

8. Sapora, A. V. and Mitchell, E. D. <u>The Theory of Play and Recreation</u>. New York: The Ronald Press Company, 1961. 558 p. (This book was published first in 1923 by Bowen and Mitchell, and the revised edition, written by Mason and Mitchell, was published in 1934.)

1936

9. Larkin, Richard A., "The Influence of John Dewey on Physical Education." Master's thesis, The Ohio State University, 1936.

1937

10. Sharman, Jackson R. <u>Modern Principles of Physical Education</u>. New York: A. S. Barnes and Company, Inc., 1937. 208 p.

1938

11. Cassidy, Rosalind. New Directions in Physical Education for the Adolescent Girl in High School and College. New York: A. S. Barnes and Company, Inc., 1938. 231 p.

12. Esslinger, Arthur A., "A Philosophical Study of Principles for Selecting Activites in Physical Education." Ph.D. thesis, State University of Iowa, 1938.

13. Wayman, Agnes R. A Modern Philosophy of Physical Education. Philadelphia: W. B. Saunders Company, 1938. 231 p.

1939

14. Staley, Seward C. Sports Education. New York: A. S. Barnes and Company, 1939. 325 p.

1940

15. Cureton, T. K., Jr., "The Philosophical or Group Thinking Method of Research," Research Quarterly, Vol. XI, No. 3:75-83, October, 1940.

16. McCloy, C. H. Philosophical Bases for Physical Education. New York: Appleton-Century-Crofts, Inc., 1940. 211 p.

1941

17. Cahn, L. Joseph., "Contributions of Plato to Thought on Physical Education, Health, and Recreation." Ed.D. dissertation, New York University, 1941.

1943

18. Clark, Margaret C., "A Philosophical Interpretation of a Program of Physical Education in a State Teachers College." Ph.D. dissertation, New York University, 1943.

19. Cobb, Louise S., "A Study of the Functions of Physical Education in Higher Education." Ph.D. dissertation, Columbia Teachers College, 1943.

1944

20. Lynn, Minnie L., "Major Emphases in Physical Education."
    Ph.D. dissertation, The University of Pittsburgh, 1944.

1945

21. Pope Pius XII, "Physical Culture and Youth," Catholic News-
    letter, No. 288, May 26, 1945.

1948

22. Nash, Jay B. Physical Education: Interpretations and Objec-
    tives. New York: The Ronald Press Company, 1948.
    288 p.

1949

23. Cobb, Louise S., "Philosophical Research Methods," in Re-
    search Methods Applied to Health, Physical Education,
    and Recreation. Washington, D. C.: American Associ-
    ation for Health, Physical Education, and Recreation,
    1949, pp. 136-147.

1951

24. American Association for Health, Physical Education, and Rec-
    reation, Democratic Human Relations. Washington,
    D. C.: AAHPER, First Yearbook, 1951. 562 p.

25. Brownell, Clifford L. and Hagman, E. P. Physical Education
    - Foundations and Principles. New York: McGraw-Hill
    Book Company, Inc., 1951. 397 p.

26. Scott, H. A. Competitive Sports in Schools and Colleges. New
    York: Harper & Row, Publishers, Inc., 1951. 604 p.

27. Shepard, Natalie M., "Democracy in Physical Education: A
    Study of the Implications for Educating for Democracy
    through Physical Education." Ed.D. dissertation, New
    York University, 1952.

1953

28. Pope Pius XII, "Sports and Gymnastics," Catholic Mind, No.
    51:569-576, September, 1953.

1954

29. National Education Association and American Association of
School Administrators, Educational Policies Commission.
<u>School Athletics, Problems and Policies</u>. Washington,
D. C.: The Commission, 1954. 116 p.

1955

30. Lozes, Jewell H., "The Philosophy of Certain Religious
Denominations Relative to Physical Education, and the
Effect of this Philosophy on Physical Education in Certain
Church-Related Institutions." M.S. thesis, Pennsylvania
State University, 1955.

1956

31. Bair, Donn E., "An Identification of Some Philosophical Beliefs
Held by Influential Professional Leaders in American
Physical Education." Ph.D. dissertation, University of
Southern California, 1956.

32. Downey, Robert J., "An Identification of the Philosophical Beliefs of Educators in the Field of Health Education."
Ph.D. dissertation, University of Southern California,
1956.

33. Moolenijzer, Nicolaas J., "Implications of the Philosophy of
Gaulhofer and Streicher for Physical Education."
Master's thesis, University of California, Los Angeles,
1956.

34. Pope Pius XII, "Christian Conduct Towards Athletics," <u>Catho-
lic Mind</u>, No. 54:309-417, July, 1956.

35. Spears, Betty M., "Philosophical Bases for Physical Education
Experiences Consistent with the Goals of General Educa-
tion for College Women." Ph.D. dissertation, New York
University, 1956.

36. Wilton, W. M., "Comparative Analysis of Theories Related to
Moral and Spiritual Values in Physical Education."
Ed.D. dissertation, University of California at
Los Angeles, 1956.

1957

37. American Association for Health, Physical Education, and Recreation, Division for Girls and Women's Sports. "State of Policies and Procedures for Competition in Girls' and Women's Sports." JOHPER 28:6:57-58; September, 1957.

1958

38. Ellfeldt, Lois E. and Metheny, Eleanor, "Movement and Meaning: Development of a General Theory." Research Quarterly 29:264-273, October, 1958.

39. Krug, Orvis C., "The Philosophic Relationship between Physical Education and Athletics." Ed.D. dissertation, New York University, 1958.

40. Morland, Richard B., "A Philosophical Interpretation of the Educational Views Held by Leaders in American Physical Education." Ph.D. dissertation, New York University, 1958.

41. O'Brien, Joseph P., "A Basis in Catholic Thought for Physical Education." Master's thesis, The Ohio State University, 1958.

42. Sanborn, Marion A., "Major Issues in Physical Education." Ph.D. dissertation, The Ohio State University, 1958.

43. Shivers, Jay S., "An Analysis of Theories of Recreation." Ph.D. dissertation, The University of Wisconsin, 1958.

44. Twomey, J. J. Christian Philosophy and Physical Education. Liverpool 6: Kilburns (printers) Ltd., 83-85 Shaw Street, 1958. (See also "Mens Sana in Corpore Sano," The Clergy Review, No. 169:11-12, 24, n.d.)

1959

45. Armstrong, Joanna N., "The Theory of Play: A Study of Its History and Philosophy Based on Original Texts by Schiller, Froebel, Compayre, and Piaget." Doctoral dissertation, University of Houston, 1959.

46. Friermood, Harold T. (editor). A New Look at YMCA Physical Education. New York: Association Press, 1959.

47. Hess, Ford A., "American Objectives of Physical Education from 1900-1957 Assessed in the Light of Certain Historical Events." Ed.D. dissertation, New York University, 1959.

48. Metheny, Eleanor, "Philosophical Methods," in Research Methods in Health, Physical Education, and Recreation. Washington, D. C.: American Association for HPER, Second edition, 1959, pp. 482-501.

49. Taggart, Gladys M., "A Study of the Relationship Between the Goals of Physical Education and Higher Education." Ph.D. dissertation, New York University, 1959.

1960

50. Char, Pusthakama, "An Introduction to a Comparative Study of the Philosophies of Education of the United States of America and India as Related to Physical Education." Master's thesis, The Ohio State University, 1960.

51. Forsythe, Eleanor, "Philosophical Bases for Physical Education Experience Consistent with the Goals of American Education for High School Girls." Ph.D. dissertation, New York University, 1960.

52. Nash, Jay B. Philosophy of Recreation and Leisure. Dubuque, Iowa: Wm. C. Brown Company, Publishers, 1960. (This book was published originally by the C. V. Mosby Company, St. Louis in 1953.)

53. Paplauṣkas-Ramunas, Antoine, L'Education physique dans l'Humanisme integral. Ottawa, Canada: Les Editions de l'Universite d'Ottawa, 1960. 115 p.

54. Shepard, Natalie M. Foundations and Principles of Physical Education. New York: The Ronald Press Company, 1960. 352 p.

55. Zeigler, Earle F., "A True Professional Needs a Consistent Philosophy," Australian Journal of Physical Education, No. 18:15-16, Feb.-March, 1960. (This article appeared also in The Physical Educator, Vol. 19, No. 1:17-18, March, 1962.)

1961

56. Avedon, Elliott M., "A Philosophical Inquiry into the Essence
of Recreation." Doctoral dissertation, Columbia University, 1961.

57. Brightbill, C. K., Man and Leisure: A Philosophy of Recreation. Englewood Cliffs, New Jersey: Prentice-Hall,
Inc., 1961. 292 p.

58. Davis, Elwood C. The Philosophical Process in Physical Education. Philadelphia: Lea & Febiger, 1961. 301 p.
(Includes several excellent analyses by Roger Burke.)

59. Frederick, Mary M., "Naturalism: The Philosophy of Jean
Jacques Rousseau and Its Implications for American
Physical Education." 1961. D.P.E. dissertation,
Springfield College.

60. Lewis, Clifford G., "Expressed Values of College Women at the
University of Georgia Concerning Selected Social Factors
Related to Acceptance of and Participation in Physical
Education." Ed.D. dissertation, Columbia University,
1961.

1962

61. Athletic Institute, The, Report of the National Conference on
Interpretation of Physical Education. Chicago, Illinois:
The Athletic Institute, Inc., 1962, 65 p.

62. Oberteuffer, D. and Ulrich, C. Physical Education. New
York: Harper & Row, Publishers, Second edition, 1962.
466 p. (First edition published in 1961, 374 p.)

63. Onaga, Takeomo, "Philosophical Concepts of Selected Leaders
in Physical Education." Master's thesis, Los Angeles
State College, 1962.

64. VanderZwaag, Harold J., "Delineation of an Essentialistic
Philosophy of Physical Education." Ph.D. thesis, The
University of Michigan, 1962.

65. Zeigler, Earle F., "Naturalism in Physical, Health, and Recreation Education," The University of Michigan School
of Education Bulletin, Vol. 34, No. 2:42-46, December,
1962.

66. _____., "Philosophy of Physical Education in a New
Key," The Australian Journal of Physical Education, No.
26:5, 7-8, October-November, 1962.

<u>1963</u>

67. American Association for Health, Physical Education, and Recreation, Division for Girls and Women's Sports and Division of Men's Athletics. Value in Sports. Washington,
D. C.: AAHPER, 1963. 130 p.

68. Brackenbury, Robert L., "Physical Education, An Intellectual
Emphasis?" Quest, I, Winter, December, 1963. pp. 3-
6.

69. Brown, Camille and Cassidy, Rosalind. Theory in Physical
Education. Philadelphia: Lea & Febiger, 1963. 244 p.

70. Cowell, Charles C., "Interpreting Physical Education Through
Contrasting Philosophies," The Physical Educator, Vol.
20, No. 4:147, December, 1963.

71. _____ and France, Wellman L. Philosophy and
Principles of Physical Education. Englewood Cliffs, New
Jersey: Prentice-Hall, Inc., 1963. 236 p.

72. Davis, Elwood C. (editor). Philosophies Fashion Physical
Education. Dubuque, Iowa: Wm. C. Brown Company,
Publishers, 1963. 136 p. (Five of the papers in this
book were first presented by Elwood C. Davis, Roger K.
Burke, Delbert Oberteuffer, Leona Holbrook, and
Deobold Van Dalen at the American Association for
Health, Physical Education, and Recreation Convention,
Atlantic City, New Jersey, March 19, 1961.)

73. _____., "The Power of Beliefs," Quest, I, Winter,
December, 1963, pp. 7-12.

74. Holbrook, Leona, "The Teleological Concept of the Physical
Qualities of Man," Quest, I, Winter, December, 1963.
pp. 13-17.

75. Huelster, Laura J., "The Body of Knowledge in Physical Edu-
cation--Philosophical." A paper presented to the American Academy of Physical Education Annual Meeting, 1963.
(This article appeared in The Physical Educator, Vol. 22,
No. 1:6-8, March, 1965.)

76. Keating, James W., "Winning in Sport and Athletics," Thought (Fordham University Quarterly), Vol. XXXVIII, No. 149: 201-10, Summer, 1963.

77. Oberteuffer, Delbert, "On Learning Values Through Sport," Quest, I, Winter, December, 1963. pp. 23-29.

78. Pullias, Earl V., "The Education of the Whole Man," Quest, I, Winter, December, 1963. pp. 37-42.

79. Slusher, Howard S., "Existentialism and Physical Education, A paper presented to the American Association for Health, Physical Education, and Recreation Convention, May 3, 1963. (An abridged version appeared in The Physical Educator, Vol. 20, No. 4:153-156, December, 1963.)

80. Steinhaus, Arthur H. Toward an Understanding of Health and Physical Education. Dubuque, Iowa: Wm. C. Brown Company, Publishers, 1963. 376 p.

81. VanderZwaag, Harold J., "Essentialism and Physical Education." A paper presented to the American Association for Health, Physical Education, and Recreation Convention, May 3, 1963. (This article appeared in The Physical Educator, Vol. 20, No. 4:147-149, December, 1963.)

82. Wagner, Ann L., "The Concept of Physical Education in Selected Liberal Arts Colleges." Master's thesis, State University of Iowa, 1963.

83. Zeigler, Earle F., "The Implications of Experimentalism for Physical, Health, and Recreation Education." A paper presented to the AAHPER Convention, May 3, 1963. (An abridged version appeared in The Physical Educator, Vol. 20, No. 4:150-152, December, 1963.)

84. _____., "Philosophical Foundations and Educational Leadership," The Physical Educator, Vol. 20, No. 1:15-18, March, 1963.

85. _____., "Values in Physical Education--A Philosophical Dilemma," Journal of the Canadian Association for Health, Physical Education, and Recreation, Vol. 29, No. 3:10-12, February-March, 1963.

86. Bucher, Charles A. Foundations of Physical Education.
St. Louis: The C. V. Mosby Company, 1964. (The first
edition was published in 1952.)

87. Carver, Julia, "A Study of the Influence of the Philosophy of the
Church of Jesus Christ of Latter-day Saints on Physical
Education in the Church Schools." Ph.D. dissertation,
University of Oregon, 1964.

88. Kaelin, Eugene F., "Being in the Body." A paper presented to
the National Association of Physical Education for College
Women Conference, National Music Camp, Interlochen,
Michigan, June 14, 1964.

89. Keating, James W., "Sportsmanship as a Moral Category,"
Ethics, Vol. LXXV, No. 1:25-35, October, 1964.

90. Kleinman, Seymour, "The Significance of Human Movement--a
Phenomenological Approach." A paper presented to the
National Association of Physical Education for College
Women Conference, June 17, 1964.

91. Mijatake, H., "Mao Tse Tung's 'The Study of Physical Education'," Japanese Journal of Health, Physical Education,
and Recreation, Vol. 14, July, 1964.

92. Sanborn, Marion A. and Hartman, Betty G. Issues in Physical
Education. Philadelphia: Lea & Febiger, 1964. 256 p.

93. Slatton, Yvonne L., "The Philosophical Beliefs of Undergraduate and Graduate Physical Education Major Students and
the Physical Education Faculty at the University of North
Carolina at Greensboro." M.S. thesis, University of
North Carolina at Greensboro, 1964.

94. Society of State Directors of Health, Physical Education, and
Recreation, The, "A Statement of Basic Beliefs: The
School Programs in HPER." A pamphlet prepared by the
Society and available through its Secretary-Treasurer,
Simon A. McNeely, President's Council on Physical Fit-
ness, 441 G. Street, N.W., Room 4820, GAO Bldg.,
Washington, D. C. 20548.

95. Van Dalen, D. B., "Philosophical Profiles for Physical Education," The Physical Educator, Vol. 21, No. 3:113-115,
October, 1964.

96. Zeigler, Earle F., "An Analysis of the Implications of Reconstructionism for Physical, Health, and Recreation Education." A paper presented to the American Association
for Health, Physical Education, and Recreation Convention in Washington, D. C., May 7-11, 1964. 28 p.

97. _____., "A Brief Analysis of the Educational Philosophy Underlying Five Men's Instructional Physical
Education Programs," Journal of the Canadian Association for Health, Physical Education and Recreation, Vol.
30, No. 3:23-26, 31, February-March, 1964.

98. _____., "The Dilemma of Many Faces and a Blurred
Image." A paper presented to the Wisconsin Association
for Health, Physical Education, and Recreation Convention, May 1, 1964.

99. _____., "A Philosophical Analysis of Amateurism in
Competitive Athletics," School Activities, Vol. XXXV,
No. 7:199-203, March, 1964.

100. _____. Philosophical Foundations for Physical,
Health, and Recreation Education. Englewood Cliffs,
New Jersey: Prentice-Hall, Inc., 1964. 356 p.

1965

101. Austin, Patricia, "A Conceptual Structure of Physical Education." Ph.D. dissertation, Michigan State University,
1965.

102. Bronzan, Robert T., "Attitudes of University Publics Toward
the Contributions of the Intercollegiate Football Program
to General Education." Ed.D. dissertation, Stanford
University, 1965.

103. Cassidy, Rosalind, "The Cultural Definition of Physical Education," Quest, IV, Spring, April, 1965. pp. 11-15.

104. Cavanaugh, Patric L., "An Essentialistic Approach--Moderate
Realism." A paper presented to the History and Philosophy Section of the Physical Education Division of the
American Association for Health, Physical Education,
and Recreation Convention, Dallas, Texas, March 22,
1965.

105. Huelster, Laura J., "New Meanings and Emphases in Physical Education," Illinois News (IAHPER), Vol. XII, No. 3:2-6, March, 1965.

106. Jokl, Ernst, "Sport as Leisure," Quest, IV, Spring, April, 1965. pp. 37-47.

107. Keating, James W., "Athletics and the Pursuit of Excellence," Education, Vol. 85, No. 7:428-431, March, 1965.

108. _____., "The Heart of the Problem of Amateur Athletics," The Journal of General Education, Vol. 16, No. 4:12 pages, January, 1965.

109. Mason, M. G., "Some Philosophical Aspects of Physical Education," in Conference Papers, Vol. 1, Nos. 1&2:4-8, November, 1965. (This is a publication of the Carnegie Old Students Association, Carnegie College, Leeds 6, England.)

110. McIntosh, Peter C., "Means and Ends in a State of Leisure," Quest, IV, Spring, April, 1965. pp. 33-36.

111. McPherson, Francis A., "Development of Ideas in Physical Education in the Secondary Schools in the United States Between 1884 and 1920." Ph.D. dissertation, The University of Wisconsin, 1965.

112. Metheny, Eleanor. Connotations of Movement in Sport and Dance. Dubuque, Iowa: William C. Brown Company, Publishers, 1965. 220 p.

113. _____ (editor). "This is Physical Education." A statement published by the American Association for Health, Physical Education and Recreation, 1201 Sixteenth St., N. W., Washington, D. C. 20036. 1965. 24 p.

114. Mordy, Margaret A., "Physical Fitness--A Progressivistic Analysis--Reconstructionism." A paper presented to the American Association for Health, Physical Education, and Recreation Convention, March 22, 1965.

115. Murphy, Gardner, "Education of the Will," Quest, IV, Spring, April, 1965. pp. 1-9.

116. Oberteuffer, Delbert, "Some Contributions of Physical Education to an Educated Life," in <u>Background Readings for Physical Education</u> (Ann Paterson and Edmond C. Hallberg, editors). New York: Holt, Rinehart and Wins Winston, 1965, pp. 109-119. (Reprinted from a 1945 JOHPER article.)

117. Stone, Gregory P., "The Play of Little Children," <u>Quest</u>, IV, Spring, April, 1965. pp. 23-31.

118. Webster, Randolph W. <u>Philosophy of Physical Education</u>. Dubuque, Iowa: William C. Brown Company, Publishers, 1965. 227 p.

119. Weiss, Paul, "A Philosophical Definition of Leisure," <u>Quest</u>, V, Winter, December, 1965. pp. 1-7.

120. Williams, Jesse Feiring, "The Destiny of Man," <u>Quest</u>, IV, Spring, April, 1965. pp. 17-21.

121. Williams, John, "William Ellery Channing's Philosophy of Physical Education and Recreation," <u>Quest</u>, IV, Spring, April, 1965. pp. 49-52.

122. Zeigler, Earle F., "Current Trends in the Philosophy of Physical, Health, and Recreation Education," in the <u>Proceedings</u> of the Illinois Association for Professional Preparation in Health, Physical Education, and Recreation, Allerton House, Monticello, Illinois, March 5, 1965.

123. _____., "A Philosophical Analysis of Recreation and Leisure," <u>Quest</u>, Monograph V, Winter Issue, 8-17, December, 1965.

124. _____., "The Role of Physical Education in the Educational Structure," <u>The Australian Journal of Physical Education</u>, No. 35:5-11, October-November, 1965.

1966

125. Banks, Gary C., "The Philosophy of Friedrich Nietzsche." Master's thesis, The University of Wisconsin, 1966.

126. Caldwell, S. A., "Conceptions of Physical Education in Twentieth Century America: Rosalind Cassidy." Ph.D. dissertation, University of Washington, 1966.

127. Fawcett, Donald F., "Analysis of John Dewey's Theory of Experience: Implications of Physical Education Methodlogy." Master's thesis, The University of Southern California, 1966.

128. Fraleigh, Warren P., "The Perplexed Professor," Quest, Vol. 7, December, 1966. pp. 1-13.

129. Gerber, Ellen W., "Three Interpretations of the Role of Physical Education, 1930-1960: Charles H. McCloy, Jay B. Nash and Jesse F. Williams." Ph.D. dissertation, University of Southern California, 1966.

130. Huelster, Laura J., "The Physical Educator in Perspective," Quest, VII, Winter, December, 1966. pp. 62-66.

131. Keating, James W., "Sartre on Sport and Play." A paper presented to the History and Philosophy Section, Physical Education Division, AAHPER, Chicago, March 21, 1966.

132. Kleinman, Seymour, "Phenomenology--The Body--Physical Education." A paper presented to the History and Philosophy Section, Physical Section Division, AAHPER, Chicago, March 21, 1966.

133. Pelton Barry C., "A Critical Analysis of Current Concepts Underlying General Physical Education." Ph.D. dissertation, University of Southern California, 1966.

134. Slater, Morris B., "An Identification and Comparison of Some Philosophical Beliefs in the Area of Physical Education Held by Elementary School Teachers." Master's thesis, University of Oregon, 1966.

135. Smithells, Philip A., "The Physical Educator as Professor," Quest, Vol. 7, December, 1966. pp. 53-56.

136. Spence, D. W., "Analysis of Selected Values in Physical Education." Ed. D. dissertation, Louisiana State University, 1966.

137. VanderZwaag, Harold J., "Does Existence Precede Essence in Physical Education?" A paper presented to the History and Philosophy Section, Physical Education Division, AAHPER, Chicago, March 21, 1966.

138. Zeigler, Earle F., "The Educational Philosophy of Existentialism," Illinois News HPER, Vol. XIV, No. 1:9-10, November, 1966.

139.   _____, "Philosophy of Administration," Journal of the Canadian HPER, Vol. 32, No. 6:19-24, August-September, 1966.

140.   _____ and VanderZwaag, Harold J. Physical Education: Reconstructionism or Essentialism? Champaign, Illinois: Stipes Publishing Company, 1966.

1967

141.   Brooks, Betty, "Views of Physical Fitness foom Four Educational Philosophies," The Physical Educator, Vol. 24, No. 1:31-32, March, 1967.

142.   Davis, Elwood C. and Miller, Donna Mae. The Philosophic Process in Physical Education. Philadelphia: Lee & Febiger, Second edition, 1967.

143.   Felshin, Janet. Perspectives and Principles for Physical Education. New York: John Wiley and Sons, Inc., 1967.

144.   Hileman, Betty Jean, "Emerging Patterns of Thought in Physical Education in the United States, 1956-1966." Ph.D. dissertation, University of Southern California, 1967.

145.   Leavitt, Gordon F., "A Philosophical Study of Interscholastic Football in the Area of Sacramento, California." Master's thesis, Sacramento State College, 1967.

146.   Metheny, Eleanor, "How Does a Movement Mean?" Quest, VIII, Spring, 1967. pp. 1-6.

147.   Paddick, Robert J., "The Nature and Place of a Field of Knowledge in Physical Education." Master's thesis, University of Alberta, 1967.

148.   Shults, Frederick D., "The History and Philosophy of Athletics for Men at Oberlin College." P.E.D. dissertation, Indiana University, Bloomington, Indiana, 1967.

149.   Shvartz, Esar, "Nietzsche--Philosopher of Fitness," Quest, VIII, May, 1967. pp. 83-89.

150.   Slusher, Howard S., Man, Sport and Existence: A Critical Analysis. Philadelphia: Lea & Febiger, 1967.

151. Thomson, P. L., "Ontological Truth in Sports: A Phenomenological Analysis." Ph.D. dissertation, the University of
Southern California, 1967.

152. VanderZwaag, Harold J., "Pitfalls in Philosophical Recearch,"
Illinois News HPER, XIV, No. 3:4-6, May, 1967.

153. Zeigler, Earle F., "Christian Idealism and YMCA Physical
Education (Part I)," Journal of Physical Education, Vol.
64, No. 6:163-165, July-August, 1967.

154. _____., "Christian Idealism and YMCA Physical
Education (Part II)," Journal of Physical Education, Vol.
64, No. 7:28-31, September-October, 1967.

155. _____., "The Need for Consensus and Research,"
The Physical Educator, Vol. 24, No. 3:107-109, October,
1967.

156. _____., "A Riddle for Tomorrow's World: How to
Lead a Good Life," Parks & Recreation, Vol. 11, No. 9:
28, 47-49, September, 1967.

1968

157. Cavanaugh, Patric., "A Delineation of Moderate Realism and
Physical Education." Ph.D. dissertation, The University of Michigan, 1968.

158. Dorman, Jacquelyne L., "Creativity as a Significant Concept
in Sport, Dance, and Physical Activity." M.S. thesis,
University of Massachusetts, 1968.

159. Fogelin, R., "Sport: The Diversity of the Concept." Unpub-
lished paper presented at the 13th Annual Meeting of The
American Association for the Advancement of Science,
Dallas, Texas, December 28, 1968.

160. Fraleigh, Warren P., "Meanings of the Human Body in Modern
Christian Theology," Research Quarterly, Vol. 39:265-
267, May, 1968.

161. Kaelin, E. F., "The Well-Played Game: Notes Toward an
Aesthetics of Sport," Quest, X, Spring, May, 1968.
pp. 16-28.

162. Kleinman, Seymour, "Toward a Non-Theory of Sport," Quest,
X, Spring, May, 1968. pp. 29-34.

163. Loy, John W., "The Nature of Sport: A Definitional Effort," Quest, X, Spring, May, 1968. pp. 1-15.

164. Meier, Mila H., "Play as a Way to Know." Ed.D. dissertation, Boston University, 1968.

165. Schmitz, Kenneth, "Sport and Play: Suspension of the Ordinary," Unpublished paper presented at the 13th Annual Meeting of The American Association for the Advancement of Science, Dallas, Texas, December 28, 1968.

166. Shadduck, Ione G., "A Philosophical Base for a Physical Education Program Design." Ph.D. dissertation, Michigan State University, 1968.

167. Sheehan, Thomas J., "Sport: The Focal Point of Physical Education," Quest, X, Spring, May, 1968. pp. 59-67.

168. Walsh, John H., "A Fundamental Ontology of Play and Leisure." Ph.D. dissertation, Georgetown University, 1968.

169. Zeigler, Earle F., "The Employment of Philosophical Analysis to Supplement Administrative Theory and Research," The Journal of Educational Administration, Vol. VI, No. 2:132-151, October, 1968.

170. _____., "The Idea of Physical Education in Modern Times," The Australian Journal of Physical Education, No. 43:17-24, June-July, 1968.

171. _____., Problems in the History and Philosophy of Physical Education and Sport. Englewood Cliffs, New Jersey: Prentice-Hall, Inc., 1968.

172. _____., "A Tale of Two Titles," JOHPER, Vol. 39, No. 5:53, May, 1968.

173. _____ and VanderZwaag, Harold J. Physical Education: Progressivism or Essentialism? Champaign' Illinois: Stipes Publishing Company, Second edition, 1968.

174. American Association for Health, Physical Education, and Recreation (Division for Girls' and Women's Sports), "Philosophy and Standards for Girls' and Women's Sports," Washington, D. C.: The Association, 1969. 54 p.

175. Bookwalter, Karl W. and VanderZwaag, Harold J. _Foundations and Principles of Physical Education_. Philadelphia: W. B. Saunders Company, 1969.

176. Carlistle, Robert, "The Concept of Physical Education," in the _Proceedings_ of the Philosophy of Education Society of Graat Britain, The Annual Conference, 1969. pp. 5-35.

177. Cramer, Carolyn Ann, "John Dewey's View of Experience for Education: Implications for Physical Education." M.S. thesis, Drake University, 1969.

178. Fraleigh, Warren P., Meanings of the Human Body in Modern Christian Theology," in _Research Quarterly_, Vol. 39, No. 2:265-277, May, 1968. (Reported in _Completed Research_ for 1968 which appeared in 1969.)

179. _____., "A Prologue to the Study of Theory Building in Physical Education," _Quest_, No. XII, May 1969, 26-33.

180. Gerber, Ellen W., "Identity, Relation and Sport," _Quest_, No. 8, 1967, 90-99. (This listing is out of chronological order.)

181. Harper, William A., "Man Alone," _Quest_, No. 12, May, 1969, 57-60.

182. Kleinman, Seymour, "The Significance of Human Movement: A Phenomenological Approach," _Dimensions of Physical Education_ (editors, Charles A. Bucher and Myra Goldman). St. Louis: The C. V. Mosby Co., 1969. pp. 150-153.

183. Kretchmar, R. Scott, "A Phenomenological Reduction: The Unity of Sport and Dance." Unpublished manuscript, Kansas State Teachers College at Emporia, 1969.

184. _____ and Harper, William A., "Must We Have a Rational Answer to the Question Why Does Man Play?" _JOHPER_, Vol. 40, No. 3:57-58, March, 1969.

185. Lutz, Helen S., "Philosophical Foundations of the Movement Form, Modern Dance." M.A. thesis, Drake University, 1969.

186. Metheny, Eleanor, "This 'Thing' Called Sport," JOHPER, Vol. 40, No. 3:59-60, March, 1969.

187. Powell, Suzanne M., "Meaning in a Dance Form." Ph.D. dissertation, University of Southern California, 1969.

188. Remley, Mary L., "Twentieth Century Concepts of Sports Competition for Women." Ph.D. dissertation, University of Southern California, 1969.

189. Rosentsweig, Joel, "A Ranking of the Objectives of Physical Education," Research Quarterly, Vol. 40, No. 4:783-787, December, 1969. (Descriptive method and accompanying technique is employed.)

190. Siedentop, Daryl, "What Did Plato Really Think?" The Physical Educator, Vol. 25, No. 1:25-26, March, 1969.

191. Spencer-Kraus, Peter, "The Application of 'Linguistic Phenomenology' to the Philosophy of Physical Education and Sport." M.A. thesis, University of Illinois, Urbana, 1969.

192. Stone, Roselyn, "Meanings Found in the Acts of Surfing and Skiing." Ph.D. dissertation, University of Southern California, 1969.

193. VanderZwaag, Harold J., "Sport: Existential or Essential," Quest, XII, Spring, May, 1969, 47-56.

194. Weiss, Paul, Sport: A Philosophic Inquiry. Carbondale, Illinois: Southern Illinois University Press, 1969.

195. Wilson, Clifford, "Diversities in Meanings of Physical Education," Research Quarterly, Vol. 40, No. 1:211-214, March, 1969.

196. Zeigler, Earle F., "Philosophy of Administration," Illinois Journal HPER, Vol. 16, No. 1:9-12, Winter, 1961.

197. _____., "Vigorous Physical Education and Sport as Essential Ingredients in America's Pattern of Physical Education," The Physical Educator, Vol. 26, No. 1: 14-17, March, 1969.

1970

198. Allard, Ronald J., "Sport: Tyranny of the Mind." M.S. thesis, University of Massachusetts, 1970.

199. Bend, Emil, "Some Functions of Competitive Team Sports in American Society." Ph.D. dissertation, University of Pittsburgh, 1970.

200. Daly, John A., "An Identification of Some Philosophic Beliefs Held by Australian Physical Educators, with Implications for Administration." M.S. thesis, University of Illinois, Urbana, 1970.

201. Fraleigh, Sondra Horton, "Dance Creates Men," Quest, No. 14, June, 1970, 65-71.

202. Fraleigh, Warren P., "Theory and Design of Philosophic Research in Physical Education," in Proceedings of the National College Physical Education Association for Men, Portland, Oregon, December 28, 1970.

203. Glader, Eugene A., "A Study of Amateurism in Sports." Ph.D. dissertation, University of Iowa, 1970.

204. Harper, William Arthur, "Human Revolt: A Phenomenological Description." Ph.D. dissertation, University of Southern California, 1970.

205. Hein, Hilde, "Performance as an Aesthetic Category," Journal of Aesthetics and Art Criticism, 28, Spring, 1970, 381-386.

206. Houts, Jo Ann, "Feeling and Perception in the Sport Experience," JOHPER, Vol. 41, No. 8, October, 1970, 71-72.

207. Kelly, Darlene A., "Phenomena of the Self-Experienced Body." Ph.D. dissertation, University of Southern California, 1970.

208. Kleinman, Seymour, "Physical Education and Lived Movement." Proceedings of the NCPEAM. 74:60-65, 1970.

209. _____, "Sport as Experience." Unpublished paper presented at the Annual Convention of the AAHPER, Seattle, Washington, April, 1970.

210. _____, "Will the Real Plato Please Stand Up?" Quest, No. 14, June, 1970, 73-75.

211. Kretchmar, Robert Scott, "A Phenomenological Analysis of the Other in Sport." Ph.D. dissertation, University of Southern California, 1970.

212. Lowe, Benjamin, "The Aesthetics of Sport: The Statement of a Problem," Sport Psychology Bulletin, Vol. 4, No. 1, February, 1970, 8-13.

213. Miller, David L. Gods and Games: Toward a Theology of Play. New York: World Publishing Company, 1970.

214. Nelson, Emogene A., "Value Patterns of Physical Educators in Colleges and Universities of the United States." Ph.D. dissertation, University of Minnesota, 1970.

215. Oberteuffer, Delbert, and Ulrich, Celeste. Physical Education: A Textbook of Principles for Professional Students, Fourth edition. New York: Harper & Row, Publishers, Inc., 1970.

216. Rickard, R. S., "Distinction--or Extinction?" The Physical Educator, Vol. 27, No. 2, May, 1970, 75-76.

217. _____., "An Explication of the Role of Aesthetic Value in American Physical Education: A Conceptual Analysis of Physical Education Literature." Ed.D. dissertation, Stanford University, 1970.

218. Sanborn, Marian A. and Hartman, Betty G. Issues in Physical Education, Revised edition. Philadelphia: Lea & Febiger, 1970.

219. Spicker, Stuart F. (editor). The Philosophy of the Body. Chicago: Quadrangle Books, 1970.

220. Stewart, Mary Lou, "Why Do Men Play?" JOHPER, Vol. 41, No. 9, November-December, 1970, 14.

221. Updyke, Wynn F. and Johnson, Perry B. Principles of Modern Physical Education, Health, and Recreation. New York: Holt, Rinehart and Winston, Inc., 1970.

222. VanderZwaag, Harold J., "Sports Concepts," JOHPER, Vol. 41, No. 3, March, 1970, 35-36.

223. Warren, William E., "An Application of Existentialism to Physical Education." Ed.D. dissertation, University of Georgia, 1970.

224. Zeigler, Earle F., "An Analysis of an Approach to Teaching: Mosston's Spectrum of Styles," The Australian Journal of Physical Education, 48:29-30, February-March, 1970.

225. _____., "A Philosophy for the Private Agency," Journal of Physical Education, Vol. 67, No. 3:67-81, 1970.

226. _____., "The Rationale for Philosophical Analysis with Implications for Physical Education and Sport," Illinois Journal of HPER, 1:17-18, Winter, 1970.

227. _____., "A Reaction to Fraleigh's Assessment of Philosophic Research in Physical Education," in Proceedings of the National College Physical Education Association for Men, Annual Meeting, Portland, Oregon, December 28, 1970, 52-56. (Published in 1971).

1971

228. Aldrich, Virgil C., "Art and the Human Form," Journal of Aesthetics and Art Criticism, 29:295-302, Spring, 1971.

229. Bell, James W., "A Comparative Analysis of the Normative Philosophies of Plato, Rousseau, and Dewey as Applied to Physical Education." Ph.D. dissertation, The Ohio State University, 1971.

230. Fahey, Brian W., "Basketball: A Phenomenological Perspective of Lived-Body Experience." M.S. thesis, University of Washington, 1971.

231. Gregg, Jerald, "A Philosophical Analysis of the Sports Experience and the Role of Athletics in the Schools." Ed.D. dissertation, University of Southern California, 1971.

232. Keating, James W., "The Urgent Need for Definitions and Distinctions," The Physical Educator, 28, 1:41-42, March, 1971.

233. Keenan, Francis W., "A Delineation of Deweyan Progressivism for Physical Education." Ph.D. dissertation, University of Illinois, Urbana, 1971.

234. Kovich, Maureen, "Sport as an Art Form," JOHPER, 42, October, 1971, 42.

235. Meier, Klaus V., "An Existential Analysis of Play." M.A. thesis, The University of Western Ontario, 1971.

236. Osterhoudt, Robert G., "A Descriptive Analysis of Research Concerning the Philosophy of Physical Education and Sport." Ph.D. dissertation, University of Illinois, Urbana, 1971.

237. Paddick, Robert J., "The Nature and Place of Knowledge in Physical Education." M.A. thesis, University of Alberta, 1971. (Mentioned also under 1967 ??)

238. Patrick, George, "Verifiability of Physical Education Objectives." Ph.D. dissertation, University of Illinois, Urbana, 1971.

239. Pearson, Kathleen, "A Structural and Functional Analysis of the Multi-Concept of Integration-Segregation (Male and/or Female) in Physical Education Classes." Ph.D. dissertation, University of Illinois, Urbana, 1971.

240. Sundly, Jerry A., "The Desire to Win: A Phenomenological Description." Ph.D. dissertation, University of Southern California, 1971.

241. Toyama, Judith S., "The Language of Sport: A Study of the Knowledge of Sport Terminology as a Function of Exposure to the Mass Media." M.S. thesis, University of Wisconsin, 1971.

242. Zeigler, Earle F., "A Comparative Analysis of Educational Values in Selected Countries: Their Implications for Physical Education and Sport," in Proceedings of the National College Physical Education Association for Men, Minneapolis, Minnesota, 1971, 169-174. (Appeared also in Gymnasion, Vol. 8, No. 1:13-16, 1971.)

243. _____., "The Health Teacher Needs a Philosophy," in New Directions in Health Education (edited by D. Read). New York: The Macmillan Company, 1971, 65-94.

244. _____., "The Need for Some Basic Agreement in Physical Education and Sport," Missouri Journal of HPER, Vol. 1, No. 1: 3, 13, Spring, 1971.

245. _____., "Putting the Greek Ideal in Perspective," Illinois Journal of HPER, 3:8-9, 1971.

246. _____, Howell, M. L. and Trekell, Marianna. Research in History, Philosophy, and International Aspects of Physical Education and Sport. Champaign, Illinois: Stipes Publishing Company, 1971.

1972

247. Broekhoff, Jan, "Physical Education and the Reification of the Human Body," in Proceedings of the 2nd Canadian Symposium on the History of Sport and Physical Education, Windsor, Ontario, Canada, May 1-3, 1972.

248. _____, "Sport and Ethics in the Context of Culture." A paper presented at the 2nd Annual Meeting of the Philosophic Society for the Study of Sport, SUNY, College at Brockport, New York, October 26-28, 1972.

249. Gerber, Ellen W., "Arguments on the Reality of Sport," in Sport and the Body. Philadelphia: Lea & Febiger, 1972.

250. _____ (editor). Sport and the Body. Philadelphia: Lea & Febiger, 1972.

251. Hyland, Drew, "Athletic Angst: Reflections on the Philosophical Relevance of Play," in Sport and the Body. Philadelphia: Lea & Febiger, 1972.

252. Keating, James, "Athletics: Ethical Problems of Competition." A paper presented at the 2nd Annual Meeting of the Philosophic Society for the Study of Sport, SUNY, College at Brockport, New York, October 26-28, 1972.

253. Lenk, Hans, "Perspectives of the Philosophy of Sport," in The Scientific View of Sport. New York: Springer-Verlag, 1972.

254. Papkins, Michael, "An Analysis of the Values Asserted by Roger Bannister Concerning Running: Essentialistic - Progressivistic." M.S. thesis, University of Western Illinois, 1972.

255. Roberts, Terry, "The Fiction of Morally Indifferent Acts in Sport," in Proceedings of the 1st Canadian Symposium on the Philosophy of Sport and Physical Activity, Windsor, Ontario, Canada, May 3, 1972.

256. Scott, Jack, "Ethics in Sport: The Revolutionary Ethic." A paper presented at the Annual Convention of the AAHPER, Houston, Texas, March 28, 1972.

257. Slusher, Howard S., "Ethics in Sport: The American Ethic." A paper presented at the Annual Convention of the AAHPER, March 28, 1972, Houston, Texas.

258. Suits, Bernard, "The Grasshopper: A Thesis Concerning the Moral Ideal of Man." A paper presented at the 2nd Annual Meeting of the Philosophic Society for the Study of Sport, SUNY, College at Brockport, New York, October 26-28, 1972.

259. Thomas, Carolyn, "Do You 'Wanna' Bet: An Examination of Player Betting and the Integrity of the Sporting Event." A paper presented at the 2nd Annual Meeting of the Philosophic Society for the Study of Sport, SUNY, College at Brockport, New York, October 26-28, 1972.

260. Ulrich, Celeste, "Ethics in Sport: The Christian Ethic." A paper presented at the Annual Convention of the AAHPER, Houston, Texas, March 28, 1972.

261. VanderZwaag, Harold J. Toward a Philosophy of Sport. Reading, Mass.: Addison-Wesley Publishing Company, 1972.

262. Zeigler, Earle F., "The Black Athlete's Non-Athletic Problems," Educational Theory, Vol. 22, No. 4:42-426, 1972.

263. _____., "A Model for Optimum Development in a Field Called 'X'," in Proceedings of the 1st Canadian Symposium on the Philosophy of Sport and Physical Activity, Windsor, Ontario, Canada, 1972. pp. 73-85.

264. _____., "The Pragmatic (Experimentalistic) Ethic as it Relates to Sport and Physical Education." A paper presented at the 2nd Annual Meeting of the Philosophic Society for the Study of Sport, SUNY, College at Brockport, New York, October 26-28, 1972.

265. _____., "Teaching Methodology in Philosophy," in Proceedings of the 1st Canadian Symposium on the Philosophy of Sport and Physical Activity, Windsor, Ontario, Canada, 1972. pp. 73-85.

Note: In 1973 the C. C. Thomas Publishing Company of Springfield, Illinois published The Philosophy of Sport, edited by Robert G. Osterhoudt of Minnesota. In this book Osterhoudt included certain papers mentioned above from the 1972 Annual Meeting of the Philosophic Society for the Study of Sport. The authors of these papers were as follows: Jan Broekhoff, James Keating, Bernard Suits, Carolyn Thomas, and Earle Zeigler.

266. Fraleigh, Warren P., "The Moving 'I'," in The Philosophy of Sport (editor, R. G. Osterhoudt). Springfield, Illinois: C. C. Thomas, Publisher, 1973. pp. 108-129.

267. _____., "On Weiss on Records and on the Significance of Athletic Records," in Osterhoudt's The Philosophy of Sport. pp. 29-38.

268. _____., "Some Meanings of the Human Experience of Freedom and Necessity in Sport," in Osterhoudt's The Philosophy of Sport. pp. 130-140.

269. Keenan, Francis W., "The Athletic Contest as a 'Tragic' Form of Art," in Osterhoudt's The Philosophy of Sport. pp. 309-325.

270. _____., "The Concept of Doing," in Osterhoudt's The Philosophy of Sport. pp. 141-148.

271. Kretchmar, Scott, "Ontological Possibilities: Sport as Play," in Osterhoudt's The Philosophy of Sport. pp. 64-77.

272. Kuntz, Paul G., "The Aesthetics of Sport," in The Philosophy of Sport by Osterhoudt. pp. 305-308.

273. Morgan, William, "An Existential Phenomenological Analysis of Sport as a Religious Experience," in Osterhoudt's The Philosophy of Sport. pp. 78-107.

274. Osterhoudt, Robert G., "An Hegelian Interpretation of Art, Sport, and Athletics," in his The Philosophy of Sport. pp. 326-359.

275. _____., "The Kantian Ethic as a Principle of Moral Conduct in Sport and Athletics," in his The Philosophy of Sport. pp. 282-290.

276. _____., "On Keating on the Competitive Motif in Athletics and Playful Activity," in his The Philosophy of Sport. pp. 192-197.

277. Roberts, Terence J. and Galasso, P. J., "The Fiction of Morally Indifferent Acts in Sports," in Osterhoudt's The Philosophy of Sport. pp. 274-281.

278. Sadler, William A., Jr., "A Contextual Approach to an Understanding of Competition: A Response to Keating's Philosophy of Athletics," in Osterhoudt's The Philosophy of Sport. pp. 176-191.

279. Schacht, Richard L., "On Weiss on Records, Athletic Activity and the Athlete," in Osterhoudt's The Philosophy of Sport. pp. 23-28.

280. Stone, Roselyn E., "Assumptions about the Nature of Human Movement," in Osterhoudt's The Philosophy of Sport. pp. 39-47.

281. Suits, Bernard, "The Elements of Sport," in Osterhoudt's The Philosophy of Sport. pp. 48-63.

282. Weiss, Paul, "Records and the Man," in Osterhoudt's The Philosophy of Sport, pp. 11-12.

283. Zeigler, Earle F., "Five Stances That Have Got to Go., JOHPER, 44, No. 7:48-49, 1973.

284. _____., "Intramurals: Profession, Discipline, or Part Thereof?" in Proceedings of the NCPEAM, Minneapolis, Minnesota. pp. 85-90.

Selected References

Aldrich, Virgil C. Philosophy of Art. Englewood Cliffs, New Jersey
Jersey: Prentice-Hall, Inc., 1963.

Alston, William P. Philosophy of Language. Englewood Cliffs, New
Jersey: Prentice-Hall, Inc., 1964.

Archambault, Reginald D. John Dewey on Education. New York:
The Modern Library, 1964. (The "Selected Writings" were
edited by Professor Archambault.)

_____. Philosophical Analysis and Education.
New York: The Humanities Pres, 1965. (Nine contributors to
this book edited by Professor Archambault.)

Aron, Raymond. Introduction to Philosophy of History. Boston: The
Beacon Press, Revised edition, 1948. (English translation,
1961.)

Barker, Stephen F. Philosophy of Mathematics. Englewood Cliffs,
New Jersey: Prentice-Hall, Inc., 1964.

Bayles, Ernest E. Pragmatism in Education. New York: Harper &
Row, Publishers, 1966.

Beck, Robert N. Perspectives in Philosophy. New York: Holt,
Rinehart and Winston, Inc., 1961.

Bernstein, Richard J. John Dewey. New York City: Washington
Square Press, 1966.

Bigge, Morris L. Positive Relativism. New York: Harper & Row,
Publishers, 1971.

Black, Max. Critical Thinking. Englewood Cliffs, New Jersey:
Prentice-Hall, Inc., 1952.

Boas, George. The Major Traditions of European Philosophy. New
York: Harper & Brothers, 1929.

Bochenski, I. M. Contemporary European Philosophy. University
of California Press, Berkeley and Los Angeles, 1966.

Boodin, John E., "Philosophy of History," in Twentieth Century Philosophy (D. D. Runes, editor). New York: Philosophical Library, 1943.

Brameld, T. Philosophies of Education in Cultural Perspective. New York: The Dryden Press, 1955.

_____. Toward a Reconstructed Philosophy of Education. New York: The Dryden Press, 1956.

Brauner, Charles J. and Burns, Hobert W. Problems in Education and Philosophy. Englewood Cliffs, New Jersey: Prentice-Hall, Inc., 1965.

Breed, Frederick S., "Education and the Realistic Outlook," in Forty-first Yearbook of the National Society for the Study of Education (Part I, "Philosophies of Education"). Chicago, Illinois: The University of Chicago Press, 1942.

Brinton, Crane. The Shaping of Modern Thought. Englewood Cliffs, New Jersey: Prentice-Hall, Inc., 1964.

Bronstein, D. J. and Schulweis, H. M. Approaches to the Philosophy of Religion. Englewood Cliffs, New Jersey: Prentice-Hall, Inc., 1954.

Broudy, Harry S. Building a Philosophy of Education. Englewood Cliffs, New Jersey: Prentice-Hall, Inc., Second edition, 1961.

_____. Paradox and Promise. Englewood Cliffs, New Jersey: Prentice-Hall, Inc., 1961.

Brown, L. M. (editor). Aims of Education. New York: Teachers College Press, Columbia University, 1970.

Brubacher, J. S. Eclectic Philosophy of Education. Englewood Cliffs, New Jersey: Prentice-Hall, Inc., 1962.

_____. Modern Philosophies of Education. New York: McGraw-Hill Book Company, Inc., Fourth edition, 1969.

Burtt, E. A. In Search of Philosophic Understanding. Toronto, Canada: Mentor Books, The New American Library of Canada, Limited, 1967.

Bury, J. B. The Idea of Progress. New York: Dover Publications, Inc., 1955.

Butler, J. Donald. <u>Four Philosophies</u>. New York: Harper and Row, Publishers, Revised edition, 1957.

_____. <u>Idealism in Education</u>. New York: Harper & Row, Publishers, 1966.

Caton, Charles E. <u>Philosophy and Ordinary Language</u>. University of Illinois Press, Urbana, Illinois, 1963.

Chazan, Barry I. and Soltis, Jonas F. <u>Moral Education</u>. New York: Teachers College Press, Teachers College, Columbia University, 1973.

Chisholm, Roderick M. <u>Theory of Knowledge</u>. Englewood Cliffs, New Jersey: Prentice-Hall, Inc., 1966.

Cohen, "Modern Philosophies and Education." <u>54th Yearbook</u>, National Society for Study of Education, Part II, University of Chicago Press, 1955.

Dray, William H. <u>Philosophy of History</u>. Englewood Cliffs, New Jersey: Prentice-Hall, Inc., 1964.

Durant, Will. <u>The Lessons of History</u>. New York: Dover Publications, Inc., 1955.

_____. <u>The Story of Philosophy</u>. New York: Garden City Publishing Co., Inc., Revised edition, 1938.

Educational Policies Commission, "The Central Purpose of American Education," Washington, D. C.: National Education Association, 1961.

_____. <u>Moral and Spiritual Values in the Public Schools</u>. Washington, D. C.: National Education Association, 1951.

Ekirch, A. A. <u>The Idea of Progress in America</u>. New York: Columbia University Press, 1944.

Frank, Philipp. <u>Philosophy of Science</u>. Englewood Cliffs, New Jersey: Prentice-Hall, Inc., 1957.

Frankena, William K. <u>Ethics</u>. Englewood Cliffs, New Jersey: Prentice-Hall, Inc., 1963.

_____. *Philosophy of Education*. New York: The Macmillan Company, 1965.

_____. *Three Historical Philosophies of Education*. Chicago, Illinois: Scott, Foresman and Company, 1965.

Geiger, George R., "An Experimentalist Approach to Education," in *Modern Philosophies and Education* (edited by N. B. Henry). Chicago: The University of Chicago Press, 1955.

Greene, Theodore M., "A Liberal Christian Idealist Philosophy of Education," in *Fifty-fourth Yearbook* of the National Society for the Study of Education (Part I). Chicago, Illinois: The University of Chicago Press, 1955.

Harvard Educational Review. Volume 26, Number Two. Spring, 1956.

Hawton, Hector. *Philosophy for Pleasure*. Greenwich, Conn.: Fawcett Publications, Inc., 1961.

Heinemann, F. H. *Existentialism and the Modern Predicament*. New York: Harper & Brothers, 1953.

Hempel, Carl G. *Philosophy of Natural Science*. Englewood Cliffs, New Jersey: Prentice-Hall, Inc., 1966.

Hick, John. *Philosophy of Religion*. Englewood Cliffs, New Jersey: Prentice-Hall, Inc., 1963.

Horne, Herman H., "An Idealistic Philosophy of Education," in *Forty-first Yearbook* of the National Society for the Study of Education (Part I, "Philosophies of Education"). Chicago, Illinois: The University of Chicago Press, 1942.

Hospers, John. *An Introduction to Philosophical Analysis*. Englewood Cliffs, New Jersey: Prentice-Hall, Inc., 1953.

Huxley, Julian. *New Bottles for New Wine*. New York: Harper & Brothers Publishing, 1957.

_____. *Tomorrow and Tomorrow and Tomorrow*. New York: Signet Books (The New American Library, 1964.

Johnson, A. H. *Experiential Realism*. London: George Allen & Unwin, Ltd., 1973.

Kalish, Donald and Montague, Richard. *Logic*. New York: Harcourt, Brace & World, Inc., 1964.

Kaplan, Abraham. The New World of Philosophy. New York: Random House, 1961.

Kaufmann, Walter. Existentialism from Dostoevsky to Sartre. New York: World Publishing Company, 1956.

_____. Without Guilt and Justice. New York: Peter H. Wyden, Inc., 1973.

Kneller, George F. Existentialism and Education. New York: Philosophical Library, Inc., 1958.

Knight, Thomas S. William James. New York: Washington Square Press, 1965.

_____. Charles Peirce. New York: Washington Square Press, 1965.

Kolatch, Jonathan. Sports, Politics and Ideology in China. Middle Village, New York: Jonathan David Publishers, 1972.

Krikorian, Yervant H. (editor). Naturalism and the Human Spirit. New York: Columbia University Pres 1944.

Langer, Susanne K. Philosophy in a New Key. New York: Mentor Books (The New American Library), 1948.

McGucken, William J., "The Philosophy of Catholic Education," in Forty-first Yearbook of the National Society for the Study of Education (Part I, "Philosophies of Education"). Chicago, Illinois: The University of Chicago Press, 1942.

Morris, Van Cleve. Existentialism in Education. New York: Harper & Row, Publishers, 1966.

_____. Modern Movements in Educational Philosophy. Boston: Houghton-Mifflin Company, 1969.

_____. Philosophy and the American School. Boston: Houghton-Mifflin Company, 1961.

Muller, Herbert J. Religion and Freedom in the Modern World. Chicago, Illinois: The University of Chicago Press, 1963.

Nevins, Allen. The Gateway to History. Garden City, New York: Doubleday & Company, Inc., 1962.

Ozmon, Howard. Dialogue in the Philosophy of Education. Columbus, Ohio: Charles E. Merrill Publishing Co., 1972.

Rand, Ayn. For the New Intellectual. New York: The New American Library, Inc., 1961.

Rosten, Leo (editor). Religions in America. New York: Simon & Shuster, 1963.

Rudner, Richard S. Philosophy of Social Science. Englewood Cliffs, New Jersey: Prentice-Hall, Inc., 1966.

Russell, Bertrand. Education and the Good Life. New York: The Hearst Corporation, (Avon Book Division), 1926.

Salmon, Wesley C. Logic. Englewood Cliffs, New Jersey: Prentice-Hall, Inc., 1963.

Spencer, Herbert. Education: Intellectual, Moral and Physical. London: Watts & Co., 1949.

Stroll, Avrum and Popkin, Richard. Introduction to Philosophy. New York: Holt, Rinehart & Winston, Inc., 1961.

Taylor, Richard. Metaphysics. Englewood Cliffs, New Jersey: Prentice-Hall, Inc., 1963.

Tesconi, Charles A., Jr. and Morris, Van Cleve. The Anti-Man Culture. Urbana, Illinois: University of Illinois Press, 1972.

Toynbee, Arnold J. A Study of History. (Abridgement of Volumes I-VI by D. C. Somervell). New York and London: Oxford University Press, 1947.

Van Loon, H. W. The Arts. New York: Simon & Schuster, 1937. Englewood Cliffs, New Jersey: Prentice-Hall, Inc., 1953.

Warnock, Mary. Ethics Since 1900. London: Oxford University Press, 1960.

Weiss, Paul. The Making of Men. Southern Illinois University Press, 1967.

White, Morton. The Age of Analysis. Boston: Houghton-Mifflin Company, 1962. (Also available in paperback from Mentor, 1955.)

_____. Pragmatism and the American Mind. New York: Oxford University Press, 1973.

Whitehead, Alfred North. The Aims of Education. New York: The Macmillan Co., 1929.

Wild, John, "Education and Human Society: A Realistic View," in the
Fifty-fourth Yearbook of the National Society for the Study of
Education (Part I, "Modern Philosophies and Education").
Chicago, Illinois: The University of Chicago Press, 1955.

Williams, J. Paul. What Americans Believe and How They Worship.
New York: Harper & Row, Publishers, 1952.

Zeigler, Earle F. An Introduction to the Philosophy of Religion.
Champaign, Illinois: Stipes Publishing Company, 1965.

Education, philosophy of –
reconstructionism
(continued):
  procedure, 126, 127
  purpose of study, 126
  school and community relationship, 133
  self-evaluation check list,
   202-214
  spectrum: 125, 215
   progressivism to
    essentialism, 126
  sub-discipline, 303
  teacher-education in, 333,
   334
Eiseley, Loren, 251
Electroligarchy, 35
Elliott, Ruth, 329
Ellis, M. J., 383
Encyclopedia of Physical Education, 367
Encyclopedists, 84
Ervin, Samuel, 35
Essentialism, 224, 333, 334,
335, 336, 338, 339
Ethics: 81, 82
  historical perspective, 81,
   82, 83, 84, 88, 89
  metaethics, 82, 88, 90
  normative ethics, 90
  problems, 88, 89
  values, role of in Parson's
   action system, 85, 86,
   87, 88
Exercise, remedial, 12
Existentialism, 65, 333 (see
  also Education, philosophy
  of, and Sport and physical
  activity)
Experimentalism, 225 (see
  also Philosophy, and
  Physical, health, and
  recreation, philosophy of)
Eyler, Marvin, 46, 378

Fairs, John R., 47, 232
Feigl, H., 419
Fein, Leonard, 252
Fishwick, Marshall, 38

Fitness schools, summer, 27
Flexner, Abraham, 326
Ford, Henry, 38
Fordham, Sheldon, 361
Fraleigh, W. P., 287
France, Wellman, 359
Frank, Lawrence K., 151
Frankena, William K., 38,
403, 424, 425
Frederick the Great, 327
Freedom:
  change, need for, 260
  concept of, 249, 250, 255
  education, philosophy of:
   approaches, philoso-
    phical, 258
   bureautechnocracy, 259,
    260
   new conservatism, 259
   students today, 257, 258
   super-industrial revolu-
    tion, 257
  future, 268
  in philosophy:
   coercion, 256
   education, importance
    of, 256
   freedom of, to, in, and
    from, 256
   life without choice, 254
   strategies to avoid, 255
  man and his relationship
   to freedom today, 250-
   254
Freedom in competitive sport
  (see sport, competitive)
Freeman, Kenneth J., 230
Freud, Sigmund, 43
Friermood, H., 176
Fromm, Erich, 252
Furberg, Mats, 287

Galasso, P., 348
Gallup, George, 142, 268
Gardiner, E. Norman, 231
Glaser, William, 466
Glassford, R. G., 47, 380,
385
Gochnauer, M. L., 427

- 511 -

"Good life", The, 49, 50
Goodwin, Richard, 254
Gordus, Adon A., 43
Gordy, J. P., 328
Gough, Harrison G., 150
Gould, Samuel B., 35
Greece (see Athletics)
Greenberg, P. J., 154
Greene, Theodore M., 438
Gustad, John W., 153

Hall, Ann, 47
Hanna, David, 149
Hare, R. M., 91
Harper, R., 182
Harris, Harold A., 232
Harvard Guide to American
    History, The, 40
Harvard Summer School of
    Physical Education, 332
Health and safety education:
    6, 11, 18
    graduate study, 320
    philosophy:
        self-evaluation check
            list, 202-214
        spectrum, 215
        values in school health
            education, 207, 208,
            209
    physical education, split
        from, 394
Health education: 30
    aims and objectives under
        reconstructionism, 136
Health, physical education,
    and recreation:
        programs, suggested,
            in junior and senior
            high schools, 412, 413
Health, Y.M.C.A. (see
    Y.M.C.A.)
Hegel, G., 65
Heine, Heinrich, 456
Heinemann, F. H., 196
Henry, Franklin, 350
Henry, Jules, 141
Heraclitus, 410

Hess, Ford A.: 404
    objectives, physical educa-
        tion, 4
Heywood, Robert W., 39
Historiography (see History)
History:
    advances, twenty-five
        years prior to 1961, 33,
        34
    as a bridge, 40
    changing nature of, 42, 43
    contemporary history,
        place of, 45
    corroborative detail, 45
    as a "happening", 38, 39
    historiography: 40
        the term, uses for, 37
    humaneness of, 40
    interdisciplinary aspects,
        39, 43, 44
    interpretation, historical:
        approaches to, 41, 42
    language, ordinary, 42
    philosophy of, 41, 42
    psychology, role of, 43
    social and behavioral
        sciences:
            credentials, lack of,
                43, 44
    study of, 39
    subjective element: 40
        value judgments, 41
    teaching, professional
        responsibility: 45
            case study, 46
    the term, uses for, 36
Hobbes, Thomas, 83
Hook, Sidney, 183
Horne, H. H., 258
Howell, Maxwell, 47
Huelster, L. J., 286
Hume, David, 83
Hunsicker, Paul, 361
Hutton, Daniel C., 154
Huxley, Aldous, 276, 369
Huxley, Julian, 251, 456

Osterhoudt, Robert:
"A Descriptive Analysis of
Research concerning the
Philosophy of Physical Edu-
cation and Sport", 423, 424

Parsons, Talcott: 101, 379,
385
values, role in action
system: 85, 86, 87
need for change, 87
Partridge, P. H., 255, 262
Patrick, George: 94, 288, 292
"Verifiability (meaningfulness) of selected Physical
Education Objectives,"
422
Pearson, Kathleen: 288, 292
conceptual analysis (philosophy of language), 422
Pearson, Lester B., 460
Peirce, C., 84, 93, 183
Penny, W., 317
Pestalozzi, 327
Philosophies of fitness, sports,
and physical recreation:
common denominators,
68, 69
essentialism, 67, 68
existentialism, 65, 68
idealists, 68
language, philosophy of,
65, 68
naturalistic realists, 68
need for a philosophy, 64
progressivism, 67, 68
value reassessment by
society, 64
Philosophy:
analytic:
language analysis, 199
logical atomism, 199
logical positivism, 199
branches of, chart, 128
ethics: 81, 82
history, 81, 82, 83, 84,
88, 89
meta ethics, 82, 88, 90
normative ethics, 90

Philosophy - ethics
(continued):
problems, 88, 89
values, role in Parson's
action system, 85,
86, 87, 88
existentialism, 180, 185,
186, 187, 188, 189
experimentalism, 76
a "family resemblance"
term:
meaning, 418
freedom, 254, 255, 256
function of philosophers,
88, 89, 92
idealism:
philosophers, 168
importance in physical
education and sport, 13
justification for: 451
existentialism, 452
philosophical analysis,
451, 452
methods of analysis, 3
naturalism, 71, 92, 93
philosophical analysis:
existentialism, 421
logical atomism, 419,
420
logical positivism, 419,
420
ordinary language
philosophy, 420
twentieth century de-
velopment, 418
pragmatism (ethical
naturalism): 91
axiology: 96, 97, 98
aesthetically, 97
ethically, 97
religiously, 97
socially, 98
epistemology, 94, 95
experimentalism, 93
instrumentalism, 96
logic, 95, 96
metaphysics, 98, 99
naturalism, 92, 93
progressivism, 93

Physical, health, and recreation education, philosophy of (continued):

  naturalism:

    growth and development, child's, 74

    health, 72, 73

    physical education, 72, 74

    women, 73, 74

  need for a basic philosophy, 53

  need for a logical, consistent philosophy, 57, 58

  phases of society: 466

    communication, 467

    cooperation, 468

    diversity, 467

    place of physical education and sport, 468

  philosophy of life, importance of, 216-218

  realism:

    aims and objectives, 162, 163

  reconstructionism, implications:

    aims and objectives: 123

      physical education, 135, 136

      recreation education, 136

      school health education, 136

    comments, general, 133, 134

    conclusions, 154, 155

    educational aims and objectives, 122

Physical, health, and recreation education, philosophy of (continued):

    empirical data, 139, 140, 141, 142, 143

    epistemology, 122

    metaphysics, 122

    methodology, 137, 138

    scientific data, 143-154

  rungs on "philosophical ladder", 58, 59, 60

  sub-philosophies and parent discipline relationship, 54

  values from, 53, 54

Plato, 82, 232

Platt, John, 110

Play:

  definition, 457

  naturalism, influence of, 458

  theories of, 383

Politics, influence on education and physical education, 16, 192

Pooley, John, 245

Popp, James, 152

Pragmatism: (see also Philosophy, and Physical education and sport, philosophy of)

  relation to reconstructionism, 127, 129

President's Council on Physical Fitness, 25, 74

Pressey, S. L., 149

Professionalism in sport:

  implications of existentialism, 195

  new role for athlete, 227, 228

Professional preparation,
physical education and
sport - philosophical
positions, etc.
(continued):
    curriculum,
    special-
    ization or
    general-
    ization, 335,
    336
    "disciplinary
    emphasis"
    versus "pro-
    fessional
    preparation"
    approach,
    337
    evaluation by
    students, 338
    language
    analysis and
    competency
    approach,
    335
physical education,
historical review,
U. S., 329
physical education,
problem areas,
1927, 330, 331
physical education,
twentieth century,
U. S., 329, 330
professions, histori-
cal review:
    meaning of
    term, 326
    teachers, pre-
    paration of,
    326, 327
    teachers, status
    of, U. S.,
    327, 328
teacher education,
twentieth century,
328, 329

Progressivism, 224, 333, 335,
336, 338, 339 (see also
Philosophy)
Publications:
    Journal of Canadian Sports
    History and Physical Edu-
    cation, 47

Rand, Ayn, 236
Rarick, Lawrence, 150
Realism (see also Education,
philosophy of, and Physical,
health, and recreation education, philosophy of), 225
    foundations, 409, 410
Reconstructionism (see Edu-
cation, philosophy of)
Recreation: 6, 31
    definition, 457
    recreation education,
    unique role, 462
    split from physical educa-
    tion, 394
Recreation and park adminis-
tration, graduate study,
320
Recreation education, philoso-
phy of:
    aims and objectives
    under reconstruc-
    tionism, 136, 137
    self-evaluation check
    list, 202-214
    values, 210-212
Reich, Charles A., 233, 236,
254, 299
Reid, Thomas, 83
Religion, influence on physical
education and sport, 16, 18
Research Quarterly:
    "The Contribution of Physi-
    cal Activity to Human
    Well-Being", 366, 440
Rice Institute, The, 280
Roberts, Oral, 263
Robertson, 253
Rousseau, Jean-Jacques, 84,
458
Rovere, Richard, 253

World today (continued):
  White House Conference on
    Youth, 1971, 442
World War I, 330

Yale University, 303, 304
Y.M.C.A.:
  characteristics, 167
  goals, original, 167
  idealism:
    background, 168
    physical education,
      idealistic concept,
      168, 169
  idealism, protestant
  Christian:
    aims and objectives,
      educational, 170,
      171
    conservative versus
      liberal positions,
      173
    development stages,
      178, 179

9 21 112

Y.M.C.A. - idealism, protestant Christian (continued):
  epistemology, 171
  influence today, 169,
    170
  metaphysics, 170
  physical directors,
    responsibilities, 172
  teaching method, 177
  values:
    health education, 171
    physical education,
      172
    recreation education,
      172
international influence:
  174
    World Y.M.C.A.
    Consultation on
    Health and Physi-
    cal Education,
    Rome, 1960, 174,
    175, 176